Survey of
Modern Fantasy
Literature

Survey
of
Modern Fantasy
Literature

Edited by
FRANK N. MAGILL

Volume One
A – Fac
1 – 510

SALEM PRESS
Englewood Cliffs, N.J.

Library of Congress Cataloging in Publication Data

Survey of modern fantasy literature.

   Includes bibliographies and index.
   1. Fantastic literature—History and criticism—
Addresses. essays, lectures. I. Magill, Frank Northen,
1907-
PN56.F34S97 1983   808.8'015   83-15189
ISBN 0-89356-450-8 (set)
ISBN 0-89356-451-6 (volume 1)

Printed in the United States of America

PUBLISHER'S NOTE

Survey of Modern Fantasy Literature provides a library reference to those forms of fantastic literature broadly grouped under the designation Fantasy Literature: high fantasy, low fantasy, horror, Gothic fantasy, science fantasy, psychological fantasy, avant-garde experiments, and various unclassified fantastic works. Works representative of all these categories have been included in this set, allowing a broad and acceptable definition of the genre.

The list of titles and the length of each article were determined with the assistance of staff consultants, all professors, writers, or critics of fantasy literature. Each essay was written and appears signed by a member of the writing staff, all of whom represent an informed and established body of serious critics and students of fantasy as a literary genre.

Five hundred Essay-Reviews treat individual works, as well as trilogies, series, collections, and the short fiction of numerous authors, all of which are arranged alphabetically. (See "Short Fiction of" and the author's last name to locate these entries.) Individual essay-reviews vary in length from 1,000 to 10,000 words. Titles of historical and critical value are covered in approximately 2,000 words; those of lesser importance receive a 1,000-word treatment; important series, trilogies, and benchmark titles receive 3,000 words or more.

The standard format first presents useful ready reference: author's name with birth and death dates, date of first book publication, type of work, time, locale, a brief description of the work, and a list of principal characters accompanied by a brief descriptive phrase. The essay-review which follows combines story digest with critical commentary to introduce the reader to the work from an objective perspective. A selected bibliography lists works or articles that specifically discuss the title. In some cases, no significant secondary literature was available, and the phrase "No listing" was inserted. (Sources about the author in general or other works by that author have been excluded from this selective bibliography. For general reference, see the "Annotated Bibliography.")

Throughout the work, dates of first book publication appear in parentheses following the first mention of a title; foreign titles also are accompanied by the title of the English translation. All titles are alphabetized by the English title when one exists; foreign titles are cross-referenced in the Index, as are the individual works in a trilogy or series.

A general "Annotated Bibliography" covers extensively the critical material available about the genre and individual writers. A "Bibliography of Anthologies" provides access to many important collections in which the works of various writers can be found. A "Chronology" permits each of the titles discussed in the set and additional works of fantasy literature to be put in historical perspective.

Nineteen topical essays appear in volume 5. These extended discussions address topics of importance and interest to both the casual reader of fantasy and the serious student. Together with the essay-reviews, they involve each reader in the complex task of defining fantasy literature.

A comprehensive Index allows access to information contained in the five-volume set by author, title, or term. Foreign titles, pen names, and series titles are all cross-referenced in the Index.

Survey of Modern Fantasy Literature has been designed to fill two library needs. It can assist library patrons in selecting authors or titles they would enjoy reading. It also provides students with an objective reference tool for reviewing works or conducting research on an author, title, or theme.

PREFACE

THE TITLE of this work has been the occasion of considerable discussion among staff members because of the broad policy obvious in the preparation of the list of titles. The purist element wanted to limit the works discussed to high fantasy and title the work *Critical Survey of Modern Fantasy*. There were, however, those who believed that the set would be more appealing and useful if the list were expanded to include works in dark fantasy and Gothic, with even some experimental works (leaning more toward science fiction than fantasy)—meanwhile changing our title to, perhaps, *Critical Survey of Modern Fantastical Literatures*. The suggested title change was not adopted since it is well recognized that horror literature, at least, is often subsumed under the broad title of "fantasy." While it is true that specific scholarly definitions of "fantasy literature" vary greatly, it is also true that many fantasy authors are active in related genres as well, and despite our confining title, some genre crossovers are inevitable. Daniel Defoe and Jonathan Swift have already showed the way to spread out a title, but we thought better of that. We have retained the title originally selected and yet have allowed some genre crossovers in our concern for broadened coverage.

What is far more important than our title is the fact that this work surveys an extensive body of imaginative literature representing the creative output of 341 authors who have contributed to the development of the genre to its present high level of artistry. There are five hundred separate works represented in this five-volume set and nineteen additional essays that cover areas of special interest to the student of modern fantasy literature.

The element of fantasy when introduced into a story is often cerebral but primarily appeals to the sensibilities; all emotions are elevated to a higher level because the tale, while it may not be true to life, is invariably exotic and perhaps threatening. Indeed, one of the most popular themes in Western literature is built on the threat—that of Faust, the story of whose pact with the Devil has intrigued readers of the fantastic for centuries. For an analysis of this phenomenon please see "The Faust Figure" essay on page 2316.

Fantasy literature, however, is not all "magic and witchery." Some of the language and concepts are especially beautiful and appealing, for here an author may take advantage of his unrestrained imagination to create situations and characters whose emotional outpourings might ordinarily violate conventional proscriptions against sentimentality. James M. Barrie's *Dear Brutus* is a good example to consider. The playwright has persuaded the audience to go along as he gives Will Dearth all the emotions of a fond father doting on his lovely daughter Margaret—although she exists only in his imagination. When this relationship finally ends and the stage lights go down at the end of the first act, Margaret fades from view calling: "Daddy, come back; I don't want to be a 'might-have-been.'" Because the audience had accepted the fantasy as real, their emotion of sadness over Will's loss is also real. By its very nature, fantasy enables an author to drop all inhibitions and express emotions—sadness, for example—without seeming sentimental.

Another example of potential sentimental risk is Friedrich de La Motte-Fouqué's *Undine*, the lovely story of a water sprite who has assumed human form and with whom Huldbrand has fallen in love. They marry but eventually quarrel and Undine loses her human form and returns to the water, though still in love with her human husband. Her water guardian, however, is offended that Huldbrand has mistreated Undine, and he causes Huldbrand's death. When her beloved is buried, Undine returns as a small spring to surround his grave in her arms forever. This German Romantic *Kunst-märchen*, which has its roots in the Middle Ages, to some may seem maudlin; others, voluntarily enmeshed in the story and involved all the way, will accept the ending as a genuine expression of eternal devotion. In such cases, it is incumbent upon the author to guide the reader so skillfully that the story, when crowned with the freedom of fantasy, is irresistible.

For a contemporary example, one might consider *So Love Returns*, a beautiful fantasy about love and loss and eternal sadness by Robert Nathan, whose fantasy novel *Portrait of Jennie* was made into a superb 1948 motion picture. *So Love Returns* tells of a writer living at the beach with his two small children after his young wife, Trina, has suddenly died. One day a "lady from the sea" appears to comfort him and help with the children. When they fall in love, however, the spell is broken and she must obey the interdiction against human romantic involvement and return to her sea environment. Even so, her presence has helped the young father adjust to his loss and reach for a new future.

Survey of Modern Fantasy Literature is replete with examples of highly fanciful flights into the fantasy world, each with its own special view of the scene beyond the norm. The Arthurian legend, for example, has provided more than its share of imaginative literature in the West from the sixth century on down to the late twentieth. Citations here are unnecessary since a representative—though by no means exhaustive—collection of selected titles may be found in the essay "Arthurian Legend and Modern Fantasy," beginning on page 2299.

Another extensive work of fantasy is James Branch Cabell's *The Biography of the Life of Manuel*. Its Storisende edition of eighteen volumes surpasses—in scope if not in imagination—any other work of fantasy by an American author. The story line recites the history of two lineages from the twelfth century, with its proper share of medieval fantasy; it ends in the mind of a romantic twentieth century husband who believes that he has discovered the sigil of Scoteia, that magic device which will transport him back to his medieval land of illusion. The sigil, alas, turns out to be only the broken top of his wife's cold cream jar—a spell-breaker of shattering disillusionment for the dreamer. Meanwhile, however, the reader has been provided with a highly entertaining experience.

There are many prototypes among imaginative literary works. Bram Stoker's *Dracula* may not be the best vampire story ever written, but it is doubtless the most influential and most often emulated. Mary Shelley's *Frankenstein* is a similar example of a work that far surpassed its author's expectations in appeal and influence. Many critics consider that H. Rider Haggard's *She* novels fall in the same sort of category because the works immediately caught the fancy of a large reading audience, who were mainly attracted to the exoticism inherent in the story line. J. R. R. Tolkein's *The Hobbit* set a style and provided a challenge to the imagination, that appealed to readers everywhere and resulted in a fantasy mode that has since been copied repeatedly— even by the author himself in his trilogy *The Lord of the Rings*.

There are simply too many outstanding writers represented in this set to allow individual comments; it is incumbent upon the user to examine his own preferences. Each must determine whether, say, Hermann Hesse's *The Glass Bead Game* or Ursula K. Le Guin's *The Earthsea Trilogy* or Stephen King's *The Shining* should take precedence over the 497 other works analyzed in *Survey of Modern Fantasy Literature*. With the plethora of selections available, some of the flights of imagination represented throughout will surely reward those who choose to become engaged.

I wish to thank all Staff members, and particularly Professor Keith Neilson, for the dedication obvious in the preparation of this work. Fantasy literature deserves such attention; it represents the creative mind uninhibited.

FRANK N. MAGILL

CONTRIBUTORS

Writing Staff for Essays

Mike Ashley
Neil Barron
Peter Brigg (Canada)
John Clute (England)
Joan DelFattore
Steve Eng
Donald P. Hasse
H. G. Haile
Walter E. Meyers

Donald Palumbo
Stephen Prickett
Franz Rottensteiner (Austria)
Roger C. Schlobin
Brian Stableford (England)
Raymond H. Thompson
 (Canada)
Robert Weinberg
Gary K. Wolfe

Writing Staff for Title Articles

Brian W. Aldiss
John Algeo
Mike Ashley (England)
Richard Astle
Brian Attebery
Melissa E. Barth
Barbara L. Berman
Peter Brigg (Canada)
Douglas A. Burger
Mary A. Burgess
Donald R. Burleson
Fran E. Chalfant
Edgar L. Chapman
Judith A. Clark
John Clute (England)
Alfred L. Cobbs
F. A. Couch, Jr. (Canada)
Gary William Crawford
Elizabeth Sikes Davidson
Thomas Franklin Deitz
Mike Dickinson (England)
Grace Eckley

Wilton Eckley
Greta Eisner
Jeffrey M. Elliot
Elizabeth Elchlepp
Richard D. Erlich
Mary Ferguson
Benjamin Franklin Fischer IV
R. E. Foust
Frederick S. Frank
Robert Frazier
Beverly Friend
Linda S. Gilbert
Penrith Goff
Stephen Goldin
Donald P. Haase
William H. Hardesty III
Ina Rae Hark
Donald M. Hassler
Charles Heffelfinger
Lillian M. Heldreth
Don Herron
Jane Hipolito

Richard Kopley
Brooks Landon
George P. Landow
Amy C. Lawler
Donald L. Lawler
Russell Letson
David Lewis
Kent P. Ljungquist
Kathleen Massey
Richard Mathews
Peter Mauzy
Clark Mayo
Roderick McGillis (Canada)
James M. McGlathery
Patrick L. McGuire
Willis E. McNelly
Douglas J. McReynolds
Walter E. Meyers
Miriam Youngerman Miller
Francis J. Molson
John C. Moran
Chris Morgan (England)
Katharine M. Morsberger
Robert E. Morsberger
Keith Neilson
Peter Nicholls (England)
Donald Palumbo
John R. Pfeiffer
Stephen Prickett

Julia R. Reed
Robert Reginald
Franz Rottensteiner (Austria)
David N. Samuelson
Joe Sanders
Roger C. Schlobin
William M. Schuyler, Jr.
A. Langley Searles
Roberta Sharp
T. A. Shippey (England)
Mark Siegel
Louisa A. Smith
Elisa Kay Sparks
Kathleen L. Spencer
Paul Spencer
John D. Squires
Brian Stableford (England)
Vivien Stableford (England)
David Stevens
C. W. Sullivan III
J. E. Svilpis (Canada)
Frank H. Tucker
Samuel H. Vasbinder
Robert Warburton
Christine Watson
Robert Weinberg
Gary K. Wolfe
Carl B. Yoke
Jules Zanger

LIST OF TITLES IN VOLUME ONE

SURVEY OF MODERN FANTASY LITERATURE

ADAM AND EVE

Author: John Erskine (1879-1951)
First book publication: 1927
Type of work: Novel
Time: The prelapsarian period
Locale: Paradise

An alternate version of the Adam and Eve story that reveals much about men and women

Principal characters:
ADAM, the first man
LILITH, the first woman
EVE, Adam's wife

In America during the 1920's, there was a trend toward idol-breaking, tearing down ancient, often revered figures and seeing them in a different, perhaps more believable, light. With the publication of *The Private Life of Helen of Troy* (1925), John Erskine established himself as one of those idol-breakers. This widely popular novel was followed two years later by *Adam and Eve*, an amusing and perceptive look at mankind's original forefathers, but more particularly, at all men and women.

The story begins with Adam's first days on Earth, as he courageously struggles to survive the murderous thorns on berry bushes, to drink from a pond like a dog, to escape the wrath of a stampeding bull, and to withstand the danger of a caterpillar crawling on his back. Adam longs for a companion, and, conveniently, Lilith appears. She and Adam are blissfully happy together in their ideal natural surroundings, eating, talking, playing, and loving together. Soon, however, Eve, the second woman, enters the scene and connivingly pulls Adam away from Lilith, forcing him to remain with her out of duty and guilt. She succeeds in completely trapping and tying him down when she gives birth to their son, for whom Adam takes much responsibility.

The dominant characteristic of Erskine's style is irony. With this device, he creates the cleverly humorous tone and scenes of the novel, most of which revolve around the bumbling main character, Adam. Early in the novel, Adam sees a dog drinking water from a pond and decides to try it himself. Getting down on all fours and sticking his tongue in the water, he attempts to drink but discovers instead that his hair gets wet and that he cannot breathe. His rational conclusion from this experience is that water is something to be avoided. Much of this humor also arises from the dialogues between Adam and Lilith. During their conversations, she is constantly exposing Adam's ignorance. When they are discussing the order in which life forms appeared on Earth, Adam declares that it is proper that he came after the animals, because "Life ought to be better as it goes along. The animals first—then man." Lilith cleverly replies, "And then woman." Adam is dumbfounded at this thought, and his pride will not let him acknowledge that a woman could be better than a man. Perhaps the ultimate irony of the saga is that Adam leaves the open-minded Lilith for the conniving, selfish Eve. Appropriately enough, when Adam makes his final decision to stay with Eve in Part Five, Erskine entitles the section, "The Fall of Man."

As the central character, Adam is the one around whom most of the action revolves. He is a study in the ignorance, pride, and folly of man. Adam's chief flaw is that he is too analytical. Although he tries, he cannot justify the dog's killing of the rabbit and the existence of snakes. Lilith, however, warns him that he will never fit into the world if he goes through it so timidly and critically. Instead, he should accept the actions of nature and not question their justness. Adam's analytical mind tells him that since there is a road intended for travel, man should stick to it and not wander across the fields, but Lilith explains to him that he lives only in his brain, lacking the spontaneity and adventurousness of his emotions. Another flaw in Adam is his pride. After he and Lilith are reunited following a short separation, he is too proud to let her know he missed her, for he does not want to appear weak.

Diametrically opposed to Adam is Lilith, whose primary purpose is to educate Adam. While Adam believes there is a planned reason for every occurrence, Lilith argues that most things are a result of accident. She calls her arrival after Adam an accident of nature, but he disagrees, saying that he arrived first because he must be responsible for everyone else. While Adam tries to analyze and change the sometimes cruel world, Lilith is totally accepting of it, vowing to relish the good things without complaint about the bad things. She is eager to branch out and experiment, while Adam prefers to "stick to the road" and do things the traditional, safe, expected way. She must educate Adam in the art of lovemaking and of enjoying life in general. Lilith is also intuitive, having been born with experience. The moment she sees the world, she is familiar with it and knows how things are to be used, how people will act, and what will happen to her. Thus, from the beginning, she knows about love and knows Adam will one day leave her for another women. Adam, on the other hand, is naïve and ignorant, not believing something exists or will happen until he sees or experiences it. In short, Lilith is an ideal woman. She is totally accepting of the people and things around her and has an ability to enjoy and appreciate life. She wants Adam to remain with her only out of love and not out of a sense of duty and habit.

Eve, on the other hand, is superficial, prudish, selfish, and conniving. She explains to Adam that eating should be an art; the process of satisfying hunger should be hidden by manners. She is insulted the first time Adam kisses her, yet she insists that he remain to protect her. While Lilith genuinely enjoys making love to Adam, Eve is disgusted and merely tolerates it (only after marriage, of course), because it is a wife's duty. She even invents clothes to cover the "shameful" parts of the body. To Eve, everything in life is a duty. Duty is what keeps a husband and wife together, and children are merely an extension of this duty. It is through this sense of duty, guilt, and responsibility that she forces Adam to live with her. While Lilith leaves nature as it is, Eve insists on a planned, disciplined garden, not containing vegetables which they might eat, but only flowers to improve appearances. She also insists that Adam build a wall around their house so that she can selfishly keep her property to herself. In short, Eve is concerned with superficial appearances and guilt-induced duty; Lilith is concerned with spontaneous nature and love. Although always feeling happier with Lilith, Adam decides, against his instincts, to remain with Eve, rationalizing that since Eve came after Lilith, perhaps she really is better and perhaps all her talk about duty and soul is a step beyond Lilith's passionate love of nature and sensual delights.

Thus Adam is caught between the life of nature (Lilith) and the life of civilization (Eve). He realizes that when he is with Lilith, he is happy, but when he is with Eve, he is aware of his faults. He admits that one experience is pleasant; the other is good for him. Suddenly he comes up with the idea that the best arrangement would be "to have the woman you loved the same person as your wife—Lilith and Eve in one. . . . If he had begun in time, perhaps he could have persuaded Lilith to treat him like a husband, or Eve to make him her lover." Adam dismisses the thought as being impossible, but certainly Erskine believes it should be a possibility.

An amusing, clever story on the surface, *Adam and Eve* is, in fact, a wise, sometimes sad, exposé of the nature of men and women. The reader may initially find himself laughing at the dialogues and actions of the characters, but soon he realizes that he is also laughing at himself. The only hope for the reader is that perhaps Adam was wrong: perhaps it is really possible to have a lover and a wife, a Lilith and an Eve, in the same person.

Elizabeth Elchlepp

Bibliography
No listing.

ALADORE

Author: Henry John Newbolt (1862-1938)
First book publication: 1914
Type of work: Novel
Time: An idealized Middle Ages
Locale: The city of Paladore; its paradigm, Aladore; and the surrounding countryside

A weary knight in search of an unknown desire encounters an enchanting lady and, with her help, enters an alternate world

> *Principal characters:*
> YWAIN, the knight errant
> AITHNE, his enchanted lady love
> THE CHILD, his guide, "desire"
> THE HERMIT, his mentor
> THE RHYMER, the magician who built Aladore

Aladore is, on its most elemental level, a fairy tale, a story so limpid and gentle in the telling that one is tempted to read it simply for pure enjoyment. Sir Henry John Newbolt's pastiche of the style made popular by William Morris employs a rich though archaic language which contributes greatly to the beautiful flow of this tale of a medieval quest for love and the meaning of life.

Ywain is the jaded administrator of an unnamed medieval state who is so overcome with ennui that he renounces his rights and turns over his lands and appurtenances of office to a younger brother, takes up the cloak and staff of a pilgrim, and sets off to follow his "desire," a will-o'-the-wisp in the guise of a child. He first encounters a hermit in the wilderness who teaches him the joys of the aesthetic life: solitude and peace. They break bread together and bathe in a mountain stream (the first of many such allusions to Christian fellowship). Ywain is soothed, but torn between the fellowship and peace of the hermitage and the lure of the child, his desire. This tension is reminiscent of the pull between the saintly life and the knightly quest depicted so well in Geoffrey Chaucer's *The Canterbury Tales* (1387-1400), and it is never resolved here completely.

Ywain leaves the hermit's solitary paradise and is directed toward Paladore, a walled city. There he encounters a beautiful lady, Aithne, who entreats him not to desert her as other knights have done in the past. He is distracted by the nearby sounds of battle and, overcome with a strange compulsion, joins the Eagles who are attacking the besieged Tower and helps to win the day. The warring parties converge at the end of the battle, and both sides honor Ywain as a hero. They explain that the battle is part of an age-old custom whereby the Eagles (who represent the liberal forces for change) challenge the Tower (the bastion of conservative power). Ywain is given a house and welcomed to the community. He has an inexplicable interlude with the lady Aithne, whose supernatural powers enable her to travel at will to the magical city of Aladore. He cannot "see" the city when she asks him to look for it, and she turns away in resignation. Meanwhile, the Tower, although outwardly friendly, secretly conspires to rid itself of Ywain's influence. He is challenged with three adventures which he accepts. Each time, when he is confounded by seemingly overwhelming odds, the lady Aithne appears in the guise of another and saves him.

Finally, Ywain is lured to join a band of knights who seek the City of Saints. Although the company's motives are varied and suspect, Ywain still longs for fulfillment and so elects to join the group. After much travail, Ywain and his companion Bartholomy happen upon the city and think they have completed their quest. The city is both lovely and unusual, but it is governed by ringing bells. A caretaker, Vincent, asks what they hope to find. "Peace," responds Bartholomy, but Ywain says, "I look only to love and to seek." Subtly, both men succumb to the lure of the bells which lull them into a state of forgetfulness. They think they have found peace, but the bells are really their captors. After a period of time, Ywain stumbles upon a garden where he meets again the lady Aithne. Suddenly, he remembers all that has gone before and realizes that she is the image of all that he desires. She asks him to forswear the bells and follow her on a new pilgrimage. At this point, they are startled by a spy for the city slithering away in the grass, like a serpent invading the lovers' Edenic paradise.

Ywain agrees to break the bonds of the city and follows his lady to the Lost Lands of the South. Here they encounter oreads, naiads, and fauns in a magical kingdom of milk and honey. Ywain falls in with the fauns and is enchanted by their rough pursuit of earthly pleasures. Together with Aithne (in the guise of a shepherdess), he spends blissful days in pastoral harmony. Gradually, Ywain becomes fearful of the fauns and their madcap antics. One evening, he has a vision of the city of Aladore, and the longing for his desire overcomes him once again. He begs Aithne to leave with him and aid him in casting off the animal trappings which make him kin to the fauns.

The fauns, growing bolder, follow the lovers in their flight. Suddenly, Aithne and Ywain are taken up by a strange creature with wings and flown to the city of Doedala, where a race of men carry on the tradition of Daedalus. Ywain is then taught the art and flies off to seek Aladore, leaving Aithne behind. He falls to the ground and is rescued by his old friend, the hermit. Here he bides, again renewing his strength and purpose. The hermit counsels him to return to Paladore and seek his desire among men. Ywain returns and discovers the Tower and the Eagles still at odds. He speaks to them and pacifies them temporarily, although the Tower has grown to hate him and resolves to destroy him.

One afternoon, Ywain follows the sound of many children frolicking and singing. There, on the Sherperdine Sands, he discovers again the city of Aladore. This time, he is permitted to cross through the mist and over the sea to its gates. He is taken to the chamber of the Rhymer's Hall, where he finds a book containing a picture of Aithne; he turns and finds that the image has become reality and follows her to their bridal chamber. They are wedded, and she tells him he has become the master of his dream, which is her dream as well. They begin an idyllic existence, as Aithne shows Ywain the Rhymer's magic, wherein all the seekers and lovers of times past, of myth and of history, are brought to life before their eyes. Ywain visits the scene of Aithne's childhood, Castle Kerioc, where he sees her as a child and there experiences with her all the warmth and love of her childhood years.

Ywain has forgotten that his pilgrimage must also take him past the gates of death. Aithne releases the key to a crypt wherein an old man dwells. The man warns Ywain that the time will come when he will be recalled to the world of man, and with the sounding of the midnight bells, Ywain finds himself in Paladore once more. Aithne follows him and together they are drawn into the final climactic battle for mastery of the city. Ywain is offered the principality but refuses when he realizes that the offer is an illusion; the real prince is a captive of the archbishop and subject to the wishes of the Tower. Instead, he elects to sacrifice himself, like Christ, to purchase the freedom and salvation of his brothers and companions in arms, the Eagles.

Ywain sees the child of his desire one last time and follows him to the sanctuary where Aithne awaits him. There he sees a bier carried in by knights, and, as he pulls back the pall, discovers his own face. Aithne calls him and they depart hand-in-hand through the battle. They are never seen in Paladore again, but the effigies of a knight and his lady are discovered on the tomb of the altar in the sanctuary. Ywain's friend Hubert explains: "They are not here but otherwise, and their sleep is but a semblance. And doubtless the pilgrim hath achieved his pilgrimage for he learned of this lady: and she came and went of her own magic, and had from her birth the Rhymer's heritage."

This allegory of Christian love is notable for the fact that it is (except for the somewhat juvenile Greenwood tales of G. P. Baker) the only medieval fantasy published between the death of William Morris in 1896 and the twenty-year interlude between World War I and World War II. Newbolt is clearly familiar with Morris' work and uses the same style of language, indefinable time period, and medieval trappings. That such a novel, with its emphasis on love and companionship at all levels, should appear on the eve of World War I is indeed ironic; Newbolt, who later wrote the official history of the navy in that conflict, never wrote another novel.

Robert Reginald
Mary A. Burgess

Bibliography
No listing.

ALICE'S ADVENTURES IN WONDERLAND
and
THROUGH THE LOOKING-GLASS

Author: Lewis Carroll (Charles Lutwidge Dodgson, 1832-1898)
First book publications: Alice's Adventures in Wonderland (1865); *Through the Looking-Glass* (1871)
Type of work: Novels
Time: Probably 1862
Locale: Wonderland and the world beyond the looking-glass

The fantastic adventures of Alice, a Victorian girl who meets many bizarre creatures in two of the most famous children's books ever written

Principal characters:
Alice's Adventures in Wonderland
ALICE, a young Victorian girl
A WHITE RABBIT
THE CATERPILLAR
THE DUCHESS
THE CHESHIRE CAT
THE MARCH HARE
THE MAD HATTER
THE DORMOUSE
THE MOCK TURTLE
THE KING AND QUEEN OF HEARTS

Through the Looking-Glass
THE WHITE KNIGHT
THE RED QUEEN
THE WHITE QUEEN
TWEEDLEDUM AND TWEEDLEDEE
HUMPTY DUMPTY

Lovers of children's literature have had difficulty in recent years trying to reclaim *Alice's Adventures in Wonderland* and *Through the Looking-Glass* for children. A perusal of the table of contents in the 1971 Norton Critical Edition of the Alice books should indicate why, since the essays listed are formidable: the cult of the romantic child or the sublimation of Charles Lutwidge Dodgson's obsession with little girls; a psychoanalytic-ironic pastoral reading that sees death and sex as major concerns; chess and theology in the Alice stories; nonsense as an inexorable linguistic and logical game; Carrollian nonsense and its relation to Ludwig Wittgenstein; nonsense and modernism; and the Alice books as an expression of the psychological development of Charles Dodgson. Not only are nearly all of the essays sophisticated, sometimes daring interpretations, but they also, with the possible exception of two brief essays that situate the Alice books in the history of the fairy tale, clearly reflect their authors' assumption that they are dealing with adult literature.

Thus, when to the witness of the essays anthologized in the Norton Critical Edition is added that of still other essays—Alice and William Wordsworth's "Ode to Immortality"; Alice and James Joyce's *Finnegans Wake* (1939); Carroll and surrealism; Alice and the "nightmare" of Victorian society; Alice and time; Alice and non-Euclidean mathematics—it is no wonder that a person should feel trepidation at reclaiming Alice for children's literature. Nevertheless, the reclamation can be done; first, however, it will be helpful to survey the current status of the Alice books.

When *Alice's Adventures in Wonderland* was first published in 1865, there was no doubt that the book was meant to be a children's story. Several years earlier, to entertain his very good friends, seven-and-a-half-year-old Alice Liddell and her two sisters, Charles Dodgson began making up stories about underground adventures enjoyed by a child also named Alice. On the occasion of a boat trip on the Thames in mid-1862, Dodgson delighted the Liddell girls by telling a sequence of stories about the fictional Alice. The next year he presented Alice Liddell with a manuscript copy of a completed, book-long narrative about the second Alice, "Alice's Adventures Under Ground." Sometime in 1864, George MacDonald, soon to be acclaimed as an author of children's fantasy and presumably capable of recognizing a children's story when he heard one, urged his friend Dodgson to publish a still further expanded version of "Alice's Adventures Under Ground" which he had read to the entire MacDonald family and which was still in manuscript. This Dodgson finally did in 1865, but with a different title. Upon publication, *Alice's Adventures in Wonderland* was immediately accepted by children and praised by adults as a delightful children's fantasy.

Shortly afterward, Dodgson, utilizing more stories that he had told Alice Liddell, began putting together a second fantasy narrating the further adventures of Alice in Wonderland; and in 1871, he published *Through the Looking-Glass*, which was also praised as a delightful children's fantasy. With the publication of the Alice books, furthermore, astute observers began to realize that literature written expressly for children would never be the same again; a creative force had been unleashed which would make impossible the reimposition of the severe restrictions that heavy-handed didacticism and moralism had foisted upon children's books.

Today the status of the Alice books is dramatically altered. For one thing, whether they are children's books is problematic in the eyes of many adults. Some wonder whether children today will be interested in fantasy that is heavily dependent on one hand upon verbal nonsense and mental games and on the other hand upon an acquaintance with Victorian culture. In other words, these adults maintain that the Alice books as children's books lack interest—a quality essential to a book if children are to read it and like it. Other adults go further, questioning whether children today possess the linguistic skills they believe are necessary to comprehend the manifold verbal richness they claim for the Alice books. These adults argue that the books are too difficult for a normal child to read and hence lack another essential quality of a children's book—readability. Undoubtedly, both groups of adults would agree that if copies of the Alice books circulate among young readers, they do so far more as gifts from adults than as items selected off a library shelf or purchased by the youngsters themselves. Finally, a third group of adults, taking a different tack, suggests that attempts to classify the Alice books as children's literature are unnecessary, if not actually restrictive, since the books are obviously literature and as such open to anyone, regardless of age, who is sufficiently interested and verbally skilled to read them. (Incidentally, acceptance of the third position validates the view that the Alice books, regardless of whether they are children's books, are at least adult literature.

Another important shift in the status of the Alice books concerns their critical reputation. Whether they were extensively popular with the general reading public in the last decades of the nineteenth century is doubtful, but there is no evidence that any segment of that reading public was judged incapable of comprehending or enjoying the books. Further, they never became the object of critical adulation. Today the Alice books continue to be not especially popular; in spite of their fame and reputation, most of the reading public (and this includes children) have not read them. Moreover, a sizable part of whatever popularity the books enjoy is probably due to the various stage and film adaptations, especially the Walt Disney film (1951), that have achieved success and have made the major characters and situations of the Alice narratives recognizable to many people. Today, *Alice's Adventures in Wonderland* and *Through the Looking-Glass* have become literary classics—an achievement that even the reticent Dodgson would have deemed an honor, but still, paradoxically, an achievement that is a mixed blessing. For not only are the Alice books, like many other literary classics, more venerated than read, but they also attract studies and analyses that have shifted attention away from the author's original intent to tell a children's story entertainingly.

It may be countered as evidence for the popularity of the Alice books that they are often quarried, so to speak, as a source of quotations and allusions that are humorous, either per se or when applied to people and situations. A substantial number of people, for example, like to quote snatches of Carrollian verse that are nonsense—"'Twas brillig and the slithy toves/ Did gyre and gimble in the wabe"—or seem to have no point—"How doth the little crocodile/ Improve his shining tail." Others apparently simply enjoy using phrases from the Alice narratives such as "Off with his head," "curiouser and curiouser," "Wow! Wow! Wow!" or "No room! No room!" Finally, there are even people who delight in referring to themselves or to others as characters from the Alice stories—for example, Cheshire Cat, a beamish boy, a Mad

Hatter—or in describing situations in which they find themselves as similar to those in the stories—for example, a mad tea-party, a caucus race, or stopping a Bandersnatch. Unfortunately, that people allude to passages, characters, or situations ostensibly from the Alice books does not conclusively demonstrate the popularity of the books. This familiarity may stem from film and stage adaptations or comic books and cheap reprints that are actually rewritten or digested, as well as from the books themselves.

Contributing to and at the same time feeding off the transformation of the Alice books into literary classics has been a remarkable boom in criticism and research concerning Dodgson and his writing. One part of this boom is textual; over the years, bibliographers have established the history of each edition and printing of the two books. They point out, for example, that the very first printing of the first edition of *Alice's Adventures in Wonderland*, defective in Sir John Tenniel's eyes because of the poor reproduction of his illustrations, was dumped onto the American market; or that a handful of copies of the second printing—bound in vellum, given to the royal family, and hence called the Royal Alice—is the rarest of all the book's issues. Bibliographers were delighted with the discovery in 1974 of the suppressed and presumed-lost episode, "The Wasp in a Wig" from *Through the Looking-Glass*. Significantly, the newly found chapter was first published as a private edition for the Lewis Carroll Society of America before it was made available to the general public.

An offshoot of the textual study of the Alice books concerns the annotating of the many allusions, jokes, tricks, games, parodies, and puzzles found in them. So extensive has this practice become that Martin Gardner was able to publish *The Annotated Alice* (1960). By bringing together in one volume all that has already been discovered or surmised, Gardner's edition has proved to be very helpful to readers seeking, for example, clarification of the chess moves that explain Alice's movement in *Through the Looking-Glass*, or speculating about the possible sources and meaning of the Jabberwocky verses, or desiring information about the original poems that Dodgson parodied in his inimitable style, or even looking for solutions to the Mad Hatter's famous riddle, "Why is a raven like a writing desk?" It is likely that the phenomenon of annotated editions of his books would have pleased Dodgson, who relished games, puzzles, and mental problems whose solutions and answers were not immediately apparent.

Also likely is that another phase of the boom in Carrollian research would not have pleased Dodgson: the effort and ingenuity expended in scrutinizing everything he ever wrote in hopes of uncovering every scrap of information about his life and finding possible correspondences between it and the Alice books. Thus, readers are told that the transformation of the Ugly Duchess' baby boy into a pig is not surprising since the dislike of young boys implied in the scene corroborates a dislike of young boys manifest in Dodgson's other works and correspondence. Readers are also cautioned that, based on the evidence of contemporary meteorological records, the famous "golden afternoon " of which the prefatory verses speak, when Dodgson first recited the stories about a girl named Alice, could not, as he said years after the publication of the book, have occurred on July 4, 1862. Such discoveries, in spite of their relatively meager results as far as a literary appreciation of the Alice books is concerned, are at least objective.

The same cannot be said, however, about some of the psychological probings and analyses of Dodgson that have been published in recent decades. In highly speculative fashion, they have sought to demonstrate that in the fantasy of Alice's adventures Dodgson sublimated much of the sexual desire and tension he allegedly experienced in his private life. For example, it has been argued that the adoption of a pseudonym and the obvious affection for Alice Liddell incorporated in the Alice narratives were ways of expressing strong sexual attraction to a young girl, which Dodgson could declare openly in his own name only at the risk of catastrophe. It has been further maintained that the hobby of photographing naked girls constituted for the celibate Dodgson a socially acceptable medium whereby he could vent deep sexual frustration. The force of these arguments must be weighed, however, against the substantial evidence that Dodgson enjoyed the celibate state and seemed at peace with himself and against the fact that he photographed naked girls with the approval of their parents, who, all the evidence attests, would never have permitted their daughters to pose for any man about whom there was the slightest doubt regarding his intentions. Another example of how highly speculative psychological studies of Dodgson can be is the suggestion that the pool of water in which Alice swims—the result of her tears of frustration, it will be recalled—after she has fallen into Wonderland represents the amniotic fluid of the womb. This representation, along with references to a birthday in the opening scenes, supposedly points not only to the initial stages of Alice's transformation from a child who lacks control over her destiny to one who does, but also, and more significantly, to Charles Dodgson's "rebirth" as Lewis Carroll.

If the Norton Critical Edition is to be believed, the Alice books are only historically interesting "entertainment for Victorian children" and hence important in the history of children's literature, but, presumably, of little consequence in children's literature today. On the contrary, there are many reasons for contending that the Alice books remain today, as they always have been, highly attractive literature for children. First of all, there is Alice herself, a most engaging protagonist. Although she is modeled upon a Victorian child, Alice is still immediately recognizable as a young girl. No miniature adult, she is a *bona fide* child: her actions, her perceptions, her mental categorizing of what she encounters in Wonderland, and her strategies of accommodation and survival are all plausibly childlike; in short, there is no contradiction between Alice's physical appearance as a child and her behavior.

Thus, the protagonist of the Alice books is a believable child and easily meets the first requirement of a children's book: that it contain a protagonist with whom children can readily identify.

Second, much of the inspiration for the characters and paraphernalia of the Alice books Dodgson found in the actual lives of Victorian children; also, most of the situations in which he places his protagonist are ones with which any child is familiar, often at first hand. To mention some obvious examples, there are babies, mischievous boys, pets, small animals and their characteristic behavior, caterpillars and other insects, Mother Goose rhymes and characters, pots and pans, winding balls of worsted, flowers, games of all kinds (especially chess, croquet, and cards), toys, parties, invitations, paper hats, dancing, jokes, puns, riddles, slapstick, etiquette, school, lessons, recitations, competing for prizes, being curious, inventions, railroads, eating, sweets, tea, treacle, food, eggs, violence, rough language, accidentally tripping over a hole in the ground, falling, dreaming, crying, make-believe, false accusations, getting revenge, falling asleep over a boring book, pretending to be a queen, getting punished, and, by no means to be overlooked, physically large persons who order one about, raise their voices, shout, threaten bodily harm, and often seem to act arbitrarily.

The point of this lengthy list is to show that the Wonderland that Alice enters—both its pleasant daydream of wish-fulfillment, escape, and loafing around wasting time and its nightmare of confusion, turmoil, and noise—strongly resembles the day-by-day living that children actually experience and contemplate. Commentators on the Alice books do not have to go to modernism or surrealism to find analogies to Wonderland that supposedly deepen its meaning or extend its range of implications. All they need to do is abandon sentimental, overrationalized notions of childhood and make the effort to recall what being a child is actually like—in particular, the child's growing realization that too many grown-ups control his or her life not because they are loving and wise but because they are physically larger and stronger than children. For the commentators, then, the "felt experience" of childhood will become palpable once more in the Alice books. This "felt experience," characteristic of an authentic children's book, is another reason why the Alice books are children's books.

A good number of adult readers, perhaps as a consequence of their tendency to intellectualize the Alice books, fail to appreciate the emphasis on physical activity and movement in the plots. Consider that of *Alice's Adventures in Wonderland*. From the initial quiet of falling asleep, the reader is moved quickly, abruptly, via Alice's falling down a hole in an attempt to catch up with a running rabbit, into a world where physical activity is paramount and everything seems in flux. In the first three chapters, for example, the reader encounters, in addition to the act of falling and plummeting downward, the physical contortions of trying to curtsy while falling, the thump of coming to

the end of a fall, jumping, running, walking, kneeling, shrinking and enlarging, climbing, swimming, and running a race. All of this physical activity, it must be recalled, is not incidental but central to the plot in the beginning of the book and throughout. Who can forget, for example, the wildly active tea-party scene which ends with the Dormouse being shoved into the teapot, or the absurdly solemn dancing of the lobster-quadrille?

This emphasis on physical activity and movement is one more feature of the Alice books that makes them readily accessible to children and hence attractive children's literature. Children, because they are both very active physically and sensitive to motion, are often immediately responsive to what may be termed the kinetic quality of a literary work. Consequently, children are open to the many appeals the Alice books make to the reader's sensitivity to physical activity and motion. On the other hand, adults, who tend to become increasingly sedentary as they age and less spontaneously sensitive to the totality of sensuous appeal in literature, are simply less responsive to the kinetic quality of the books and may need to be reminded of it. Accordingly, it is understandable that some adults do stress the cerebral aspects of the books, focusing, for example, on the aptness of the various moves and implied strategies in the mammoth chess game of *Through the Looking-Glass* rather than responding to the walking, running, and jumping from space to space that accompany the game. Yet at the same time, skewed interpretations resulting from a failure to respond adequately to the kinetic quality of the Alice books should not be permitted to go unchallenged as the only valid approaches to Dodgson's masterpieces.

It is a commonplace of children's literature that children are very interested in books that allow them to confront vicariously the myriad confusions and tensions of growing up. One phase of the latter that is very unsettling is the phenomenon of the rapid growth and change brought on by puberty. Part of the distinctive fantasy of *Alice's Adventures in Wonderland* (and to a lesser degree, of *Through the Looking-Glass*) is an especially striking, imaginative rendering of this phenomenon of growth and change: another reason why *Alice's Adventures in Wonderland* is a *bona fide* children's book. Unable to enter the lovely garden she sees because she is too big and wishing she could "shut up like a telescope," Alice finds a bottle labeled DRINK ME. Carefully drinking from it, she inexplicably shrinks. Believing that she is now adapted to her new surroundings, Alice discovers instead that she will need the golden key that she had found earlier to open the door to the garden; however, she is now too short to reach the key on a table. Noticing a small cake upon which are the words EAT ME, she once more follows instructions, eats, and—quite as inexplicably as before—changes, this time into a giant. Indeed, her body begins to act like the telescope she had wished she might be.

In the presentation of Alice's transformations, Dodgson reflects a keen understanding of children. Alice initiates her various changes through an act of eating—corroboration of the child's accepting as fact that putting food into the mouth both tastes good and makes one grow. Alice's next change is also caused by eating—further corroboration. A third change, however, she precipitates by touching a fan; subsequent changes are again brought about by eating. In this way, Dodgson imaginatively renders the strange and confusing growth of puberty which results not only from eating but also from forces seemingly outside the understanding or control of children. Thus, Alice begins to think of her limbs as entities acting independently of her will. Dodgson is also correct in having Alice fret about her size and her ability to fit into her new surroundings, since children often do not feel secure until they have made for themselves a special place into which they can fit. Alice's physical transformations can be viewed in other ways, but an obvious interpretation— at least to those who can recall their own childhood—is that they represent the preadolescent's struggle with the strange phenomenon of physical growth and change.

In his classic, "On Fairy-Stories," J. R. R. Tolkien distinguishes as one of the values of fairy stories their capacity to assist readers and listeners to escape the prison of their humdrum, daily lives. This capacity the Alice books also possess, and it is both one of their greatest assets and yet another reason why they are attractive to children. To begin with, the Alice books are escapist in the sense that anything which is fun or entertaining is escapist because it aids in alleviating boredom. Consider, for example, the slapstick of Bill's being kicked up the chimney, the boisterous commotion of the Pig and Pepper chapter, the antics of the tea-party, the droll preparations for the fight between Tweedledum and Tweedledee, the struggle between the Lion and the Unicorn over the King's Crown, the Punch-and-Judy jousts between the White and Red Knights, and the Knights' unique method of coming to a stop by falling off their horses. The fun of these scenes and others is apparent to anyone, old or young. Granted, a particular child may not perceive all the humor; it is even possible that some children, seeking quiet in their reading, may find some of the fun too rowdy for their needs. Still, for most young readers there is enough fun available in the Alice books to enliven many otherwise dull and slow-moving hours.

The Alice books are escapist in another positive sense, providing opportunities not only to run away *from* but also to run away *to*. That is, children, through these books, can escape into an imaginative world where they can test roles and options not readily available to them in real life. By identifying with Alice, for example, a child can take on the role of the person who successfully resists the manipulative pressure of authority figures and society and, as a result, can triumph on his or her own terms. In *Alice's Adventures in Wonderland*, after a period of turmoil and confusion that causes her, among other things, to question her own identity and to begin adopting some of the values and attitudes of Wonderland (for example, the scolding and rudeness she exhibits during the tea-party), Alice does eventually refuse to be judged by the standards of Wonderland, recognizes her judge and jury as a mere "pack of cards," and escapes with her freedom. In *Through the Looking-Glass*, Alice, older and more experienced because of her previous sojourn in Wonderland, is gradually able to accommodate herself without compromise. Becoming a queen herself, she gains her freedom from the irksome Red Queen (surely an outstanding example of the adult who orders children about and tries to control them). Moreover, Alice manages to hold her own in the various games and word matches in which she finds herself.

There remains one more point to be made about the continuing attractiveness of the Alice books as children's literature. In all likelihood, Dodgson intended, in addition to entertaining the Liddell girls, to help free children's books from the constraints imposed upon them by the contemporary dictum that, since children should use their time for self-improvement, what they read must teach. Evidence of Dodgson's intention is so pervasive in the Alice books that they, especially *Alice's Adventures in Wonderland*, seem to celebrate the joy of wasting time rather than improving it—in particular, the reader assumes, by listening to or reading stories that make no sense, urge no obvious moral, and present no explicit instructions.

This celebratory note is sounded at the very beginning of *Alice's Adventures in Wonderland* when the prefatory verses describe a scene of leisurely activities: "All in the golden afternoon/ Full leisurely we glide." In the first chapter, the joy of wasting time is celebrated primarily through Dodgson's making fun of the insistence that children should always improve their time. Alice is put to sleep by her sister's earnest book which has no "pictures and conversations." Alice is determined not to waste time while falling down the hole, so she recites her lessons. "Wise" Alice will not be like the "foolish children" peopling didactic children's books who drink from bottles labeled dangerous. Subsequent chapters contain many more incidents in which Alice learns lessons, morals, and manners, but in unexpectedly funny or absurd forms, and in which inhabitants of Wonderland waste time. Two incidents in particular need to be mentioned. One is the marvelous parody, "How doth the little crocodile/ Improve his shining tail," of Isaac Watt's famous didactic poem, "How doth the little busy bee/ Improve each shining Hour." The other is the mad determination to "kill" time on the part of the participants in the tea-party. Without a doubt, Dodgson's high-spirited and clever assault on didactic, moralistic children's books with their incessant talk about improving time was amusing to Alice Liddell and her sisters. This assault can also be amusing to children today once they realize what Dodgson is doing. When this occurs, they too find escape from the plethora of contemporary books that tediously and blatantly teach and moralize about a host of current social problems.

Obviously, Charles Dodgson was not completely successful in liberating children's literature from the constraints placed upon it by many well-intentioned but misguided adults; otherwise, there would be no need today to defend the Alice books as children's books. Ironically, the very works Dodgson created to show how excitingly fresh and imaginative children's books can be may be falling victim today to new constraints that other well-intentioned but equally misguided adults wish to place on children's literature—constraints of interest and readability levels set as low as possible to satisfy the least interested and least skilled of young readers. The Alice books do possess, however, as has been argued, many qualities that are very attractive to children. The truth of the matter is, finally, that the Alice books are indeed children's literature in the best sense of the term: literature that both children and adults can read and enjoy, each group comprehending in its appropriate way and each finding that for which it is looking.

Francis J. Molson

Bibliography
Carroll, Lewis. *Alice in Wonderland. Authoritative Texts of Alice's Adventures in Wonderland, Through the Looking-Glass, The Hunting of the Snark, Backgrounds, Essays in Criticism*, 1971. Edited by Donald J. Gray.
_____. *The Annotated Alice*, 1960. Introduction and notes by Martin Gardner.
_____. *The Wasp in a Wig: A "Suppressed" Episode of Through the Looking-Glass and What Alice Found There*, 1977. Preface, Introduction, and Notes by Martin Gardner.
Hudson, Derek. *Lewis Carroll: An Illustrated Biography*, 1977.

ALL HALLOWS' EVE

Author: Charles Williams (1886-1945)
First book publication: 1945
Type of work: Novel
Time: 1945
Locale: London

In London immediately after World War II, a sorcerer prosecutes his designs of gaining power over the world and making himself into a new Messiah, but he is opposed and finally frustrated by the ghost of a dead woman

> *Principal characters:*
> LESTER FURNIVAL, a dead woman
> RICHARD FURNIVAL, her living husband
> EVELYN MERCER, her dead companion
> SIMON THE CLERK, an evil archmage
> BETTY WALLINGFORD, his illegitimate daughter and intended agent
> JONATHAN DRAYTON, an artist, Richard's friend and Betty's fiancé
> LADY WALLINGFORD, Betty's mother

When this last of Charles Williams' seven metaphysical romances was reprinted in 1948, it was prefaced by an Introduction by T. S. Eliot containing a memoir of the author, who had been a personal friend. The Preface is particularly appropriate, for *All Hallows' Eve* appears to spring from a few lines near the end of the first section of Eliot's *The Waste Land* (1922). Here the poet stands on London Bridge, watches the crowds of hurrying commuters, and says: "Unreal City . . . / A crowd flowed over London Bridge, so many,/ I had not thought death had undone so many." The last line is a translation from Dante's *Inferno* (c. 1320), and in the mind of Williams—who of course knew Eliot well, and who had published a study of Dante only two years before *All Hallows' Eve*—the joint image of London as the Silent City of the Dead seems to have acted as the stimulus and center for his novel.

The image is especially prominent in the first scene. A young woman is standing on Westminster Bridge. She is dead, killed the moment before in a plane crash, but she has not yet realized it. Indeed, the reader realizes before she does, alerted by the ghostly City's ominous stillness and by the blank in the young woman's memory. Her main feeling, though, is of anger at having been kept waiting, and when she finally recognizes her husband's footsteps walking toward her, she bursts out at him with, "Where have you been? what have you been doing? I've been waiting." He replies with shock, throws out his hand to touch her, fails, and fades. Then the word "dead" does enter Lester Furnival's mind, for the meeting is so evidently one between a person and a ghost. Still, for a while, she thinks *she* is the person.

The opening scene adds to the novel something unusual in fantasy: a weight of regret and sorrow. When realization does dawn on Lester—the reader has also realized by this time that Lester's whole life and marriage have been marked by displays of imperiousness and bad temper—she is oppressed above all by the sense that she has behaved in death as in life: harshly and abruptly. Now she will never have the chance to improve or to apologize. She must bear the guilt of a separation in anger. In fact, Lester is wrong in imagining that she has no future. During the action of *All Hallows' Eve*, she manages to meet or to contact her husband, Richard, four more times, and they are on an ascending scale of charity, building up indeed to mutual forgiveness and to their final, resigned acceptance of separation. Her initial remorse also becomes the start of a process of repentance and self-denial, which leads Lester from her normal, not very admirable state to something one can only call salvation.

This internal drama is further counterpointed by the existence (in "the City") of Evelyn Mercer, Lester's friend, killed with her in the plane crash. At the moment of their death, most people would have found it hard to tell the two apart in terms of morality or spiritual development. Both are ordinary, obedient to the conventions of their society, capable of little acts of selfishness, but meriting their actions so far neither very clear spiritual reward by nor punishment. By the end of the novel, however, Lester has experienced repentance and compassion, becoming fit for a life in Heaven, while Evelyn has been reduced to a gibbering shape of malice which can only be called damned, and for all the initial similarity of the two women, the reader is persuaded that this distinction is just. Little as either did in life, it was enough to make a distinction and death has made the distinction clearer.

One of Williams' aims, it can be said with some confidence, was to emulate John Milton and "justify the ways of God to man." Hell and Heaven seem harsh and arbitrary concepts to people nowadays. Williams denies the popular idea of an external Power that sends the sheep to the right and the goats to the left and that sees sheep and goats where man sees only people. He insists on and restates the idea of salvation and damnation, but with this unorthodox modification: that even after death, the decision to go one way or the other remains in the individual's own hands. More orthodox is Williams' demonstration, with great novelistic skill, of how even the petty actions of everyday life contain within them the seeds of eternal reward or eternal degradation. Lester is imperious, but she can feel remorse. Evelyn is a gossip and a "clutcher": all through life, she has tried to get *hold* of people, physically or emotionally, and in the end, this urge to dominate and frighten is her bane. In a sense, the world of the dead women—silent, eventless, introspective— is dull and slow, checking the pace of the novel at many moments. Williams presents it obstinately, however, as of the first importance: the fate of a soul, even an ordinary one, is eternal and so outweighs any amount of political or physical excitement in the "real" world of life.

Besides saving herself, besides apologizing to her husband, Lester Furnival (as it happens) also saves the world. This act of external salvation provides the novel's other main strand, which is dominated by the evil archmage, Simon the Clerk. His goals are never entirely clear. One can say that the City of Williams' imagination, like the *Inferno* of Dante, can be visited under certain circumstances by the living. Into it, Simon sends his daughter and agent, Betty Wallingford, to exploit its timelessness and bring him back news of the future. Lester and Evelyn knew Betty in life and are drawn to her by memories of regret or of exploitation, following her back through the silent streets to her home and to the mage. Simon's intentions, however, do not end there.

It should be noted that in the whole of this novel there are almost no explicit mentions of the Christian faith—Lester and Evelyn both use words such as "God" and "Hell," but purely conventionally, with no sense that they have a meaning, and although Lester has a vision of the Cross at one moment, she does not recognize it. Still, Christianity is strongly present in the mind of Simon in distorted form. Through these distortions, it appears that he is trying in some way to make himself God. He knows of the Annunciation to Mary and of her impregnation by the Holy Ghost. In the tradition of his sorcerers' college, though, this was all a trick played by Joseph, who was no carpenter but a mage of great cunning. Joseph was attempting to create a child with mystic powers, as Simon does in his deliberate conception of Betty on Lady Wallingford. In Simon's view, the attempt was a failure, for the child Jesus could not protect himself from death, and though by power He managed to hold together body and soul for forty days after the Crucifixion, in the end that, too, came to nothing. Simon knows of, but reinterprets, the events of the Annunciation and Crucifixion. He has never grasped the point of Atonement, and he has no sense at all of love. What he is scheming, one cannot be sure, but apparently he aspires to rule the world, to make mankind into his worshipers, and to extend his power (via the body and soul of Betty) into the City and beyond.

He fails because Lester will not let him kill Betty, obstinately holding her friend's soul within its body; and also because Richard Furnival and Jonathan Drayton, the husband and fiancé of Lester and Betty respectively, are alerted by their increasing web of contacts with the living and the dead to watch and to interfere. One of the strong points of the novel is its series of animated descriptions of magical operations: the conception of Betty, Simon's creation of two *Doppelgängers* to send to other parts of the world (both presented in flashback), the sending-out of Betty, the first contact between Simon and Lester, and the two attempts to murder Betty. Possibly the most gruesome and convincing is Simon's creation of a body in which Lester and Evelyn are to live, when he still hopes to use the one and master the other. It is an ugly and crippled shape as befits the already disintegrating personality of Evelyn, but it brings the women from the City into London, and in a sequence of macabre scenes, they hobble awkwardly around the real world, undead but unrecognized.

One of Lester's five contacts with her husband comes when she speaks to him from the dwarf-body—and over the crazy croaking of Evelyn—*on the telephone*. Before she can do that, she has to master her own "unflesh" enough to beg the coins necessary from a passerby: an incident that takes place a million times a day, with varying blends of fear and charity, but one that is raised from insignificance to a scene of the greatest moment. The man who gives the two pennies will never know what he has done. He may, however, have "saved the world" with his awkward gallantry even to an old beggar-woman. One is allowed to think, moreover, that the action may have saved his soul. Such actions repeated as a habit certainly would.

In his double-plot of Lester and Evelyn and of Simon the Clerk and the kingdoms of the world, Williams is making a statement about the sources of true power and true significance. *All Hallows' Eve* was written in 1944 and is set in a world where the war has recently finished, seemingly in October, 1945 (for Halloween is October 31st). Its characters are therefore marked by wartime and are disposed to think that what is really important is politics. Jonathan Drayton is a serving officer, although also an artist, and Richard Furnival works for the Foreign Office, being given at one time the job of contacting Simon the Clerk and asking him to head a multigovernmental peace initiative, an evident parody of the moment when Christ in the wilderness is offered power over the kingdoms of the world.

Ironically, the war is less significant than Simon, and Simon less so than Lester Furnival, though she is but one of T. S. Eliot's faceless, commuting millions. If one were to sum up the intention of *All Hallows' Eve* in a phrase, it would be that it attempts to "sacramentalize the everyday." Williams emphasizes tiny gestures, such as apologizing, fetching a glass of water, raising one's hat like a gentleman even if approached by an old, ugly, shabby beggar-woman. A word he uses frequently is "courtesy." One of the better moments of Lester's life, in his view, is when she is pressed by what might be called mild "sexual harassment" by a man in a taxi but allows him to clutch at her for a while because she senses the fear and anxiety beneath the approach. Consideration for others, reluctance to be provoked, a certain ceremony of gesture: these mild and uncompetitive virtues, Williams urges, are signs of strength rather than weakness. The fact that Simon seeks for power and false advantage is a sign, in reality, that he needs protection.

In the novel, there is indeed what Eliot would have called an "objective correlative" of the view expressed above, in two paintings by Jonathan, Betty's fiancé. One is of Simon and his congregation, seen by some insight of the artist as a horde of beetles flying to a crack in a rock wall with everlasting nothing behind it. This is a great work, declares Simon, which has caught his own essence even in its apparent mindlessness; for as he says with approval, *"scientia adepti stultitia mundi"* ("the knowledge of the adept is foolishness to the world"). The world is right, however. The world is also seen in Jonathan's other painting, of which Simon does *not* approve, which shows the real city of London after an air-raid, a symphony of light radiating from a "hidden sun." The hidden sun, one has to say, is Christ, the Son, whose presence is always felt in the novel but never stated; the shattered beam in the foreground is the Cross, and the devastated city which nevertheless continues to live and to grow must be an image of mankind. What, though, is the artist's skill that enables him to penetrate Simon and to create a religious meaning of which he is not aware? Is it the secret power of Simon (as Simon, looking at Jonathan, seems to think)? No, declares Jonathan, and the rest of *All Hallows' Eve* backs up his answer. In a phrase of Joshua Reynolds, the secret of great art is "common observation and a plain understanding." For all his dealings with the supernatural, Charles Williams would be glad to have that phrase applied to his own writing. The important things are all in daily life.

T. A. Shippey

Bibliography
Carpenter, Humphrey. *The Inklings: C. S. Lewis, J. R. R. Tolkien, Charles Williams, and Their Friends*, 1978.
Eliot, T. S. "Introduction," in *All Hallows' Eve*, 1948.
Glenn, Lois. *Charles W. S. Williams: A Checklist*, 1975.
Hadfield, Alice Mary. *An Introduction to Charles Williams*, 1959.
Hillegas, Mark R., ed. *Shadows of Imagination: The Fantasies of C. S. Lewis, J. R. R. Tolkien, and Charles Williams*, 1979.
Moorman, Charles. "Myth in the Novels of Charles Williams," in *Modern Fiction Studies*. III (1957-1958), pp. 321-327.
_____ . *Precincts of Felicity: The Augustinian City of the Oxford Christians*, 1966.
Morris, Lawrence Allen. *Charles Williams' Novels and Possibilities of Spiritual Transformation in the Twentieth Century*, 1978 (dissertation).
Shideler, Mary McDermott. *Charles Williams: A Critical Essay*, 1966.
_____ . *The Theology of Romantic Love: A Study in the Writings of Charles Williams*, 1962.

THE ALLAN QUATERMAIN SAGA

Author: H. Rider Haggard (1856-1925)
First book publications: King Solomon's Mines (1885); *Allan Quatermain* (1887);
  Allan's Wife (1887); *Maiwa's Revenge* (1888); *Allan's Wife, and Other Tales* (1889);
  Marie (1912); *Child of Storm* (1913); *The Holy Flower* (1915); *The Ivory Child*
  (1916); *Finished* (1917); *The Ancient Allan* (1920); *Smith and the Pharaohs and*
  Other Tales (1920); *She and Allan* (1921); *Heu-Heu* (1924); *The Treasure of the*
  Lake (1926); *Allan and the Ice-Gods* (1927)
Type of work: Novels and short stories
Time: The late nineteenth and early twentieth century
Locale: Africa and England

Allan Quatermain, an African hunter and explorer, is continually drawn into a num-
ber of adventures, most of them dealing with the lost race theme and involving beautiful
women, often possessed of supernatural powers

> *Principal characters:*
> ALLAN QUATERMAIN, a white hunter and explorer
> HANS, his Bushman companion

Allan Quatermain's saga, recorded in some sixteen novels and a handful
of short stories, is, next to Edgar Rice Burroughs' Tarzan books, the most
detailed and inventive fantasy series that uses in such large measure the theme
of the lost race. *King Solomon's Mines* and its sequel *Allan Quatermain* made
the name of its hero a household word and forced Henry Rider Haggard to
return to the days of Quatermain's youth to find the stories that his public
demanded. Quatermain became the prototype for many subsequent fantasy
heroes: Tarzan of the Apes shares many qualities with him; John Carter of
Mars and the Barsoom novels owe a debt to his saga, as do Jimgrim and Tros
of Samothrace in the novels of Talbot Mundy; several of Arthur Conan
Doyle's novels, notably *The Lost World* (1912), and the more modern Gor
series of John Norman also exhibit characteristics of the Quatermain saga.

Haggard's hero is distinguished above all by strength of character. Time
after time, Quatermain demonstrates his moral fiber, his stubborn endurance.
He never gives up, even when nature is doing her worst. In *King Solomon's*
Mines, he and his companions cross formidable deserts to reach Sheba's
Breasts and the country beyond; in *Allan Quatermain*, he penetrates the most
dense and forbidding country that Africa possesses; in *King Solomon's Mines*,
he serves with courage and daring as a warrior in a Zulu impi; he faces with
nerves of steel many an elephant charge, and, in *Heu-Heu*, he negotiates with
cold courage a deep cavern at night in the company of his bushman companion
Hans simply to view the petroglyph of the devil-god Heu-Heu. In the trilogy
Marie, Child of Storm, and *Finished*, he shows what an extraordinary fighter
he is in scenes of terrible carnage and violence.

The sequence of the saga is curious and a bit difficult to follow. *King*

Solomon's Mines was written first, with no idea that it would initiate a chain of similar adventures all starring Allan Quatermain. The enormous success of *King Solomon's Mines* prompted Haggard to write a sequel, *Allan Quatermain*, in which he decided to kill his hero off. The last words in the book are written by Quatermain's best friend and companion on this adventure, Sir Henry Curtis, after Quatermain's death. The public was greatly disappointed at this turn of events, however, and Haggard understood that he was not yet finished writing about this character whom he had brought to such vivid life and fame.

In order to find material for more novels about Allan Quatermain, Haggard needed to return to the days of Quatermain's youth. *Allan's Wife* introduces the reader to Quatermain's early adolescence, his growth to rugged manhood, and his middle age. Several subsequent novels, including *Marie* and *Child of Storm*, are sandwiched into time periods covered in *Allan's Wife*. It is clearly impossible to regard the saga as a coherent, well-planned whole. As new events occurred to Haggard, he found a time period in which he could place them. The resulting inconsistencies and improbabilities make it impossible to work out a neat chronology for the saga.

Quatermain's adventures vary considerably, as novels within the sequence differ greatly in their atmosphere and evocative power. Novels such as *Marie*, *Child of Storm*, and *Maiwa's Revenge* are simple adventure stories, chronicles of the white man's invasion of the Zulu world and of the great Boer struggle. In these works, there are no grand civilizations of the past and few occult phenomena. These novels are similar to many other novels set on the South African veldt and to Haggard's own histories. They are filled with hardship, bloodshed, cruelty, and adventure on the grand scale. These, however, are not the novels for which Haggard is remembered.

Haggard's fame depends in large measure on the novels within the saga which are set in the rugged, unknown interior of Africa. Some of these novels are charged with occult or supernatural events, such as the visions of future events brought on by the fumes of the drug Taduki; the complete adventure set in the past, in which Allan and his companions participate through prehistoric alter-egos; and the uncanny visions in the Zulu wizard's hut in *Heu-Heu*. Most of the novels feature the lost race motif which Haggard made his trademark. The ancient map, the dead explorer, an unknown region, a select circle of fellow adventurers, and physical actions that tax the courage and strength of all participants: this formula is very old, but Haggard made it his own.

The circle of select companions is a particularly important ingredient in these adventures. Some of the companions, such as Hans, Sir Henry Curtis, Good, and Lady Ragnall, appear in several novels. The blond Sir Henry Curtis, fighting man without peer, is one of Haggard's finest characters, but the black African for whom he had such a high regard is given his moment as well. The redoubtable warrior Umslopogaas and his equally redoubtable counterpart Imbopa are warriors of the highest courage and valor. The bushman Hans is another of Quatermain's valiant companions; when the bushman dies in *The Ivory Child*, a victim of the elephant god Jana's fury, Quatermain writes "I wept." In the next chapter, he tells the reader that the death of the bushman was so distressing that it caused him to lose interest in everything. The fellowship and camaraderie among the adventurers, like the friendship between Doyle's Holmes and Watson, was one key to the popular success of the saga.

The women who inhabit the saga are all of a type, less individualized than the male characters. Unbearably beautiful, they are, with the exception of Marie Marais and Stella Carson, not touched. Quatermain preserves a deep and abiding love for his wives, and despite the charms of women such as Luna (Lady Ragnall), he remains outside any love relationship with them. Marie died for him, wearing a disguise of Quatermain's own clothing so that she was mistaken for her husband and shot by his enemies. Of Stella Carson, Quatermain writes in *Allan's Wife*: "I was broken-hearted, and broken-hearted I must wander to the end. Those who have endured my loss will know my sorrow; it cannot be written. In such peace and at such an hour may I also die!" Despite the appeal of the erotic creatures with whom he is continually thrown into intimate association on long and lonely treks, Quatermain cannot forget the loss of Stella and Marie.

Another essential element of the Quatermain saga is the lure of the "Dark Continent." Although expeditions were constantly being mounted into the interior of Africa, in Haggard's time the interior was still largely unknown. What lay in these regions was open to the imagination. Haggard's Africa is a mixture of fantasy and realistic description; he had spent some time in Africa himself and had seen the country and the peoples of which he wrote firsthand. Unlike Burroughs, whose Africa is entirely the work of a fertile imagination, Haggard buttresses his fantastic plots with closely observed detail which lends the novels a rich, authentic sense of place.

The charm of authenticity is not restricted to Haggard's description of the African settings. The weapons of the hunt and of the fight are described with loving care. No trek is attempted, no adventure begun unless the party is suitably armed. One is aware that the rifles and shotguns chosen are the right ones for such an occasion. Just as in Ernest Hemingway, one is sure that all descriptions of hunting and fishing equipment are accurate. It is such attention to detail that give the entire range of the African novels a richness of texture, providing an effective backdrop for the fantasy element.

Haggard is often attacked by his critics for his glaring solecisms, yet such errors did not diminish the interest and enthusiasm of his readers. Particularly in the Allan Quatermain saga, the writing suits the character of the narrator. Quatermain, who is for the most part presented as the author, is a bush hunter and cannot be expected to write with the precision of an Oxford man. The saga will still reward the reader with some of the greatest fantasy romance ever written, and the best of the Quatermain novels, *King Solomon's Mines*, will remain a standard work in the genre for generations to come.

Samuel H. Vasbinder

Bibliography

Cohen, Morton. *Rider Haggard: His Life and Works*, 1980.
Ellis, Peter Beresford. *H. Rider Haggard: A Voice from the Infinite*, 1978.
Haggard, Lilias Rider. *The Cloak That I Left: A Biography of the Author Henry Rider Haggard, K. B. E.*, 1951.
Menville, Douglas. "Introduction," in *Allan's Wife*, 1980.

ALRAUNE

Author: Hanns Heinz Ewers (1871-1943)
First book publication: 1911
English translation: 1929
Type of work: Novel
Time: Approximately 1870-1911
Locale: Germany, principally the Rhine region

In the decadent society of imperial Germany, Professor Jacob ten Brinken challenges God and Nature by creating a human through artificial impregnation in fulfillment of the ancient mandrake legend, resulting in the child Alraune, who appears to be the soulless incarnation of the myth, bringing easy wealth and ultimate destruction simultaneously to those around her

Principal characters:
> JACOB TEN BRINKEN, acting privy councillor, university professor, and researcher in artificial impregnation
> FRANK BRAUN, ten Brinken's nephew, a wild university student who becomes a world-traveling seeker of life
> ALRAUNE TEN BRINKEN, Jacob's adopted daughter and heir, the offspring of his experiment

Hanns Heinz Ewers was first introduced to the English-speaking public in 1917 when his 1905 essay "Edgar Allan Poe" appeared in New York literary circles. Introducing her translation of this essay, Adèle Lewisohn said of Ewers: "His conclusion is that the occult is so deeply rooted in our spiritual natures that the mind is our actual body, and the imagination our real mind— that as a phenomenon of nature there exists nothing more holy or more spiritual than the carnal." Ewers believed that this perception of the true nature of existence was confined to an elite, elevated above the mass by culture, heredity, or force of will. He treats this Nietzschean theme in a trilogy of novels described by fantasist Fritz Leiber as being "among the best of weird fiction." Though *Der Zanberlehrling* (1907; *The Sorcerer's Apprentice*, 1927) and *Vampir* (1921; *Vampire*, 1934) are powerful in their own right, *Alraune* is generally considered the finest of the three and Ewers' best work of fantasy.

Ewers himself was a controversial figure. His fiction was sometimes attacked as mere sensationalism—lurid sex stories laced with horror. That characterization seems particularly true of the three short stories published in America in *Blood* (1930) and of "The Execution of Damiens," translated by the author for John Gawsworth's *Crimes, Creeps and Thrills* (1937).

More sinister than Ewers' stories, though, were his politics: he became an enthusiastic Nazi in the 1930's. His last novel to see English translation, *Reiter in deutscher Nacht* (1932, *Rider of the Night*), is the tale of an exsoldier fighting the Allied occupation forces in the Ruhr which ends with a song of praise for Adolf Hitler and the other "patriots" struggling for Germany. Subsequently,

Ewers ghosted the notorious "Horst Wessel Lied" and wrote the official party biography of Wessel (1932) and the screenplay for the film based on his life. The Nazi streetfighter was elevated partly through Ewers' work into an official Nazi martyr, and his song became a patriotic hymn. Despite his sycophantic approach to the Nazis, Ewers fell into disfavor, and his books, except for *Rider of the Night* and *Horst Wessel*, were banned as politically suspect.

In *Alraune*, Ewers' mysticism and his obsession with blood lust and sex combine to produce a minor classic of dark fantasy. A dinner party attended by Frank Braun, the unifying character in Ewers' trilogy, is disrupted by an ancient mandrake root ("alraune" in German) falling abruptly from its place among the numerous curios on the wall. One of the guests then recounts the German mandrake legend:

> [A] criminal stripped naked as a pair of tongs and hanged at the crossroads, lost . . . his final seed, the moment his neck was broken. This seed falls to the ground and there germinates. Thence results an alraune, either a little man or a little woman. . . . It brought luck in lawsuits and in war . . . and drew money into the house. . . . With all that, the manikin was nevertheless a creator of pain and misfortune. All the other members of the house were hounded by ill-luck, and the possessor himself was led into avarice, lechery and criminality. In the end it brought its owner to a miserable death and sent his soul to hell. Nevertheless, mandrakes were much desired.

His imagination fired by this account, Braun (who is a Nietzschean hero, "beyond good and evil") proposes that his Uncle Jacob ten Brinken use his scientific skills in artificial impregnation to create a living alraune. Ten Brinken is to combine a condemned criminal's last seed with the earth itself, "the eternal prostitute . . . the most shameless, the most arrogant of all. . . . Then we shall see what truth there is in an old story. We shall be able to look down into the innermost bowels of Nature."

Subsequently, ten Brinken accepts Braun's challenge, enlisting his aid in locating a suitable mother in which the creature can gestate. The "father" is a brutal rapist-murderer whose execution is arranged according to the formula in the folktale. The subsequent story of Alraune's birth and growth into a young woman is superbly handled. There are constant hints of her possible supernatural origins and influences, though if taken singly, none seems beyond coincidence. Ten Brinken comes to believe that she is the embodiment of the ancient myth and chronicles all the "coincidences" in a leatherbound journal. As predicted by the legend, he grows increasingly wealthy from all investments relating to the earth—and increasingly contemptuous of any restraints, legal or moral, upon his activities.

When Alraune returns to the ten Brinken estate from a private school (which she has attended after being expelled from a convent school), no fewer than five men successively become ensnared by her, leading to the deaths of four of them and the disgraced exile of the other. One of these victims is ten

Brinken himself. As the legend predicted, he has been led (along his natural inclinations) into "avarice, lechery and criminality." While he is distracted by his obsessive lust for his adopted daughter, his enemies combine to overthrow him. Before his suicide, ten Brinken appoints the wandering Braun as Alraune's guardian during her minority, to ensure that Braun, the originator of the idea, will share his fate.

Ewers' work is not well-known today. In his native Germany, his fiction was banned by the Nazis; many copies of his books were destroyed in subsequent firebombings. After the war, his works were banned again because of his Nazi inclinations. His greatest influence on English-language fantasy may be indirect, through the work of S. Guy Endore, the translator of *Alraune*, whose classic *The Werewolf of Paris* (1933) shows a number of thematic links with Ewers. Ewers' fiction often chronicles (in occultist terms) the journeys of twisted souls down the "left-hand path." They are not always pleasant journeys, especially in the light of the parallel path of their author. As H. P. Lovecraft said, Ewers' best work contains "distinctive qualities which raise them to a classic level."

John D. Squires

Bibliography

Kracauer, Siegfried. *From Caligari to Hitler: A Psychological History of the German Film*, 1947.

Leiber, Fritz. "Frank Braun: Modern Sorcerer, German Don Juan, Nietzschean Nazi," in *Amra*. II, no. 42 (1966), pp. 11-16.

Mills, Richard. "Caverns of the Soul," in *Nyctalops*. II, no. 3 (January-February, 1975).

Ronay, Gabriel. "Germany: Vampire Horror Fiction, Blood and the Nazi Myths," in *The Truth About Dracula*, 1974.

THE AMBER SERIES

Author: Roger Zelazny (1937-   )
First book publications: Nine Princes in Amber (1970); *The Guns of Avalon* (1972);
   Sign of the Unicorn (1975); *The Hand of Oberon* (1976); *The Courts of Chaos* (1978)
Type of work: Novels
Time: The distant past
Locale: The kingdoms of Amber and Chaos and the shadow-worlds that lie between
   them, including Earth

*Corwin, a prince of Amber, awakes on Earth with amnesia, and in his subsequent
quest for his memory, he learns not only the secret of form and chaos but also the secret
of maturity as he strives desperately to save the universe from total destruction*

> *Principal characters:*
> CORWIN, one of the many children of Oberon, King of Amber
> OBERON, the King of Amber, long absent from his throne and
>   believed to be dead
> DWORKIN, a mad dwarf who holds the secret of Amber and the
>   family
> DARA, mother of Corwin's son, Merlin
> ERIC, a brother of Corwin who claims the vacant throne
> BRAND, a brother of Corwin and an agent of Chaos
> RANDOM, a brother of Corwin who exhibits the true traits of
>   leadership

Roger Zelazny's most significant writing has frequently exhibited the characteristic of the double quest, and the Amber novels are no exception. While the physical quests he sets for his protagonists are fairly obvious, the psychological quests are not, but they do follow a typical pattern. The story often begins with the protagonist disoriented or dislocated. Usually he is suffering from some personality fault; it might be simple immaturity, as it is in the Amber novels, or vanity, or something worse. Sometimes the fault is so severe that the character can be classified as neurotic. Carlton Davits of "The Doors of His Face, the Lamps of His Mouth" and Dr. Charles Render of *The Dream Master* (1966) are such characters. Typically, as Zelazny's heroes pursue their physical goals, they must also solve their psychological problems. They do this by learning from their accumulating experiences, and they usually succeed eventually in harmonizing the disparate aspects of their personalities, best represented by Sigmund Freud's id and superego. When they accomplish this, they reach a new and higher state of consciousness which also brings them mature love and happiness.

It is the psychological aspect of Zelazny's characters which makes them believable and human. Otherwise, they would remain typical larger-than-life science-fiction characters: immortal or near-immortal, stronger, taller, and more intelligent than mortal men and blessed with some exotic gift such as telepathy. It is often this superiority that creates the characters' psychological

problems. Early and easy success breeds false pride and creates expectations
that they cannot reach, and when defeat or rejection comes, they cannot
accept it.

The beginning of the Amber story introduces the psychological journey of
its protagonist. Corwin, a character modeled on the tarot Fool, awakes on
Shadow-Earth with a case of amnesia that has lasted since the time of Elizabeth I. He has had an automobile accident which broke both his legs and
left him with a head injury, which has triggered some sort of recall. From a
psychological point of view, Corwin is the alienated hero common to the fairy
tale. Although he does not yet know it, he has been pushed out of his home
in Amber, an excruciatingly painful experience that initiates his journey toward
maturity and self-awareness. His amnesia suggests that he has undergone the
metaphoric death of an old and inadequate self and has been reborn on a
higher plane of existence. The symbol of the new moon in the arms of the
old supports this hypothesis and further suggests that he is about to undergo
a process of psychological growth. Because of the amnesia, he is forced to
begin accumulating experience anew, like the tarot Fool with whom he is
identified. They both stand at the same point of development: still id-domi-
nated but with the superego about to assert itself. Both are still immature,
their egos not strong enough to integrate these conflicting systems of personality.

Throughout most of *Nine Princes in Amber*, Corwin struggles to free himself
from the psychological slavery of the id. It is obvious from his reactions that
he is operating under the pleasure principle, that Freudian function of the id
which immediately reduces tension, whether generated internally or exter-
nally, without thought of its consequences. To some degree, this posture is
forced on Corwin by his amnesia. Without memory of the past, it is difficult
to calculate the future consequences of his actions. He is alone, and his
memory has been jogged sufficiently so that he knows not to trust anyone.
Evidence gradually emerges which shows that he has never trusted any of his
brothers and sisters, with the possible exception of Deirdre. At this point in
the story, he does not even trust Random, the eventual king. He views him
as mean and devious and remembers those incidents in their youth when
Random played tricks on him. He continues to distrust him even after Random
helps him get to Amber and leads him through several dangerous traps set
for him by Julian and the others who are supporting Eric for the throne.
Corwin admits early in the novel that he feels a terrible sense of distance
from his brothers and sisters even though some of them are physically close
to him at the time.

There is, of course, other evidence of Corwin's id-domination. Initially he
is driven by his need to recover his memory, but when he finally does remember, he becomes driven by his hate for Eric and his desire for revenge. Even
his aspiration for the throne is selfish: he simply does not want Eric to have
it. This selfish attitude is characteristic of the id and usually lasts until early

adolescence, when the person begins to put the interests of others ahead of his own and learns to love for altruistic reasons. This is when the id gives way and the superego begins to emerge.

In Corwin's case, the emergence of the superego begins near the end of *Nine Princes in Amber*, in the scene where he is forced to watch Eric crown himself King of Amber. Corwin, beaten to his knees by Julian, is told to pick up the crown and hand it to Eric. Corwin ponders the situation, and after a momentary deliberation, he refuses; then he picks up the crown and proclaims himself king. Finally he throws it at Eric, hoping to put out one of his eyes. At this point, however, Corwin suddenly remembers the face of his father beneath the crown, at which he has been staring. This memory prompts Corwin's refusal to cooperate and attests to his awareness that the crown and what it symbolizes are more important than his own interests. His refusal eventually leads Eric to punish Corwin by putting out his eyes, an expensive payment for someone only interested in himself, especially when he knew his actions were futile and that he could have avoided the pain by simple capitulation. Corwin's actions betray an interest far beyond the immediate reduction of tension.

To support and emphasize the development of Corwin's superego, Zelazny fills *The Guns of Avalon* with grail-quest and other Arthurian imagery, which continues throughout the rest of the novels. Much as he used a body of Arthurian imagery to represent Eileen Shallot's neurotically romantic point of view in *The Dream Master*, Zelazny uses it here to represent Corwin's emerging concern for the ideal and the perfect, summed up for him by the city of Amber itself. Having now solved the question of his identity, Corwin is set upon a new quest, one befitting and symbolizing his psychological state. He sets out to restore the wounded land, whose injury he believes he brought about by means of a curse he placed upon it when Eric put out his eyes. The initial intensity of Corwin's sudden surge of idealism is symbolized by a concentration of clues near the beginning of the novel. Almost as soon as he arrives in Avalon, Corwin encounters a knight named Lancelot du Lac who is bleeding from a wound in the side and is resting against an oak tree. Dead upon the ground around him are six knights he has slain, a scene taken from the Tristan legends. Further, the name of the previous king of Avalon, he discovers, was "Uther," recalling Uther Pendragon, Arthur's father. Moreover, the black and white doves which Corwin released in Amber with messages for Eric tied to their legs arrive in Avalon. They suggest the black and white sails which are so important to the Tristan legends, although doves were also frequently associated with the grail knights; and in fairy tales, as Bruno Bettelheim points out, white birds, usually doves, represent the superego. Finally, there is the inescapable clue contained in the name Avalon itself, which is the name of the isle where the fatally wounded Arthur was taken and where it was expected that he would be healed so that he could some day return to his people.

The grail-quest elements also support the emergence of the superego because they emphasize the ideal and the perfect. The elements are those identified in *From Ritual to Romance* (1920) by Jessie L. Weston, who extracted them from the numerous Perceval, Gawain, and Galahad legends. The first element is the task of the hero, which is inevitably to restore the wounded land and thus revitalize the king; the land mirrors his condition. Such is certainly the case in the Amber novels. The city is first encroached upon by a black and twisted wood in the Vale of Garnath and is then assaulted by creatures from Chaos who travel to Amber by means of a black road. This is possible because Oberon, the king, lies imprisoned near the center of Chaos and is believed to be dead. Although not physically wounded, his powers are diminished because of his distance from the primal pattern which supplies energy to the city and his children. When Corwin sets for himself the task of eliminating the dark wood in Garnath, he does so out of guilt, a typical id motive. Later, when he chooses to join forces with Eric to save Amber and (although he does not yet know it) the sick king as well, he places other interests ahead of his own tension reduction. Clearly, Corwin's task has become that of the hero, to save the land and cure the king.

The second grail element, "the freeing of the waters," consists of literally bringing water to the drought-stricken land; such an event occurs at the end of *The Guns of Avalon*. Several times during the long battle with the forces of Chaos, lightning and loud thunder are mentioned; but there is no rain. Then, at the moment that the battle ends and the creatures retreat, rain begins to fall. The land has found relief and so has Corwin, at least temporarily. Psychologically, he has been under assault from his id, symbolized by the forces of Chaos, and he has beaten it into submission.

A third grail element present in the Amber novels is called "the Medicine Man"; this is one whose function is to cure the wounded king and thus restore the land. In Zelazny's series, this role is played by Corwin, who is ultimately responsible for restoring form to his universe. Even though he does not perform the act himself, he helps Random do it, and he made it possible both by seeing that the Jewel of Judgment was delivered to the future king and by teaching him how to use it. Not only does Corwin save his own universe, but he also may have created a new one when he used the Jewel to create an entirely new pattern.

A final grail element is called "the Perilous Chapel/Perilous Cemetery" and is characterized by a strange and terrifying adventure which threatens the life of the hero. It is orchestrated by forces which are evil, supernatural, and powerful, often involving a dead body on an altar, a mysterious black hand which extinguishes the tapers, and a terrible storm. Zelazny scatters these details throughout the last part of his story. The chapel is represented by Chaos itself, the body on the altar by Oberon's funeral, the black hand by Dworkin's sudden reversion to monster form and his attempt to grab Corwin with his clawed, black hand, and the terrible storm by the great form-destroying storm sweeping toward Chaos.

The buried grail motif with its attendant imagery clearly marks the emergence of Corwin's idealism and of his superego, but he must still learn to understand his id. Near the end of the novel, Corwin begins to recognize that there are discordant aspects of personality; he even recognizes manifestations of those aspects. It is not until later, however, that he realizes the full impact of what he knows. Zelazny dramatizes the monster in man's nature in three scenes which raise Corwin's level of awareness. The first occurs on the way from Avalon when he meets a beautiful woman who quickly seduces him. He discovers that she is wearing a mask, and when he removes it, he sees absolutely nothing behind it. The experience shocks him and prompts him to remark that there is some monster in all people. This observation is reinforced at the very end of the novel when he witnesses Dara, the mother of his son, change into a tall, horned, and magnificent creature, beautiful and horrible at the same time. It is reinforced again when, in *The Hand of Oberon*, Dworkin turns from human form to monster while Corwin watches; the mad dwarf's features begin to flow, and he grows taller and longer-limbed.

Corwin does not realize the full meaning of what he has seen, however, until after he learns that Dworkin is his grandfather and that Amber is itself only an illusion torn from Chaos and capable of being destroyed. It is not until the very end of *The Courts of Chaos* that he realizes that the monster he met in the girl who seduced him, in Dara, and in Dworkin, is indeed present in his own personality in some horrible form. He eventually understands that it is the nature of the universe that form be won from chaos despite the fact that neither can be complete without the other, since they depend upon each other for definition.

For both personality components to come ultimately under the control of the ego, Corwin must grow psychologically under the prompting of his accumulating experience, as the tarot Fool does, and there must be clear signs of this growth in the story line. The first of these signs occurs in Zelazny's adaptation of the Hanged Man tarot card, which shows a youth hung upside down on a cross several feet above the ground with his hands tied behind his back. Corwin encounters such a youth in *The Guns of Avalon*, except that here he hangs from the bough of a tree by means of a knotted rope attached to his right ankle. Later in the same novel, he dreams of the youth. Then, as he is making his way to Chaos with the Jewel in *The Courts of Chaos*, he passes through a place of bright nothingness and sees a man nailed to a wall upside down. In traditional tarot lore, the T-sign made by the youth hanging on the cross upside down is interpreted as the sign of the "Great Work" which requires the overcoming of the personality and the transmutation of the lower passions into pure gold. Once encountered, the person must accomplish regeneration for himself both consciously and voluntarily. The Hanged Man has surrendered himself to spirit and sacrificed his small desires for the greater one.

This is, of course, exactly what Corwin does: he turns his attention from his petty interests to those of perfection. That is indicated when he puts aside his hatred for Eric and joins him in the fight against the forces from Chaos who have invaded Amber. It is also an indication of Corwin's ability to suspend the process of immediate tension reduction and shows that his id is coming under control. It is no accident that when Corwin encounters a figure nailed to a wall in his journey to Chaos that it is that of a man and not a youth. Putting his concern for the universe above that of Amber marks yet another level of growth. The youth has become a man.

Yet another sign of Corwin's psychological growth is seen in Zelazny's equivalent of the tarot Wheel of Fortune card. While the Wheel is mentioned several times in the novels, Corwin's most significant encounter with it in *The Hand of Oberon* is in a scene where he watches the sky, half black and half like a bottle of colored sands, spin above him. That he seems to be at the hub of the wheeling sky is significant, for symbolically he represents the Fool encountering the Wheel of Fortune. This occurrence marks the time when the Fool's apprenticeship is over; from that moment on, he must rise and fall by his own choices. It also marks the beginning of the end of Corwin's adolescence. The Wheel is connected specifically with Chaos in the novels, so Corwin's apprenticeship will not officially and completely end until he accepts the ultimate reality of Chaos and the shadow nature of Amber. Then he will come to know the finer aspects of princeship and maturity: the power of creation, the value of relationships with others, and the happiness of adult love. Most important, he will come to accept man for what he really is.

A final sign of Corwin's psychological growth is found in his evolving relationship with the primal forces of the universe. Like the tarot Fool who comes to understand all the secrets of life and how to use them, Corwin also learns the nature of the basic forces that operate in his universe. This is evident when he masters the use of the Jewel of Judgment and when he comes to understand the value of interpersonal relationships. It is also reflected in his relationships with animals. In fairy tales, animals are recurring symbols for the id. When they are tame, the id is under control; when they are wild, it is not. As Bettelheim points out, the alienated hero succeeds because he is in touch with primitive, basic things, including rocks, trees, and animals; the simpleton (equivalent to the Fool) succeeds because he can tap his inner resources, which are represented by helpful animals.

Of the several encounters Corwin has with animals in the course of his adventures, three are of particular significance. On his way to Chaos, he meets a large jackal which symbolizes his efforts to keep the id under control. Even though it appears to be friendly, he is wary of the animal, and justifiably so, for it turns on him and he has to kill it. Also in his travels he meets a bird named Hugi with whom he has a continuing dialogue about the ego and the absolute. Finally, he rejects Hugi's arguments about merging with the absolute and eventually twists off the bird's head, this act representing Corwin's rejection of the dominance of the superego. Finally, near the end of *The Courts of Chaos*, he encounters a unicorn which he has seen earlier; it delivers the Jewel of Judgment from the abyss into which it has fallen and chooses Random as king. It does not pick Corwin as successor to Oberon, but Corwin himself no longer desires the kingship. He is the one who has made it possible for Amber to survive, however, and he is the one who teaches Random how to use the Jewel to save the universe. It is the unicorn's earlier appearance to him that permits him to fulfill his quest. Psychologically, the appearance of the unicorn represents the taming of both his id and his superego. The unicorn's own evolution, from a sexually significant, pre-Christian form composed of odd parts from strange beasts to a beautiful animal associated with Christ, is a metaphor for Corwin's own psychological growth.

Neither the id nor the superego will ever disappear, just as chaos and form will not. They are indigenous to man and the universe, and to achieve mental health, man must integrate these antagonistic systems within his personality. Only then will man find true, adult love which will permit him to know the ultimate emotional security of his existence; and only then can he dissipate the fear of death. To learn these lessons is painful, as Corwin discovers, but necessary if one is to bring meaning and significance to one's life; such is the message of the Amber novels.

Carl B. Yoke

Bibliography
Sanders, Joe. *Roger Zelazny: A Primary and Secondary Bibliography*, 1980.
———————. "Zelazny: Unfinished Business," in *Voices for the Future*, 1978. Edited by Thomas D. Clareson.
Yoke, Carl B. "Personality Metamorphosis in Roger Zelazny's 'The Doors of His Face, the Lamps of His Mouth,'" in *Extrapolation*. XXI (Summer, 1980), pp. 106-121.
———————. *Roger Zelazny*, 1979.

AMBROSIO
Or, The Monk

Author: Matthew Gregory Lewis (1775-1818)
First book publication: 1796
Type of work: Novel
Time: During the Spanish Inquisition
Locale: Madrid

Ambrosio, a celebrated monk, is seduced and corrupted by the forces of evil within and around him, provoking a series of physical and emotional cruelties unleashed against innocents in this universe of pain

Principal characters:
AMBROSIO, a Capuchin monk
MATILDA, his mysterious lover
ANTONIA, an innocent girl
AGNES, a cloistered nun
RAYMOND, her lover
LORENZO, her brother
THE PRIORESS, the head of the Convent of St. Clare
LUCIFER

Matthew Lewis never meant to be a rebel. The adolescent scion of a prominent but broken home, he wrote *Ambrosio: Or, The Monk* (commonly known as *The Monk*) before he was twenty, and he never matched its quality in any of his later works. *The Monk* itself seems to have been written primarily as entertainment (even its harshest critics were unable to deny its effectiveness in that respect). Its author, a genial if rather effete minor aristocrat, probably wanted his readers to regard the novel as simply an exciting diversion. Even so, the massive popularity of *The Monk* provoked more than a touch of scandal and revolutionized the Gothic genre, taking it to a level of horror that infuriated some and hypnotized others. Lewis broke with the norm for romance, and the break never healed.

Born an Englishman in the era of the French and Industrial Revolutions, Lewis had wandered about Europe during his teens, and through his travels he absorbed a substantial amount of German and French culture. It was not in his youthful nature, however, to attempt to convey the excitement of his time through a political or social treatise; beyond inclinations, he simply did not have the intellectual ability. Instead, he tried his hand at a romance in the Gothic style of Ann Radcliffe (in truth, Mrs. Radcliffe's famous novel, *The Mysteries of Udolpho*, 1794, was only one of many literary influences on his work). Although Lewis told his mother that he had written *The Monk* in a span of merely ten weeks, it seems more likely that he had been working on something Gothic for a good while, and that many of his earlier ideas became specific episodes in the final version of the book. In any case, the new novelist quickly found a publisher and soon *The Monk*, its title page graced only by the author's initials, was enjoying a fantastic success in England, Europe, and America.

Imitations could be found everywhere as well. Among the more obvious were *Manfrone, the One-Handed Monk* by Mary Anne Radcliffe (only the name, not the novel, linked her to posterity and the famous Mrs. Radcliffe) and *The Bloody Monk of Udolpho* by T. J. Horsley Curties (who contrived in his title to borrow equally from one and all). Lewis himself was accused of plagiarizing various authors, but he had freely listed his conscious sources in an advertisement to the original edition of his romance. While his unconscious borrowings extended far beyond the given list, it is fair to say that this young traveler had adopted and assimilated these subconscious sources rather than plagiarized them. A deluge of European influences became focused in *The Monk*, making it uniquely reflective of the cultural and social developments of the time.

In the first year after its publication, *The Monk* sold exceedingly well and garnered several encouraging reviews. All the encouragement evaporated when the still very young author, then a newly appointed Member of Parliament, elected to add his name and the initials MP to the second edition of his work. Soon thereafter, he found himself at the center of a social storm which raged for years, making him the object of everything from simple literary censure to outright moral· disgust. The storm was precipitated by Samuel Taylor Coleridge, not yet famous himself but already a literary critic, in an article which sharply questioned the propriety of a Member of Parliament writing a sensational work such as *The Monk*. Coleridge saw the novel as a work of uncommon talent, but talent betrayed by vulgar taste. Although he found some merit in the book, he felt obliged to condemn it as essentially pornographic. Lewis had included a number of blatantly sexual episodes in the book, and to make matters worse, had written a passage implying that the Bible itself contained suggestive material. Although Coleridge maintained a substantial objectivity in his review, he felt it necessary to protest this hint regarding the Bible.

To many Englishmen the idea of a junior MP squandering his ability on apparently indecent scribblings was more than disgraceful; it was obscene. A spate of anti-Lewis articles thundered down on the British public, who responded by flooding the booksellers with requests for the scribblings in question. Sales expanded with the scandal. The cost, however, was high: Lewis, a man whom Lord Byron would later describe as both good-hearted and dull, found his name vilified and his character libeled. The uproar was so general that a rumor persisted for generations of an attempt by the government to suppress the sale of *The Monk*. Although untrue, the rumor served to darken Lewis' reputation permanently, so that the nickname "Monk" virtually replaced his Christian name as far as the press and the public were concerned.

A shaken Lewis responded to the outcry by deleting or purifying many of the sexual allusions in the fourth edition of his work, to the extent, as Louis F. Peck has noted, that a reference to a character's "prostitution" became a reference to "what should be her shame." The much-abused biblical passage disappeared. Nevertheless, the basic content of the book remained the same and remained emblematic not only of Lewis' name but also of Gothic literature, with its suggestions of a fundamental change in the nature of things, of a world re-created by revolution. Curiously, of all the contemporary critics of *The Monk*, perhaps the most perceptive was the Marquis de Sade, himself in fact the kind of writer Lewis was only by rumor. Sade recognized the relationship between the sensational aspects of the horror genre and the cruel chaos of real revolution. In an age in which William Wordsworth grieved over what "man has made of man," the excess of *The Monk* was not pornographic; it was representative.

The Monk was, then, much more than its author intended it to be. Lewis deliberately packed his work with melodrama, giving the Devil a featured role in the story. Lucifer leads the novel's title character, Ambrosio the Capuchin monk, down the path of damnation, a jouney referred to often in literature; however, this particular journey, while highly derivative, is still extraordinarily wild and, for the reader, pleasurably exciting. Deliberately or not, the book presents the road to hell not so much as a miserable rush toward deserved punishment as an enticing trip into sensation. Illicit sex, gratuitous violence, and all the motions of evil carry Ambrosio down a giddy spiral into irreversible sin and its inevitable aftermath, an infinity of pain. The reader, of course, may vicariously experience all the thrills of the spiral without the agony of concluding it.

Yet the monk is not really a victim. Even before Lucifer sends the demon Matilda to tempt him to break his vow of celibacy, Ambrosio has already begun his voyage to hell. Although he is known to all Madrid as "The Man of Holiness," he is secretly an egomaniac, exulting in his power and fame, drawing the Devil to him by the very enormity of his pride. When Agnes, a real victim of the evil of others, begs him to help her early in the story, he refuses not out of deliberate malice but out of simple selfishness. Ambrosio is a priest, but his clerical garb merely disguises his utter lack of true holiness.

For that matter, no one in this novel is able to depend on those who should represent holiness. The young virgin Antonia is pursued by Ambrosio, her confessor, who first kills her mother and then rapes Antonia in the crypt of a convent. Ambrosio himself is initially led into lust by Matilda, whose features are the image of a Madonna but who is actually a devil in disguise. There is irony even in the fact that the totally unsuited Ambrosio is a monk at all. Left as an infant at the door of an abbey, he was reared in the monastery, and his vocation is more a matter of environment than inspiration.

As for Agnes, she is forced to take the vows of a nun and then tortured by a sadistic prioress for giving birth to an illegitimate child. Her lover, Don Raymond, escapes from the clutches of a ghost called the Bleeding Nun, but is unable to effect Agnes' escape from the Convent of St. Clare. Her brother, Don Lorenzo (himself in love with the ill-fated Antonia), looks to the Inquisition for justice; when the prioress is arrested in the midst of an elaborate religious procession, the list of her misdeeds so enrages the crowd that they become a mob. In an instant, worshipers become killers, and the prioress dies horribly.

Nothing spiritual can be trusted in the world of *The Monk*. The supernatural exists, but only in the shape of ghastly demons and anguished ghosts. Heaven is talked about, but no angel appears to save Antonia or help Agnes. Detractors and admirers alike have always agreed that Lewis breaks away from the genteel style of Ann Radcliffe, choosing to dwell deliberately on the sensational, the grisly, and the erotic, but his refusal to affirm the positive nature of the universe is finally a much more significant break with the Radcliffean philosophy of Gothic fiction. What he presents instead is a kind of travesty of the traditional Christian quest: a movement from seeming spiritual stability and the best of hopes to uncertainty, anarchy, even complete disintegration. Ambrosio travels the whole route, but no one else in the story is allowed to escape it entirely. Something fundamental has been lost or reversed.

In a universe such as the one Lewis offers to his readers, sexual energy is not a creative force but an annihilative passion. The illicit affair between Raymond and Agnes, although bonded by true love and honorable intentions, leads only to torture for both Agnes and the baby to whom she gives birth in a dungeon. Isolated in horror, she watches the infant die and decay on her breast while she lies sick and helpless. The prioress has determined that such should be the punishment for breaking the vow of chastity, and although Lorenzo eventually rescues Agnes, both Raymond and she must live out their lives with the memory of their murdered child.

Antonia's case is even more pitiful since the passion which engulfs her is not her own but Ambrosio's. After ravaging her in the crypt, the monk turns on the girl as if she were at fault: "What seduced me into crimes whose bare remembrance makes me shudder? Fatal witch! was it not thy beauty?"

Ambrosio thus inverts even the normal relationship between criminal and victim, a reversal seemingly confirmed by Antonia, who is almost glad when the monk stabs her. Dying, she tells Lorenzo that death itself is the only relief from the dishonor of rape. Out of passion has come the loss of both virtue and order. Neither the priest nor the girl can restore that which has been lost. Ambrosio has actually lost more than he knows. It is Lucifer who later gives him some very bad news: Antonia was his sister, he her mother's long-lost son. Now included among his crimes are matricide, incest, and fratricide.

No catalog of evil deeds, however, can explain Ambrosio's character in full. The book would truly be no more than the smut it was accused of being were the monk only a cardboard villain; but he is instead a complex figure. Rationalizing away his sins one after the other, he continually puts off repentance and reform in favor of selfish impulse. His behavior is always comprehensible, contemptible, and completely, distressingly human. His resemblance to the rest of humanity makes his end all the more frightening. Taken and tricked by a gloating Lucifer, he is hurled into a slow, agonizing death—an uncreation of sorts—to be followed by an eternity of despair, the completion of his journey to hell. The story ends with his death, but the horror will go on. While the monk and the prioress have both paid brutally for their transgressions, their violent deaths seem more like vicious sport than just punishment meted out by man and God. They have been killed, after all, by a mob and the Devil, and the evil which was at the core of their existence still flourishes as the book closes.

Innocence is no protection in this novel: Antonia is proof of that. A kind of goodness does survive in characters such as Raymond and Agnes, but they are described by Lewis as living out lives as "happy as can be those allotted to mortals, born to be the prey of grief, and sport of disappointment." Left in a vale of tears, the survivors have little enough to celebrate. After all the events, the deaths, the agony, what remains is endurance in the face of pain. Nothing especially positive has been found to offset that pain or to suggest that going through it leads to an eternity of joy. Unexceptional and inoffensive, Raymond and Agnes triumph in only the narrowest sense; they are not heroes.

Perhaps Coleridge was right to worry about the effect of *The Monk*—not the effect of its sexual material but the effect of its turning away from the ordered, the expected, the necessary victory of good within the universe. Lewis, too young to understand precisely what he was doing, pushed the Gothic away from the merely intriguing toward the truly disturbing. At the last, *The Monk* suggests that evil is more prevalent than good, that no one can escape agony, and that virtue is almost meaningless in whatever scheme of things exists—if any does. The fact that such horrifying suggestions are to be found in an enjoyable format merely makes them all the more disturbing. It is ironic that the author of such a disquieting work was himself neither an anarchist nor a philosopher. In 1818, a middle-aged Lewis died aboard ship while returning from a mission of mercy in Jamaica. It is more ironic that after death, he once more illustrated the macabre: his sea-buried coffin rose in its shroud like a sailboat and billowed away from the ship on its own voyage.

Mary Ferguson

Bibliography

Coleridge, Samuel Taylor. *Coleridge's Miscellaneous Criticism*, 1936. Edited by Thomas Middleton Raysor.

Fogle, Richard Harter. "The Passions of Ambrosio," in *The Classic British Novel*, 1972. Edited by Howard M. Harper, Jr., and Charles Edge.

Kiely, Robert. *The Romantic Novel in England*, 1972.

Peck, Louis F. *A Life of Matthew G. Lewis*, 1961.

Reno, Robert Princeton. *The Gothic Visions of Ann Radcliffe and Matthew G. Lewis*, 1980.

ANDROCLES AND THE LION
A Fable Play

Author: George Bernard Shaw (1856-1950)
First book publication: 1916; presented 1913
Type of work: Drama
Time: The second or third century A.D.
Locale: In and around Rome, Italy

Androcles, a Greek tailor and a Christian, pulls a thorn from the paw of a lion and survives to be spared by the very same lion who might have killed him in the Roman Colosseum

Principal characters:
ANDROCLES, a Greek tailor and a Christian who has a way with animals
LION, a maneater
FERROVIUS, a fierce Christian soldier
SPINTHO, a degenerate, cowardly Christian
LAVINIA, a beautiful, proud Christian
CAPTAIN, a noble Roman officer attracted to Lavinia
EMPEROR, a pragmatic ruler

George Bernard Shaw asserted that *Androcles and the Lion* was a "fable" play for children based on an old story familiar to them (preserved in *Attic Nights* by Aulus Gellius in the second century A.D.) which, nevertheless, had content for the "most mature wisdom" to consider. It is one of the shorter of the fifty-odd Shavian plays that were produced, among which it was about the twenty-fifth work staged—giving it a mildly interesting halfway-mark status in Shaw's monumental corpus. He gave an autographed copy to James Matthew Barrie, whose own famous fantasy play *Peter Pan* was staged in 1904. In his will, Shaw designated *Androcles and the Lion* as the work to be first printed in the now-curious "Shaw alphabet"—so done in 1962 based on a system developed by Kingsley Read. It is one of several plays in which Shaw treated the subject of Christianity, this time as a fantasy comedy and satire.

The Preface and accessory materials in a complete edition of *Androcles and the Lion* require three times the number of pages as the script itself, constituting a major analysis of the sources and cogency of Christianity. The play includes a prologue and two acts. In the Prologue, Androcles, while walking through the jungle, comes upon a wounded lion and performs his legendary act of mercy, while his erstwhile nagging wife Megaera abandons him in terror. In Act I, Androcles is captured in a sweeping arrest of Christians in preparation for a Roman circus/persecution. Others captured are the cowardly Spintho, who looks for a painlessly quick martyr's death as a guaranteed way to Heaven; and Ferrovius, a fierce but honest, strong man for whom the meekness demanded of good Christians requires a real if dramatically comic effort, especially when the asinine Lentulus slaps him in the face and tells him to "turn the other cheek." Finally, there is Lavinia, proud and lovely, who must relinquish much of her Christian faith to preserve the integrity of her spirit and the ability to face her own death, thus providing perhaps the most profound thesis of the play.

The three scenes of Act III show the fates of the captured Christians. Terrified, Spintho decides to sacrifice to the pagan gods and is accidentally devoured by the lion under the stands. Ferrovius loses his Christian control, kills six gladiators, and accepts a position in the Emperor's Praetorian body-guard. Lavinia's Christianity gives way to her courage just as the Emperor, impressed by Ferrovius' strength, calls off the slaughter. To oblige the crowd's desire for at least a bit of a show, Androcles agrees to be the lion's meal. The lion is, of course, the one he had befriended. The lion and Androcles literally waltz out of the arena up to the Emperor's box, whereafter Androcles escapes slavery because the lion protects him, and the captain visits Lavinia for conversations about, presumably, religion.

Shaw's characters always provide amusing surprises. While the traditional Androcles story calls for some heroism, the heroism in Shaw's version is not exactly where and what one expects it to be. The lion is a prominent character, but the temptation for cheap humor with a toothless beast is resisted. The lion is a realistic animal. He does not talk; he roars. He eats people and is dangerous to the end to all but Androcles. Moreover, if the viewer looks for the heroic in Androcles, he will be disappointed. He is not so much brave as he is neurotically sympathetic toward animals to the point of being a fool, and he is extremely lucky. His way with animals is completely worthless because no one else can learn it. If anyone in the story is heroic, it is Lavinia. Ironically, her courage grows exactly at the rate that her precious Christian faith diminishes. Always alert to the opportunity for humorous amusement, Shaw, as is proper for a teller of fairy tales, has named a number of the characters allegorically. Androcles' wife Megaera is named for one of the Furies; Ferrovius means "made of iron"; Lentulus, who foolishly taunts Fer-rovius, means "somewhat slow"; and Lavinia has the name of the wife of Aeneas, the first of the Roman emperors.

Cleverly appropriate diction and sweetly rational messages are the hall-marks of Shaw's work. *Androcles and the Lion* is an animal fable, and the script is therefore studded with references to cats, rams, lambs, snakes, boars, fish, goats, leopards, turkey-cocks, mice, and horses. Spintho is a swine, a snake, and a dog; Ferrovius is an elephant and a bull; and Lavinia is a filly. Furthermore, the play's subtitle of "fable" provides the occasion for Shaw to analyze that which is proverbial and clichéd. Here he takes a famous fable and makes its characters talk realistically. There is no stilted, melodramatic diction as the characters pass through traditional episodes of terrible ordeal,

Survey of Modern Fantasy Literature

keen suspense, heart-throbbing romance, and noble destiny; they speak naturally, even colloquially. The effect is sustained understatement, a most durable comic discourse. What is true and what is false in the fable and in reality is revealed with an adroit, surprising clarity that does not frighten but rather humors the audience because it is a beneficial experience.

Androcles and the Lion has a number of messages, one of which is that it pays to be kind to animals. Shaw had a deep commitment to the cause of preventing cruelty to animals, even as he understood and approved of scientific experimentation. Otherwise, nothing very constructive happens in the story. Androcles certainly does not grow or learn, and the captain is not converted by Lavinia. People are better off at the end of the story not because they know more, but because they are in stronger social positions than at the beginning. In Lavinia, faith fails in the face of pain, suffering, and death. Christian faith and pagan faith—Christian fables and pagan fables—are of the same value; neither tells the truth or yields a reliable theology. Church and state are never separate in established civilization. Religion is a tool of propaganda for preserving civil order. Christianity was once vitally revolutionary, but when it became legitimate, it became as fraudulent and superfluous as the pagan myths of Greece and Rome. The lion's way may be best: he is without speech and therefore without myth and illusion, as is Androcles with his natural rapport with animals. There is no apotheosis of a heroic character; that traditional episode is replaced by the spectacle of a crazy little man waltzing with a lion. As long as men are men, heroism and divinity are rarely to be found in them.

John R. Pfeiffer

Bibliography
Abbott, Anthony S. "The Triumph of Laughter: *Androcles and the Lion*," in *Shaw and Christianity*, 1965.
Berst, Charles A. "*Androcles and the Lion*: Christianity in Parable," in *Bernard Shaw and the Art of Drama*, 1973.
Brophy, Brigid. "The Way of No Flesh," in *The Genius of Shaw*, 1979. Edited by Michael Holroyd.
Chappelow, Allan. *Shaw—"The Chucker-Out,"* 1971.
Pearson, Hesketh. *G. B. S.: A Postscript*, 1950.

ANIMAL FARM

Author: George Orwell (Eric Arthur Blair, 1903-1950)
First book publication: 1945
Type of work: Novel
Time: The 1940's
Locale: A farm in England

After the animals of Farmer Jones overthrow their harsh human oppressors and establish a society in which all animals are equal, the pigs take control, subvert the revolution to their own ends, and twist the democratic ideal so that "some animals are more equal than others"

>Principal characters:
>FARMER JONES, the owner of Manor Farm
>NAPOLEON, a despotic pig
>SNOWBALL, his rival
>BOXER, a cart horse
>BENJAMIN, a cynical mule

Both in his life and in his writing, George Orwell was a tireless champion of freedom and human decency. His convictions led him, for example, to fight in the Spanish Civil War (where he was wounded); his books reflect the same concern for individual freedom and dignity. As an essential part of his resistance to oppression, he fought against the corruption of language and the cant, propaganda, and jargon of political life. Thus, for Orwell, politics and literature were always integrally related.

Yet *Animal Farm* (1945), he said, was "the first book in which I tried, with full consciousness of what I was doing, to fuse political purpose and artistic purpose into one whole." His beast fable became a powerfully effective vehicle for his vision. As J. R. R. Tolkien says in "On Fairy Stories" (1938), one of fantasy's principal functions is to assist the reader past knee-jerk reactions and clichéd understandings to a truer, more realistic view of life. The device of talking animals provided Orwell with the distance and artistic economy that enabled him to convey a clear view of the political realities of his time.

Fittingly emblematic of the oppressed, the underfed and mistreated animals of Manor Farm rise from their servitude and drive away Farmer Jones (the common name suggesting an Everyman figure). They create a new society governed by the principles of "Animalism," in which all animals will have their just share in the product of their own labor. The system is governed by the Seven Commandments, most of which prohibit the human habits of their former overlords: wearing clothes, sleeping in a bed, drinking alcohol. The last and most important Commandment is "All animals are equal."

In depicting the animals and in conveying his ideas about modern society, Orwell takes full literary advantage of age-old conventional portraits of animals. The sheep, for example, are thoughtless conformists; no matter what the circumstances are, they chant, "Four legs good, two legs bad." Benjamin the mule is "stubborn as a mule," and he cynically refuses to believe that any good change is possible. Moses the Raven, like a bird trained to a language he does not understand, croaks mechanically about Sugarcandy Mountain, where all animals go when they die.

The conventional image becomes most important, however, to the characterization of the pigs. Their traditional laziness and greediness are immediately shown when they choose to do the "work" of management rather than actual physical labor. They are also not content to share power with one another. A struggle develops between Snowball, who advocates a windmill, and Napoleon, who opposes it. Before the issue is resolved, the farm is attacked by Jones, aided by his neighbors, Frederick and Pilkington; the animals are victorious, although several, including Snowball, are wounded. Notwithstanding his "war record" and his powers of oratory, Snowball is driven from the farm by savage dogs that Napoleon has raised secretly. Thereafter, Napoleon claims that he always favored the windmill, and he consolidates his power by holding trials and commanding bloody executions. Soon he and his fellow pigs start sleeping in beds and drinking alcohol, and the Seven Commandments written on the wall become strangely altered. (For example, to the words of the Fifth Commandment, "No animal shall drink alcohol," are added the words, "to excess.") The final scenes show clothed pigs walking on two legs and playing cards with human beings. The new ruling class of pigs has become indistinguishable from the old class of human beings, and the final Commandment becomes "All animals are equal, but some animals are more equal than others."

The traditional steadiness and dependability of the horse is exemplified by Boxer, the cart horse. Boxer is an indefatigable laborer, and largely through his efforts is the windmill eventually built. His consistent answer to all problems is that he must work harder. He, however, like the other animals, has a poor memory, and when the Commandments are altered, he cannot remember the original form. Consequently, the pigs are able to control the other animals because they use words to twist reality. Because of the corruptions of speech and thought, the oppressed are never capable of seeing the actual situation.

Many of the characters and episodes have parallels in the history of Russian Communism. Snowball is the expelled Leon Trotsky, and Napoleon is Joseph Stalin, whose savage secret police (the dogs), showpiece trials, and purges were notorious features of his despotism. The windmill plan is suggestive of the quixotic five-year plans. The attack of the farmers suggests World War II, and Frederick and Pilkington seem to represent Germany and the Allies respectively. As Orwell maintained, he wanted to write a "counter-myth" to the Soviet myth, to bring home a clear picture of the corruption of the revolution to his compatriots who strongly supported the Soviet system. (One should recall that the book was written in 1943, when the English were still allied with the Russians.)

To solely limit the applicability of the book to Soviet history, however, would be a mistake. Orwell's tale speaks to all times and all situations in which political ideals are subverted, in which decency and freedom are undermined by power and dishonest use of language. *Animal Farm* continues to comment on history through its searing warning of the need for that integrity in thought and word that will bring man to a clear view of the political realities around him.

Douglas A. Burger

Bibliography
Lee, Robert A. *Orwell's Fiction*, 1969.
Meyers, Jeffrey. *A Reader's Guide to George Orwell*, 1975.
_____ , ed. *George Orwell: The Critical Heritage*, 1975.
Meyers, Jeffrey, and Valerie Meyers. *George Orwell: An Annotated Bibliography of Criticism*, 1977.
Williams, Raymond, ed. *George Orwell: A Collection of Critical Essays*, 1974.

APHRODITE

Author: Pierre Louÿs (1870-1925)
First book publication: 1896
English translation: 1900
Type of work: Novel
Time: 56 or 57 B.C.
Locale: Alexandria

A classic erotic novel describing the tragic consequences of a fierce but transient passion

Principal characters:
CHRYSIS, a courtesan
DEMETRIOS, a sculptor
BERENICE, Queen of Alexandria
BACCHIS, a courtesan
MYRTOCLEIA, a young dancer
RHODIS, a young flute-player
PHRASILAS, PHILODEMOS, AND NAUCRATES, philosophers

Aphrodite is one of the most outstanding productions of late French Romanticism. The popularity that it enjoyed in its own time and the reputation it has enjoyed since are to a great extent a result of its eroticism, but it is a work of considerable quality and serious intent. The prurience of the public's interest in it was one of the factors in Louÿs' despairing retirement from the world of letters at the height of his fame. His representation of ancient Alexandria as a quasi-Utopia of sexual license was but a means to a further end, and he was disappointed by those readers who considered it an end in itself.

Although *Aphrodite* makes no use of overtly supernatural apparatus, it clearly qualifies as a fantasy. The distant past in which it is set, although certain of its details are reconstructed with academic scrupulousness, is an imaginary world, a highly decorated, lushly exotic milieu where social relations are entirely erotic in character. The essence of the story is its characterization of passion as a quasi-supernatural force. The goddess Aphrodite does not appear in the story as an actual person—although her statue plays an important role in the consciousness of the characters—but her presence is nevertheless immanent. The emotion she personifies works upon the characters as a tyrannical caprice which toys with them roughly and carelessly. "As flies to wanton boys are we to the gods," observed William Shakespeare, in one of his more bitter moments, and that is exactly the existential situation of Demetrios and Chrysis as they are driven to damnation by their wholly irrational passion, which possesses each of them momentarily but irresistibly.

As the story begins, Chrysis, a courtesan of Jewish origin, seems to be in complete accord with her environment and in complete control of her life. She has enjoyed more than two thousand lovers, of both sexes, and is entirely happy with her circumstances. She is highly regarded by everyone she knows (professional jealousies aside). The same cannot be said for her counterpart in the tragedy, Demetrios. He is the lover of Queen Berenice, but he is also an artist and suffers the congenital dissatisfactions of his calling. Having sculpted Aphrodite in the image of Berenice, his affections have been transferred from the person to the image. Countless women desire him desperately, but he spurns them all, often cruelly. It is partly for this reason that, when he sees Chrysis one day and is seized by a sudden and illimitable desire for her, she is disposed to retaliate on behalf of her sex. A perverse whim drives her to set for Demetrios a price on her favors which is beyond reason: she asks him to procure on her behalf three objects, whose attainment will require robbery, murder, and blasphemy. Demetrios, beyond reason indeed, carries out this assignment.

Demetrios' passion dies as soon as he has completed his task. Ironically, when she discovers what he has done, Chrysis is overwhelmed by an appalling desire of like magnitude. He then requires of her as *his* price that she will wear the three gifts publicly, condemning herself to death by accepting responsibility for the crimes. Chrysis duly destroys herself for the sake of her passion, but carries it to the grave willingly enough. Demetrios, cold and uncaring again, goes free.

This main narrative is complicated by a number of auxiliary scenes that complement it by offering other representations of the tyranny and treachery of love. One of these, the most horrific, provides the climax of a feast given by the courtesan Bacchis, where three philosophers have debated the nature of love. The wisest of the three (and the least popular) is Naucrates, who defines love as "the name given to sorrow to console those who suffer." He adds the observation that "There are but two ways of being unhappy: to desire what one has not or to possess what one desires. Love commences by the first and finishes by the second." This, as Louÿs observes, is an essentially masculine philosophy, but in Alexandria as in his own world, it is the males who rule. This point is emphasized in the scenes featuring the agony of the deserted Berenice, and particularly one in which Berenice is reproached by her twelve-year-old sister for allowing a lover to obsess her so. The sister keeps her own lover under lock and key and uses him like a slave—but that, the Queen observes, is hardly love. (Berenice's sister, of course, later ruled in Alexandria herself; her name was Cleopatra.)

In the Preface to his story, Louÿs defends his representation of the ancient world as a world without sexual shame, presumably intending to turn aside criticism of his interest in "vice" by pleading accuracy of description. This is not so much dissimulation as a token gesture to contemporary morality. The point that he actually makes in the story, and at which he hints in the Preface, is much more profound than the mere contention that the Hellenized culture of ancient Egypt was little bothered by sexual taboos. His argument concerns the destructiveness of erotic passion, which is no less wickedly powerful in his imaginary Alexandria than in *fin de siècle* France. The only characters in the story depicted with genuine sympathy are young girls, especially Myrtocleia and Rhodis, Chrysis' child-lovers. Their devotion is both honest and uncorrupting, but they, of course, are very young, with time in hand to discover damnation. Louÿs carefully reverses the contention of the great majority of modern stories of love and sex, that love is good and merely physical relationships are bad. He argues that the opposite is true and attributes to his declaration an almost metaphysical significance.

Not many readers, of course, would accept the authority of this argument, and it is perhaps not surprising that Louÿs' Parisian contemporaries failed to see the wood while being titillated by the trees. The fantastic nature of the story provides a ready excuse for discounting its implication. This is why such a powerful and fascinating work is so frequently considered to be no more than a decorative item of soft pornography.

Brian Stableford

Bibliography
No listing.

ARACHNE

Author: Eden Phillpotts (1862-1960)
First book publication: 1927
Type of work: Novel
Time: Hesiod's "Age of Heroes"
Locale: Lydia, in Greece

A retelling of the story of Arachne and her challenge to Pallas Athene, with a new interpretation and a new moral

> *Principal characters:*
> ARACHNE, an artist in weaving
> MOPSUS AND POLYDORUS, her suitors
> PALLAS ATHENE, the goddess of wisdom
> HEBE, the goddess of beauty

Eden Phillpotts was the author of more than two hundred books, including novels, collections of short stories, plays, poetry, and children's stories. In the early part of his career, his realistic novels of Dartmoor life brought him a reputation as the poor man's Thomas Hardy, but he later branched out into science fiction, detective stories, contemporary novels and thrillers, leaving even that reputation in ruins. Perhaps the most idiosyncratic and distinctive aspect of his work, however, is to be found in a series of semiallegorical fantasies that rework the substance of Greek legend in order to infuse the ancient myths with a new and intrinsically modern moral significance. The novellas *The Girl and the Faun* (1916) and *Circe's Island* (1925) are among the best of these stories; but the best of them all is perhaps the novel *Arachne*.

The original story of Arachne is a kind of "just-so story," providing a fanciful explanation for the spider's ingenuity in weaving. It is also a tale of hubris, the fatal pride which occasionally led mortals to defy or challenge the gods. In this case, the weaver of tapestries, Arachne, boasted that she would make a picture that would shame the artistry of the goddess Athene and made good her boast, with the result that Athene destroyed her work in a fit of jealous rage. Arachne subsequently hanged herself and was turned into a spider in order to save her life and allow her to weave webs forever.

The essence of Phillpotts' approach to the moral revision of Greek myth is that he is rather in favor of hubris and thinks that it is good for men and women occasionally to challenge the gods. His fantasies would perhaps be too simple if this were all that there were to them, but he is also somewhat enchanted with the human failings reflected in the lives of the gods, and with unparalleled condescension, he permits himself to write tolerantly and satirically of their arrogance and jealousy.

In *Arachne*, the eponymous heroine becomes the protégée of Pallas Athene, who observes her flair for color and undertakes to teach her the art of weaving.

Unfortunately, being the goddess of wisdom, Athene cannot help throwing in a generous measure of philosophical enlightenment along with the practical advice. Arachne, although grateful enough for the instruction in weaving, has little interest in the goddess' reservoir of wisdom, and she even has the temerity to be skeptical of some of the sacred truths entrusted to her ears. At first, Arachne is shielded from Athene's anger by the generosity of Hebe, who sits in on the lessons and makes diplomatic intercessions on her behalf. The attention of the goddess of wisdom is also deflected by Polydorus, a patrician and suitor to Arachne, whose appetite for authentic enlightenment is unlimited and whose talent for flattery is scarcely less so.

Polydorus is appalled by Arachne's independence of spirit and desires that she should not only show a proper humility and gratitude in her dealings with her Olympian patroness, but that she should also conform to the social expectations of the day by taking her weaving less seriously and becoming a good and dutiful wife. Even Arachne's other suitor, Mopsus—who is far from being a patrician and has no enthusiasm for enlightenment—fears that she might get into deep water and wishes that she would settle down. Arachne, however, is so headstrong that her falling out with Pallas Athene is only a matter of time. The challenge of a contest is issued, the judges chosen (Zeus, Dionysus, and Hermes), and the work begun.

Arachne suspects that the verdict will go against her, and when Athene blasts her picture, she feels sure that the divine wrath of the goddess is sanctioned by the judges. In fact, however, Arachne has won a tremendous moral victory: the judges have decided unanimously in her favor, agreeing that while Athene's weaving is *technically* perfect, it lacks the certain special something that makes great art essentially human. Arachne's picture of the gods and their amours, although it manifests a heretical view of divine prerogatives, has this spark of life.

In *this* version of the story, Arachne does not hang herself, although Hebe tells Athene that she has done so and that she has been turned into a spider by Zeus. Athene is satisfied with this story and is thus prevented from pursuing Arachne further. Arachne, meanwhile, runs away with Mopsus to live peacefully under an assumed name. By this time, Polydorus has withdrawn his suit, feeling that it is bad for his image to be mixed up with someone who has earned the disfavor of the goddess of wisdom. He becomes an academic, instead.

The story is full of digressions and philosophical asides that make it seem occasionally ponderous and silly, but these observations need not be taken too seriously and do not detract too much attention from the central story line. Phillpotts seems to have been enjoying himself in writing the book, and his enjoyment communicates itself throughout the text. The tone is always light, and the main aim is always entertainment. *Arachne* is by no means a great book; but it is an exceedingly pleasant one, frequently amusing and sometimes subtle in spite of the characters' tendency to pontificate. It has a hint of seriousness that keeps it from being inconsequential.

Brian Stableford

Bibliography
Girvan, Waveney. *Eden Phillpotts: An Assessment and a Tribute*, 1953.
Phillpotts, Eden. *From the Angle of 88*, 1951.

ARCHY AND MEHITABEL

Author: Don Marquis (1878-1937)
First book publication: 1927
Type of work: Short stories
Time: 1916
Locale: The United States

Archy and Mehitabel reflect the concerns of Americans in their stories and adventures

> *Principal characters:*
> ARCHY, a cockroach who was once a poet
> MEHITABEL, a cat of Bohemian tendencies

To those reared in the decades since the advent of comic strips and movie cartoons, the notion of a wise-cracking rabbit like Bugs Bunny or a politically sophisticated 'possum like Pogo is not uncommon. To the readers of Don Marquis' humorous column in the New York *Sun* on March 29, 1916, however, the topic of the day might have come as a surprise. For it was in this column, "The Sun Dial," that the work of a very small poet and contemporary commentator appeared. That commentator's name was Archy. According to Marquis, a cockroach was seen painfully jumping from one key to another on Marquis' old typewriter. When Marquis reads what the insect has written, he is surprised to find that Archy is the recipient of the human soul of a dead poet. Because of his dual nature of insect and poet, Archy has received a number of benefits, not the least of which is the ability to see life from both sides, from the human viewpoint as well as the animal's. This perspective insures Archy a unique view of the comedy of life. Yet another perspective is added by the character of Mehitabel, an aging but still desirable alley cat.

These two little creatures brought fame to Don Marquis; few who read and enjoy *Archy and Mehitabel* know, however, that Marquis was also the author of several novels, several collections of sketches featuring nonanimal characters, and even a play or two, including a Passion play, *The Dark Hours* (1924, produced in 1932), that had a short run on Broadway. Few know the story of his life, which was marked by illness and the tragic deaths of his two children and his two wives. Today Marquis is honored for his creation of the sensitive and gentle Archy and the free-spirited Mehitabel, whose words and stories reflect the critical view and often biting humor of the author.

Archy is a particularly adroit creation, a poet with a traditional poetic *Weltschmerz*, a Byron of the drains who suffers for his art. He even has the tragic experience of seeing a critic, Freddy the Rat, eat his poetry, expressing scorn as he munches on the verses. Archy's only hope is that in the next life he and Freddy will exchange places; then Archy will ignore the poetry and eat Freddy instead. Archy the suffering poet is also a commentator on the news of the day. In one sentence he can issue a call for volunteers in the fight against people who poison roaches and water bugs, and in the next comment on the post-World War I economy and say of the high cost of living, "it isn't so bad if you/ don't have to pay for it." When he comments on Prohibition Archy says it "makes you/ want to cry/ into your beer and/ denies you the beer/ to cry into"; while later, of repeal he says, "it may not have improved the country but it has improved the liquor."

Archy's poetry leads him into science fiction when he communicates with Mars by radio and discovers that he is the Martians' favorite poet. Later, inflamed by reading some verses by Rudyard Kipling, he launches into a burlesque:

> the cockroach stood by the mickel
> wood in the flush of astral dawn
> and he sniffed the air from the hidden
> lair where the khyber swordfish spawn.

Ever the consummate poet, Archy experiments with versification and form, limited only by his inability to use the shift key: capitalization and punctuation are impossible.

Archy the sensitive poet is balanced by the worldly-wise cat Mehitabel. A modern female, Mehitabel reflects the new morality of the 1920's; she is free-living, free-drinking, and free-loving. Her motto, *toujours gai* (in American English, "wotthehell wotthehell"), reflects her unconcern with anything but living life to the fullest today. Her attitude of breezy unconcern causes many anxious moments for her biographer, Archy. Once Mehitabel was a pampered housecat, but she grew tired of the confinement and ran away. She prefers life on the streets where she can come and go as she pleases, even though she knows that she will undoubtedly end up on the garbage scows of the Hudson River. In her personal life, Mehitabel experiments with free love, scorning traditional marriage as "one damn kitten after another"; but that is exactly what she gets from her liaisons with the battle-scarred Toms who join her on the fencetops for a midnight howl. When her kittens invariably appear she is affectionate though absentminded and inevitably loses them. Her usual reply to Archy's inquiries about the kittens is "What kittens?"

When Marquis spent a few years in Los Angeles as a screenwriter, his experiences in the movie capital provided many stories for Archy and Mehitabel to tell. Archy suffers from a black depression as he contrasts the name of the city—the City of Angels—with the moral vacuum he senses there. Frustrated in his battle against depravity, Archy hitches a ride home to New York in an airplane. Mehitabel, ever hopeful, tries to break into the movies; she is thrown out of every major studio and leaves Hollywood with her only souvenir, a litter of platinum blond kittens. After losing them in the desert, she tours the Southwest with a handsome coyote. Home in New York once again, Mehitabel has a litter of very strange kittens who prefer bones to cream and studded collars to ribbons. Undaunted, the brave little mother rents them out to the dog-and-pony show.

Despite the humor, Marquis' concern with the values that he saw in the decades of the 1920's and 1930's shows through. He portrays a self-centeredness in Mehitabel that, while funny in a cat, can lead to tragedy for the humans on whom Mehitabel is modeled.

The Archy and Mehitabel columns which Marquis wrote between 1916 and 1925, the later columns for *The Saturday Review of Literature*, and the pages written from time to time for *Collier's* filled three volumes when they were finally collected. They are *Archy and Mehitabel* (1927), *Archy's Life of Mehitabel* (1933), and *Archy Does His Part* (1935). The three volumes were anthologized as *The Lives and Times of Archy and Mehitabel* (1935), still available today. E. B. White's Introduction to that volume sums up Archy and Mehitabel's contribution: they "performed the inestimable service of enabling their boss to be profound without sounding self-important, or even self conscious."

Julia R. Reed

Bibliography
Anthony, Edward. *O Rare Don Marquis*, 1962.
Bier, Jesse. *The Rise and Fall of American Humor*, 1968.
Blair, Walter, and Hamlin Hill. *America's Humor: From Poor Richard to Doonesbury*, 1978.
Lee, Lynn. *Don Marquis*, 1981.
White, E. B. "Don Marquis," in *The Second Tree from the Corner*, 1954.
Yates, Norris. "The Many Masks of Don Marquis," in *The American Humorist: Conscience of the Twentieth Century*, 1964.

ARTHUR REX

Author: Thomas Berger (1924-   )
First book publication: 1978
Type of work: Novel
Time: The legendary early Middle Ages; traditionally, the sixth century but with the weapons and chivalric traditions of the thirteenth
Locale: England, Scotland, Wales, Ireland, and Brittany

In a legendary medieval period of chivalry and magic, Arthur and his knights reenact the classic adventures of the Round Table

Principal characters:
ARTHUR, King of Britain
GUINEVERE, his reluctant queen
UTHER PENDRAGON, Arthur's father
LANCELOT, the greatest knight of his time
TRISTAN, a mournful and ill-fortuned lover
ISOLD, a lady fated to unhappiness
GAWAIN, a cheerful lecher and valiant knight
PERCIVAL, a clumsy giant and lovable innocent
MORDRED, a malicious schemer
MERLIN, an enigmatic magician
MORGAN LA FEY, Arthur's half-sister and an enchantress
THE LADY OF THE LAKE, Arthur's supernatural patroness

Thomas Berger's *Arthur Rex* was seen by some as a parody of the Arthurian legends much in the manner of Berger's parody of the hard-boiled detective novel, *Who Is Teddy Villanova?* (1977), which immediately preceded it. This misunderstanding of the work is similar to the erroneous view that *Little Big Man* (1964), which is actually a picaresque comic novel about the West, is merely a flippant parody of the traditional formula Western. In actual fact, however, Berger began as a realist in *Crazy in Berlin* (1958), and he has maintained the tone of comic realism in the three succeeding Reinhart novels, including the recent *Reinhart's Women* (1981). It is a more accurate view of Berger to say that, far from being either a parodist or a practitioner of fashionable "fabulation," he is a novelist with a personal comic vision. In style and point of view, his work often resembles that of Henry Fielding or that of Mark Twain in his middle period (a strong influence on Berger, although Ihab Hassan has noted parallels with Saul Bellow). Berger has strayed from realism to write comic works in various genres. *Arthur Rex*, however, is not a parody of the Arthurian legends, but a comic and at times romantic re-creation of them.

In *Arthur Rex*, Berger presents the Arthurian legend in swaggering medieval splendor. Most of the familiar characters are present and reenact their ritual roles, coming to life through the charm of Berger's style, which combines fresh, modern vigor with mannered, archaic idioms. Here is Berger's description of young Arthur's first sight of Guinevere from a meadow outside King Leodegrance's castle:

> And it happened that though it was a gray day and the heavens of a color like unto dull pewter, Arthur did become aware of a golden radiance coming from one of the towers of the castle, and he looked towards it, but it was so bright that he could not distinguish its source, and he decided that it was again Merlin with some cunning alchemical device.

In Berger's vision of a timeless legendary medieval world, magic and the supernatural play almost as great a part as in Sir Thomas Malory's *Le Morte d'Arthur* (1485). That is, they intervene frequently and shape the action, but in the end, the characters reach their fates by virtue of their own choices. Sometimes magic is explained away as an illusion created by someone's advanced knowledge of science, but this shallow device is itself satirized. Magic does exist as a potent entity in the book, and the magic is not all of one kind. Merlin himself confesses that he does not fathom the feminine magic of the Lady of the Lake, the sorceress who takes on the responsibility for much of the feminine enchantment (attributed to various witches and deceitful ladies in earlier versions). Berger makes the Lady of the Lake into an archetype of the "feminine principle," and her powers constitute one of the most pervasive and subtle influences in the saga.

Berger's treatment of the Arthurian characters varies in its success. Merlin is somewhat philosophical and pedantic but not quite the eccentric, absent-minded schoolmaster of T. H. White's *The Once and Future King* (1958). Arthur is a true idealist who turns a little cynical and resigned over the years. Arthur's foster brother, Sir Kay, receives unaccustomed attention as a comic foil for Arthur and his knights. Kay, the seneschal, is a gourmet cook and connoisseur of wines, yet he longs for recognition as a knight. The result of this desire is a series of misconceived quests and amusing pratfalls.

Arthur's father, Uther Pendragon, is another comic figure, although he appears only briefly early in the tale. Berger presents Uther as a lusty, beef-eating Englishman in the mold of Fielding's Squire Western. Indeed, Uther sometimes sleeps with his hounds, and it is a running joke that his son Arthur meets Uther's bastards all over the kingdom during all the years of his reign.

Perhaps Berger's finest characterization is his Guinevere. When first seen, she is a provincial girl, angry over the fact that her canary has been killed by Arthur's falcon (a fateful overture to her unhappy marriage). Guinevere grows in majesty and stature after her marriage to Arthur, and her humanity is enlarged by her long affair with Lancelot. Although Guinevere is sometimes shrewish in her relationship with Lancelot, she merits the reader's sympathy. As in other versions of the Arthurian saga, Lancelot is characterized as longing for a moral perfection to match his skill at combat. While a sympathetic character, he is scarcely the most enjoyable person with whom to enjoy an illicit love affair, and the reader finds Guinevere's frequent displays of anger and exasperation understandable. Her ire is tempered by wit and unswerving loyalty. In fact, Berger's Guinevere is probably the most compassionate and credible treatment of this character in all the major versions since Alfred, Lord Tennyson's *Idylls of the King* (1859-1885). Moreover, in later sections of the novel, Guinevere is transformed from a lovable (if sometimes petulant) queen and mistress into a woman of tragic stature.

Of the other characters, Gawain, depicted as a combative but essentially sanguine womanizer, is impressively done. Gawain's chief fault is jealousy of other knights, a failing he rises above as he grows in maturity. Less impressive is Tristan, a melancholy lover for whom Berger has difficulty creating sympathy. In fact, the greatest failure in Berger's treatment of the saga is probably his rather tedious handling of the Tristan/Isold material, even though both of his Isolds are well drawn. Berger succeeds in restoring to passionate romantic love a sense of mystery, but it is through his Gawain and his Lancelot and Guinevere that he accomplishes this.

Berger's two triumphs of characterization in the final third of the novel are Mordred and Percival. The handling of Mordred is not unexpected: Berger gives him a certain amount of Freudian motivation—after all, Arthur is his father and his parentage is both illegitimate and incestuous—but surprisingly, part of Berger's success is in his eschewing subtlety in drawing Mordred. The usurping prince is sketched in bold strokes as a melodramatic villain, a pure combination of ambition and malice, untroubled even by personal vanity.

In contrast to Mordred, Percival is a surprise. A lumbering, ungainly knight with old, ill-fitting armor, Percival is all good-natured innocence and naïveté. Yet despite his simplicity, or rather because of it, he triumphs in one crisis after another, although he is at times subjected to comic embarrassments. The characterization of Percival is a notable achievement for Berger, one which allows him to celebrate a theme found in much of his other fiction (most notably the Reinhart novels): the "innocent triumphant" or the victory of a quixotic "holy fool" over the trials of existence.

In the last quarter of the retelling, Berger deals admirably with the tragic ending of the saga. Arthur, Guinevere, and Lancelot all acquit themselves nobly in the tragic conclusion to the experiment of the Round Table. Lancelot and Guinevere become truly repentant in cloisters, and Arthur dies heroically in his final struggle against Mordred. If Arthur's death is his payment for his early incestuous mating and siring of Mordred, it is also a victory because it destroys Mordred, the evil that Arthur's transgression had engendered. When last seen, Arthur's body is being borne away to Avalon by three ladies. The three feminine spirits are described as Guinevere, Morgan la Fey, and the Lady of the Lake, "the not-so-wicked, the not-so-virtuous, and the supernatural." Berger's final comment is that "in these fair laps we must leave King Arthur, who was never historical, but everything he did was true."

The ending underscores Berger's purpose in this retelling: his concern has not been to re-create any kind of historically plausible Arthur and Camelot, as Rosemary Sutcliff attempted in *Sword at Sunset* (1963); instead, Berger has sought to reanimate and enrich an enduring legend. Nevertheless, his version aims at a kind of truth—not the truth of history, but the truth of myth and the imagination.

Berger's *Arthur Rex* is an American homage to the Arthurian saga that ironically enough atones for Twain's debunking of the matter of Arthur in *A Connecticut Yankee in King Arthur's Court* (1889). It draws on many earlier versions to aim at an encyclopedic completeness. In its sophistication about sex, its sure narrative art, the complexity and skill of its characterizations, and its mastery of a sure comic touch, Berger's work surpasses in many ways the rival modern versions of the Arthurian epic by John Steinbeck, T. H. White, and Mary Stewart. Its sheer audacity and liveliness make it a fantasy novel likely to be read frequently in years to come.

Edgar L. Chapman

Bibliography

Cleary, Michael. "Finding the Center of the Earth: Satire, History, and Myth in *Little Big Man*," in *Western American Literature*. XV, no. 3 (Fall, 1980), pp. 195-211.

Hassan, Ihab. "Conscience and Incongruity: The Fiction of Thomas Berger," in *Critique: Studies in Modern Fiction*. V (Fall, 1962), pp. 4-15.

Hughes, Douglas. "The Schlemiel as Humanist: Thomas Berger's Carlo Reinhart," in *Cithara*. XV, no. 1 (Spring, 1975), pp. 3-21.

Schickel, Richard. "Interviewing Thomas Berger," in *The New York Times Book Review*. April 6, 1980, pp. 1, 21-22.

AT SWIM-TWO-BIRDS

Author: Flann O'Brien (Brian O'Nolan, 1911-1966)
First book publication: 1939
Type of work: Novel
Time: A manic blend of past and present
Locale: Ireland

An indolent Irish college student attempts to write a novel blending myths, themes, and characters from other works, and as he writes, he supplies ironic commentary on his own life and on the events in his fantastic novel

> Principal characters:
> THE NARRATOR, a Dublin college student who is writing a novel
> THE NARRATOR'S UNCLE, a typical Dubliner with whom the narrator lives
> DERMOT TRELLIS, a novelist character in the narrator's novel
> JOHN FURRISKEY, the intended villain in Trellis' novel
> PEGGY, a domestic servant, the intended victim in Trellis' novel
> ORLICK TRELLIS, a bastard son of Dermot, himself a novelist
> SHEILA LAMONT, Orlick's mother
> SHORTY AND SLUG, Irish cowboys

One critic has suggested that Flann O'Brien's *At Swim-Two-Birds* contains some thirty-six different prose styles and some forty-two extracts from other writers; other counts might go higher. This comic novel wildly combines Irish legends, literary spoofs, messages from horse touts, extracts from other books, lists of aphorisms, lists of irrelevant information, puns, flights of outrageous fancy, religious tracts, and all sorts of material one would never dream of finding side-by-side in any conceivable piece of writing, much less in a novel. What most complicates this work, however, is that it features a novel-within-a-novel-within-a-novel. Like James Branch Cabell's *The Cream of the Jest* (1917) or Robert Coover's *The Universal Baseball Association* (1968), O'Brien's novel develops multiple story lines, each line operating on a different fictional level. It introduces an unnamed narrator who is writing a novel in which the central character, Dermot Trellis, is a novelist whose characters write a novel in which Trellis is himself a character, subject to their manipulations as they are to his.

This circular arrangement logically follows the aesthetic credo of O'Brien's narrator, who holds that "a satisfactory novel should be a self-evident sham to which the reader could regulate at will the degree of his credulity." The narrator, himself an unmistakable parody of James Joyce's Stephen Dedalus, also states that each character in a novel "should be allowed a private life, self-determination and a decent standard of living." A third tenet suggests that the modern novel should be "largely a work of reference," borrowing its characters from other works of literature.

Accordingly, the narrator structures a novel that borrows not only characters but also prose styles from many other literary forms, interrupting his narrative with biographical reminiscences and self-conscious commentary on his own writing. The narrator's intrusions and digressions can only remind the reader of Laurence Sterne's *Tristram Shandy* (1760-1767), and, indeed, it seems to be O'Brien's intent to satirize almost every aspect of Irish and English literary history. Even American literature gets a nod from the author, both in the way his multilevel structure closely parallels that of Cabell's *The Cream of the Jest* and in his parody of the Western, featuring cowboys who do their cowpunching in Dublin.

Insofar as any single plot can be said to run through this novel, it charts the rebellion of a group of characters against an author, their despotic creator and ruler. O'Brien's narrator creates Dermot Trellis, a novelist intent on writing a book that will "show the terrible cancer of sin in its true light and act as a clarion-call to torn humanity." To do this, Trellis plans to chronicle the corruption of a virtuous woman, Peggy, by a man of great depravity, John Furriskey. He creates both characters and prepares his readers for Peggy's impending corruption and ravishment at the hands of the villainous Furriskey. What Trellis does not understand is that Furriskey has a will of his own, quite unlike that ascribed to him by the author. Furriskey is really a mild-mannered and proper man who wants only to marry Peggy, settle down, and start a family. When Trellis is awake and writing, Furriskey must act as the writer commands, but when Trellis sleeps, his characters lead the independent lives they desire, eventually drugging him to insure his sleeping.

This confusing interchange between author and characters reaches its extreme when, in one of his rare waking moments, Trellis writes into existence a second woman for Furriskey to ravish, Sheila Lamont. When Trellis sees how attractive his new character is, however, he loses control and rapes her himself. A fully grown young man, Orlick Trellis, is the immediate offspring of this rape, and as soon as Orlick realizes that he possesses literary talent, he begins writing a novel in which he can punish his father by subjecting him to various violences and indignities. Finally, determined to guarantee their independence from their novelist-creator, Orlick and the other characters place the novelist on trial for his life. The trial goes badly for Dermot, but he is "rescued" from his accusers when his maid accidentally burns the manuscript pages in which Trellis had first created his characters.

In its delightful send-up of literary forms and narrative conventions, *At Swim-Two-Birds* anticipated by some thirty years the basic techniques of the contemporary metafictional novel.

Brooks Landon

Bibliography
Clissman, Anne. *Flann O'Brien: A Critical Introduction to His Writings*, 1975.

AT THE BACK OF THE NORTH WIND

Author: George MacDonald (1824-1905)
First book publication: 1871
Type of work: Novel
Time: The nineteenth century
Locale: England

Little Diamond is taken by the North Wind on a series of journeys and adventures which culminate in a visit to the mysterious land at her back; he performs various good deeds before dying young and returning to his spiritual home at the back of the North Wind

> Principal characters:
> THE NORTH WIND
> DIAMOND, a little boy
> FATHER AND MOTHER, his parents
> NANNY, a ragged little girl
> OLD SAL, her guardian
> MR. COLEMAN, a business man
> MISS COLEMAN, his daughter
> MR. RAYMOND, a kindhearted gentleman

At the Back of the North Wind is by far the longest and most ambitious of George MacDonald's children's fantasies, combining, in a way that none of the others attempt to do, an allegorical and religious fantasy with a grim social realism. The little-boy hero, symbolically called "Diamond" (named after his father's favorite horse), is the son of a London coachman and sleeps in the hayloft over the stable where "big Diamond," the horse, lives. Through a tiny knothole in the wall, he hears the North Wind talk to him. She appears in the form of a beautiful woman and takes him on her back at night on great journeys over land and sea—sometimes on errands of mercy, but quite as often for purposes of destruction. On one such trip over London, he sees a ragged little homeless girl, Nanny, and he helps and befriends her.

Diamond is one of the child saints of Victorian literature, never behaving in a selfish or even a childish way and never losing an opportunity to do good to others; on one occasion, for example, he intervenes to stop a neighbor, a drunken cab-driver, from beating his wife. What saves this, the realistic side of the book, from complete implausibility is the way in which his friends, including Nanny, find Diamond impossibly priggish and, in the end, avoid him. A number of clues, particularly his constant ill-health, suggest that he is not long for this world, and the book concludes with his death.

Interwoven with the realistic narrative of the life of the London poor is the story of Diamond's relationship with the North Wind—his frequent references to whom the others interpret as a sign of his growing illness. Although at first sight, she seems similar to Irene's great-great-grandmother in *The*

Princess and the Goblin (1872), she is a much more disturbing and ambiguous figure; for, while she is kind and protective toward Diamond, she can also be a bearer of destruction and terror. As an avenger, she takes on the shape of a great gray wolf to frighten an evil nurse; she also sinks a ship at sea, drowning all of the innocent sailors. The reader is clearly meant to be puzzled—as Diamond himself is—by her moral significance.

When he questions her about her two sides, she enigmatically insists that she is always the same person. Most plausibly, she represents Nature both in a beneficent, Wordsworthian sense and also in the guise of an arbitrary destroyer. As the story makes clear, however, that with greater knowledge there is nothing arbitrary about her actions. The ship she sank, for example, belonged to Mr. Coleman, Diamond's father's dishonest employer, who is thereby ruined, and it is made clear that for him, bankruptcy is the first step toward moral regeneration. Nevertheless, the sailors are still drowned, and Diamond's father loses his job.

Even more mysterious is the beautiful land at the back of the North Wind. MacDonald spends some time trying to link it with other literary references; in spite of discrepancies, he insists, there really *is* a common reality to which the various symbolic accounts of previous fantasies relate. One such report, MacDonald says, is that of a young peasant girl, Kilmeny (a character from the verse tale in James Hogg's *The Queen Wake*, 1813), who had visited "a land where sin had never been." Another is a "great Italian of noble family who died more than five hundred years ago." His name was Durante, "and it means Lasting, for his books will last as long as there are enough men in the world worthy of having them." After this neat play on Dante's family name, the description that follows makes it clear that this land at the North Wind's back is the Earthly Paradise (*Purgatorio, XXVII-XXXIII*, c. 1320), a symbolic re-creation of the Garden of Eden, where man can live in an unfallen state. The use of direct reference to Dante to evoke a state of unfallen nature supports the hints that the North Wind is a personification of Nature. Her apparent cruelties can be seen through the eyes of faith (or the eyes of a child) as further ways to good.

The symbolism of the names reinforces this thesis. As MacDonald, a chemistry graduate, knew well, a diamond is a natural form of carbon, the essential element in all life and the hardest gem known. The rich man, Mr. Coleman (or "Coalman"), is also made of the same element, but coal is dirty, black, and fit only for burning. Significantly, North Wind is also the Angel of Death and thus provides the motif that gives the story so much of its power. Diamond is able to hold communion with her because he is, almost from the start, a holy child marked by Death, who eventually claims him for her own. Seen thus, the episodic action of the story takes its shape from Diamond's accommodation of death as something natural and inevitable, as he learns to accept and love her rather than fear her.

This theme of the acceptance of death is central to many of MacDonald's other fantasies, most notably *Lilith* (1895), his last book, but nowhere else in his writings does he attempt to combine such highly complex symbolism with the grim social conditions of Victorian London. The result is only partially successful. Although the initial encounter with the North Wind is as good as any of MacDonald's magical transitions between real and fantasy worlds, much of the rest of the story is too longwinded and drawn-out for modern tastes. Perhaps in recognition of this, MacDonald never again attempted the same kind of synthesis; subsequently, his two worlds were always presented as separate and distinct from each other.

Stephen Prickett

Bibliography

Faben, Aline Sidny. *Folklore in the Fantasies and Romances of George MacDonald*, 1978 (dissertation).

McGillis, Roderick. *The Fantastic Imagination: The Prose Romances of George MacDonald*, 1973 (dissertation).

Manlove, C. N. *Modern Fantasy: Five Studies*, 1975.

Mann, Nancy Elizabeth Dawson. *George MacDonald and the Tradition of Victorian Fantasy*, 1973 (dissertation).

Pierson, Clayton Jay. *Toward Spiritual Fulfillment: A Study of the Fantasy World of George MacDonald*, 1978 (dissertation).

Prickett, Stephen. *Romanticism and Religion: The Tradition of Coleridge and Wordsworth in the Victorian Church*, 1976.

——————— . *Victorian Fantasy*, 1979.

Reis, Richard H. *George MacDonald*, 1972.

Wolff, Robert Lee. *The Golden Key*, 1961.

THE ATLAN SERIES

Author: Jane Gaskell (Jane Gaskell Lynch, 1941-   )
First book publications: The Serpent (1963); *Atlan* (1965): *The City* (1966); *Some Summer Lands* (1977)
Type of work: Novels
Time: The distant past
Locale: The Northern and Southern Continents and Atlantis

The picaresque story of the travels and trials of Cija, who is born into a royal family and taken by fortune to far places until her perseverance and luck bring her back home

> *Principal characters:*
> CIJA, the daughter of the queen of an independent city-state
> SMAHIL, her half-brother
> ZERD, General of the Northern Army; later Emperor of Atlan and Cija's husband

The Atlan series by the prolific British novelist Jane Gaskell (great-grand-niece of the Victorian novelist Elizabeth Gaskell) has been inaccurately referred to in print as a trilogy, but the series contains either four or five parts, depending on which editions one examines. The original hardbound British editions included *The Serpent* (1963), *Atlan* (1965), *The City* (1966), and *Some Summer Lands* (1977). When a British paperback edition appeared, *The Serpent* was split into two volumes, entitled *The Serpent* (1975) and *The Dragon* (1975). American hardbound editions (from St. Martin's Press) have followed the five-part paperback division but with a delay of more than a decade: the American edition of *The City*, for example, was published in 1978.

In any format, the series is unlikely to be greeted with indifference: one reader may find a vivid painting of a fantastic world while another may find an overblown work verging on parody. Questions of taste cannot be resolved in a review, but some reasons for this disparity of judgment may be suggested.

The setting for the series is Earth, a very long time ago (as Gaskell reveals in a note to *The City*). The parts of the story located on familiar continents (presumably Europe and Africa) take place in regions vaguely named "the Northern Continent" and "the Southern Continent"; but the physics and biology of the setting are not those of the familiar Earth.

Many of the stories are set in Atlan, a rich and mighty land in the middle of the Atlantic. The scientists of Atlan have protected it from outside invasion by removing the air from a shell-like area doming the island continent. Note that the effect is produced by scientists, not by magicians: there is no hint of a supernatural cause for the vacuum barrier, and its dissolution is worked by ordinary means.

The fauna of the setting is clearly fantastic: military mounts may be horses or mules, but the preferred steed is something like a vicious, powerful, untiring ostrich. Some of the inhabitants of Atlan ride "saurians" (dinosaurs, that is); putting humans and dinosaurs in the same geological period is as fantastic as mixing humans and dragons. The Southern Continent also contains tribes of primates, less intelligent than humans but smarter than the great apes—they use weapons (of sorts) and possess a rudimentary form of language. Surprisingly, the human-apeman union is fertile. Finally (and even more surprising), the Northern Kingdom contains intelligent humanoid lizards kept as servants, slaves, or sometimes concubines; the warrior Zerd is the product of this unusual pairing. Other fabulous monsters move through the pages: pterodactyls fly through the air and an especially interesting creature burrows through the mud. This huge snakelike beast captures its prey alive and, like a spider, cements its victims to the wall of its burrow to ripen. There is no question that the setting of the Atlan series is colorful.

The plot—the adventures of the princess Cija—may remind some readers of Voltaire's *Candide* (1759) or perhaps of Terry Southern's *Candy* (1958). Cija runs from peril to peril, variously kidnaped, beaten, cast adrift, abandoned, chased, threatened with rape, and generally menaced by monsters, deserters, thieves, bandits, an evil high priest, a mad scientist, a pimp, a demigod, and other villains. Among her lovers, she numbers her half-brother Smahil, a half-lizard general, and an apeman with whom she lives for a season, a diarykeeping Jane to his inarticulate Tarzan. She experiences the range of social levels in her world, at one time the Empress of Atlan, at another, a scullion in a shabby inn. As this account may suggest, the novels are episodic, and if there is any overriding movement to the five parts of the story, it is simply the constant desire of Cija to find a place where her husbands, captors, lovers, persecutors of every rank and station will leave her in peace.

Gaskell's style is markedly personal. In the dialogue, one finds occasional terms of British slang coming from the mouths of the characters, who call one another "right nits," "stripey," and the like. Nor does Gaskell worry about anachronisms: the officer in charge of a detachment of soldiers is termed the "CO," roads take "hairpin bends," characters warn one another in bad weather, "We'll be bronchitic by evening." These usages must be conscious choices on the author's part: in a note at the beginning of *Atlan*, Gaskell remarks, "Although *Atlan* happens B.C., the translation Christening is used in preference to some phoney word like Dedicating-to-God." One may question the rightness of the choice, but the implication remains that the dialogue of the characters was specifically written to sound modern, supporting the fiction that the stories are translations of Cija's diary, made by a translator determined to avoid archaisms.

The fiction of the modernizing translator may be more acceptable to the reader than the passages of description, which strike one as overly florid. Gaskell likes to coin words, but all the mintings are not equally sound: "Gurgles and plashing led us to water wimpling-dimpling over a tumble of quartz rock that was honestly crystal in places." This is not an exceptional example, but rather one that is characteristic of prose that John Clute, writing in Peter Nicholls' *The Science Fiction Encyclopedia* (1979), called "occasionally overheated."

The Atlan series may not be to everyone's taste, but the books show inventiveness of incident, and the publication of the series is a testimony to the staying power of Plato's myth of the lost continent.

Walter E. Meyers

Bibliography
No listing.

ATLANTIDA
(L'ATLANTIDE)

Author: Pierre Benoit (1886-1962)
First book publication: 1919
English translation: 1920
Type of work: Novel
Time: 1896-1903
Locale: The Sahara Desert

The story of an officer in the French Foreign Legion who discovers the last remnant of the empire of Atlantis, ruled by a beautiful queen in the depths of the Sahara

    Principal characters:
        ANDRÉ DE SAINT-AVIT, an officer in the French Foreign Legion
        JEAN-MARIE-FRANÇOIS MORHANGE, a brother officer
        ANTINEA, Queen of Atlantis
        ETIENNE LE MESGE, a scholar
        CÉGHEIR-BEN-CHEIKH, a Targa tribesman

L'Atlantide was Pierre Benoit's most successful novel and became even more celebrated through its cinema versions—the first a French silent film in 1929, the second a German version in 1933. It was translated into English as *Atlantida* in the United States and as *The Queen of Atlantis* in Britain. Benoit was correctly charged with imitating H. Rider Haggard's *She* (1887), but the imitation is not very close, and there is an unmistakable Frenchness about Benoit's novel which gives it a distinctive flavor.

The novel is rather slow-moving and takes an unnecessarily long time getting its real story under way, packing it into a flashback contained within a frame narrative and further interrupting it with digressions of dubious pertinence. It is also a rather oblique tale; the author's beating about the bush extends to a seeming reluctance to allow the reader any substantial view of Antinea, the pivot on which the plot turns, so that she remains a much more shadowy figure than her prototype, Ayesha. In addition, the text is strewn with footnotes and with interminably careful pseudoscholarly references which constitute an awkward and inadequate attempt to create an atmosphere of plausibility.

The frame narrative begins with Lieutenant Ferrières of the third Spahis, stationed at Hassi-Inifel in 1903, preparing to mount an expedition into the central Sahara. It then goes painstakingly back in time some months to explain how Ferrières first met Captain André de Saint-Avit, the man he is to accompany on the journey.

The *real* story, however, is Saint-Avit's account of an earlier adventure in the Ahaggar mountains, when he undertook an exploratory mission in the company of Captain Jean-Marie-François Morhange, from which he returned alone. Saint-Avit explains how he and Morhange were drugged with hashish by their native guide, a Targa who initially gave a false name but who turned out to be Cègheir-ben-Cheikh, no friend of France. In their drugged state, they were kidnaped and taken to a lost city which proved to be the last remnant of Atlantis, where they found preserved much of the lost knowledge of the ancient world, salvaged from the library at Carthage.

In this lost city, Saint-Avit and Morhange meet three aged Europeans, including the scholar Etienne le Mesge, who explains much to the knowledgeable Morhange. They also meet Antinea, the beautiful queen whose origins are obscure, and who pursues on behalf of her sex a crusade against the male of the species, avenging betrayals committed throughout the centuries. She has Europeans kidnaped by her servants, allows them to fall in love with her, and then destroys them, keeping their corpses (embalmed in bronze) as trophies. Morhange resists her, but Saint-Avit cannot, and ultimately obeys her command to kill his brother officer before escaping to safety with the aid of the Targa (who owes him a favor) and of a captive girl from the outer world. The magnetism of Antinea's personality, however, proves so great that Saint-Avit cannot keep away forever, and he is resolved to join the crowd of bronze-clad ex-lovers.

Atlantida is, of course, an absurd story; no amount of dressing-up can possibly conceal the fact that the plot is manifestly ridiculous. What saves the book from being merely silly, however, is the fact that it recapitulates one of the most common erotic fantasies: the masochistic ideal of a cruel and irresistible femme fatale who can make any man into a willing slave by the sheer sexual power of her presence. Another writer toying with the same basic plot might have been seduced into making Morhange the hero because he almost turns the tables on Antinea, but Benoit is sensible enough to consign the erudite captain to his appropriate fate and to make Saint-Avit the real hero. It is Saint-Avit, after all, who experiences the full force of the perversely perfect infatuation. This is the one advantage that *Atlantida* retains over *She* (it is in all other respects an inferior book): it is honestly self-indulgent and refuses to let morality or masculine pride triumph over the secret desire for captivity and abasement.

Not everyone, of course, will appreciate this fantasy. It is doubtful whether Benoit's work, as a vulgar echo of Leopold von Sacher-Masoch, could ever attract as many admirers as, say, the work of Dennis Wheatley, which has equally vulgar echoes of the Marquis de Sade. Nevertheless, *Atlantida* is not for this reason a work without interest—rather the opposite, since cheap fantasies of sadism are so commonplace—and it has its place in the history of fantastic fiction.

Brian Stableford

Bibliography
No listing.

ATLANTIS

Author: John Cowper Powys (1872-1963)
First book publication: 1954
Type of work: Novel
Time: The twelfth century B.C., some decades after the fall of Troy
Locale: The Mediterranean island of Ithaca and parts of the Atlantic Ocean

Beset by change and religious argument, the aged Odysseus resolves to leave his island kingdom of Ithaca, and, with a group of varied companions, he sails to the site of recently sunken Atlantis and beyond

> *Principal characters:*
> ODYSSEUS, the aged King of Ithaca
> TELEMACHOS, his middle-aged son, priest of Athene
> NISOS, a youth of noble birth, servant to Odysseus
> ZEUKS, an elderly farmer
> ENORCHES, priest of Orpheus
> NAUSIKAA, the Princess of the Phaiakians, later the Queen
> PAN, the goat-legged god
> ATROPOS, one of the Fates, appearing as an old woman
> MYOS, a housefly
> PYRAUST, a small brown moth

John Cowper Powys is almost unknown within the fantasy genre, although most of his fifteen novels include fantasy elements, while in mainstream English literature, he is regarded as a major figure. Two of his brothers also became outstanding writers, while several others of his siblings (he was one of eleven children) achieved some degree of artistic fame. By profession, Powys was a university lecturer, spending thirty years of his career in the United States but returning home to Great Britain upon his retirement.

Atlantis is typical of his work in that it is a long and complex novel involving many characters, written in a free-flowing, rhetorical style. Its subject matter is derived from Homer's *Iliad* (c. 800 B.C.) and *Odyssey* (c. 800 B.C.), of which Powys made a lifelong study. This expertise is evident from the manner in which the material is used, even though considerable license has been taken with characters and situations. A later Powys fantasy novel, *Homer and the Aether* (1959), draws on the same source material.

Very little about *Atlantis* is simple, straightforward, or easily explained. The characters seem to dance around one another in groups of varying size, conversing, learning, and, in particular, declaiming their own philosophies of life (sometimes introspectively and often at great length). The situation of Odysseus is a pitiful one: it is seventeen years since his wife, Penelope, died, and he has become an old man, living simply and celibately in his palace, looked after by only three female servants and Nisos. He has lost the respect of his subjects. He cannot abdicate in favor of his son, because Telemachos is the leading priest on Ithaca and is disinterested in ruling. Quite suddenly, Odysseus realizes how much he hates this sedentary life and the political and religious wrangling that accompanies it. A last voyage of adventure will, he feels, bring him to life again—and this it does, restoring him physically, spiritually, and sexually to something like his former self. He seizes upon the chance to use the ship of Nausikaa, a visiting princess, and he does not care if he never returns to Ithaca. The news of his kingdom being usurped in his absence reaches him *en voyage* and leaves him unmoved.

Of the other male characters, Enorches provides much of the novel's mysticism. Contradictory in his actions and allegiances, he is certainly a revolutionary, opposing Odysseus, trying to depose Telemachos, reviling Zeuks, and imprisoning Nisos, yet he is unable to influence events significantly. Zeuks is a rambunctious, Falstaffian character. A natural rebel, he proclaims that "Prokleesis" (defiance or challenge) is the secret of life, and he acts as a mouthpiece for Powys' own views. Nisos, the strong-minded teenaged boy, is a type of character Powys had not previously used, even though he represents Powys' oft-repeated theme that the development of sexual sensation leads to self-revelation.

Powys is not regarded as a great interpreter of female character, and that is true here; none of his human females undergo much development. Nevertheless, the cause of feminism *is* advanced by this novel. Just as male supremacy is reported to have been overthrown among the gods, so female emancipation is seen to be occurring among mortals, with a state of equality being achieved even if not the promised female domination. The virgin female (young or old) is used here by Powys to represent power and a store of knowledge.

The Greek gods are so busy coping with their own troubles that only Atropos makes an appearance significant to the plot, pushing Odysseus into his westward journey, while Pan helps one of the young female characters to achieve some self-enlightenment by increasing her sexual awareness. At the same time, the ambience of the period is such that the gods are constantly in the minds of the people, with Olympian events coming quickly into public knowledge via the oracular talents of prophetesses.

Nonhuman characters play a whimsical and peculiarly important part in the novel, with Powys anthropomorphosizing a pillar, an olive shoot, the club of Herakles, a fly, a moth, a hawk, and even the separate hairs of Odysseus' beard, to the extent that they can all think and, in most cases, converse with one another. The club of Herakles is intended as a phallic symbol: ever since the death of Penelope, it has leaned against the wall in the palace's entrance corridor. During the novel, Odysseus picks it up again and carries it with him on all his adventures, on Ithaca and abroad. Most important of all these nonhuman participants are the moth, Pyraust, who is arguably the most highly developed female character in the novel, and the fly, Myos, who displays male chauvinism.

Sexual symbolism appears in several guises. Apart from the club of Herakles and the role of sexual awareness in leading to greater self-understanding, there is an identification throughout of sex with adventure and life, and the dagger given to Nisos directly before he dives to investigate Atlantis with Odysseus is a symbol of his manhood. Nor does the sex in the novel need to be fully consummated for its effects to be felt. Only the sexual attraction between Odysseus and Nausikaa is actually consummated; several other cases of sexual attraction are important to the plot, and there are many hints of bisexuality or androgyny. In addition, there is recurring life/death symbolism in the novel. The author stresses the coexistence of opposites (male/female, life/death, peace/revolution), suggesting that they can always achieve a balance in life and sometimes a fusion.

The present-day parallels can be clearly seen. The overthrow of the Olympian gods by formerly inactive Titans is a warning of the growing strength of Russia and China. The feminist propaganda is striking, written at a time when the current feminist movement had not yet been formed. When, in the final chapter, the ruler of Atlantis is killed, after attempts at genetic manipulation, Powys is warning against uncontrolled scientific advance.

Atlantis is by no means a well-known novel, even among admirers of Powys. It is at present out of print in Great Britain and has never been published in the United States. It is difficult reading; the cast of characters is perhaps too large, and their lengthy and repetitive speeches frequently impede the plot. By the time the author's narrative thrust becomes apparent, the reader may have lost interest. Despite its important qualities, *Atlantis* is likely to remain a minority taste.

Chris Morgan

Bibliography
Brebner, John A. *The Demon Within*, 1973.
Cavaliero, Glen. *John Cowper Powys: Novelist*, 1973.
Collins, H. P. *John Cowper Powys: Old Earth-Man*, 1966.
Knight, G. Wilson. *The Aturnian Quest: John Cowper Powys*, 1964.

BACK TO METHUSELAH

Author: George Bernard Shaw (1856-1950)
First book publication: 1921; presented 1922
Type of work: Drama
Time: 4004 B.C.-A.D. 31,920
Locale: The Garden of Eden, London, Galway Bay, and an unspecified location

A *"metabiological pentateuch" intended to enshrine in a series of parables the mythol-ogy of a new creed appropriate to the twentieth century*

> Principal characters:
> ADAM, the first man
> EVE, the first woman
> CAIN, their son
> FRANKLYN BARNABAS, a clerical gentleman
> CONRAD BARNABAS, a professor of biology
> BURGE-LUBIN, President of the British Islands
> JOSEPH POPHAM BOLGE BLUEBIN BARLOW, O. M., an elderly gentleman
> ZOO ENNISTYMON, a young girl
> PYGMALION, a scientist
> LILITH, the creator of life

Back to Methuselah is prefaced by a long essay entitled "The Infidel Half-Century," which comprises an attack upon Darwinism. Attacking Darwinism is, of course, a popular pastime, and for many years, it was almost a fashionable activity for slightly wayward intellectuals. Samuel Butler, Hilaire Belloc, and Arthur Koestler have led the fight on behalf of different generations and very different individual creeds, and it is assumed that others will take up the banner in future. What these people objected to in Darwinism—and in this George Bernard Shaw stood foursquare with them—is the way in which the theory gives a central role to chance and removes from man's understanding of the evolutionary process any notion of purpose or direction. It is easy to see why such a revelation seemed to many to be singularly unedifying and also easy to see why the critics have been attracted to neo-Lamarckism: the doctrine that animals and men can contribute to the evolution of their species by strategic effort and the power of the will, by striving to acquire new characteristics whose acquisition can confer some marginal advantage upon the next generation.

Shaw's own plea on behalf of neo-Lamarckism is not particularly unusual in glossing over the issue of whether man has any good reason for believing that acquired characteristics actually can be inherited. His defense assumes that such a belief may be pragmatically necessary and that man is compelled to hope that it may be true because otherwise he may be damned. "Creative Evolution," he writes, "is already a religion, and it is indeed now unmistakably

the religion of the twentieth century." He adds, however, that the development of the new religion is inhibited by the fact that it has no legends and
parables to give it popular appeal and clarify its message, and it is to fill this
need that he has embarked upon the writing of *Back to Methuselah*.

The play begins by rewriting the story of the Garden of Eden. Adam is a
farmer and Eve is a housewife: they have fallen readily enough into these
roles and acquired appropriate attitudes. They have invented marriage in
advance of discovering sex, and they have recently become acquainted with
the idea of death. Death is here represented as the result of a will to die,
brought on by the terror of immortality. Adam finds himself in something of
a dilemma, having acquired the will to die because of his fear of immortality
and then discovering that he is also afraid of death. It is in searching for a
way out of this dilemma that Eve consults the serpent, who explains that
death can be counterbalanced by birth and that the cycle of birth and death
can be productive because it substitutes for mere repetition a process of change
and renewal.

Change and renewal are not immediately attractive to the conservative-
minded Adam, but Eve takes notice anyway, and the fruit of her new wisdom
is Cain. Cain is in favor of change and renewal, but his methods are violent.
He is, of course, the first murderer, and here he becomes the inventor and
guiding spirit of the art and science of warfare. It was Adam who elected to
die, but it is Cain who fixes the eventual human lifespan. Cain's destructive
verve together with Adam's dogged materialism provide the existential brack-
ets which henceforth confine the human condition.

Act II of the play deals with the new spiritual dawn of which Shaw fondly
believed that he might be a herald. World War I having made its impact, it
was time for the gospel of Cain to be set aside. This part of the play includes
satirical portraits of the leading politicians of the day in Lubin (Herbert Henry
Asquith) and Burge (David Lloyd George). The heroes of the piece are the
enlightened Socialists, the brothers Franklyn and Conrad, Barnabas, whose
talents represent a combination of religious feeling and biological acumen.
Their new gospel is partly political and partly spiritual; their party is for both
equality and longevity, and they believe that will and necessity can keep death
at bay as well as conquer injustice.

Act III delivers an interim report on the progress of the Barnabas brothers'
dream. The political system has been superficially transformed, so that the
attributes of the rival party politicians are now amalgamated in the person
of the President of the British Islands, Burge-Lubin. Parliament is full of
lunatics (literally), but the civil service is sane and efficient, partly because
of a slow and unobtrusive revolution from within. The first fruits of the
experiment in longevity are now reaching the limits of their new term of three
hundred years, and they have done their duty by occupying a variety of offices
over the years.

By the time of Act IV, the year 3000, a Utopia of Creative Evolutionists has been established in Ireland, and the long-lived folk have largely retired from involvement with the old world. The British Commonwealth is now extended across the globe, and short-lived people constitute a community of rather absurd reactionaries. This part of the play deals with the confrontation and debate between Joseph Popham Bolge Bluebin Barlow, an "elderly gentleman" who visits Ireland with a small party sent to seek advice from "The Oracle," and Zoo Ennistymon, one of the children of the new world. They argue about matters of philosophy and morality to the general advantage of the long-lived folk.

Act V, set in A.D. 31,920, is entitled "As Far as Thought Can Reach" and is set in a new Golden Age whose oviparous inhabitants are questioning their purpose. A youth named Pygmalion has anticipated Karel Capek's Rossum in solving the technical problem of making artificial men. These androids follow tradition in turning upon their creator and destroying him, but this is not allowed to become a symbol of the defeat of humankind. It is, instead, a momentary aberration quickly set aside; the duty of these perfect people is not to begin the human story all over again by becoming degraded god-substitutes, but it is to live up to the expectations of the creator who set the whole process in motion back in Eden. This prime mover is not the Christian God but the hermaphroditic Lilith, who divided herself in two to become Adam and Eve. Having long since rejected the burden of Cain, men must now set aside the burden that Adam accepted: they must accept at last the duty of eternal life, as spiritual beings of pure intelligence.

Back to Methuselah is not, of course, designed for performance on the stage. It is far too long and rambling and is much taken up with abstract philosophical discussions. It has no theatricality despite the fact that it is full of parts for ham actors. It is a complex work crowded with ideas, and no brief summary can possibly include them all. As the handbook of a would-be religion, it naturally aspires to cover every aspect of human experience, responsibility, and potential. It can hardly be deemed a successful work by any standard—in aesthetic terms, it is rather ineffectual—but it is undoubtedly an impressive failure, and it is invaluable as a key to Shaw's political and philosophical thought. It is not a work of genius itself, but it is obviously a work written *by* a genius.

In a postscript which was added to the play in 1944, Shaw declared, "The history of modern thought now teaches us that when we are forced to give up the creeds by their childishness and their conflicts with science we must either embrace Creative Evolution or fall into the bottomless pit of an utterly discouraging pessimism." This statement may perhaps be deemed pessimistic in itself, although it is highly probable that Shaw would have considered the contemporary world to be a demoralized one. Shaw, of course, always tried to practice what he preached, but his own determined attempt to live to be three hundred failed when he was less than a third of the way there. Whether this would have required him to concede that the gospel of the Brothers Barnabas was itself a creed tainted with childish wish-fulfillment and in conflict with the lessons of empirical study, it is obviously impossible to know.

Some critics have found in *Back to Methuselah* what they interpret as a retreat from socialism to which Shaw was dedicated, largely because the fourth and fifth parts pay no attention to matters of socialist theory. The Utopia of the long-lived folk is Communist in kind, but Shaw has nothing to say about its politics or economics. The fact that it is a *post*-socialist Utopia, however, merely emphasizes the fact that Shaw saw socialism as a means to an end rather than as an end in itself. The fact that the end of human progress is declared to be transcendental in character will undoubtedly be a disppoint-ment to materialists who consider that all traffic with the metaphysical is a retreat into idle fancy, but there is no need to accuse Shaw on this account of a betrayal of his earlier ideals.

In his Preface, Shaw links *Back to Methuselah* with the sequence in his earlier play *Man and Superman* (1903) in which Don Juan visits Hell (the act is usually omitted from stage versions). He says in comparing the two works that "the exuberance of 1901 has aged into the garrulity of 1920." He observes, with wry honesty, that his powers are on the wane, but he adds with char-acteristic panache that this may be "so much the better for those who found me unbearably brilliant when I was in my prime." He was right in the first instance, and he was not altogether wrong in the second.

Shaw's hope that many more apt and elegant parables of Creative Evolution might follow his has been betrayed by time and circumstance, and if anything, it is the Darwinian doctrine whose cause has been best served by exemplary fictions. *Back to Methuselah* thus remains an eccentric and exceptional work, largely without parallel.

Brian Stableford

Bibliography
Crompton, Louis. *Shaw the Dramatist*, 1969.
Evans, T. F., ed. *Shaw: The Critical Heritage*, 1976.
Kaufmann, R. J., ed. *George Bernard Shaw: A Collection of Critical Essays*, 1965.
MacCarthy, Desmond. *Shaw*, 1951.

BARON MÜNCHHAUSEN'S NARRATIVE OF HIS
MARVELLOUS TRAVELS AND CAMPAIGNS IN RUSSIA

Author: Rudolf Erich Raspe (1737-1794)
First book publication: 1785
Type of work: Short stories
Time: The eighteenth century
Locale: Unspecified

The archetypal collection of tall stories

> *Principal character:*
> HIERONYMUS VON MÜNCHHAUSEN, a German nobleman, who was
> at one time in the Russian service

Baron Münchhausen's Narrative of His Marvellous Travels and Campaigns in Russia first appeared, written in English, in 1785 (though the title page of the first edition is postdated 1786). This first edition consisted of a series of fourteen preposterous anecdotes combined into a continuous narrative, presented as the reminiscences of an old soldier. The substance of the anecdotes appears to have been borrowed from material published in 1781 and 1783 in a German journal, *Vademecum für Lustige Leute.* Their presentation in this new form was almost certainly the work of Rudolf Erich Raspe, a German satirist and man of letters who had been forced to flee to England in 1775 after pawning valuable items (whose custodian he was) in order to keep his creditors at bay. Raspe never claimed authorship of the first Münchhausen volume, but he was later named as its originator by the biographer of the book's German translator, Gottfried Bürger, who was widely suspected of being the author.

The original collation, which corresponds to Chapters II to VI in most modern editions, was an instant success. Several more editions were issued in 1786, two of them by the same bookseller who issued the first. The later of these added a new section (corresponding to Chapters VII to IX in most modern editions). It is possible that these new anecdotes were the work of Raspe, but there is a marked difference in style, implying that they may be by another hand. It is virtually certain that all other additions to the canon were done by other writers.

The second bookseller to become involved with Münchhausen was G. Kearsley, who issued a new augmented edition under the title *Gulliver Revived: Or, The Singular Travels, Campaigns, Voyages, and Adventures of Baron Munikhouson, commonly called Münchhausen* (1786). Here the text of the original editions has been extensively rewritten, making it both more pompous and more cumbersome. Virtually all modern editions follow this text, although it is in no way preferable to the original and should properly be regarded (as far as the previously written chapters are concerned) as corrupt. The Cresset Press edition published in 1948 gives the earliest versions of all the different sections of the text and should be regarded as the proper source for interested readers.

Kearsley issued several more editions of *Gulliver Revived* between 1786 and 1792, occasionally adding new sections. In 1792, the situation was complicated by the issuing by a rival publisher of *A Sequel to the Adventures of Baron Münchhausen Humbly Dedicated to Mr. Bruce the Abyssinian Traveller*. The rivalry appears to have been quickly settled, and by the turn of the century, the two works were being issued in a combined edition. The sequel now represents Chapters XXII to XXXV of most modern editions; its author is unknown.

Editions of the Münchhausen stories published in Germany and France also took on lives of their own, being augmented by native writers (Théophile Gautier was rumored to have written some of the French additions). The Baron became common property, adopted as a source and authority by tellers of tall tales everywhere. The real Baron Münchhausen found himself briefly famous, much to his surprise and (apparently) not altogether to his liking. He had been a *raconteur* of considerable ability and style, but by the time Raspe's anecdotes appeared, he was sixty-five and past his prime. The vulgar and often scurrilous tales which were appended to Raspe's original contribution certainly did no service to his reputation and moved on from relatively innocent mockery to ridiculous parody and occasional obscenity (though some of the obscenities are edited out of the familiar modern editions). The authentic Baron died in 1797, reportedly embittered and miserable.

The idea of Münchhausen transcends the actual anecdotes. The original booklet taken in isolation is a relatively stylish piece of work and contains all the really good stories. Here the Baron recalls how he hitched his horse to a "tree-stump" after a heavy snowfall and went to sleep, only to wake to find the snow gone and the poor animal dangling from a church steeple. Here, too, is the story of the stag with the cherry tree growing between its antlers, and the story of the horse bisected by a falling portcullis—not to mention the story of the exploding bear, the story of the pregnant greyhound which gives birth while chasing a pregnant hare, and the account of the Baron's first trip to the moon. These tales, in their original version, are narrated in a straightforward and laconic style which fits them perfectly.

Everything else added to the canon is inferior in quality and seems to prove that preposterous anecdotes, which can be charming if taken in moderation, become painfully tedious if sampled to excess. To read Münchhausen's adventures as if they were a novel, starting at the beginning and reading through to the end, is extremely difficult—the catalog of silly incidents rapidly ceases to be funny and becomes boring, while the mysterious sly digs at long-forgotten eighteenth century personages make hardly any sense to the average reader. If, as one suspects, Raspe washed his hands of the matter once he had published his first small book, one can only applaud his good judgment in so doing.

Brian Stableford

Bibliography
Carswell, John. "Introduction," in *The Adventures of Baron Münchausen*, 1948.
_____ . *The Prospector: Being the Life and Times of Rudolf Erich Raspe, 1737-1794*, 1950.

THE BEGINNING PLACE

Author: Ursula K. Le Guin (1929-   )
First book publication: 1980 (published in Great Britain as *The Threshold*)
Type of work: Novel
Time: The twentieth century
Locale: A suburban American town and a fantasy world variously called the "ain"
  (Scottish for "own") country, Tembreabrezi, or the Mountain Country

Hugh Rogers and Irena Pannis find their separate ways into another country, where
citizens of a feudal town need a hero to slay a monster that cuts them off from their
mountain country; after slaying the monster, Hugh and Irena return to their own world,
becoming first lovers and then friends as they struggle home

> *Principal characters:*
> HUGH ROGERS, a checkout clerk at Sam's Thrift-E-Mart
> IRENA PANNIS, a delivery girl for an engineering firm
> LORD HORN, the old Lord of the Mountain and feudal lord of
>   Tembreabrezi
> MASTER DOU SARK, the leader or mayor of Tembreabrezi
> ALLIA, Lord Horn's fair daughter

Ursula K. Le Guin's distinguished career as a writer has been marked by versatility; she has received awards for her Earthsea trilogy for children, earned a major reputation for science-fiction novels such as *The Left Hand of Darkness* (1969) and *The Dispossessed* (1974), and achieved successes in the political-historical-mythical ethos of *Orsinian Tales* (1976) and *Malafrena* (1979). In *The Beginning Place* (1980), she has moved to a different mode, creating a delicate and complex domestic fantasy with intricate psychological overtones of the rite of passage into maturity.

Not least among the unusual features of *The Beginning Place* is the vital function of the outside world, portrayed in a brief portrait of the common lives of ordinary young people in the United States in 1980. While many fantasy tales have starting places from which white rabbits in waistcoats with pocket watches may lead the reader, few tales delineate these "normal" worlds in realistic detail to demonstrate the need for a world of the imagination to which humans may escape. Hugh Rogers and Irena Pannis, however, do not "escape" to the "ain" country; their exploits are absolutely necessary to their growth as dignified human beings, and they return from these fantastic exploits transfigured.

The opening chapter of *The Beginning Place* establishes the banality of Hugh Rogers' smothered existence. He is obviously unhappy with his limited life as a supermarket checker and lives with his irritable yet possessive mother, who is never satisfied with him and who is constantly threatening to disown him. He flees this claustrophobic world, blindly running through the dusk to collapse in a glade beside a stream. For several weeks, he explores this quiet, safe place, discovering that the time he spends there is somehow stretched. He also discovers a desperately needed tranquillity in contrast to his mother's constant nagging, curiosity, and interference in his life. He is drawn so strongly to the glade that he buys simple camping equipment to enable him to stay there overnight.

Irena, coming back to the "beginning place," discovers Hugh sleeping in the glade and tries to drive him away. She, too, escapes to the glade but then walks on into the mountain country. Her escape is from a family situation dominated by a stepfather who seeks to seduce her, and by her mother, a woman for whom the domestic world is sufficient. When Irena walks past the sleeping Hugh and on to Tembreabrezi, she finds to her horror that the town is waiting for a hero to free it from the thrall of a monster they cannot describe. Two things are made painfully clear to her: she cannot be the hero, and they expect that the stranger she has seen will be that hero. She is reluctantly forced to bring Hugh to the town and to act first as his translator and later as his guide on his quest.

Le Guin's intent becomes clear when the reader considers the source of the fantasy world of the "ain" country. As Irena's private world, it is pure, free, and simple, a feudal model of quiet order governed by Dou Sark, the dark, powerful mayor whom she can adore from afar, and providing domestic tranquillity through the family to which she attaches herself. Into this world, which is, of course, the converse of Irena's situation "outside," Hugh is thrust against Irena's will. Yet the townspeople, Dou Sark, and Lord Horn recognize Hugh's role before they set eyes on him. Le Guin presents Hugh's acceptance of both his task and the sword given him by Lord Horn with a mixture of gnomic riddles and unclear mysteries typical of the dream quest. After Hugh and Irena slay the monster and find their painful way to each other's affection and out of the forest, the reader realizes that the whole of Tembreabrezi has been an insubstantial dream, a metaphor for the experience of beginning adulthood.

The adventures on the quest are told in a strangely and consciously ambivalent fashion. Finding the dragon's cave, Irena challenges the beast, and Hugh suddenly, almost accidentally, slays it and is gravely injured when it falls upon him. Irena pulls him free, and as they flee, they become lovers, again suddenly and almost accidentally. All of these actions happen in the fantasy land, but Le Guin does not transform Hugh and Irena into the hero and lady found in typical fairy tales. They remain young, twentieth century Americans puzzled by the fairy-tale atmosphere, yet sensing that they must follow its pattern. The monster they slay is female, representing for Hugh the pervasive domination of his mother (with its unexplored incestuous aspect) and his lack of sexual experience, and for Irena, the disgust at the advances of her stepfather and the discrepancy between her mother's fecundity and the blighted relationship of the couple with whom she has shared an apartment. The monster also represents much more for them: it is all that has held them back from beginning the adult life of choosing and loving. They kill the monster together, Irena pulling Hugh free, just as earlier, Irena (despite her fears) was forced to abandon her false, sexless adoration of Master Sark and the father figure of Lord Horn for an active encounter with Hugh.

The Beginning Place is a most surprising book. Perhaps Le Guin's point of departure is best expressed in Irena's thoughts: "'You never think of going on past the dragon,' Irena thought. 'You only think about getting to it. But what happens afterwards?'" Afterward, of course, the fantasy myth engenders action and meaning in the lives of the characters who experience it. The novel uses myth and fantasy to explain a complex life experience by lifting it from the mundane to another world. *The Beginning Place*, therefore, focuses on the need for the "ain" country, a birthplace and a refuge amid the tangled thickets of ordinary life.

Peter Brigg

Bibliography
Bucknall, Barbara J. *Ursula K. Le Guin*, 1981.
Le Guin, Ursula K. *The Language of the Night: Essays on Fantasy and Science Fiction*, 1979. Edited by Susan Wood.
Olander, Joseph D., and Martin H. Greenberg, eds. *Ursula K. Le Guin*, 1979.

A BELEAGUERED CITY

Author: Margaret Oliphant (1828-1897)
First book publication: 1880
Type of work: Novel
Time: July, 1875
Locale: The town of Semur, in Burgundy

The inhabitants of a small French town are temporarily banished from their homes by the spirits of the dead

> *Principal characters:*
> MARTIN DUPIN, the mayor of Semur
> FELIX DE BOIS-SOMBRE, a hotelier
> PAUL LECAMUS, an old man, reputedly a visionary
> JACQUES RICHARD, a dogmatic materialist
> M. LE CURÉ, the custodian of the faith in Semur

Margaret Oliphant was one of the most prolific Victorian writers, publishing more than 120 books and several hundred magazine pieces. Although she drew faint praise from Henry James, among others, she is now almost forgotten. The only thing she wrote that remains widely familiar is "The Open Door," the best of her several ghost stories. She wrote three fantasy novels, which are part of the strong late-Victorian tradition of fiction speculating about the afterlife. *A Little Pilgrim of the Unseen* (1882) is a reassuring fantasy set in Heaven; *The Land of Darkness* (1888) is a companion piece set in hell. These two conventional romances of the afterlife are, however, completely overshadowed by *A Beleaguered City*, which is the most striking and most original of all her literary endeavors.

The novel takes the form of a series of documents; in this respect, its method seems to be modeled on that of Wilkie Collins. The main testament is that of Martin Dupin, M. le Maire of Semur, a minor Burgundian town which lays claim to the title of "city" by virtue of its cathedral and its surrounding wall. Although Dupin's is the leading part in the strange history which it is his duty to record, he scrupulously calls upon the testimony of other witnesses to supplement his own account and fill out the picture. This manner of presentation not only cultivates verisimilitude but also adds a subtle gloss of irony, for M. le Maire is more than a little pompous and his narrative tells the reader more than he imagines.

The introductory chapter explains Dupin's disillusionment with the people of his town, who have largely forsaken the worship of God for the pursuit of money, storing up treasures on Earth rather than in Heaven. Although only the ill-mannered braggart Jacques Richard is willing to advertise his preference, his elevation of Mammon above Christ is symptomatic of a much more widespread apostasy. Twice in one day Dupin hears good people lament that "it is enough to bring the dead out of their graves"—and so, as things turn out, it is.

Semur is beset by a strange mist that brings darkness to the daytime. With Paul Lecamus, an old man reputed to be something of a visionary, Dupin steps outside the city wall and finds himself terror-stricken by the immanent presence of something he can neither see nor feel. In letters of fire upon the cathedral door, there appears a supernatural command bidding the citizens of Semur to leave their homes, and they find themselves helpless to disobey. Once outside, the children and most of the women are sent to Dupin's estate to wait, while the men stay and discuss the possibility of repossessing the city.

Searching for a scapegoat, the people turn on Dupin, blaming him for having invited the wrath of the dead by closing the chapel in the Hospital of St. Jean (after patients complained that the sound of the nuns praying disturbed their convalescence). This charge is false, but Dupin recognizes the futility of persuading the citizens that they themselves have brought the visitation. He gets the chance to redeem himself, though, when Paul Lecamus brings a message from the city. Not forgetting to deputize Felix de Bois-Sombre lest he should not return, M. le Maire goes into the mist-shrouded city to placate the friendly dead with assurances that their visit has not been in vain and to offer promises of renewed attention to spiritual matters on behalf of all. M. le Curé, as the official responsible for liaison between Earth and Heaven, goes with him.

In the city, they find one man left behind: Pierre Plastron, confined to his sickbed in the hospital. He does not even know that anything untoward has happened, though he complains bitterly about the negligence of his nurses. Dupin sees—as Lecamus has already seen—abundant signs of the return of long-lost loved ones, though the ghosts remain invisible. As he and the curé walk through the streets, however, the visitation ends.

The final chapter describes the aftermath of the visitation, and it is here that the irony of the tale takes full hold. The people stick by their promises of renewed faith, but in their own fashion. Jacques Richard is converted, but his new piety is as monstrously aggressive as his old atheism and is simply another vehicle for his domineering character. Paul Lecamus, the authentic visionary, rejoins his lost wife among the dead, but his place is taken by Pierre Plastron, who begins "remembering" all kinds of supernatural wonders experienced during the siege and becomes a fount of fake and platitudinous wisdom. No one takes any notice of M. le Maire's protestations—for, after all, was it not he who was responsible for waking the dead, when he closed the chapel of the sisters of St. Jean?

Mrs. Oliphant took good care to distance her narrative from her immediate audience by setting it in another country and gently satirizing her "viewpoint" character. In a way, though, this merely serves to emphasize that the readiness with which one is inclined to shift the novel's burden to the follies of other people is merely one more example of the bad faith that comes so easily to the people of Semur. The moral of the story is that it hardly matters that the Age of Miracles is long past, because modern men have their own psychological strategies for dealing with potential revelations, protecting themselves from any threatening implications. (It is possible that Mrs. Oliphant had in mind the most recent visit of the Blessed Virgin to Earth, which supposedly occurred at Lourdes in 1858; by the time she wrote *A Beleaguered City*, the spiritual and commercial exploitation of that alleged miracle was well established.)

A Beleaguered City, as an allegorical moral fantasy, is perhaps too esoteric to enjoy wide popularity, and it suffers somewhat from the pertinence of its own irony. Those at whom it is directed—"semi-lapsed Christians"—are exactly those who, as the final chapter points out, are least likely to see the point. The novel is, however, a subtle and elegant work which should help to preserve the memory of its author among the cognoscente.

Brian Stableford

Bibliography
Colby, Vineta, and Robert A. Colby. *The Equivocal Virtue: Mrs. Oliphant and the Victorian Literary Market Place*, 1966.

BEYOND THE GOLDEN STAIR

Author: Hannes Bok (1914-1964)
First book publication: 1970
Type of work: Novel
Time: The 1940's
Locale: The Everglades and Khoire (an alternate world)

An ill-assorted quartet of criminals escapes from prison, flees into the Everglades, and finds a staircase which leads to a world in another dimension

> *Principal characters:*
> JOHN HIBBERT, an unwitting criminal who dreams of greater things
> SCARLATTI, a bullying criminal who drags Hibbert along on his escape from prison
> BURKS, Scarlatti's partner who helps him to escape from prison
> CARLOTTA, Scarlatti's girl friend
> PATUR, the Keeper of the Gate in Khoire
> MARETH, a Watcher of the Qsin who patrol Earth

Specialized societies have been founded by fans and scholars alike to popularize, honor, and study the lives and works of quite a few fantasy authors. Some of these writers—J. R. R. Tolkien, for example—are widely recognized even among the general public, while others have a much more limited following. Of these, Hannes Bok is perhaps the least renowned. Primarily an illustrator whose art work appeared on the covers of pulp fantasy magazines from the early 1940's to the early 1960's, Bok wrote fantasy as well. He so admired the writings of Abraham Merritt that he completed two novels, *The Fox Woman* (1946) and *The Black Wheel* (1947), from notes left by Merritt, who died in 1943. This project—carried out in Merritt's style—partially accounts for the style of Bok's own later work. While Bok's *The Sorcerer's Ship*, which appeared in *Unknown Stories* in 1942, before he had completed the Merritt novels, shows only limited Merritt influence, *Beyond the Golden Stair*, originally published in a severely shortened version in *Startling Stories* in 1948 as *The Blue Flamingo* and later published in a more complete version in Ballantine Books' Adult Fantasy Series in 1970, is much more like a Merritt novel.

Beyond the Golden Stair opens like several Merritt stories: a group of average people from the contemporary world stumble on a preternatural site in an actual remote or unexplored locale. In Bok's book, four people, two of whom have just escaped from prison with the help of the other two, are fleeing through the Everglades when they come upon an ancient ruin. At first, they think it is an old Spanish ruin, but in the center, they find an old staircase built of coral and looking as if "it was made a million years ago," stretching up to the tops of the surrounding palmettos. When they reach the top of the stair, they find a platform, thirty feet square, with a pool in the

center. In the pool stands a blue flamingo. After speculating about the legendary Fountain of Youth (and other, more sinister tales), Burks, one of the
criminals, steps into the pool. The flamingo appears to attack him, and he
shoots it. At this point, another stairway appears, and the four climb it and
find themselves in Khoire.

In most fantasy novels in which people are preternaturally transported from
this world to another, the process is completed within the first few pages.
Bok, however, spends approximately fifty pages (almost a quarter of the
novel) completing the process. Bok's intent, it seems, is to develop his four
characters as identifiable individuals before their entrance into another world.
Scarlatti is a big, tough criminal. He is a rather insensitive man who, because
of his size and strength, bullies the others and generally gets his own way.
Carlotta, Scarlatti's girl friend, is a tough, back-country woman who sticks
with him because she respects the very strength by which he dominates her.
Burks is the coolly efficient criminal, but where Scarlatti enjoys being brutal,
Burks is a criminal because he feels that it is the only way he can exist in
contemporary society—and he maintains that he could be different in a different place. Hibbert is in the group by chance. He was "left holding the
bag" by some dishonest business partners and found himself in a prison cell
with Scarlatti. When Burks helps Scarlatti to escape, the big man drags Hibbert along, often referring to him as a toy or a baby that "papa" might break
or discipline.

It is important for the reader to know what sort of person each character
is because in Khoire each will undergo a change. Shortly after they arrive at
the top of the second stair, a great voice tells them that, in Khoire, "what
you are within your hearts holds sway over whatever you may pretend to
be." Later, after having thoroughly acquainted themselves with Khoire, they
realize that the statement is meant to be taken literally. Burks says to their
guide, Patur, "We simply wait around until the nature of this place works on
us, and we turn into what our minds really are—right?" Patur's response is
simply a nod.

Khoire is thus an ultimate fantasy world, a world where a person is quite
literally able to become what he deserves to be. The bullying giant, Scarlatti,
finds that his body shrinks to match his mean-spirited nature, and Carlotta,
who has slavishly followed him, is transformed into "something not quite yet
very like a black and hairless dog!" Hibbert, the sympathetic main character,
finds his crippled and undersized body growing to match his great and giving
spirit. He then returns to his own world to study and become worthy of full
citizenship in Khoire and of the love of Mareth, a beautiful Khoirian woman.
Although Hibbert's transformation is the one appropriate to the main character in the story, Burks's transformation is much more interesting. After
learning about Khoire, Burks volunteers to become a flamingo, take the place
of the one he shot, and earn his Khoirian citizenship that way—even though

it will take thousands of years. His request is honored, and he earns the sincere admiration of the Khoirians, who regard themselves as far superior to the people of Earth. Burks's determination gives Mareth the evidence she needs to believe in Hibbert's love for her and determination to return to her.

Beyond the Golden Stair is much more a metaphysical fantasy than an action/adventure tale. In addition to the concept of internal reality determining physical form, Bok interjects—often briefly—quite a few other ideas. When the humans speak aloud in Khoire, colors stream from their mouths. Hibbert suggests that this happens because both light and color are "manifestations of the same basic energy. Theoretically, it's possible to convert one into the other by speeding up or slowing down their wave lengths." The poltergeists of Hibbert's world are creatures from the "world-under-men," and the Watchers from Qsin who patrol the Earth have been seen by some sensitive people, giving rise to reports of "fox-spirits, vampires, goblins, angelic visitations, demonic possessions, and various *genii locorum.*"

It is perhaps because Bok was a painter that *Beyond the Golden Stair* is such a richly pictorial book. The colors, shapes, and textures of both the earthly Everglades and the other worldly Khoire are vividly presented. In addition to specific episodes of the plot, the reader will certainly remember Bok's pictures—Scarlatti's transformation from giant to dwarf; the gravity-defying, dark corridors between worlds; and the blue flamingo standing in the "impossibly blue pool." Bok's literary reputation may rest on only two books, *Beyond the Golden Stair* and *The Sorcerer's Ship*; but they are enough.

C. W. Sullivan III

Bibliography
Carter, Lin. "About *Beyond the Golden Stair*, and Hannes Bok: The Gate of Khoire," in *Beyond the Golden Stair*, 1970.

BID TIME RETURN

Author: Richard Matheson (1926-   )
First book publication: 1975
Type of work: Novel
Time: November, 1971, and November, 1896
Locale: Coronado, California

A writer, dying of an inoperable brain tumor, falls in love with the portrait of a turn-of-the-century actress and transports himself to her time to join her

Principal characters:
    RICHARD COLLIER, a television writer
    ELISE MCKENNA, an actress
    WILLIAM FAWCETT ROBINSON, her manager
    ROBERT COLLIER, Richard's brother

Richard Matheson opens his novel with a quotation from William Shakespeare's *Richard II* (1595-1596), Act III, Scene ii: "O call back yesterday, bid time return." This passage, the latter part of which is also the novel's title, conveys the yearning the protagonist of *Bid Time Return* feels, while gently misleading its readers about the action that yearning will cause. This same kind of ambiguity, present throughout the book, keeps the novel from falling too easily into any one of the categories it touches. It could be described as a story of time travel, a romance, a psychological study—and, because of Matheson's deft intermixing of the three, a mystery.

Richard Collier, from his earliest appearance, is shown as a man obsessed with time. There is ample reason for this: at the age of thirty-six, he has been told that he suffers from an inoperable brain tumor and has only months to live. The pressure of that knowledge, coupled with the desire not to spend those months as a burden on his family, drives Collier out of his brother Robert's home. He takes to the road abruptly, with no particular destination in mind, and he lets the toss of a penny determine the direction his flight will take.

His first day's journey ends in Coronado, a small town near San Diego. The Hotel del Coronado, built in 1887, seems to Collier to be saturated with time, laden with the atmosphere and experiences of the decades during which it has operated. The feeling of so much time intoxicates him as much as the graciousness of the establishment charms him. He decides to lodge, at least temporarily, at the hotel.

Collier's mesmerization becomes truly complete when he enters the hotel's Hall of History and finds a photograph of Elise McKenna, an actress who appeared on the Hotel del Coronado stage in November of 1896. Irrationally, without reserve, Collier falls in love with the woman whom he knows must be long dead and buried, and comes to believe that he can somehow travel across the seventy-five years which separate them. He goes about researching his trip in the same methodical manner he employed as a college student and, later, as a television writer. Once he has familiarized himself as completely as possible with McKenna's biography, he turns to a volume entitled *Man and Time*, using its author's definitions of time to form his own approach to it.

In brief, the young man decides that in order to transport himself to 1896, he must accomplish two things. First, he must make himself as much a part of the time, physically, as he can. To do this, he shuts himself away in his hotel room, dressed in a costume appropriate to 1896, with money from that time; he also puts everything out of his sight that will remind him that he is actually in 1971. Second, he must convince himself, consciously and unconsciously, that he has indeed made the transition to that long-ago year. Using a form of self-hypnosis to meet this second requirement, Collier first dictates, then writes a series of instructions to himself: "Today is Thursday, November 19, 1896. . . . Elise McKenna is in the hotel now. . . . Every moment brings me closer to Elise."

His determination is eventually rewarded. Collier finds himself—initially for only brief intervals—in the Hotel del Coronado circa 1896. After several of these short visits, he manages to fix himself firmly in the new time.

Unfortunately, as he later discovers, this mind-over-matter approach to time travel works in both directions. Much later, when the possibility of his being drawn back into his own time has ceased to concern him, the sight of a 1971 penny he accidentally carried back with him breaks Collier's hold on 1896 and snaps him back to the present he has fought so hard to escape.

Considered as a romance, *Bid Time Return* offers a pair of lovers who must overcome not only the massive obstacle of time which separates them, but also a number of other obstacles as well. McKenna is a woman most unusual for her time: as an actress, she functions as a career woman during a period in which such a creature was viewed with considerable suspicion, if not outright amazement. Even for such a woman, however, the social mores of 1896 present a less than favorable climate for a whirlwind love affair.

McKenna's professional stature and her omnipresent manager, William Fawcett Robinson, present further impediments. When Collier appears at the hotel—a loner, with neither professional nor social ties to legitimize him, and with an odd unfamiliarity with the most mundane conventions—he presents the very image of the kind of fortune-hunter against whom both the actress and Robinson must be on their guard.

Obstacles notwithstanding, there is an inevitability, a *fatedness* about their encounter which overcomes all other considerations. Collier speaks of this constantly while attempting his jaunt into time, often referring to his biographical readings about McKenna. Noting the many references made to her never having married, as well as her own veiled remark about a "Coronado scandal" which occurred in 1896 and somehow changed her life, he argues that their coming together has already taken place and thus cannot be prevented.

McKenna also senses this inevitability. Like Collier, she has never found a person whom she could truly love, and while she lacks his certain knowledge of her own future, she has twice been offered glimpses of it by women who claim occult powers. On each occasion, the fortune-teller told her that she would meet a man who would come to her in some mysterious fashion and become her lover. The second prediction included the time and place of their meeting, setting it in the month of November, on a beach.

Both Collier and McKenna are so absorbed by what they believe to be foreknowledge of their destinies that each new development seems laden with *déjà vu*. They sense one another's feelings and thoughts with an ease more common to lovers of much longer standing, and even their first words together are not those of strangers: "'Is it you?' she asked."

From this first meeting, their intimacy increases at a speed which astonishes McKenna as well as the people closest to her. Her mother, who travels and often appears in productions with her, makes it obvious that she finds her daughter's behavior peculiar. Beyond making her puzzlement known, however, Mrs. McKenna interferes hardly at all; Collier attributes this to the older woman's theatrical background, noting that even the most rigidly moralistic actresses of the period were suspected of wilder behavior than that of other women.

Robinson, on the other hand, does not stop at mere astonishment. McKenna's manager, who obviously cares very deeply for her but considers himself unworthy of her attentions, is wounded and infuriated by his client's sudden change in behavior. He attributes every aspect of the change to Collier and will stop at nothing to prevent the younger man from so much as speaking to the actress. He even goes so far—when rudeness, threats, and bribery have failed to eliminate Collier's unwanted presence—as to have Collier kidnaped during McKenna's performance by a pair of thugs who knock him unconscious and leave him trussed up in a shed miles from the Hotel del Coronado. This attempt to keep Collier from his newfound love long enough for her to be whisked off on a train toward her next performance fails as miserably as each of Robinson's earlier efforts. Collier manages to free himself and makes his way back to the hotel, where McKenna is waiting for him. There, untroubled by any further interruptions, they finally become lovers.

The joy they discover in their lovemaking astonishes and elates them both. McKenna, who has repressed her emotions throughout her adult life for fear that they would compromise her acting if given free rein, finds that she feels stronger and more capable for having let herself go; Collier, on the other hand, sees the consummation of his love as the last tie he needs to fix him permanently in his new time. So convinced is he that his last contacts with

1971 have been broken that he leaves McKenna to sleep alone for a few moments while he goes to destroy the record he has been keeping of his spatial and temporal travels.

Since the beginning of his adventure, Collier has steadfastly refused to give the evidence of the tragic nature of McKenna's "Coronado scandal" the same credence he has given the happier proofs. Now, after a last brief encounter with Robinson—made brief by his telling the older man the precise manner of his approaching death—Collier discovers that past sorrow is as inevitable as past joy. Upon returning to McKenna's room, he finds the penny, hidden in a coat pocket, which wrenches him back to 1971. He has fulfilled his part in McKenna's past and has been removed from it as abruptly as he entered it.

There is another somewhat troubling interpretation of the story which has little to do with the possibility of time travel or the pain and pleasure of romance. *Bid Time Return* is represented as Collier's single novel and his last piece of written work and is bracketed by a preface and afterword, ostensibly written by his brother. According to Robert Collier, the manuscript of the book was written when his brother was undergoing tremendous grief and stress and is most likely the product of an unhinged mind.

Because of certain ambiguous clues which Matheson has taken care to place in different sections of the book, the elder Collier's hypothesis is arguable. On more than one occasion, prior to his entry into the past, Collier questions his own sanity as well as the sanity of the thing he was attempting to do. He also refers, throughout his tenure in the past, to the fantastic nature of his journey and to the unbelievable order of events which have followed his arrival.

This hint of unreality (omitted from the filmed version of the story, *Somewhere in Time*, 1980, which Matheson scripted) is provided most strongly by an almost offhand mention of a change Collier undergoes after his arrival in 1896. He makes frequent references, during the section of the novel set in 1971, to his excruciating headaches. These headaches drove him to see his doctor in the first place, and they are an increasingly painful symptom of the tumor that is killing him. Collier's first mornings in the Hotel del Coronado, despite his fascination with the place, are made miserable by the headaches, which will not respond to any cure but slowly fade during the day.

From his first morning in 1896, however, Collier finds that the headaches have completely vanished; he rises from his sleep refreshed, without the slightest twinge of pain. Only this symptom—and, by extension, the tumor itself?—has been affected by Collier's temporal shift. Physically and mentally, he remains in all other ways unchanged. If a man were so set on escaping the terrors that his own time held for him that he could hallucinate a trip into the past, it seems prudent to assume that he would also hallucinate the disappearance of his greatest burden.

Matheson has drawn a careful balance here, providing his readers with all of the information needed to draw a conclusion, yet stopping short of making *any* conclusion inescapable. He has, however, made it difficult for anyone reading *Bid Time Return* not to agree with the final words of Robert Collier's postscript, written after his brother's death:

> It would make my grief for my brother's passing immeasurably lighter if I could convince myself that he really went back and met her. Part of me wants very much to believe that it was not a delusion at all. That Richard and Elise were together as he said they were. That, God willing, they are, even now, together somewhere.

Christine Watson

Bibliography

Nicholls, Peter. "Richard Matheson," in *Science Fiction Writers*, 1982. Edited by F. Everett Bleiler.
Sammon, Paul M. "Richard Matheson: Master of Fantasy," in *Fangoria*. Nos. 2 and 3, 1979.

THE BIOGRAPHY OF THE LIFE OF MANUEL

Author: James Branch Cabell (1879-1958)
First book publications: The Eagle's Shadow: A Comedy of Purse Strings (1904); *The Line of Love* (1905); *Gallantry* (1907); *Chivalry* (1909); *The Cords of Vanity: A Comedy of Shirking* (1909); *The Soul of Melicent* (1913, later published as *Domnei: A Comedy of Woman Worship*); *The Rivet in Grandfather's Neck: A Comedy of Limitations* (1915); *The Certain Hour* (1916); *From the Hidden Way* (1916); *The Cream of the Jest: A Comedy of Evasions* (1917); *Jurgen: A Comedy of Justice* (1919); *Beyond Life* (1919); *Figures of Earth: A Comedy of Appearances* (1921); *The Jewel Merchants* (1921); *The Lineage of Lichfield* (1922); *The High Place: A Comedy of Disenchantment* (1923); *Straws and Prayer Books* (1924); *The Music from Behind the Moon* (1926); *The Silver Stallion: A Comedy of Redemption* (1926); *Something About Eve: A Comedy of Fig Leaves* (1927); *The White Robe* (1928); *The Way of Ecben* (1929); *Sonnets from Antan* (1929)
Type of work: Novels, short stories, essays, and poetry
Time: The late twelfth century to the early twentieth century
Locale: Primarily Western Europe (real and imaginary) and especially France

The history of two men and their principal descendants from their origins in the imaginary kingdom of Poictesme in the twelfth century to the modern world

Principal characters:
DOM MANUEL, a twelfth century swineherd who rises to become Count of Poictesme, redeemer, and patriarch
DAME NAIFER, his wife, the matriarch of "Domestic Women"
MIRAMON LLUAGOR, a wizard and dream master of Poictesme
HORVENDILE, an archetypal poet and demiurge, also the alter ego of Felix Kennaston
QUEEN FREYDIS, Manuel's mistress and a witch whose magic gives life to the clay figures of Manuel
SESPHRA, the first of Manuel's animated figures and a pagan spirit of self-indulgent pleasure
COUNT EMMERICK, Manuel's son and heir
SUSKIND, a prelapsarian daughter of Eve, who is, for Manuel, the archetypal, unattainable first love
KOSCHEI THE DEATHLESS, the chief demiurge of the universe
GLAUM, one of the Sylan, a spirit who must occasionally assume the body of a human being in order to perpetuate his own life
MELICENT, one of Manuel's daughters
DEMETRIOS OF ANATOLIA, the son of Miramon Lluagor, a pagan champion, and the first husband of Melicent
PERION DE LA FORÊT, the chivalrous lover and second husband of Melicent
AHASUERUS, Demetrios' aide-de-camp who saves Melicent for Perion
JURGEN, a cashiered poet and pawnbroker, whose legend in Poictesme epitomizes the gallant mode of life
DOROTHY LA DÉSIRÉE, Manuel's daughter and Jurgen's lover, the symbol of the sexually alluring woman
FLORIAN DE PUYSANGE, a descendant of Jurgen who persists in

realizing his dream of possessing the ideal woman

PRINCESS MELIOR, the enchanted princess who is Florian's ideal

GERALD MUSGRAVE, an early nineteenth century Virginian descendant of Manuel who trades places with Glaum

ETTARRE, Manuel's daughter, who becomes the symbol of the ideal, unattainable woman

MADOC, the legendary poet and husband of Ettarre

FELIX KENNASTON, an early twentieth century Virginian descendant of Manuel and, like Gerald Musgrave, a writer involved in the genealogy of Manuel

KATHLEEN KENNASTON, Felix's wife and an incarnation of the spirit of Ettarre

RICHARD FENTNOR HARROBY, a friend of Felix Kennaston

COLONEL RUDOLPH MUSGRAVE, the putative author of *The Lineage of Lichfield*

The Biography of the Life of Manuel is arguably the best and most ambitious work of fantasy conceived and carried out by an American writer. The premise as outlined by Queen Freydis at the end of *The Silver Stallion* is simple enough on the surface: Manuel will live through his descendants, "in all the inheritors of his foiled being . . . wanting always what he has not ever found . . . and without which he may not ever be contented." Carrying out that plan occupied James Branch Cabell as a writer for more than fifty years. The Storisende edition collected eighteen volumes of his work up until 1930; although Cabell was to write several more titles in the series, all the major works of the biography are included in this edition, which is regarded as the standard edition.

The Biography of the Life of Manuel is comic fantasy; the formal premise is genealogy. Cabell actually worked for several years as a professional genealogist, an experience that shaped his creative imagination by suggesting an approach to the creation of a comic universe. The eye of the genealogist looks for both progressive change or advancement and repeated patterns of action and behavior. Each modifies the other so that human affairs are neither entirely the same nor entirely different. What becomes most obvious to the trained eye is the recurrent type, the pattern of behavior and response in the genealogical history of a family. As a history, it portrays the artist's interest in the forms in which history is preserved and transmitted. Thus, the biography also includes essays, genealogies, poems, plays, and short stories, as well as prose romances. Cabell even creates the illusion of nonfiction rhetoric among the works of the biography in a manner that owes something in form and style to Oscar Wilde.

In addition to Wilde, Cabell's comedy owes something to George Bernard Shaw, especially in its stylistic preferences for paradox, wit, elegance of manner, and ornament. Cabell also admired such eighteenth century wits as Richard Sheridan and the Restoration playwrights William Congreve and William

Wycherley. His literary debts to William Shakespeare may well exceed all others, but his penchant for absurd and bawdy humor certainly owes something to François Rabelais and probably to Geoffrey Chaucer. Other notable influences are found in *The Arabian Nights' Entertainments* (fifteenth century) and the work of late Victorian philosophers such as William James, Friedrich Nietzsche, and George Santayana. These influences suggest not only a broad and eclectic range of reading but also an equally broad spectrum of comic interests. Cabellian comedy is rich and varied, ranging from philosophic comedy to puns. It is also historically progressive in style, subject, and treatment in real time, observing standard conventions of fiction. Hence, the comedic flavor in real time is distinctly different in *Something About Eve* and *The Cream of the Jest*, set respectively in the nineteenth and twentieth centuries, compared with *Figures of Earth* and *The Silver Stallion*, set in the thirteenth and fourteenth centuries. Nevertheless, there is both an ironic detachment and an energy that is characteristic of nearly all Cabellian comedy.

The great virtue dramatized in nearly every work in *The Biography of the Life of Manuel* is tolerance. While there is a generous sufficiency of satire directed at Cabell's contemporaries, from revivalists to literary critics, the groundwork of the satire is both a modernist and an eclectic viewpoint, which refuses to take human beings, their ideas, institutions, taboos, and beliefs at their own valuation. There is, however, together with the skepticism that leads to satire, a naïveté that leads to irony. Cabell's sources of naïve forms are concentrated in the traditions of the literary romance from Chrétien de Troyes to Nathaniel Hawthorne, in folklore, and in mythology.

Cabellian comedy portrays human behavior as predetermined by biologically inherited traits and influenced by the recurrent cycles of historical changes. These traits endlessly combine and recombine as long as the genealogical line is intact, producing new and interesting permutations as implied in the life of the original patriarch—in this case Manuel—but never fully realized in either his character or his life. Intervention, by whatever gods may be, is commonplace in Cabell's world and its history, not only because intervention is a clear marker of the fantastic but also because such intervention symbolizes the equally commonplace encounters with chance and irrational events in both the microcosm and the macrocosm.

Cabell's persistent irony reinforces the comic potentials of the difference between human expectations of order and their actual experience of and participation in the disorder and disarray of life. Order is presented in Cabell's works as a structure imposed by the mind or the imagination on the crude, imperfect, unfinished, and recalcitrant materials of nature. Science, the author insists, requires more faith than modern man is capable of providing. Pursuit of order, in one of its many forms, occupies almost all of Cabell's major characters from the domestic woman to the demiurge, which makes for many occasions of irony and satire and a wry expectation by the mature characters of an imperfect management of life's affairs.

In his prefaces and in many of his essays, Cabell has devoted considerable attention to his scheme of character presentation. In *The Biography of the Life of Manuel*, Cabell sees Manuel and Jurgen defining opposing types of personality between which oscillate their descendants; Manuel is the man of action and Jurgen the man of thought. Moreover, each appears to be the prototype for attitudes from which grow the terms of Cabellian comedy. Manuel exemplifies the chivalric attitude and Jurgen the gallant attitude toward life. If the former is more characteristic of the medieval mind, the latter is more like the modern outlook. Together with the poetic attitude, these two make up the traditional structure of the comic life.

The chivalrous attitude is essentially an allegorical view of life in which the person believes himself directed by supernatural forces. The code according to which the chivalrous person lives is, therefore, perceived to be a divinely ordained guideline of action. Moreover, the chivalrous person conceives himself as representing divine will on Earth and identifies his goals and purposes with the larger goals of Heaven. For the chivalrous person, therefore, the familiar world and its life are less important than what lies beyond them. These characters are motivated by abstract ideas which have for them a greater force than present needs.

The gallant attitude, epitomized by Jurgen and Rudolph Musgrave (*The Rivet in Grandfather's Neck*), is the one that receives the most attention from Cabell and seems closest to his own viewpoint. Gallantry takes the world on its own terms and makes the best of it, however ruefully. The gallant character is content to keep his own place, to prefer comfort to martyrdom, and to be tolerant of both himself and of the inconveniences of an imperfect world. The gallant person is a "well-balanced sceptic, who comprehends that he knows very little, and probably amounts to somewhat less, but has the grace to keep his temper." The gallant person is characterized by the virtue of urbanity, which is Cabell's palliative for the deficiences of life, the world, and the illusions or dreams provided by the proponents of the third attitude, the poetic.

The poetic attitude is the code of the artist who lives detached from, and therefore above, life. He shares with the chivalrous person a sense of transcendence, but, for the poet, that sense proceeds from the power of art to take the incoherent substances of life, including the artist's own experiences, and to shape them into meaningful and satisfying patterns. The poetic attitude is represented by Felix Kennaston (*The Cream of the Jest*) and supremely by his alter ego, Horvendile, who appears in several stories as a demiurgic character. The poetic attitude expresses itself in one of two modes, as explained in *Beyond Life*: the realistic and the romantic. The extreme pursuit of each betrays both truth and art. The realistic poet or artist makes his art serve the vulgar and the commonplace, and this leads to triviality or despair. The romantic poet, on the other hand, enslaves his art to dreams and wish fulfillment, regardless of their effect on potential human understanding of truth.

In addition to these three attitudes, defined in *Beyond Life* and mentioned elsewhere in his prefaces and essays, Cabell presents within the romance framework the practical or pragmatic attitude, defined by an unheroic, utilitarian approach to life, one in which survival is often the principal end of action. Parents and older-generation rulers and wardens of the status quo fill up this classification, illustrated by Richard Fentnor Harroby in *The Cream of the Jest*.

Since Cabell devoted his attention to predominantly male stereotypes in his essays, female stereotypes have been given less critical attention, perhaps because they are more stock characters than allegorical attitudes. There are three main types of woman in the Cabellian universe as counterparts to the three types of man. The first is the "Princess": young, beautiful, desirable, and often innocent, she is basically passive, waiting to be claimed by an appropriate champion. In the world of romance, she is, if not literally a princess, at least highborn. The Princess remains the ideal not only of hot-blooded young men (and middle-aged *roués* like Jurgen) but also of women as well. More often than not, however, this ideal lacks intellect, possessing the allure of the mysterious and ineffable. The Princess is the ideal of all other women to the degree that all wish to be treated and paid court to as though they were princesses. Melior (*The Silver Stallion*), Melicent (*Domnei*), and Ettarre symbolize the major types of princesses in Cabell's world.

Sooner or later, Princesses marry, and when they do, they turn almost immediately into the "Domestic Woman." The rapidity of the transformation process from Princess to Domestic Woman is always a source of surprise and then chagrin to the husband, whose typical reaction is either some form of escape or armed truce. The Domestic Woman is concerned with the practical affairs of keeping house, rearing children, preparing meals, managing the servants, and so on, and she therefore has neither interest in nor patience with any foolishness of her husband that would jeopardize the smooth and orderly management of things. Since the Domestic Woman is the end product of the pursuit of the Princess and the ideal woman, Cabell has the formula for both satiric and ironic sexual comedy; and it is this comic dynamic that is at the heart of his novels.

The third type of woman is rarer and more interesting: the "Witch Queen" of mysterious, superhuman power. Because she is unpredictable, the Witch Queen can be as dangerous as she can be helpful. Her weakness usually lies in her feminine susceptibility to the flattering attentions of a younger man. Alianora, a Witch Queen, seemingly could not wait to be transformed into a Princess and thereafter into a Domestic Woman. Remaining a queen, however, she never achieved nor attempted the kind of respectability characteristic of Dame Naifer. Melusine remained a dangerous enchantress, while Freydis, also a dangerous enchantress, gave up her immortality and other supernatural prerogatives for a time in order to be with Manuel. Whether this was done out of love, as she later insisted, or vanity, as Manuel suspected, remains moot and in Cabell, delightfully so. Of the Witch Queens in the biography, the most powerful and mysterious is Sereda, sister of Koshchei the Deathless and one of the Aenseis—the demiurgic spirits who control a portion of Cabell's universe.

The three principal types of woman correspond closely to the three historic attitudes: the Princess is the equivalent of the chivalrous viewpoint, or is at least a corresponding virtue; the Domestic Woman seems to be the counterpart of the gallant attitude; and the Witch Queen finds her equivalent in the poetic approach. As is the case with the historic attitudes, the qualities of the three types combine to produce the potentially endless variety of incarnations of female life in the series.

The unifying theme of the series is the life of Manuel as it finds new expression in the generations of his descendants. The key to that life is its dissatisfaction with the world and its desire to discover that which truly and completely satisfies the spirit. There are many tokens and symbols of the heart's desire but none proves final or absolute, even those that come from the realm of the gods, who confess themselves as perplexed with man's apparent congenital dissatisfaction with the workings of the world as the Domestic Woman, who is forever exasperated with his eternal hankering after he knows not what. The impression that men are of the spirit and women of the earth is produced in Cabell's comic world at almost every level. From this dichotomy comes the basis for the eternal battle of the sexes. According to Koschei, the chief demiurge, it is a tension which is at the very heart of his creative design of the universe.

Not surprisingly, religion is one of the major recurrent themes of *The Biography of the Life of Manuel*. Cabell's approach to religion is both skeptical and naïve. It is skeptical in an anthropological sense, meaning that Cabell portrays religion as the product of man's mythmaking powers, driven by the passion to find meaning and solace in life. Cabell wishes to present the paradox he finds at the heart of all faith: the desire for coherence, meaning, and purpose in life, a unity that the evidence of the world and its history seems to deny.

In addition to religion, other important themes are those of courtship, romance, and sex, which represent the means by which Manuel's descent is managed. Courtship, in its various phases and mutations across the ages, is the focal point for the development of all the other themes and for the presentation, development, and analysis of character and narrative. The treatment is comedic, heavily spiced with satire and irony. The arena is the battle of the sexes from courtship and/or seduction to parenthood and beyond. It is the central fact of life in Cabell's genealogy of Manuel.

Cabell's approach to fantasy and the fantastic in *The Biography of the Life of Manuel* is an inventory of the potential range of narrative comedy in the fantastic mode. Cabell deliberately seems to challenge one of the most basic assumptions about fantasy, that the fantastic illusion, once established, must be maintained. Cabell invites the reader to see beneath the illusion as he constantly moves the reader back and forth between the world of fantasy and the mundane world. In using this approach, Cabell seems interested in illusion as the product of something like natural selection in both life and art. As an artist, Cabell wishes to create not one level of fantastic effect or illusion but many, one within the other, fantastic history merging with authentic history, each deconstructing and reconstructing the other in the mind of the reader. The great illusion is to erase the horizon line between the worlds of the real and the fantastic so that the reader can no longer tell where one begins and the other ends. Cabell's creation of the imaginary province of Poictesme should be understood in that context, as it exists at the crossroads of historic and fantastic reality. In Cabell's work, therefore, both dimensions seem to be enhanced by the presence of the other.

The Biography of the Life of Manuel is an essay in mythopoesis. It is also, by virtue of its comedic rationalism, a critique of the same. Surely one of Cabell's outstanding achievements as an artist is the ability to create the illusion of legend growing out of history and into myth, while at the same time creating sufficient comic distance from the process to afford the reader a new point of view regarding myth. The comic undercutting makes it impossible to invest what J. R. R. Tolkien terms "secondary belief" in the mythology of Manuel the Redeemer, which Miramon Lluagor orchestrates and which other characters promote for various reasons. Since the world of *The Biography of the Life of Manuel* is, so to speak, half mythic and half historic, Cabell does not need to underline the realization that the myth of Manuel the Redeemer dies out in time to be recalled only in the pages of history or romance or both combined. The point is made, and it is a recurrent motif of the biography, that myths have their day, and when they die, they move on into another world of thought: Antan (French for "yesteryear" or "from times past"), the world of romance and fantasy, to which the myths of the past are repatriated. In *The Biography of the Life of Manuel*, mythopoesis also makes the mundane world fit for human habitation. Myth brings order, a sense of purpose and meaning to life. Cabell's characters are always bumping into these mythic props supporting their culture and their minds. In one way or another, their response to these encounters defines their character for the reader as well as their position in the comedy in which they participate.

It is obvious from the dates of the books' publications that Cabell did a fair amount of backing and filling in putting together the entire genealogical patchwork. The work that stands now as a preface to the biography is *Beyond Life*, a work that would almost certainly discourage any new reader otherwise unfamiliar with the other fiction in the series. *Beyond Life* is conceived of as an elaborate literary exercise on the argument between realism and romance with suitable digressions on some of Cabell's favorite authors, who represent key values and points of view which he later develops. Readers are introduced to the three historic attitudes around which Cabell is to build the biography, together with explanations and illustrations. Many of the prevailing themes are also considered and discussed, such as woman worship, economy (especially the economy of poets as they create permanent works out of borrowed materials of life experience), the relation between mythmaking and religion, and the preferred virtue of urbanity recommended by the character John Charteris as the wanted palliative of the pathetic deficiencies of life and the world.

The first novel in the series, although not the first written, is *Figures of Earth*, which treats the life and legend of Dom Manuel of Poictesme. (The first work in the series to be written was *The Line of Love*; but the first published work was *The Eagle's Shadow*.) It is useful to recall that *Figures of Earth* was written after *Jurgen* and *The Cream of the Jest*, the latter being chronologically the last work of the genealogy. Cabell was therefore able to work back and forth across time and art in more ways than one, establishing premises for types, themes, motifs, objects, and characters later to appear in fictional time in the series but already abroad in previously published titles. This is one of the ways Cabell achieved the internal consistency of his genealogy as well as the internal frames of reference within the series that create the special pleasures of privileged knowledge and recognition which are among the most cherished rewards of series readership.

Figures of Earth is subtitled "A Comedy of Appearances," from which one expects that the comic vision would reveal the differences between appearances and reality; but Cabell is an ironist and rarely plain. The history of Manuel's rise from swineherd to Dom Manuel, Count and Redeemer of Poictesme, is undercut so often by the conflicting intentions of the principal characters that the reader is left with as much skepticism about reality as about appearances. The story of Manuel suggests that while realists may have truth on their side, the heroic man refuses to accept a mere factual economy of life without an accounting of dreams and desires that produces discontentment with things as they are. Manuel himself no more understands this discontentment than do the gods themselves, but it is the force which drives him until he denies it and is prepared to accept things as they are as the best bargain with fate that could be managed before he passes out of Poictesme and into legend. At the end, Manuel has certainly changed in many respects as the direct result of the obligations he has incurred willy-nilly pursuant to his attainments. One may see each fresh duty as a constraint, gradually choking the joy of life until he is willing to answer the call of Grandfather Death, even when the latter offers Manuel the right of refusal. It seems at this point that the boundary marker of Cabell's comic vision lies very close to tragedy, as disillusionment lies close to despair.

The story of Manuel is mock-heroic, treating with ironic and comic ambiguity the legendary history of Manuel the swineherd who becomes through a series of tricks, swindles, and deceptions, Redeemer of Poictesme. Manuel, however, is caught gradually in the toils of the legend he helps to create and becomes, in time, a worthy patriarch and redeemer figure despite his shortcomings and failings. At least, that appears to be the judgment toward which the reader is moved as the comedy draws to its end. Manuel begins and ends an ambiguous figure, and the transparency of the growth of his legend only enhances that ambiguity.

Miramon Lluagor, "Lord of the Nine kinds of sleep and Prince of the Seven Madnesses," presents Manuel the swineherd with the magic sword Flamberge and encourages him to undertake the quest of rescuing Gisele, the Count of Arnaye's daughter, held in durance vile atop the gray mountain Vraidex. Flamberge alone can break the enchantments of the mountain and rescue the princess from her dreaded captor, who is Miramon Lluagor himself. Miramon has three reasons for his patronage of Manuel. First, he claims that it is the will of the Norns (Fates). This reason sounds feeble in comparison to his other motives until the reader discovers Miramon later acting the part of Manuel's Merlin, making it possible, with the help of Horvendile, for Manuel to become the first ruler of Poictesme by conquering the Northmen and later to become the Redeemer by performing the requisite actions to qualify for that godlike office. Just what those actions are, Cabell leaves to his reader's fancy. Second, Miramon wishes to be rid of Gisele, who has settled down to become a Domestic Woman almost immediately after Miramon had abducted her. Finally, Miramon is anxious to dispose of Flamberge, the magic blade destined to come to the hand of King Arthur, which makes its bearer invincible, and which has been predicted to be the weapon with which Miramon's son will eventually kill him. However, Miramon's designs are frustrated when Gisele refuses to be rescued, since she is satisfied to be mistress of Vraidex. Meanwhile, Manuel has taken a fancy to Naifer, a rather homely girl who first introduced him to the art of encouraging others to deceive themselves, and he finds her wonderfully clever.

That which follows parodies the formulas and conventions of the heroic romance in the development of the young hero into the man of legend. Manuel begins absurdly, molding clay statuettes because his mother had placed a geas on him to "make a figure in the world." Each time he encounters an influential person, he remolds an idealized self-impression, including the features of that person with his own (King Helmas, King Ferdinand, Alianora) until he wins the secret of incarnating his figures of Earth from Queen Freydis. In the end, Manuel leaves Freydis even as he has eased his way out of marriage with Alianora, because each in her way wished him to live sensibly, while he insisted that he would "follow my own thinking and my own desire" and "see this world and all the ends of this world that I may judge them." These statements, often repeated by the younger Manuel, serve as a kind of refrain throughout the story, gaining ironic significance as Manuel gradually becomes the domesticated figure he refuses to acknowledge in his youth.

He may be said to be trapped by fate (the decrees of the Norns), by his pursuit of his geas, by Cabellian poetic justice (which flourishes in every novel), but the means by which Manuel is caught after escaping the traps of Alianora and Freydis are of his own making. Having encouraged Naifer to go in his place with Grandfather Death so that he might fulfill his geas, he chivalrously wishes her back from the pagan underworld where she had been taken. In order to do so, he must serve Beda, goddess of Misery, for a month of years, and so he forfeits his youth in order to reclaim the compliant Naifer whose figure he shapes out of Earth from memory—a fair likeness of the original but imperfect in several ways: she limps because Manuel failed to make her legs equal. No sooner does Naifer materialize than she, too, begins acting the part of the Domestic Woman and in time manages to establish a tolerable amount of control over the now middle-aged man whose intention of seeing and judging the world and all things in it is lost amid a series of indefinite postponements. He finds himself having to live up to popular expectations of a man in his position as both husband and nobleman, for Naifer is assiduous in pressing his obligation to maintain appearances (if not for his sake, then for hers and the children's). Thus Manuel sees the gradual exchange of his mother's geas, which led him into egoism and adventure, for the common geas of Naifer and that which seems expected, which leads him into role-playing, loss of self-identity, and eventually despair.

From this novel, Manuel leaves behind three lines of descent. Because of an earlier obligation involving the rescue of a stork from an eagle, Count Manuel was able to make the necessary arrangements for the stork to deliver five children to his wife, Dame Naifer. Of the five, four were delivered to Naifer, but one was transferred to Queen Alianora of England because she was childless. Hence, the line of Manuel descended through the English child (Edward Longshanks), through his four children delivered to Naifer (Melicent, Emmerick, Dorothy, and Ettarre), and through the figures of earth later animated by Queen Freydis, including Sesphra (a god of the Philistines), Alessandro de Medici, Shakespeare, Robert Herrick, Wycherley, Alexander Pope, Sheridan, John Charteris, and the ancestor of Rudolph V. Musgrave, compiler of *The Lineage of Lichfield* and thereby reputed author of *The Biography of the Life of Manuel*.

Cabell's fantastic gamesmanship includes prominently the question of authorship: literary, creative, biological, metaphysical, and cosmological. Throughout the biography, characters come face to face with figures (usually demiurges such as the Leshy Horvendile) who reveal, sometimes boastfully,

that the characters' lives are merely fictions invented by the enigmatic per-
sonage. However disconcerting these revelations prove, the characters continue about their business, dismissing, discounting, or ignoring them as
embarrassing, unaccountable aberrations in their daily routines.

Cabell's pantheon of phenomenological deities stretches from the gods to
men with poets as the last links in the chain of creation. In *Figures of Earth*,
this chain involves several orders and types of beings: the highest are the
three Norns, or the Fates; below the Norns and subject to their decrees are
the Leshy, an order that includes the magician Miramon Lluagor and Horvendile; and slightly below are the two witch demigoddesses, Alianora and Freydis, both queens, and each the lover of Manuel during his youth. Of the two,
Freydis is the more powerful and important, for it is she who teaches Manuel
the secret of animating his clay figures. It is through her power that the first
of the figures, Sesphra of the Dreams, is animated. Later, Sesphra is nearly
able to lure Manuel away from Poictesme to become a supreme artist, a kind
of demiurge; but although Manuel loves his own creation and yearns for a
life of greater excitement and personal fulfillment, he rejects Sesphra's
requirement that he slaughter his family so as to free himself from worldly
obligations.

The reader observes in the novel the process of Manuel the swineherd
becoming Manuel the Redeemer with the help of gods, men, and women,
high and low, each of whom, in one way or another, he betrays. Readers
watch the spectacle of Manuel's dealings with the world and how he becomes
one whom the gods choose to favor because he eventually becomes dependable. While it is true that "all kissed women turn to stupid figures of warm
earth and all love falls away with age into the acquiescence of beasts," it is
also true that Manuel has become a kind of redeemer despite the superstition
of the masses. Sentiment is served by the fact that the Manuel who sacrifices
his dreams for his children and his wife is a better and more admirable figure
than the charming young egoist who begins the story. Perhaps that is the key
to understanding the reappearance of the youthful Manuel, after his own
disappearance and death as the famous Dom Manuel of Poictesme, sitting by
the side of the road, modeling figures of clay, and waiting for Miramon Lluagor
to offer him the benefit of Flamberge. Thus, in a way, the story turns back
upon itself as Miramon comments upon the lock of hair missing from Manuel's
head, a sure sign of the Alf Charm of Suskind, since shortly before he murders
Suskind, an older Dom Manuel has had a lock of gray hair taken, and it is
to restore the missing lock of Melicent that Dom Manuel slays Suskind, the
"unkissed," and the only truly unattainable woman of the story.

This pattern of development is characteristic of the series, and it is, moreover, one of the chief ingredients in Cabell's special brand of fantasy. *Figures
of Earth* is a representative illustration of the main tendencies of this fantasy
and the means of achieving the effects which distinguish a Cabell fantasy from

that of another writer. The Cabellian intent includes the means by which the reader may experience, understand, and perhaps adopt an appropriate attitude toward life and the human comedy. The chief fantastic effect is the special sense of dislocation that comes from this very sophisticated trick of creating the illusion of a lost horizon between reason and vision, history and fiction, and primary and secondary realities. The difficulties of this Cabellian method become apparent in the question of simply which is the real Manuel: the one with or without the lock of hair. To what extent, for example, are readers encouraged to imagine an earlier Manuel, forelock intact, who went along perhaps another path to become Manuel the Redeemer, only to give birth to a figure of Earth whose adventures readers encounter in the book by the same title? Not only does Cabell eclipse the distinctions between reality and fantasy, but he also delights in playing with the implications of his own method. He successfully invites the reader to see through the fantastic world and characters he has created.

The third volume in the biography, *The Silver Stallion*, is subtitled "A Comedy of Redemption," and the comedy has a familiar cast. The motif that seems to dominate this collection of tales covering the adventures of the Fellowship of the Silver Stallion is "at a price," a motif that lies close to the heart of Cabellian ethics. Following the departure or death of Manuel, the members of the Fellowship go their separate ways at the direction of Horvendile, who persuaded Naifer to call a last meeting of the Fellowship and who somewhat cryptically directs each hero to a different point of the compass. As in *Figures of Earth*, the comic inventions revise the familiar expectations of heroic fantasy; the reader observes the growth of Manuel's myth, often despite rather than because of the adventures and preoccupations of the Fellowship.

The sagas of Dom Manuel's knights end as Horvendile had predicted. Necessarily, each contributed his share to the legend of Manuel the Redeemer. Gonfal became Holy Gonfal who repulsed the pagan queen; Pious Miramon resisted the Devil in the form of bees with the help of Manuel; and so on. When Radegonde calls upon Jurgen, the pawnbroker, to arrange replacing the gems adorning the statue of Manuel at the redeemer's tomb, Jurgen discovers that the jewels are nothing more than glass, and so ends the gest of *The Silver Stallion*.

Jurgen's story is told in the novel of 1919, *Jurgen*, which had the good luck of being banned and the target for Comstockery. As the natural result, *Jurgen* became a rare commercial success for its author, a cause around which enlightened authors and critics could rally, and for a generation, the benchmark of Cabell's achievement as a comic satirist. Rarely in the body of apologetic critical literature supported by *Jurgen* since the 1920's has there been much interest in the work as comic fantasy or in its place as part of *The Biography of the Life of Manuel* until the recent renaissance of fantasy has made it once again critically respectable.

Jurgen is by no means the most bawdy of Cabell's sexual comedies; nevertheless, Jurgen's career in search of justice takes him into the arms of the most famous temptresses in the best bowers of bliss known to myth and legend, both pagan and Christian. The theme of the battle of the sexes is one that Cabell never tired of chronicling in the lives of the descendants of Manuel, and it marks perhaps the most persistent theme and interest of the entire series. Manuel's descendants, male and female, represent various reincarnations of the patriarch and of Jurgen as well. In these progressive incarnations, their descendants try to work out anew the problems that define the human comedy of the biography; and none is more seriocomic, more vexatious and shot through with paradox than the relations between the sexes, characterized by Koschei, the eternal and chief demiurge of the universe, as a mixture of love and disliking. Yet, each generation begins by believing that it has the chance to conduct life in an entirely satisfactory manner only to discover that the very virtues which make for civilized life—compromise, self-sacrifice, and deference—lead to isolation, unhappiness, and even despair. Those who escape such a melancholy fate among the descendants of Manuel and Jurgen must either retain their illusions or lose them entirely in favor of gallantry. Even then, disillusionment brings sorrow, however mitigated it may be by the sense of self-possession that gallantry creates.

It is surely one of the cultural markers of the present era that Cabell's witty comedy of the sexes seems to have such little appeal to the rising generation of young readers whose reputed sexual mores would appear to make them candidates for easy identification with a character like Jurgen. Nothing, however, could be further from actual experience. The comedy is too sophisticated, and Jurgen is, after all, a middle-aged pawnbroker and former poet who knows both the price and the value of nearly everything. He cultivates no illusions, although he has the wisdom to permit those who have them (especially if they are young and comely) to retain them against the disagreeable compromises of life. The reader is reminded that the Society for the Suppression of Vice did not have much of a sense of humor when it came to sex, proving that comedy and pornography are incompatible ventures. Pornography is one thing, indecency is another. Cabell never claimed that his work was not indecent. It is one of the keys to his handling of sexual comedy.

Jurgen begins his adventure a fortnight before his last meeting with Dame Naifer at the tomb of Manuel recorded in the closing chapters of *The Silver Stallion*. The adventure lasts a little more than a full solar year of "out" time and less than a day of "in" time. Cabell designs the adventures of his hero as a parody of the mythic solar hero (Hercules is the chosen satiric reference) as Jurgen proceeds in his adventures from one house of the zodiac to another. An important object of Cabellian satire in *Jurgen* are those critics of myth for whom solar gods and heroes were the key which unlocked the secrets of mythic consciousness. In the "Foreword: Which Asserts Nothing," Cabell indulges some good-natured deconstruction of the inflated readings of the so-called "Jurgen legend" by myth critics whose "solar theory" is invoked in order to reveal the "esoteric meaning of these folk-stories." Such jibing is in part self-mockery because Cabell profited from his own readings in cultural anthropology, with special emphasis on folk legends and myths. Indeed, early modern scientific studies of myth and its place in human culture form a matrix for the entire biography. Sometimes this material expresses itself as an organizing device of narrative motifs and at other times as the basis for characterization, burlesque, self-parody, and most often for deflating criticism of middle-class cultural views based upon unexamined survivals of Victorian notions of propriety and respectability derived from reactionary religion and public opinion. These were, for the author, especially deserving targets of the full arsenal of comic deflation, including a studied but consistently lively indecency which owed as much to Aristophanes and Rabelais as to James Frazer and Sigmund Freud. One of Cabell's more potent weapons is to adopt something of his own idiom, against prudery.

Jurgen begins his apotheosis by reproving a passing monk for cursing the Devil after stubbing his toe. In gratitude, an apparent devil has Jurgen's wife, Dame Lisa (born Adelais, daughter of Ninzian), disappear into a cave. Jurgen follows and meets Nessus, the centaur, who carries him off on his quest "in search of justice, over the grave of a dream and through the malice of time." It is Nessus who gives Jurgen his shirt, identifying the latter as an authentic hero. Jurgen's progress begins at the "Garden between Dawn and Sunrise," where he encounters his grand illusion, the idealized woman, Dorothy la Désirée, his onetime sweetheart, restored to her bloom of youth. Dorothy is Manuel's daughter, sister of Count Emmerick, whom Jurgen lost to Heitman Michael (son of Guivric of Perdigon) during the exile imposed by Jurgen's father, Coth of the Rocks. Despite Nessus' counsel that the Dorothy of Jurgen's youthful dreams was but the fantasy of a poet, Jurgen cajoles Mother Sereda, who controls Wednesdays and whose task is the bleaching of all things, to give him a special Wednesday in August of 1256, on which day a masque, "The Birth of Dionysos," was enacted at Bellegarde, the castle of Count Emmerick. At the masque were Dame Melicent and Perion de la Forêt, little Ettarre, and the principals involved in the night Jurgen regarded as the turning point in his life, the night in which Heitman Michael returned triumphantly to Bellegarde. This event also turns out to be the point at which Melicent and Perion begin their passion recorded in *Domnei*.

Domnei, Cabell's comedy of woman worship, originally appeared in 1913 as *The Soul of Melicent* and was later revised and lengthened. The Author's Note touches upon the reputed authorship by Nicolas de Caen of the story of Melicent, Manuel's daughter. The same Nicolas de Caen, an actual historian, is credited by Cabell (fictitiously) with the authorship of the gests of

The Silver Stallion. The sense of dislocation produced by the Chinese box puzzle of tales within tales, authors writing within the works of other writers, is another one of the persistent tensions within separate works of the biography. The theme culminates in the two final titles of *The Biography of the Life of Manuel*.

In *Domnei*, the chivalrous attitude is revealed in the conduct of both the male and female characters, but especially in Perion and Melicent. Woman worship, or domnei, as it is called, is a manifestation of the chivalrous attitude. Each chief male figure demonstrates an aspect of chivalry. Even schemers such as Ayrart de Montors and Ahasuerus, who do not seem initially to be chivalrous, prove to be, in a sense, the most chivalrous of all as devoted admirers of "The Soul of Melicent." All the lovers of Melicent, the archetypal heroine of romance, worship her in an appropriate but distinctive way. Perion loves the Melicent he idealizes as the object of a heroic quest. She becomes for him, therefore, an incarnation of the dream woman no man may ever possess. Theodoret, the king Melicent was destined to marry, loves her qualities of youth and beauty. Montors, a bishop and later a Pope, loves her essential beauty, which he takes for wisdom. Demetrios, son of Miramon Lluagor, scourge of Christian Europe, and captor of Perion, whom Melicent ransoms with her own body, loves the integrity and fidelity of her spirit. Demetrios, moreover, knows that these are illusions and that Perion is something of a fool. Ahasuerus, the counselor and servant of Demetrios, loves the beauty of Melicent but above all, perhaps, the craft that fidelity and innocence employs in its service. By offering herself to save Perion, first to Demetrios and then later to Ahasuerus, Melicent places obligations of chivalry on those who would otherwise force her without her consent.

Cabellian comedy in *Domnei* is of two kinds. The first defines the illusions of youthful love and chivalry, exemplified in the episodes involving Perion and Melicent. The second aspect of the comedy of woman worship is the discovery in cynics—men of the world, ambitious self-servers, villains, and dictators—manifestations of the chivalrous attitude. This aspect is seen in all of Melicent's lovers, who prove to be not only woman worshipers but also admirers of the illusions of Melicent and Perion, because they find those illusions impossible and fragile.

The Music from Behind the Moon is a much shorter work and deals with the fortunes of Ettarre, the youngest daughter of Manuel, as the object of the woman-worshiping of both Sargatanet, a fallen angel, and Madoc, the great poet who composed with a quill from the wings of Lucifer, the father of all lies. As in most of the biography, however, the woman's point of view is represented only from the perspective of the obviously male narrator and the other males involved. In this tale, Ettarre remains the ideal woman, as it seems to be her destiny in such later works as *The Cream of the Jest*. Her chief quality is to be desirable and elusive, hence the true Ettarre seems to have the bad luck of being desired but never possessed. *The Music from Behind the Moon* is, therefore, more the story of Madoc, the poet to whom Ettarre appears and plays her music, and his search for Ettarre and her music.

Despite its length, readers following the development of the biography will learn numerous worthwhile pieces of the overall design of the cosmology of Cabell's fantastic universe from *The Music from Behind the Moon*, including Ettarre's apprenticeship, some hints on true and false poetry and their origins, the identity of Maya of the Fair Breasts (who returns in *Something About Eve*), and the Book of the Norns. The Norns were given responsibility for writing the history of the world, called "Earth's Epic." In writing the history, of course, the Norns were creating it, and since it was one of their first efforts, they admit to having written a great deal of balderdash as the result of their inexperience: "So we put poets in that book and death, and God, and common sense, and I can hardly remember what other incredibilities."

The next major work in the series is *The High Place*, which Cabell intended as a deconstruction of *Jurgen*, showing the effects of mixing gallantry with egoism. In Jurgen's character, gallantry was mixed with the poetic attitude, keeping him always detached enough from himself and his experiences to save him from the disillusionment of attempting the fulfillment of his dreams. Whereas Jurgen committed himself to the attitude of gallantry in a provisional way (as Cabell indicates in his Author's Note to *The High Place*), Florian's pursuit is more wholehearted than tentative; and it is marred by three defects of his character. Florian is an egoist with loyalties to none but himself and the code of Puysange. His desire for both beauty and holiness, doubtless expressions of his era (the late seventeenth century), is compromised by his egoism. Moreover, the pursuit of those virtues with the object of somehow possessing or controlling them is compatible with the pursuit of gallantry. Beauty is the proper object of the poetic attitude and holiness of chivalry, but neither is proper to gallantry, which instead demands self-possession. When Jurgen was given the opportunity to test his dream of ideal beauty, he refused to unveil Helen, prferring instead the illusion. Florian, as an egoist, is determined to satisfy his ambitions and his desires, seizing the opportunity to lift the enchantment on Brunbelois in order to possess his dream princess, Melior.

In *Something About Eve*, Cabell shows that paternity can lead to love and self-sacrifice rather than rivalry and combat. There is also a fantastic condition to such lately found devotion for Gerald Musgrave, the hero of the story: his son is imaginary, and as soon as Gerald declares himself contented, he loses everything that made him so. *Something About Eve* is the last novel of the biography to be written. It was published one year after *The Silver Stallion*, which it resembles in style, spirit, and theme.

Gerald is a descendant in the nineteenth generation of the life of Manuel, and he also traces his descent from Madoc, the poet in *The Music from Behind the Moon*. As such, there is a division in his nature between the poetic and the chivalrous. Gerald's failure to reach Antan and fulfill his quest of a poetic or heroic destiny, however, is to be regarded as a victory of his humanity over his ambition, according to Cabell in the Author's Note. How such a state of affairs came about is the argument of the novel.

The last major novel in *The Biography of the Life of Manuel* and in the series is *The Cream of the Jest*, in which Cabell's genius for metafictional illusion is given its most sophisticated expression. The novel is presented in the form of a reminiscence by Richard Fentnor Harroby, an author, whose last book, *The Cream of the Jest*, concerns the career and the double life of Felix Kennaston, who appears earlier in *The Eagle's Shadow* as the author of *Men Who Loved Alison*, the book which marked him as a genius. Harroby's account of Kennaston is self-consciously ambiguous: Harroby is torn between dislike for the man and admiration for the author. Harroby's attitude is an indicator underlining Cabell's sense of values expressed first in *Beyond Life* and throughout the works of the biography about the relationship between life and art. Indeed, Kennaston wins Cabell's highest accolade as a writer in the former's "ultimate success as an economist." The terms of Kennaston's success and the price he must pay for it are the subjects of the novel.

The Cream of the Jest completes *The Biography of the Life of Manuel* in both primary and secondary senses. The biography on which Gerald worked in the nineteenth century also occupies Kennaston in the twentieth. That work, left incomplete by Kennaston, is presumably completed by Harroby in his last book, which bears the current title. Readers learn, however, in *The Lineage of Lichfield*, that the story of Kennaston as told in *The Cream of the Jest* is itself part of the biography of Harroby contained in *The Musgraves of Matocton*, written by the noted genealogist Colonel Rudolph Musgrave. This pattern of one fictional life, genealogy, and order of reality leading into another is at the very heart of the biography and of this last novel. Cabell never sends the reader on wild goose chases or into dead ends; rather, the metabiography always leads back into itself in ways typical of the primary world. Cabell's world unites the artificial and natural in relationships designed to exercise the reader's sense of imagined awe and wonder while producing the illusion of a displacement of reality in the intersection of history and fantasy. Hence, real and imaginary characters rub shoulders in the biography of Manuel's lives, and even the historical characters are given imaginary genealogies or roles to play in the comedy.

The illusion is as satisfying as it is complex and depends on the contrived disorientation of the reader's sense of the differences between primary and secondary history and finally between primary and secondary realities. Cabell does not intend that his reader accept a fantastic secondary reality nor does he propose that the reader disbelieve in the primary world. Rather, they both exist simultaneously: in Cabellian fantasy, readers find the primary world implicated and modified as much as the fantastic appears to be potential in the real. The conventional boundaries between primary and secondary disappear, and distinctions between real and imagined are redefined. The reader experiences a special kind of dislocation which has later come to be associated with the fantasy of writers such as Jorge Luis Borges and postmodern metafictionists such as John Barth.

The story of Felix Kennaston is modeled after Cabell's own life, making this the most autobiographical of the novels in the biography. Kennaston is the twenty-second and last of the generations of Manuel. He adopts toward life the poetic attitude and is a spiritual descendant of Madoc (*The Music from Behind the Moon*). While not a direct descendant of Gerald Musgrave, being rather collateral, Kennaston should be seen as his spiritual descendant. Kennaston is, in the phrase of John Charteris, an economist, the most successful of the entire biography. He lives the life of a Southern gentleman in Lichfield (Richmond) during the late nineteenth and early twentieth centuries, thanks to his wife's fortune. His fame rests upon an early novel, *Men Who Loved Alison*, augmented by *The Tinctured Veil* and *The King's Quest*, works in which Kennaston's experiences in Poictesme as Horvendile find their artistic expression. Kennaston finds the entire business of his double life both satisfying and·perplexing. As his imaginary life develops, his biological life becomes more commonplace, conventional, and trite.

The key to Kennaston's double life is the Sigil of Scotia, the amulet Kennaston finds upon his garden path. To Harroby, for whom *Men Who Loved Alison* is miraculous, the Sigil is nothing more than half the lid of a cold-cream jar (Harroby's Crême Cleopatre). Its origin is, therefore, hopelessly commercial and commonplace. For Kennaston, the Sigil originates elsewhere, in the world of romance and legend, being the amulet of Ptolemy which came to Manuel as spoils of his wrestling victory over his father Oriander the Swimmer and thence to Ettarre as a portion of her inheritance. Ettarre in turn gave Horvendile half the broken Sigil, which had the power to transport him from his country (Kennaston's twentieth century America), "an inadequate place in which to live," to the world of Poictesme. The relationship between Kennaston and Horvendile is foreshadowed in the relationship between Glaum and Gerald Musgrave in *Something About Eve*, but Horvendile is the romantic extension of the poet's self in the world of his imagining where he meets Ettarre, the archetypal woman. The law of that imaginary world is such, however, that whenever Horvendile attempts to touch Ettarre, the dreamworld disappears and Ettarre with it. The paradox of the Grecian urn is obviated, however, by two conditions of Kennaston's divided life. The first is that the Sigil offers him a sure passage into the world in which he is fulfilled as Horvendile and in which Ettarre is his Beatrice. As his life at Storisende increases, his life at home with his wife Kathleen diminishes. As Horvendile discovers, however, the world of his making has its own laws and his characters their own lives, even though he believes he has created them. In this belief, Horvendile appears to be mistaken, at least regarding Ettarre, and he comes to realize that she represents something fundamental that is beyond and outside his power to invent or to control. Ettarre becomes, as Beatrice was for Dante, Kennaston's link with divine authorship, a power that transcends secondary creation and promises a primary creation in which the aspirations of the heart for beauty and truth may be fulfilled.

The key to the fantasy in *The Cream of the Jest* is the Sigil of Scotia, with its dual history symbolizing the duality of the world and the dual lives of Felix and Kathleen Kennaston. Felix discovers the other half of the Sigil in his wife's dresser drawer and realizes that the woman with whom he lives on such comfortable but unheroic terms must be Ettarre. However, Kathleen refuses to discuss the matter, and when confronted by Felix with both halves of the Sigil, she laughs and throws them away as worthless trash. The ideal woman can be known only through art, but even there her mystery cannot be solved, and she can never be possessed. If such knowledge and possession is portioned for humans, it must lie in a world beyond art, a world that Cabell implies only art can glimpse.

In the Storisende edition of *The Cream of the Jest*, the reader will find a drawing of the Sigil done by Cabell in a curious script of his own. The drawing is reproduced in the Ballantine edition, albeit dimly, and is translated as follows: "James Branch Cabell made this book so that he who wills may read the story of man's eternally unsatisfied hunger in search of beauty. Ettarre stays inaccessible always and her loveliness is hid to look on only in his dreams. All men she must evade at the last and many are the ways of her elusions." Notwithstanding the implied disclaimer of the inscription, Kennaston rejoins the separate halves of the Sigil and finds the way back to Storisende, thus returning the life of Manuel to his home and effectively closing the circle of *The Biography of the Life of Manuel* into a work of art. The testimony of Harroby, the skeptical friend and grudging admirer of Kennaston, reminds the reader that what may be lost in life is to be gained in art, but only if one adopts the fantastic attitude.

In the genre of fantasy literature, James Branch Cabell occupies a distinguished position. The size and extent of his work in *The Biography of the Life of Manuel* make him unique in American letters, and he ranks with the greatest writers of comic fantasy in world literature. Although his influence has been thus far less pervasive, he can be paired with Tolkien in achievement. Within the limits of the comic, ranging from puns to serious and philosophic comedy, Cabell knows no peers in modern fantasy.

Viewed in the larger perspective of world literature, Cabell is seen as the author of a series that is of uneven merit and perhaps of inordinate length. Judging his art by its highest achievement in the major works of the biography, Cabell excels in three areas. First, he is a rare comic genius in the tradition of Aristophanes, Rabelais, and Congreve. Although more classical and European than American, Cabell shares much in common with Mark Twain and has influenced comtemporary writers from Peter S. Beagle and L. Sprague de Camp to Kurt Vonnegut, Jr. Perhaps more than any other major comic writer, Cabell's work deliberately and thoroughly includes the full scope and history of comic invention.

It is equally remarkable that he achieves this sweeping comic perspective in the fantastic mode, and his second area of achievement is as a comic fantasist emerging from the aesthetic tradition and moving into experimentalism. Cabell is both antirealist and anti-idealist, roles he shares with many of his better-known contemporaries writing in the comic mode, such as James Joyce and George Bernard Shaw. As a fantasist, Cabell is as experimental as Joyce and Shaw in their chosen modes. Readers of the biography may be surprised to find a persistent and informed interest in the sciences, particularly anthropology and biology, complementing his mastery of language, history, and especially genealogy.

The third area of supreme achievement for Cabell is as a moral allegorist. A contemporary of H. L. Mencken, Sinclair Lewis, and Sherwood Anderson, Cabell reveals a keen sense of the shortcomings of American culture in the first third of the twentieth century. While many authors, like Joyce, were stung and moved to invective and retort by obtuse reviewers, pragmatic publishers, and an indifferent public, few writers were able to turn their personal disappointments to such witty and comic benefit as did Cabell in his prefatory Author's Notes. Beyond American provincialism and the contemporary state of arts and letters, Cabell addressed himself to such universal moral ailments as triumphant pragmatism and hypocrisy as special targets for mockery, ridicule, and correction.

Cabell wrote for a world lacking a sense of absolutes and inherent values. He insists in his work that human imagination can supply what intellect does not discover and therefore denies. The medieval world of Poictesme, while far from Utopian, is protected by its sense of universal allegory. Gradually, as that allegorical consciousness diminished during the post-Renaissance, science and art provided the matrix which held together the Western world view. Since the Renaissance, art has been creating anthrocentric experiences and has been preserving the sense of human value in an increasingly chaotic and complex universe. In the modern era, art itself has become the vassal of science's obsession with facts that cannot either explain themselves or the world of which they are presumably an integrated part. Romance and fantasy resist the vulgarity and hopeless matter-of-factness of realism and naturalism, but they too must have a check or restraint on their tendency to ignore or worse, in Cabell's view, betray truth. The check is the comic view that corrects excess because it constantly reminds the poet that illusions are imagined and not objective realities, that the gods are projections of a human need for meaning in life. The comic element also gives expression to the chaos of nature and the incoherence of history, both of which continually overwhelm human self-deceptions about the everyday affairs of life. Yet the comic view consoles as it corrects, because, in the end, it realizes the good in some things, if not everything, human; in that vein, the comic view is hopeful without necessarily being self-deceived.

Cabell is a comic fantasist who sees the world historically and essentially in human terms. If the comic spirit is a necessary corrective to the romance of fantasy, the latter is also a necessary corrective to the mundane and commonplace world in which the human spirit is in danger of being forgotten or suppressed.

Donald L. Lawler

Bibliography

Cabell, James Branch. *Letters*, 1975. Edited by Edward Wagenknecht.

Davis, Joe Lee. *James Branch Cabell*, 1962.

Duke, Maurice. *James Branch Cabell: A Reference Guide*, 1979.

Glasgow, Ellen. "The Biography of Manuel," in *Saturday Review of Literature*. VI (1930), pp. 1108-1109.

Hall, James N., and Nelson Bond. *James Branch Cabell: A Complete Bibliography*, 1976.

Mencken, H. L. *James Branch Cabell*, 1927.

Teaford, Ruth R. *Southern Homespun*, 1980.

Wagenknecht, Edward. "Cabell: A Reconsideration," in *College English*. IX (1948), pp. 238-246.

Wells, Arvin. *Jesting Moses: A Study in Cabellian Comedy*, 1962.

THE BIRTHGRAVE TRILOGY

Author: Tanith Lee (1947-   )
First book publications: The Birthgrave (1975); *Vazkor, Son of Vazkor* (1978); *Quest for the White Witch* (1978)
Type of work: Novels
Time: The eclectic past of the sword-and-sorcery genre
Locale: The various lands of an earthlike planet

Among a complex group of societies ruled by violence and magic, a superhuman woman seeks her identity; her abandoned son, grown to manhood, seeks her

> *Principal characters:*
> KARRAKAZ, ALIAS UASTI, UASTIS, AND RESSAVEN, the last survivor of a lost race of superhuman beings
> DARAK, a brigand, her first consort
> VAZKOR, a scheming politician and warrior, her second consort
> VAZKOR, ALIAS TUVEK, son of Vazkor and Karrakaz
> SOREM, royal prince of Bar-Ibithni, friend of the younger Vazkor
> MALMIRANET, his mother, the younger Vazkor's mistress
> LELLIH, an old woman rejuvenated by the younger Vazkor

Imagine a planet very like Earth, with earthlike seas, mountains, and plains. Imagine it inhabited by people like the people of Earth, working and dealing, brawling and fornicating, scheming and loving, in sparsely populated agrarian societies. Imagine its cities and empires, with their haunting similarities to Rome, to medieval Islam, to European peasant cultures and central Asian (or North American) nomadic ones. Imagine its technologies: cannon and paper, steel forging and clock making, its witchcraft and slavery. Then imagine the sudden arrival in the midst of these of a member of the Lost Race, godlike superpeople who once ruled all that world. Imagine that she, like her lost forebears, has no need of food or drink; heals miraculously from all wounds, including fatal ones; and has no limitations on her Power, a pure mental energy which can, at her will, either heal or destroy. The sum of these imaginings is the world and the narrator of Tanith Lee's *The Birthgrave*, first of a sprawling trilogy of novels dealing with that world, that woman, and her son. The two remaining novels, *Vazkor, Son of Vazkor* and *Quest for the White Witch*, constitute a single sequel narrated by the son.

The woman—whose real name neither she nor the reader knows until the end of *The Birthgrave*—awakes, fully grown but amnesiac, in a cavern within a volcano just beginning to erupt. A mysterious voice identifying itself as Karrakaz the Soulless One tells her of the evil of her race and the curse upon her (to leave the cavern will be to ensure that the volcano will destroy the surrounding countryside). She deserves to die, the voice tells her: she is evil and hideous, kin only to Jade, not humankind. Terrified, she flees Karrakaz, surviving the eruption and embarking on a quest to find herself and her people.

Throughout it, she is pursued by the memory of Karrakaz, haunted by the vision of Jade, disgusted by her physical ugliness (a preternatural whiteness of hair and flesh which she hides behind a series of veils and masks, and worshiped as a goddess for her strange powers and extraordinary talents.

This very large novel—402 pages of text—is basically a picaresque quest. The goal of the search, as often in such fiction, is knowledge of self. More than anything else, the narrator wishes to establish who she is and, perhaps even more important, why she is in her current circumstances. She is aided in succession by three men to whom she becomes attached. The first, Darak the brigand, teaches her about sex (and perhaps love) and about the ways of those who live by their wits and their swords. The opening third of the novel recounts her few weeks with Darak, from the time he snatches her from the town she woke in as it is being destroyed by the volcano to his death at the very moment of his greatest triumph. This section is a splendid freewheeling adventure, climaxing in the grand festival chariot race of the Sirkunix, which Darak wins, in part because of the narrator's skill at archery. Lee uses a large, crowded canvas to depict an age not unlike the Roman Empire two millennia ago; against this backdrop, the narrator learns something of her Powers and hears a few supernatural hints about her origin and nature.

She learns much more in the company of her second lover, Vazkor, whom she meets after a time of trial in the wilderness (including her own death by violence and her resurrection two or three days later). Vazkor purports to be of her race, and has indeed mastered some of its Powers. He is mostly interested, however, in using her to further his ambitious scheme to unify all the surrounding city-states under his rule. He therefore makes her appear to be the incarnation of the goddess Uastis, and has her married to the ruling Javhovor, a boy named Asren. Vazkor then removes Asren, marries the goddess himself, and has himself declared Javhovor. Overwhelmed by his energy, his resemblance to Darak, and his sexuality, the narrator plays along as he begins a war of conquest and unification. After Vazkor deliberately impregnates her, however, she loses her patience and her temper. Unable to abort the child, she crushes Vazkor by willing the destruction of his forces in a storm, then escapes the ruin of his schemes by joining a nomadic band. Among them she secretly gives birth to a son, whom she exchanges for the chieftain's son, born the same day and dead soon afterward from natural causes.

Fleeing, she reaches the sea in the company of a band of nomadic blacks. At the coast are evidences of her race—an abandoned and haunted tower, a faded and illegible book. On the verge of despair, threatened by the apparent nearness of Karrakaz, the Soulless One, she is attacked by a dragon and rescued by a passing starship, which she boards. The captain, third of her male mentors, persuades her to undergo analysis by the sentient computer on the ship, a brain which she had called from space to assist her with the dragon. She learns that she is the sole surviving princess of the Lost Race, the last members of which had retreated before a plague to an underground temple. There the priest Sekish berated them, convincing them that the plague was visited on them for using their Power corruptly. Despite their contrition, they continued to die from the plague; even Sekish succumbed. Only the narrator lives. Surviving in a cave but deep in a coma, she is awakened by the impending eruption of the surrounding volcano. (The cavern is thus her intended tomb and a protecting womb—her birth grave.) Having learned all this, she removes her veil and finds that she has been seeking outside herself what has all along been within. The Jade is implanted in her forehead as a caste sign and is indeed her kin (for she is not really human); she is incredibly beautiful, not hideous; and her own name is Karrakaz. As the novel ends, she leaves the ship, alone, possessing an identity and seeking a destiny.

In the sequels, the son of Karrakaz—known first as Tuvek—embarks on a quest not unlike hers. His goal is the mysterious woman who bore him and left him on the day of his birth. Like his mother, he begins in ignorance of his true identity and of his special talents. Of the latter, he begins to learn when the ritual tattoos marking his entry to manhood heal without a trace. Of the former, he begins to learn when, at nineteen, he leads a raid on a nearby city and is mistaken for Vazkor come back from the dead. Some months later, he learns of his true mother and her desertion of him; taking his true father's name, he kills his foster father with his Power and is taken to the city. Upon arrival, however, he is thrown into a dungeon when he tries to claim his heritage. After being tortured by agents of the current Javhovor, Vazkor is rescued by Demizdor, a city woman he had captured in his earlier raid. He escapes from the city through a long tunnel, at the end of which he meets the black tribe that had once sheltered his mother. With the young witch Hwenit, Vazkor goes to an offshore island, where he learns witchcraft and counsels the girl and her brother, who are struggling against their incestuous passion for each other. The moral problem is interrupted by the arrival of a raiding party seeking Vazkor. He defeats them, heals Hwenit (killed in the melee), and goes off in a small boat to seek his mother. His departure is the end of *Vazkor, Son of Vazkor*, shortest and least successful of the novels. A shapeless work without a real climax, it serves primarily as a bridge between the two longer works.

The final novel of the series, *Quest for the White Witch*, is—like *The Birthgrave*—the record of a search for the identity of the mysterious albino woman who profoundly affects societies through which she passes. Vazkor, in his quest, uses his Power from the first—to heal himself and his retainer when they are injured in a storm at sea; to defend himself aboard the ship that rescues them, and then to capture it; to establish himself as a powerful healer, a force to be reckoned with, in the city of Bar-Ibithni to which the ship sails. The two most important public actions of his first few days in the Masrian empire set in motion all the events of his stay there. First, he makes Lellih, an obscene old hag, young again; this hubristic healing leads to much trouble, including Vazkor's death. Lellih, it turns out, both despises and worships her savior, who spurns her sexual favors. Since she has read Vazkor's mind during the healing incident, she uses his quest against him, feigning his mother's Powers, luring Vazkor to her, and finally attacking him with supernatural Power stolen from him during her rejuvenation. Vazkor is required to drain his energies in opposing her so that he dies in killing her with his psychic force.

This confrontation occurs well along in the sequence of events set in motion by his other public action, the embarrassing of Sorem, son of the emperor. As Vazkor and Sorem attempt to settle their differences by a duel, they are attacked by forces loyal to another son of the emperor. Fighting side by side, the two discover an affinity which leads to friendship and to Vazkor's taking part in a coup staged by Sorem. Vazkor gives up much—he betrays people who worship him as their long-lost god. He also gains much, not least the sexual favors of Sorem's mother Malmiranet; a jealous Sorem plans to punish Vazkor after the coronation. The ceremony is disrupted, however, by a plague of flies, sent by Lellih and carrying a deadly disease which kills much of the population of Bar-Ibithni—including Sorem. Vazkor seeks out Lellih, to their mutual death; Malmiranet kills herself, not wishing to be subject to Sorem's rival, whose mother is another wife of the late emperor.

Rising from the dead a month later, then, Vazkor finds nothing to keep him in Bar-Ibithni, and resumes his quest. The search, by land and sea, takes months, but he finally arrives at the snowbound southern city of Kainium, where Karrakaz rules. He finds pale, blond children using Powers irresponsibly to tease his mother's worshipers; he finds, also, their mentor, the incredibly beautiful Ressaven, who tries to intercept him. Vazkor and Ressaven experience immediate psychic communion and, soon, sexual union—the latter despite Vazkor's qualms about intercourse with a sister, and over Ressaven's own protests. The morning after their lovemaking, Vazkor overcomes the resistance of Karrakaz's retainers and of Ressaven and enters his mother's citadel. After a long conversation, he matches Power with her and wins, only to discover that he has been conversing with an illusion. Stunned, he realizes that Ressaven is Karrakaz: his mistress is his mother. In despair at his Oedipal crime, he flees, but after five months of exile he returns, intending to beget a new race upon his lover and mother.

It would be a mistake to take the three Karrakaz novels too seriously. Basically, they are rousing sword-and-sorcery adventures, mixing violent excitement with a series of power fantasies and with more than a little eroticism. At this level, their only remarkable feature is the unusual female protagonist of the first novel and her domination of the consciousness of the more conventional protagonist of the other two. Their obvious aesthetic kin ranges from *The Three Musketeers* (1844; young Vazkor is a kind of D'Artagnan) through *Ben-Hur* (1880; especially the chariot race in the 1959 film version by William Wyler) to the Marvel Comics versions of Robert E. Howard's Conan and Red Sonja. In common with these works, the "Birthgrave" books are burdened by contrived plotting, stereotyped characters, and a style seemingly composed of equal parts of clumsiness and pretention. Lee, for example, insists that people are "birthed," not "born," and "concussed," not "knocked unconscious." A sensitive reader needs too often to ignore such sentences as this one, referring to the Boys' Rite of Vazkor's adoptive tribe: "No male became a warrior without he had undergone it." Lee discusses some topics—especially botanical ones—in an anachronistically technical vocabulary, and she will occasionally stop her narrative dead with a passage so purple it blinds the reader: "The sea, pebbled and scythed by the deluge, blended into an auburn distance." Clearly, the volumes were written rapidly; they need editing.

Equally mistaken, however, would be a failure to take the books seriously enough. Lee is grappling with major themes; power, who shall wield it, and what its effects are on both user and target. The unbridled power of the lost doomed them; their descendants, Karrakaz and Vazkor, must learn the responsible use of their inheritance, and both carry a heavy weight of guilt for the transgressions committed before the lesson was learned. Moreover, there is the recurring question in the novels of the sources and use of power in sexual relationships. Indeed, *The Birthgrave* is probably the first major feminist critique of sword-and-sorcery cast as a novel within the genre itself; as such, it deserves careful comparison with John Norman's antifeminist Gor books.

Lee's trilogy has other virtues as well. The principal structuring of the books, within each individual work and between works, is by parallelism of event and character. This technique, rather than the linked-variations-on-a-theme of a true trilogy, unifies the work. Thus, Karrakaz meets and loves a series of men who turn out to be avatars of the priest Sekish, dimly remembered from her childhood; thus, she repeatedly attracts to herself sets of three male retainers who serve as her bodyguards. Thus, also, Vazkor meets some who knew her as he retraces her path across the world. Lee further structures the novels by using powerful sexual motifs; each principal character is identified with a particular form of aberrant sexual behavior. In the case of Karrakaz, it is rape: she herself is violated several times, particularly by those whom she later comes to love; she also observes several rapes, performed on other women as expressions of either sexual need or dominance. In the case of Vazkor, it is incest; he moves from observing brother-sister sex through sexual liaison with a friend's mother to congress with his own mother, first under the impression that she is his sister, and then deliberately. Lee's dramatizations and analyses of these situations increase the power of the novels.

   The Birthgrave launched Tanith Lee's meteoric career in adult speculative fiction. The novel and its two successors are not lacking in flaws; they are too long, overwritten, and somewhat implausible. These weaknesses, however, are those of heroic fantasy at large, which tends to an annoying tendency to shrug off inconsistencies in logic. Lee's strengths are also those of the genre— stunningly described action, engaging mythopoesis. Beyond those, however, Lee offers a fresh view of an old sort of fiction and a pair of believable protagonists. In this she shows a talent and a craft which promise even better works to come.

William H. Hardesty III

Bibliography
Schweitzer, Darrell. "Interview: Tanith Lee," in *Fantasy Newsletter*. IV (November, 1981), pp. 12-15.

BLACK EASTER
and
THE DAY AFTER JUDGMENT

Author: James Blish (1921-1975)
First book publications: Black Easter (1968); *The Day After Judgment* (1970)
Type of work: Novels
Time: The late 1960's
Locale: Italy and the United States

In an alternate present, representatives of man's curiosity and destructiveness use black magic to bring about Armageddon, after which they discover its meaning and the responsibility that falls upon mankind

Principal characters:
FATHER DOMENICO, a Jesuit priest and white magician
THERON WARE, a black magician who controls eighty demons
BAINES, a billionaire munitions merchant
JACK GINSBERG, Baines's secretary
ADOLPH HESS, a scientist for Baines's Consolidated Warfare Service
D. WILLIS McKNIGHT, a Strategic Air Command general for the United States Air Force
DR. JOHANN BUELG, adviser to McKnight from the RAND Corporation
DR. DŽEJMS ŠATVJE, adviser to McKnight and "godfather of the selenium bomb"

Most widely known for his prose adaptations of the television program *Star Trek*, James Blish was an accomplished writer and critic of science fiction. Educated in science (he received a B.S. in biochemistry from Columbia University) and modern literature (Blish also published critiques of James Joyce's *Finnegans Wake*, 1939), he took both the artistic and scientific dimensions of his writing seriously. In numerous critical essays (collected in 1964 as *The Issue at Hand* and in 1970 as *More Issues at Hand*, using the pseudonym William Atheling, Jr.), he took himself as well as other writers to task for failures in design, research, and imagination. In addition to a number of shorter works, his major achievements in science fiction are a loosely structured "tetralogy," collected in 1970 as *Cities in Flight*, and the award-winning novel *A Case of Conscience* (1958), itself part of the trilogy to which his black magic work belongs.

Blish's major contribution to modern literature is the trilogy "After Such Knowledge," which consists of a science-fiction novel (*A Case of Conscience*), a fictionalized biography, and a pair of fantasy novels: *Black Easter* and *The Day After Judgment*. Written in that order, they can also be read, as Blish preferred, in terms of their fictional chronology, except that the cataclysmic events of *Black Easter* and its sequel do not seem to have taken place before

A Case of Conscience. The overall title, taken from T. S. Eliot's poem "Gerontion" ("After such knowledge, what forgiveness?"), appears as an epigraph to *The Day After Judgment*, but its implications are present in the earlier books as well; they are united thematically by questions which divide the Catholic Church from the spirit of modern science over what Blish and his characters call the "Problem of Evil." A declared agnostic, Blish focused on Roman Catholic teachings for aesthetic and historical reasons. In the fantasy mode, he was able to depict, and confront directly, problems for which the images and metaphors of Church teachings were more appropriate than those of historic actuality or scientific extrapolation.

In the 1953 novelette version, *A Case of Conscience* tells the story of four explorers from Earth on the planet Lithia who are excited by its similarities to and differences from their home world. Convinced by its Edenic qualities and its reptilian inhabitants' apparent programming for ideal Western and Christian values, Father Ramon Ruiz-Sanchez sees Lithia as a "special creation" of Satan to trap unwary humans. A Lithian child, Egtverchi, is introduced into Earth society as a "stranger in a strange land." Called a "snake" by many earthmen, Egtverchi enjoys a hellish "coming out" party and serves as a focal point for neurotic dissenters in Earth's postnuclear underground "shelter society." Unwanted by either world, he stows away on a ship bearing a special communications device and the last supplies needed by the scientist Cleaver to test Lithia's potential for producing nuclear weapons. Cleaver's experiment and Ruiz-Sanchez's long-distance exorcism suggest alternate explanations for the planet's sudden disintegration.

Science and religion are also at odds in *Doctor Mirabilis* (1964). The life story of Roger Bacon, the twelfth century monk who anticipated later empirical thinking and technological forecasting, this novel is less ambitious in design and invention but more ambitious in terms of research and the details of everyday life. The economic, political, philosophical, theological, and scientific activities of the times are subordinated in the work to the development of Bacon's character and his consuming need to separate science from mere authority and superstition. Blish's longest novel, it is arguably his best, in part because of the editorial assistance he received from Faber and Faber and the great amount of time and effort he expended on the work.

Having arrived at the root of the separation between science and religion in the West, Blish could then wholeheartedly take up a fantasia on the problem of evil. Having flirted in earlier fiction with both fantasy and apocalypse, he finally confronted the apocalyptic fears of 1950's America by making them explicit. Modern science and modern society proceed, not without guilty twinges, on the basis of an assumption that God does not matter, if in fact He exists. Using magic in lieu of science, therefore, Blish probes the moral consequences of that assumption by fictionalizing its effectuation and results.

Black Easter is a veritable countdown to Armageddon, proceeding by means

of increasingly consequential ritual acts of destruction, underscored by epigraphs for the entire novel as well as for each major section. In "Preparation
of the Operator," which precedes the numbered chapters, Father Domenico
catches and identifies a "smell of demons," despite his historical skepticism
and scientific materialism appropriate to the age.

"The First Commission" (Chapters 1-5) introduces the other major characters. Theron Ware has few illusions about his power and its source, which
is under the control of demons. Baines, for whom ordinary warfare has lost
its thrill, requires proof: gold tears on a mirror pass the first test; then he
orders the undetected murder of the Governor of California. Ware agrees to
instruct his secretary, Jack Ginsberg, in the limited magic needed to summon
a succubus to meet his "special" sexual needs. To keep tabs on Ware, Baines
recruits Adolph Hess to become a kind of "sorcerer's apprentice."

In "Three Sleeps" (Chapters 6-13), Domenico goes to Ware's palazzo to
act as an official observer, forbidden by "the Covenant" to interfere in any
way. Described in detail, Ware's second conjuration eventually drives the
antimatter theorist Albert Stockhausen to suicide by working not on his vices
but on his virtues: the nihilism underlying his research drives him mad. With
the completion of this test, however, Baines reveals his true purpose: releasing, "for aesthetic purposes," all the major demons out of hell for one night.
Recognizing the danger that even his best-chosen fifty can bring, Ware permits
Father Domenico to hold a conference with his colleagues, and sets the date
that is least propitious for the adversary. The monk is not comforted by this
Easter message.

In "The Last Conjuration" (Chapters 14-17), the forces of good are in
disarray. With less than half the world's white magicians in attendance, the
Celestial Princes are convoked to no avail on Monte Albano, but their confusion is a pale harbinger of the chaos to come. Ware's conjuration echoes
the black masque in Christopher Marlowe's *The Tragedy of Doctor Faustus*
(1592), which is followed at first by only sporadic radio reports of the usual
quota of battles and disasters. The news picks up with the burning of William
Blake's Dante illustrations at London's Tate Gallery, the nuclear bombing of
Taiwan, and the napalming of the late United States President's widow. Hess
tries to rationalize the incidents, Baines takes full responsibility, and a mushroom cloud over Rome convinces Domenico that things have gone too far.
Awakened, Ware tries futilely to put the jinni back in the bottle, only to raise
the "Judas Goat," Baphomet or Put Satanachia. Denying the demon's existence, Hess is swallowed by it. Attempting an exorcism, Domenico sees his
cross explode. In answer to his question "Where did we fail?," the monk
receives the book's last words: "God is Dead."

Ostensibly independent, the sequel begins with a five-page synopsis of its
predecessor. Consisting of four "Stations," *The Day After Judgment* begins
with an unnumbered section, "The Wrath-Bearing Tree," in which the Goat

does not return and the principals react in characteristic ways. Domenico denies the demon's message, Ware muses on his continuing usefulness, Baines contemplates his next move, and Ginsberg, sent to pack, has one last fling with his succubus.

"So Above" (Chapters 1-5) focuses mainly on Death Valley, California, where the central fortress of Dis, from Dante's *Inferno* (c. 1320), has surfaced. Seen from Strategic Air Command headquarters in Colorado, its identity is only gradually and partially accepted by McKnight and his science advisers, a cartoonish counterpoint to the debaters in Italy. Amid discussions of "humane" bombs, "escalation ladders," Chardinian dreams of progress, and the benefits of a European education, they confirm their speculation by computer and plan to attack whatever portion of the "invaders" that may be material. Meanwhile, the "pilgrims" are on their way. Baines and Ginsberg travel to Colorado by plane. Ware sees little difference between Armageddon and World War III and resolves not to commit himself fully to Satan. Father Domenico returns to Monte Albano for another desultory conference, concluding that hope "is all we have . . . ever had."

"Come to Middle Hell" (Chapters 6-10) brings the four main characters to Death Valley by various routes, while McKnight continues to battle the invaders. Nude on a broomstick, Ware is brought down over Pennsylvania by tolling church bells. Seeing a demon installed as Pope, Domenico crosses the sea more or less "on foot." Participating in the Strategic Air Command debate, Baines sees the attack on Dis fail, then is summoned directly to Satan's headquarters.

"The Harrowing of Heaven" (Chapters 11-13) assembles the pilgrims as allegorical sins of upper hell: lust (Ginsberg), gluttony (Ware), wrath (Baines), and hoarding (Domenico). Within the fortress, they find a "Utopian" city with clonelike people, public obscenities, and no children or animals. At the center of this epitome of postindustrial man's striving, they try to justify their missions to Satan. In Miltonic blank verse, he replies that he has been forced to occupy God's throne as a force for good, until man himself can become a god. A fragmentary dramatic Epilogue shows the pilgrims in an unscarred desert, each about to take a new and complementary position: the man of faith to think, the destroyer to believe, the magician to hope, the seducer to love.

Like *A Case of Conscience* and *Cities in Flight* before it, *Black Easter* and *The Day After Judgment* form an eccentric composition. Introspection, debate, parody, satire, levity, adventure, horror, awe, and scholarship vie for attention to the detriment of character, balance, continuity, and verisimilitude. Yet even this inconsistency may serve its purpose in a fantasia as deliberately misshapen as the moral values it depicts.

A book about man rather than individual men (women are conspicuously absent), *Black Easter* and *The Day After Judgment* employ allegorical characters verging on caricature. The most likely force for good, Father Domenico is compromised from the start as a white monk supposedly given a dispensation to practice magic. As an observer, he refrains from interfering with Ware until it is too late, adhering to a vague "Covenant" over the dictates of his conscience. A "hoarder" by profession (white magic is used to find treasure for the Church), he is defined by Ware in terms of his attempt to use the crucifix only to prevent danger to his person. It even takes the installation of a demon as Pope to get him to confront Satan on his own, and even then only because Satan makes it possible.

Domenico's opposite number is Ginsberg, the "Reformed Orthodox Agnostic" who follows Baines for his leavings. Similarly, he employs Ware's magic for his own needs, ignoring the knowledge that if it works, so does the metaphysical framework from which it descends. Although he is properly at odds with his German counterpart in Baines's employ, Ginsberg is not far from an anti-Semite's stereotype: smug, fawning, greedy, and lecherous. There is little for him to do, however, except ogle girls and bed his succubus, providing each volume with a soft-porn scene until he can be recognized as the allegorical representative of "lust."

There is nothing explicitly Nazi about Adolph Hess other than his name (a composite of Adolf Hitler and Rudolph Hess). Like Ware, he is a fanatic in quest of knowledge; like Baines, he is committed to destructive inventions. In contrast to both, and to a greater degree than Ginsberg, he refuses to believe that through the magic, he has helped to bring about a supernatural force. Swallowed by Baphomet (whether literally or figuratively is a subject for debate), he reappears at least in spirit in the Strategic Air Command bunker in the second volume.

Least convincing, perhaps, is Baines, unable to surmount the pulp fiction position of the one man responsible for war, both before and after hiring Theron Ware. Frustrated by nuclear weapons that make his job more difficult and by the loss of excitement, he seeks the ultimate in "controlled destruction" for the sheer exercise of power. Even after Armageddon, he visualizes himself as useful, but he is perhaps the only one at the Strategic Air Command base to recognize the hubris of attacking Dis (and foreseeing the next step as a war on Heaven), and to recognize the demons' Utopia as a man-made hell.

The most believable character is Ware, whose name comes from a fictional clergyman who lost his faith (in *The Damnation of Theron Ware*, 1896, by Harold Frederic). His self-consciousness and erudition permit Blish to demonstrate his knowledge of conjuring and theology (some of it gained from research on the earlier two books). This solidity of detail in turn gives Ware a dimension the other characters lack. An American in Italy (evading United States government regulation), he is introspective, proud, and somewhat apprehensive, although he believes he can outwit the Devil. Having literally sold his soul for knowledge, he epitomizes Faustian man, incorporating and extending the others' desires.

The little dignity and stature these characters have in *Black Easter* is effectively stripped from them in *The Day After Judgment*: Ware rides a broomstick nude, Domenico walks on water, Baines is dragged through a window by a force toward a giant television screen from which Satan beckons. Strategic Air Command's three "wise men," to be sure, are even more absurd. If Buelg and Šatvje are unrealistic in advising material attack on a spiritual enemy, General McKnight is downright silly, seeing treason under the bed, America as invincible, the invasion as caused by the "yellow peril," and Baphomet himself as Fu Manchu. *Black Easter* has its moments of levity, chiefly in the confused conclave of white magicians bearing names of science-fiction writers and editors (including Father Atheling—Blish himself), but its mood is primarily one of high seriousness, even as its structure is orderly, based on widening circles of horrific action leading to the final announcement. *The Day After Judgment* is closer to self-parody, with its gallows humor and a rambling structure that counterpoints military satire with the gathering of pilgrims, regardless of the pattern of its chapters and "stations," and it concludes with fragments of Miltonic epic and closet drama. No doubt the shift is appropriate to Satan's reign, with its ironic reversals, one of which is that he must be a force for good (echoing *The Revolt of the Angels*, 1914, by Anatole France) and give way in turn to man. *Black Easter*'s last section is also preceded by an epigraph from C. S. Lewis' *The Screwtape Letters* (1942); this is apposite, however, pinpointing the twin dangers of ignoring demons and being too fascinated by them.

Blish's major problem is aesthetic distance, since he wants his readers to take his message more seriously than its vehicle. To this end, he employs as alienating devices not only allegory and parody but also structural discontinuities which underscore the modern world's loss of meaning and pattern provided by a metaphysic (in this case, the Catholic Church). Discontinuities of another sort are given by allusions to other writers. Among them, of course, are John Milton, Dante, and Lewis, as well as Roger Bacon, Leo Tolstoy, Oscar Wilde, Herman Kahn, Teilhard de Chardin, Sax Rohmer, and the science-fiction establishment. Epigraphs to each volume and each major section obtrude more on the action, but they also highlight the "Problem of Evil," suggesting (among other things) that this is hell (*The Tragedy of Doctor Faustus*); Christian teaching is more competent than Aristotle (Albertus Magnus); Theurgy provides a "wonderworld" (A. E. Waite); it is hard work to be or to recognize a devil (*Sayings of Tsaing Samdup*); and woe is coming to man (Revelation). Others suggest that greatness lost can be restored (Job) and that sinners have an aesthetic place in the universe (St. Augustine). The medieval witch-hunt text, *Malleus Maleficarum* (1486), scorns heretics who disbelieve in the greatest of evils, a position reiterated by Screwtape, who regards as the demons' "perfect work" the "Materialist Magician" who worships "Forces" but denies the existence of "spirits." And all of these are to some extent subordinated to the question of T. S. Eliot's which Blish adopted as the overall title for his trilogy: "After such knowledge, what forgiveness?"

The kind of knowledge Blish has in mind is not the arcane pattern and ritual of black magic but the materialist imperative of modern science. The world described is a world of nuclear warfare, unlimited scientific investigation, essentially untrammeled pursuit of one's desires, and spiritual emptiness, pointing toward the "Utopian" vision within the walls of Dis. Yet, it is also a fictional world in which magic functions, both its ends and its means bearing "evil" significance. Ware has sold his soul literally, but the others have sold theirs too, at least figuratively. Ware had already concluded that they were damned—even Father Domenico, and, in fact, everyone in the modern world—before the announcement that "God is dead." The orthodox position that Satan cannot create anything material, that only by illusion can he encourage man to do evil, is supported by the rationalist position which Hess is not alone in asserting. The tests that Ware and his demons passed for Baines are not conclusive; the damage of Armageddon is no worse than that anticipated for World War III; Death Valley is unmarked after the pilgrims emerge from their tête-à-tête with the Prince of Darkness.

"The Problem of Evil" is not solved by the invention of devils to take the blame, but neither is it eliminated by the rationalist's position, based in the material successes of science and technology. This is a difficult position to maintain in a science-fiction framework, especially for one with Blish's scientific outlook. In *A Case of Conscience*, only Father Ruiz-Sanchez can see the moral dimension not only of the existence of Lithia, but also of human's amoral attitudes toward it. As a result, his position becomes that of a fanatic. In *Doctor Mirabilis*, the positions are reversed, the "fanatic" being Bacon who thought some scientific knowledge could be separated from moral considerations. Only in an outright fantasy could Blish let the apocalyptic vision flourish and follow the question to its source. Just as the evil springs from man, so does the forgiveness. The damnation of this Faust is to be responsible for his own actions.

David N. Samuelson

Bibliography
Atheling, William, Jr. "Cathedrals in Space," in *The Issue at Hand*, 1964.
Rickard, Bob. *"After Such Knowledge*: James Blish's Tetralogy," in *A Multitude of Visions*, 1975. Edited by Cy Chauvin.
Stableford, Brian. *A Clash of Symbols: The Triumph of James Blish*, 1979.

THE BLESSING OF PAN

Author: Lord Dunsany (Edward John Moreton Drax Plunkett, 1878-1957)
First book publication: 1927
Type of work: Novel
Time: The 1920's
Locale: England

Lured by wild reed music, inhabitants of an English village turn from following God to following Pan

Principal characters:
ELDERICK ANWREL, the vicar of Wolding
TOMMY DUFFIN, the piper of Pan
PERKIN, the madman of Snichester

The Blessing of Pan is one of a great number of modern fantasies that champion paganism against Christianity. The novel's protagonist is the rather complacent vicar of Wolding, Elderick Anwrel. Anwrel becomes concerned with the enchantment of certain young women of the parish when they follow the piping of a notably unintelligent young man named Tommy Duffin. Anwrel appeals to his bishop for aid against the strange powers of that wild music, but the bishop merely counsels a vacation. Mrs. Tichener, the wise woman of Wolding, hints at some spell cast by the absconded Reverend who had performed the marriage ceremony for Tommy's parents and concluded it with a strange utterance in a foreign tongue.

What has happened to Tommy, no one can exactly put into words. Seeking explanations of the great mysteries of the universe, he had gone to the woods. Something whispered by the wind among the reeds responded to his needs, and without knowing why he did so, he fashioned a musical instrument. Somewhat frightened of his own new powers, Tommy keeps them secret until unaccountable urgings make him bolder.

Returned from his holiday, Anwrel finds conditions have worsened, and he himself is "the only enemy of that victorious music." Anwrel, seeking to fix the blame on Tommy, sees him change visibly in appearance as evening nears, and he takes from his pocket the crude musical instrument that Anwrel recognizes as Pan's pipes. Now the young men as well are following the piping of Tommy Duffin.

Anwrel's second journey in search of aid takes him to Hetley, the Greek scholar who had replace him during his vacation. Anwrel describes his parishioners as people who attend church but who are spiritually "little better off than many that missionaries travel far to convert," but Hetley knows little more than the Peloponnesian War. On the cathedral of Snichester, Anwrel finds a gargoyle, a likeness of Pan, and decides that it proves incontrovertibly that Pan has continued in the consciousness of simple artisans, even while they were building a cathedral to a rival God. The bishop, whom he consults, urges him to sane occupations; only Perkin, a wandering madman who has "lost his illusions," agrees to come to Wolding in search of another illusion. Perkin describes an astral journey during which he talked with angels and saw Heaven, but Anwrel suspects some deep wisdom in him.

The village of Wolding seems to be under a curse, evidenced in the gradual encroachment of pagan ways, and Anwrel questions why it should happen to his vicarage. Duffin has forgotten to harvest the hay, the teacher has dismissed the school children, and young men wear circles of roses on their bare heads. As if the Christian God has retreated, the tomb of St. Ethelbruda no longer cures warts. Anwrel, half-conscious of divine rivalries, knows that, should the villagers place burnt offerings to their heathen god at the Old Stones outside the village, they will never come to church again. Then, inside the circle of Stones, he sees a fire left to burn all night and recognizes in it the last rite of Pan, which the Greeks observed as the other rites faded. His wife Augusta mentions that something peculiar about Wold Hill had drawn to it, years before, a wandering goat. Likewise, he decides that the brainless Tommy Duffin is merely the "halting place of some strayed power." Whether ancient memories linger for thousands of years or the powers invade certain personalities, Anwrel overhears Mrs. Duffin, supposedly conducting the Sunday school, chanting childish nonsense syllables. "Egg, oh, pan, pan, tone, tone, lofone, R. K. D.," he recognizes as Greek, "ego pan, panton, ton lophon Arcadiou basileus," or "I Pan, of all the Arcadian valleys, King"—not a curse but the blessing of Pan.

Attempting to fortify his people against the encroaching paganism, Anwrel on one last Sunday preaches stirringly and holds the attention of his congregation until Tommy begins piping directly outside the church. Then, one by one, all the members of his congregation leave, including his wife Augusta. He and Perkin, his last hope for Christian aid, follow the crowd, going to the Old Stones, where Anwrel himself, drawn into the ceremonies, kills the sacrificial bull with his own flint ax. Thereafter the villagers sacrifice a bull each year on the Old Stones, Anwrel retires from his vicarage to a hut near the Old Stones, vegetation thrives wildly around the community, and Wolding— self-sufficient in primitive retreat—closes itself off from the rest of the world's commerce.

Lord Dunsany draws on very little of the vast store of mythology that could have been brought to bear on the novel's theme. Instead, he concentrates his talents in description of the inexplicable and imponderable stirrings within the soul: Tommy's music, for example, makes him "one of a fellowship to which the hush of the night, the deep of the woods, or mysteries bold in the moonlight, reported all their secrets." At no point does Dunsany make Pan himself appear. The Old Stones, set in a circle that the Irish call a fairy ring, suggest the strange rites of Stonehenge, but Dunsany reduces those rites to a simple march around the Stones and the sacrifice of the bull. The bulrushes or "some such reeds" of which Tommy Duffin makes "the pipes of Pan," Pan as the goat that wanders into the community (although it dies there), and the ancient chant reduced to English nonsense syllables—these bare doctrinal attributes support the entire novel.

Dunsany remains gentle, also, about the status of the Church, left in the hands of a bishop who refuses to consider a problem and a visiting vicar who, as a Greek scholar, studied war instead of theology. Only the "madman" Perkin partakes of the visions of Emmanuel Swedenborg and, in discussing the jealousies among angels, suggests a rivalry among deities. When the Church proves incapable of concerning itself with powers which it believes do not exist, then the "great occasions of Nature" triumph once more.

Grace Eckley

Bibliography
Amory, Mark. *Biography of Lord Dunsany*, 1972.
de Camp, L. Sprague. "Two Men in One: Lord Dunsany," in *Literary Swordsmen and Sorcerors*, 1976.

THE BLUE HAWK

Author: Peter Dickinson (1927-   )
First book publication: 1976
Type of work: Novel
Time: The distant future
Locale: A primitive kingdom

Tron, a boy in a priest-ridden society, interrupts a ceremony by removing the hawk intended for sacrifice, under instruction from a god, thus propelling himself into a struggle between church and monarch and a series of perils and responsibilities which force him to mature

> *Principal characters:*
> TRON, a boy priest
> THE YOUNG KING
> ODAH, the village priest
> ONU OVALAKU, a messenger from the Felathi
> THE ONE OF SINU, the god of death
> THE ONE OF O,
> THE ONE OF AA, and
> THE MOUTH OF SILENCE, the major priests
> GDU, a god

Peter Dickinson is the only writer to have won Britain's Silver Dagger Award (for crime novels) in successive years. His first prizewinner, and perhaps the best known of his several works in that genre, is *The Glass-Sided Ants' Nest* (1981, originally published in Britain as *Skin-Deep*, 1968). That novel demonstrates a fascination with ritual and an exploration of the interaction between ritual and freedom which is also evident in *The Blue Hawk*. Dickinson is also the author of a single science-fiction novel, *The Green Gene* (1973), which was runner-up for the John W. Campbell Award. Despite this success in other spheres, he is best known for his young-adult fiction, which almost invariably includes some element of science fiction or the fantastic, but which is also rooted in historical or contemporary realism. Dickinson's young-adult fiction is of sufficient maturity to appeal strongly to adults; there is certainly never any question of talking down to an audience. *The Blue Hawk* is particularly complex, combining elements of the historical novel, science fiction, and, by its elliptical manner, the mystery genre.

Because of the novel's complexity, and the interlocking of its themes and action, it is necessary to summarize the main details of the story before looking at it in greater detail. Tron, a thirteen-year-old priest of Gdu (the god of hawks and healing), has been chosen as "Goat," which allows him to break the Temple ritual without incurring the displeasure of the gods. He chooses to abduct, in mid-ceremony, the blue hawk that was to have been sacrificed to renew the soul of the King. The major priests, for their own undisclosed reasons, send him to the remote House of Tan (a minor god) to train the hawk. Here he meets the new King, son of the one he doomed, who befriends him. The King reveals that his training is a plot by the priests designed to cause his own death at the funeral of the old King. Together they contrive Tron's escape from the funeral in a coffin, which is floated downriver to the Jaws of Alaan, a massive waterfall. Tron manages to escape, a previous rescue attempt having failed, on the very brink itself and becomes for several months priest of Upper Kalakal. While there, he meets Odah, a priest who was crippled for refusing to conform, but who invents new rituals.

On an exploration of the wilderness, hunting with his blue hawk, Tron encounters a tribe of primitive hunters who retain enough memory of his civilization to be impressed by his priesthood. They have a prisoner from another land, Onu Ovalaku, who gives Tron a red spear. This, he explains, is the symbol of an ancient treaty whereby his people, the Felathi, can invoke the aid of Tron's King when under attack, as they are in this case by the Mohirrim, a barbaric horde. Tron conveys him to the King, who calls for the Horn of War, which should signal the predominance of the House of Sinu, the war god. The major priests attempt to stop this by drugging the One of Sinu, destroying the red spear, and sacrificing both the messenger and Tron. They only succeed in the former two aims and despite bitter opposition the King raises an army. The Kingdom's exits have long been closed, however, at the behest of the gods, by an ancient curse which can only be lifted by three major priests. When the major priests refuse, Tron, Odah, and the One of Sinu successfully perform a long and arduous ceremony, dictated by Odah. The King's army defeats a large band that has come through the pass, but Odah and Tron, while blessing the dead Mohirrim, are shot by one who was lingering. Tron miraculously recovers and is recuperating in Upper Kalakal when news comes that, at great cost, the King has defeated the numerically superior main Mohirrim army.

One of the most immediate problems to confront the reader is that of the nature of this novel. The heavily ritualistic opening, fraught with the danger of a false word or move, gives the impression that this is a historical novel. Dickinson supports this view by his deft use of language. With a poet's feel, he manipulates a style that is simple, almost biblical, but one that avoids too direct an imitation of the Bible and the awful anachronistic fusion which this metier can produce in less skillful hands. Identification at first suggests Ancient Egypt as the setting because of such correspondences as the Dawn Hymn, the sun god, the treatment of the dead, the great stress placed on the power of the gods, and the consequent dominance of the priestly hierarchy. Even outside the Temple, the agriculture, the importance of its central river, the deserts, and, most of all, the sport of hawking are redolent of Egyptian civilization. Odd jarring dissonances, however, indicate that this is not a merely historical re-creation. The geography is subtly but crucially different from that of Egypt. This country is trapped between desert, marsh, and vast mountain ranges, a land doomed by its rulers' desire for stasis as much as by the dwindling fertility of its salt-choked fields.

Even more important dissimilarities are presented in the nature of the gods. Here Dickinson is at his most subtle, for, faced with this sort of absolutist theocracy, bound only by its own fossilized laws for the placation of the deities, the twentieth century mind is most likely to regard it as mere superstition. Thus the fact that this theology contains a great, and fundamentally un-Egyptian, opposing duality between O and Aa—sun and moon, light and dark—seems of little import initially, but conditions the whole flow of the narrative, as does the close involvement of Tron with his patron god, Gdu. Moreover, the gods are important not merely because of their priests but because of their very nature. Throughout the book there are small, insubstantial mentions of the "Wise," who set down the hymns which stored wisdom in dealing with the gods and built roads, bridges, and the dam across the Jaws of Alaan, the remnants of which helped to save Tron. Finally, it becomes apparent at the end of the novel that Tron's is a future society, the socially devolved remnants of the "Wise." The gods emerge as aliens, immensely powerful but reluctantly tied to the Earth, captives of the "Wise" unable to free themselves. Thus the power of the gods emerges as something tangible and Tron's recurrent sensation of possession as nothing other than the truth.

Dickinson's choice of point of view is particularly well-adapted to the story he wishes to tell. His protagonist Tron has been brainwashed by his upbringing, having spent all but his first year of life in the Temple. Although he is close to the real power in the Kingdom, his interest in finding out about himself and the real state of the Kingdom enables the author to give facts in a naturalistic way without resorting to neatly packaged items of information. His shock at discovering the elaborate system of secret passages, spyholes, drugs, and poison by which the priests manipulate not merely such as himself but the whole Kingdom cannot but affect the reader. Tron, however, is more than an author's tool. Central to the book is his growing maturity, his development of self-reliance as well as his recovery from his early conditioning.

The maturing of a young person forced to develop under stress is an essential theme in juvenile literature, and one which Dickinson has always handled with dexterity. Tron's character is developed as his loyalty is stretched between the priesthood, the gods, his hawk, and the new King, whose generosity and character he appreciates. This loyalty, though, is not a malleable thing and there is a constant, believable hedging against the forces pushing him into radical change. Among the most telling passages in the early part of the book is the one in which Tron and the King examine the ruined House of Tan, forcing Tron to recognize what devastation the King's aims could bring to the safe world of his childhood. The stages by which Tron moves from this position to that, near the end of the book, when he realizes the meaninglessness of the life of a priest who had helped them earlier, are set out with consummate craftsmanship and conviction. Similarly Tron's willingness to risk his life in blessing the fallen enemy during a vicious war shows not only bravery but also an individual moral code.

Character rather than action predominates, and Tron's development, revealed in small, telling details, proceeds with the logic of life. At several instances, when he is sent out into the desert to train his hawk, when he is first exiled in Upper Kalakal, and after the ritual for the opening of the Kingdom, he is isolated from main events and has time to ponder his situation, each time with added experience. There is no sense that these great events have stopped, merely that he is at least temporarily not involved. He is the key to crucial developments, but the author does not make the illogical move of developing him into a figure of conventional heroism.

If there is a hero in the book it is the King. He has the bravery to attack the hierarchy that killed his father and made his predecessors mere tokens. Since the point of open conflict is the King's wish to combat foes of utter ferocity, superior numbers, and great military skill, this courage takes on true heroic timber. The King in the event possesses craft and sufficient strategic gifts to channel the Mohirrim into the desert and defeat them. His boundless energy, though, is the thing that most impresses Tron, and is the most necessary quality for his long-term task. The portrait of the King is rounded. His offer of friendship to Tron, in the circumstances, shows largeness of soul, and his relationship with Tron is conducted as between equals. The patience he shows in the face of Tron's loyal reservations is matched by his use of Tron's knowledge of the priesthood and by the profound gloom which can come to energetic people, when he believes that Tron has perished in the coffin.

The journey downriver in the coffin has, in fact, given Tron the opportunity to observe the decay in the Kingdom, convincing him that the King's purge is vital. The closure of the Kingdom has led to an inward-looking sickness, exacerbated by the actions of the priests in poisoning desert wells—and any monarch who has shown spirit. Dickinson stresses this tyranny of tradition by such details as the Keeper of Rods' worry that any mistake in one day's records (inscribed on Rods) will result in incorrectly timed sowing of the fields and similar disasters. Like an intricate clock, the mechanism of the Kingdom is shown as being worn by time. The King's ideas and the verve with which he applies them provide the needed corrective, adding narrative thrust to the novel and complementing the central theme of Tron's growing up.

Just as Tron is often accidentally instrumental in the growth of the political struggle but peripheral to much of its action, so the Kingdom itself is involved in the concerns of the aliens, whose main purpose is beyond human comprehension for most of the story. Here, too, Tron's potential as an instrument attracts one of the aliens, who watches him from the beginning of the story until his journey to the King with Onu Ovalaku, instructing him from time to time, as in the original command to take the bird, and sending him signs, often through the hawk, to encourage or persuade him. Twice the god also possesses him, once focusing an alien eye on the hawk and, on the journey mentioned above, sending a vision which Tron interprets as his removal from continual scrutiny now that the balance of the Kingdom is irrevocably tilted.

At the ritual for the freeing of the Kingdom, all three participants sense first the presence of the gods, then their departure. Tron alone, however, can sense the completeness of their withdrawal, and only later can surmise that the original enclosure of the Kingdom and the gods' subsequent actions were directed towards forcing humans to find some way of releasing them from their bond to the Earth. Just how inconceivably different they were from the anthropomorphic human gods is shown by the exceptional involvement of Tron's personal god, who, obviously uncharacteristically, restores Tron's life after the Mohirrim attack and then needs Tron to free his hawk to release him, as if prolonged mental contact with a human had imprinted his nature.

All in all, this is a most complex book, with its intertwining of three major themes, shifting conflicts, and changing protagonist. It is to Dickinson's great credit that the result is eminently readable and tenaciously memorable.

Mike Dickinson

Bibliography
No listing.

THE BLUE STAR

Author: Fletcher Pratt (1897-1956)
First book publication: 1969
Type of work: Novel
Time: A period similar to the late eighteenth century
Locale: The queendom of Dossola, chiefly Netznegon City; the Eastern Sea; the city
of Charalkis in the dominion of Mancherei

On orders from the subversive Sons of the New Day, clerk and would-be revolutionary
Rodvard Bergelin first seduces young Lalette Asterhax, seeking control of her magical
Blue Star jewel, then becomes disillusioned with radicalism and realizes that he truly
loves her

> *Principal characters:*
> RODVARD BERGELIN, a clerk in the Office of Pedigree and member
>   of the Sons of the New Day
> LALETTE ASTERHAX, his mistress and a witch
> COUNT CLEUDI, a powerful royalist political figure
> MATHULIN, the Count's manservant, secret leader of the Sons of
>   the New Day
> MARITZL OF STOJENROSEK, Rodvard's unfulfilled love, later Cleu-
>   di's mistress
> DAME DOMIJAIEK, a widowed seamstress and an Amorosian

Most works of modern fantasy take place in barbarian or feudal cultures;
a sizable number are set in some version of the contemporary present; most
of the remainder occur in some variant of a decadent futuristic society. In
The Blue Star, Pratt passes over all of these options and instead sets his story
in a fantasy world which somewhat resembles Europe on the eve of the French
Revolution. As Pratt explains in the story's frame (three men discuss philosophy over port, and that night all dream the same dream, which is the body
of the book), the chief differences between the novel's world and the real
world are that there gunpowder was never invented; instead, magic works,
operating chiefly through the women of certain bloodlines. Pratt's plot deftly
combines both the similarities and the differences between his imagined world
and the real world.

In the queendom of Dossola, the feudal order is drawing toward its close.
One group hoping to pull it down is the Sons of the New Day, a conspiratorial
group of idealists and malcontents drawn chiefly from the middle classes.
Their main goal is to remove the barriers of class so that individual effort
and merit can find their true reward, and they are convinced that all means
are justified in pursuit of this glorious end. Rodvard Bergelin, an ambitious
but credulous and somewhat muddled clerk in the government Office of
Pedigree, is ordered by the conspirators' mysterious High Center to seduce
one Lalette Asterhax, who belongs to an impoverished witch family, and

whose chief inheritance will be a Blue Star jewel and the genetic ability to activate it. All Lalette's witchly talents remain latent so long as she is a virgin; the most important of these, the Blue Star, will serve not Lalette herself but her husband or lover, for so long as he remains faithful to her. The Blue Star enables its bearer to read the thoughts of almost anyone into whose eyes he stares—obviously a useful ability for a revolutionary.

Rodvard is reluctant to go ahead with the seduction, both because of a few twinges of conscience and because he is in love from afar with Maritzl of Stojenrosek, a young noblewoman who has repeatedly visited the Office of Pedigree. Rodvard realizes, however, that daughters of the nobility are not available to lowly clerks, and in the end he obeys his instructions. His characteristic ineffectuality is demonstrated in the fact that he almost bungles the seduction, very nearly turning it into a rape—which would not advance the Sons' interests. Fortunately, at the last minute Lalette consents; at least it seems to be a way to avoid being sold by her mother into concubinage to Count Cleudi, a powerful figure at court. Indeed, so upsetting does Lalette find the Count that at their next meeting she inadvertently reveals that her witchly powers are now active. Witchcraft is illegal and forbidden by the established Church, a fact which itself does not much disturb the Count, but which will now serve as an excuse to avenge the fact that Lalette has preferred another man to him. Lalette appeals to Rodvard, and the two flee together, taking refuge with Mme. Kaja, a faded former opera singer and courtesan, now one of the revolutionaries. No sooner has the couple settled in and begun to thrash out their difficulties (Lalette, quite properly, feels used; Rodvard, with less objective reason, also feels put upon) than they are forced to flee again, betrayed by Mme. Kaja.

Desperate, Rodvard knocks on an apartment door at random and asks for help. Luckily, the occupants turn out to be Dame Domijaiek and her son, who are Amorosians, members of a persecuted religious minority, and who are willing to help others in similar straits. Pratt has lifted the theology of the Amorosians virtually unaltered from medieval Catharism, but the religion has been transplanted into a later social setting where it is in some ways more like Protestantism. (Pratt is less specific about the theology of the state church of Dossola, but it seems analagous to an extremely corrupt Catholicism.) Rodvard again makes contact with the Sons, who pack him off to Sedad Vix (analogous to Versailles) to make use of his Blue Star. Lalette is left behind, and for unexplained reasons the Sons even fail to deliver the note Rodvard has sent her. Cleudi's manservant Mathulin is a Son, and apparently through his offices Rodvard has been placed as a secretary to the Count, from which office he is soon able to provide useful political intelligence to the conspirators. Dossala is suffering financial woes, and the court is discussing new revenue measures. Rodvard finds the politics of the court and the tactics of the Sons equally distressing, but he is not beyond a little double-dealing of his own.

Separated from Lalette, and with his Blue Star enabling him to find out women's true desires, the feckless Rodvard finds himself attracted to various females from the dissolute Countess Aiella to his own chambermaid, Damaris. Concupiscence triumphs without much of a battle, Rodvard lies with Damaris, and the Blue Star goes dead. This is only the beginning of Rodvard's troubles, for he is soon run out of town for his attentions to Countess Aiella, then "rescued" by an elderly couple who eke out their income by robbing and murdering travelers. Meanwhile Lalette, who is still staying with Dame Domijaiek, senses Rodvard's betrayal and later, through some residual link, the fact that his life is in danger. She casts counterspells, saves Rodvard, and, apparently through the sheer force of her own loyalty, reactivates the Blue Star. In so doing, however, Lalette has broken her promise to Dame Domijaiek not to use magic while under her roof; moreover, she despairs of Rodvard, both because of his recent betrayal and because she has discovered his revolutionary connections.

Accordingly, Lalette decides to accept Dame Domijaiek's suggestion that she emigrate to Mancherei, where Amorosianism is the established religion and where there are hospices for friendless young women. Lalette takes ship, and is put in touch with a secret Amorosian among the crew who is supposed to see to her initial religious instruction. All goes well until this Amorosian insists that he has a claim on her body and, when she refuses him, tries to rape her. She saves herself by bewitching him, accidentally killing him in the process. She comes under grave suspicion aboard ship, but fortunately the Manchereians raise no questions and admit her on her promise to forswear future witchcraft. Meanwhile, Rodvard's captors, not daring to kill him since the display of Lalette's magical defense, instead sell him to a sea captain, so that he too finds himself crossing the Eastern Sea to Mancherei. Also like Lalette, he finds his virtue threatened—by the homosexual captain—and is finally saved only by the intervention of the Manchereian authorities, who grant him asylum.

Despite these timely rescues, Mancherei proves to be something less than the promised land. Life is drab, regulated, and work-oriented. Even so, Rodvard soon obtains a job as a clerk and shortly is dallying with his landlord's daughter. At the hospice, Lalette finds that things are not quite as they seemed. The Amorosians, like the medieval Cathars, hold that everything in the material world, including sexuality and marriage, is evil, and Amorosian initiates, like Cathar Perfecti, are celibate ascetics. Short of this perfection, all conduct is more or less of equal taint. Accordingly, when diaconals training for initiatehood find themselves overcome by earthly lust, they are invited to cohabit with a hospice girl until they are again able to set their minds on spiritual things. Lalette refuses to accept any diaconal, and for this she faces "instruction" in prison. Fortunately, the relevant paperwork crosses Rodvard's desk, and he hurries off to rescue her. Rodvard proves as ineffectual as ever, and the couple is caught trying to flee the country and are cast into prison.

Fortunately, they are soon rescued from jail by the Sons of the New Day; Rodvard and his Blue Star are needed back in Dossola. Worsening domestic conditions have led to the convening of the Dossolan equivalent of the Estates General, and the Sons, led by the former servant Mathulin, have gained control of the assembly. The reader soon perceives that all that has happened is that one tyranny has been replaced by a worse one; the hated provosts have merely been retitled the people's guards. A purge is already thinning the ranks of the Sons themselves. Rodvard, lacking the reader's historical perspective and not being very perceptive anyhow, feels no more than vaguely uneasy and consents to place his Blue Star at the service of the new order, first in the national assembly and then in a revolutionary tribunal. The process of his disillusionment continues, but it is very slow. Lalette has come to an earlier realization of the truth, but her nature is passive, and the most that she can do is to resist the Sons' pressure to use her witchcraft on their behalf.

Finally, Rodvard's old love Maritzl comes before the tribunal. Since Rodvard last saw her she has become Cleudi's mistress and has recently been caught bearing a letter from Cleudi requesting foreign intervention in the royalist cause and promising territorial concessions in return. Although she no longer loves Rodvard, Maritzl tries to seduce him into arranging her escape. Thanks to his Blue Star, Rodvard recognizes her duplicity, but for old times' sake he attempts, apparently successfully, to get her acquitted. By now Rodvard is disillusioned with the revolution, and the romantic image of Maritzl that had been estranging him from Lalette has been shattered. The two agree to flee once more, and again they turn to Dame Domijaiek for help. She arranges safe conduct out of the city. As they depart, Rodvard, with Lalette's approval, throws away the Blue Star, and the two presumably disappear from the stage of great affairs.

Certain aspects of *The Blue Star* are extremely well done. The major characters come across in all their psychological complexity, and even the minor ones are deftly sketched. Pratt's imagined world melds a historical progression with the existence of magic into a plausible whole. The intended parallels with the French Revolution are considerably less obvious than the above summary may have suggested; indeed, they have been overlooked by more than one critic. Pratt's adaptation of Catharism to altered social circumstances is brilliant. The portrayal of the contradictions of Amorosianism, which, despite a generally repugnant theology, can produce a near-saint such as Dame Domijaiek, and which shows such mixed results when institutionalized in Mancherei, shows considerable insight into the workings of religion in society.

At the same time, it cannot be said that the novel is entirely successful. There appear to be a number of minor problems and one major one. Among the minor difficulties are style and pacing. The mildly archaic language used, combined with brisk pacing and a determination to show rather than explain, may sometimes leave the reader confused. Certain turning points, such as Lalette's reactivation of the dead Blue Star, are not properly highlighted. Next, there is some confusion about the true nature of witchcraft. At the beginning of the novel, it seems to be in truth a morally neutral, or even beneficial "science," with the religious condemnation of it being mere prejudice. By the end of the novel there is a hint, but no more than that, that the Blue Star, like the Ring in J. R. R. Tolkien's then unpublished trilogy, inevitably corrupts its bearer. The portrait of the Sons of the New Day is not successful. The very existence of such a body in Dossola—authoritarian, conspiratorial, ruthlesss—is rather difficult to accept; analogous bodies did not evolve in Europe until the nineteenth century, in response to monarchies which were newly vigilant and oppressive after the object lesson of the revolution in France. Still, it is not surprising that an author writing in the early 1950's would wish to make his fanatics resemble the Communists and other modern fanatics more than the Jacobins, and the anachronism might have been acceptable had it been done tellingly.

Instead, Pratt settles for easy caricature. It is amply clear, and was clear even in 1952, that one of the most powerful appeals a conspiratorial group has for its members is that it provides them with both a sense of purpose and of fellowship. Rodvard's revolutionaries seem to be devoid of both feelings. They gratuitously insult Rodvard and keep him ridiculously short of funds; despite their desire to control the Blue Star, they betray Rodvard to the royalist police (later explaining only that they knew he would escape one way or another), and then separate Rodvard from Lalette and fail to provide for her, despite knowing that if Rodvard is unfaithful the usefulness of the Blue Star will be gone. This facile and not particularly telling satire might have provided an amusing moment in one of Pratt's humorous collaborations with de Camp, but here it is central to the plot of a fairly serious novel, and indeed the reader is asked to believe that such a party could actually seize power and hold it for months.

The greatest difficulty of all, however, lies in the characterization of Rodvard and Lalette. It is almost as if Charles Dickens had decided to populate *A Tale of Two Cities* (1859) with characters drawn from Henry Fielding's *Tom Jones* (1749). Rodvard is hopelessly credulous, weak-willed, and ineffectual, his only redeeming quality being a capacity for halfhearted and generally fleeting repentance. When the novel opens, he is too far sunk into the ideology of the Sons to win much sympathy from the reader. By the novel's end he has learned nothing positive through all his experience—merely that "somewhere I have lost the line," and that he has been playing out of his league. His final discarding of the Blue Star seems not so much a rejection of evil as a decision to scurry away into a corner of the world scaled to small creatures such as himself. Lalette is in some ways more appealing; at least her sense of right and wrong is more nearly intact. At the same time, she is generally content to be forced along by events, acting only to defend herself from the most pressing dangers. Such a cast of character may be entirely reasonable in a young woman of her culture and position, but that does not serve to make her any more interesting to the reader. Rodvard and Lalette are not caricatures; they come across as real people, but unfortunately the wrong people to interest the reader in this story. Once again, Pratt's general predilection for the unheroic hero served him better in his humorous collaborations than it does in a serious work.

Still, although not a complete success, *The Blue Star* is worth reading. Moreover, the causes of its relative failure discussed above seem to be difficulties that could have been solved while preserving the novel's freshness of approach as embodied in its realistic characterization, its sophisticated treatment of religion and politics, and its unusual cultural setting. Since Pratt's day, an occasional writer, possibly under *The Blue Star*'s influence, has occupied something like the same territory. Roland Green's Wandor series, for example, is set in a post-medieval world lacking gunpowder where magic works, and much of the action centers about the formation of the sort of centralized monarchy readers see being destroyed in *The Blue Star*. Even so, many of the thematic breakthroughs of *The Blue Star* have not been followed up in later works of fantasy. That this should be so is fantasy's loss.

Patrick L. McGuire

Bibliography
de Camp, L. Sprague. "Parallel Worlds: Fletcher Pratt," in *Literary Swordsmen and Sorcerers: The Makers of Heroic Fantasy*, 1976.

THE BOATS OF THE "GLEN CARRIG"

Author: William Hope Hodgson (1877-1918)
First book publication: 1907
Type of work: Novel
Time: The early to mid-eighteenth century
Locale: The Sargasso Sea area in the North Atlantic

Three lifeboats from the shipwrecked "Glen Carrig" encounter monstrous life forms and unexpected dangers as they explore the weed-clotted waters and mysterious islands of the Sargasso Sea area

> *Principal characters:*
> THE NARRATOR (JOHN WINTERSTRAW), a shipwrecked passenger
> THE BO'SUN, leader of the shipwrecked crew
> MARY MADISON, the narrator's sweetheart

Handsome, energetic, gregarious, a bit of a daredevil, William Hope Hodgson was the antithesis of the popular image of the horror-story writer. The third of twelve children of a nonconformist minister, he ran away to sea in his early teens. Eight years later, he returned home to start a body-building school and to explore writing as a way of supplementing his seasonal income. His first efforts were articles on body-building, illustrated with his own photographs (he was an excellent photographer), but it was obvious from the beginning that the readership for such efforts was quite limited. He turned to fiction, drawing upon the most extreme experiences of his young life for his material—his time at sea.

Although Hodgson the boy may have run off, impelled by a romantic vision and love of the sea, the man who returned eight years later loathed it, both because of the harshness and brutality of the sailor's life and because of the awesome, inexplicable dangers, real and imagined, to body and soul that it harbored. His first writing attempts were in short fiction, most of which follow a simple, effective pattern. The sailor narrator encounters a mysterious situation in the ocean or on an uncharted island, which he then explores. The menace grows as the enigmatic phenomenon—a rat-infested derelict, a voice in the night, a ship made of stone, "mermaids" with claws—is revealed, leading to a climax from which the narrator and his associates may or may not escape.

This same pattern structures his first novel, *The Boats of the "Glen Carrig"*; indeed, the first third of the novel can stand alone as a separate story. After drifting for five days through weed-glutted waters, the shipwrecked crew of the *Glen Carrig* at last come upon land, where they first encounter strange, ominous sounds ("a curious, low, sobbing note"), then a derelict boat occupied by a monstrous sea creature, and finally the land itself, an island bereft of sounds or animal life, but filled with strange plants that seem, upon close examination, to have animal and human forms embedded in them. The plants attack the men. When the sailors slash at them, the plants wail and bleed. Are they half-plant, half-animal, or are they plants that capture and absorb animals and humans? The reader cannot be sure, but the latter seems likely. As the men row away from the island, one of the sailors produces a letter found on the abandoned ship. "But I hear my lover's voice wailing in the night, and I go to find him; for my loneliness is not to be borne." Were the two faces the crew found embedded in a single tree those of the woman and her beloved?

The remainder of the novel follows a similar pattern, although the sequence of events is more complex. After barely surviving a severe storm at sea, the men find themselves drifting through another weed-choked sea, this one dotted with derelict ships, where they encounter sea beasts—a giant crab, an even more gigantic devilfish, and, most harrowing, "a white demonic face, human save that the mouth and nose had greatly the appearance of a beak" staring up from beneath the water. Finally sighting an island, the men cautiously land on it, pausing briefly to inspect a large boat covered by odd battlements. The island, of course, conceals dangers that slowly emerge as the men explore it. Gradually it is revealed that the island and surrounding waters are inhabited by hordes of the bizarre semihuman forms they had sighted under the water. The Narrator describes one of the "Weed Men" as being "a human slug . . . great eyes, so big as crown pieces . . . the bill like to an inverted parrot's . . . slug-like white and slimy body . . . two short and stumpy arms . . . the ends divided into hateful and wriggling masses of small tentacles." Initially the Weed Men hide in the shadows, attacking individual sailors under cover of darkness. One injured sailor is carried off and drained of blood. At last the Weed Men attack *en masse*, and the ensuing battle, with the small group of sailors fighting off the mob of human slugs in the dark with broad swords and homemade torches, is one of the most horrific action scenes in the literature.

While exploring the island, the crew of the *Glen Carrig* discover that the barricaded ship is occupied. For the balance of the book, they divide their time between defending themselves from the Weed Men and trying to make contact with those stranded aboard the *Seabird*. They flash messages printed on large canvases back and forth; they attempt, and fail, to shoot a line to the ship by constructing a huge bow; and finally they succeed with a very simple idea, flying a kite to the ship.

Much of the strength of the book lies in Hodgson's concrete, believable handling of everyday life. Like all important writers of weird fantasy, Hodgson was a master realist. Only by creating a carefully realistic environment can a horror writer make his otherworldly intrusions seem convincing and shocking. His years at sea gave Hodgson a thorough understanding of shipboard routine and he very adroitly merges the details of the sailors' lives with the exotic dangers that surround and harass them. In like manner, their attempts to contact the survivors of the *Seabird* are described in precise detail. It is only after that contact is made that the book flags somewhat. Once aboard the *Seabird*, the Narrator meets and falls in love with Mary Madison, a passenger stranded on the ship. Thus Victorian sentimentality intrudes on nautical horror and dissipates some of its effects.

The damage is minor, however (unlike the sentimentality that badly mars Hodgson's most ambitious work, *The Night Land*, 1912). *The Boats of the "Glen Carrig"* is an exciting, powerful, scary book, probably the best extended introduction to Hodgson's writing, although it does not really seem to have the "seriousness" its author somewhat retroactively attributed to it in his Preface to *The Ghost Pirates* (1909). In that later novel, he cited *The Boats of the "Glen Carrig"* as the first in a trilogy of novels (with *The Ghost Pirates* and *The House on the Borderland*, 1908): "though very different in scope, each of the three books deals with certain conceptions that have an elemental kinship." That "kinship," as explained at great length in *The Ghost Pirates*, is that certain areas of the world are borderlands between dimensions, through which strange creatures from other realms can enter the familiar world. Thus, Hodgson retrospectively provided a kind of science-fiction rationale for a novel that works quite well as one of the most effective horror stories of the sea ever written.

Keith Neilson

Bibliography
Ashley, Mike. "The Essential Writers: William Hope Hodgson," in *Twilight Zone*. VII, no. 1 (April, 1982), pp. 69-72.
Hodgson, William Hope. "Preface," in *The Ghost Pirates*, 1909.
Koenig, H. C. "William Hope Hodgson: Master of the Weird and Fantastic," in *The House on the Borderland and Other Novels*, 1946.
Lovecraft, H. P. *Supernatural Horror in Literature*, 1945.
Moskowitz, Sam. "William Hope Hodgson," in *Out of the Storm: Uncollected Fantasies by William Hope Hodgson*, 1975.
Stableford, Brian. "*Deep Waters*," in *Survey of Science Fiction Literature*, 1979. Edited by Frank N. Magill.

THE BOOK OF PTATH

Author: A. E. van Vogt (1912-   )
First book publication: 1947 (later published as *200 Million A.D.*)
Type of work: Novel
Time: Two hundred million years after the twentieth century
Locale: The fictional world of Gondwanaland

> *The god Ptath is challenged for supremacy by his first wife and archenemy, Ineznia, the golden goddess, who seeks to destroy Ptath and become the supreme divinity for all eternity*

Principal characters:
> PTATH, a god who does battle against the wicked Ineznia
> INEZNIA, Ptath's first wife and mortal enemy
> PETER HOLROYD, a deceased American soldier who occupies the superhuman body of Ptath
> L'ONEE, Ptath's second wife and chief ally

A. E. van Vogt sold his first story to *True Story* magazine in 1932; similar stories in the true-confessions genre followed. After a period of writing radio plays and business-news articles, he sold his first science-fiction story to *Astounding* late in 1938 and his second in January, 1939; this second science-fiction novel, "Black Destroyer," was the first to be published and appeared in the July, 1939, issue. (The earlier story was not printed until later, under the title "Vault of the Beast.") During these formative years, when van Vogt made his home in Canada, he and *Astounding* editor John W. Campbell, Jr. struck up a correspondence. When Campbell found that his publisher, Street and Smith, was planning to launch a companion magazine to be called *Unknown*, he urged van Vogt to study the new magazine's contents and submit stories that would reflect its particular slant. Although fantasy was never van Vogt's métier, he wrote his first successful fantasy story, "The Witch," as a result of Campbell's suggestion that the Granny character of his science-fiction novel *Slan* (1940) would make an interesting witch. In the tale, therefore, the old aunt who arrives to live with the main character and his wife proves to be a genuine old and villainous sea witch. "The Witch" was later turned into a script for one of Rod Serling's television series and was entitled "When Aunt Ada Came to Stay." When *Unknown* (or *Unknown Worlds*, as it was later called) began to feature a lead novel in every issue and Campbell again asked van Vogt to contribute, the latter's first effort was *The Book of Ptath*.

Long before the tale opens, the god Ptath (pronounced "Toth") has merged with the human race; "merging," as defined by van Vogt, means that he reacquaints his deep, inner self with the human condition of mortality by living from birth to death the lives of countless human beings. Ptath orders seven protective spells to ensure that he will eventually be able to return to his state of godhood, an action typical of the arrogance of gods and goddesses. Meanwhile, his first wife, the golden goddess Ineznia, sets out to become the supreme divinity for all eternity; she devises numerous plans and traps whereby she seeks to overcome Ptath's spells and ultimately to destroy him. Her first act is designed to confuse the divinity of Ptath by reviving the last human identity which he had assumed prior to returning to Gondwanaland. Thus, Peter Holroyd, an American soldier who was killed in World War II, finds himself transported two hundred million years into the future, occupying the seemingly human but actually superhuman body of the god Ptath. Thereafter, it is Holroyd's task to save Ptath and himself from the beguiling schemes of Ineznia. In the subsequent struggle, the principal ally of Ptath and Holroyd is Ptath's second wife, L'onee; unfortunately, she is not a particularly strong ally, since years earlier she was imprisoned in a cold dungeon and divested of most of her power as a goddess by Ineznia.

One of the protective spells is broken by the act of lovemaking. Holroyd, who was young, dashing, and unattached in 1944, has no moral qualms whatsoever about vanquishing a beautiful, seductive temptress. Unfortunately, the spell is broken before L'onee can adequately warn him. In similar, devious ways, each of the other six spells has its own Achilles' heel built into it; the exultant Ineznia works her wiles while Holroyd visits the imperial palace in the spectacular capital city of Ptath, where he witnesses dazzling marvels of a fantastic future.

Several of the disasters that befall the Holroyd/Ptath body are in themselves masterpieces of inventiveness. Early in the tale, for example, a spear is impaled in Ptath's chest, whereupon, still bound hand and foot, he is transported on the back of a huge one-horned "dottle" with the spear still buried deep within him while he pretends to be dead. It is not compassion that compels someone to remove the deadly spear from his chest, but rather that the problem of keeping him balanced on the back of the mammoth beast is made more difficult because of the unbalancing force of the swinging spear shaft.

One by one, Ineznia overcomes the protective spells that Ptath conjures up until only one is left. This seventh and final defense focuses on the throne chair of the Nushir of Nushirvan. To obtain it, Holroyd/Ptath must find a way to cross the treacherous river of boiling mud, something which the golden goddess herself has never been able to do. In order to succeed, she must invent a devious plot involving vast armies and a variety of psychologically odd creatures called "screers."

As it turned out, *Unknown* died with *The Book of Ptath*, which proved to be one of the better book-length novels of its kind. It was published in the very last issue of the magazine in October, 1943. Subsequently, in 1947, a small special editions publisher, Fantasy Press, printed a beautiful hardcover edition of one thousand copies—which are now collectors' items. *The Book of Ptath* has since been reissued in a series of paperback editions, most recently by Zebra Books under the title *200 Million A.D.*

Jeffrey M. Elliot

Bibliography
Drake, H. L. "A. E. van Vogt," in *Algol*. XXVIII (Spring, 1977), pp. 17-19.
Elliot, Jeffrey. "Interview: A. E. van Vogt," in *Science Fiction Review*. XXIII (November, 1977), pp. 19-23.
Knight, Damon. "Cosmic Jerrybuilder: A. E. van Vogt," in *In Search of Wonder*, 1956.
Moskowitz, Sam. *Seekers of Tomorrow: Masters of Modern Science Fiction*, 1966.
Wilson, Colin. "A. E. van Vogt," in *Science Fiction Writers*, 1982. Edited by E. F. Bleiler.

THE BOOK OF THE DUN COW

Author: Walter Wangerin (1944-   )
First book publication: 1978
Type of work: Novel
Time: Before Adam and Eve
Locale: The fictional world of the medieval beast fable

Chauntecleer the rooster and his coop (a community of hens and animals) successfully combat the dreadful evil of Wyrm, Cockatrice, and a brood of basilisks, thereby proving themselves worthy Keepers of the world

Principal characters:
    CHAUNTECLEER, a rooster, the Lord of his coop
    PERTELOTE, a hen, his wife
    JOHN WESLEY WEASEL, the devoted friend of the chickens
    MUNDO CANI, a humble, self-sacrificing dog
    COCKATRICE, a monster, half-rooster and half-reptile
    WYRM, the immense World-Snake living in the bowels of the Earth

In *The Book of the Dun Cow* (1978), Walter Wangerin taps a venerable tradition by writing a tale of talking animals—a beast fable. Popular from the time of Aesop, the form was particularly favored by preachers of the Middle Ages, who found animal fables well-suited for teaching morality, while at the same time delighting congregations with the antics of wily foxes, gentle lambs, and voracious wolves. Wangerin is likewise a preacher with deeply moral concerns which thoroughly permeate this tale of the Keepers of the Lord God's Earth. As were his medieval predecessors, he is centrally concerned with entertaining, the marks of which are everywhere present: in the rousing plot, in the full-blooded characterization, and in the energy of his zesty style.

Yet Wangerin does not merely supply another typical beast fable. *The Book of the Dun Cow* is a full-scale novel incorporating the vision of the world implicit (although seldom fully expressed) in the medieval tales of animals. First, there is a fully imagined, richly detailed cosmology wherein the Lord God has fixed the round, unmoving Earth in "that holy place" at "the absolute center of the universe"—precisely where medieval science, following Ptolemy, said it was. In those days before the creation of man, the animals had dominion over the land; they were the "Keepers" who maintained the natural harmonies and guarded the land from ill. The source of evil in this universe is Wyrm, a gigantic serpent whom God has imprisoned under the "face" of the world; it gnaws the innards of the Earth and longs to be free so that it can smash all of God's creation. The name *Wyrm* suggests, at once, the biblical "worm that dieth not," the Old English name for the dragons who traditionally lay waste to their fictional lands, and the Midgard Serpent of Norse myth, who is destined to wreak universal destruction on the cosmos of the Northmen. In *The Book of the Dun Cow*, it is as if the medieval world of the beast fable had sprung to vital and manifold life.

One beast fable in particular serves as a source of Wangerin's inspiration, a tale, interestingly, told by another preacher—Geoffrey Chaucer's wise and witty Nun's Priest. Chauntecleer, the chief character, is the cocky rooster who falls from pride in both stories. Pertelote, his lovely and gracious wife, likewise derives from Chaucer, although Wangerin's has none of the "henpecking" qualities of the Priest's chicken. In Chaucer, the antagonist is the treacherous fox, Dan Russell, who nearly kills the foolish cock. In *The Book of the Dun Cow*, Dan Russell also appears, but he is not the antagonist; the fox here is a beloved member of Chauntecleer's community or coop. In him, the fox's traditional slyness modulates into a comic trickiness, and the usual duplicity and double-tongued speech becomes a loopy, ludicrous double-talk. Rather, the antagonist here is Cockatrice, a distorted rooster with the head and wings of a cock, but with reptilian scales on his grotesque body, and the tail of a serpent. To Chauntecleer, especially in the later scene where they meet in battle, Cockatrice appears as a "mirror," a monstrous double, a hideous perversion who is an appalling version of Chauntecleer himself as he might be if he were to succumb to evil.

As in "The Nun's Priest's Tale," the impetus for the plot is a dream. In another coop, many miles upriver from Chauntecleer's, an evil dream insinuates itself into the mind of a lonely old rooster appropriately named Senex. No longer does the aged leader crow the hours correctly; he has sired no heirs; the hens scorn and humiliate him. The dream gives him the strange and absurd hope of begetting himself as his own son and of killing one hundred hens. Falling prey to the dream, he calls the evil suggestion "good" and wills it into existence with the words "Let it be!" Thereafter, the entire episode is rife with distortions of the natural processes. He, the leader, bloodies his hens and drives them from the coop. He, the male, feels a tearing of his old loins and lays an egg which a toad incubates. Thus the new egg represents, not life and the continuance of the natural cycle, but unnaturalness and death. From the egg comes Cockatrice.

Chauntecleer is shown as an admirable contrast to Senex. He also is attacked by a dream in a chapter entitled "The First Engagement with the Enemy." The dream tries to take insidious advantage of the feeling of loneliness that inevitably accompanies Chauntecleer's position of authority. Suggesting that the hens are ungrateful and ignore him, the evil voice rouses Chauntecleer to resent them. When the dream shows him the necessary conclusion of unchecked resentment, however, when it shows him Senex's "hope"—a vision of dead hens—all of Chauntecleer's instincts rebel. He defies the dream, calls it evil, and turns with renewed love to Pertelote and the other beloved animals of his community. His compassion and care have saved him.

Also in contrast to Senex's unnatural behavior is Chauntecleer's role as protector of the natural cycles. Unlike Senex's cockeyed crowing, Chaunte-cleer's canonical crows make the day familiar and blessed to the hens and other animals by marking precisely the movement of the natural rhythms. Unlike Senex's unnatural egg, Chauntecleer maintains the natural reproduction of his coop by saving the eggs of his hens. When it is discovered that Ebeneezer Rat has been secretly eating the eggs, he removes the menace, but not, significantly, by killing the rat. Rather, he makes the rat's stealth impossible in the future by plucking two feathers from his own wings, driving them permanently into Ebeneezer, thus marking him forever. The act is characteristic of Chauntecleer's self-sacrificing nature, for without two of his "primary feathers . . . the Rooster's flight would be a grievous desperation."

Thus, taking the central characters, some hints of plot, and the implied world view of "The Nun's Priest's Tale," Wangerin has fashioned a new, gloriously vivid depiction of the struggle between good and evil, the natural and the unnatural. Although his emphasis is completely original, what could be more wholly fitting for an animal story than a pervasive concern with the natural world and natural behavior? It is Wangerin's literary gift to detect the rich possibilities inherent in the genre and exploit them in a moving and significant way. As the story develops, he strengthens the great theme of nature and antinature and interweaves it with an exploration of the nature of true leadership, the basis for a sound and wholesome community, and the temptations of pride.

Under Cockatrice, who soon kills the bewildered Senex, the old community disintegrates and natural order decays. Cockatrice refuses to crow, to keep the natural hours; thus, all life becomes strange and alien to the animals and the hens. His stench makes it impossible for them to eat. They quarrel and withdraw from the community in mutual distrust and blame. Throughout all this time, Cockatrice, in a frenzy of mechanical lust, rapes the hens and makes them lay eggs which hatch a progeny of poisonous basilisks: "Black, licorice long, damp, each with two burning eyes in its head and teeth already in its mouth, they were small, curled serpents." With his death-dealing brood, Cockatrice utterly destroys the coop. The triumph of Wyrm comes nearer.

In Chauntecleer's coop, death and destruction are replaced by love and life. In a variant of the biblical vision of the lion and the lamb lying down together, John Wesley Weasel (a wonderfully feisty, loyal character) woos the Widow Mouse, a refugee from Cockatrice's coop. Instead of rape, there is the poignant love which develops between Chauntecleer and Pertelote (another refugee) in a beautiful vision of mutual trust and understanding. They are married amidst the animals' rejoicing; and the river, the channel between the two coops, freezes over. Soon three chicks are born to Chauntecleer and Pertelote. Nevertheless, the safety and security of winter does not last. Spring comes, ironically not with the promise of new life but with the danger of death from the thawing river. The children of Cockatrice penetrate the land and kill the children of Chauntecleer, and the future and the natural cycle are thwarted.

The challenge to Chauntecleer is overwhelming. Yet, like the good leader he is, he knows he needs help. Pertelote heartens him as do the other animals; and the Lord God himself does not leave them comfortless in their trouble— he sends them the Dun Cow. The "Book of the Dun Cow" is the name of an early Irish manuscript which includes even earlier Irish legends, in particular the heroic tales of Cuchulain. As well as being appropriate here for the concern with heroic behavior, the presence of the Dun Cow suggests the deep-seated belief of the early Celts that the Divine was immanent and often manifested by animals (as shown, for example, by Epona the Horse Goddess and Cerunnos the Horned God). The Dun Cow comes among the animals with the Divine gift of compassionate understanding. Chauntecleer is crushed with sorrow for his sons and utters his terrible version of "My God! My God! Why hast Thou forsaken me?" She then appears and "the miracle takes place": "His grief had become her grief, his sorrow her own."

To quell the evil, Chauntecleer must fight three major battles in quick succession, each of which calls upon different aspects of leadership. In the first, he must prove his good generalship. He marshals all the animals, enspirits them, and delegates duties. When their spirits flag before battle with the basilisks, he calls the animals each by name and continues his crowing, lending the comfort of order. In the fighting itself, Chauntecleer takes the lead by killing the basilisks with his crows *potens*. In this, as elsewhere, Wangerin makes full use of the old legends about basilisks, which tell that crowing cocks and weasels are the serpents' traditional enemies (thus the central role of John Wesley Weasel). The legendary protection against their poison is rue, and the animals here guard themselves by rubbing the herb on one another and on the coop. Against the appalling menace, the animals win, and they return to the coop, covered with wounds but victorious.

In the second major battle, Chauntecleer must prove his own worth and courage alone. He puts on battle spurs and fights in single combat with Cockatrice. Again, Chauntecleer triumphs: he kills his archfoe, although he emerges from the fight with a mass of bloodied feathers and broken bones. Still a third enemy remains, Wyrm, and in that more subtle challenge to his leadership, he fails. All great leaders must know when to step aside, and this final battle is not his to fight; it is the duty of the dog, Mundo Cani. Chauntecleer, however, cannot swallow his pride, and when he sees the Dun Cow sympathetically talking with Mundo Cani, he is filled with resentment and jealousy. The Cow, he thinks, should be talking to *him*, and he succumbs to pride.

Mundo Cani begins the novel with a whining, obsequious, spaniel-like fawning which Chauntecleer finds difficult to control. Feeling marooned in an ungainly body, the dog is continually howling "marooned" and groveling before the rooster. Yet it is he who is chosen for the last battle. The Dun Cow breaks off her horn, which the dog places in his mouth. Just as the seemingly invincible Wyrm is about to burst through a crack in the Earth, the dog calls, "Wyrm! Look on me!," then leaps down and blinds the solitary eye of the terrible foe. The fissure in the Earth closes, and the Keepers are at last wholly victorious. Mundo Cani, however, is trapped with Wyrm. In his self-sacrificing humility, the dog has shown utter obedience. By his act of love, he has become the true guard dog of the universe—in a profound sense, the cosmos is "Mundo Cani," Latin for the "world of the dog."

Through Pertelote's guidance, Chauntecleer recognizes his pride and is healed, and the story ends with Chauntecleer and John Wesley Weasel vying to be the first to go down to visit Mundo Cani in the underworld. As in "The Nun's Priest's Tale," the rooster has learned his lesson.

Chaucer himself says that great writers put "new wine in old bottles." Walter Wangerin's strikingly original achievement is to take an old form and invest it with new and burgeoning life—to explore age-old human concerns and Christian themes in a fresh and highly moving way. In *The Book of the Dun Cow*, the old is transfigured into a new fantasy of unusual potency and meaning.

Douglas A. Burger

Bibliography
No listing.

THE BOOK OF THE NEW SUN

Author: Gene Wolfe (1931-   )
First book publications: The Shadow of the Torturer (1980); *The Claw of the Conciliator*
   (1981); *The Sword of the Lictor* (1982); *The Citadel of the Autarch* (1982)
Type of work: Novels
Time: The unimaginably remote future
Locale: A continent in the Southern Hemisphere of Earth

> *Severian, orphan and apprentice torturer, finds that both his feelings and his fate remove him from the profession he had thought would be his, and after a series of adventures, he becomes both the ruler of his country and the herald of a new age for the planet*

> *Principal characters:*
> SEVERIAN, a journeyman-torturer, Lictor of Thrax, later Autarch
> DORCAS, his lover, of mysterious origin
> AGIA, a woman who becomes his nemesis
> JASON, Severian's friend, a former space-voyager
> DR. TALOS, the apparent head of a company of players
> BALDANDERS, the giant companion of Dr. Talos

Gene Wolfe's tetralogy, the Book of the New Sun, has been praised as highly as any recent work of fantasy or science fiction, and perhaps better than any other shows how indistinct is the dividing line between the two fields. For example, the first volume, *The Shadow of the Torturer*, was nominated for a Nebula award as the best science-fiction novel of 1980, and also took the honors at the World Fantasy Convention for best fantasy novel of the same year. The second volume, *The Claw of the Conciliator*, was again nominated for the Nebula in 1981. Those who find a clear and unmistakable line between fantasy and science fiction will have much to discuss about the Book of the New Sun.

One way out of the difficulty of classification that the work presents would be to endorse Arthur C. Clarke's dictum that a sufficiently advanced science is indistinguishable from magic. The problem with this answer is that Clarke most probably meant "indistinguishable from magic *by the characters in the story*" (italics added), not by the readers of the story. Even though the question of genre is settled, the categorization of the Book of the New Sun remains tentative: the work contains many of the trappings of science fiction—spaceships, time travel, alternate futures, intelligent aliens, genetic engineering (much reminiscent of the works of Cordwainer Smith), drug-heightened consciousness, and robots.

The work also contains many of the ingredients of myth, both bright— miraculous cures (even the raising of the dead) and the intrusion of the divine into the human sphere—and dark: a character much like a fury, unwitting incest, ritual cannibalism, ghosts, and necromancers. Finally, the work has what might be called the atmosphere of fantasy, the sensation that the world is not completely explicable by a mechanical materialism.

Certainly the time of the work favors fantasy: it is set in an immensely remote future, when Earth (called "Urth" by the characters) is in the same melancholy position as it is in Jack Vance's *The Dying Earth* (1962). The sun has dimmed noticeably, and the stars are visible in the daytime; winters are becoming colder, marking the approach of a final, unending ice age. In *The Citadel of the Autarch*, Severian meets a visitor from the future—actually, a student of the Earth of Severian's time—who comes from a possible future in which even the atmosphere has frozen and lies covering the planet in a miles-deep blanket.

The passing of geologic ages has had other effects, too. Moonlit nights are now brightly illuminated with a greenish light. Long in the past, the moon has somehow been equipped with an atmosphere and is covered with forests. Their verdure gives a greenish tinge to the light, a light which is stronger because the moon is closer. At one point, Severian casually notes its distance from the earth as 50,000 leagues. In *The Claw of the Conciliator*, Wolfe translates *league* as about three miles. Thus the moon orbits the Earth at a distance of 150,000 miles rather than its present 238,000 miles.

When a span of time that can produce such effects is applied to human affairs, the depth of history behind the setting becomes so great that it is almost unimaginable. Through the millennia, a city may expand to enormous size. For example, Nessus, the principal city of the Autarchy, appears to be the size of whole counties; although millions live in it, it contains more houses than people. For ages, Nessus has grown northwards. Its southern parts become slums, then are abandoned altogether. By the time of the story, huge regions of the city lie deserted, some for thousands of years. Looters operate a whole industry of marginal legality, prowling about the ruins, salvaging furniture and valuables from empty houses and taking them north for resale.

Yet even this example—a future analogue of tomb-robbing—does not adequately suggest the sense of the immensity of human time conveyed in the tetralogy. A company of players present a drama about the beginning of a new age, the coming of the New Sun, supposed to produce apocalyptic changes in the Earth, with the sea bottoms rising to become dry land. A character speaks of the riches of rare metals that will be brought to light when they rise, and among the metals he names not only gold and silver, but also iron and copper. Although the original veins of ore have been exhausted, an industry of "mining" continues, excavating the scrap of civilizations without number, buried one below the other. Although the date of the setting is nowhere given, it must be millions upon millions of years in the future. Imagine the time needed for the Tigris-Euphrates delta to be heaved up into mountains by the buckling of the Earth's crust, so that along a fault line, centuries of human culture lie vertically exposed: such is the imaginative scope of time in the Book of the New Sun.

A vivid account of the burial of eons of history occurs in *The Sword of the Lictor*, when Severian descends a cliff. As he does so, he passes a layer of fossils of men and animals in the face of the mountain. Below this lie the petrified limbs and trunks of some long-dead forest. Still lower, he sees "buildings and mechanisms," and he is not yet halfway down. Even below the midpoint, he passes decorated tiles in the strata and compares himself to a fly descending a portrait, but it is a portrait of the past on which he is perched.

Across such an extent of time, it is perhaps pointless to speak of the setting of the tetralogy, since continents themselves may have moved. Still, Severian speaks of seven continents, and the story is clearly set in the Southern Hemisphere: he moves northward to the equator, and the Southern Cross is visible in the heavens. Whether the scene is South America, Africa, or even Australia is difficult to say; new mountain chains have grown up and new river systems descend from them. A closer identification of the setting of the story would only be guesswork.

Although the characters of the books know that human history stretches for eons behind them, they are unaware of its details. The past is lost, or at least lost to Severian; as an apprentice and later a journeyman in the torturer's guild (officially, the "Seekers of Truth and Penitence"), his training has been mostly the practical refinements of his craft, and his grasp of history is sketchy. Since most of what the reader knows about the intervening eons comes from Severian, only a clue here and there about the future of mankind is provided. From those hints, it appears that at some remote time in Severian's past, humanity gained interstellar transportation and, in the process, met with many an intelligent race. For reasons unknown, that period of expansion and empire is long past. No longer do earthmen visit the stars in ships of human manufacture and direction, although they may sign as crew members on the ships of aliens (called "cacogens" in the story). Urth no longer has the resources to build, guide, and maintain starfleets. Even the heavier energy weapons which both sides employ in the war between the Autarchy and the Ascians are imported from offworld.

Urth is a poor planet: it lacks both minerals (after thousands of years of extraction) and energy (as the sun dims). Consequently, human endeavors are a strange mixture of advanced and obsolete technology. A soldier mounted on something like a warhorse may carry a laser, while the man or woman next to him has only a sword.

Because Severian is a torturer, questions of crime and its punishment fill much of the books, but the story is not about law and its search for justice. Because Severian becomes a soldier, there is many a battle scene, but the story is not one of conquest or government. Rather, the books tell of prophecy and its fulfillment.

At the center of the story is Severian, first met in *The Shadow of the Torturer* as an apprentice in the guild of Torturers. Like his fellows, he does not know who his parents were; apprentices come from the children orphaned by the execution of the guild's "clients." From the beginning, Severian is unusual, having been chosen for involvement in higher matters. Along with other apprentices, he swims for recreation in the great river Gyoll, which runs through the city near the Citadel in which he lives. Once, while swimming, he becomes entangled in river weeds. He struggles to escape, but to no effect; then he has an unmistakable sense of being rescued by a woman—huge, supernatural, yet somehow familiar.

His special qualities include a perfect memory (a useful attribute for the narrator of a first-person story). This gift makes him a favorite pupil of the masters of the guild. He also has a strong sense of beauty (although there is little to stimulate it in the Citadel), and, most important, he has a kindness bred of sympathy and reflection. His compassion is first evident in his healing of an injured dog, although pets are forbidden to those in his position. After he becomes a journeyman and has prisoners in his keeping, his yearning for beauty and his strong affections unite to cause him to fall in love with one of the inmates, an aristocratic woman named Thecla.

Thecla's imprisonment also offends Severian's sense of justice, because she has done nothing wrong herself. Thecla's sister has recently joined a rebel band. The authorities hope, through pressure on Thecla, to force her sister to return and thereby to gain intelligence about the rebel movement. Severian's involvement with Thecla becomes known, and only his masters' affection for him and their fear of embarrassing the guild save him from death. A discreet banishment is the chosen penalty, so he is sent to the provincial capital of Thrax, far to the north and close to the war zone, to take the position of Lictor, chief official of law enforcement and punishment under the governor of that city.

There is little urgency to Severian's journey, and indeed, the leisurely pace of the narrative leads one at first to expect a blend of *Bildungsroman* and picaresque novel. Yet the incidents that occur in his travels have a significance that becomes clear only much later, for at this point, in the second volume, the theme of prophecy begins.

In the world of the Book of the New Sun, God (called the Increate) had long before sent a mediator, a wonder worker known by many names, but most often called "the Conciliator," perhaps meaning one who reconciles man to God. A religious order of women, the Pelerines, have preserved a relic of the Conciliator, a sapphirelike gem which has at its center a claw-shaped brilliance that gives it its name. Severian comes into possession of the Claw of the Conciliator, and almost at once, strange things begin to happen. Sometimes, but not always, he can work miracles with it, healing the sick and wounded and even, a few times, raising the dead. Here the legends of the Conciliator begin to take on meaning.

On his way north, Severian falls in with a traveling company of actors. This strange band consists primarily of only two people: Dr. Talos, the playwright, and the giant Baldanders, who seems as simple as he is strong. With the addition of Severian and two women, the company travels together, stages a play, separates for a while, and is eventually reunited for a performance at the fabled House Absolute, the palace of the Autarch. They perform the play of the coming of the New Sun, which is one of the names by which the Conciliator is remembered. Adam and Eve figures appear, and they struggle against the authorities of the old order (including the Autarch), who seek to prevent the passing of their mode of existence, poor though it is. The meaning of "New Sun" and the nature of the changes it will bring, however, are not clear. The Conciliator is much in Severian's mind after the play, and through the center part of the tetralogy, he tries to return the Claw to the Pelerines. The difficulty is caused by the fact that they are a wandering order, and first he must find them.

At the end of the third volume, *The Sword of the Lictor*, Severian must leave Thrax, once again for dereliction of duty involving kindness to a condemned woman. After escaping from Thrax, he meets with a band of lake-dwellers oppressed by a local tyrant, and he agrees to lead them in battle against the tyrant, a self-corrupted monstrosity whose misuse of science is aimed at preserving his own existence. In battle with the monster, both objects symbolic of Severian's personality are destroyed: the Claw of the Conciliator is lost, and *Terminus Est*, the executioner's sword presented to him on leaving the Citadel, is destroyed. Both his identity as a torturer and his growing ability as a miracle worker seem ended; some change is surely at hand, but the question of what kind of change is not answered until the fourth volume.

The fourth book, *The Citadel of the Autarch*, is in some ways both more and less science-fictional than the others. In this volume, Severian comes into closer contact with the cacogens than he has experienced before, and he discovers them to be sympathetic and helpful rather than hideous. The cacogens are observing the war between the Autarchy and the Ascians with interest though without preference, for it seems they offer more than only victory in a local war. Severian enlists in a cavalry troop, sees action at the front, and finally encounters the Autarch himself.

This shadowy figure has been the subject of gossip throughout the story, but not until Severian meets him does the reader learn that the Autarch shares Severian's desire to bring about the advent of the New Sun. One learns as well what the nature of the New Sun is: the cacogens have the ability to create a *white hole* at the heart of the sun, through which the energy of a counter-universe will be channeled, restoring the sun to its former splendor and utility. For some reason, the cacogens insist on an earthman's passing a test of some kind as a condition of the renewal. The Autarch was the last one since antiquity to attempt the test, and he failed, at personal loss to himself. Now, in a desperate situation, he offers Severian the chance to become not only the next Autarch, but also the repository of the consciousnesses of all the former ones. A similarity has been noted between the works of Jack Vance and the Book of the New Sun, but this twist of the plot, this recapturing of the memories of the past, recalls Frank Herbert's *Dune* books. In the Book of the New Sun, there is more than a hint that the process may be somewhat diabolical; not only is it achieved through a grisly operation, but also the name by which some servants address the former Autarch is "Legion," the name of the New Testament band of devils whom Jesus drives from a possessed man into a herd of swine. Nevertheless, Severian accepts the challenge. At the story's end, he has established himself as the new Autarch and looks forward to trying the test himself, full of confidence that he will succeed.

What is here presented is only the sketchiest outline of a highly convoluted plot, and a brief mention of only a few of the characters whose actions intertwine throughout the story. It omits many conflicts—for example, the unwearying tracking of Severian by a woman named Agia, lusting for personal revenge. It omits the tale of Dorcas, a woman with whom Severian falls in love after her appearance under very strange circumstances, and the unraveling of that mystery, leading to Severian's discovery of his ancestry. It fails almost entirely to capture the tone of the story, by which, more than anything else, the work's classification as fantasy is justified: the frequent talk of spells and enchantments, the frequent appearance of numinous objects and persons—even ghosts—all lend an atmosphere to the story that removes it far from the realm of the hard science fiction of, for example, *Analogue*.

Finally, a brief essay such as this cannot consider in any detail the skill with which Gene Wolfe puts his words in order. The Book of the New Sun is too rare a thing: a work that can be enjoyed and appreciated for its style. Consider, only as one brief example, a short paragraph from *The Shadow of the Torturer*, in which Severian describes a dream:

> I bestrode a great, leather-winged being under a lowering sky. Just equipoised between the rack of cloud and a twilit land we slid down a hill of air. Hardly once, it seemed to me, the finger-winged soarer flapped her long pinions. The dying sun was before us, and it seemed we matched the speed of Urth, for it stood unmoving at the horizon, though we flew on and on.

Wolfe adds to his style a depth of time, deepening the texture of his imaginary society by bringing forward folktales, legends, and poems to increase its verisimilitude. This is, of course, the method that writers such as Richard Adams, Ursula K. Le Guin, and above all J. R. R. Tolkien have used to bring a dimension of historicity to their stories.

If the Book of the New Sun is science fiction, then it is science fiction of a rare kind; to the sense of wonder found in almost every chapter, Wolfe brings understandable, well-rounded characters, characters in whose story one takes an interest and in whose fates one is involved.

Time and the judgments of readers will assess the worth of the Book of the New Sun more carefully than it is possible to do here, but it will come as no surprise if the work finds a permanent place in the canon of twentieth century fantasy literature.

Walter E. Meyers

Bibliography

Gordan, Joan. "An Interview with Gene Wolfe," in *Science Fiction Review*. X (Summer, 1981), pp. 18-22.

THE BOOK OF WONDER

Author: Lord Dunsany (Edward John Moreton Drax Plunkett, 1878-1957)
First book publication: 1912
Type of work: Short stories

This collection of brief and beautifully written tales represents the finest achievement of one of the best, and certainly the most influential, of all writers of short fantasy fiction

The eighteenth Baron Dunsany was an Irish peer, a flamboyant character who enjoyed hunting, shooting, and fishing and who served as an officer with the British Army in the Boer War and World War I. It is surprising that he should also have found the time for (or been interested in) intellectual pursuits. He was the Irish chess champion and a prolific writer of novels, plays, poetry, and, in particular, short stories.

Lord Dunsany published approximately sixteen volumes of stories, and while his later efforts from the 1930's and 1940's—mainly tall tales related by Mr. Jorkens and his friends—are entertaining, they are less important than his early fantasies. Between 1903 and the time of World War I, Dunsany wrote more than 150 tales which are of the utmost importance to the fantasy genre. While William Morris is undoubtedly the founding father of, and major influence upon, modern heroic fantasy novels, Lord Dunsany fills the same role for fantasy tales.

The Book of Wonder was the fifth of Dunsany's eight collections of heroic fantasy stories, and it is generally regarded as his best. The stories are very short—only two or three thousand words each—with disproportionately long titles. The first edition contains fourteen stories; subsequent editions have as many as thirty-four stories. Those tales deal with queens and princesses, with dragons and hippogriffs and splendid palaces, with precious jewels and those who try to steal them, and with terrible monsters, all the more terrifying because they are never fully described. The plots are somewhat sparse, often anecdotal or unresolved, yet this is unimportant in context. It is the exquisite and poetical language in which the stories are written that counts, marking them as something original. Written in London and Ireland during 1910 and 1911, most of the original fourteen stories were based on pictures by Sidney Sime rather than the pictures being based on the stories. Sime was an English artist whose atmospheric black-and-white paintings had complemented Dunsany's previous collections. Ten of these bizarre, darkly moody, and occasionally humorous illustrations are included in the first edition of *The Book of Wonder*.

The subtitle of *The Book of Wonder* is "A Chronicle of Little Adventures at the Edge of the World." Some of the stories, such as "The Bride of the Man-Horse" and "The Distressing Tale of Thangobrind the Jeweller, and of the Doom That Befell Him," are set completely in a fantasy world which seems to be compatible with the hemisphere of Pegana, the setting for the stories in Dunsany's previous four collections: *The Gods of Pegana* (1905), *Time and the Gods* (1906), *The Sword of Welleran* (1908), and *A Dreamer's Tales* (1910). He seems to have invented the names of countries and cities whenever he needed them, however, with little regard for any intricate fitting-together of places or events.

Quite often "the edge of the world" is used as a locale (in "The Probable Adventure of the Three Literary Men," "The Injudicious Prayers of Pombo the Idolater," and, by implication, in "The Hoard of the Gibbelins") with the suggestion that it can be reached from the familiar world ("the fields we know," as Dunsany calls it). Indeed, several of the stories in the collection are at least partly set in the familiar world. One such is "The Loot of Bombasharna," in which Shard, a pirate captain, raids the city of Bombasharna, carrying off the Queen of the South to a floating island "on the wrong side of the Sargasso Sea." "Miss Cubbidge and the Dragon of Romance" opens in the London of 1910, from which its eponymous heroine is carried off by a golden-skinned dragon to live with him outside the normal confines of space and time in a marble palace beside the mystical sea. Mr. Nuth, in "How Nuth Would Have Practised His Art Upon the Gnoles," is an upper-class burglar living in London's Belgrave Square, though his expedition to rob the gnoles of only two of their emeralds is surely beyond the boundaries of the familiar world.

It is difficult to convey the style of these stories without quoting extensively. While almost completely descriptive, the stories are carefully pruned of all unnecessary words. The diction is slightly archaic (Dunsany acknowledged the King James Bible as an influence) though not affectedly so. Dunsany's secret is that he was writing prose poems, carefully maintaining the mood and rhythm of each story by using the right word, and reinforcing the fantastic by means of frequent strange names. There are gods such as Chu-bu and Sheemish, characters such as Alderic, Shepperalk, Slith, and Ackronnion, places as curiously named as Zretazoola, Tlun, Moung, and the Dubious Land.

The tone of the stories is not unremittingly heroic. Dunsany is more humorous, ironic, and even sarcastic than in earlier or later volumes. The last few lines of "The Distressing Tale of Thangobrind the Jeweller, and of the Doom That Befell Him" provide an excellent example of this ironic tone: "and [she] became aggressively dull, and called her home the English Riviera, and had platitudes worked in worsted upon her tea-cosy, and in the end never died, but passed away at her residence."

The stories also contain highly moral implications, though with a male chauvinist bias; thieves are almost always thwarted and usually killed nastily as they ply their trade, while heroes frequently seize beautiful women by force and carry them off as brides with no sign of retribution and the author's full approval. "The Coronation of Mr. Thomas Shap" and "The Wonderful Window" can be interpreted as cautionary tales, warning against daydreaming or concerning oneself too much with fantasy worlds. "The Wonderful Window," though, is the odd one out in the collection; like H. G. Wells's "The Crystal Egg" (first published in 1897, some fifteen years earlier), it describes a gadget, of mysterious origin which is later lost, giving a view of another world.

Dunsany's influence upon later writers has been immense. The effect is most noticeable in the work of American writers. H. P. Lovecraft, Robert E. Howard, L. Sprague de Camp, and Fritz Leiber, to name only four of the most eminent, all owe much to Dunsany's style in his short fantasy fiction, while many other writers have borrowed freely from Dunsany before their own styles evolved.

Chris Morgan

Bibliography
Saul, George Brandon. "Strange Gods and Far Places: The Short Stories of Lord Dunsany," in *Arizona Quarterly*. XIX (Autumn, 1963), pp. 197-210.

THE BORROWERS SERIES

Author: Mary Norton (1913-   )
First book publications: The Borrowers (1952); *The Borrowers Afield* (1955); *The Borrowers Afloat* (1959); *The Borrowers Aloft* (1961)
Type of work: Novels
Time: The recent past and Victorian England
Locale: Firbank Hall, an English country house in Bedfordshire, and the surrounding countryside

A series of novels documenting the exploits of a family of tiny people who live by "borrowing" the essentials of life from human beings

> *Principal characters:*
> POD CLOCK, a Borrower
> HOMILY CLOCK, his wife
> LITTLE ARRIETTY, their daughter

Pod, Homily, and Little Arrietty live under the floorboards of Firbank Hall in the English Home Counties. This is true in one sense, but in a broader literary context, the Borrowers inhabit the familiar but undefined fictional hinterlands of England's past, a locale familiar to readers of P. G. Wodehouse, Agatha Christie, and Jane Austen, as well as, to a lesser extent, readers of children's books.

In the Borrowers series, Mary Norton has devised a fascinating variation on the familiar fairy-story concept of "the little people," and with something approaching genius, she has renewed the magic of this concept by rooting it firmly in the mundane. The first two volumes of the series, which are by far the best, chronicle the adventures of Pod, Homily, and Little Arrietty, at first in Firbank Hall, and then, in *The Borrowers Afield*, in the surrounding countryside. (*The Borrowers Afloat* and *The Borrowers Aloft*, while perfectly adequate, suffer from those weaknesses inherent in sequels when the impact of the original idea has become diluted by familiarity.)

The appeal of the Borrowers series as children's books probably lies not only in the meticulous detail with which Mary Norton describes the day-to-day lives of the Borrowers but also in the analogy of Borrowers and children, which is never overstressed, but which must be obvious to the child reader, especially in passages where Arrietty engages in dialogue with Mrs. May's brother and the young Tom Goodenough. Children and Borrowers regard adults with puzzlement and suspicion but are ultimately in their power and depend upon them for survival. This is the message, although Pod, Homily, and Little Arrietty ultimately confound its truth by surviving in the wild and becoming self-sufficient.

The world of the Borrowers is restricted in both artistic and physical terms. Pod, Homily, and Little Arrietty are not Lilliputian figures; their activities have no deeper political or symbolic significance. Their appeal lies more in the absolute conviction and authenticity with which Norton describes life in the English country house in terms of the tiny people who parasitize "Human Beans"—the decadent Overmantels who had to leave the morning room when the Master died, because there was no longer food or warmth for them when the morning room was closed; the Harpsichords whose children grew up peaked because they had to subsist entirely on a diet of afternoon tea, the only meal served in the drawing room; the Broom-Cupboard boys, the Sinks, and the Rain-Pipes. These are all names which evoke vividly the lost but not forgotten era of the English country house.

The delightful domestic descriptions are one of the best features of *The Borrowers*. In *The Borrowers Afield*, the action is transferred to the English countryside, after the Clock family has fled from Firbank Hall, having been discovered by Mrs. Driver and Crampfurl, the housekeeper and gardener. The descriptions of a Borrower's-eye view of long grass, full of choking pollen and made perilous by its sharp blades; a confrontation with a spider; and a climb up a hedge all contrive to open the reader's eyes, if not to a whole new world, at least to a new perspective on the old one. This is as much as one can reasonably hope to gain from a work of art.

The Borrowers Afloat and *The Borrowers Aloft* are both satisfying books, although neither has the freshness of the earlier volumes. Perhaps this is, in part, due to the chronological progress of the books. The adventures described in *The Borrowers Aloft* take place in a more modern, more commercial, less appealing society. Also, the Borrowers' removal from the ordered, structured Victorian/Edwardian world in which they were first located and transferal into more recent times makes difficult the reader's suspension of disbelief. Borrowers do not belong to a technological world, and although Norton assures the reader at the end of the last volume of the Borrowers' adventures that "Stories never really end," it seems artistically appropriate that the end of the Borrowers' chronicles comes when it does.

Vivien Stableford

Bibliography
Green, Roger Lancelyn. *Tellers of Tales*, 1965.

BRAK THE BARBARIAN

Author: John Jakes (1932-   )
First book publications: Brak the Barbarian (1968); *Brak the Barbarian Versus the*
  Sorceress (1969, also known as *The Sorceress*); *Brak the Barbarian Versus the Mark*
  of the Demons (1969, also known as *The Mark of the Demons*); *Brak: When the*
  Idols Walked (1978); *The Fortunes of Brak* (1980)
Type of work: Novels, novellas, and thematically related short stories
Time: The distant past
Locale: Various locations in an alternate world

Cast out by his own people for blaspheming the gods, Brak, a barbarian from the
North, attempts to reach the fabled city of Khurdisan, only to find his progress thwarted
by the evil forces of the Dark One, Yob-Haggoth, especially through the activities of
a master wizard named Septegundus

Principal characters:
BRAK, a barbarian from the North country
SEPTEGUNDUS, an evil wizard, representative of Yob-Haggoth
ARIANE, the beautiful, wicked, and lustful daughter of Septegundus

Heroic fantasy, a subgenre of speculative fiction, has developed its own
special characteristics since it crystallized in Robert E. Howard's "Conan the
Cimmerian" stories of the mid-1930's. A hero walks exotic worlds where men
are mighty, women are beautiful, problems are few, and life is adventurous.
Shining cities cast their spires to the skies, and various witches, wizards, and
sorcerers cast their spells. Spirits stalk crumbling ruins, and strange monsters
lurk in forest, air, and stream. Kingdoms rise and fall on the sword and the
courage of a larger-than-life hero. The stories are colorful, vigorous, and
action-filled, and the hero who dominates them is usually a "noble savage"
type who prevails over the forces of evil more by his sword and innate sense
of good than by his wits. Occasionally, the hero is of a different type. Henry
Kuttner's Elak, for example, is a suave and witty prince of Atlantis.

John Jakes's Brak the Barbarian, however, falls into the "Conan" mold.
Jakes has admitted his debt to Howard and does not apologize for it, nor
should he, for Brak is an excellent imitation of the original. A grim and silent
barbarian from the North country, he wields a sword named "Stormbringer"
(a gift from rebels of the kingdom of Toct) and dresses in a lion-skin. He is
of a simple and practical nature, instinctive rather than intellectual, cunning
but never devious, physical, ethical, moral, and sexually appealing. Alienated
from his own people for blaspheming the gods, he does not seem to have
suffered any psychological damage. Rather, he is buoyed in spirit by his
dreams of success in the fabled, golden city of Khurdisan far to the South.

Brak's world, on a plane parallel to the modern reader's, is a dichotomous
one in which both evil and good are active forces. Evil seems to have the
upper hand, however, and is represented by a powerful god named Yob-

Haggoth, who seeks to corrupt man and to subjugate him. He works through a number of agents, the most powerful of whom is a wizard named Septegundus. Called an emissary of evil and Yob-Haggoth's army on Earth, Septegundus is a man who has no eyelids and whose skin is covered with the living, writhing figures of those whose souls he has captured for the Dark One. He is aided by his beautiful but wicked daughter, Ariane, who lusts after Brak. Through his various "on-the-road" adventures, Brak encounters analogues of both Septegundus and Ariane. Nordica Fire-Hair, of *The Sorceress*, for example, is actually possessed by Ariane. As Friar Pol, a Nestorian priest in *The Mark of the Demons*, explains to Brak, "evil seems forever more skilled in presenting itself attractively." Implemented by a host of wizards and sorceresses who are armed with enchantments and spells, Yob-Haggoth's plan to subjugate the world of Brak seems well on its way to success.

Resisting it are only a few Nestorian priests, followers of the Nameless God, and several people who still hold good above the evil that is enveloping them. While good is an active force (note that Ambrose the Pillarite does call up help for Brak in *The Sorceress*), the Nameless God seems indifferent to the plight of men, and his priests have only limited powers. Nevertheless, there is a kind of abstract power present in the stories which helps defeat evil. In "The Unspeakable Shrine," for example, Brak sets Yob-Haggoth's temple to crumbling, even though the presence of evil is so great that he can feel it, by sticking his sword into a fissure in the rocks. Perhaps Brak's assertion that there is no spirit in hell that can bind a man's will unless he wills it is also a statement of the manner in which the Nameless God works, through man himself.

Brak's world is filled with brooding evil, and the imagery of the stories often amplifies and symbolizes it. *The Sorceress*, for example, is laden with images of rot and decay, often presented in the form of various odors. Brak, in fact, seems able to smell evil instinctively. "The Courts of the Conjurer," to cite another example, is filled with dripping, plopping, dank images. Moreover, the presence and active quality of evil are amplified by a pathetic fallacy; dark clouds scud across the skies, cold winds rip and tear travelers, and fog, smoke, and mist reduce the sun to a silver-white disk at noon. Nature broods as evil broods. Landscapes also enhance the presence of evil. They are often referred to as wastelands, as in *The Sorceress*' "Storm in a Bottle" (which clearly uses elements from the "Grail Quest" motif) and "The Barge of Souls."

Many of the characters also support the concept of active evil. Some are possessed, like Nordica Fire-Hair. Some are actual creations of Yob-Haggoth, like Ky and Kya, the beautiful twin "blood-eaters" of *The Mark of the Demons*. Most, however, show the result of active evil by succumbing to human weaknesses such as greed, lust, and selfishness. This is best shown by the many times that Brak is betrayed. In "Flame-Face," Jath, his cell-mate, informs on Brak in an attempt to save himself. In "The Courts of the Conjurer,"

Princess Jardine betrays both Brak and her father in her fascination with the power displayed by a wizard named Ankhma-Ra. In *The Sorceress*, Runga, a smith marked for sacrifice, betrays Brak because of his lust for Nordica, and in "Ghosts of Stone," Zama Khan breaks his word and tries to kill Brak so he will not have to share a treasure with him. Balanced against those who have been corrupted is a group who somehow manage to maintain ethical principles despite the temptations placed before them. This balance is often manifested by the many father-and-daughter teams that Brak encounters. Inevitably, one is evil and the other either a victim or someone who helps Brak.

Within the context of heroic fantasy, the Brak stories are excellent. They follow a predictable formula: Brak meets a beautiful woman (who may be either good or evil), loses his sword, gets knocked unconscious several times, encounters a fantastic and evil creature that he must slay (such as Fangfish, Scarletjaw, Doomdog, Manworm, T'Muk, or Rock Beast), defeats evil, and marches stalwartly on to Khurdisan. Jakes is too skilled a writer simply to hammer out the same formula always in the same way, however, and while the formula does tend to make the stories wearisome, Jakes's inventiveness saves them. His attention to detail, his successful efforts to imbue standard characters with qualities that raise them above the level of the stereotypes of other heroic fantasies, as well as his imaginative monsters and situations, serve to make the adventures of Brak interesting and entertaining.

Carl B. Yoke

Bibliography
Greenberg, Martin Harry, and Joseph D. Olander. "Introduction," in *The Best of John Jakes*, 1977.

THE BREAST

Author: Philip Roth (1933-   )
First book publication: 1972
Type of work: Novella
Time: 1971
Locale: New York City

David Allen Kepesh, a thirty-eight-year-old English professor, wakes up one morning to discover that he has turned into a 145-pound mammary gland

> *Principal characters:*
> DAVID ALLEN KEPESH, a giant breast
> CLAIRE OVINGTON, his mistress
> DR. GORDON, his physician
> DR. KLINGER, his psychiatrist

The Breast is the only major work of fantasy that the contemporary American writer Philip Roth has attempted. Since his first book, *Goodbye, Columbus* (1959), earned him the National Book Award, Roth has been hailed as a major American writer, and his subsequent novels, often about young or middle-aged Jewish-American men who are sexually obsessed, self-conscious, and solipsistic, have usually attracted considerable attention: *Letting Go* (1962), *When She Was Good* (1967), *Portnoy's Complaint* (1969), *The Great American Novel* (1973), *My Life as a Man* (1974), *The Professor of Desire* (1977), *The Ghost Writer* (1979), and *Zuckerman Unbound* (1981). Roth is also the author of a number of prizewinning short stories and highly regarded critical essays, many of which discuss his own writing. Only *Our Gang* (1971), his lone political satire, and *The Breast* deviate radically from his basically realistic comedy, and they have been the least favorably received of his works.

The Breast is a self-consciously Kafkaesque novella that reverses Roth's normal approach to his material. Instead of beginning with realistic, often common-place situations in which rather neurotic characters act and react in increasingly exaggerated ways, here a perfectly sane character is placed in an impossible situation. Roth begins *The Breast* with a brief description of the events immediately preceding David Allen Kepesh's transformation, bluntly announces the outcome, and then attempts to relate this incredible event to the reader's reality by surrounding it with normal, credible events and Kepesh's sane and intelligent self-analysis. Kepesh, without sense organs but still able to speak, hear, and to an exacerbated extent, feel, reposes in a private room in Lenox Hill Hospital. He is visited periodically by his mistress, his father, and his psychiatrist. The first piece of narrative, describing the night just previous to the metamorphosis (an "endocrinopathic catastrophe" that takes place in four hours), vaguely implies a series of possible associations but no real causes for the particular transformation: fear of venereal disease, castration anxiety, and guilt for sexually neglecting Claire. The "scientific" explanations for his change that soon follow are descriptive rather than explanatory, and, as in Franz Kafka's "Die Verwandlung" (1915, "Metamorphosis"), the impossibility of ever really ascribing a cause to the problem suggests that any meaning that the event may have exists at a symbolic, metaphysical level.

The fantastical and probably metaphorical qualities of *The Breast* might normally be expected to produce a number of disparate readings. Roth, however, like most of his protagonists, is obsessed with self-analysis and provides a reading of the text in a collection of essays appropriately entitled *Reading Myself and Others* (1975).

The metaphor functions on three major levels: the sexual, the psychological, and the artistic. Faced with his inexplicable disaster, Kepesh ransacks his imagination for some sort of justification to make his ordeal psychologically bearable. In a sense, Roth makes one's problems in interpreting the metaphor Kepesh's problem as well, suggesting that solving the impenetrable mystery of man's existence is a heroic, perhaps necessary, and ultimately frustrating task in both life and art. Roth does his best to make the horror of his protagonist's situation real; but it is horror recollected in a stunned tranquillity. Since there seems to be little hope of changing his (or humanity's) situation of grotesque isolation, Kepesh must devote all his energies to accommodating himself somehow to the metamorphosis, on a psychological as well as a physiological level.

Kepesh first reflects that he has in fact regressed to a state equivalent to infancy—erotic, solitary, and self-absorbed; but his psychological needs quickly push him toward maturity and the reestablishment of an adult identity. Since his identity as a breast is an apparent, grotesque absurdity, he clings to his former sense of propriety and his identity as an English professor, wondering if the college will somehow allow him to continue to teach. His urge to remain alive and to maintain a sense of self hangs in precarious balance, and he next wonders if he is being punished by God or, like Jonah, being taught to recognize His will. During his quest for meaning, Kepesh perceives his situation from a variety of perspectives from the banal to the sublime, and he notes that, despite the alteration of his appearance, his mode of "apprehending" and valuing himself does not change much. He recognizes the absurdity of any fixed identity, but he also notes the apparent human need for at least some sense of such. He passes from religious interpretations to fairy-tale morals ("Beware of what you wish"), finally returning to a more existential and aesthetic perspective ("Reality has style"). Briefly overwhelmed by the horror of his situation, he fantasizes about receiving continuous sexual gratification, a mindless but pleasurable escape. Because Kepesh clings to vestiges of his propriety, however, he cannot wholeheartedly pursue this course; instead, he concludes what any sane person would: he is insane, only imagining himself a breast. He assumes that, in his insanity, he must be transposing the words of his psychiatrist and other visitors, and only after months of failing to convince himself that he is not a breast does he confront the fact that his sanity depends on his accepting his apparently insane situation.

Of course, since Kepesh teaches literature, the literary parallels of his situation with Kafka's "Metamorphosis" and Nikolai Gogol's *Nos* (1836, *The Nose*) do not escape him. Just as he had applied psychoanalysis to his situation, he now applies the tools of his scholarly trade, concluding at one point that, having inadequate talent as a writer, he has yet "one-upped" Kafka by making the word flesh and his life a living metaphor. He rehearses the death scene from *Othello*, and even suggests that his story is meaningless entertainment— although he insists that it is true, if not for the reader, at least for himself. In the end, he accepts the absurdity of his situation and, in what Roth has said is one of the most heroic actions in his fiction, begins to plan a future for himself.

The sexual implications of Kepesh's situation are perhaps the most obvious, since, like several other Roth heroes, Kepesh has one of his personal obsessions realized in a horrible fashion. Life can be pleasurable since, Roth implies, it is first and foremost man's apprehension of physical experience; however, total surrender to the pleasure principle is, in the end, a failure.

The psychological and aesthetic implications of *The Breast* are far more complex. In a way, Kepesh represents the human condition: man trapped in a grotesque and absurd situation from which there is no release but death and of which there is no satisfactory explanation. Dr. Klinger's supportive admonitions to rely on one's "will to live" and "strength of character" are, says Kepesh, the therapeutic equivalent of lame jokes that do nothing to ease the horror of his life. Kepesh notes that his transformation has occurred a year after he has finished a "successful" psychoanalysis—in other words, after he has exhausted the possibilities for self-dramatization that psychoanalysis provides. Only "self-dramatization" gives true meaning to life, and even then, Kepesh learns, man can never expect anyone else to understand him on his own terms.

Such conclusions complement Roth's attitude toward art. In *Reading Myself and Others*, Roth maintains that the particular difficulty faced by contemporary writers is how to make fiction seem credible when reality itself is incredible. If reality has style, as Kepesh says, that style is not necessarily realism. Although *The Breast* begins "It began oddly," Kepesh is quick to add that he knows all about the perspective from which everything appears awesome and mysterious. Man is isolated and alienated, although to some extent able to accept this fate. *The Breast* is many things; but most consistently it may be read as a combined statement on the problem of contemporary man, in both life and literature, of maintaining a healthy perspective on his absurd and often grotesque relationship to his inevitably solipsistic cosmos.

A critic of the novella once complained that, on a metaphorical level, the fantasy remained rather opaque, but Roth has since chided himself for not ending with exactly that statement. As in much contemporary fiction, ambiguity here is not the failure to convey a clear assessment of reality; it is an accurate assessment of the only honest conclusion about reality that is possible.

Mark Siegel

Bibliography
Jones, Judith Paterson, and Guinevera A. Nance. *Philip Roth*, 1981.
Rodgers, Bernard F., Jr. *Philip Roth*, 1978.
Roth, Philip. *Reading Myself and Others*, 1975.
Sabiston, Elizabeth. "A New Fable for Critics: Philip Roth's *The Breast*," in *International Fiction Review*. II (1975), pp. 27-34.

THE BROKEN SWORD

Author: Poul Anderson (1926-   )
First book publication: 1954
Type of work: Novel
Time: The ninth century
Locale: Primarily the east coast of England

As part of a witch's curse of revenge, a human baby, Skafloc, is stolen and brought up by elves, while Valgard, the changeling left in his place, brings about the ruin of that cursed family before going off to join the trolls

> *Principal characters:*
> SKAFLOC, a human baby stolen by elves
> VALGARD, the changeling left in his place
> FREDA, sister of Skafloc, who believes herself to be the sister of Valgard
> A WITCH, who tries to revenge the death of her family
> IMRIC, elf-earl, foster father to Skafloc
> LEEA, elf, sister of Imric
> ILLREDE, king of the trolls

Poul Anderson is best known as a writer of science-fiction novels, of which he has produced more than forty, yet his few fantasy novels are generally more original and of a higher standard than his science fiction. *The Broken Sword* was first published in the same year as his first science-fiction novel, *Brain Wave*. At the time, Anderson was only twenty-seven, and there was no recognized market for adult fantasy novels. Anderson's relative youthfulness led him to write with such enthusiasm that, in its original published form, *The Broken Sword* was florid and purple in style and unrelievedly grim and cruel in content. A more mature Anderson could not and would not have written such a book, but the few fantasy novels published in the early 1950's were aimed at juveniles, marketed under the umbrella of another genre (such as science fiction or historical fiction), or simply dropped out of sight. *The Broken Sword* was not reprinted for seventeen years. It is ironic that, also in 1954, the first two volumes of J. R. R. Tolkien's *The Lord of the Rings* were published, paving the way for the eventual rise of adult fantasy during the late 1960's.

Before *The Broken Sword* was reprinted in 1971, Anderson revised it, cutting some of the more embarrassingly overwritten descriptions, tightening historical details, and eliminating inconsistencies. This process and the reasons for it are explained by Anderson in the Foreword to the 1971 edition.

Even so, *The Broken Sword* remains a curious novel, atypical of Anderson's work. Its style is often florid despite revision, with frequent use of archaic words, some of them Scottish or Scandinavian, such as "byrnie" for a coat of mail. Such words reinforce the novel's setting simply by their alien quality;

they are not necessarily words which were extant in ninth century England. This alien quality is increased by the behavior and expectations of the novel's human characters—and by the major participation of the nonhuman races of faeries, with their magical powers. Nor is the plot what one might expect, for there is much horror and little happiness, and certainly no happy ending, with no winners but the Norse gods.

Anderson's sources are some of the Norse sagas, but he has deliberately not kept to any one of them (as he did to produce his novel *Hrolf Kraki's Saga*, 1973). Instead, he has adapted elements from various sagas and ballads (including the c. thirteenth century works *Völsunga Saga*, *Poetic Edda*, *Hervara Saga*, and *Aage and Else*), combining them with his own leaping imagination. The result is a novel that is strongly plot-oriented. Mingled together are the main story line, concerning bitter wars between the elves and the trolls, and a subplot concerning the revenge taken by a witch upon a Viking and all his family in retribution for the killing of her family. Intruding upon both series of events (especially where they intersect) are the machinations of the gods, who play games with all lesser beings. It is to Anderson's credit that he succeeds in controlling these plot complexities.

Tolkien's sources were the same original sagas, which accounts for any apparent similarities between *The Broken Sword* and *The Lord of the Rings*. Anderson develops his material with great originality, carefully avoiding the heroic fantasy prototypes of William Morris, Lord Dunsany, and E. R. Eddison. In particular, Anderson's descriptions, though overwritten, are very brief in comparison with those of his three predecessors, while he manages to further his plot or show action on almost every page.

Although *The Broken Sword* is set largely in England, most of the plot concerns elves and trolls (and their slaves and allies, including dwarfs, imps, and goblins). How so many thousands of these creatures manage to live in England and engage in violent and bloody wars without being noticed by humans is never satisfactorily explained. Even though humans need to be granted "witch-sight" in order to see the faerie creatures or their constructions, one would imagine that the occurrence of large-scale battles and the consequent piles of rotting corpses could not exist entirely unnoticed by the human populace. A more credible representation of elves living unseen beside humans is given by Sylvia Townsend Warner in *Kingdoms of Elfin* (1977), in which the elves (few in number) live mainly below ground, in very lonely places, and do not normally indulge in any activities likely to bring themselves to the notice of humans.

The elves, as depicted by Anderson, are slightly smaller than humans, very slim and physically attractive. Yet he is careful not to paint them as being wholly good. In fact, they are shown as being amoral in all things—not recognizing marriage, and frequently practicing trickery or deceit. For example, Imric, the elf-earl of Elfheugh (which seems to be the most important elf stronghold in England), is quite willing to steal a human baby and leave a changeling in its place, while his sister Leea will share her bed with any handsome male. These elves are very long-lived, with enormous reserves of life-force (Imric survives many months of hanging by his thumbs over hot coals after the trolls capture Elfheugh), yet they cannot bear to touch iron. Also, they are very remote and ethereal creatures, never knowing the emotion of love. Anderson's trolls are green-skinned, very broad and gross. They far outmass an elf, or even a human, and they seem to have no redeeming features. Native to Scandinavian caves, they are the sworn enemies of the elves, against whom they conduct intermittent warfare with immense cruelty. The only other faerie members who are at all important to the plot are the Irish Sidhe, the half-divine race of heroes, who give limited help to the elves. They are without doubt the most human and most honorable of all the faerie creatures shown here.

To a greater or lesser extent, all of these faerie creatures employ magic. Apart from using it to conceal their doings from humans, they use it to fool one another and to help themselves against the elements. This magic can be learned without much trouble, even by humans, since Skafloc is shown using it, occasionally as a reflex action. In particular, he changes shape, becoming a wolf, an eagle, and an otter in quick succession when he enters the troll-held castle of Elfheugh to recover the broken sword. Imric uses magic in the creation of a changeling. The unnamed witch enchants several people, including Valgard, persuading them that she is a beautiful young woman in order to enjoy their lovemaking. Further, she gives Valgard a leather bag containing a steady wind that will blow his ship to the northeast.

That the faerie inhabitants do not perform more magic is attributed (by Illrede, the troll king) to fear of the gods. In particular, humans who feel that sorcery is being practiced against them might ask the gods for help. If the old Norse gods—the Aesir—are called upon they will take a more active part in the struggle between trolls and elves, not aiding one side against the other so much as increasing their own hold upon Britain and Europe. For this reason, and because they have been tricked by the Aesir in the past, the elves and trolls fear and distrust them. (Yet, as the occasional appearances of Odin indicate, many of the events in *The Broken Sword* are being controlled by the Aesir.) Even more do they fear "the great white god" (as Illrede calls the Christian God). The spread of Christianity is an interesting aspect of *The Broken Sword*, especially as Illrede, at least, recognizes its power and realizes his own *fin de siècle* situation. Anderson returned to this problem of Christianity eclipsing faerie in *The Merman's Children* (1979).

The most crucial event of *The Broken Sword* is that the firstborn son of Orm the Strong is stolen by Imric and replaced by a changeling. The stolen baby, renamed Skafloc, and the changeling, Valgard, are the two main characters in the novel, both for their own sakes and for the similarities and

contrasts between them. They could so easily have been hackneyed figures—
the good guy and the bad guy—but Anderson is subtle in his treatment of
both. Skafloc is, to a certain extent, the archetypal hero, being big, strong,
handsome, pleasant, and a great fighter. His elfin upbringing leaches away
some of his humanity, though, and he becomes a less emotional and less moral
figure than a hero should be. Also, he is dogged by fate throughout his short
life, affected both by the witch's curse and by the Aesir's naming-gift of the
broken sword. When Skafloc falls in love with Freda, he believes he has found
true happiness and tells her (Chapter XVIII) that her influence is banishing
his elfin upbringing and making him human again. This happiness is short-
lived, however, because Skafloc and Freda soon discover that they are brother
and sister. Then, once Skafloc has journeyed to Jötunheim—the land of the
giants—to have the broken sword repaired, its evil influence grips him, making
him cruel and forcing him to kill each time he draws the blade from its
scabbard. In the end, the sword fulfills its prophecy by killing him.

Valgard, the changeling, has been magically produced to take Skafloc's
place, and they look remarkably alike throughout their lives, so that friends
and relatives mistake one for the other. Yet from the start, Valgard is unpleasant, a cruel and solitary boy who mocks Christianity and grows up to become
a heartless and untrustworthy warrior. His great fighting skill and bravery are
not in doubt, but he is disliked for his berserk fits. He is the perfect weapon
of revenge for the witch, whose sexual influence causes him to kill Ketil (whom
he believes to be his brother) and leads directly to his killing of Orm and of
Orm's other son, Asmund. Valgard realizes that he cannot help himself—
that these killings have been planned for him. At this point, he evokes some
reader sympathy, which is strengthened when he turns on the witch in an
attempt to kill her, but dissipates when he decides to join the trolls, taking
two of Orm's daughters with him as a gift for Illrede. Perhaps Valgard achieves
something like happiness when he controls Elfheugh and beds Leea, though
this is a brief spell. In the end, his short, tragic life is taken by the evil within
the enchanted sword.

Most of the other characters are unimportant except as plot elements. The
only one to be developed at all during the course of the novel is Freda. Her
great strength of will (presumably because of her Christian beliefs) enables
her to overcome the horror of seeing most of her family and a sweetheart
killed by the man she believes to be her brother. It is not surprising that she
should fall in love with the heroic Skafloc (who has, after all, rescued her
from the clichéd fate worse than death). Then, not once but several times,
the person that she loves most is taken from her: she loses her love for Skafloc
on discovering that he is her brother, sees her new sweetheart killed by
Skafloc, is tricked out of her newborn baby by Odin and, at the end, realizing
that Skafloc is all she has left, succeeds in distracting him at just the wrong
moment in his battle with Valgard. There is a suggestion that she renounces

her Christian faith as a consequence of these tragedies (and would not otherwise have returned to Skafloc at the end). The elves (of whom Imric and Leea are almost the only ones named) are essentially unchanging, nor are any of their characters explored. To them, the two decades or so which span the novel's plot are as a few months to humans. Still, they are able to recognize their own emotional inadequacies. Right at the end, Leea sees Freda cradling the dead Skafloc and remarks, "Happier was her fate than mine."

The Broken Sword is a remarkable novel, particularly in its stronger, revised form. Its faults of commission (mainly stylistic) and of omission (the lack of character development) are not serious. They are more than balanced by narrative drive, complexity, finely controlled tragedy, and fascinating mythic elements (the changeling, the witch's revenge, the invincible sword that controls its wielder, and so on). Since 1954, many heroic fantasy novels have appeared, most of them pale imitations of the work of either Tolkien or Robert E. Howard. It says much for *The Broken Sword* that it is derived from neither author yet manages to combine the best aspects of both.

Chris Morgan

Bibliography

Anderson, Poul. "Foreword," in *The Broken Sword*, 1971.

Carter, Lin. "A Changeling in Elfland," in *The Broken Sword*, 1971.

McGuire, Patrick L. "'Her Strong Enchantments Failing,'" in *The Book of Poul Anderson*, 1975. Edited by Roger Elwood.

Miesel, Sandra. "Afterword—An Invitation to Elfland," in *Fantasy*, 1981.

_____ . *Against Time's Arrow: The High Crusade of Poul Anderson*, 1978.

BROOD OF THE WITCH QUEEN

Author: Sax Rohmer (Arthur Sarsfield Ward, 1883-1959)
First book publication: 1918
Type of work: Novel
Time: The twentieth century
Locale: London, its environs, and Egypt

With the help of his father, Robert Cairn penetrates the evil world of a satanic sorcerer, Anthony Ferrara, and after many dangers and astonishing difficulties, he thwarts the magician's plans

Principal characters:
ROBERT CAIRN, a journalist
DR. BRUCE CAIRN, his father
SIR MICHAEL FERRARA, an Egyptologist
MYRA DUQUESNE, Sir Michael's niece and ward
ANTHONY FERRARA, an evil sorcerer

Few authors can claim to have invented a character whose name became a household word, but Sax Rohmer (Arthur Sarsfield Ward) is without doubt in that select circle. As the creator of Dr. Fu Manchu, Rohmer gave the world of fantasy literature one of its immortal villains, and in the character of Nayland Smith, he created the type of archnemesis of evil whose character and style of action have been much imitated.

Rohmer was uniquely qualified by both temperament and training to write novels involving the use of occult ceremonies and paraphernalia. As a young man, he was unable to function in the world of business and failed at a number of ventures, including journalism. His father, an engineer with a narrowly practical mind, despaired of his son's making a living at all; but Arthur Sarsfield Ward dreamed of being not only a writer of arcane experiences but also a serious student of the occult. He was a member of the well-known occult group, the Golden Dawn, whose members included such luminaries as William Butler Yeats, Arthur Machen, and Arthur Edward Waite; he may also have been a member of the British Rosicrucian Society. The knowledge gained from these groups and from his own reading culminated in his study of the occult, *The Romance of Sorcery* (1914), and also found its way into nearly every novel and story he wrote. He was particularly fond of Oriental culture and acquired much of his knowledge of this subject by reading and rereading Sir Richard Burton's entire *The Arabian Nights' Entertainments* (1885-1886).

Brood of the Witch Queen was the result both of Rohmer's studies and of the honeymoon trip he made to Egypt in 1913 with his wife Elizabeth. Its plot is based on the idea of the survival of Egyptian sorcery in the modern world, but it is an entirely evil sorcery, a black art without any redeeming qualities. The novel begins slowly. Robert Cairn, a student, witnesses the violent death of a swan on the estuary of a river. Some powerful although invisible force lifts Apollo, the male swan, out of the water and breaks its neck, a feat of considerable difficulty even for a strong and quite visible man. Later, a similar force kills the eminent Egyptologist Sir Michael Ferrara as he sleeps. This brings into the story the strange and evil adopted son of Sir Michael, Anthony Ferrara, who is responsible for both of these supernatural killings.

Ferrara is a type to be found in all of Rohmer's fiction. Imbued with superhuman strength of mind and will and placed within exotic, Oriental settings, they are egomaniacs who attempt to rule the world. The author's most famous and well-developed examples of this type of character are Dr. Fu Manchu, the Chinese scientist, and Sumuru, the beautiful but evil woman who wants to be the empress of the world. Like Fu Manchu, who is depicted in various exotic Oriental environments, or Sumuru, who also lives in elegant Eastern settings, Ferrara has fitted out his rooms in London's Piccadilly in an extravagantly Eastern style. It includes a table

> . . . with its nameless instruments and its extraordinary silver lamp; the mummies were there; the antique volumes, rolls of papyrus, preserved snakes and cats and ibises, statuettes of Isis, Osiris and other Nile deities were there.

Ferrara himself is as unusual as his surroundings; in the heat of summer, he wears a fur coat and gloves and has a hot fire constantly burning in his rooms. At their first meeting in these rooms, young Cairn and Ferrara initiate their battle, which is to take them to the pyramids of Egypt and several solitary British settings. Ferrara is the perfect type of the archsorcerer whose magic is dedicated to egomaniacal ends and who suborns all good to those ends.

Robert Cairn is forced to seek the help of his father, Dr. Bruce Cairn, an eminent Egyptologist, medical doctor, and learned student of the magic arts. Cairn is able to rescue his son from Ferrara's long-range attempt to drive Robert mad with giant, although impalpable, insects that crawl around Robert's room and over his body. Ferrara practices here, as he did in the murder of his adopted father and Apollo the swan, a kind of magic that uses an image of the victim and a lock of his hair or a fingernail paring to cause bodily harm—even death—at great distances. Interlocked with Robert Cairn's troubles is his deep concern for Ferrara's stepsister, Myra Duquesne, whom Ferrara is attempting to kill, so that he can control the entire estate. One of the powerful subplots of the book is the rescue of Myra from her brother's evil designs.

In order to gain power and to strengthen his knowledge, Ferrara journeys to Egypt where he carries out a demoniac ceremony deep in the heart of a step pyramid. (This part of the novel grew out of Rohmer's own journey into a pyramid, an experience that worked powerfully on his imagination.) Dr.

Cairn and his son, as well as a friend known as Sime, barely escape with their lives.

The chapters of the book that involve the Egyptian witch-queen, the black sorceries in the pyramid, and the bizarre, hypnotic experiences in a Cairo hotel are not only the best in the novel but are also scarcely surpassed in any novel of a similar kind. Rohmer was writing about what he believed in, what he loved best, and what his entire personality sought out as satisfying; consequently, he is at his most effective here. These chapters are exciting in their action, powerful in their evocation of atmosphere, and accurate in their depiction of magic rituals. *Brood of the Witch Queen* overflows with supernatural lore and supernatural experiences; no other novel or story written by Rohmer uses so much background material.

After the father and son return to England, they understand how Ferrara can be defeated. Dr. Cairn locates the hidden building in which Ferrara performs his magical ceremonies. The heart of these ceremonies is the infamous *Book of Thoth*, which they steal from its iron casket hidden in a pit below the floor. Without this book to protect him, Ferrara is helpless, and the demons he has raised from the infernal regions turn on him and destroy him; thus, good prevails and evil perishes. *Brood of the Witch Queen* contains almost every theme with which Rohmer occupied himself in a long and successful writing career. Despite occasional dated prose, the novel remains one of the best pictures of the evil sorcerer, his equipment, his attitudes, and his methods of operation, and shows the difficulty the ordinary human being has in dealing with someone adept in the black arts.

Samuel H. Vasbinder

Bibliography
Ash, Gay Van, and Elizabeth Sax Rohmer. *Master of Villainy: A Biography of Sax Rohmer*, 1972. Edited by Robert E. Briney.

BURN WITCH BURN!

Author: Abraham Merritt (1884-1943)
First book publication: 1933
Type of work: Novel
Time: The 1930's
Locale: New York

A medical man and expert on abnormal psychology named Lowell discovers a science immeasurably old when he encounters a witch who animates dolls and uses them as assassins

Principal characters:
> DR. LOWELL, a medical doctor who learns that witchcraft is real
> JULIAN RICORI, a notorious underworld chief
> McCANN, Ricori's most trusted bodyguard
> HARRIET WALTERS, a nurse who continues to fight the forces of evil even after her death
> MADAME MANDILIP, a dollmaker and practitioner of witchcraft
> LASCHNA, allegedly Madame Mandilip's niece

Lush, verbose, sentimental, dreamy, overheated, and suffocating are some of the terms used by modern critics to describe the style of Abraham Merritt's stories. Indeed, it seems fashionable for sophisticated modern readers to deprecate his work, especially those who are devotees of hard science fiction. Merritt nevertheless has a large following even today. Five of his books, *The Moon Pool* (1919), *Seven Footprints to Satan* (1928), *The Face in the Abyss* (1931), *Dwellers in the Mirage* (1932), and *Burn Witch Burn!*, have been printed many times since they first appeared in book form. Moreover, *The Metal Monster* (1920), *The Ship of Ishtar* (1926), thought by many to be his best book, and *The Fox Woman and Other Stories* (1949), have been reprinted several times. Even *The Black Wheel* (1947), which was finished by Hannes Bok, has been reprinted to capitalize on Merritt's continuing popularity. Total sales of his books in the United States and abroad are estimated at more than ten million copies.

As Sam Moskowitz noted in *Explorers of the Infinite* (1963), the pattern for Merritt's stories was set in his extremely popular novel *The Moon Pool*, which pits light against darkness, includes a beautiful priestess of evil, and incorporates villains memorable for their brilliant characterizations. Moreover, traditionally repulsive symbols are reversed by connecting them with sympathetic and admirable characters. Such is the pattern, with slight variations, for *Burn Witch Burn!*, Merritt's next-to-last completed novel.

In this book, a simple and clear-cut equation is established. Light is set against darkness when science is set against witchcraft, or "the dark wisdom," as Lowell often calls it. Lowell is a prestigious medical doctor, connected with two of New York City's foremost hospitals, who becomes embroiled in a series of strange deaths when the gangster Julian Ricori recruits him to save the life of a good friend. At first Lowell believes that a new disease is about to sweep the city, and he attempts to solve the mystery of its origin and nature in a logical way. He applies the scientific method to the problem. This approach quickly leads him to a factor common to all of the cases—a doll shop operated by Madame Mandilip. Unfortunately, Lowell makes a fatal error. His confidence in the power of science lulls him into a false sense of security. He believes that all can be explained logically, if he can but find the answers, and that once he does he will be able to handle Madame Mandilip. This self-deception leads first to the death of Dr. Braile, a friend and colleague, and then nearly to the deaths of Ricori, McCann, and himself. In the end, in fact, it is not science that defeats Madame Mandilip's witchcraft; rather, her destruction is self-generated. Her continuous torture of one of her dolls, made in the likeness of Nurse Harriet Walters, causes it to rebel against her inhumanity, and it turns on her and kills her. So, in this novel, evil falls by its own weight, as it often does in fantasies. In Merritt's stories, evil is a powerful and active force, not merely the absence of good, which threatens at any moment to topple the forces of light. While light does inevitably triumph over darkness, it is a battle not easily won. Even though defeated, evil often has tragic consequences.

The motif of the beautiful priestess of evil is given a unique twist in *Burn Witch Burn!* Unlike *The Moon Pool* or *Dwellers in the Mirage*, where evil is presented attractively as a real and beautiful woman, this novel presents the beautiful and evil priestess as an illusion cast by Madame Mandilip so that she can manipulate people. She uses this device, for example, to disarm Ricori, McCann, and Lowell when they come to kill her near the end of the novel. By projecting the image of a naked young woman of such extraordinary beauty that it astounds them, she gains a psychological advantage which permits her to take control of the situation. Madame Mandilip's normal appearance is both strange and repulsive. Although not fat, she is a heavy woman with enormous breasts, close to six feet tall, and powerful. She has a long face, brown skin, a distinct mustache, a mop of iron-gray hair, and eyes that are large, black, and vital. The change is not only shocking but also establishes the strength and extent of her powers.

Like other memorable Merritt villains, Madame Mandilip is skillfully characterized. To generate a feeling of her mystery and power, Merritt withholds her actual appearance in the novel until near its end. Instead of learning about her directly, therefore, the reader learns about her indirectly. She is known through the effects she produces and the products she creates, through the strangely beautiful and animated dolls, through the peculiar symptoms of her victims, and through the fear and neurosis of Laschna, her alleged niece. The reader learns of her through the reports of those who have seen her and through the diary of Nurse Walters. While the mystery of how the killings are effected gradually becomes clearer, the mystery of who Madame Mandilip is and how her powers work grows each time science fails. While she does not change during the course of the story, her presence increases dramatically. It becomes apparent that the stories of her generosity and kindness are simply masks for her diabolic nature, and the reader comes to feel that evil lurks just below the surface. Horror is generated by the fact that evil is insidious and masks itself in beauty.

Burn Witch Burn! also contains the typical Merritt device of reversing the traditional value of a symbol. Since frogs, spiders, snakes, and gangsters are normally thought of as negative, the frogmen of *The Moon Pool*, the spider-men and snakewoman of *The Face in the Abyss*, and the gangster Ricori of *Burn Witch Burn!*, one would assume, would be evil, vile, or repulsive. Yet this is not the case. On the contrary, Ricori is a sensitive and honorable man, as appalled as Lowell is by the diabolic looks that appear on the faces of Madame Mandilip's victims. Superstitious by nature, he is the first to suspect a witch, and he is the first to recognize the extent of the danger. He balances out Lowell's science with his intuition, and without him Lowell would easily have been destroyed by Mandilip, for through Lowell's trust of him, he is able to convince the doctor of the reality of the dark wisdom. What terrifies Ricori most about the witch's victims is the look on their faces betraying complete loss of their humanity, for he is the most human, the most compassionate man in the story. He mitigates the hard and unfeeling nature of science and embodies the theme of the novel—humanness. For the purposes of this work, Merritt translates diabolic as inhuman.

Burn Witch Burn! is a classic. Filmed as *The Devil Doll* in the early 1930's with Lionel Barrymore, it well displays one of Merritt's greatest and most appealing characteristics as a writer—his ability to transcend the coldness and dehumanization that frequently accompany pure fantasy.

Carl B. Yoke

Bibliography
Atheling, William, Jr. [James Blish]. "Exit Euphues: The Monstrosities of Merritt," in *More Issues at Hand*, 1970.
Bleiler, E. F. "A. Merritt," in *Science Fiction Writers*, 1982.
Moskowitz, Sam. "The Marvelous A. Merritt," in *Explorers of the Infinite*, 1963.

THE BURNING COURT

Author: John Dickson Carr (1906-1977)
First book publication: 1937
Type of work: Novel
Time: The spring of 1929
Locale: Crispen, a small town near Philadelphia

The ultimate detective fantasy novel

> *Principal characters:*
> EDWARD STEVENS, a young editor
> MARIE STEVENS, his young wife, who has a mysterious background
> MARK DESPARD, Stevens' neighbor, who is obsessed with the
> thought that his uncle was sadistically poisoned
> LUCY DESPARD, Mark's wife
> GAUDAN CROSS, an impressively amoral man who is a longtime
> student of crime
> MYRA CORBETT, a nurse

Given the definitions of fantasy and detective fiction, it would seem unlikely that the two could be combined effectively. The job of the detective, after all, is to assemble facts to clarify baffling circumstances, while fantasy by its nature unravels certainties. Nevertheless, there is a long history of works with elements of both genres—or of works in one genre that sometimes pretend to be in the other. In particular, beginning with Ann Radcliffe, there is a long tradition of mystery fiction that appears to be fantasy until the conclusion explains that the frights had natural origins; the reader gets the frisson of the supernatural, then is restored to a rational world.

The best modern writer of fantasy detective fiction is John Dickson Carr. Beginning with his first book, *It Walks by Night* (1930), Carr utilized outrageously Gothic trappings in scrupulously constructed puzzle plots. The early novels are filled with blood and mutilation, madness, rotting corpses, and so forth, but Carr's detectives always find a natural explanation for events that at first seem supernaturally horrifying to the reader. *The Burning Court* is Carr's only exception to this pattern, and it is the more effective for being only one of Carr's numerous detective novels. The novel subjects a reader to extreme emotional and mental swings, from its commonplace beginning to a state of mind in which everything appears threatening and grotesque, back to a rational world view—then abruptly presents an understated conclusion that transforms everything that has gone before into something rich, strange, and frightening.

Carr's manipulation of mood is immensely skillful. The novel's opening pages stress Edward Stevens' ordinariness, and settled, pleasantly routine life. Then Stevens looks at the manuscript of Gauden Cross's latest study of notable criminals and sees a photograph of a female poisoner who was guillotined in

1861: it is his wife. Immediately Stevens' mood changes; ordinary things become ominous. When a friend stops to chat with him, the innocent conversation touches on sickness and food. When Stevens steps off the train, he sees the brightly lit sign of the village druggist. Carr does not overstress these suggestions, but they register at least subliminally in Stevens' (and the reader's) mind. Moreover, Stevens and the reader are suddenly aware of suspicious activities that otherwise would have been overlooked.

After a large number of sinister events have occurred, including a body vanishing from a sealed tomb, Stevens is relieved to find that there are natural explanations for everything that has happened, and the reader relaxes as well. This is, after all, a detective novel, and it seems to fall into the familiar, safe pattern of that genre. For the seemingly familiar conclusion, Gauden Cross, a man who has had immense experience with human crime, thanks to his criminal past, gathers all the characters together and explains how the crime could have been accomplished. It does not matter that one of the suspects is missing and that the other refuses to confess. It does not even matter that Cross immediately dies, a victim of poison. The police take this as evidence that the person Cross accused is guilty, and everyone in the book is satisfied.

The reader is satisfied as well, until the last chapter, "Verdict," changes everything in an unnerving fashion. Marie Stevens gently meditates on how she and Cross fooled everyone. They are really the reincarnated spirits of evil humans who have managed to inflict pain on others for centuries. Now, thanks to human incredulity at the supernatural, they have won again. Even more disturbing is Marie's thought concerning her husband: "I did not wish my husband to guess, not yet. I love him, I love him; he will be one of us presently, if I can transform him without pain. Or too much pain." Earlier, telling of Marie's reaction to a description of a man dying of poison, Myra Corbett says that she looked "like a woman suffering from sexual excitement." This helps to explain Marie's motivation in making people die in agony; it also strongly qualifies her love for her husband. The more one thinks of the implications of the last chapter, the more disturbing the story as a whole becomes.

Carr wrote other short detective fantasies, which appear in the collection *Department of Queer Complaints* (1940) and two of which were reprinted in *The Magazine of Fantasy and Science Fiction*. Still later, he wrote several novels that combine time travel and detective fiction, including the superb fantasy *The Devil in Velvet* (1951). *The Burning Court*, however, is his only full-length horror novel, and it is a memorable one, unexpected and devastating in the context of his other work. Carr's later books have been criticized for mechanical plotting and emotional flatness. That certainly is not true of *The Burning Court*, in which he exploits detective-story conventions masterfully to deliver a stunning shock.

Joe Sanders

Bibliography

Herzel, Roger. "John Dickson Carr," in *Minor American Novelists*, 1971. Edited by Charles A. Hoyt.

Sheridan, Daniel. "Later Victorian Ghost Stories: The Literature of Belief," in *Gothic*. December 2, 1980, pp. 33-39.

CAMINO REAL

Author: Tennessee Williams (1911-1983)
First book publication: 1953
Type of work: Drama
Time: Indefinite
Locale: The plaza of a seaport in a mythical Latin American country

A group of fugitive romantics assert their love and honor against the harsh realities of the walled city at the end of the Camino Real

> *Principal characters:*
> DON QUIXOTE, a would-be knight
> KILROY, a young American former boxer and GI
> JACQUES CASANOVA, a weary, would-be lover
> LORD BYRON, a poet
> BARON DE CHARLUS, an elderly, foppish deviate
> LA MADRECITA, a blind female singer
> MARGUERITE GAUTIER, an aging courtesan
> THE GYPSY, a fortune-teller
> ESMERALDA, her young daughter
> GUTMAN, dictator of the walled city

Although Tennessee (Thomas Lanier) Williams pushed theatrical realism to the very edge with his lyrical intensity, extreme situations, and exaggerated, often grotesque characters, only one of his major works, *Camino Real*, can be classified as a fantasy. When Williams made this stylistic departure in 1953, it surprised and baffled the critics, and even today *Camino Real* probably remains Williams' most controversial work. Whatever the merits of the play when compared with his other works, one frequent criticism is unwarranted, that of obscurity. As many artists have discovered, Williams found that the freedom of fantasy allowed him to express his ideas in language and images with a directness and clarity difficult on a purely realistic stage. These qualities are apparent if one pays close attention to what is actually being said and done on stage and is not distracted by the literary and theatrical trappings that do, at times, make the play seem overly complicated and agitated.

One important indication of Williams' intentions and methods is the play's epigraph taken from Dante's *Inferno* (c. 1320): "In the middle of the journey of our life I came to myself in a dark wood where the straight way was lost." Thus the "walled city" at the end of the Camino Real is Williams' contemporary hell, which is, like Dante's, also an elaborate poetic image of the familiar world, and the denizens—or "sinners"—of Williams' hell, similar to those in the Dantean version, are both real people and types or literary figures, whose plight on the Camino Real reflects their factual or literary careers.

The play begins when a bedraggled Don Quixote stumbles onto the stage, followed by Sancho Panza. As soon as the latter realizes that he has come to a place where, according to the map, "the spring of humanity has gone dry," he rushes out. Nonplussed, Don Quixote settles down to sleep and dream the action of the play, at the end of which he will "choose one among its shadows to take along with me in the place of Sancho."

Gutman, dictator of the walled city, enters and begins the play proper. Throughout the drama, Gutman both oversees the action and comments on it in passing, while he announces the sixteen "blocks," or units of action, to the audience. Gutman, the fat villain of Dashiell Hammett's *The Maltese Falcon* (1930), represents the *Camino Real*—the "real" road—as against the "*Camino Real*"—the royal road. Against him and his collaborators are arrayed the "romantics," who are victimized, exploited, persecuted, mocked, and killed, but whose tenacious resistance and defiance give the play its drive, tension, and meaning.

The action takes place in a plaza, in the center of which is the dry fountain and the sleeping Quixote. On one side is an expensive hotel, the Siete Mares, populated with elegant, mindless guests; across the street is Skid Row, with a Gypsy's stall, a Loan Shark's office, and the "Ritz Men Only," a fleabag hotel. The street itself is a no-man's-land, periodically patrolled by Street-cleaners who sweep up, not dirt and debris, but mysteriously dead guests, such as the Baron de Charlus (from Marcel Proust's *À la recherche du temps perdu*, 1913-1927, *Remembrance of Things Past*), an elderly, elegant, foppish deviant.

By and large, Gutman seems content to let the burned-out romantics dissipate themselves slowly, as he enjoys the spectacle of their emotional and creative impotence, but his security is threatened by the arrival of Kilroy, an all-American youth, ex-boxer, and GI with "a heart as big as the head of a baby." Kilroy is, of course, the ubiquitous World War II GI whose huge nose hung over fences all over the world ("Kilroy was here!"). Along with him come the five things Gutman most fears: innocence, hope, brotherhood, honor, and love. Kilroy's innocent eagerness, energy, and vulnerability threaten Gutman, as well as stirring new feelings and hopes among the desperate romantics.

To thwart this danger, Gutman first has Kilroy robbed, then tries to demean him by forcing him into the role of the "Patsy," in clown costume, able to talk only by honking the horn in his illuminated nose. Even as the Patsy, Kilroy is defiant, and that defiance becomes infectious. Lord Byron renounces his "passion for declivity" and, after making a stirring speech on the death of Percy Bysshe Shelley, strikes out across the Terra Incognita, a forbidding desert that borders the walled city, shouting, "Make voyages! Attempt them! There is nothing else!" Jacques Casanova, reduced to despair and begging until he finally accepts the antlers of the cuckold in a mock ceremony, finds new meaning and hope in Kilroy. In a climactic act of defiance and brotherhood (a word that Gutman has banned), Casanova and Kilroy remove each other's symbols of subjugation (from Casanova, the horns; from Kilroy, the Patsy's nose).

The strongest weapon against Gutman's world is love. Old lovers Casanova and Marguerite Gautier, the aging courtesan, win out over time and despair when they find that their love is more powerful than humiliation and lethargy. Young love between Kilroy and Esmeralda (from Victor Hugo's *Notre Dame de Paris*, 1831, *The Hunchback of Notre Dame*) renews innocence and commitment, even when it destroys the lovers. Kilroy knows that "love" will kill him, given his weak heart, but he defies fate to take Esmeralda's "veil" in a scene that is moving, coy, sensual, and somewhat corny. Even after he is seized by the Streetcleaners and sent to the laboratory, where his heart is removed, Kilroy remains defiant. He seizes the heart—made of gold—and races to join the newly awakened Don Quixote in an exploration of the Terra Incognita.

Written at a time when Williams was producing some of his bleakest realistic plays, *Camino Real* is surprisingly affirmative. Despite the power of Gutman and his cohorts—the Old Gypsy, A. Ratt, the Streetcleaners, the Policeman—the defiant romantics win real victories through love, brotherhood, hope, honor, and daring; as Marguerite Gautier says, "the violets are breaking the rocks!" These desperate romantics are, of course, the same characters who are defeated by life in Williams' realistic plays. Perhaps Williams made this one serious foray into fantasy to give his "fugitives" a chance to escape from the rigidly deterministic psychological, social, and metaphysical logic of his bleak realistic melodramas.

Keith Neilson

Bibliography
Cohn, Ruby. "The Garrulous Grotesques of Tennessee Williams," in *Tennessee Williams: A Collection of Critical Essays*, 1977. Edited by Stephen S. Stanton.
Falk, Signi. *Tennessee Williams*, 1978.
Jackson, Esther Merle. *The Broken World of Tennessee Williams*, 1965.
Tischler, Nancy. *Tennessee Williams: Rebellious Puritan*, 1961.
Williams, Tennessee. *Memoirs*, 1975.

"THE CANTERVILLE GHOST"

Author: Oscar Wilde (1854-1900)
First book publication: 1891 (in *Lord Arthur Savile's Crimes and Other Stories*)
Type of work: Short story
Time: The late nineteenth century
Locale: Canterville Chase, a rural English estate

The haunting of Canterville Chase by the wry ghost of Sir Simon de Canterville produces only indignation on the part of the American family that had bought the historic place, and their efforts to be rid of the unwelcome tenant and his strategies of retaliation set the stage for a surprise ending

Principal characters:
> SIR SIMON DE CANTERVILLE, a ghost
> MR. OTIS, an American minister
> MRS. OTIS, his wife
> VIRGINIA, their daughter
> WASHINGTON, their eldest son
> THE OTIS TWINS, adolescent boys

"The Canterville Ghost" is a delightfully witty confabulation calculated to horrify absolutely no one but the humorless, who are in any case always easily dismayed by irreverence. The surface satire in this elegant romance, which is about an old British ghost inhabiting ancestral premises newly purchased by an American clergyman and his family, is pointedly evenhanded and good-natured. In addition, and with peculiarly Wildean irony, the reader is treated to a comic situation exploiting the confrontation between aesthetic and pragmatic values, and the resolution of this conflict makes a telling point about the nature of art itself.

The story pits the resourcefulness, pragmatism, and infectious ingenuousness of the Otis clan against the proud determination and artistic inventiveness of the blue-blooded ghost haunting Canterville Chase. The ghost of Sir Simon de Canterville, having been about his disreputable business for more than three centuries, has a social position and reputation to uphold. The Reverend Mr. Otis and family, being "modern" Americans, have enough skepticism and brisk common sense to put a strain on even the hardiest of British spirits, and British custom and credulity as well. The colonials have come to stay, and with Yankee efficiency, they set about cleaning house, starting with the unsightly bloodstain on the floor left by Sir Simon's first victim.

Since Americans characteristically never say die, the Otises attack every incident of supernatural visitation with a dose of Yankee know-how; if it is not Pinkerton's Champion Stain Remover and Paragon Detergent, Tammany Rising Sun Lubricator (for oiling clanking chains), or Dr. Dobell's Tincture (for curing spectral moaning attributed to indigestion), then it is the frightening efficacy of a primitive pea-shooter or a simple game of trip-the-ghost.

On one occasion, the American minister confronts the bedeviled ghost with a revolver, ordering him to raise his hands in a scene reminiscent of the frontier desperado cornered by a marshal and his posse. Naturally, the horrified ghost promptly vaporizes; though shaken in spirit, he is firm in his resolve to deliver a nasty comeuppance to these disrespectful Americans.

American ingenuity, coupled with sublime naïveté and the spirit of republicanism, refuses to bend to either the reputation or the shenanigans of a bothersome house ghost. Indeed, Mr. and Mrs. Otis come to regard their phosphorescent visitor as a star attraction that has unaccountably escaped the discerning eye of America's enterprising impresarios. On the other hand, Sir Simon's treatment at the hands of these vulgarians who refuse to take him seriously reduces him to a fever, later to desperate plans of revenge, and finally to invalidism and ignominious retreat. He even stoops to oiling his chains with Tammany Lubricator.

Of the four Otis children, only the twins (called "The Stars and Stripes" in honor of the punishment they receive for acts of unrelieved mischief) are relentless in the subversive attacks on the ghost's demoralized person. The very thought of that demonic twosome is so terrifying to him that Sir Simon will not leave his room, even for a chance to impersonate his favorite character—the Bloodless Vampire Monk, otherwise called the Bloodless Benedictine.

Predictably, Sir Simon is a wonderful creation, both engaging and sympathetic. His trouble is his respectability; he has solid expectations of his own nightly performances and he works hard to achieve continuing excellence of effect in the various roles that have contributed to his fame. He delights in boasting of his greatest impersonations and enumerating a long list of successes he has had with scaring people to death. He relishes past achievements with the "enthusiastic egotism of the true artist." Like any professional player, the ghost is a passionate exhibitionist whose appearances are executed with exquisite malice and forethought. He is the writer, producer, director, and star of his own little horror shows, a consummate theatrical personality, a veritable bard of the supernatural circuit.

Sir Simon has a problem, however, with his current audience. The irrepressible Americans will not observe the proprieties and conventions of the situation. Sir Simon's nightmare is realized: an audience jeering, laughing, and throwing things instead of swooning in the aisles, prostrate with fear. The Otises simply will not enter into the spirit of the occasion. Since they refuse to play their part, his delicate art is lost entirely on stiff-necked Yankee pragmatism.

Foiled at last, the ghost of Sir Simon finds a friend in fifteen-year-old Virginia, the only Otis who "had never insulted him in any way." Here "The Canterville Ghost" takes a grave turn. The innocent American girl befriends this ghost of a man, doomed to his awful state as atonement for a cardinal sin. Sir Simon wistfully longs for death and entreats the "Golden girl" to weep for one who has no tears and pray for one who is without faith. In return for her trust and belief in him, the ghost tells Virginia, Death will grant him peace and a permanent resting place. So Virgin(ia), the pure of heart, undergoes the trials of unselfish love in order to redeem Sir Simon's soul. The ghost of Canterville Chase is laid to rest when the bones of Sir Simon are placed in a proper grave with all due pomp and circumstance.

Thus, the wily old codger has moved out of melodrama at last and into high tragedy, with himself as both subject and lead player. By enlisting the participation of the ideal ingenue, Sir Simon manages to have both Virginia and Death for a supporting cast. In her new role, Virginia moves from audience to center stage, the heroine of the ghost's final, but surely most enduring, production.

As her reward, Virginia receives from the ghost a valuable casket of antique jewels and the secret of "what Life is, and what Death signifies, and why love is stronger than both." As befits a "Hylo-Idealistic Romance" as the play is subtitled, with its theatrical stage whisper that belief and truth are inextricably intertwined, the American girl eventually marries a young duke, thus merging new-world courage and heart with old-world wisdom and experience. While she has always been the American minister's true daughter, Virginia, by the story's end, is Sir Simon's child as well, possessing a ducal coronet, the Canterville heirlooms, and an otherworldly secret. Although she lacks blue blood, her husband has enough of that to ensure that their progeny will keep a firm foothold on both sides of the Atlantic.

Art does indeed redeem life. With a superb flair for the unlikely but inevitable end, Wilde provides the life and ghost of the notorious Sir Simon with a permanent showcase (to the endless delight of admiring audiences everywhere), frees the resident Americans of one unwelcome proprietary guest (rather like the colonists winning independence all over again), and grants Virginia a fairy-tale future with her royal duke. If one dares to believe that tying up loose ends settles the matter, then one is teasingly reminded of the secret Virginia possesses. Whatever that secret is, one must divine it for oneself.

Greta Eisner

Bibliography
Ellman, Richard. *Oscar Wilde: A Collection of Critical Essays*, 1969.
Hyde, H. Montgomery. *Oscar Wilde: A Biography*, 1975.
Kronenberger, Louis. *Oscar Wilde*, 1976.
Nasser, Christopher. *Into the Demon Universe: A Literary Exploration of Oscar Wilde*, 1974.

CARNACKI THE GHOST-FINDER

Author: William Hope Hodgson (1877-1918)
First book publication: 1910
Type of work: Short stories
Time: The late nineteenth and early twentieth centuries
Locale: Great Britain

Thomas Carnacki, a professional psychic investigator, probes unusual cases of supernatural manifestation, of which some prove to be hoaxes and others genuine instances of arcane forces breaking into material reality from outside

Principal characters:
THOMAS CARNACKI, a ghost-hunter
DODGSON, the narrator and a friend of Carnacki
JESSOP,
ARKWRIGHT, and
TAYLOR, Carnacki's friends

William Hope Hodgson is critically acclaimed for his fantasy novels, in particular the brilliantly original books *The House on the Borderland* (1908) and *The Night Land* (1912). His stories set at sea have occasioned comparison with those of Joseph Conrad, yet most commentators agree that Hodgson was second to none in his power to evoke the mystery of seafaring and to paint the horrors that may rise from ocean deeps. Hodgson spent eight years at sea, beginning as an apprentice at sixteen years of age and finally passing his tests for a ship's mate. He detested life at sea, however, with its loneliness and bullying. In self-defense, Hodgson became a physical culture enthusiast, eventually setting up gymnasiums in England after leaving the merchant navy. To promote his business, he wrote a series of articles about body building, illustrated with photographs he took of himself, and realized his desire to become an author. His interests in fiction ran to the bizarre, and he admired the fantasy writing of such authors as Edgar Allan Poe and H. G. Wells. As a child, he had an interest in the occult and in the possibilities of terror; his younger brother Chris once stated in an interview that Hodgson would chase his brothers and sisters about the house brandishing a kitchen knife. Naturally, Hodgson's early fiction dealt with the fantastic and horrific; these remained his major themes until his untimely death in World War I.

The series of stories about Carnacki the ghost-finder came late in Hodgson's career, appearing serially from 1910 through 1912, and apparently intended only as hackwork ground out to pay the bills while Hodgson prepared for his major creative effort, the epic novel *The Night Land*. The framing device of the series is minimal. Carnacki, a professional occult investigator, invites his cronies Jessop, Arkwright, and Taylor, as well as Dodgson, the putative author of these stories, to dinner. After eating, he gives them the details of one of his cases; then, the narrative finished, he abruptly ushers them out into the night. Carnacki, of course, is inspired in part by Arthur Conan Doyle's Sherlock Holmes; the influence of Algernon Blackwood's psychic sleuth, *John Silence, Physician Extraordinary* (1908), can also be detected. *Fin de siècle* England was fascinated with the occult, and such figures as Aleister Crowley and Madame Blavatsky were world renowned. Carnacki fit easily into this milieu, and perhaps Hodgson felt he needed no extensive introduction.

Six tales of Carnacki's adventures were published in Hodgson's lifetime and collected in the 1910 edition; the Arkham House edition of 1947 added three more tales, apparently discovered among Hodgson's papers. Mystery critic Peter Christensen has suggested that the original book may have had more conscious artistry than many people have realized, and that the stories, alternating between accounts of genuine instances of supernaturalism and stories of elaborate hoaxes ferreted out by the detective, have a fascinating structure that "is the product of a carefully contrived interplay between the world of supernatural horror and the world of logical explanation." Christensen even credits the repetitive framing device for creating a sense of order around the disruptive nature of the forces unleashed in the course of Carnacki's narrative.

"The Thing Invisible" has Carnacki investigating a chapel attached to the ancestral castle of the Jarnocks. Tradition has held the chapel to be haunted, but little is made of this reputation until the family butler is stabbed one night by a dagger hurled by an invisible agency. Sir Alfred Jarnock's son summons Carnacki, and the investigator sets up his camera in the chapel. He grows apprehensive while waiting, although he wears armor against the spectral dagger and has a pistol for use against run-of-the-mill foes. The dagger strikes as he crosses the chamber; Carnacki is saved by his precautions. Once the excitement of the incident passes, the sleuth deduces that the dagger is thrown by a mechanical system set in action by opening the altar gate. Old Sir Alfred himself, a bit unhinged since the death of his wife, has set the trap to protect jewels hidden in the chapel. The mystery is solved and the solution kept confidential. In "The Gateway of the Monster," Carnacki sets up his esoteric Electric Pentacle, suggested by a passage in the occult Sigsand Manuscript to check into the haunting of the Grey Room. An actual "ab-normal" power manifests itself and almost destroys Carnacki, but he manages to escape and figures out a way to prevent the monstrous force from reappearing.

The next tale returns to a mundane explanation for its weird occurrences, yet "The House Among the Laurels" has several frightening moments as Carnacki and a group of men find themselves besieged in an old manor house in west Ireland. "The Whistling Room" revives the truly supernatural in the form of another haunted room, which transforms itself into a huge face with hungering, whistling lips—an image that one critic calls the "most imaginative of the Carnacki series." "The Searcher of the End House" relates an incident that happened to Carnacki himself when he was younger and was living with his mother in a cottage. The explanations offered for the visions of a spectral woman and child roaming the upper floors are part mechanical and part supernatural, and the story gives the impression of having been written in haste.

In "The Horse of the Invisible," Carnacki brings to light the mechanical effects by which a man has reenacted the legendary hauntings of a monstrous ghost horse, only to have the man in custody as the actual horse thunders invisibly down the hall to slay the hoaxer. In "The Haunted 'Jarvee,'" Carnacki explores a strange mystery aboard a ship at sea. "The Find" is a routine detective story about a missing book, bearing more resemblance to one of August Derleth's tales of Solar Pons, written in imitation of the Holmes stories, than to any of the other Carnacki investigations. "The Hog" is the last in the series, a frightening adventure in which the sleuth confronts a horrible hoglike entity that is forcing its way from the "ab-" into the "normal" world, possibly the greatest menace of Carnacki's career. In fact, Hodgson suggests that if Carnacki had failed to stop the Hog, the material universe itself would have been disrupted.

Whatever Hodgson's artistic intentions in the Carnacki stories, the fact remains that when the occult manifestations are proven to be rigged, the reader is disappointed. It is true that many of the cases that an actual psychic investigator would probe would turn out to be hoaxes; Hodgson met Harry Houdini, a great debunker of professional occultists as well as an escape artist, and knew well enough the percentage of charlatans at work in the field. His efforts to be authentic, however, to wrap the tales in the jargon and methods of genuine occultists, only weigh the stories down. After an effective and horrifying encounter with the Hog, the reader must wade through several pages of occult-oriented explanation; it is a case in which verisimilitude, instead of aiding the willing suspension of disbelief, undermines it.

Another factor working against the artistic impact of the Carnacki tales is the series format. A character who habitually rubs shoulders with ghosts makes a less satisfying victim of terror than an unsuspecting initiate. Supernatural horror is an odd art form, requiring careful arrangement of mood and incident to be effective. "Ancient Sorceries" is the strongest of Blackwood's John Silence tales because Silence himself takes no part in the action, and yet few would rate that story equally with Blackwood's nonseries masterpieces, "The Willows" and "The Wendigo." Likewise, the Carnacki tales are not as effective as some of Hodgson's independent narratives, and they in no way approach the best work in his novels; in fact, they leech off his other writing, as seen in "The Hog," which recalls the assault of the dreadful swine-things in *The House on the Borderland*. Similarly, "The Haunted 'Jarvee'" is not on a par with the stories set in the weird wastes of the Sargasso Sea. Even within the series, the frequent recurrence of invisible monsters and haunted rooms becomes monotonous.

Ultimately, the reader must be grateful that Hodgson's innate talent in evoking supernatural terror raises the hackles here and there in *Carnacki the Ghost-Finder*, even when the source of terror is eventually dispelled, and be grateful, too, that the series funded Hodgson so that he could write that unique epic of romance and terror, *The Night Land*.

Don Herron

Bibliography

Christensen, Peter. "William Hope Hodgson: Carnacki the Ghost-Finder," in *The Armchair Detective*. XII, no. 2 (Spring, 1979), pp. 122-124.

Lovecraft, H. P. *Supernatural Horror in Literature*, 1945.

Moskowitz, Sam. "William Hope Hodgson," in *Out of the Storm: Uncollected Fantasies*, 1975.

CARRIE

Author: Stephen King (1947-   )
First book publication: 1974
Type of work: Novel
Time: April through May, 1979, with references to 1966, 1980, 1981, 1986, and 1988
Locale: Chamberlain, Maine

When Carrie White, a much-abused high-school girl with telekinetic talents, is cruelly humiliated at the school prom, she uses her powers to devastate her tormentors

> *Principal characters:*
> CARRIE WHITE, an unpopular high-school girl with telekinetic powers
> MRS. MARGARET WHITE, her mother, a religious fanatic
> SUSAN SNELL, a fellow student, sympathetic to Carrie
> TOMMY ROSS, Susan's boyfriend
> CHRISTINE HARGENSEN, another female student, hostile to Carrie
> BILLY NOLAN, Christine's boyfriend
> MISS RITA DESJARDIN, the girls' physical education teacher at Ewen High School

Discouraged by his inability to sell his short fiction to any but the low-paying "men's magazines," and unhappy with his general progress as a novelist, Stephen King tossed the first draft of *Carrie*, his first novel, into the trash. His wife, Tabitha, retrieved it and convinced her husband to finish the book, an act for which King later dedicated it to her: "This is for Tabby, who got me into it—and then bailed me out of it." The rest of the story, of course, is the stuff of Horatio Alger. *Carrie* was accepted for publication by Doubleday & Company and was published in 1974. *Salem's Lot* appeared a year later and became a best-seller. In 1976, Brian DePalma filmed *Carrie*, with Sissy Spacek (physically the antithesis of King's "heroine") in the title role. The movie was an enormous popular success and its author's name became a household word, at least among those with a taste for the violent and macabre.

That King has been dubbed the "King of Horror Fiction" is, however, a bit ironic in view of the fact that only one of his novels, *Salem's Lot*, can be labeled a traditional horror story and one other, *The Shining* (1977), an unorthodox one. Among the others, *The Stand* (1978) and *The Dead Zone* (1979), in very different ways, fall into that ambiguous territory between science fiction and horror; *Firestarter* (1980) is a blend of science fiction, horror, and intrigue; *Cujo* (1981) is a realistic suspense narrative with some largely unsuccessful gestures in the direction of supernatural horror.

Carrie is a mix of science fiction and horror. Technically it should be categorized as science fiction; in mood and feel it is horror. The science-fiction elements include a future setting (published in 1974, the book is set in 1979 with references as far ahead as 1988) and an unusual phenomenon, telekinesis, which is "explained" in the course of the novel. Nothing "supernatural" happens in the narrative; everything is a logical extension of the conflicts between the characters, considering their personalities, needs, prejudices, and fears—given an added push, of course, by Carrie's "wild talent."

The plot line is simple and direct. Carrie White, an unhappy sixteen-year-old girl, is caught between the pressures of snobbery and vindictiveness at Ewen High School and the fanatic discipline imposed by her fundamentalist mother. Carrie yearns to belong and feel "normal"; she also wants to please her mother and is afraid to cross her. This conflict is brought to a head by Carrie's belated first menstruation, which takes place in the shower during a physical education class. The girls mock her and pelt her with tampons. When she returns home, her mother is distraught, not by her daughter's traumatic experience, but by the fact that Carrie has "become a woman," thereby becoming ripe for sin. The intensity of this experience also unleashes Carrie's telekinetic talents, which have been latent since childhood. As she becomes aware of them, Carrie consciously attempts to master these powers and finally succeeds.

Two of Carrie's classmates take a special interest in her development. The first, Susan Snell, feels guilty about her behavior toward Carrie, and decides to give her an opportunity to "join the group." She induces her boyfriend, Tommy Ross, to invite Carrie to the junior-senior prom. The second girl, Christine Hargensen, irritated by the disciplinary actions taken against her for the shower incident, and especially annoyed by Sue's actions on Carrie's behalf, plots a cruel and dramatic revenge. Helped by her boyfriend, Billy Nolan, she plans to rig the "King and Queen of the Prom" selection in favor of Tommy and Carrie and then to humiliate the couple by dumping two buckets of pig's blood on them during the coronation. Christine's plot succeeds too well, provoking the crowd to hysterical laughter and Carrie to violence. Using her newly perfected telekinetic powers, she destroys the gym, killing most of the students, and then wreaks havoc on much of the town. As soon as she reaches her home, Carrie is stabbed by her mother, not for her violence, but for the evil act of attending the prom. Badly wounded, Carrie then kills her mother and wanders back toward the ravaged town, encountering and killing Chris and Billy before dying from loss of blood. The novel ends on a slight note of reconciliation, however, as Sue Snell, having followed Carrie at a distance, attempts to comfort the moribund girl in her last moments and gains, if not forgiveness, at least an insight into her own responsibility and mortality.

If the plot of *Carrie* is straightforward, King's manner of telling the story is not. All of King's subsequent novels have been traditional in narrative technique, the story moving logically and chronologically from beginning to end. In his first novel, however, King chose to break up his direct presentation with a series of excerpts from various "analyses" of the events, published long after they took place. These documents include *The Shadow Exploded*, a scientific analysis of Carrie White's life and powers; "The Black Dawn of TK," an *Esquire* article; the "White Commission Report," a congressional inquiry on the disaster; and *My Name Is Susan Snell*, Sue's defense of her role in the catastrophe. Thus, the reader knows from the beginning that Carrie's powers will lead to mass disaster, and that she will be killed in the final conflict, but the reader does not know the exact shape of the final event from the beginning. As the story progresses, King periodically supplies hints and details of the finale, but it is not until the book's end that all the gory pieces fit into place.

This documentary device is effective for a number of reasons. It gives a kind of "scientific" authenticity to the events and it allows King to "explain" his central plot device, telekinesis. There is also a provocative tension created between the distant, analytical fragments of books and articles and the intense, immediate story itself. Suspense is not blunted by knowing what will happen. Rather, it is heightened as the reader's curiosity about the exact shape of the pending events vies with concern for the doomed characters.

This narrative technique becomes especially effective during the descriptions of the final catastrophe. The documents act as an effective counterpoint—almost an "alienating device"—to King's vivid, detailed descriptions of the violence and carnage. Since King's lifelong addiction to film is well known, it is not surprising that cinematic qualities permeate his writings, and they are particularly successful in the final sequences of *Carrie*. As the climactic moments approach, King sets up several lines of action—Carrie and Tommy at the prom, Carrie's mother's murderous plans for her daughter, Christine and Billy's vengeful plot, and Sue Snell's solitary reflections at home—and cross-cuts between them, while also interspersing bits of documentation along the way. In the best motion-picture tradition, these scenes become shorter and shorter, the cross-cutting more rapid, and the juxtapositions more extreme, until the moment when Carrie, drenched with blood and mocked by the group, retaliates violently. After Carrie's explosion and her subsequent destruction of the gym and surrounding area, the cross-cutting technique is continued, the scenes becoming longer and progressively less visceral, the pace gradually slackening until, by the time Carrie dies, a sense of relative calm has been restored.

Everything that happens in *Carrie* is the logical result of characters in conflict, and this believable characterization is complemented by the accuracy and vividness of King's setting. His ability to create realistic contemporary environments, filled with the minutiae of everyday American life, even to brandname details, has become one of his trademarks. King's Ewen High School seems thoroughly real although, despite its 1979 dating, the atmosphere feels more like that of the 1950's or early 1960's. One might even lump *Carrie* into the "1950's revival" of the early 1970's. It is the dark side of

"Happy Days"; Billy Nolan, acted by John Travolta in DePalma's cinematic adaptation, is a more sinister, more realistic version of Danny Zuko, the character Travolta played years later in the film *Grease*. While there are few topical references, aside from some casual allusions to the Vietnam War (hardly likely in 1979), the songs, manners, language, preoccupations, and life-styles all suggest that self-indulgent but tense period stretching from the early 1950's to the death of John F. Kennedy.

Beneath this realistic surface, King also precisely delineates the social, psychological, and economic pressures of the high-school setting. Personal, social, and economic tensions underlie the characters' behavior and give validity to their actions and responses. Although the characters are stereotypes—the bright, popular girl; the all-American boy; the spoiled brat; the greaser; the religious fanatic; and, above all, the scapegoat—each of them, with varying degrees of complexity, is a real individual. The tensions between the stereotypical roles they have assumed and their personal needs provide much of the impetus for their actions. "We were kids," Sue Snell tells the readers of her apologia; "We were kids trying to do our best." Given the rigid social roles and moral assumptions imposed upon them within the closed environment of a small-town high school, and their personal immaturity, their persecution of an "outsider" such as Carrie White was inevitable.

Sue Snell's decision to induce her boyfriend to take Carrie to the junior-senior prom is the gesture that sets the terrible sequence of events into motion. Her reasons for doing so are clear. She is sincere in her desire to help Carrie, but she does so in a patronizing way. She feels guilty about the shower incident, and beyond that she feels guilty about her situation—her good looks, her perfect boyfriend, her popularity, her recent experiments with sex—and therefore the befriending of Carrie White appears to be the perfect way to assuage her guilt. She enjoys the conspiracy itself; she is, with the best intensions, a devout manipulator, who enjoys managing things and people, not least her boyfriend, Tommy Ross. In her liberal arrogance, it never occurs to her that her plan might fail and damage the girl she is so intent on helping. Tommy's willingness to take Carrie to the dance is less complicated. He loves Sue, probably feels that he has taken advantage of her sexually, and is confident enough to be seen with the class joke. Christine Hargensen, the spoiled daughter of a rich, successful domineering lawyer, initially sees Carrie as a subhuman plaything. When Christine is punished for her lead in the shower-room incident, she is angered, affronted, and embarrassed. Learning that her father's power cannot alter the situation, her thoughts of vengeance turn vicious, especially when she learns about the magnanimous gesture that her major rival, Sue Snell, has made toward the hated person.

Christine's accomplices, Billy Nolan and his gang, are lower-class "machine-shop types." After a steady diet of Ivy League men, Christine has found a new experience in Billy. His rough, crude speech and manners, his direct, almost violent actions, especially in sex, even his smells and his broken-down automobile fascinate her. For his part, Billy has responded to Christine's good looks, her sexuality, her sophistication, and her status as an "upper-class" beauty. They are, of course, both using each other; mixed with her attraction to Billy's animalism is a snob's contempt; despite his pleasure in her beauty and sexuality, Billy feels a deep hostility toward Christine as a representative of the arrogant, respectable, "good" kids. As their plot develops, Chris vents her rage against Carrie and Sue; Billy's anger is directed toward the whole class of "richies"—best represented by Chris herself—that keep themselves aloof from the greasers. It is Billy's antagonism that carries the plan along, as Chris begins to realize the implications of her actions. In the end, it is Christine's fear of Billy more than any hatred of Carrie and Sue that pushes the plot to its completion. (Interestingly, DePalma altered this emphasis in his film adaptation, keeping Billy firmly under Chris's thumb throughout the story. Thus, he substituted a "matriarchal" system for the class-oriented society in King's novel, a fact that King himself noted admiringly in commenting on the film in *Danse Macabre*, 1981).

Carrie is, of course, the most important and interesting character in the novel. Her character is believable owing to King's adroit balancing of the conflicting forces, internal and external, that buffet her. King does a remarkable job of making a character who is a mass of contradictions and extremes both likable and, despite the destruction she causes, sympathetic. He dramatizes her humiliation so forcefully that one is compelled to identify with her, and then he excuses her immoral actions by suggesting that she is temporarily insane.

Carrie's relationship with her mother is complex and ambiguous. Mrs. White's religious fanaticism has imbued her daughter with visions of hell-fire and apocalypse, as well as a distorted image not only of herself but also of all womanhood. On the practical level, the clothing that Mrs. White gives her daughter to wear would be enough to guarantee the girl's outsider status, and the failure to give her any information regarding the development of her own body has set her up for the emotional shock attendant upon her first menstruation. Carrie has accepted all of her mother's beliefs and disciplines, including an acceptance of her own essential sinfulness. She genuinely loves her mother and wants to please her, though she fears her for purely physical reasons. At the same time, Carrie has rebelled against her mother in many little ways from childhood up until the shower incident. Once the development of her telekinetic powers gives her self-confidence, she makes this rebellion overt in her determination to attend the prom with Tommy.

As Alex Alexander has pointed out, there is a fairy-tale quality to Carrie's transformation at the prom. Not only does she become attractive with the help of cosmetics and nice clothes, but she also suddenly acquires poise, social grace, and even some wit. Carrie's scenes with Tommy Ross are reminiscent of Laura Wingfield's encounter with the Gentleman Caller in Tennessee Williams' *The Glass Menagerie* (1945). All this is shattered when the buckets of blood fall on the couple. Carrie's explosion is inevitable. From the beginning, she suspected that she was being set up, but it was a risk that she was tenaciously willing to take. To be given a glimpse of wholeness and acceptance only to have it viciously snatched away and replaced by public scorn and laughter was a shattering vindication of her mother's hellish vision. Thus, given the powers of a god, she strikes back with the wrath of a god. Yet she knows her powers are demoniac, a final proof of her personal damnation, a damnation she cannot resist. As she destroys her enemies, she punishes herself.

Two hundred deaths and the destruction of an entire town are the result of a teenage girl's almost whimsical decision to loan her boyfriend to the ugly girl in the class. The incongruity between terrible consequences and their seemingly trivial causes is a theme that runs throughout King's fiction. Petty mistakes, jealousies, and conflicts can have enormous and awful results, consequences all out of proportion to the initial causes. Careless, casual malice, even well-intentioned blundering, can unleash forces which, once set in motion, cannot be stopped until they have worked out their terrible repercussions. That is, in fact, one of the basic tenets of horror fiction: the dark powers, be they supernatural or human in origin, need only the slightest provocation to break loose and wreak their terror.

Keith Neilson

Bibliography

Alexander, Alex E. "Stephen King's *Carrie*—A Universal Fairy Tale," in *Journal of Popular Culture*. XIII, no. 2 (Fall, 1979), pp. 282-288.
King, Stephen. *Danse Macabre*, 1981.
—————— . "Foreword," in *Night Shift*, 1978.
Winter, Douglas E. *Stephen King*, 1982.

THE CASE OF CHARLES DEXTER WARD

Author: H. P. Lovecraft (1890-1937)
First book publication: 1943
Type of work: Novel
Time: The early twentieth century
Locale: Providence, Rhode Island

A sensitive young scholar, investigating an ancestor who lived unnaturally long and developed methods for raising the dead, is engulfed in horror when he brings the ancestor back through his own methods, as he has been predestined to do

Principal characters:
CHARLES DEXTER WARD, the protagonist
JOSEPH CURWEN, Ward's ill-famed ancestor
DR. WILLETT, the Ward family doctor
EZRA WEEDEN, Curwen's sworn enemy

In 1927, H. P. Lovecraft wrote one of his most intriguing and most auto-biographical works, *The Case of Charles Dexter Ward*, a novel set in the author's own native Providence, Rhode Island. The novel's theme is one of the central notions in the canon of Lovecraft's fiction—that the present time is no refuge in which one can hide from the past, which reaches forward with ineludible tentacles to ensnare the hapless mortal whom it has resolved to overwhelm.

The novel opens with the information that a person who "bore. the name of" Charles Dexter Ward has disappeared from a private sanitarium. With that wording, Lovecraft has already played an ironic joke on the reader, who only later learns that the patient indeed bears the name of Charles but in fact is not Charles at all. The reader gradually learns of the youth's circumstances. Charles is diagnosed as suffering from "a peculiar change in the apparent contents of his mind"—he has the mentality and the diction of an eighteenth century person and, like Lovecraft himself, is an outsider in the twentieth century. The psychologists tend to explain the problem by speculating that Charles, an avid antiquarian scholar, has simply been mentally overwhelmed by familiarity with the past that he knows and loves so well; but this explanation is simply a wedge in the reader's mind, a created tension in the novel, for one realizes that the problem is of far deeper and more bizarre origin.

Young Ward, who lives with his parents in an old Providence house corresponding to the Halsey Mansion in the real city, and who is in many respects a fictive image of the author himself, discovers quite by chance—for the pertinent records have been deliberately but imperfectly expunged—that he has an eighteenth century ancestor named Joseph Curwen (the name being derived from a Salem witchcraft judge, Corwin), a reputed sorcerer who in his day maintained a farm south of the city, in Pawtuxet, Rhode Island. In a flashback of sorts, the reader is made privy to what Charles, through sedulous research, discovers about his strange ancestor. Curwen in his time has aroused the suspicions of his fellow townspeople by living too long (scarcely seeming to age at all over the span of a century, providing an eerie counter-example to William Shakespeare's dictum, "Youth's a stuff will not endure") and by his furtive activities at the farm, from which strange sounds issue at night. Rumors spread to the effect that Curwen, who turns out to be able to traffic with the long-dead, has knowledge of past events and family affairs that no one could naturally possess; he often uses such knowledge for blackmail.

Earning the enmity of one Ezra Weeden by breaking up Weeden's engagement to the daughter of a prominent citizen to marry her himself and thus reestablish his name in a community distrustful of him, Curwen oversteps his bounds. Weeden, with the help of a friend, spies on Curwen's activities and finally organizes a raiding party, which stages a surprise raid on the Pawtuxet farm and dispatches the nefarious Curwen. Lovecraft handles this episode masterfully, mixing fantasy with details of Rhode Island history, and having the young scholar discover the episode through the surviving diary of Weeden's friend. By making the diarist (who is stationed far from the farm during the raid) the sole conduit of information, Lovecraft emulates the tradition of Greek drama in keeping the violence and carnage "offstage," at an extra remove from the reader, who is left to speculate about the horrific details of what the raiding party found and did.

Charles Ward, in the process of researching his ancestor, discovers that an old Providence house well known to him is in fact the house in which Curwen lived before moving his ghastly activities to the Pawtuxet farm. Investigating the house, he uncovers a mural portrait of Curwen—whom Ward atavistically resembles to an uncanny degree—and discovers, in a recess in the wall, the journal of Joseph Curwen and various other papers, including one in cipher and one significantly inscribed *To Him Who Shal Come After, And How He May Gett Beyonde Time and Ye Spheres*. The motif of finding and working out messages left in cipher is a common one with Lovecraft, who apparently imbibed an early interest in cryptography from Edgar Allan Poe by reading "The Gold Bug" at an early age.

Thus the reader learns that Ward is caught up in a demonic kind of fate or determinism. He is predestined to do what he does, delving into the Curwen affair until he is drawn in beyond hope; for young Ward is, of course, "him who shal come after."

Ward begins working on the cipher text, which apparently holds clues to Curwen's mode of sorcery, and begins searching for Curwen's unrecorded grave. He embarks on a long stay abroad to consult on arcane subjects with certain aged authorities (who turn out to be contemporaries of Curwen, still alive through unnatural means); when he returns, the description of his reentry into the College Hill area in Providence is closely autobiographical, faithful in detail to Lovecraft's joyous real-life homecoming after his unhappy residence in New York.

Soon thereafter comes a memorable scene in which the reader learns that Ward has found and exhumed Curwen's remains, for a heavy and ominous box is brought up to Ward's attic laboratory in the dead of night. Over the following days, Ward performs shocking incantations, in spite of the complaints of his parents, who have enlisted Dr. Willett to reason with the youth. (Dr. Willett in the novel lives at 10 Barnes Street, which in real life was Lovecraft's 1927 home, around the corner from the Halsey Mansion, or "Ward house." Lovecraft also uses a former Providence residence of his, 598 Angell Street, as the home of Ezra Weeden's descendants.) After one of the incantations, Ward's parents are shocked to surmise that Ward, in apparent dialogue behind his closed attic door, no longer seems to be alone; in a most powerful scene the mother, listening at the door, hears Ward exclaim, "*Sshh!—Write!*" Ward has succeeded, by Curwen's own methods of employing the bodily "essential salts," in having Curwen up from the dead; Lovecraft has made bizarre use of the mythic motif of death and rebirth.

Dr. Willett receives a letter from Charles expressing the desire to extricate himself from the whole affair; Curwen has rifled the tombs of the world's sages to gain power from them, but Ward's motive has expressly been the innocent pursuit of knowledge as such. It is too late, however; his double Curwen murders him and masquerades as him. Willett and Ward's father have the impostor, whom they believe to be a deranged Charles, committed to an asylum, and Willett investigates the Pawtuxet bungalow which Ward has rented on the site of Curwen's demolished farm. In a scene perhaps unexcelled in the Lovecraft canon for sheer potency of horror, the heroic Willett explores a vast underground vault on the site, discovering hideous and still living things at the bottoms of wells in the floor—Curwen's unsuccessful experiments. Willett finally realizes the truth and returns to the asylum to put Curwen down by means of his own incantations. The ending is no surprise to the reader, who has gleaned the truth long since; but it comes with awesome force nevertheless.

Lovecraft did not think highly of this novel, but his self-criticism is unduly harsh, for the work stands as one of the finest exercises in the psychology of fear in all of fantasy literature.

Donald R. Burleson

Bibliography

de Camp, L. Sprague. *Lovecraft: A Biography*, 1975.

Joshi, S. T. *H. P. Lovecraft and Lovecraft Criticism: An Annotated Bibliography*, 1981.

_____ , ed. *H. P. Lovecraft: Four Decades of Criticism*, 1980.
St. Armand, Barton Levi. *The Roots of Horror in the Fiction of H. P. Love-craft*, 1977.
Shreffler, Philip A. *The H. P. Lovecraft Companion*, 1977.

THE CASTLE
(DAS SCHLOSS)

Author: Franz Kafka (1883-1924)
First book publication: 1926
English translation: 1930
Type of work: Novel
Time: The timeless present
Locale: A village

K., a Land Surveyor, claims he has been summoned to the village ruled by Count Westwest and the authoritative bureaucracy housed in the Castle; although neither the Castle nor the village will accept the legitimacy of his claims, he persists in attempting to present his case and resolve his now untenable position

Principal characters:
    K., a Land Surveyor
    KLAMM, Chief of Department X
    FRIEDA, the barmaid
    BARNABAS, a Castle messenger
    OLGA, sister of Barnabas

Franz Kafka's unfinished novel *The Castle* can permit of no resolution, either metaphysical or aesthetic, because the human condition itself, symbolized by the plight of a nameless protagonist, is one of agonizing uncertainty. Living in the midst of the incomprehensible, paradoxical, and inexplicable, man is caught in a solitude so profound, an apartness so vast, that he seeks comfort in any sign that will acknowledge the validity of his existence and proclaim it meaningful. Kafka's faceless K. prophetically prefigures the special dilemma of modern man, who, having proclaimed himself master of the world, feels alienated from it, from himself, and from his own kind.

K., a Land Surveyor, believes he has been summoned to the village ruled by Count Westwest, in order to fulfill some unspecified assignment. His arrival there seems both unexpected and even undesired; he is not received at the Castle, owned by Count Westwest, nor is he treated hospitably by the villagers. Indeed, his very identity is called into question. The plot revolves around K.'s persistent efforts to present himself to the authorities of the Castle. Occasionally encouraged and led on by mystifying communications from the powers on high, he is nevertheless uncomfortably positioned, caught as he is between the overt hostility of the villagers and the crushing indifference of the Castle.

Certainly the conditions under which K. enters this strange world (a world which he, incidentally, makes no attempt to leave) are not auspicious. A stranger to the place, he arrives late one evening when the village is "deep in snow." The Castle is hidden in mist and darkness, and there is not so much as "a glimmer of light" anywhere. In order to reach the village, he has had to leave the main road, which is a risky venture under the circumstances. Standing on the wooden bridge connecting the village with the world outside, K. gazes "into the illusory emptiness above him." All the signs are threatening.

In fact, the darkness, solitude, and emptiness are not to remain illusory. In reaching for human contact, K., the stranger, admits his awful loneliness in confiding to the village teacher: "I don't fit in with the peasants, nor, I imagine, with the Castle." Indeed, the Count's Land Surveyor will continually find the seemingly endless village street deserted, the cold and snow interminable, the tiny cottages monotonously alike, and the rooms he enters claustrophobically small. He is at once shut out and shut in. He walks the narrow streets past houses whose small, dark, cramped spaces reflect a community where "hospitality is not the custom." Thus, seeking refuge at one or another of the two village inns, K. resorts to sleeping in foul corners, or already inhabited places, or cupboards, or dank beer barrels—but always at the sufferance of those who are both in awe and contemptuous of him.

From the beginning, when the peculiarity, even absurdity, of his situation dawns on him, K. aggressively contends with the powers that be, that beehive of Authorities, Secretaries, and Deputies controlling the lives of the villagers. He sends messages, demands meetings, invites confrontation. Yet there is no substantive communication possible on his relentless trek through the claptrap, the tangle of cross-purposes, double-talk, and secondary meanings. Beset on all sides, K. persists in hoping that his defiance will win him a meeting with Klamm, Chief of Department X at the Castle.

K. clamors for recognition and acceptance in a world where he is a stranger, insisting on exerting his will and using whatever power he can muster, given his ambiguous position. Obsessive in his resolve to obtain some sign from the Castle, he bruises himself against a cold and indifferent universe, suddenly lacking in any discernible meaning. All the while, he carries his questions about like a burden that he cannot be permitted to discharge. Searching for a "yes" or "no," he is granted only a "maybe" in a provisional world crowded with replies such as "perhaps" and "probably." Faceless, nameless, without history or past, and facing an endless future of avoidance and uncertainty, K.'s fatigue begins to wear him down. While at the start he is contentious, impatient, and obstinate, later the seeds of futility and despair make even his desire for resolution "uncertain."

Indeed, the extent of K.'s flagging energy is drawn with comic brilliance in the scene at the inn where he mistakenly enters the bedroom of a Castle functionary named Bürgel. With K. perched at the end of his bed, it being the middle of the night and there being nowhere else to sit, Bürgel promises to settle K.'s affairs and solve his case. In this accidental encounter, K. unintentionally achieves what he has sought for so long: a face-to-face encounter with an official, a mediator between village and castle. Yet K.'s response is to fall asleep, "impervious to all that was happening."

In the transition from pugilistic applicant to passive supplicant, K.'s awareness and powers of observation are sharpened; and so also is the undefinable aura of guilt that surrounds him. A hilarious episode reminiscent of the lunatic happenings in a Marx Brothers movie has K. observing an absurd bureaucratic ritual called "file distribution" which "nobody was allowed to watch." Although his presence at the scene is quite innocent and random, he is nevertheless branded as someone who, riding "roughshod over everything," is without human consideration. Human consideration, however, is barely to be found in this world bounded on one side by the village and on the other by the Castle. Although K.'s vocation is to survey, to establish boundaries and assess parameters, he finds himself in a no-man's-land, a maze without apparent exit. What if there is no way out? To ascertain the "lay of the land," so to speak, is denied K. since the village does not want him and the Castle will not accept him; he is therefore condemned to flounder in uncertainty and eventually accept mystery and doubt as a condition of life itself. He must shuttle back and forth through the narrow streets of his existence seeking solace and certitude. Not even sleep is a consolation, for in this nightmare place rest is to be found only fleetingly, in temporary and solitary corners.

Often rejected and rebuffed, sometimes deserted, but always driven, K. stubbornly refuses to give up wanting *to know*. If the desire to know puts him in jeopardy with Count Westwest, whose very name signifies meaninglessness and menace (little children are protected from hearing it), then so be it. K. comes inevitably to accept the propositional world ruled by the likes of Westwest. His options are, after all, limited. Running in every direction, pushed to the extremity of self-doubt, and undermined by forces that subvert his reason and spirit, K. nevertheless searches for meaning in a seemingly absurd and arbitrary universe. The village, darkened by the long shadow of the Castle, is almost devoid of light or understanding, of pity or compassion. Terrible as that acknowledgment is for him, K. does not forfeit hope.

The Castle should remind the reader, albeit painfully, that only in the certainty of the human capacity for laughter, even if that laughter be bitter as gall, can individuals pick their uncertain way through the dark. Like K., humans are left to cling tenaciously to the fragile hope that there is someone out there, somewhere, who will redeem them from laughing themselves to death.

Greta Eisner

Bibliography
Eisner, Pavel. *Franz Kafka and Prague*, 1950.
Emrich, Wilhelm. *Franz Kafka: A Critical Study of His Writings*, 1968.
Gray, Ronald. *Franz Kafka*, 1973.

Heller, Erich. *Franz Kafka*, 1975.
Kuna, Franz, ed. *On Kafka: Semi-Centenary Perspectives*, 1976.

THE CASTLE OF OTRANTO
A Gothic Story

Author: Horace Walpole (1717-1797)
First book publication: 1764-1765
Type of work: Novel
Time: c. 1245, during the era of the Sixth and Seventh Crusades
Locale: A medieval castle in southern Italy

The retributive forces of Gothic architecture fulfill an ancestral curse and fantastic prophecy by crushing the castle's wrongful heir and expelling its usurper in a spectacularly supernatural fashion

Principal characters:
MANFRED, a despotic prince and usurping proprietor of Otranto
HIPPOLITA, his infertile wife
CONRAD, their sickly son
MATILDA, Manfred's despised daughter
BIANCA, her faithful maidservant
ISABELLA, a girl vigorously pursued by Manfred
FREDERIC, Marquis of Vicenza, her righteous father
RICARDO, Manfred's grandfather, a ghost
ALFONSO THE GOOD, the legitimate owner of Otranto, whose gigantic body imbues the castle's superstructure
FATHER JEROME, a benign but inept priest
THEODORE, a noble peasant and the rescuer of Isabella, eventually revealed as the proper heir to the house of Otranto

The first Gothic novel was the invention of Horace Walpole, dilettante, socialite, and enthusiastic patron of the medieval revival which permeated the arts of painting, architecture, and literature in the 1750's. Reacting to the rigidities of reason and aesthetic decorum dictated by neoclassicism, Walpole's *The Castle of Otranto* accommodated the new romantic impulse to indulge the strange, the weird, the savage, and the ghoulish. These repressed pleasures of the imagination had already manifested themselves in the morbid imagery and supernatural musings of the poets of the Graveyard School as well as in the passion for ruins that had begun to displace the taste for neat, symmetrical building styles. The fashion in mortuary landscaping, with its collapsed walls, ruined turrets, and moss-grown façades, appealed strongly to an imagination like Walpole's in quest of an outrageous new concept of the sublime.

The literary foundations of *The Castle of Otranto* were laid in 1749 when Walpole sequestered himself at his newly purchased Strawberry Hill estate for the purpose of constructing a fully equipped medieval dreamworld. His eccentric stucco fortress at Strawberry Hill became the architectural predecessor of the bizarre and novel tale of flying helmets, mobile portraits, subterranean flights and pursuits through "vaults totally dark," and supernatural alarms and diversions. Although Walpole's original haunted castle (the model setting and floorplan for innumerable Gothic novels to come) is not itself a sublime ruin at the outset of the book, it would nevertheless become Gothic literature's first decayed world. At the novel's architectural denouement, the colossal specter of Alfonso the Good shatters the castle's foundations and in doing so obliterates the rational security of the reader as well. Walpole's motives for writing *The Castle of Otranto* were an extension of his motives for converting an elegant country house into a crazy castle at Strawberry Hill; he wished to challenge the artistic norms of the day by releasing forbidden imaginative energies.

The novel was an expression of the buried emotional life of its creator and an example of his revolt against the tedium of probability and common sense. It was also a means of protest against Isaac Newton's well-regulated and orderly universe, for Walpole's diverse gadgetry of shock, incredible and sometimes incoherent plotting, and melodramatic characterization all reflect a desire to achieve a vision of chaos. Walpole himself best articulated his intention to disturb, offend, and finally elevate a readership grown weary of the neat couplets of the Augustan writers when he observed that "The great resources of fancy have been dammed up by strict adherence to the common life."

Walpole's plea for the liberation of fancy appears in the pair of informative Prefaces to the first two editions of *The Castle of Otranto*. Here he sets forth the behavioral laws of the Gothic world as well as the technology and psychology of future tales of terror. Uneasy over the novel's public reception, Walpole counterfeited his authorship in the fake Preface to the first edition. Readers were told that the book had been recovered from an Italian manuscript set down by the monastic chronicler, Onuphrio Muralto, Canon of the Church of St. Nicholas at Otranto, and later rendered into English by that scholarly gentleman, William Marshal, whose antiquarian zeal closely resembled Walpole's own exuberance for things medieval. In the Preface to the second edition, Walpole abandoned these poses, declared his authorship, invoked the invulnerable examples of William Shakespeare and Voltaire to justify his melodramatic procedures, and added the eye-catching adjective "Gothic" to the subtitle of the novel. Because of its pejorative connotations for the eighteenth century mind, Walpole's description of his novel as Gothic was a bold and brilliant choice, for it both enticed the curious reader and captured the quintessence of the form in a single word.

Walpole's Prefaces offer important criteria for the construction of catastrophic narrative. In an expertly chosen metaphor, Walpole designates terror as "the author's principal engine," thus fixing the useful notion that the high Gothic operates most effectively as an infernal machine composed of interworking preternatural parts. The friction and motion of such weird machinery installed throughout the castle would generate the level of terror required to place the inmates of the castle in "extraordinary positions." When skillfully manipulated, the apparatus of anguish would have the additional effect of keeping the emotional lives of the entrapped characters in "a constant vicissitude of interesting passions." Cleverly and deliberately, Walpole did not define the term "extraordinary positions," just as he did not specify precisely what was meant by "interesting passions." Henceforth as the Gothic form emerged, an "extraordinary position" for a Gothic victim might be either physical or psychological. The lethal predicament might place a sickly young man in the landing zone of an enormous flying helmet or it might locate a tormented consciousness within a contracting pit and then threaten that mind with the metronomic descent of a razor-sharp blade.

Walpole's positions and passions furnished a standard for measuring the relative Gothicity of later works in the horror/terror tradition. A supernatural novel or tale does not merit the Gothic label unless it displays some of the remnants of Walpole's engine of terror in some form. Chief among these Walpolesque props is the central, claustrophobic setting of a haunted castle or some viable architectural equivalent of that fiendish edifice, such as a dilapidated mansion resting precariously at the edge of a tarn. The castle or its surrogate must be intricately wired with Walpole's terrifying appliances and inhabited by frenzied characters who resemble Manfred, Isabella, Frederic, Matilda, and others in the original cast of *The Castle of Otranto*, whose postures of victimization and dreadful architectural dilemmas are nothing if not extraordinary.

As would be the case with all true Gothic novels to follow from Walpole's prototype, the most potent and determined personality in *The Castle of Otranto* is the sentient castle itself. More than simply a receptacle for the absurd or an atmospheric framework for the containment of the villain's persecution of the maiden, the castle has a superbiology and a willful intelligence of its own. It responds to Manfred's erotic villainy and concealment of paternal crime with all the sexual vigor of a revitalized human body and all the moral vigor of a wronged human soul. The symbolic layout of the castle with its own heaven and hell and its interior honeycombed with secret corridors spiraling inward and downward to various compartments of peril and salvation are features that suggest the structure of the human brain. Commenting on the rich symbolic properties of the haunted castle, Elizabeth MacAndrew has drawn the analogy between the interior of the castle and the interior of the mind under stress:

> A dire and threatening place, it remains more than a dwelling. It starts out as a stone representation of the dark, tortured windings in the mind of those eminently civilized, and therefore unnatural vices, ambition and cruelty; it bears the whole weight of the ages of man's drift away from an ideal state; and it becomes a lasting representation of the torments of the subconscious pressing upon the conscious mind and making a prison of the self.

Taking the castle as character, its subterranean portions can easily be equated with the subconscious aspects of the self. To the idea of the castle as emblematic of the imprisoned romantic self may be added the historical view which sees the castle as a configuration of a doomed social structure, seemingly solid but approaching collapse.

Next in importance to the character of the mighty castle in Walpole's Gothic cast is his sinister superman, Manfred. He is a figure of great potential virtue, warped spiritual magnificence, and perverted moral energy of similar stature to Satan in John Milton's *Paradise Lost* (1667, 1674) or one of the sexual monsters of Elizabethan-Jacobean blood tragedy. Never absolutely repulsive or totally degenerate, Manfred seems to have inherited his evil tendencies through a corrupt genealogy, and his maliciousness seems to be a result of a divided nature continually at war with itself. Although he lacks the contorted brow and diabolic glance of later Gothic villains, Walpole's Manfred exhibits most of the psychological characteristics of the Gothic's half-evil protagonists. Walpole endeavored to give his tormented tormentor something like tragic status when he carefully described Manfred as a man who was "naturally humane when his passions did not obscure his reason." During most of the story, this psychological dichotomy inclines toward Manfred's base passions, making him the ancestor of the Byronic hero whose vices are often virtues in reverse and whose commitment to crime has heroic if not quite tragic overtones. When Walpole allows Manfred to use the phrase "a man of many sorrows" to expose the causes of his heroic villainy, he touches upon the *Angst, Weltschmerz*, and metaphysical exasperation later to be noted in Johann Wolfgang von Goethe's Faust and Herman Melville's Ahab. Almost never delighting in his evil, Manfred is the progenitor of Gothic literature's strangely fascinating race of fallen creatures whose bondage to a mouldering feudal building signifies both their twisted inner conditions and their enslavement to exhausted ideals of power and self. Although Manfred may appear to possess Otranto and to control its interior affairs, it is really the castle which owns and torments this potentially noble being.

Manfred's acts of sadism are directed against the two Gothic virgins condemned to reside in perpetual suspense in the gloomy chambers of Otranto. Isabella and Matilda are the hysterical forerunners of the menaced maidens of countless Gothic thrillers who spend most of their lives as cryptomaniacal sufferers in the Gothic underworld. Little more than a focal point for Manfred's erotic urges, Isabella's main duty in the novel is to give Manfred the opportunity to fulfill his legacy of evil by pursuing the distressed maiden through the Gothic darkness. The underground chase is a repeated pattern of emergency for Isabella, but Walpole's rhetorical lampoons of her Gothic panics sometimes disclose a sardonic sense of the ridiculous. Descending through a series of trapdoors and screaming on cue, Isabella's histrionic dialogue during her flight from Manfred shows crisis dissolving into comedy:

"'Oh, heavens!' cried Isabella, 'it is the voice of Manfred! Make haste, or we are ruined! And shut the trap-door after you.'" The Gothic tradition originates with the melodramatic interplay of villain and maiden and with Isabella's desperate series of subterranean gropings to find an egress from the primordial darkness of the castle to a domestic Eden for herself beyond its walls.

The grotesque collision of villain and maiden in the castle's depths is matched by the conflict between Manfred and the forces of supernatural retribution which oppose his hereditary ownership of the castle. All later disastrous events at Otranto are preceded by the initial spectacular event: the arrival from the sky of Alfonso's Brobdingnagian helmet which crushes Manfred's son Conrad and causes in the novice Gothic reader both a shudder and a titter. Walpole's technique of immediate shock at the outset of the novel was calculated to shatter his reader's faith in a controllable universe of empirical cause and effect and to stimulate their irrational expectations. If the reader can tolerate the compound of the lurid and the ludicrous found in the unidentified flying helmet of the novel's opening page, he is then in a position to enjoy the unremitting series of Gothic shocks and marvels to come. Future Gothics will owe much to Walpole's first law of Gothic motion as demonstrated by the huge helmet; this law states that the deader or more inanimate an object is, the more likely it is to move, to feel, to think, and to exert its own peculiar supernatural jurisdiction over events in the natural world. Statues which bleed, pictures which desert their frames to converse with the denizens of the castle, mirrors whose reflections yield macabre images of the past or future, and chambers which change their shape without warning derive from the incident of the helmet and establish the total aliveness and unnatural instability of the Gothic world.

The novel's hardware of horror was accompanied by Walpole's ingenious designing of several type-scenes which would prove useful to his Gothic successors. Although it is related very obscurely to the Manfred-Isabella plot, a fine example of one such type-scene is Frederic's astonishing encounter with the hooded monk. The scene illustrates the moment of transition from terror to horror when a character crosses over from something dreaded to the appalling confrontation with the thing itself. Exploring the forbidden chambers of Otranto in search of the missing Hippolita, Frederic's fears are transformed into horror when he discovers a robed figure kneeling before an altar. The encounter that follows is a familiar moment in Gothic fiction and can be labeled the terrible turn or the ghastly rotation, a very useful implement for jolting the skeptical reader out of his disbelief in the horrid reality of the supernatural. Unlike the skillful presentation of the terrible turn in the horror film *The Phantom of the Opera* (1925), Walpole's management of this versatile Gothic contraption is done with too much flippancy to produce a serious horrific effect; yet the contraption itself is completely installed and ready for adaptation by later Gothics.

> The marquis was about to return, when the figure rising, stood some moments fixed in meditation, without regarding him. The marquis, expecting the holy person to come forth, and meaning to excuse his uncivil interruption, said, "Reverend Father, I sought the Lady Hippolita."—"Hippolita!" replied a hollow voice, "camest thou to this castle to seek Hippolita?" And then the figure, turning slowly round, discovered to Frederic the fleshless jaws and empty sockets of a skeleton, wrapt in a hermit's cowl.

With its versatile contraptions and weird contrivances, *The Castle of Otranto* rapidly came to be regarded as the indispensable dynamo to which later Gothic writers could connect their own plots to electrify the reader and supercharge the melodrama with high-voltage emotions. From Mrs. Ann Radcliffe and Matthew G. "Monk" Lewis in Walpole's own age to Victoria Holt, H. P. Lovecraft, and Stephen King in the twentieth century, Walpole's power plant remains a steady producer of Gothic energy. Yet it would be a misinterpretation of Walpole's significance to the rise of the Gothic tradition to see his contributions as merely mechanical or technical innovations. In erecting his dark castle, Walpole was also acknowledging the disturbing psychic reality that the human mind is a place of darkness haunted by the demon of the unknown self. Beyond the exaggerated acoustics created by the fall of the House of Otranto may be heard the reverberations of what a later and greater master of the Gothic, Edgar Allan Poe, would call the "terrors of the soul."

Frederick S. Frank

Bibliography
Bleiler, Everett F. "Horace Walpole and *The Castle of Otranto*," in *Three Gothic Novels: "The Castle of Otranto" by Horace Walpole, "Vathek" by William Beckford, and "The Vampyre" by John Polidori*, 1966.
Conger, Syndy M. "Faith and Doubt in *The Castle of Otranto*," in *Gothic: The Review of Supernatural Horror Fiction*. I (December, 1979), pp. 51-59.
Ehlers, Leigh A. "The World as Stage: Providence and Character in *The Castle of Otranto*," in *Wascana Review*. XIV, no. 2 (1980), pp. 17-30.
Lewis, Paul. "*The Atheist's Tragedy* and *The Castle of Otranto*: Expressions of the Gothic Vision," in *Notes and Queries*. XXV (1978), pp. 52-54.
Quennell, Peter. "The Moon Stood Still on Strawberry Hill," in *Horizon*. XI (Summer, 1969), pp. 113-119.
Riely, John. "*The Castle of Otranto* Revisited," in *Yale University Library Gazette*. LIII (1978), pp. 1-17.

THE CENTAUR

Author: Algernon Blackwood (1869-1951)
First book publication: 1911
Type of work: Novel
Time: 1910
Locale: Narrated in London but with flashbacks to a ship in the Mediterranean bound for the Black Sea and the Caucasus mountains

A "panpsychic" novel exploring man's spiritual affinity and union with the Earth's consciousness

Principal characters:
TERENCE O'MALLEY, a reporter and foreign correspondent in his thirties
DR. HEINRICH STAHL, a German doctor formerly in a mental hospital but now a ship's doctor
A NAMELESS RUSSIAN AND HIS SON
THE NARRATOR

All of Blackwood's stories grew out of events experienced either directly by him or by someone he knew. *The Centaur* arose from a trip that Blackwood took, sometime around 1909, through the Caucasus. "The stupendous grandeur of those almost legendary mountains made a profound impression upon a young and sensitive mind," he wrote forty years later in "The Birth of an Idea" (1950); but "after an extended tour I came home charged with a thousand storms of beauty and wonder, only to find that I could not write a line about it all." Ideas and possibilities remained latent in Blackwood's mind for more than a year, during which time he encountered *A Pluralistic Universe*, William James's Hibbert Lectures on the Present Situation in Philosophy delivered at Manchester College and published in book form in 1909. It is entirely possible that Blackwood had attended the Hibbert Lectures; in any case, he was certainly already well acquainted with most of James's facts and theories. Evidently the book struck a responsive chord; Blackwood quotes from it profusely throughout *The Centaur*, especially the fourth lecture, "Concerning Fechner," which he uses as the connecting thread throughout the novel. Thus Gustav Fechner's theories are, in effect, the *modus operandi* of the novel, and an understanding of those theories is essential for an appreciation of *The Centaur*. Blackwood unravels them through the medium of Dr. Stahl in several of the early chapters.

Gustav Fechner (1801-1887) was a German professor of physics who became famous through his championing of the theories of the experimental psychologist Ernst Weber, which led to the establishment of the quasiscience of psychophysics. Fechner was as much a mystic as a scientist, and he developed the theory that the Earth had its own collective consciousness. With simple logic he explained those aspects of the Earth that are analogous to the heart, the eyes, the brain, and other vital organs, emphasizing the fact that humans should not take these comparisons too literally. Instead humans must regard the Earth as a totally different conscious being, one of a much higher class than either man or animal.

This theory held strong appeal for Blackwood, who, since his early years, had been a disciple of Nature. The concept of planets as living organisms has become a common theme in science fiction, from Arthur Conan Doyle's "When the World Screamed" (1929) to *Solaris* (1961; 1971) by Stanislaw Lem to John Varley's *Titan* (1979), but no one before or since Blackwood has used the theme in quite the same way. Blackwood united it with the idea that, just as the human personality can extend itself under certain conditions, so the Earth-soul may project portions of itself and become manifest in the form of gods and mythical beings in the past. Over the millennia man has lost contact with these emanations through the dulling effect of civilization, but occasionally there are psychic throwbacks, *Urmenschen*, who respond to the true lure of Nature, the *Urwelt*.

Thus Blackwood had his premise for *The Centaur*: the response to the ultimate lure, the *Urwelt*. In this sense the plot of the novel is deceptively simple, but the implications are vast. The hero of the novel, if he can be described as such, is an itinerant Irish newspaperman, Terence O'Malley, who is described as a man "of vigorous health, careless of gain" who believes that "Civilization . . . [has] blinded the eyes of men, filling them with dust rather than vision." O'Malley relates his experiences to a friend who subsequently tells the story, pieced together from memories of conversations long into the night with O'Malley, and from scattered notes and papers left behind after O'Malley's physical death.

The story actually begins with the departure of a steamer from Marseilles with O'Malley aboard on a roving commission for his newspaper among the tribes of the Caucasus. Also on board as the ship's doctor is Heinrich Stahl, with whom O'Malley is already acquainted as a result of past meetings and correspondence in connection with two books of "curious tales" that O'Malley had written. Stahl has a contradictory nature, for while he occasionally drops remarks "that [betray] a belief in all kinds of things, unorthodox things," after having "led the Irishman into confessions of his own fairy faith, he [will] abruptly rule the whole subject out of order with some cynical phrase that [closes] discussion." Stahl thus has a dichotomous role in *The Centaur*: at one moment he is encouraging and inspiring O'Malley with theories and ideas that inflame his vision, and in the next he rapidly tries to extinguish that passion by advising O'Malley against his heart's desire, at times actively intervening.

Also on board is a large blond man, whom Stahl and O'Malley deduce to be Russian, and his son. Both Stahl and O'Malley find themselves entranced by them, Stahl because of a traumatic experience years earlier when he encountered the Russian in his mental hospital, and O'Malley because he recognizes one of his own kind in the Russian. The big man makes a sympathetic response. Particularly fascinating is the fact that the pair seem much larger than they really are. O'Malley's first impression when looking into the eyes of the Russian is of "a hunted creature that at last knows shelter." O'Malley learns from Stahl that the Russian is one of the *Urmenschen*, a true child of Nature. As the doctor explains,

> He is not a human being at all in the sense in which you and I are accustomed to use the term. His inner being is not shaped, as his outer body, upon quite human lines. He is a Cosmic Being—a direct expression of cosmic life. A little bit, a fragment, of the Soul of the World, and in that sense a survival—a survival of her youth.

O'Malley observes a few strange events when the Russian and his son are alone on deck, not least a visitation by a "messenger—from the sea"; but his whole future is decided when through a set of circumstances he comes to share a cabin with the *Urmenschen*. That night, as O'Malley lies awake, he is aware that although the man and boy are asleep, their spiritual selves are active within the room, and O'Malley's own spirit becomes enveloped by their presence. He begins to experience sensations of beauty and rapture and is overwhelmed by a yearning for spiritual freedom. Entranced by the sleeping face of the Russian, O'Malley finds himself spiritually hypnotized with only a slender thread of his conscious mind anchoring him to the everyday world, which has become remote and trivial. Even so, O'Malley knows that if the man's eyes open he will be "beyond recall."

> The narrow space of that little cabin was charged already to the brim, filled with some overpowering loveliness of wild and simple things, the beauty of stars and winds and flowers, the terror of seas and mountains; strange radiant forms of gods, heroes, nymphs, fauns and satyrs; the fierce sunshine of some Golden Age unspoilt, of a stainless region now long forgotten and denied—that world of splendour his heart had ever craved in vain, and beside which the life of To-day faded to a wretched dream.

After a violent internal struggle O'Malley extricates himself from the cabin, but he is now firmly under the spell of the Russian and determined to follow him to seek spiritual peace and harmony. The feeling of oneness with the Earth-soul increasingly overwhelms O'Malley as the steamer carries them through the Isles of Greece toward the Black Sea and the Caucasus. On arrival at Batoum, in Georgia, O'Malley, through the machinations of Dr. Stahl, loses track of the Russian, but he knows that they will find each other again; indeed, O'Malley later experiences the effects of the Russian's spirit as it searches for him. At length, they are reunited after O'Malley has traveled as far as "a little Swanetian hamlet beyond Alighir" where he was planning to penetrate deeper into the mountain recesses "and feed his heart with what he found of loneliness and beauty." Suddenly he becomes aware that the Russian is watching him. "O'Malley saw him for a full minute before he understood. The man seemed so absolutely a part of the landscape, a giant detail in keeping with the rest—a detail that had suddenly emerged."

Hitherto O'Malley's journey has been a physical one in search of psychic rejuvenation; now, with his rediscovery by the Russian, it becomes a spiritual odyssey. For O'Malley "there seemed no definite line that marked off one state of consciousness from another, just as there seems no given instant when a man passes actually from sleep to waking," but together now, fired by the *Urwelt*, the two venture farther north where "the Irishman knew in his heart that they in reality came nearer to the Garden long desired, and to those lofty Gates of horn and ivory that hitherto he had never found— because he feared to let himself go." This is no physical Garden of Eden, but the psychic, primeval nexus of the Earth-soul's projected consciousness. O'Malley is enraptured: "He was everywhere; in everything; shining, singing, dancing."

At length in a distant valley, they encounter their heart's desire. Beyond them is the Garden, separated by only a barrier of shadow built by the Night from "her masses of silvery architecture." As night settles and the moon rises, the barrier trembles "like a line of wavering music" and a gateway forms. O'Malley hears the sound of simple, old-time piping, and the "moon-blanched Gate of Horn and Ivory swung open. The consciousness of the Earth possessed them. They passed within." Thus O'Malley enjoys the ultimate transmogrification, a spiritual apotheosis into the form of those spirits of perfect primeval power, the centaurs. "The absorption was absolute."

The novel does not end here, however, for although O'Malley has achieved his goal, there has been no purpose beyond self-attainment. Although in his short fiction, such as "The Man Whom the Trees Loved," Blackwood often concluded a story at such a climax, his novels work on a different level. Early in his life, Blackwood desired to be a great teacher, and it was only in his novels that he found the medium by which he could express his beliefs and put forward his suggestions and remedies.

Suddenly there shimmers through O'Malley's unfettered spirit the desire to share his experiences and knowledge with the world, and as his thoughts return to worldly matters, so the gates of horn and ivory close behind him, and abruptly he is back at the hamlet where the Russian had rediscovered him. O'Malley's journey has transcended both time and space. His attempts to convert the world are doomed from the outset, for although he has all the fervor and conviction of the neophyte, the world is not receptive. In time, he realizes his error: "I shall never reach men through their intellects. . . . I must get at them *from within*. To reach their hearts, the new ideas must rise up from within. . . . I must do it *from the other side*." With a spirit that is strong and vibrant, O'Malley happily allows his physical body to die so that his psychic self can continue to direct his desires into the hearts of men.

Mike Ashley

Bibliography

Blackwood, Algernon. *The Collected Essays, Journalism, and Letters*, 1968.

Briggs, Julia. *Night Visitors: The Rise and Fall of the English Ghost Story*, 1977.

Colombo, John Robert. *Blackwood's Books: A Bibliography Devoted to Algernon Blackwood*, 1978.

Sullivan, Jack. *Elegant Nightmares: The English Ghost Story from Le Fanu to Blackwood*, 1978.

THE CENTAUR

Author: John Updike (1932-   )
First book publication: 1963
Type of work: Novel
Time: 1947; 1962; the mythological ancient past of Greece
Locale: Olinger, Pennsylvania and environs; ancient Greece

A high-school science teacher comes to accept the inevitability of failure and death during a three-day period he and his son spend separated from home; later his son tries to capture in art this time in which he came to understand his father, partially by means of transmuting it into mythological terms

Principal characters:
> GEORGE CALDWELL, a science teacher, also the wise centaur Chiron
> PETER, his son, also the Titan Prometheus (and Chiron's daughter Ocyrhoe)
> CATHERINE (CASSIE), his wife, also Ceres (mother of Persephone)
> "POP" KRAMER, her father, also Chronos (father of Zeus)
> PENNY FOGELMAN, Peter's girl friend, also Pandora (wife of Epimetheus, Prometheus' brother)
> AL HUMMEL, a garageman, also Hephaestus
> VERA HUMMEL, a girls' gym teacher, also Venus
> LOUIS ZIMMERMAN, an autocratic and lecherous principal, also Zeus

John Updike's third novel, *The Centaur*, is also his most explicitly mythic, so drenched in obvious allusions and nonrealistic angles of vision that it can legitimately be called a "fantasy" despite the fact that its narrative consists entirely of everyday events taking place in 1947 suburban Pennsylvania, the setting of so many of the author's naturalistic fictions. Several modes of narration involving fantasy give cosmic significance to a series of ordinary events important on the realistic plane only to George Caldwell, his son Peter, and their immediate family and acquaintances. Controversial because of the explicit mythological scaffolding, underscored by an Index to classical allusions, *The Centaur* is Updike's most complicated novel, even praised as his best by some critics, despite problems of formal consistency.

Seen as a realistic story, the book concerns Caldwell's confrontation in the dead of winter in his fiftieth year with the fear of death, possibly from cancer. More likely "battle fatigue," an accumulation of self-deprecation and unrequited love for his students, the "snake" in his guts is represented metaphorically as an arrow in his ankle, possibly poisoned, at the very start of the novel. Fused into Chiron, exceptional among the brutish centaurs of Greek myth for his wisdom, nobility, and prowess as an educator, Caldwell has the arrow removed by the garageman, Hummel (paralleling the centaur's body with the teacher's car), but the sense of being poisoned remains. Caldwell is later examined by Dr. Appleton (Apollo) and the X-rays prove to be negative.

In the meantime, Caldwell and his son have spent three days in town, prevented by car trouble (physical and mental problems) from getting him home to suburban Firetown. Finally welcomed home by mother and grandfather, Peter is put to bed with a fever and, seeing his father framed in the window, vows someday to make permanent this vision. Just out of sight, Caldwell (Chiron once more) shovels snow and comes to terms with his mortality (as Chiron once gave up his immortality for Prometheus).

Just before the three days of exile, George has a horrendous class period in which he strikes a student during the principal's visitation. During the three days, moreover, he watches the swimming team he coaches get beaten by the high school in neighboring Alton, discovers that 140 tickets in his care for the next night's basketball game are missing, observes Mrs. Herzog of the school board emerging from the principal's office with her lipstick smeared (possibly giving her reason to want to fire him), has a theological dispute with the Reverend March, and has brief meetings or confrontations with dozens of other minor characters.

From Peter's standpoint, occasionally represented in the first person, these days are important because they give him a chance to get closer to his father, to come to terms with both the clumsy and the saintly aspects of his character. He sees George's self-pity, his carelessness about his person and appearance, his apparent neglect of his son's feelings, but also his selflessness, his interest in other people, his giving to others from inner resources he does not believe that he has. Moreover, the adventure feeds Peter's longing for the City (Alton and its hotel New Yorker) and the Future, from whose vantage point he will look back as a self-confessed second-rate abstract expressionist painter, committed to a life of secular sensuality symbolized by his black mistress. Recognizing their responsibility for each other, he will nevertheless be unable fully to grasp the nature of things which gives meaning to the lives and sacrifices he and his father have made.

On one level, then, the novel presents an attempt by Peter to understand, to find the cosmic dimensions according to which human lives have meaning in a world that science has made seem orderly but irrelevant. George Caldwell's science teaching sets up this secular framework of chance which Peter has internalized, although as an artist he may be out of step with it. As Chiron, however, George explains the mythological basis which informs the novel and Peter's memories to the students. Seen as Peter's retrospective attempt to reproduce that meaningful moment in his art, the mythological level is primarily a device that charges with supernatural values the adventures and encounters of those three days of winter exile. Thus George is ennobled as Chiron, as is Peter himself as Prometheus, his anxiety over his father's health being the rock to which the fire-bringer was chained, his affliction of psoriasis the daily devouring of the Titan's liver by the eagle sent by Zeus as punishment. The capable auto mechanic becomes Hephaestus, his sensuous wife Venus (Updike mixes Greek and Roman names somewhat at random), the doctor Apollo, the language teacher Artemis, the principal Zeus, Peter's mother Ceres, his grandfather Chronos, and his girl friend Pandora, whose unattainable "box" offers hope to sustain the still-untried artist and lover. Similarly, others met by George and Peter in their travels become Hermes (a foul-mouthed hitchhiker who steals George's gloves), Dionysus (a drunk who accuses George of sodomy and challenges him to accept death), Hades (the school janitor), Charon (the hotel clerk), Hera (the school board lady), Minos (the luncheonette owner), Dedalus (a recent graduate, now a pinball wizard with pornographic playing cards), Heracles (the school jock), and Ares (the minister), among others.

The parallels are not always ennobling, however; more often they are comic, giving the book a "mock epic" quality perhaps explainable in terms of Peter's vision if he is seen as consciously unable to realize fully the values he needs by means of a system of outmoded correspondence. Committed to the City and the Future, he can hardly grasp ultimate reality in terms of the pastoral and the past. An abstract expressionist and a hedonist, he can hardly be content with continuity and coherence in art or altruistic dedication to others in life. Much of the narrative, moreover, takes place away from Peter's sight and hearing and is not rendered to him by others, but rather to the reader as from an omniscient narrator. This, too, may be explained as Peter's chosen methodology, perhaps a neo-cubist combination of various modes of narration, realistic and surrealistic, first and third person, past and present tense, formally disjointed as an abstract canvas, collage, or poem. Such an explanation, however, makes the older Peter's problems of narration those of Updike, all but dissolving the distance between character and author.

There are similarities to be sure: Updike went to art school and freely acknowledges George Caldwell as a tribute to his own father. The differences are far greater, however, and a creator greater than Peter must be acknowledged in the degrees of fantasy applied to the story, extending it from earth toward an unreachable heaven, adumbrated in the book's epigraph by the theologian Karl Barth. Whereas Peter, like his father, is rather distanced from religious thinking, Updike, in this book as in others, employs a Christian perspective throughout, surrounding as it were one mythology with another, just as one fantasy encapsulates another in the technique of his narrative.

Chapter Two (like Four and Eight) shows Peter's first-person view of his present, incorporating and perhaps embellishing his memories of George Caldwell. Fantasy here turns primarily on symbol and allusion. Peter dreams, for example, of Penny turning into a tree, an image which comforts him although Chiron in Chapter One was troubled when Venus reminded him that his mother had done the same thing. Peter views his skin, which looks as if it had been pecked by a great bird, as a curse of God to make him a man (to grow up in Olinger, to lose his immortality in Greek myth). George observes that Pop Kramer will outlive him, which is inevitable if Kramer is Chronos, or time. George's electric clock on the wall keeps faster time than the one handed down by Kramer's father (Uranus, or heaven). Cassie's insistence on moving to the country (Firetown incorporates the starry heaven of medieval cosmology as well as the place from which Prometheus stole the fire) is inevitable for the spirit of grain and nature ("mama" even to George; in other words, Mother Earth). Pop Kramer seems to subsist entirely on bread (the Christian "staff of life"), his mouth consuming whole slices (as Chronos swallowed his children). When the trip to school gets under way, the car passes the Jewish cemetery, then the town of Galilee, and the hitchhiker (Hermes) suggests transition to the land of death.

Chapter Seven is similar, except that the viewpoint is omniscient, shifting back and forth between Peter and George; all of the other chapters involve greater doses of fantasy. Chapter Five is a fictionalized obituary of George as if he had died in 1947 at the age of fifty, written in a conventional, if florid, newspaper style, glorifying him as Peter might like him to be remembered. Chapter Three is also relatively straightforward, except that Caldwell is all but totally obscured in a rendering of Chiron among his students (including his daughter, Ocyrhoe, who foresees the day when Zeus will be seen as a toy manufactured by men).

Chiron and Caldwell coalesce in Chapters One and Nine, as do Peter and Prometheus in Chapter Six, in Updike's most daring "experiments," dissolving scenes and styles into one another. After Caldwell has the arrow removed from his leg, for example, he returns to class by cutting through the basement of the school, where he remembers once coming upon Vera Hummel nude in the girls' gym. In his memory, he becomes Chiron, and she Venus, in a scene using formal diction for both narrative and dialogue. On his return to the classroom, his lecture on scientific cosmology and evolution, foreshortening both time and space for easier understanding, is interrupted by a surrealistic fantasy in which objects come to life and the latent sexuality of the students (and the principal) becomes manifest. Similarly, Peter's agony "on my rock," as he worries about what his father's X-rays will show echoes Aeschylus' *Prometheus Bound* (date unknown) as various characters come to visit him—not separated by a chorus, however, but blending into one another. Although he also attends classes, having trouble in Latin with a scene in which Aeneas recognizes the true divinity of Venus, his mother, and learning about entropy in his father's class (where the sun is credited with being the author of all life and death is anticipated as a welcome rest), scenes flash by as if Peter were static, unable to move. At one point, his ostentatious red shirt is said to disintegrate, betraying his affliction to the ridicule of everyone. At another, he is visited by a character called "The Town" who finds it all but impossible to remember his father and says that they should never have moved away.

Framed by the Caldwell-as-Chiron chapters, the wanderings of George and Peter approximate the traditional form of the "romance" (labeled "the secular scripture" by Northrop Frye). After reaching Olinger, George faces Hades, Hephaestus, Minos, Charon, Dionysus, and other denizens of the underworld, while Peter finds the city of Alton and its seedy hotel a substitute for paradise. Before their return, Peter challenges Zimmerman (Prometheus versus Zeus), George confronts Marsh (Chiron versus Ares, or Mars), and Peter finally discovers the "nothing" between Penelope's legs which represents the central force of creativity (as well as all the evils of the world Pandora's box presumably contained). Confronting the snow on their second day of wanderings, both sense a purification, but Peter also fears its ghostly quality, and their car is once again disabled by it. Seen through the later Peter's recollection of the Alton museum, incorporating all levels of romance from heaven to hell, Vera Hummel (Venus) presents her warm, maternal side, and in her house Peter comes to see that he cannot expect miracles. Finally, on their return, although George is criticized by his father-in-law for not having brought back the *Sun* (newspaper), he has brought the groceries and a sense of acceptance, while Peter (whose psoriasis also badly needs the sun and the spring) goes back up the stairs to his bedroom, as welcome to his mother as Persephone (another unacknowledged parallel) was to hers.

The three-day exile corresponds to the traditional rite of passage (the kernel of the "monomyth" to Joseph Campbell), one important variant of which in man's world is the Crucifixion and Resurrection of Christ. Although the Christian world view is not as explicit and intrusive as the Graeco-Roman, it is never far away in an Updike fiction. The epigraph from Karl Barth, Updike's favorite theologian, informs the whole novel, pointing up the inability of man ever to comprehend the universe and its maker. The gap in distance and in magnitude is too great, whether it be viewed in terms of the endless numbers of modern science, the fables of ancient Greece, or the faith-demanding postulates of Christian theology. A leap of faith is required in any context to claim for man a place between heaven and earth, god and beast. Fusing these contexts and concepts in the centaur (Chiron, Caldwell and his car) and *The Centaur*, Updike has created a multileveled fantasy in which the distance is mediated in three ways. George Caldwell surrenders all claim to fame and success so that Peter (and others) may grow to surpass him; Chiron gives up his immortality so that Prometheus may live, however punished, after making his own gesture toward man; and Christ abandons his mortal life on behalf of all that accept Him. While the continued existence of the first and last of these outside the book is problematical, within the text the Epilogue makes certain that the reader knows the fate of Chiron, elevated by Zeus to the stars.

David N. Samuelson

Bibliography

Burchard, Raphael. *John Updike: Yea Sayings*, 1971.

Hamilton, Alice, and Kenneth Hamilton. *The Elements of John Updike*, 1970.

Hunt, George W., S. J. *John Updike and the Three Great Secret Things: Sex, Religion, and Art*, 1980.

Markle, Joyce B. *Fighters and Lovers: Theme in the Novels of John Updike*, 1973.

Uphaus, Suzanne Henning. *John Updike*, 1980.

Vargo, Edward P. *Rainstorms and Fire: Ritual in the Novels of John Updike*, 1973.

CHANGELING
and
MADWAND

Author: Roger Zelazny (1937-   )
First book publications: Changeling (1981); *Madwand* (1981)
Type of work: Novels
Time: An indeterminate future
Locale: Earth and a parallel world governed by magic rather than science

The changeling Pol Detson, reared on Earth as Daniel Chain, must return to his home world and reclaim his family powers in order to restore the balance of the universe

> *Principal characters:*
> POL DETSON, a changeling and wizard
> DANIEL CHAIN, OR MARK MARAKSON, the earth-child exchanged for Pol
> MOR, the white magician who exchanges them
> MOUSEGLOVE, a clever thief befriended by Pol
> MOONBIRD, the father of dragons
> HENRY SPIER, the Madwand
> BELPHANIOR, a demon-spirit created by Det Morson to protect his son Pol
> DET MORSON, father of Pol Detson, son of Mor

Changeling and *Madwand* are further attempts by Roger Zelazny at exploring the nature and destiny of man through the vehicle of fantasy. By focusing on the question of personal and social identity in a context of the interrelation of fate or destiny, free will, and chance or accident (much in the spirit of Greek drama), he is able to dramatize these themes. Zelazny is primarily concerned with external religious and cultural dimensions in *Changeling* and with internal psychological and emotional ones in *Madwand*. The shift in point of view from a totally external third-person perspective to a significantly internal first-person point of view brings an immediacy to the second work which is lacking in the first.

Pol Detson is a character in the mold of Zelazny's other characters, including the Jack of Shadows and Corwin of Amber; the parallels with Corwin are particularly interesting. As Corwin grows in consciousness throughout the Amber series, the novels themselves improve dramatically. There is a richer texture, both of language and image, and a much fuller sense of character, with expanded psychological and emotional dimensions, as the drama shifts from an external to an internal one. This same shift makes *Madwand* a more interesting and complex novel than *Changeling*.

Like many of Zelazny's earlier works, these novels are set in two parallel worlds. One world is governed by the principles of magic and is afraid of science; the villagers try to kill Mark Marakson for his creation of a steam engine and then a solar car, to replace the horse and buggy. The other world is governed by the principles of science but is afraid of magic. Yet the cosmic "law of symmetry" requires that the Balance be kept between the two worlds, as well as between magic and science and good and evil. When this Balance was upset in the past, an evidently atomic cataclysm occurred, nearly destroying both worlds and deforming many of their inhabitants. The two worlds have been split, one now totally governed by magic, the other by science. In the world without science, fearful villagers live in primitive conditions; on the other hand, science without magic has created an Earth-world which is totally artificial, composed of synthetic trees and grass. The plot of *Changeling* revolves around the need to replace one child with another, since the people fear the possibility that Pol performs black magic. Mor must walk a shining, golden road between the alternate worlds of magic and science to exchange Pol and Dan. It is a passage through time as well as space, reflected in the comic touch of Pol later meeting the March Hare as he walks the road himself. In ridding their world of one threat, the villagers bring upon themselves a greater one, the intrusion of the feared science through Mark. Mark is eventually destroyed by Pol at the end of *Changeling*, or at least is defeated and disappears. *Madwand* focuses on Pol's pilgrimage to discover his full powers, and the plot of the Madwand, Henry Spier, to tip the Balance forever by opening the Gate to Hell and letting out black powers that no one will be able to control.

Changeling begins with an ending, as many of Zelazny's novels do. The people and the white wizard Mor are in the process of overthrowing the black sorcerer Det Morson and destroying the Keep of Rondoval, because Det has tipped the Balance between good and evil. The problem of the relationship between authority and power is a central issue in the family struggle here. Det is Mor's son, as his name reveals; Pol will later do battle both with his stepbrother Mark and his brother Larick. Though the dramatic opening is somewhat weakened by inappropriately colloquial contemporary American slang, the essential conflict is made clear. The forces of white magic will strive to keep the Balance intact, both between good and evil and between magic and science; the forces of black magic will seek to tip the scales, perhaps permanently. Though Det is defeated and killed, his scepter of power cannot be destroyed. Mor's breaking it into three pieces, thus separating the magics of fire, earth, and air and banishing the pieces to the three corners of the Magical Triangle of Int, provides Pol with the quest which begins to unlock for him the mystery of his identity.

Pol (known as Daniel Chain on Earth) and Daniel Chain (known as Mark Marakson in Pol's home world) are alter egos, each embodying the dominant characteristics of his own world. Pol is intuitive and uses both music and words of power to control the fabric of reality. His music, in fact, at one point brings centaurs dancing in a growing pattern, as did Conrad Nomikos' music in *This Immortal* (1966). Pol's allies are the figurines, black sorcerers imprisoned in small statuettes by his father. The figurines suggest that fate, rather than free will, rules the universe and that all are pawns in a cosmic chess game. Dan-Mark is logical, and his ally-mentor is the "teaching machine," a computer-library which is his source of power. He provides a classic example of the traditional problems of the artist and society, with the added ironic twist that he is rejected for his science but not his art. The villagers, who in the postcataclysmic age have rejected science and kept magic, look on him as villagers everywhere have looked on Dr. Frankenstein figures. They curse him, stone him, and drive him away for awakening the "forbidden things" of science. Both Pol and Mark are rejected by the villagers for being out of the ordinary, and both desire revenge on them for killing their fathers. Each has a great power over others, and each struggles with the corrupting aspect of his power. Pol is able to let go of his desire for vengeance; Mark is not. Yet in this "undying conflict" between magic and science, the figurines are nearly able to convince Pol (and the reader as well) that science is the agent of insurgency and must be destroyed by magic, the agent of preservation. Instead, both magic and science are balanced parts in the cosmic dance.

Changeling ends when Pol, with the help of Mouseglove and Moonbird, wins a Pyrrhic victory: Mark has seemingly been destroyed by Pol, and Pol has "won" the girl Nora, whom they both desire, by throwing away his scepter of power. (One of the flaws in *Madwand* is that Nora is dropped from the plot with only a brief sentence and no dramatic reason.)

The structure of *Madwand* is framed by a device that makes it considerably more complex and interesting than *Changeling*. The novel opens with a "spirit" which is searching for its identity, making explicit a central underlying theme in the first book, the quest for self-knowledge, and acting as counterpoint to Pol's continuing quest for himself. This spirit is Belphanior, the Curse of Rondoval, a demon-spell created by Det out of the raw material of creation to protect Pol. The process by which the spirit comes to realize its power and purpose closely parallels Pol's and is akin to that of Jack and his soul in Zelazny's *Jack of Shadows* (1971). *Madwand* ends with Belphanior's choosing to identify with Pol, and the realization that Pol contains within himself a mirror image, his own dark, sorcerous side, reflected in the image of the father Det. The novel's "ending," in fact, is not an ending at all; Spier the Madwand has escaped with one of the figurines, which are the keys that will open permanently the Gate to Hell, and there is jealousy between Pol and Larick over the love of Ryle Munson's entranced daughter, Taisa.

The structure of *Madwand* is that of a *Bildungsroman*, its subject being Pol's education as a madwand magician. His flight has become a quest, and he must progress through ten stages of initiation into his full power. During the process, he is imprisoned by his brother Larick (though neither of them realizes that they are brothers at this point), who fears that he is a black sorcerer—black not only for using "morally objectionable" forces, but also because the use of those forces inevitably warps the character of the magician himself.

Madwand is a novel of unexpected twists and turns, both of character and of plot. The figurines, which were crucial allies of Pol in *Changeling*, and Henry Spier, who aids him here, both turn out to be evil enemies; the wizards Munson and Larick, with whom Pol fights and whom he believes to be evil, turn out to be good and his allies. The indications are that Pol will continue to develop as a character, perhaps on the order of Corwin in the classic Amber novels.

Clark Mayo

Bibliography
Sanders, Joe. *Roger Zelazny: A Primary and Secondary Bibliography*, 1980.
_____ . "Zelazny: Unfinished Business," in *Voices for the Future*, 1978. Edited by Thomas D. Clareson.
Yoke, Carl B. *Roger Zelazny*, 1979.

THE CHARWOMAN'S SHADOW

Author: Lord Dunsany (Edward John Moreton Drax Plunkett, 1878-1957)
First book publication: 1926
Type of work: Novel
Time: The Christian Middle Ages
Locale: A tower and an enchanted wood in Spain, near Aragona

Sent by his father to learn the Black Art of making gold, a young man first loses his shadow to his magician-teacher and then wins it back, together with that of his helper, the magician's charwoman

> *Principal characters:*
> RAMON ALONZO, the young hero
> GONSALVO, Lord of the Tower and Rocky Forest, his father
> MIRANDOLA, his sister
> THE DUKE OF SHADOW VALLEY, Mirandola's eventual husband
> THE MAGICIAN, Ramon's instructor in the Black Art
> ANEMONE, ALIAS DOCKWEED, the magician's charwoman

The central fable of *The Charwoman's Shadow*, Lord Dunsany's third full-length fantasy, is a simple one. A young man, Ramon Alonzo, is sent by Gonsalvo, his father and Lord of the Tower and Rocky Forest, to learn from a magician the art of making gold, which is needed for the dowry of Mirandola, Ramon Alonzo's sister. The young man finds that the fee for this knowledge is his shadow. It seems a trivial price, but before long, he meets the charwoman who sweeps the magician's house and who counsels him very forcefully against the exchange; she sold her shadow long ago for the rest of her life and regrets the bargain bitterly. Nevertheless, the family's need for gold drives the young man to surrender his shadow, and he discovers that alienation from humanity, weariness, and eventual damnation must indeed be the result. He therefore determines to steal back his shadow, together with the charwoman's, from the box where the magician keeps them. In the end, he succeeds, and also by this time, his sister has arranged her marriage without a dowry by means of the love-potion he has sent. Furthermore, the charwoman's rescued shadow is that of a young girl, and when she and it are fitted together, she is rejuvenated, substance conforming to shadow instead of the other way around. All live happily ever after, even the magician, who retires to the strange "Country Towards Moon's Rising," taking with him, like a Pied Piper, the imps and elves and magic creatures of the world, so that the story concludes with the end of "the Golden Age."

By comparison with most fantasies, *The Charwoman's Shadow* has a very narrow scope. The setting, for the most part, is restricted to the magician's house and Gonsalvo's tower; there are few characters; and the peculiar creatures in the background (apart from the imps whom the magician catches to cook his food) are not described in any detail. Perhaps especially surprising is that, unlike many "sorceror's apprentice" stories, this novel offers little discussion of the rules and nature of magic; at the same time, it contains practically no symbolism or covert meaning. For example, one might expect the "shadows," of which so much is made, to symbolize personality or humanity or some other abstract quality, but they do not; the world of *The Charwoman's Shadow* is exactly as it appears to be, with no external connections, hidden meanings, or grand designs. Instead, the appeal of this slight and whimsical fantasy lies in the author's highly distinctive, even idiosyncratic, style.

The most obvious feature of Dunsany's style is its grave and elaborate courtesy. This fits the setting, the aristocratic Spain of grandees and hidalgos before Don Quixote was invented to expose it to satire. All the characters in the book assume, or at least pretend to assume, that anyone can do anything and that failure can only be the result of some willful quirk or decision. The magician gravely commends Ramon Alonzo's grandfather for his philosophy—in the field of boar-hunting, as it happens—and regrets "that his studies gave him no time for that last erudition which would have ensured his survival to these days and beyond them." In fact, as the reader suspects, Ramon's sporting grandfather pursued no studies and had no erudition; but this will never be admitted. Similarly, on calling for Father Joseph to write his letter, Gonsalvo remarks that in youth he learned the art of writing in case occasion for it should ever arise; however, he is out of practice, which explains the need for Father Joseph. Words such as "forgotten" or "illiterate" would be condemned by all as mere barbarisms. The story's setting, then, demands a stiff ceremoniousness.

One example of this formality is Ramon's request to the magician to teach him to read. This the magician does, at the price of half of Ramon's eyesight, taking him through consonants, vowels, commas, colons, the reason the "j" is dotted, and "many another mystery." All this is expounded before Ramon's "awed and wondering eyes." He would detail the mystery further, Dunsany explains, "but the thought comes to me that my reader is necessarily versed in this mystery, and for that reason alone I say no more on this magnificent theme." He leaves the scene instead, but he remarks as he does so that while the young man and the magician worked together, "they heard outside in the passage the doleful sweeping of the shadowless woman that minded that awful house."

There is heavy irony in words such as "mystery," "awed," or "magnificent," since the modern reader does not regard literacy as a mystery; on the other hand, he does not know about shadows, and the presence of the "shadowless" charwoman keeps the magician at least in a position of threat. Therefore, if this knowledgeable person regards reading as a "mystery," could he not be right? Finally, there is an overall sense almost of conspiracy; as the author, like a Spanish grandee, persists in treating his reader with an elaborate courtesy which assumes that both are on the same exalted level, he invites the reader to suspend disbelief, to accept even writing as a part of the Black Art.

Both the style and the content of *The Charwoman's Shadow* continually present and challenge concepts of naïveté. Ramon is a young man with no experience of anything but hunting; his family is poor and credulous, but full of absurd pretensions; and the charwoman is a nobody. Against all of these figures, the magician seems to be a figure of power and knowledge whose art has suggestive connections with modern science that give it legitimacy for the reader. For example, he teaches Ramon that transmutation starts with the perception that all elements are of the same fundamental nature, an idea relatively advanced for 1926, let alone for "the Golden Age." The magician sees subtlety where the reader sees simplicity, as in Ramon's grandfather's skill in boar-hunting, which the magician describes as one of "the four great branches of learning," since it leads infallibly to happiness—an argument not easy to refute. It is also true that the instinctive courage of the young hero opens the shadow-box, which all the magician's art cannot keep locked; and his sister does not seem to need a love-potion to get her way. Perhaps naïveté is wisdom; perhaps the author's dignified misapprehensions contain some sense; perhaps fantasy contains insights barred to sober realism.

Such is the tacit argument underlying Dunsany's carefully chosen authorial personality. It works so powerfully that one of the story's charms is indeed its many didactic passages, or pauses, in which the author slowly lectures his readers on youth and age, ambition and oblivion, self-centeredness and detachment, and much more. Few writers achieve sufficient moral authority to be able to do this successfully.

One final aspect of Dunsany's art also demands recognition, for in it, he has never been matched. This is his ability to suggest, suddenly and with extreme economy, wholly new vistas as if on the edge of vision. In *The Charwoman's Shadow*, it becomes increasingly clear that the Black Art is opposed to Christianity and that even Ramon's minor traffickings with the former must lead to his damnation, unless he wins back his shadow. When Ramon dares to ask the magician about salvation one day, he receives the indignant and contemptuous reply that salvation is "a thing common to countless millions," containing neither knowledge nor preeminence. He would prefer to flame "beside the Count of the Mountain, who held the Chair of Magic at Saragossa," declares the magician, than share a vulgar Heaven. Before that Count, kings in hell abase themselves on the sulfur. The reader has never before heard of "Chairs of Magic," still less of continuing fame after death; the image of burning greatness, known to all but the reader and Ramon, extends the scope of the story with a sudden flash. In the same way, brief glimpses are given of the strange journeys into interstellar space on which the magician sends his captive shadows and of the arcane researches he pursues; these whet the appetite without satisfying it.

Perhaps the most powerful of all the story's sudden disclosures is that of the "Country Towards Moon's Rising." It is mentioned by one member of a suspicious crowd looking at Ramon and the rejuvenated charwoman, after their escape from the magician; and when he says its name, all open their eyes wider:

> That land lies not only beyond salvation, but the dooms of the Last Judgement cross not its borders either; so that those who have trafficked in magic and known the Black Art walk abroad there boldly, unpunished; a most dreadful sight. Only they must come to it before ever they die; for then it is too late.

The desire for a land which is neither Earth, Heaven, nor hell, and where the bitter choice of good obedience or evil independence need not be made, is old in folklore. Nevertheless, Dunsany's vision of it is entirely original, although presented once more as something everyone knows and of which everyone disapproves—"a most dreadful sight." Nor can this vision be interpreted as mere wish-fulfillment because of the words "too late"; they hint at a set of rules and constraints outside common knowledge, but nevertheless exploitable by one who understands them. It is a particularly successful ending, therefore, to have the magician decide after the loss of his shadows that he is too old to carry on, so that he retires not to the flames of hell with the Count of the Mountain, but to the glittering rampart and welcoming trumpets of the country where magic is at home and where his true worth is recognized.

In this fantasy, realism and common humanity are, in the end, victorious; but the novel creates a yearning for what has been irrevocably lost, whether shadow-journeys, Black Art, or the Golden Age.

T. A. Shippey

Bibliography
Amory, Mark. *Biography of Lord Dunsany*, 1972.
de Camp, L. Sprague. "Two Men in One: Lord Dunsany," in *Literary Swordsmen and Sorcerors*, 1976.

CHIMERA

Author: John Barth (1930-   )
First book publication: 1972
Type of work: Novel
Time: The pre-classical era, the Middle Ages, and the early 1970's
Locale: Greece, Samarkand, and coastal Maryland

An unsung heroine, a major hero, and a minor antihero turn the crucial events in their lives into stories, the telling of which becomes possibly even more fantastic than the events themselves

> *Principal characters:*
> SCHEHEREZADE, the legendary teller of *The Thousand and One Nights*
> DUNYAZADE, her younger sister, who has a story of her own
> THE GENIE, a present-day writer who materializes in Samarkand
> PERSEUS, a mythical demigod who slew the Gorgon, Medusa
> CALYXA, a "priestess" who cares for Perseus and his shrine
> THE "NEW" MEDUSA, reborn to become Perseus' lover in the sky
> DELIADES, OR BELLEROPHON, a mortal who thinks he is his demi-god brother, Bellerus
> MELANIPPE, an Amazon warrior who becomes Bellerophon's lover
> POLYEIDUS, a tutor of Bellerus and Deliades

Co-winner of the 1973 National Book Award for Fiction, *Chimera* was the logical culmination, to that date, of John Barth's "experiments" with story-telling. After two basically realistic novels, *The Floating Opera* (1956) and *The End of the Road* (1958), *The Sot-Weed Factor* (1960) was considerably more involved, a pseudohistory of colonial Maryland in which one character makes up a biography of another who may never have existed. On the fringe of fantasy, this historical romance drew the attention of critics who saw it fulfilling the pattern of traditional heroic myth and legend.

After reading Lord Raglan's *The Hero* (1936) and Joseph Campbell's *The Hero with a Thousand Faces* (1949, both cited in *Chimera*), Barth deliberately set out to ring all the changes on the traditional pattern in *Giles Goat-Boy: Or, The Revised New Syllabus* (1965), a surprise best-seller. Mixing allegory, satire, science fiction, fantasy, epic, and farce, this "Revised New Syllabus," a mock-scripture on computer tape, ostensibly edited (if not plagiarized) by Barth, fulfilled the metaphor of the universe as university. Story forms continued to multiply, metamorphosize, and intermingle in *Lost in the Funhouse* (1968), a collection of fictions, several for oral performance. Narrators include a sperm, an echo, a tape recorder; one narrator has to cope with seven separate, telescoped tellings of the same story. Point of view and other technical matters move so far into the foreground that the hero of the book becomes the artist.

These matters and more are bound up in *Chimera*, which, like the mythical monster from which it takes its name, is tripartite, monstrous, and specifically literary in origin. Part lion, part goat, part serpent, winged and fire-breathing, the chimera is monstrous in the sense of "misshapen" as well as "threatening." Where it appears in the third story, both its existence and its slaying are matters of hearsay, its female gender is a matter of contention, and the weapon used to kill it—a lump of lead on the end of a spear—is suspiciously metaphorical. Problems of hearsay, anachronism, and metaphorical and documentary form distort all three stories from the standpoint of traditional storytelling. Their convoluted construction, as stories about stories about storytelling, in which narrators literally become their narratives, threatens the mental comfort of the reader.

Third in order of composition, and originally placed third in the sequence, the *Dunyazadiade* begins the collection with two heroines whose lives parallel *in extremis* the situation of the modern writer as Barth sees it. Scheherezade must literally publish or perish. Her sister, Dunyazade, faces on her wedding night an "audience," her husband, reputed to have done and heard everything that her sexual and narrative "performance" could possibly offer. She holds his attention by tying him up and threatening his vital parts with a razor. Before their position as narrator and audience is revealed, however, she tells the "real" story of how Scheherezade got the stories that she told. Dunyazade claims that a Genie from the future recited them orally, having memorized them from a book collecting what her sister was reported to have told. This time travel was originally precipitated when both Scheherezade and the Genie were unable to produce, and they came simultaneously to the conclusion that "the key to the treasure is the treasure." The Genie, a novelist blocked in the middle of writing three long stories about storytelling, is of course a fictional analogue of Barth himself.

Considerably longer, the *Perseid* continues the legend of Perseus beyond the traditional stories. Narrated by Perseus from two vantage points in time and space, it opens with his discovering himself in a shrine, being cared for by Calyxa, a combination of nymph, priestess, caretaker, and graduate student. Suffering a mid-life crisis, like the Genie of the first tale, Perseus is better able to perform orally, recounting his adventures to date, than sexually, his premature ejaculations corresponding to his premature giving up on adventure in his life. Having found something missing in his middle years, he has tried to restore it, first by revisiting the places of his saga and second by retelling his legend and trying to find what went wrong. Finally, he redirects his actions in the sequel, gradually becoming less self-centered. His life story thus spirals around itself, not only in his telling of it, but also in the shape of his shrine, on whose walls Calyxa is painting low-relief murals representing his feats. The whole of his story, including what he relates to Calyxa, Perseus nightly tells Medusa in their roles as stellar constellations, circling each other and the Earth, whose population thus becomes his ultimate audience.

Longer still, by the same ratio, the *Bellerophoniad* elaborates still further on the problems of storytelling and the difficulty of knowing what to do; for this "hero as artist," moreover, his heroism is as much in doubt as his artistry. Self-acknowledged as "a perfect imitation of a mythic hero," Bellerophon is even confused as to who he is; ostensibly "Bellerus the killer," his name turns out to mean "killer of Bellerus"; that is, his brother, Deliades. Successful as a provincial administrator, doted on by his wife, Philonoë, in contrast to Perseus' nagging Andromeda, Bellerophon longs in middle age to complete the "pattern" of the mythic hero described to him by his tutor, Polyeidus.

Trying to do so, he assaults Mount Olympus on his winged horse but, like his mythological namesake, Barth's hero falls when Pegasus is bitten by a gadfly. Instead of wandering the Earth alone like his model, as he would in fact prefer to do, this version of Bellerophon floats in the marshes of Maryland, home of Barth (and the Genie), in the form of a bundle of letters comprising his story and considerable commentary on it. Both document and gadfly are Polyeidus, a minor shape-shifting deity whose other guises include such documents as the *Perseid*, the heroic pattern (adapted from Campbell), letters from characters in previous Barth novels, and a lecture by Barth himself on his own past, present, and future books and characters.

Self-consciousness personified, Bellerophon lacks the spontaneity and the above-average gifts of the true heroic personality. His story's title emphasizes his "phoniness," as does the fact that his heroic feats depend almost entirely on Pegasus. A traditional symbol for artistic inspiration, the winged horse in later years cannot get off the ground without a dose of "hippomanes," identified by the story (but not elsewhere) as an aphrodisiac herb. Bellerophon's life and story are similarly grounded, the former in part by a regard for women's rights somewhat unseemly for a classical hero, the latter seemingly by whatever happens to come to Barth's mind. Bellerophon's own judgment on the result is given in his next-to-last speech, in which he terms his narrative a "beastly fiction, ill-proportioned, full of longueurs, lumps . . . lacunae, a kind of monstrous mixed metaphor." His last words declare "It's no *Bellerophoniad*. It's a."

Originally, the *Dunyazadiade* would have concluded the sequence, its optimistic ending on "Good morning" being followed by an auctorial epilogue. With "Good evening" central to the *Perseid*, when the constellation Medusa rises in the sky, and "Good night" beginning the *Bellerophoniad*, the sequence is still preserved by starting over, but then the first word met is "Chimera," characterizing the entire book as a document, a figment of the imagination, a phantasia, a veritable treasure trove of what might be called "chimerical engineering." Although it contains fantasies and fantasizing, the book also concerns the positions of the storyteller and the audience participating in such acts. As content and technique are inseparable in fiction, so are they in life, especially in the emotion and act of love. As the stories explore varied relations between speaker and hearer, so do they delineate varied relations between male and female, striving, if not for absolute equality, at least for a dynamic state of equilibrium. As the narrators grapple with their material and the form in which to present it, they also come to realize the need to live in the present without constantly making comparisons with the fabled past or the idealized future.

The book abounds in fantasies, of course, not only mythic heroes and heroines, but also such impossible creatures as a flying horse and a chimera, as well as such concepts as time travel and metamorphosis. Sheer physical impossibility may not strain the reader's credulity as much as the anachronisms, particularly the conceit that all the narrators are afflicted with mid-twentieth century self-consciousness. Like the Genie, Perseus and Bellerophon are middle-aged and balding; like these three males, Dunyazade is also floundering in memories and indecision. They all try to tell the stories of their lives in order to arrive at some sort of understanding about themselves, while they realize that neither the life nor telling the story is simple. Moreover, telling one's story is recycling one's life, not getting on with it, and the story cannot end until the life does, at which point a pattern may emerge, but one is normally not around to tell it. Thus Perseus' story is ultimately recycled in the sky, Bellerophon's in the swamp, his voice one of many in a document subject to commentary and misinterpretation; long since committed to writing in the Genie's time, Scheherezade's stories are now opened to doubt regarding their authorship, and Dunyazade's story is preserved only in Barth's invention.

The difficulty each narrator has with expression is as much the content of the narrative as the story each has to tell. Matters of technique—the only thing writers can talk about, Scheherezade and the Genie agree—become the story, holding the reader's attention with the problems of how to hold the reader's attention. This situation is perhaps best embodied in the image of a snail in the Maryland marshes mentioned by the Genie (who says he may have invented it). This creature picks up bits and pieces everywhere it goes and from them secretes its shell, each new chamber being as large as the last two combined. This spiral image is repeated in Perseus' shrine, and in the relative length of the stories in the book, while the pace of the snail is also appropriate to Barth's self-conscious narratives.

Problems of self-consciousness stem from education, with which Barth has some anachronistic and self-contradictory fun. Saving the lives of the kingdom's maidens, for example, is a task not comprehended by Scheherezade's university studies in psychology and political science, while Calyxa, a graduate student in mythology, finds that her studies have not prepared her for coping with a real live mythic hero. Philonoë has also studied mythology at the local university, while Bellerophon has learned the subject from his tutor. Education need not depend on literacy, of course; documents may in fact be more suspect than the living tale. Indeed, Scheherezade gets her stories and relays them orally, while her sister learns about both literature and sex by living illustration. Perseus rehearses his life story endlessly; his reeducation at the hands of Calyxa unfolds in murals. His telling of the story in the sky, however, is punctuated by references to pages and paragraphs, suggesting a paradox that is deepened in the third story. Bellerophon is explicitly illiterate, barely able to write his initial, but he also reads the *Perseid* and the written version of the mythic pattern, and in later years, he endlessly scribbles his memoirs to the despair of his mistress Melanippe, an Amazon used to somewhat more action.

Like any heroic yarn, these narratives do concern feats of daring and sexual adventures, but they also feature elements of prudence and sexual failure. To talk of storytelling, Barth maintains, is almost by definition to use sexual metaphors—rising action, climax, falling action—but he is also parallelling relationships between male and female with those between narrator and listener. Neither is complete without the other, but neither is superior or inferior, either. Variations on the theme of equality occur throughout the book.

After the king has held Scheherezade's life by a thread for 1,001 nights, he arranges for himself and his brother to marry her and her sister. As Dunyazade tells her story, however, she holds her king's life at razor-point until he tells her he is not the rake and murderer his brother is. Unsure whether to trust him—he may be able to spring his guards on her, despite his protestations—she is asked to do so, to act *as if* they were equals.

Perseus regards sex as his due as a mythic hero, though failure is not a complete stranger to him before Calyxa. Her avidity upsets his balance; like storytelling, potency cannot be rushed or forced. Deserted by Andromeda for living in the past, adopted by Calyxa (as one among three demigods she serves), he finds happiness with the "New" Medusa after he has learned to trust. Their eternal happiness, however, is restricted to the night sky, where it can never be consummated and never grow stale, even as his story can never end.

Bellerophon is troubled not so much by his sex drive as by his concern with sexual relations. After raping the Amazon Melanippe in his youth, he repents of forcing anyone against her will. Retracing his steps (emulating Perseus and the pattern), he resists attempted seduction by Anteia, who rails against the "impossibility" of rape *by* a female. Philonoë lets him leave a fruitful and prosperous marriage in search of his destiny, and another Melanippe (no relation) takes him up, willingly forsaking her Amazon upbringing for the sake of home and family. His situation is summed up in his most memorable feat, a triumph of uncertainty: he may or may not have slain the Chimera, which may or may not have existed, and may or may not have been female.

Given the parallels offered between the Genie and the heroes, not to mention Barth's own circumstances during the writing of *Chimera*—he divorced his wife and married a younger woman—there are obviously elements of autobiography present, but they are in a sense universalized, just as the writer's block he suffered during the composition was turned to good use in the composition itself. Embodied in the Tragic View of Sex and Temperament, enunciated by Dunyazade's king, and the Tragic View of Marriage and Parenthood, alluded to by Bellerophon's mistress, is the realization that nothing lasts and one must make the best of what one has. The problems of life and love, like those of storytelling, can best be solved simply by getting on with it, accepting the answer arrived at by Scheherazade and her Genie: "The key to the treasure is the treasure."

David N. Samuelson

Bibliography

Glaser-Wöhrer, Evelyn. *An Analysis of John Barth's Weltanschauung: His View of Life and Literature*, 1977.

Jones, Steven. "The Legends of Perseus and John Barth's *Chimera*," in *Folklore*. XI (1978), pp. 140-151.

MacKenzie, Ursula. "John Barth's *Chimera* and the Strictures of Reality," in *Journal of American Studies*. X (1976), pp. 91-101.

Morrell, David. *John Barth: An Introduction*, 1976.

Powell, Jerry. "John Barth's *Chimera*: A Creative Response to the Literature of Exhaustion," in *Critique*. XVIII (1976), pp. 59-72.

Tharpe, Jac. *John Barth: The Comic Sublimity of Paradox*, 1974.

Warrick, Patricia. "The Circuitous Journey in John Barth's *Chimera*," in *Critique*. XVIII (1976), pp. 73-85.

CHRISTMAS STORIES

Author: Charles Dickens (1812-1870)
First book publications: A Christmas Carol (1843); *The Chimes* (1844); *The Haunted Man* (1848)
Type of work: Novellas
Time: The mid-nineteenth century
Locale: London

Novellas written for publication as Christmas booklets, combining sentimentality with a fierce concern for the plight of the London poor

Five times within a span of six years, Charles Dickens wrote a "Christmas Book." The fourth of the series, *The Battle of Life* (1846), is entirely non-fantastic, and in the third, *The Cricket on the Hearth* (1846), the supernatural plays only a peripheral role. In the other three, supernatural visitations provide the means by which the plots are moved and their resolutions secured. The first of these is, of course, *A Christmas Carol*; the others are *The Chimes* and *The Haunted Man*. Later, when Dickens at last managed to launch his own periodical successfully with *Household Words* (first issued in 1850), he followed a policy of issuing an extra Christmas number every year, but the fiction featured there was mostly short, insignificant, and nonfantastic.

All three of the major Christmas fantasies share the same structure. Each one is organized around a crisis in the affairs of a protagonist, which is precipitated by supernatural intervention. The reader is first presented with a description of the life-style and world view of each protagonist and then is made to share with him a dreamlike supernatural experience. As a result of these experiences, the protagonists learn to see the world through new eyes and to evaluate their lives and actions in different terms; each undergoes a powerful and drastic moral renewal. This formula allowed Dickens to pack his narratives with emotive writing, to plumb the depths of horror and despair, and to return precipitately to dizzy heights of exaltation in a fashion which would have seemed inappropriate in his lengthier novels.

There is hardly any need to summarize the plot of *A Christmas Carol*; it is one of the rare stories which *everyone* knows in some detail, regardless of whether he has ever read the text. The names of the characters, the events of the plot, and even some snatches of dialogue have become part of the common currency of modern folklore. Ebenezer Scrooge has become a literary archetype, the most renowned character invented by a man who specialized in the production of memorable characters.

A Christmas Carol is by far the best of the Christmas stories; it is superior to the others on every count. It is a fast-moving story, packed with incident and written with a descriptive economy which Dickens never matched in any of his other works. The human characters are sharply drawn, while the supernatural visitors who take Scrooge traveling through time and space are magnificent allegorical figures: the first an embodiment of idealized childhood, the second a jovial merrymaker, and the third a shrouded avatar of Death. The urgency of the call for social reform through the exercise of charity and goodwill is emphasized by its clarity; the neat description of Christmas with the Cratchit family is juxtaposed with the moment of stark symbolism in which the second spirit draws back the hem of its opulent robe to reveal man's feral children, the boy who is Ignorance and the girl who is Want. It is a story remarkable for its sensitivity as well as its sentimentality. Significantly, it has no villains, and the scenes snatched from Scrooge's past life provide an unusually elegant account of the slow compounding of injurious circumstances which have made him what he is, unable to accept the lifelines thrown to him all too rarely by those who have his best interests at heart.

That none of the other Christmas stories measures up to such a high standard is hardly surprising, but even considered in isolation, they have their disappointing aspects. In *The Chimes*, Dickens attempted to follow up his tour de force with a more dramatic and demanding appeal for the cultivation of a better social conscience. It is a magnificently angry story that presents with scalding intensity an image of the horrible desperation of the London poor. The story's protagonist, Trotty Veck, is a more vulgar Bob Cratchit, an essentially decent man squeezed nearly to death by constricting circumstance. He clearly belongs to the social group that the Victorian mythology of careful philanthropy dubbed the "deserving" poor; he is scrupulously honest and knows his place. Also featured in the story is Will Fern, a paradigm of the kind of poor man considered undeserving—a vagrant jailbird—and the plea which Dickens utters on his behalf is scarcely less strong. He is shown as a helpless victim of circumstance with no available escape even to the steady wretchedness of the likes of Trotty Veck.

Trotty Veck is a ticket-porter whose pitch is in the shadow of an old church whose wind-buffeted bells measure out the time of his life. His daughter Meg is engaged to be married, but the marriage has been frequently postponed because of their poverty. In the course of a typical day's work, Trotty is confronted with a number of gentlemen who take time out to offer observations on the condition of his kind. Alderman Cute believes that the city poor are a new and threatening race who must be controlled by relentless oppression in order to preserve the order handed down from the "good old times." Mr. Filer is a devotee of political economy for whom the poor themselves and the goods which supply the necessities of their lives are simply statistics to be juggled within a Malthusian equation. Sir Joseph Bowley is an archetype of the discriminating philanthropist who doles out meager charity in return for extravagant demonstrations of deference, gratitude, and moral probity.

Trotty is himself a victim of the propaganda which these poseurs distribute.

He interprets his own situation and the world he reads about in the yellow press in the light of these theories, accepting that the poor are "born bad," that they are a burden on society to be patiently borne by the rich, and that they have a duty to be content with a lot that includes no right to life or liberty. He is disillusioned by an enchantment, when the bells in the church tower call him into a vision of possible futures, in which the doctrines which he has been prepared to accept impose their logical consequences upon his own situation and those of his friends and loved ones, grinding them implacably to destruction.

Trotty Veck is not called upon to repent, as Scrooge was. He belongs to the poor and has neither Scrooge's power to hurt others nor his power to help others. He is called upon instead to realize the extent to which he has been betrayed by his own gullibility—to become clear-sighted in his justified resentment. Dickens intended *The Chimes* to be "a great blow for the poor," and he threw himself so fervently into the writing of the story that he made himself ill. In doing so, however, he somewhat lost control of his literary skills, and the story moves more awkwardly the further it progresses. It is more of a tract than a parable, and as such, it tends to fit rather badly into its narrative frame. It is both too serious and too frenetic in its argumentative aspect to belong to the literary form which it adopts.

The Cricket on the Hearth is subtitled "A Fairy Tale of Home," but the fairy cricket actually does nothing within the story except to symbolize the calming effect of lovely domesticity upon the rawer emotional impulses. The crusading reformism is here abandoned entirely, while the sentimentality overflows to such an extent that the story leaves a saccharine aftertaste. Significantly, it was the most successful of the Christmas books in its own time. *The Battle of Life* is less sentimental and contrasts oddly with *The Chimes* in parading a kind of world-weary defeatism.

In 1847, Dickens produced no Christmas book, and the one further addition to the group, *The Haunted Man*, seems to be a deliberate attempt to return to the beginning by recapturing the whole spirit of *A Christmas Carol*. In a sense, it is almost a self-conscious copy and anticipates the fact that *A Christmas Carol* was to become one of the most copiously copied stories of all time. (The closest imitations are Tom Gallon's *The Man Who Knew Better*, 1901, Marie Corelli's *The Strange Visitation*, 1912, and Richard Ganthony's play *A Message from Mars*, 1923.) *The Haunted Man* is the story of Mr. Redlaw, a professor of chemistry whose past life has been dogged by the vicissitudes of evil circumstance. Unlike Scrooge, he has not been soured by these experiences into adamantine selfishness but has retained his essential benevolence and sympathy for others. However, he is defeated by life and falls prey to an aching sadness and wholehearted self-pity. The sin of which he must repent is not avarice but the more private and personal moral disease of despair.

One Christmas Eve, Redlaw is visited by a ghost: a phantom of himself, offering a bargain. The phantom proposes to banish Redlaw's "sorrow, wrong and trouble," leaving him with his memory intact but insulated from the strong emotions which make remembrance unbearable. For *his* part, Redlaw must accept the provision that the gift will not affect him alone, but will also be bestowed on all others with whom he comes in contact. Redlaw believes that this will make him a benefactor to others as well as securing his own release from private pain, and he accepts.

It soon becomes clear, however, as he goes forth into the world, that his gift is a blight. Everyone touched by it, in becoming insensitive to his or her own pain, becomes insensitive to the pain of others. Redlaw takes away their powers of empathy and makes them selfish in making them immune to sorrow. He realizes that in destroying the power of poor people to love one another, he is obliterating the last worthwhile thing in their appallingly difficult lives. He agonizes over the effects which he has on others, particularly in regard to the threat which he poses to Milly William, the wife of one of his servants, who is the very personification of goodness and generosity. His sojourn in this curious hell, however, is short-lived. The phantom returns in response to his call, and Milly becomes the instrument by which normality is restored, spreading goodwill by her presence just as Redlaw destroyed it by his. Redlaw is left a much wiser man.

The Haunted Man lacks the moral simplicity of *A Christmas Carol* and attempts a much greater subtlety. Potentially, at least, it was a daring and complex project for Dickens to undertake. It is more a comment on human nature than a demand for moral reform, and that is perhaps the key to its failure. Like *The Chimes*, it is a type of work ill-fitted to the form of a Christmas story. It has not the narrative simplicity of *A Christmas Carol*, partly because it has to deal with more sophisticated concepts, and its style is surprisingly awkward. It is as if Dickens became the victim of his own self-consciousness; the whole story is manifestly artificial. It has in its favor, of course, that even a failed Dickensian enterprise can outshine most works by lesser writers, and it also has a moral seriousness which elevates it above *The Cricket on the Hearth* and *The Battle of Life*. Nevertheless, it remains a trick which fails to come off.

Christmas ghost stories became a Victorian institution. The Victorians were fascinated by fantasy but felt a curious guilt concerning their fascination. Indulgence in metempirical fancy was seen as a kind of moral failure, a willful desertion of utilitarian pragmatism. It was all right for children, who knew no better, to be amused with fantasies, provided that the correct moral tone was preserved; but as far as adults were concerned, fantasy was something that could be adequately sanctioned only at Christmas, when all standards could be relaxed a little.

Yet it is not surprising that Dickens became impatient with the format of the Christmas books. In the General Preface that he wrote for a collected edition of the stories in 1852, he made the following observations:

> The narrow space within which it was necessary to confine these Christmas Stories when they were originally published, rendered their construction a matter of some difficulty, and almost necessitated what was peculiar in their machinery. I never attempted great elaboration of detail in the working out of character within such limits, believing that it could not succeed. My purpose was, in a whimsical kind of masque which the good humour of the season justified, to awaken some loving and forbearing thoughts, never out of season in a Christian land.

Dickens eventually came to the conclusion that the combination of serious purpose with amusing tales of the supernatural and the sentimental required an alchemy beyond his powers. Perhaps he underestimated himself or the inherent flexibility of supernatural fiction, but the stories give adequate testimony of his developing discomfort. He came to feel that the appropriate place for his reforming tendency was in his major novels and that supernatural apparatus was neither necessary nor desirable in the pursuit of such a cause. This is why his subsequent Christmas stories, written for *Household Words*, are given over to lighthearted social comedy of a Pickwickian stripe and are possessed of a calculated triviality. He was happy enough to let other writers produce most of them.

One may deduce from these observations that the Christmas books are not to be regarded as belonging among the most important of Dickens' literary productions. Indeed, most critics ignore them, although most make token concessions in favor of *A Christmas Carol*. The issue is more complicated than this, however, for one may also discern that in the Christmas books, Dickens was trying to do something which *was* important to him—so important, in fact, that he abandoned the form because he could not achieve the blend of levity and seriousness that he sought. For that reason, the stories are of some importance in the history of his career, and it does not serve the cause of understanding the man and his work to ignore them. Consideration of these works is important both for gaining an insight into Dickens' ambitions and for tracing in the history of fantastic fiction the development of methods of deploying supernatural apparatus in the service of some kind of moral purpose.

English fantastic fiction in the age of Dickens was almost entirely trivial. When the Gothic novel entered its penny-dreadful decadence, there began a long interregnum in the career of the fantasy novel which did not end until the 1880's, when many writers made the discovery that the apparatus of the supernatural could indeed be exploited in the service of various serious purposes. In that interim, there were a number of historically significant trials and experiments which laid the groundwork for the subsequent revival of the fantasy tradition. The fact that many of these trials were at best only half-successful should not be allowed to obscure the fact that they played a significant role in the evolution of strategies which were later to be exploited productively. *A Christmas Carol*, of course, needs no apology along these lines—it is a masterpiece in its own right—but *The Chimes* and *The Haunted Man* both stand in need of rescue from virtual obscurity because their faults have unhappily been allowed to obscure their merits. They are not great stories, but they are interesting stories, in the context of Dickens' work and in the context of the tradition of fantastic literature.

Brian Stableford

Bibliography

Butt, John. "Dickens' Christmas Books," in *Pope, Dickens and Others: Essays and Addresses*, 1969.

Chesterton, G. K. *Appreciation and Criticism of the Work of Charles Dickens*, 1911.

Collins, Philip, ed. *Dickens: The Critical Heritage*, 1971.

Hobsbaum, Philip. *A Reader's Guide to Charles Dickens*, 1972.

Howells, William Dean. "Dickens' Christmas Books," in *My Literary Passions*, 1895.

Kotzin, Michael C. *Dickens and the Fairy Tale*, 1972.

Stone, Harry. *Dickens and the Invisible World*, 1980.

THE CHRONICLES OF NARNIA

Author: C. S. Lewis (1898-1963)
First book publications: The Lion, the Witch and the Wardrobe (1950); *Prince Caspian*
(1951); *The Voyage of the "Dawn Treader"* (1952); *The Silver Chair* (1953); *The*
Horse and His Boy (1954); *The Magician's Nephew* (1955); *The Last Battle* (1956)
Type of work: Novels
Time: From the Creation to the Last Judgment
Locale: Narnia, Archenland, and Calormene, three countries in a world reachable
only by magic

In successive adventures, small groups of children are drawn from this world and
time in to the parallel world of Narnia, where they assist the inhabitants in repelling
magical assaults or temptations, under the direction of Aslan, the Lion, an alternative
image of the Son of God

      Principal characters:
          ASLAN, the Lion, son of the Emperor-Beyond-the-Sea
          PETER, SUSAN, EDMUND, AND LUCY PEVENSIE, children in England
            and kings and queens in Narnia
          EUSTACE SCRUBB, their cousin
          JILL POLE, his friend
          PUDDLEGLUM, a Marshwiggle
          KING CASPIAN THE TENTH, also called the Navigator
          THE WHITE WITCH, formerly Jadis of Charn

    Between 1950 and 1956, Clive Staples Lewis published annually a new
volume in his Chronicles of Narnia. He wrote them quicker even than this,
however, keeping the later volumes back for a while so as not to "flood the
market." A junior colleague of his, who had the rooms opposite Lewis' in
Magdalen College, Oxford, during 1950, remarked much later that Lewis was
at that time the worst conceivable company for a man struggling to write his
first book. He seemed to announce a completion almost every other week,
and when asked the secret of his productivity, he would say only, "If it's clear
in your own mind, it'll be all right." The thought that there might be difficulties
of expression apparently never crossed his mind.
    This fluency had bad as well as good effects. The Narnia books contain
failures of logic and of inner consistency. One of these (quite enough by itself
to motivate J. R. R. Tolkien's recorded dislike of the whole series) is that
there is no consideration of what language might be spoken in the "parallel
world" of Narnia. When Lucy first enters Narnia through the magic wardrobe,
the first creature she sees is a Faun carrying parcels; when it sees her, it drops
the parcels and says, "Goodness gracious me!" Lucy and the Faun then carry
on a conversation without the slightest difficulty, and there is never any
mention afterward of translation problems. Lewis does give an explanation
of sorts in the sixth volume of the Chronicles, *The Magician's Nephew*, revealing that at the moment of Narnia's creation, the roles of Adam and Eve were

taken by a London cabby and his wife, transported by magic from Victorian England to the dawn of time in Narnia. Naturally their descendants would speak English and teach it to the Talking Beasts, Fauns, Nymphs, Centaurs, and Satyrs. Why the language should not have changed, why it should have had a "medieval" phase also recorded in *The Lion, the Witch and the Wardrobe*, why Lucy and the Faun should be so much on a linguistic level—these are questions and discrepancies which Lewis ignored.

In similar style, one could add that the Faun is carrying parcels as if he had been doing his Christmas shopping, while further on in that first story, Father Christmas himself makes an appearance. The Narnians know all about Christmas, but they have never heard of Christ, or at least not under that name. The inconsistency is evident to anyone but a child. One could say charitably that after all, Lewis intended his books for children and saw no reason to distract them with adult logic. To this, Lewis' friend Tolkien would have replied that logic is neither "adult" nor "childish," but fixed in the nature of reality and that writing "down" to children never works. Lewis himself would probably in principle have agreed. The tone of his books changes as they progress, moving from the cozy and jocular scenes of Father Christmas and the Faun at the start to the much more detailed, serious, and internally consistent works in the middle, and finally to *The Magician's Nephew* and *The Last Battle*, where Lewis seems to be taking stock of his own earlier works and also edging back again from adventure to allegory.

The initial impulse for *The Lion, the Witch and the Wardrobe* does indeed seem to have been allegorical, even theological, although Lewis might not have liked the terms. Narnia itself, the world to which the Pevensie children go, is a relatively familiar wonderland which gratifies the ancient urges to imagine talking animals and to have figures of mythology become real. Narnia is dominated (if not ruled), however, by Aslan, the Lion, and anyone but a very young or ignorant child will soon realize that Aslan "is" Jesus, or is an avatar of Jesus, or another image of a universal Divinity—it is hard to pick a phrase without seeming blasphemous. At the end of *The Voyage of the "Dawn Treader,"* Lewis simplifies matters by introducing a Lamb, which turns into Aslan and tells the children (English, Christian children) that just as they find the Lion in Narnia, so they can find the Lamb in England. They have been brought to Narnia, says the Lion, so that "by knowing me here for a little, you may know me better there," but the "me" of Narnia and of England is one and the same. One could paraphrase by saying that Lewis wrote his stories to give children a glimpse, in fable, of the truth they might reject or be bored by if it were presented as religion.

There is a danger in this, in that the fable Lewis invented contains elements of grandeur and aggression which have quite consciously been rejected by the Christian tradition of humility. One has more than a suspicion that Lewis (a Protestant Ulsterman known to his friends as "Fighting Jack") intrinsically preferred lions to lambs; also that, like Tolkien, what he wanted to do more than anything was to reconcile heroic literature with the religion of love. Beneath these uncertainties, however, a clear purpose remains visible in the Narnia Chronicles and most of all in the first volume. Once one looks closely, it is surprising how much of *The Lion, the Witch and the Wardrobe* is based directly on the Gospels.

To summarize the plot: as the four Pevensie children reach Narnia, a division is already present among them. Both Lucy and Edmund have been there before, Lucy to be warned of the White Witch who holds the land in endless winter, Edmund to be bribed and recruited by her. Edmund, aggrieved at being caught lying, slips away from the others and joins the Witch. His reward is to be prepared for sacrifice. Although he is rescued by Aslan and the forces of good, the Witch then appears and claims him back, saying that by the Deep Magic of Aslan's father, the Emperor-Beyond-the-Sea, all traitors are hers to kill. Aslan acknowledges that this is so, talks to her privately, and then declares she has renounced her claim. The price is that he has to die in Edmund's place, as Lucy and Susan find that night when they follow him leaving their camp, secretly and despairingly. Aslan is taunted by the Hags, killed on the Stone Table, and left there dead. The girls try to tend his body, but as the dawn comes and they walk away, the Stone Table cracks, and behind them the girls see Aslan—not a ghost (as they at first think), but returned to life by the Deeper Magic of the willing and innocent victim, something which the Witch had never understood.

The parallels with the Crucifixion are obvious: not only the death and the taunting, but also the scene of despair (which recalls the Garden of Gethsemane), the role of Lucy and Susan (compare with the two Marys at the Cross), and the breaking of the Stone Table as a sign of resurrection (parallel to the rolling of the stone from Christ's tomb). Even more striking are the elements of doctrine contained in the narrative. What Lewis says about the Deep and the Deeper Magic corresponds very well to the medieval theory of the "Devil's rights," which explained that after the Fall, all mankind belonged by right to the Devil and could not be rescued until the Devil himself broke the contract by taking a victim who was not his—in this case, Christ, whose humanity the Devil perceived without also recognizing His divinity. In this view, what the Deep Magic says is that God is Law (a point Lewis repeats elsewhere); the Deeper Magic says that God is Love; as for Edmund's treachery, it can only be called "original sin." These are deep waters for a children's book. Still, there can be no doubt that all these parallels were intended and little doubt that Lewis meant his allegory to teach readers Christian truth.

One can hardly imagine that Lewis, at this stage, meant the series to continue. The idea of translating or metamorphosizing the central doctrine of Christianity cannot be followed with any force by a second and inevitably lesser allegory. Lewis, however, had come under the spell of his own imagined world. In the succeeding four volumes, one can see the element of adventure and exploration increasing but always blending, in some proportion, with the element of morality or education.

Thus, the second volume, *Prince Caspian*, contains a strong heroic plot concerning animals loyal to Aslan pitted against skeptical, conquering men; but it also seems in essence to be a homily on faith. The kernel of the book is in Chapters 9 and 10, where the Pevensie children, called once again into Narnia by a magic horn, are trying to join the disinherited Prince Caspian to reestablish him on his throne. As they struggle in their search for Caspian, Lucy sees Aslan walking in what appears to be the "wrong" direction. She appeals to the others to follow him, but they think she has merely deluded herself. As the journey goes more and more astray, Lucy realizes that it is her duty to follow Aslan, alone if necessary. *Then* the others agree to go with her, and as they follow, Aslan becomes slowly visible even to the doubters. One could say, blessed are they who see and believe (as Lucy does); yet more blessed are those who do *not* see but still believe. Lewis is stating quite openly that one should not be deterred from belief in God by others' skepticism or by a lack of physical evidence.

To this thematic center, much of the rest of the book is related. Caspian's cause is just but several of his allies are unreliable, especially Nikabrik the Dwarf, a character unequivocally against human usurpers and invaders but without the slightest belief in Aslan and one prepared to make alliance with strength of any kind—including the Hags, the werewolves, and the Witch. The twentieth century is familiar with such cases: those who, despite their rejection of Christian and humanist values, fight against open evil but do so for their own (perhaps equally evil) purposes. Lewis might have thought of Stalin; of the Allied strategic bombing offensives a few years before; or naïve believers in scientific progress. The "allegory" is by no means as close as that of *The Lion, the Witch and the Wardrobe*, and Tolkien, for one, would not have called this allegory at all but rather "applicability." Still, a doctrinal point about faith and a moral one about ends not justifying means lie very close beneath the surface adventure of *Prince Caspian*.

Even "applicability" has faded in volume three, *The Voyage of the "Dawn Treader,"* perhaps the most lighthearted of the seven Chronicles. This volume could be called a dramatized map, for in it the two younger Pevensies, with their repulsive cousin, Eustace Scrubb, are propelled into the Narnian ocean to be taken on a voyage of quest by Prince Caspian, now established as King Caspian. One island follows another. On one, they find a living star; on another, a spring that turns everything to gold; on a third, a magician tended by the invisible (and idiotic) Dufflepuds. Much of the time, Lewis seems to be writing only out of a sense for the visual, as in his compelling description of the merpeople, glimpsed by the crew of the *Dawn Treader* at the bottom of the sea as they ride from their castles in the warm shallows to do battle with a kraken or a sea serpent in the deeps. One little sea-shepherdess (or fish-herdess) stares straight into Lucy's face for a second as the current sweeps Lucy past. They cannot speak or meet, but they become friends on the instant. If ever they see each other again, says Lewis, they will rush together with their hands outstretched. There is no "point" in a scene such as this; it appeals to pathos or to loneliness, rather than to morals or logic, but that does not mean it should not be there.

In spite of this pastoral or romantic quality, however, *The Voyage of the "Dawn Treader"* does contain a theme, although one still less organized or allegorical than that of the previous volume. It is the theme of the education of Eustace Scrubb, at first an epitome of all that Lewis disliked in modern children: smug, soft, equating machinery with civilization, contemptuous of all former times and respectful only of classroom intelligence. His trip teaches him humility and manners, the turning-point coming when he lies down on a heap of gold, thinking thoughts of greed, to discover when he wakes up that he has become a dragon. This is a folk-motif from Icelandic saga which Lewis probably learned from Tolkien, and the transformation points to the shared belief of the Oxford "Inklings" that modern civilization had gone astray through a fascination with metal, whether riches or machines. Few readers are likely to draw this precise moral from the story, however, seeing instead only the more general satire aimed at Eustace and, through him, at themselves. *The Voyage of the "Dawn Treader,"* one could say, is good fun but episodic. Lewis is in danger of moving too far away from allegory toward mere "travelogue."

The Silver Chair, however, redresses the balance most successfully and is perhaps the best volume of the sequence. It too is a quest, in which the reformed Eustace and a new friend, Jill Pole, are sent to find the lost Prince Rilian, Caspian's son. It contains particularly strong characterization, with a major role played by Puddleglum the Marshwiggle, a kind of amphibious human being whose affectation it is always to believe the worst, to take a dim view of everything, and beneath it all (rather like Tolkien's Sam Gamgee) to remain undaunted and not even noticeably depressed. The book has fine, separate, fantasy sequences in Harfang, home of the Gentle Giants (their true nature is discovered by Jill when she finds MAN next to MARSHWIG-GLE in a Giant cookery book) and in the Underworld of the gnomes, where Prince Rilian sits bemused and bewitched. Its strongest point, however (one which has, as it were, been incubating through the previous volumes of the series), is its thorough and careful presentation of sin and of the way in which the roots of sin are present in what appears too often to sinners to be "mere" carelessness or entirely forgivable error.

Error of course *is* forgivable, as indeed is sin, and Lewis had already stated as much by his presentations of Edmund, the saved traitor, and Eustace, the improved malcontent. Nevertheless, Lewis was at all times eager to distinguish charity and tolerance from license. He thought the twentieth century entirely too slack at identifying evil. *The Silver Chair* opens accordingly with Eustace and Jill in a dreadful school called Experiment House, in which liberalism rules, vice is never punished, and as a result, cruelty and bullying are rampant. Eustace and Jill arrive in Narnia impelled by despair. Once there, however, their bad training continues to work. First, Jill's efforts at "showing off" lead to Eustace's falling from a precipice. He is saved by Aslan, but his perhaps natural ill-temper—he uses the word "murder"—leads to his taking no notice when Jill gives him an urgent message from the Lion. One could say, harshly but truthfully, that already the children have jeopardized their quest by indulging in two of the Seven Deadly Sins: Pride (from Jill) and Anger (from Eustace). They, of course, call these sins "showing off" and "being sulky," which sound much less serious, but the *results* are serious, and one is made to see, with Lewis, that the results are both natural and deserved.

As the quest for Prince Rilian continues, other Deadly Sins make their appearance, albeit in at first an innocuous form. In the strange land (not Narnia) where the children first appeared, Aslan gave Jill four precepts or directions to help them find the Prince. The first is broken by Eustace's anger. The second and third are ignored in a highly credible scene in which the children, with Puddleglum, are struggling to reach shelter across a ruined city. They were told by Aslan to *look* for a ruined city, and if they had been concentrating, they would have noticed it; but they were not concentrating, because a few days before, they had met a lady who described Harfang to them so glowingly that all they could think about was fires, beds, and dinner. Jill has furthermore stopped her habit (Lewis was a believer in rote-learning) of saying Aslan's directions to herself to keep them word-perfect. The sins committed, in fact, are Sloth and Gluttony, with possibly a touch of Envy added. These leave the questers trapped, first in Harfang, and then in the Underworld, the latter being the realm of the serpent-witch who has trapped Prince Rilian, and who of course was also the seductive lady they met in the wilderness.

Fortunately, the children learn in time, remember the fourth direction, and rescue Prince Rilian from his enchantments and the silver chair to which he is tied. The witch is killed, and all escape. The crisis of the book, however, is perhaps the scene in which the children, Puddleglum, and Rilian, all marooned in the Underworld, are almost persuaded by the witch to abandon belief in Narnia and stay below. The witch's arguments are persuasive, practical, evidential. Down in the earth, she asks, what first-hand evidence is there for a sun? for an Overworld? for Aslan? Are these not fairy tales, imaginative metaphors? What proof is there for their reality, other than fallible memory? Her logic has analogues in the real world and reminds one of agnostics arguing that God is a human invention, a scaled-up Father set in the "Overworld" of Heaven. In this crisis, Puddleglum saves them all, first by putting his webbed foot in the fire, so that enchantment is dissolved by pain (and by the nauseating smell of charred Marshwiggle), and second by declaring that even if there is no Narnia and no Aslan, he proposes to believe in both, because they are intrinsically superior conceptions. His defiance lies close to Lewis' heart. It has parallels in Lewis' adult fiction, especially in *That Hideous Strength* (1945). What it says is that even if wrong is bound to triumph, it will still remain forever wrong, beyond the reach of compromise.

"Uncompromising" is indeed the word for *The Silver Chair*, with its insistence that even children are sinners, that evil must always be fought (however hopelessly), and in the end, that all sin must be paid for in grief and pain. Rilian loses his father, King Caspian, and Aslan has to shed blood to wipe out Eustace's fault. Although the children have a highly satisfying revenge on their return to Experiment House, even that is only temporary. The surprise is that this tale of blood, toil, sweat, and tears remains attractive.

After *The Silver Chair*, the pattern of the Chronicles seems once more to change. *The Horse and His Boy* is a tale of Narnia alone, with no intruding characters from the familiar human world. It deals with four refugees (boy, girl, mare, and stallion) escaping from the cruel empire of Calormene to the northern lands where talking beasts are accepted. In it, Lewis amuses himself with comic caricatures of despotism, pomposity, and pretension, while centering the book on the theme of the beauties of discipline—again a harshly attractive notion.

The Magician's Nephew, as has already been suggested, is preeminently a work of tidying-up, which explains *inter alia* how the wardrobe of the first book came to be magic, why there was an English lamp-post growing in Narnia at the point where Lucy met the Faun, and where the White Witch originated. It is also notable for its heavy borrowings from John Milton's *Paradise Lost* (1667, 1674) as is Lewis' adult novel *Perelandra* (1943) and perhaps especially for its introduction of the "Deplorable Word." This is a magic spell spoken by the Witch back in her own world, from which she is unfortunately transported to Narnia; it wiped out all other inhabitants. It is perfectly clear that Lewis meant his readers to draw the parallel with the atomic bomb and the chance of human civilization destroying itself. Throughout the novel, the temptation is once more to use bad means for good ends.

This edging back toward allegory culminates in *The Last Battle*, a work which (rather disappointingly) abandons narrative for description at its midpoint. It tells the story of the destruction of Narnia, precipitated by selfish cunning on the one hand and irresponsible weakness on the other. This latter, incarnated in a donkey called Puzzle, seems Lewis' final comment on the vices of his own time. Puzzle means well, but he does ill; his own decency makes him a prey to bandits. The last king of Narnia also surrenders tamely, and Narnia runs down very nearly to a whimper. "Is there any virtue left?" asks Lewis, and he answers "Yes" in a daring speculation which finds hope for salvation even among worshipers of Tash, the false god of Calormene. As each person dies—and in *The Last Battle*, everybody dies—he or she looks in the face of Aslan and in that instant loves or fears him. It is their reaction, not their religion, upbringing, or circumstances, which determines their fate in the afterlife. This doctrine of the *clara visio* is in fact an ancient one, propounded by the fourteenth century friar Uhtred of Boldon. By so strangely reviving it, Lewis seems to be saying that perhaps even Christians will be surprised on Judgment Day. Certainly *The Last Battle* makes a strange mingling of hope for the future with despair at the here-and-now. The theology is no longer orthodox and central but personal and even (for Uhtred's doctrine was rejected by the Church) heretical, but Lewis was a Protestant and therefore free to speculate.

The Chronicles of Narnia are not democratic works, being full of praise for kingship, hierarchy, ceremoniousness, and other archaic qualities. Their child-heroes and heroines also seem to have grown very rapidly outdated, with their slang, their pieties, and their total innocence of sex. Nevertheless, the seven books as a whole do express a powerful ideology which embraces religion, philosophy, and a code of manners. At the end of the series, the reader may look back to *The Voyage of the "Dawn Treader"* and remember the book in the magician's house which contains the loveliest story Lucy ever read or would read in the whole of her life. Like a dream, it fades as soon as she has finished; Aslan says he will tell it to her for many years once she is dead. This magical book seems to be Lewis' image of what narrative should ideally be: not ideology, allegory, or social comment, but simply a tale "for the refreshment of the spirit." This was Lewis' goal, and he must be said to have achieved it often.

T. A. Shippey

Bibliography

Carpenter, Humphrey. *The Inklings: C. S. Lewis, J. R. R. Tolkien, Charles Williams and Their Friends*, 1978.

Christopher, Joe R., and Joan K. Ostling. *C. S. Lewis: An Annotated Checklist of Writings About Him and His Works*, 1973.

Green, Roger Lancelyn, and Walter Hooper. *C. S. Lewis: A Biography*, 1974.

Hannay, Margaret Patterson, *C. S. Lewis*, 1981.

Hillegas, Mark R., ed. *Shadows of Imagination: The Fantasies of C. S. Lewis, J. R. R. Tolkien, and Charles Williams*, 1969.

Shippey, T. A. *The Road to Middle-earth*, 1982.

Smith, Robert Houston. *Patches of Godlight: The Pattern of Thought of C. S. Lewis*, 1981.

Walsh, Chad. *The Literary Legacy of C. S. Lewis*, 1979.

THE CHRONICLES OF PRYDAIN

Author: Lloyd Alexander (1924-   )
First book publications: The Book of Three (1964); *The Black Cauldron* (1965); *The Castle of Llyr* (1966); *Taran Wanderer* (1967); *The High King* (1968)
Type of work: Novels
Time: The medieval world of heroic fantasy
Locale: Prydain, a land vaguely resembling Wales

   Calling together his allies to stem Arawn's encroachment upon Prydain, Dallben eventually succeeds in cleansing Prydain of Arawn's baleful magic; essential to Dallben's victory is young Taran, whose passage from Assistant Pig-Keeper to High King parallels the victory over Arawn both in difficulty and ultimate success

> *Principal characters:*
> TARAN, an Assistant Pig-Keeper
> DALLBEN, a great wizard
> PRINCE GWYDION, an already legendary hero
> EILONWY, a princess and enchantress
> GURGI, a half-animal/half-human friend of Taran
> FFLEWDDUR FFLAM, a bard and friend of Taran
> DOLI, a dwarf and friend of Taran
> ARAWN, the king of the dark forces
> COLL, a retired hero and teacher of Taran

   Lloyd Alexander's Chronicles of Prydain have won critical praise since the publication of *The Book of Three*, the first volume in the series. Both *The Book of Three* and *The Castle of Llyr* were designated among the Notable Books of the Year by the American Library Association. *The Black Cauldron* not only was an ALA Notable Book but was also selected as runner-up for the prestigious Newbery Medal, awarded to the best children's book of the year. Fittingly, *The High King* later won the Newbery Medal. The Chronicles of Prydain have enjoyed a wide readership as well as critical esteem; Dell has released paperback editions of the series under both the Yearling and Laurel Leaf imprints: the former, with large print and wide margins, is explicitly aimed at elementary-grade readers; the latter, with smaller print and narrow margins, is designed to attract readers in junior high school and above.
   The Chronicles of Prydain are heroic or high fantasy replete with conflict, quest, ordeal, loyalty, treachery, ambition, and intrigue, all taking place in a world where honor is an ideal affirmed but not always realized and where magic and enchantment exist. The Chronicles are also an ethical fantasy which underscores the importance of choices and decisions in a youth's life and the necessity of accepting the consequences of those choices and decisions if growth is to occur. On the other hand, the Chronicles of Prydain have a freshness uncommon in contemporary heroic and ethical fantasy. One source of this freshness is Prydain itself, which, although resembling Wales and

borrowing from *The Mabinogion* (c.1100), the collection of Welsh legends, has little to do with actual Welsh geography, history, or literature. Prydain represents an attempt to suggest the ambience of Wales and its legends with an impact that is contemporary and not bookish or nostalgic. A second source of freshness in the series is Alexander's attitude toward his characters. He clearly likes Taran and his friends, but he presents them honestly, often even poking fun at them and their behavior.

Although he acknowledges that Prydain does resemble Wales, Alexander has denied that he intended any close identification between the two; moreover, he insists that the Chronicles of Prydain should not be read and judged as a retranslation or retelling of *The Mabinogion*. Perhaps the relationship between Wales and *The Mabinogion* on one hand and Prydain and the Chronicles on the other may be best understood as an instance of Alexander's use of what he calls in his essay "High Fantasy and Heroic Romance" the "Cauldron of Story," his term for what J. R. R. Tolkien called the "pot of story." That is to say, Wales and *The Mabinogion* are among the "most nourishing bits and pieces" bubbling in the great "Cauldron of Story" into which fantasists are free to dip, ladling up whatever they can assimilate into their storytelling. Accordingly, Alexander has incorporated into the Chronicles "bits and pieces" of Welsh names, places, objects, and situations: for example, Caer, a manor or castle; Dallben, an old enchanter; Gwydion, the legendary hero; Arawn, the Dark Lord; Hen Wen, the oracular pig; and the Black Crochan from which the living/dead soldiers, the Cauldron-Born, magically emerge. Prydain, then, is an original secondary world conceived and given form by Alexander's imagination and storytelling craft.

Within Prydain can be found mortal humans: rich and poor, powerful and weak, lordly and servile—social classes and ranks so differentiated that an Assistant Pig-Keeper dare not hope to marry a princess. There, too, are the Sons of Don, originally from the Summer Country (where there is no death), who have come to Prydain to help free it from Arawn. Also in Prydain are the Fair Folk, whose realm is subterranean and still accessible to mortals. There are such exotic animals as the gwythaints, huge, rapacious, evil birds; such rare creatures as shaggy Gurgi, half-human, half-animal; and mysterious, powerful entities such as Medwyn, whose secret valley shelters animals but turns away all else. Finally, because there is magic in Prydain, ordinary objects sometimes can act extraordinarily—a ball that shines, a food wallet that never runs out, or harp strings that break whenever the harpist stretches the truth.

In many respects, Prydain is the typical world of high or heroic fantasy. Hierarchical class distinctions, feudal social obligations, castles, the kinds of food and clothing, modes of transportation, methods of warfare, and reliance on physical strength are all reminiscent of the medieval world. Atypical is the absence of merchants, marketplaces, towns, and inns. More significant is the absence of priests and priestly castes, organized religion, and either a single god or gods. Consequently, there is no supernaturally revealed or sanctioned code of behavior. Furthermore, good and evil do not exist as independent forces which make Prydain an arena in which they contend for mastery. Readers sense, however, that the desirability and superiority of good deeds and behavior are assumed, along with the necessity of combating and, if possible, controlling evil. Therefore, in Prydain, a tension exists between good and evil deeds, characters, and magic.

When the Chronicles of Prydain begin, evil forces led by Arawn, the chief practitioner of black magic, are poised to take over Prydain; with the aid of a new war lord, the Horned King, the Cauldron-Born (who cannot be killed by ordinary means), the gwythaints, and secret allies among the Cantrev Lords who have been lured by the promise of power, Arawn seems invincible. Opposing him are the forces led by Dallben, the powerful 359-year-old wizard, including the Sons of Don (in particular, Prince Gwydion) and their associates and those Cantrev Lords and their followers who remain loyal to the High King Math. As is expected in high fantasy, especially that intended to attract young readers, the good forces eventually do win, thanks, in particular, to Taran, who displays qualities of leadership normally not found in an Assistant Pig-Keeper.

Paradoxically, the defeat of Arawn, achieved in part by magic, brings to an end the presence of magic in Prydain. The tools of magic are forever destroyed; Dallben, the remaining Sons of Don, and those few who have greatly assisted them must return to the Summer Country. Even Eilonwy, if she wishes to remain with Taran, must forever renounce her powers as an enchantress. At the end of *The High King*, Dallben underscores the end of magic's involvement in the affairs of Prydain when he wryly remarks that the only enchantment of which Eilonwy is capable, now that she has renounced her magic powers, is that which all women, because they are women, have over men. If white magic can no longer operate in Prydain, however, black magic cannot either. Correcting the notion that because Arawn is conquered Prydain will be free of evil, Dallben points out that it is only the enchantments of evil that have been eliminated. Thus, mortal men and women, no longer able to rely on white magic to combat evil, must face the future trusting in themselves and in their own resources. Whatever good they will achieve will come about through their own decisions and behavior; conversely, whatever evil they may do cannot be blamed on some outside force. The inhabitants of Prydain must take over the determination of their own fate and whether it will be good or evil is up to them.

The Chronicles of Prydain could easily be called Taran's Chronicles, inasmuch as their central story concerns Taran's becoming High King. Because that story is about a youth who dreams of doing heroic deeds and then in unexpected and sometimes inglorious ways becomes a hero and king, Taran's story is heroic fantasy. On the other hand, it also is about a youth's belated recognition that to be Assistant Pig-Keeper is not to be confused with being "pig-boy"; the former is honorable and requires accepting responsibility for one's own actions and for others, while the latter does not. Taran's story is also about a youth's slow and painful discovery that his destiny is to be himself and no one else. Hence, the Chronicles are an ethical fantasy that concerns a boy's passage into adulthood—a passage demanding both physical and ethical maturation.

Alexander focuses his portrayal of Taran's maturation upon the youth's learning what growing up and heroism actually entail. When the Chronicles begin, Taran is anxious to get on with the training he thinks is required to become a hero; he complains to Coll and Dallben that he is never allowed to "know anything interesting, go anywhere interesting, or do anything interesting." In response, the two appoint him Assistant Pig-Keeper. The boy immediately fails his new charge when Hen Wen, frightened and unattended, runs away from Caer Dallben. Impetuously rushing off to track down the pig, the boy imagines himself a hero, only to learn that his rash behavior simply compounds his initial mistake. Thus, he begins to see that the acceptance of responsibilities, even seemingly inconsequential ones, is what is expected of adults and heroes.

One of the distinctive features of the Chronicles of Prydain is the frankness of Alexander's portrait of Taran, who is shown at times to be weak, afraid, confused, and ineffectual, and at other times to be strong, brave, confident, and resourceful. Perhaps Alexander depicts Taran most candidly in *Taran Wanderer*, when the young man sets out on a quest to find his parents, hoping they are nobly born so that he can openly profess his love for Eilonwy. During the quest—in particular his search for the Mirror of Llunet that will reveal "something of interest"—Taran comes across as very human and hence a vulnerable and accessible character. Surely the most poignant moment of his quest is the shock and dismay he suffers when the herdsman, Cradoc, claims that the young man is his long-lost son. Forced to abandon his dreams of noble birth and of wedding Eilonwy, Taran refuses to return to Caer Dallben and to what he thinks will be further humiliation. He decides to remain with his newly found father, hoping thereby not only to inure himself to his ignominious fate but also to play the dutiful son.

Some time later, when the herdsman falls on the icy rocks, Taran hastens to aid him. Although tempted for a brief moment to abandon the man who has destroyed his dreams, Taran tries to bring him up from the rocks. Becoming very concerned for Cradoc's life, Taran uses his magic horn, which can—but only once—summon the Fair Folk's help. The dying Cradoc admits that he is not Taran's father after all; resenting, if only briefly, the "waste" of the magic horn, Taran is overwhelmed with shame and self-disgust, later falling dangerously ill. His slow recovery is predictable yet convincing. Because Taran's decision to save Cradoc through the magic horn demonstrates once and for all that the young man can rise unselfishly above his own interests and do what he perceives to be his primary duty regardless of personal cost and suffering, Taran deserves to live. Yet, Taran does not owe his "new" life only to his own inner resources; he also lives because Gurgi and Fflewddur Fflam, out of friendship offered unconditionally, have nursed him back to health.

Taran begins to travel aimlessly. His wandering takes him into the Free Commots, where he meets several artisans—Hevydd the Smith, Dwyvach the Weaver, and Annlaw Clay-Shaper—and decides he would like to master these skills. Dissatisfied with his attempts and unwilling to become a "hired sword," Taran complains to Annlaw, "What then shall I do?" What he does not yet grasp is that in seeking to emulate the three artisans, he is not only trying out possible occupations but also persisting in defining himself in terms of what he does instead of what he is. Returning to his quest and eventually finding the Mirror of Llunet—which is merely a small, clear pool of water— Taran looks into it and sees his image reflected upon the surface. In that instant, he at last knows that his destiny is simply to be himself. He understands that all he has seen and experienced has been saying to him that manhood is earned and not given by birth, the mere passing of time, or magic; living does not have to be complicated or worrisome; life can be shaped and given meaning by circumstances, self-discipline, and purpose; destiny is character; and life is good because there are good and honorable people. This moment of insight Taran does not attribute to magic, as Annlaw suggests; he has earned his insight through his own labors, pain, and intelligence, even if he has been slow to attain that insight. Moreover, whatever prompts his goodness is within himself and in the sustaining good example and encouragement of his many friends. Although Taran is destined to become High King, his worthiness is not the result of magic but stems from his unselfishness, his willingness to help, his sense of duty and loyalty, and his capacity to learn from experience.

The Chronicles of Prydain are never simplistic, naïve, or sentimental. Dallben cautions that the end of black magic in Prydain does not mean the end of evildoers. Evil people do exist; they harm other people; and they often seem to prosper. Yet there are also good people, and they, working by themselves or in concert with others, can control and even sometimes overcome evildoers. The Chronicles of Prydain are thus realistic as well as hopeful. In the introductions to the five novels, Alexander reminds readers that they are Assistant Pig-Keepers at heart; they too, if they so desire, can be like Taran— not Taran the High King, but the Taran who realizes that his destiny is to be himself and not anyone else and that in striving to be himself, he becomes heroic.

Francis J. Molson

Bibliography

Alexander, Lloyd. "The Flat-heeled Muse," in *The Horn Book Magazine.*
  XLI (April, 1965), pp. 141-146.
—————— . "High Fantasy and Heroic Romance," in *The Horn Book
  Magazine.* XLVII (December, 1971), pp. 577-584.
—————— . "Wishful Thinking—Or Hopeful Dreaming," in *The Horn
  Book Magazine.* XLIV (August, 1968), pp. 383-390.
Colbath, M. L. "Worlds as They Should Be: Middle-earth, Narnia, and Pry-
  dain," in *Elementary English.* XLIL (1971), pp. 937-945.
Stuart, Dee. "An Exclusive Interview with Lloyd Alexander," in *Writer's
  Digest.* LIII (April, 1973), pp. 32-35, 58-59.
Zahorski, Kenneth J., and Robert H. Boyer, eds. *Lloyd Alexander, Evange-
  line Walton, Kenneth Morris: A Primary and Secondary Bibliography*, 1981.

CHRONICLES OF THE CANONGATE
and
"WANDERING WILLIE'S TALE"

Author: Sir Walter Scott (1771-1832)
First book publications: "Wandering Willie's Tale" (1824, in *Redgauntlet*); *Chronicles of the Canongate* (1827)
Type of work: Short stories
Time: The seventeenth and eighteenth centuries
Locale: Scotland

Short stories that reflect both Scott's literary fascination with historical fantasies and his skepticism of the supernatural

Sir Walter Scott's position in the development of fantasy literature is a paradoxical one. Although as a critic and historian he was extremely influential in the acceptance of the fantastic tale and the ancient ballad as legitimate literary forms, he remained skeptical of literal belief in ghosts, spirits, and apparitions. Such belief in the spirit world as he had was grounded in his devout Christian faith in the soul and in life after death.

From his youth, Scott had been fascinated by the past, listening to family recollections that melted imperceptibly into history, tall tales, legends, ghost stories, and tales of the "second sight." At thirteen, he discovered Bishop Thomas Percy's *Reliques of Ancient English Poetry* (1765) and realized that established and reputable authorities shared his interest in and respect for the old ballads and tales. Yet with the acute sense of history that he developed as one of the first writers to discern the relationship of humankind's past and beliefs to actions in the present, Scott also became aware of the dangers inherent in romantic fantasy and in the political and religious fanaticism that often accompanies it. Scott realized, from the perspective of the late eighteenth and early nineteenth centuries, that this preoccupation with the past had often led to bloody and bitter clashes of clan with clan and eventually to the Jacobite Rebellion. *Waverley* (1814), Scott's first novel, depicts both the attraction of legend and romantic passion and their destructiveness when they influence political decisions and lead to warfare.

Scott's attitude toward the supernatural was equally complex for many of the same reasons. His point of view is exemplified in his finest short story, "Wandering Willie's Tale," particularly when it is considered in its context. The story appears in *Redgauntlet* (1824), a novel that deals, like *Waverley*, with the disastrous intrusion of the romantic past upon present action; but it is much more critical of that past than is *Waverley*. Brought up by his mother with no knowledge of his family history, Darsie Latimer is actually the son of the executed Jacobite Redgauntlet. His search for his identity acquaints him with a range of Scottish characters, from his harsh uncle who holds him prisoner to Wandering Willie, a blind fiddler and former retainer of the Redgauntlets.

Willie tells Darsie a tale about the Redgauntlets and his "gudesire," Steenie the piper, who is woefully in arrears in his rent to Sir Robert Redgauntlet. Finally able to borrow money, Steenie appears at Redgauntlet Castle. Sent with his old friend the butler to have a dram while Sir Robert can count the money and write out a receipt, Steenie is only too glad to quit the room, for he, like others, finds Major Weir, Sir Robert's pet ape, not only as menacing as his master but also somewhat demoniac. Scarcely out of the room, Steenie and the butler hear Sir Robert screaming in agony that his feet hurt from the gout like the fires of hell, and there were those, Willie says, who claimed that the tub of water brought to cool his feet bubbled like a cauldron. Steenie flees, terrified, hearing the laird's death cries as he runs down the stairs. Unfortunately, Sir Robert had not yet written out the receipt. Before Sir Robert's son arrives, the butler, who is the only witness of the transaction, also dies. Steenie's money is nowhere to be found. Questioned beyond endurance by the laird's son (a man more refined but even more coldly cruel than his father) as to the whereabouts of the rent money, Steenie finally shouts, "In hell! with your father, his jackanape, and his silver whistle."

On his way home through the woods at night, the desperate Steenie meets a stranger, who, on learning of Steenie's situation, offers to help him. Steenie asks for a loan, but the stranger assures him that he would not like the terms. Saying, however, that he knows for a fact that the Devil is disturbed by the curses of the laird and the wailing of the family, the stranger tells Steenie that the return of the receipt, rightfully his, will mend matters if he is willing to seek it underground. Frightened but determined, Steenie follows the stranger's directions and arrives at a place much like Redgauntlet Castle. Admitted by his old friend the dead butler, who cautions him not to take anything from the place but the receipt that is his own, Steenie enters the banquet hall. The hall is filled with the dead, the darkest villains of Scottish history, and the roll call of their deeds is terrifyingly disillusioning about the historic past. Steenie, as cautioned, refuses to eat, drink, or play the pipes. As he finally gets his receipt, he utters the name of God; all goes dark, he loses consciousness, and he awakens many hours later to find himself in the churchyard cemetery by the Redgauntlet escutcheon, clutching Sir Robert's receipt. The signature proves to be genuine, although the date is the previous day. The money is found where Sir Robert had said it was, and with it is the body of Major Weir and other missing items. Although the laird's son clearly believes that the receipt indeed came from hell, he cautions Steenie not to mention the fact for the sake of the family honor.

"Wandering Willie's Tale" is Scott's only self-contained narrative entirely in the Scottish vernacular and thus gains the immediacy of the spoken word, even more pronounced in contrast to the formal style of Darsie Latimer's epistles, in one of which it is recorded. Throughout *Redgauntlet*, Scott re-creates the rational daylight atmosphere in which most events take place and offsets it with Highland language that often evokes a past both mysterious and tragic. "Wandering Willie's Tale" is the most striking example of this contrast, an eerie tale interspersed with retellings of all the legends about Sir Robert, such as his making a pact with Satan so that "bullets happed aff his buff-coat like hailstanes from a hearth" and the circumstances of his death when he swore that he had been given "blood instead of burgundy" to drink and "sure aneugh, the lass washed clotted blood off the carpet the neist day."

In his Introduction to *Chronicles of the Canongate*, his only collection of short stories, Scott himself comments on the heightened credibility the tales gain when related aloud around the fire of an evening. The defect of these tales of Highlanders and the legendary past is that they are told in conventional and overly elaborate English. In the case of "The Highland Widow," a tale about a mother who causes her only son to be shot as a deserter when she deliberately delays his return to the hated British Army, is drawn out at tedious length, blunting the impact of the apparition that warns the son not to return home again before rejoining his regiment. "The Two Drovers" is also a tale of second sight, in this case an unheeded warning not to carry a dagger, with an ensuing tragedy. In "My Aunt Margaret's Mirror," a wife's attempt to learn her husband's fate in battle by means of an enchanted mirror leads to the deaths of two members of her family. The best of these tales, "The Tapestried Chamber," gains its effectiveness from brevity and a style suited to the narrator, a courageous and skeptical army officer with many years of service, who is completely terrified by a midnight apparition.

Some of Scott's ballads and poems deal with legend, and some have shadings of the supernatural. In these and in his novels, Scott often creates a ghostly, eerie atmosphere through the blend of vernacular tale and recollection of events made mysterious by being obscured in Highland mists, dress, legends, customs, and superstitions far removed from the tidy realities of early nine-teenth century Britain.

Despite his fantasy tales in both poetry and prose ("Wandering Willie's Tale" being one of the finest examples of the genre), it is as a critic that Scott made his greatest, albeit indirect, contribution to the acceptance of the fan-tastic in literature. In addition to his *Letters on Demonology and Witchcraft* (1830), originally written to his son-in-law and biographer John Gibson Lock-hart and based on thorough research; his critical essays such as "Essay on the Fairy Superstition" (the Preface to *Minstrelsy of the Scottish Border*, 1802-1803) and "Essay on Chivalry and Romance"; and the Prefaces to *The Anti-quary* (1816), *Waverley*, *Redgauntlet*, and *Chronicles of the Canongate*, Scott wrote numerous reviews or essays on individual works, establishing some critical principles for fantasy literature.

Of greatest interest to readers of this genre are Scott's reviews of Horace

Walpole's *The Castle of Otranto* (1764) and Mary Shelley's *Frankenstein* (1818). In the former, Scott elaborates on the roots of humankind's "secret feeling of love of the marvellous," pointing out, though not in Samuel Taylor Coleridge's words, that the essence of success in this sort of tale is not to intrude on the reader's suspension of disbelief. Scott judged that works such as Ann Radcliffe's *The Mysteries of Udolpho* (1794) make the reader feel "cheated" by rational explanations of the mysteries at the conclusion of the novel. Scott was one of the first critics (in the prestigious *Blackwood's Magazine*) to recognize the merit of *Frankenstein* (although he incorrectly identified the author as Percy Bysshe Shelley). Beginning his review with a detailed and perceptive analysis of different types of fantastic narratives, Scott set down the basic ground rule for criticism of fantasy and science fiction: once the reader has accepted the fantastic premise, the story must proceed "according to the rules of probability, and the nature of the human heart."

Edgar Johnson (Scott's major biographer), in summing up the "Wizard of the North" as his contemporaries referred to him, observed that "Scott's very rationalism was . . . rooted in an awareness of the power of tradition on men's minds and hearts." It is this combination of awareness and distance that makes Scott both an effective storyteller and a judicious critic.

Katharine M. Morsberger

Bibliography
Daiches, David. *Sir Walter Scott and His World*, 1971.
Johnson, Edgar. *Sir Walter Scott: The Great Unknown*, 1970.
Pearson, Hesketh. *Sir Walter Scott*, 1954.
Scott, Sir Walter. *Demonology and Witchcraft: Letters Addressed to J. G. Lockhart, Esq.*, 1970.
_____ . *Sir Walter Scott on Novelists and Fiction*, 1968. Edited by Joan Williams.

THE CHRONICLES OF THOMAS COVENANT
THE UNBELIEVER
and
THE SECOND CHRONICLES OF THOMAS COVENANT

Author: Stephen R. Donaldson (1947-   )
First book publications: The Chronicles of Thomas Covenant the Unbeliever (includes
  Lord Foul's Bane, 1977; *The Illearth War*, 1977; *The Power That Preserves*, 1977)
  The Second Chronicles of Thomas Covenant (includes *The Wounded Land*, 1980;
  The One Tree, 1982)
Type of work: Novels
Time: Primarily the late 1970's, also the distant future
Locale: The United States and the Land

Thomas Covenant, a leper, is magically transfered from America to the Land, a
fantasy world the survival of which is intimately linked to his capacity as a leper to
survive without fatal commitment to human passions

> *Principal characters:*
> THOMAS COVENANT, a leper, ur-Lord of the Land
> LORD FOUL, an embodiment of the principle of Evil
> ELENA, Covenant's daughter, High Lord
> MHORAM, High Lord after Elena
> SALTHEART FOAMFOLLOWER, a Giant, companion to Covenant
> HILE TROY, an American resident in the Land, its Warlord, and
>   later a Forestal
> LINDEN AVERY, an American doctor in the second trilogy who has
>   come to the Land with Covenant

One must enter the dark metaphysical domain of the Chronicles of Thomas
Covenant the Unbeliever without knowing the nature of the exit, nor how
long one will remain imprisoned within Stephen R. Donaldson's unrelenting
imagination. In late 1982, the sequence of novels remains unfinished. One
cannot yet know whether the central conflict between Thomas Covenant and
Lord Foul will end in the restoration of health to the Land, or in its final sick
dissolution: the reader shares Covenant's nescience.

The first trilogy, comprising *Lord Foul's Bane*, *The Illearth War*, and *The
Power That Preserves*, stands as an aesthetic whole; with two-thirds of the
second trilogy available, *The Wounded Land* and *The One Tree*, it seems
highly probable that Donaldson's ultimate goal is to publish three extended
novels, each comprising three separate volumes, and that his readers have
accomplished barely more than half the journey.

The series to date, however, is far more than a mere beginning. The Chronicles of Thomas Covenant the Unbeliever, the first trilogy in the sequence,
is self-sufficient and a formidable accomplishment in its own right. The Second
Chronicles of Thomas Covenant, presently two-thirds complete, carries the
tale into *terra incognita*; by the end of *The One Tree*, one is greatly distanced

from the world of the first trilogy.

Given the fact that no ambitious high fantasy can be written in the latter half of the twentieth century without invoking J. R. R. Tolkien's *The Lord of the Rings* (1954-1955), it is not surprising to note that Donaldson's fantasy shows signs of its author's immersion in the earlier work. Indeed, it has become a critical truism that the first trilogy shows too many signs of this immersion, and that only with *The Wounded Land* has Donaldson managed to escape an excessive dependence on the earlier epic. Donaldson's use of Tolkien's mythopoeic method and plot structures, and his inept habit of giving his characters names which are heavy-handed paraphrases of the functions of similar characters in Tolkien, give weight to this charge. Without Tolkien's precedent, Donaldson's work is inconceivable, yet his achievement is essentially his own, fundamentally different from Tolkien's in tone, texture, and spirit.

The Chronicles of Thomas Covenant the Unbeliever (hereafter simply the Chronicles) is high fantasy mainly by virtue of its surface paraphernalia. Stripped of these elements, the Chronicles reveals itself as a work of Gothic horror, though expanded and deepened far beyond any models within that genre. In most high fantasy, the legitimacy of the alternate domain is never fundamentally subverted, though heroes are generally permitted to wonder whether they are dreaming; Faerie or Middle-earth are autonomous in the end, and require of their inhabitants—who are usually all too eager to oblige— that they behave as though the high fantasy world existed in a reality transcending that of the mundane world. The high fantasy world is the *real* world, the mundane world is a corruption or blurred aspect of Faerie, and if Faerie is attainable only through dreams, it is because dreams must be portals to a higher world. In the Chronicles, however, the only legitimacy the Land can claim is that it exists in the mind of Thomas Covenant. His conviction that he is dreaming, however fatally he may be involved in his dream, never slides into the delusion that this dream has served as a portal to a better reality. For Covenant, the dream of the Land he is enduring is not a portal but a mirror, and the Land and all within it can only survive as an aspect of the redemption of his threatened soul.

Again and again the story underlines this central relation, in all its Gothic sublimity. On Earth, in contemporary mundane America, a young and successful writer of popular novels named Thomas Covenant finds that he has become a victim of leprosy. Before the disease is checked he loses two fingers on his right hand. He is maimed. Sent to a leprosarium for treatment, he sees in the fates of his fellow lepers the inevitable and unrelenting shape of his own life to come. In order to survive, he comes to understand that he will have to come to terms with his disease and concentrate solely on being who and what he is.

First, he must master the physical dangers of his affliction; because leprosy numbs the parts of the body it afflicts, the sufferer lives in constant danger of sustaining damage wherever his nerves are dead, and once scraped or penetrated by the sharp edges of the world, the deadened parts of the body of a leper heal slowly, if at all. Second, he must realize that, as a leper and despite his great need for human contact and assistance, he will be a pariah. The more he needs help—the more "loathsome" he becomes—the more isolated will be his essential situation as a human being. Every moment must be devoted to the prolongation of this numbed, vulnerable, execrated, solitary existence. Whenever he surrenders to human passion, to the seductions of the human or natural world, he will die a little further. The leper cannot touch a thing, not at the level of significance that makes for human meaning. Physical or psychic contact with the world is suicide.

Covenant refuses to commit suicide. He holes up in his isolated farm near a shabby country town whose inhabitants loathe the thought of his nearness. His wife has divorced him and taken their child. He concentrates on his task in life, that of being a leper. Faithfully, and indeed obsessively (as he must), he performs the VSE—the Visual Surveillance of Extremities—that is the leper's main technique for checking on whether he remains as whole as he was the day before. Of obvious prime importance to any leper, the VSE is of general significance throughout the Chronicles, for if there is a model for perception within the text—a central image for the way the world is seen— that model is the VSE. The seemingly glamorous world of the high fantasy, with its Stone folk and Wood folk and sprites and High Lords and cavewights and giants, is perceived throughout the Chronicles as though it were the face of a leper caught in the mirror of a dream.

In fantasy terms, Covenant's transference to the Land is as traditional as one could hope. After being mysteriously warned by an aged man who refuses to accept from him the wedding ring which represents Covenant's essential nature, he is knocked over by a police car and awakens in another place. His presence in what turns out to be the Land has been invoked by a semi-independent minion of Lord Foul, a cavewight by the name of Drool Rock-worm—the first but by no means the last of Donaldson's appalling coinings— who has discovered the Staff of Law in its underground hiding-place, and threatens to destabilize the Land by misusing—under Foul's indirect control— his newfound power. As a transition to a secondary universe where Good and Evil forces are in eternal conflict and there is no doubt as to who is who, this beginning seems perhaps all too satisfactory. It is, of course, not as simple as all that.

The reader beginning the Chronicles will certainly find Drool Rockworm and his Staff of Law mechanically reminiscent of Tolkien. Drool is remarkably similar to Gollum, the creature who is corrupted by his discovery of and obsession with the One Ring, though if there is any awareness on Donaldson's part of the close resemblance between Gollum and the Alberich of Richard Wagner's Ring cycle, and of the implications Tolkien allows this resemblance to bear for his own text, then this awareness is well-concealed. Drool is indeed a comically mechanical recasting of Gollum, the Hobbit who has gone wrong—both discover an icon of power, both are progressively poisoned by their usurpations, both finally die in a deep crevice, overmastered by their metaphysical loads. It is too similar for mere coincidence, nor can there be any doubt that the surface of Donaldson's saga suffers radically from any comparison with the surface of Tolkien's more considerable work.

Donaldson's intentions, however, are very much unlike Tolkien's. Tolkien's Middle-earth is a fully realized secondary universe, and its every detail works the reader further and further into comprehending its felt reality. There is no conflict. The more the reader knows of Tolkien's universe, the more he is capable of imaginative marriage with the implications of that universe. Nothing like that detailed marriage of surface and depth can occur in the Chronicles. Covenant is acutely aware of the lure of treating Drool Rockworm as real—as an integral gesture of the imagination of a concerned Maker— and it is his refusal to treat Drool as bearing autonomous reality that lies at the heart of the structure of the Chronicles. The mechanical and parodic similarity between the various contingent creations in the Chronicles and the autonomous beings of *The Lord of the Rings* functions as a kind of lure, and the reader can easily fall into the trap of fastening his attention upon this similarity. If he does so, his sympathy with Thomas Covenant—Doubting Thomas—will be exiguous at best.

In terms of the lure of belief, Covenant is a deeply unattractive figure; all in all, he is a most extraordinary character to take the leading role in a heroic fantasy, or in a fantasy of any sort, because his chill refusal to go along with the world constantly violates the delicate decorum of shared belief that makes most fantasies work for their creators, their characters, and their readers. Covenant violates the sense of awe. His presence negates the possibility of any sense of that secular nostalgic immanence, reminiscent of one's childhood visions of God, that so often provides more traditional fantasies with their moments of epiphany. One senses all of this in the opening pages of the Chronicles, and as the plot of the trilogy unfolds, one's intuition clarifies: Covenant becomes less and less tolerable as an inhabitant of the Land. Woebegone, diseased, haggard, obsessed, self-pitying, weak, violent, ungrateful, and choked with ire, he is anything but a willing and usable vessel or conduit for immanence on the cheap. Everything he touches turns to ashes.

The working out of this obsessive refusal of belief constantly serves to monitor the traditional heroic fantasy environment within which Donaldson immures his protagonist. At the heart of the surface tale there is a traditional conflict between the forces of good and the forces of evil, which are eternally opposed and, as usual, always recognizable. The reader knows from the first that Drool Rockworm is a minion of evil, and that Saltheart Foamfollower is ultimately destined to serve good. The Land's inhabitants believe that their world has been created out of Nothing by a traditional Bored Creator, and that He was originally unaware that His eternal Opponent had somehow introduced evil into the new universe. On discovering His error, the Creator in rage casts Lord Foul out of Heaven and binds him to existence, so that Foul is immured in the world and time, intrinsic with the Land. By nature, he loathes his imprisonment and the Land's abundant, radiant health, but can only escape if the Law that binds existence to itself can be dissolved. To dissolve his bonds, he needs outside intervention, a "wild card." Thomas Covenant embodies the random dissolving power required, and it is for this reason he is called to the Land.

Covenant must enact his own Despite against the world, however; he cannot be coerced. The thrust of the story of the Chronicles and of The Second Chronicles of Thomas Covenant (hereafter the Second Chronicles) lies in the dramas of moral trickery arranged by Foul so that Covenant will of his own volition destroy the Creator's prison. That this prison also represents to Covenant the humanity he must constantly refuse is the underlying paradox, the underlying dilemma that causes him such extraordinary anguish, making him, in the end, despite his repellent personality, a figure with whom the reader can sympathize deeply.

Covenant is called to the Land by Drool. Foul appears to him, tells him that everything he does will only make the trap tighter, the outcome more certain, and sends him on his way into the traditional high fantasy venue with a dire message for the High Lords in distant Revelstone. Covenant is to tell them that their long benevolent rule is doomed to collapse within a certain number of years, regardless of what they do to alter their fate. After raping a young girl in a kind of delirium occasioned by the Land's cruel capacity to regenerate his dead leprous extremities, Covenant travels across landscapes familiar to readers of the genre in the direction of far Revelstone, meeting on the way a kindly and radiant Giant by the name of Saltheart Foamfollower, who ferries him up a vast river to his goal. He rouses the High Lords to action, becoming himself ur-Lord. Drool Rockworm, exercising his skewed powers by virtue of his possession of the Staff of Law, begins a mighty campaign against the Land. Covenant and a select party travel to Mount Thunder, at the roots of which they hope to confront Drool. They do so. Drool is defeated. The Staff of Law is in the hands of the High Lords.

With the death of Drool, who has summoned him, Covenant fades from the Land back to contemporary America, where he is persecuted viciously by ignorant people as a leper, but is soon recalled to the Land, this time by the daughter of the woman he had raped. The reader is now in the second book of the Chronicles, *The Illearth War*. Forty years have passed in the Land (dreams cover more territory at a greater rate than anything that passes for significant action in the "real" world—revealingly, in most high fantasy, it is in the "real" world that time passes swiftly), and Covenant's daughter Elena is now High Lord; his actions have had consequences; the dream is biting very deep indeed. After defeating Drool Rockworm, the inhabitants of the Land have spent the past four decades trying to prepare for Lord Foul's next assault, the next stage of the leprosy. A warlord by the name of Hile Troy has been acquired. He claims also to have been transferred from America to the Land, a claim which, if verified, would seem radically to undermine the binding relation between the Land and Covenant. However, on his next return to the "real" world, Thomas Covenant fails to trace any Hile Troy, so the difficulty is passed over in the first trilogy.

The Illearth War is constructed in the form of two dovetailing narratives, each obdurately detailed and slow-moving, each building a very considerable momentum. It is a structure not entirely dissimilar to that of the second volume of Tolkien's trilogy, and is handled by Donaldson with great skill. *The Illearth War* is perhaps the strongest single volume of the five published to date. In one narrative strand, Hile Troy leads the forces of the Land on a grueling forced march in an attempt, only partially successful, to divert Foul's legions from Revelstone. Ultimately, in battles of an unrelenting ferocity, he is forced to retreat through terrible country into what seems a cul-de-sac, to Garroting Deep, which lies at the heart of the primeval, semisentient forest that once covered the entire Land, and remains inimical to man.

In the second narrative strand, Elena, Covenant and an artificial being called Amok, ride toward the great mountain, Melenkurion Skyweir, in an attempt to recover the long lost Power of Command, along with many other magic paraphernalia of the sort endemic to heroic fantasy. When the Power of Command is rediscovered, Elena takes its burden onto herself but proves incapable of wielding it wisely; she calls up one of the old Lords to do battle with Foul, and his inevitable defeat causes her death at the end of the volume. The battle in which she is mortally stricken casts Covenant downward from Melenkurion Skyweir to Garroting Deep. There, Hile Troy has bargained his life away with the spirit of the forest, who destroys Foul's army and its leader, one of Foul's three Ravers, beings not dissimilar to Tolkein's Nazgul, though comically ill-named. In the great, dubious, anguished convulsions that end *The Illearth War*, Covenant is cast back to America.

In the third volume, *The Power That Preserves*, Covenant, once again is summoned into the savage psychomachia of his inward state, finds the Land profoundly diseased. Covenant faces his final defeat, with nothing available to save him from this tenebrous frozen night of the soul but his own refusal to abandon his determination to survive as a leper. He finally confronts Foul himself—the disease has obligingly manifested itself in human garb for the encounter—and defeats him, with the cleansing aid of Saltheart Foamfollower's sane dying laughter, and by his refusal to lose himself in Despite. In effect, by remaining a self-ostracized leper, he refuses the lure of becoming leprosy himself. By refusing to become fatally human, he saves the Land, though it remains seamed with disease, for there is no remission: Foul lives within. Covenant is cast back to the "real" world. However precariously, however thinly, he is alive. He will walk the tightrope of his condition.

Because the Chronicles and the Second Chronicles are horror stories, rather than high fantasy, for many readers it is impossible to come to terms with the radical strength of Donaldson's creation, nor can it be said that its author does much to make things easy for an audience accustomed to prose styles whose high moments, whose greatest intensities, tend to the palpably melodious. Writers such as Lord Dunsany and Tolkien chastely and wisely aspire to epiphanies whose verbal melodies seduce and comfort the reader with the lure of the daydream of transcendence. It is otherwise with Donaldson. Like the story he is telling, his style is rebarbative, clenched into spasms, its imagery a constant—and often confused—act of wrestling with the raw material of vision. It is a style whose highly visual musculature thrusts without respite at the reader's perceptions; clumsy, humorless, dogged, tone-deaf, its triumphs are triumphs of the will to expose the true binding connectives within each image. Donaldson has mounted—one could not say mastered—a way of writing that constantly seems to be telling its readers: This, here, is the truth. Rather than any of the pantheon of fantasy writers to whom he has been likened, or that pantheon of "mainstream" writers to whom he might well wish to be likened, Donaldson as a stylist resembles no one more closely than Theodore Dreiser, the author of *Sister Carrie* (1900) and *An American Tragedy* (1925), though Donaldson's works are dense, even muscle-bound, with metaphor, and Dreiser's are certainly nothing of the sort. What links them so closely together is that air of relentless, gauche sincerity they both bear, and the solitude both convey. It is a solitude of the creator, and of the created. Despite its large cast of characters, the Chronicles is—horrifically—the massively detailed story of one soul in Gothic anguish.

It cannot be denied that in its juggernautlike momentum the telling of the Chronicles has its moments of unconscious humor. Many of the images topple inward on themselves like black holes, letting no light out whatsoever. With adequate editing, Donaldson might have been shifted out of his conviction that one's "mien" was synonymous with one's "face," or that "sojourn" was a synonym of "journey." Some of the more esoteric vocabulary, too, has an unexamined feel, as though it had not been perceived in any other context than an etymological dictionary—much of the difficulty of Donaldson's use of words lies in a recurring tendency to commit the etymological fallacy, to define a word in terms of its original root-meaning, rather than the meaning established for it over the centuries. Nor does it help the reader to select meanings for words which—though they are in the dictionary, such as the use of "gloaming" to describe dawn rather than twilight—are significantly at variance with normal usage. Blemishes of this sort pockmark a style of quite extraordinary strength, even ferocity, and provide fuel for Donaldson's disparagers. This is perhaps one of the liabilities of a solitary talent.

At the same time, blemishes and all, the style of the Chronicles expresses with very great eloquence the gnarled, difficult, obsessive anguish of Thomas Covenant's passion to remain alive. It is less clear, certainly at the half-way point, how successful it will prove in the full telling of the Second Chronicles, with its broader canvas, its large cast of significant characters, its change of venue from the Land to outlying territories, and its relegation of Thomas Covenant to the sidelines for significantly long periods.

A decade has passed in America. Covenant has survived. A woman doctor, Linden Avery, quite similar to Covenant in that her personality is complexly bound to her obsessive accusing guilt at the death of her parents, comes unwillingly onto the scene through the insanity of Covenant's wife, who has returned to him. She has been coerced by Lord Foul. She is possessed. To redeem her, Covenant permits himself to be drawn back to the Land, and Linden Avery is drawn along with him. Unlike Hile Troy, she is a figure of incontrovertible reality. The Land is no longer definable as an objective correlative of the sciamachies within Covenant's tortured mind. In the Second Chronicles, it is something more and less. It exists with an objective density not to be found in the Chronicles, but it exists without any intimate bondage to the meaningfulness Covenant himself conveyed, a bondage which transfixed the reader and drew him through the gauche, extravagant, Gothic telling of the tale. With the arrival of Linden Avery, the Land is emancipated. It has become secular.

Four thousand years have passed, at least half of that period in a time of tranquillity consequent upon Covenant's defeat of Lord Foul. Through treachery and subversion, however, Foul has returned. The Land is diseased, its lifeblood being literally drained by Foul's minions. That which was healthy is abhorred; only obscenities remain in the body politic. A poison atmosphere envelops the Land, transmogrifying the light of the sun into dreadful plague-like visitations of Drought, Rain, Pestilence, on a strict rotation, so that the Land and its people eviscerate themselves frantically at fixed intervals to adjust to sudden floods, sudden sick fecundities, sudden droughts. *The Wounded Land*'s considerable length is spent mostly in dramatized expositions and in recapitulations of the Chronicles. By the end of the volume, Covenant and Avery are about to leave the Land in search of material to reconstruct the lost Staff of Law; they are accompanied and crewed by a large cast of Giants who had come across the seas in search of their brethren of the Chronicles—dead now for millennia, victims of Foul's soul-perversions. Much of *The One Tree* takes place at sea. The description of one violent hurricane in the middle of the volume is perhaps the most extended *tour de force* of the entire saga to date. Covenant is himself mostly dormant. Avery is alive, but gnawed internally by helplessness and love. (In the entire saga, sexual encounters are remarkably few, and dauntingly punitive in their consequences.) The Staff of Law turns out to be with them after all, in the shape of the semianimate Vain, a creature quite similar to the Amok of the earlier sequence; his final role remains dubious. As the volumes of the Second Chronicles progress, in their vivid, secular, populous way, it is possible to regret the relegation of Covenant to unconsciousness or impotence and to fear his moments of uncontrollable ire, when he seems to come closer and closer to acts of power that will utterly dissolve the fabric of the Land and free Foul. The third volume of the Second Chronicles is to be entitled *White Gold Wielder*, a reference to Covenant's wedding ring, which signalizes his rogue and corrosive essential nature in the Land. It is to be seen whether Stephen Donaldson allows his creation to dissolve and his leper die. At this juncture it seems unlikely. There seems to be a great deal left to tell, and almost all of it, with a conviction both moving and relentless, will be about surviving.

John Clute

Bibliography
Bacon, Jonathan. "Interview with Stephen R. Donaldson," in *Fantasy Crossroads*. No. 15 (1979), pp. 11-16.
Wilgus, Neal. "An Interview with Stephen R. Donaldson," in *Science Fiction Review*. VIII (March/April, 1979), pp. 26-29.

THE CHRONICLES OF TORNOR

Author: Elizabeth A. Lynn (1946-   )
First book publications: Watchtower (1979); *The Dancers of Arun* (1979); *The Northern Girl* (1980)
Type of work: Novels
Time: The third through the sixth century
Locale: The land of Arun

A trilogy tracing the rise, flourishing, and decadence of a major cultural institution, the Warriors of the Dance, or the cheari in a land called Arun

> *Principal characters:*
> **Watchtower**
> RYKE, the watch commander of Tornor Keep
> ERREL, the rightful Lord of Tornor
> COL ISTOR, the conqueror of Tornor
> SORREN, a member of the messenger clan, Errel's half-sister
> NORRES, another messenger; Sorren's partner and lover
> VAN, founder of Vanima, the teacher who revives the art of the cheari
>
> **The Dancers of Arun**
> KERRIS, a one-armed scribe and a witch, also the nephew of the Lord of Tornor
> KEL, his elder brother, a cheari
> RINIARD, a member of Kel's chearas
> SEFER, the founder of the first school for witches; Kel's lover
>
> **The Northern Girl**
> SORREN, a bondwoman to Arré Med; the "Northern girl" of the title
> ARRÉ MED, the head of one of the ruling houses of Kendra-on-the-Delta
> ISAK MED, her brother, the finest living dancer
> PAXE, the Yardmaster of the Med household and Sorren's lover
> KADRA, a crippled ex-messenger and a "ghya" (hermaphrodite)
> MERITH, the Lady of Tornor
> KEDÉRA, her daughter

Elizabeth A. Lynn, as her nomination in 1977 for the John W. Campbell Award suggests, is one of the most promising young writers in science fiction and fantasy. She is also prolific: since 1978, when her first novel, *A Different Light*, was published, she has produced the Chronicles of Tornor; a collection of stories, *The Woman Who Loved the Moon and Other Stories* (1981); and the novel *The Sardonyx Net* (1982). At the 1980 World Fantasy Convention, Lynn won two World Fantasy Awards, one for "The Woman Who Loved the Moon" and one for *Watchtower*, the first volume of the Tornor trilogy.

In the trilogy, each volume is complete in itself, with separate casts of characters and different cultural/historical settings more than one hundred years apart; yet an intricate network of references and structural and thematic patterns link the three volumes together. The events of *Watchtower*, for example, have become in *The Dancers of Arun* a part of history, fading rapidly into legend. By the time of *The Northern Girl*, 120 years later still, even the legends are all but forgotten, fables of the race too old and dim to be quite credited. Yet Sorren, in the third volume, inherits a mysterious deck of fortune-telling cards that has the same designs as the deck owned by Errel of Tornor in the first volume (and, in fact, as the genealogy in Volume II reveals, Sorren is descended from Errel). Sorren ties the third volume to the preceding two in another way as well: she has visions of the past, seeing scenes and figures from *Watchtower* and *The Dancers of Arun* which she does not, of course, recognize.

In addition to such referential links, the trilogy is connected by a series of larger structural and symbolic patterns. Arun is a land whose cultural divisions run north and south. The North is mountainous and rugged, the land of the Keeps, which guard Arun against the attacks of Anhard, her aggressive neighbor still farther north. In the Keeps, war is a constant threat, a way of life. On the southern coast is the ancient city of Kendra-on-the-Delta, Arun's cultural center and place of origin, where the fundamental patterns of life are mercantile and urban. In between is the Galbareth, the agricultural heart of the land. The trilogy describes both a cultural and a geographical cycle: the first volume, detailing the origins of the Red Clan, the cheari, centers its action in the North; the second, studying the institution of the cheari at the height of its influence and the organized beginnings of the White Clan, the witches, takes place almost entirely in the Galbareth; while the final volume, revealing the end of the cheari and the approaching decadence of the White Clan, begins in Kendra-on-the-Delta but ends with a return to the North, to Tornor Keep where the trilogy began.

Finally, overarching all these other unifying devices is the thematic unity of the trilogy. Each volume concerns a member of the house of Tornor who is in some profound way out of place. Like a *leitmotiv*, one song echoes through all three volumes: "For I am a stranger in an outland country, I am an exile wherever I go; The hills and stars are my companions, And all I do, I do alone." These lyrics tell only half the truth, however; for if the trilogy explores the exile of these characters, it also explores their ultimate discovery of a new home, a place to belong. The trilogy is, then, in its final effect, fundamentally and satisfyingly hopeful.

Watchtower opens in winter, with Tornor Keep dead and burning. Lord Athor has been surprised by an attacker from the South, Col Istor; Athor himself is dead, and Errel, his son and heir, is a captive. To save Errel's life, Ryke, Athor's watch commander, is forced to aid the conqueror. Col Istor does not harm the Prince, but he turns him into a jester, a cheari, and sets him to tumble and fool for his dinner, which angers and humiliates Ryke almost more than Errel himself.

Soon after, two messengers arrive with a truce offer from a neighboring keep. The messengers, known as the Green Clan, are an important institution in Arun; they are the acknowledged mediators of all conflicts and are unimpeachably neutral. By luck, Errel knows these two, Sorren and Norres, who provide the opportunity for escape which he and Ryke have been awaiting. Since a war against Col in winter and without allies is unthinkable, Norres and Sorren invite the exiles home with them until spring—home to Vanima, Van's Valley. Ryke is skeptical and uneasy; Vanima, "the land of always summer," is supposed to be mythical. Errel, however, is intrigued by the idea, and they accept the messengers' offer.

As they travel, Errel becomes more eager, while Ryke, the viewpoint character, grows increasingly embittered and defensive. He has been a soldier for fifteen years; first losing to Col Istor and then running away (however necessary) have seriously shaken his sense of self. When Van asks him what he can do, he replies, "I lose wars." The only stability in his life is his fealty to Errel as Lord of Tornor; but the Prince is changing in some mysterious way. Errel's Cards of Fortune indicate transformations, unorthodox ideas, testing, change; but Ryke does not like change. His gift is not for mutability, but for steadfastness, for the stubborn staying power that is characteristic of a soldier. Even more upsetting to Ryke are the messengers Sorren and Norres. At first he assumes they are, like most messengers, ghyas—something like hermaphrodites, although no one is quite sure what they are like. Sorren turns out to be a woman (she is Errel's half-sister, in fact, Athor's daughter); and, they discover later, so is Norres, leaving Ryke uncomfortable and off-balance. Both the obvious physical intimacy of their relationship and their rejection of traditional female roles baffle him.

Van of Vanima is the most disconcerting character of all, however; the big man is the best fighter Ryke has ever met, but he does not put these skills to their normal use. Instead, he talks about chea, or balance, from which the word cheari derives. Although it has been corrupted to mean juggler or fool, it once meant something much more powerful—the Dancer, like the first of Errel's Cards of Fortune. As Van explains to Errel and Ryke, "Dance is sacred, because the dancer represents the chea, the balance of the world." As the word cheari has been corrupted, however, the chea also can be corrupted, the balance destroyed, especially by making war, and killing. Vanima is "the place that restores the balance. . . . I teach a way of fighting that does not break the balance because it does not kill." (What Van teaches is, in fact, very much like the Japanese martial art *aikido*, in which Lynn herself holds a brown belt.)

Both Ryke and Errel begin to train in the Yard with Van, Ryke in a kind of dogged homesick misery, Errel learning to dance with the growing sense

Survey of Modern Fantasy Literature

that for him Vanima may be home rather than Tornor. He does finally return north with Ryke and Van, Sorren and Norres, and others of Van's people; and with help from the one unconquered keep, he manages to defeat and kill Col Istor. Then, having reclaimed Tornor, Errel abdicates in favor of his sister Sorren. Whereas Sorren is by nature and inclination a fighter, Errel has discovered that his own calling is to be a cheari. *Watchtower*, then, sees the birth of the cheari, the Red Clan (from their identifying red scarves), as a self-aware social organization bound by a common philosophy—the fighting that is a kind of dancing is preferable to killing.

The second volume of the trilogy, *The Dancers of Arun*, opens again at Tornor Keep, but 120 years later. Seventeen-year-old-Kerris, although the nephew of the Lord of Tornor, is an outcast: since he lost his right arm as a baby, he cannot be a fighter; and even worse, he suffers from fits. These "fits," however, are actually episodes of telepathic contact with his older brother Kel, who is a cheari. One day, Kerris' prayers are answered when Kel arrives with his whole chearas—six or seven chearis living and dancing together as a kind of family—to take him away with them. His adventures with them on the road make up the rest of the novel.

Several major issues are discussed in the book. First is the position and function of chearis in Arun society (here at the height of their power and visibility) and the problems of warfare and killing, which are kept alive by border conflicts with the fierce Asech. Next is the growing number of witches—people with certain kinds of extrasensory powers, such as telekinesis and telepathy—who eventually will organize into the White Clan. This, too, concerns the Asech, who fear their witches so much that they kill or drive them into exile, for the Asech witches come in desperation to the witch town of Elath to demand instruction in their powers. A third issue, linked to Kerris' training as scribe and historian, is the problem of understanding the past and knowing the truth of history from records that are incomplete, inaccurate, or elliptical.

The novel is also about Kerris' coming of age. He must learn how to control and direct his gift of witchcraft, inspeech, and he must decide how best to use it. Sefer, the man who founds the school for witches (and who has been Kel's lover from childhood), wants him to stay in Elath and teach; Kel and Kerris' uncle also want him to stay, offering the home and family for which Kerris has always longed. Kel, however, offers his brother another option. Although Kerris cannot ever be a cheari, his presence turns out to be valuable to the chearas. As Kel, who is also a witch—a patterner—tells Kerris, the pattern feels right when he is with them; Kerris' inspeech on several occasions proves essential to the group. When Riniard's propensity for getting into trouble nearly causes a rift between himself and Kel, Kerris is able to help them resolve the quarrel constructively. Later, when Sefer is brutally murdered, Kerris helps his brother survive the initial overwhelming grief. The chearis in turn teach Kerris by their love of him to accept himself as he is. In the end, Kerris decides that, no matter how many good reasons he has to stay in Elath, his real place is with the chearas, and he joins them on the road as they are preparing to dance. Like Sorren and Errel in *Watchtower*, the exile has found his home.

By the time *The Northern Girl* opens, 120 years later, circumstances have changed greatly. The White Clan, the witches, have become an acknowledged power all through the southern half of Arun and are even beginning to compete with the traditional ruling households of Kendra-on-the-Delta. As the city grows, so does the threat of bloodshed among its heavily armed populace; the White Clan bans edged weapons within the city gates in order to promote peace and the chea. The two functions that the cheari had previously united into a balanced whole are thus split: chearis would dance and soldiers would fight. *The Northern Girl* explores the breakdown, a generation or so later, of this decision, as edged weapons are reintroduced to the city through a legal loophole. The weapons are brought back as part of a power play by a rising city family, which ultimately leads to senseless bloodshed as the established leaders struggle with aspiring ones for control of the city.

A second interwoven plot concerns the personal conflict between Arré Med and her brother Isak for control of their household. Isak is the greatest living dancer, but he is not a cheari; this separation from the ideal of supporting the chea has helped to make of Isak an embittered, duplicitous, power-hungry man, who is finally reduced to sending assassins after his sister in an effort to gain control. His plot fails, however, because of the efforts of Sorren, Arré's bondwoman; but Sorren's most pressing concern for most of the novel is to find her true place. Many factors conspire to draw her attention to the North, and to Tornor particularly—her blonde northern coloring, the Cards of Fortune left her by her mother, and especially her visions of Tornor. Her friendship with Kadra, the hopelessly drunken ex-messenger who draws her a map of the road north and teaches her to shoot a bow, also contributes to her dreams. When her uncovering of Isak's plot wins Sorren her release a year early, she immediately heads for Tornor. Once there, however, she does not find the home she had been looking for, because Tornor is dying of poverty. What she finds instead is a mission—to save Tornor, with Arré Med's help—and a companion, Kedéra, daughter of the Lady of Tornor. Home, for Sorren as for Kerris, thus turns out to be not a place but a person, as the two young women joyously take to the road for Kendra-on-the-Delta.

The movement of the trilogy, then, is not so much circular as helical: in the two hundred years since the beginning of the Chronicles, Tornor and Arun have changed in ways that cannot be reversed. Conditions of the future may resemble in some ways those of the past, but will not reduplicate them: the chearis are gone. Yet, there is some hope; where there is change, there is always the possibility of improvement, and even when society changes for the worse, there is room for individual happiness.

The Chronicles of Tornor prompts two different kinds of responses, aesthetic and political, because it is both a well-told story about characters who
command the reader's sympathy, and a feminist fantasy—although both these
latter terms are problematic. The trilogy is billed as a "fantasy" largely for
lack of a more accurate term. It tells the story of a very humanlike culture
and is full of realistic anthropological and biological details and convincing
portrayals of believable social change. It differs from realistic fiction in that
there never has been a culture exactly like this on Earth. It differs from
science fiction in that the setting is not identified either as some future or
parallel Earth, or as an Earth colony on some other planet: it is simply Arun,
a self-contained world somewhere. So, even though there is no magic (ESP
and Cards of Fortune are not the same thing), "fantasy" is the only label
currently available for this work.

As for "feminist," that label both is and is not accurate. Aside from *Watchtower*, where one of the issues is indeed the limits on women's roles, Lynn's
vision might be more appropriately described as "post-feminist." That is, in
the world of *The Dancers of Arun* and *The Northern Girl* (especially the
latter), the traditional feminist issues seem to have been solved; there appear
to be no gender-linked job restrictions at all. Not only are the heads of the
great city households as likely to be women as men, but Paxe, Arré Med's
Yardmaster (the commander and trainer of her soldiers), is also a woman.
The reader is surprised, not by the sex of the Yardmaster, but by the lack of
attention the novel gives it; in that world, it is ordinary for a woman to be a
soldier, even a Yardmaster. Indeed, so casually egalitarian has this world
become that the generic "he" has been in some cases replaced quietly by a
generic "she," even when the referent word is something traditionally male,
like "soldier." Or, for another example: "Any child, anywhere, if she were
good enough, quick enough, graceful, and disciplined, could be a cheari."

This same lack of ostentation applies to the trilogy's uncommon sexual
relationships, in *The Dancers of Arun* between men—Kerris and Kel, Kel
and Sefer; and in *The Northern Girl* between women—Paxe and Sorren, Paxe
and Arré, Sorren and Kedéra. No doubt some readers will find the erotic
scenes between these couples upsetting, for they are relatively explicit,
although within the bounds of acceptable portrayals of heterosexual eroticism.
What makes these relationships so remarkable is, first, how sympathetically
and yet undogmatically they are portrayed; and second, how ordinary they
seem, for both the narrative voice and the societies around these couples
accept their relationships without comment on their homosexual nature. The
result for readers may very well be an increased tolerance and understanding
of people who choose such alternatives.

Lynn's approach to characterization and detail is satisfyingly realistic. Not
only are Lynn's heroes sympathetic and believable, but her villains are also.

All have some good qualities, as well as understandable human motivations for what they do. Lynn also enriches the texture of her invented world by paying more attention to the details of ordinary life than is usual for fantasy. Indeed, the reader may hear rather too much about chamber pots and the women's menstrual hygiene arrangements, since these items and activities are in all cases incidental to the story; but it is rather refreshing to find characters worrying about real things such as laundry and sunburn. It adds to the verisimilitude.

The most unusual element of the trilogy—Lynn's conception of the cheari— is also the heart of the work's appeal. Not only are the cheari themselves profoundly attractive, but their activity also fits into a consistent philosophy that forms one of the most important themes of the trilogy, and hence a major source of the trilogy's unity. In following the changing fortunes of the cheari, one understands the society of Arun as a whole and the way cultural change occurs. The creation of a culture so fully developed, with such richness of character and history and such a sense of being a living thing, is a noteworthy achievement: the Chronicles of Tornor is well worth serious attention.

Kathleen L. Spencer

Bibliography
Barr, Marlene. "The Chronicles of Tornor," in *Extrapolation*. XXIII (Spring, 1982), pp. 109-112.
McIntyre, Wonda N. "Elizabeth A. Lynn: An Interview," in *Berkley Showcase 4*, 1981. Edited by Victoria Schochet and John Silbersack.

THE CIRCUS OF DR. LAO

Author: Charles G. Finney (1905-   )
First book publication: 1935
Type of work: Novel
Time: The 1930's
Locale: Abalone, Arizona

Dr. Lao, a mysterious Chinese, brings to the quiet town of Abalone his circus of creatures from myth and legend, touching the lives of the residents in a variety of ways

> *Principal characters:*
> DR. LAO, a very old Chinese
> APOLLONIUS OF TYANA, a magus and soothsayer
> THE SERPENT, an exhibit in Dr. Lao's circus
> MR. ETAOIN, proofreader for the Abalone *Tribune*
> AGNES BIRDSONG, a high-school English teacher
> JOHN ROGERS, a plumber
> ALICE ROGERS, his wife
> MRS. HOWARD T. CASSAN, a widow
> FRANK TULL, a lawyer
> LARRY KAMPER, a veteran
> SLICK BROMIEZCHSKI and
> PAUL CONRAD GORDON, college students

Published originally at the height of the Great Depression, Charles G. Finney's first and most famous work of fiction has achieved a somewhat misleading cult reputation in the last quarter century, fueled in part by a lame 1964 film adaptation and in part by association with the work of Ray Bradbury, the book's most famous champion. This is not to suggest that the novel went unrecognized upon its original appearance; in fact, it received an award in 1935 from the American Bookseller's Association as the year's "most original novel"—an award it almost certainly must have deserved. In the years that followed, the book developed a considerable word-of-mouth reputation among fantasy readers, but did not really attain a wide audience until 1956, when it was featured as the title story of an anthology edited by Ray Bradbury. Bradbury's own later novel, *Something Wicked This Way Comes* (1962), gave further evidence of the considerable influence of Finney's work. Like Bradbury, Finney was concerned with the dynamics of small-town life and with the dark, mythical underside of the traveling circus.

In many ways, however, Finney is closer in temperament to James Branch Cabell than to Ray Bradbury (Cabell is in fact the only author directly alluded to in *The Circus of Dr. Lao*). His characters in the small town of Abalone, Arizona, bear more resemblance to those of Sherwood Anderson than to the tradition of Midwestern innocence; and his tone of uncompromising, sometimes bitter irony calls to mind Ambrose Bierce and Sinclair Lewis. Before moving to Tucson, Arizona, to work on a newspaper, Finney had spent three years stationed with the Fifteenth U.S. Infantry in Tientsin, China (an experience assigned to Larry Kamper in the novel), and his work not only reflects a strong Oriental influence, but also reflects a heavily satiric dissatisfaction with the hypocrisies and complacencies of the life to which Finney returned.

This satirical edge sometimes surprises readers expecting a more traditional confrontation between small-town innocence and outside evil. Further complicating the work is its fragmented, episodic structure (complete with a catalog of names and even a quiz at the end, anticipating some of the metafictional experiments of the 1960's), its lack of a clearly identifiable central character or point of view, its unpredictable tone ranging from slapstick to pathos to blatant eroticism, and its apparent inconsistency of characterization (sometimes Dr. Lao speaks in pidgin Chinese-English, while at other times he holds forth like an Oxford scholar). In a work as short as this, these techniques can be disorienting, but they also give the work a texture and density rare among short fantasies, and there is rarely a sense that the author is not in control of his material. "The world is my idea," says Dr. Lao at one point, and the importance of such a point of view stressed here and at other points in the novel (such as a repeated joke about people disagreeing as to whether a particular creature is a bear or a Russian) reminds the reader of the similarities between the world and a work of fiction: in both cases, man derives meaning by assigning names and categories to what he perceives and by recreating the experience according to his own biases. For this reason if for no other, *The Circus of Dr. Lao* stands as a remarkably modern work of fantastic fiction, a novel whose technique seems more familiar today than when it was originally published.

The basic story is rather simple. An advertisement filled with apparently wildly exaggerated claims appears in the *Abalone Morning Tribune*, announcing a circus but offering no clue as to whose circus it is. There follows a series of brief vignettes (which will prove to be the basic structural units of the story) describing the reactions of various townspeople to the ad and revealing how some particular aspect of it appeals to each of them at some primal level; the reactions to the ad provide a kind of foreshadowing of the main action of the story by introducing the general theme of temptation and the technique of multiple points of view. This technique is made more explicit in the description which follows of the circus parade down the main street of Abalone: the parade consists only of three small beast-drawn wagons, but the discussions and arguments that arise over what is in the wagons, or what is drawing them, reveals the extent to which people attempt to deal with the unusual by accommodating it to their own narrow spheres of experience. These introductory episodes concerning the advertisement and the parade also serve to introduce a surprisingly large cast of characters representing a cross-section of American middle-class life: a newspaper proofreader, a sexually repressed high-school

English teacher, an aging widow who deludes herself into believing that her life may become interesting once again, an unemployed plumber and his family, a recently discharged Army veteran-*cum*-hobo, and a pair of obstreperous college students on vacation. Acting as a kind of Greek chorus to these major characters are a number of recurring "extras": an elderly gentleman in golf pants, a team of quarantine inspectors, and two police officers.

The bulk of the narrative consists of a dozen or so episodes in which these characters interact with the circus performers and exhibits. In the first of these, the young high-school teacher, Agnes Birdsong, arrives at the circus to hear a curiously lame and ill-informed spiel delivered by an aging magician who is not even quite sure which exhibit is in which tent. This speech, like the earlier anonymous newspaper ad, raises questions about why the circus exists at all and reinforces the notion that each visitor must seek out what he is looking for; he is certainly not going to get much help from the ballyhoo. What Miss Birdsong is seeking, apparently, is sex. She wanders into the tent housing a real satyr, and, in a scene of surprising frankness and detail, is nearly seduced by his wild, erotic dance. In a radical shift of style that is to prove one of the hallmarks of Finney's technique, Dr. Lao enters the tent delivering a learned scientific lecture on the history and habits of satyrs. The lecture brings the episode to an end without any further reference to Miss Birdsong at all.

Radical contrast of another kind characterizes the second major episode, in which the Rogers family visits the magician Apollonius. Their limited view of the world prevents them from being at all impressed by his magic, however—they assume it is all "tricks"—and Apollonius is led to perform ever more spectacular feats of magic, even to resurrecting a man from the dead. Even the restored dead man seems to have no time to ponder this miracle, however, and rushes off to attend to some unspecified business. In the following episode, this characteristic lack of imagination on the part of the townspeople has somewhat darker results, as a disbelieving housewife confronts the Medusa and is promptly turned to stone. Repeatedly, the townspeople encounter one authentic marvel after another—the part-vegetable hound of the hedges, a mermaid, a sphinx, a chimera—but in each case they seem to refuse resolutely to have their horizons expanded or to change their simple views of the world. Just as an abalone clings tenaciously to its rock, the citizens of Abalone refuse to modify their preconceptions.

This obstinance is illustrated most poignantly in what is perhaps the most affecting episode in the narrative. Mrs. Howard T. Cassan, a widow, visits Apollonius (now a fortune-teller) to hear the kind of bromidic forecasts she is accustomed to hearing from such people. Apollonius can speak only the truth, however, and the truth he tells her is brutal: nothing of any importance will ever happen in her life, and there is no apparent reason whatsoever for her existence. Mrs. Cassan lamely attempts to shift the focus of the discussion to Apollonius' own background and motives, but he dismisses her. Upon leaving the tent, she tells her friend that he has been "frightfully encouraging."

Another erotic episode follows, with the two college students visiting the peepshow and witnessing a group of nymphs molesting an innocent faun in a kind of reversal of the sexual fantasy experienced by Miss Birdsong earlier. Mr. Etaoin engages in a dialogue with the sea serpent, presented in dramatic form, which touches upon the contrasts and similarities between its mythical history and his own mundane life (notable here again is Finney's use of style and content to create a sense of disorientation; despite the wildly romantic nature of the serpent's story, he delivers it in a diffident manner reminiscent of a Damon Runyon narrator). Larry Kamper, the drifter who is the only character to have experienced much of the world outside Abalone (and the character whose background most resembles that of Finney himself), witnesses the transformation of the werewolf into an old woman; but even he expresses disappointment when the shape-shifting fails to result in a nubile young maiden.

The final episode of the story brings all the characters together for the main performance of the circus, which one of the spectators describes as "the dance of life." The performance very nearly descends into chaos as the beasts turn on one another; but Apollonius commands the center of attention by staging a witches' Sabbath with real witches and a culminating appearance by Satan himself, who threatens to take over until Apollonius vanquishes him with a crucifix. Dr. Lao himself narrates the final spectacle: a re-creation of the ancient city of Woldercan and its attempts to end a drought by staging a virgin sacrifice to its stone god Yottle. Even this myth is undercut by a heavy sense of irony—the difficulty of finding twelve attractive girls in Woldercan who are also virgins, for example—but when the pageant ends with the stone god collapsing over priest, virgin, and the lover who attempts to rescue her, so does the story, with surprising abruptness. The "catalogue" which follows, listing and commenting on virtually every person, place, or thing mentioned in the text, no matter how trivial, raises more questions about the meaning of the narrative than it answers.

The Circus of Dr. Lao is not a difficult book to read, but it can be a frustrating one. One comes away with the feeling that Finney himself is Dr. Lao, and his story the circus; certainly the way the text calls attention to itself through such devices as the catalog suggests this interpretation. With its narrative fragmentation, inconsistency of style, and variations in tone, the novel seems to taunt the reader constantly: should one accept the reality of the circus and risk becoming victims of romance, or reject it and risk becoming as staid and unimaginative as the townspeople? The novel never quite settles into being a satire, a psychological drama, a nonsense work, or a myth fantasy, and yet it partakes of all these genres and exhibits as wide a range of influences. Sometimes Finney appears to be spinning a tall tale in the tradition of Southwestern literature; at other times he is a social satirist, at still others a player with words and narrative tricks. It may be that not all of this is quite conscious; certainly some episodes work more effectively than others, and the overall unity of the work suffers from these various pyrotechnics. For all its puzzles, however, *The Circus of Dr. Lao* remains a unique work in modern American fantasy and one deserving of the readership that it has only recently begun to receive.

Gary K. Wolfe

Bibliography
Hoaglund, Edward. "Introduction," in *The Circus of Dr. Lao*, 1982.
Lee, L. L. "Fantasy as Comic American Morality: *The Circus of Dr. Lao*," in *The Markham Review*. X (Summer, 1981), pp. 53-56.

THE CITADEL OF FEAR

Author: Francis Stevens (Gertrude Bennett, 1884-1939?)
First book publication: 1970
Type of work: Novel
Time: The early twentieth century
Locale: A remote region of Mexico and the suburbs of an American city

After escaping from a lost city in Mexico where the Aztec gods are still worshiped,
a young Irish-American meets for a second time the ancient evil which he found there

> *Principal characters:*
> COLIN O'HARA, a soldier of fortune
> ARCHER KENNEDY, an explorer and man of science
> SVEND BIORNSON, an archaeologist "gone native" in Tlapallan
> CLIONA RHODES, O'Hara's sister
> ANTHONY RHODES, her husband
> MACCLELLAN, a detective

The Citadel of Fear was the second of seven pulp novels that Gertrude Bennett wrote under the pseudonym Francis Stevens between 1918 and 1923. It appeared serially in *Argosy* in 1918. Although it was not reprinted in book form until 1970, it also appeared in the magazine *Famous Fantastic Mysteries* in 1942 and, along with *The Heads of Cerberus* (1952) and *Claimed* (1966), has always been one of the most highly regarded works of one of the best of the early pulp fantasists. Stevens' career was short; she took up writing in order to support her mother and her infant daughter after the death of her husband, and her writing stopped as soon as she no longer needed the money. Apart from the seven novels, she wrote four short stories; and this represents the sum total of her literary production. According to Donald Tuck's *The Encyclopedia of Science Fiction and Fantasy* (1974 and 1978), she disappeared in California in 1939 and was never heard of again—a kind of fate which is, one feels, singularly appropriate to writers of menacing fantasies.

The Citadel of Fear starts as a conventional lost-race romance, with two explorers thrown together by chance surviving the rigors of a desert wilderness to stumble upon the city of Tlapallan, where the Aztec gods Quetzalcoatl and Nacoc-Yaotl (a dark avatar of Tezcatlipoca) are still worshiped. The followers of the two gods are mutually hostile, but peace in the city is maintained partly through the agency of Svend Biornson, an American archaeologist who has settled in the valley and married one of its women. The lost race is pale-skinned, and the women are almost supernaturally beautiful.

Events move at a relentlessly fast pace, with O'Hara and Kennedy, the two explorers, stirring up a good deal of trouble as they escape from prison and meddle in matters that were better left alone. O'Hara is quickly banished from the realm, but Kennedy, who has encountered the living god Nacoc-Yaotl, is condemned to death.

The story resumes fifteen years later, with O'Hara returned to America from one of his many expeditions in order to visit his recently married sister Cliona. While he and Cliona's husband, Anthony, are absent from the house, something breaks in and smashes up the furniture. Cliona empties a revolver through a closed door as it tries to break through, catching a glimpse of a terrible claw before it flees. Other visitations follow apace, and O'Hara tracks a giant gray ape to a mysterious house—a "fortress of fear"—where a man named Chester Reed, accompanied by an albino servant and a girl he claims is his insane daughter, is conducting sinister experiments. Ultimately, O'Hara learns that Reed is Archer Kennedy, reprieved from a sentence of death because Nacoc-Yaotl had a purpose for him; he is now a corrupt but unknowing servant of the evil god. With the aid of a compound which causes strange metamorphoses, he is planning to conquer the world.

The beautiful girl with Reed is, of course, no part of the hideous plot, and is in fact Svend Biornson's daughter. She helps O'Hara (who loves her) in the climactic confrontation in the mysterious house, where Anthony Rhodes and two detectives from the local police force also take a hand. The climax is not merely a battle between men and monsters but a duel between ancient gods, and it is conducted in suitably melodramatic fashion.

It is easy enough to see why contemporary readers loved *The Citadel of Fear* and cherished its memory. It is a crowded and eventful narrative which combines all the key elements of the fantastic fiction of its period into an extravagant thriller. There are stylistic echoes of Abraham Merritt and thematic echoes of Sax Rohmer. The novel has all the faults as well as all the virtues of pulp exotica, but that hardly matters to the connoisseur of the species—indeed, it helps to make the story almost archetypal. Mrs. Bennett was to some extent an imitative writer, but she had qualities of her own as well as a marvelous sensitivity to the qualities of other writers that were worth borrowing. She knew what kind of fiction was likely to please her relatively specialized audience, and she produced it. *Weird Tales* was founded just in time to provide a home for the last of her long stories, and there is little doubt that if she had continued to write she would have become one of the stalwarts of that magazine.

The Citadel of Fear is a book to be read rather than dissected, and afterthought only serves to accentuate the clichés and incongruities which congregate in its plot; but it is nevertheless a fine example of the popular fiction of its day.

Brian Stableford

Bibliography
Eshbach, Lloyd Arthur. "Introduction," in *The Heads of Cerberus*, 1952.

THE COLLECTED GHOST STORIES OF M. R. JAMES

Author: M. R. James (1862-1936)
First book publication: 1931
Type of work: Short stories

Ghosts and other malign spirits lurk in the fields and buildings of England, to be brought to the fore by the innocent probings of historical scholars, collectors of antiques, or meddlers, usually to the detriment of both the antiquarian and the bystanders

Montague Rhodes James wrote his first ghost story in 1893. His work in the genre over the next several decades was published in four small volumes: *Ghost-Stories of an Antiquary* (1904), *More Ghost Stories of an Antiquary* (1911), *A Thin Ghost and Others* (1919), and *A Warning to the Curious, and Other Ghost Stories* (1925). These books contain twenty-six tales; four others, previously uncollected, were added to form *The Collected Ghost Stories of M. R. James* (1931), which has remained in print continuously on both sides of the Atlantic since its publication. Thus James wrote, on the average, less than one story a year over a long career—a much smaller output than such Victorian masters of the supernatural as J. Sheridan Le Fanu or William Hope Hodgson.

Yet James's name has become significant in the history of the supernatural tale, despite his slender contribution. Three facts account for this high reputation. First, James was a widely known scholar of antiquity, both classical and British; moreover, his long career as teacher and administrator at Cambridge and Eton (where he was Provost for the last eighteen years of his life) secured this reputation among the educated and influential. His first ghost stories were written to be read aloud to some of these people and were printed because their reputation had spread among those who knew him, or knew of him; hence the tales had a presold initial audience. Second, James acquired a reputation—based on his edition of some Le Fanu tales and his thoughtful introduction to the Oxford World's Classics volume of ghost stories—as a theorist of the genre. Neither of these facts would be of any importance, however, without the third: the stories are generally of high quality. Narrowly focused, delicately fashioned, and ironic, they are finely wrought miniatures of fright.

Central to James's most successful ghost stories is setting. He wrote in the Preface to the collected stories that his inspiration tended to come from places rather than from dreams, from experiences (his own or others'), or from books. The stories bear this out: one-third have a place or building mentioned in the title, and another one-third depend on the author's ability to render the effect of the setting. Not that these locations are exotic or conventionally "spooky"; on the contrary, they are far more likely to be ordinary. The reader is presented with the marvelous in the midst of mundane surroundings—

churches, country houses, hotel rooms, libraries, even open fields. The decaying castle of the Gothic tale and the crumbling Victorian haunted house are missing, but the terror is all the greater for their absence, for it is underlined by its contrast to the security the protagonists have a right to expect. Moreover, the places in the stories are not merely backgrounds: often, a James tale involves the investigation (or disruption) of a seemingly ordinary place. The modern attitudes of the investigator contrast sharply with the antiquity of the locale, which even seems to have a personality and to fight the intruder. The conflict thus becomes one between an antiquary and the ghosts of those who wish him not to disturb their rightful homes. A professor blows on an ancient bronze whistle, to his peril; a country gentleman acts on clues to treasure found in old churches, to his mortal danger; a travel writer jokingly calls forth the inhabitant of an old tomb, to his own destruction.

The first volume demonstrates the conventions of the Jamesian ghost story. The story's form is ratiocinative; the protagonist, often a middle-aged antiquary, is looking for something (or, sometimes, he simply finds something mysterious). The seeker, it turns out, is asking the wrong question: the object or artifact is not what it seems. Worse yet, its nature is related in some way to an ancient evil that still retains some connection with it or power over it. The investigator may be imperiled by a ghost, a lingering malignant spirit, or a curse. Usually, the peril is unexpected; ordinary activity by an intellectual gentleman leads to an unpleasant surprise, as dark forces are unleashed through sheer naïveté. Generally, the tale is told by, or from the point of view of, the investigator and focuses on his mental and emotional states. Women are few in the tales, and are seen only in subordinate roles (housekeepers, daughters, loving mothers) or as ghosts; the even fewer children are either ghosts or potential victims. Rarely, the principal character is no innocent scholar, but a necromancer; James depends far more often on the shock of an unanticipated danger.

The three stories alluded to above are typical. The professor in "Oh, Whistle, and I'll Come to You, My Lad" who finds the whistle is Parkins, a skeptic who is on holiday from teaching ontography. He picks up the whistle in some Roman ruins near the seaside town where he has gone to play golf. Idly, he blows it—and is visited by a terrifying disembodied spirit which takes a horrible form in the bedclothes in Parkins' hotel room and attacks him. Only the action of gruff, practical Colonel Wilson saves Parkins: Wilson exorcises the professor by flinging the whistle into the sea. This story is among James's most celebrated, perhaps because of the effective contrast between the sleepy seaside resort and the fussy bachelor professor on the one hand, and the eerie ruins and horrible visitation on the other. Certainly the very namelessness, formlessness, and mystery of the ghost are part of the story's stunning effect.

The country gentleman, Mr. Somerton, has decoded the stained-glass windows which are clues to the location of treasure, buried centuries before in a well near Steinfeld. The extraction of the treasure from its hiding place arouses the supernatural guardian set over it by its original owner. William Brown, Somerton's manservant, has the presence of mind to write to the rector at home, an antiquary named Mr. Gregory, who comes to Germany, finds out what has happened, and (with Brown's help) returns the treasure to its home, lifting the curse from Somerton. "The Treasure of Abbot Thomas" also works through contrasts—the sleepy German town and the alert English treasure-hunter; the shy rector and the gruff manservant; the intellectual quest and its horrifying consequences; and the terror of the situation and the humor also implicit in it.

In "Count Magnus," Mr. Wraxall is in Raback, Sweden, to do a travel book. He is intrigued by the tales he hears about Count Magnus de la Gardie, a sixteenth century local tyrant who was also an alchemist and, perhaps, a necromancer. Wraxall impetuously calls up the Count's spirit from his elaborate triple-locked tomb; nothing happens, except that one lock is broken open. Foolishly, Wraxall repeats the summons twice on later visits to the tomb, and one more lock breaks each time. Wraxall realizes too late what he has done and flees, but something pursues him and, on the ship home, destroys him. The clear implication is that the evil place in which an evil man is buried has possessed an empathetic soul and forced it to do the bidding of the dead, now loosed again on an unsuspecting world. Wraxall is a sort of guilty bystander manipulated by forces of unexpected power and underestimated malignancy.

What synopses like these cannot convey is the emotional quality of the tales. In part their impact results from the rendering of place by a few well-chosen details—the way the light falls, the shape of a tree or building, the sound of the wind. In part, too, it stems from the identification on the part of the reader with a very ordinary man plunged suddenly into extraordinary circumstances. In large measure, however, the effect is created by verbal style—by the voice of the narrator, speaking slowly and softly, allowing the surprises to speak subtly for themselves, being deliberately vague about all things except when precision is what is needed, remaining calm and gentlemanly even when telling of horrors and outrages. His style is a perfect vehicle for the contrasts by which James achieves his effect. Here lies the principal result of the tales' being written to be read aloud; the reader hears a genuine voice, speaking alertly but often with ironic amusement of things about which even it has doubts and reservations.

Two other tales in the first volume deserve comment. In "Lost Hearts," the ghosts are those of two young children murdered in 1792 and 1805 by a gentleman named Abney, who consumed the ashes of their hearts (mixed with a pint of port each) in an experiment based on ancient necromantic writings. Abney believes that he will thereby gain supernatural powers, including flight, invisibility, and perhaps immortality; his experiment will be completed with the ritual of his twelve-year-old cousin and ward, Stephen Elliott. Young Elliott, although alerted to the possibility of danger by mysterious apparitions (the ghosts), is almost used by Abney in his rituals; but at the last moment the ghosts attack Abney and take vengeance by ripping out his heart as he had theirs. Some years later, Elliott reads his cousin's papers and discovers the truth of the danger into which he had innocently walked.

The tale is told from young Stephen's point of view, with the reader given little more information than the boy possesses; but the reader is less naïve and therefore able to interpret the clues that Stephen misses. For example, the reader notices that Abney repeatedly and oddly asks the boy's age; the reader guesses the truth behind the housekeeper's tale of the mysterious disappearances of the children who had lived in the house years before; the reader deduces the agency responsible for the apparitions that Stephen experiences; the reader suspects with horror the meaning of the ritual tools—incense, brazier, silver cup—assembled by Abney. The boy misses all of these clues in his innocence. At the end, the reader's suspicions are confirmed (and Stephen's eyes opened) when an adult Stephen reads Abney's papers. This climactic device brings together again the reader's and protagonist's perceptions, which had diverged early in the story; it also makes the tale fit the standard Jamesian pattern of antiquarian research.

A more thorough use of the pattern is "The Mezzotint." The picture of an unknown manor house comes into the hands of a Mr. Williams, curator of an art museum at a British university. The mezzotint dates from the early nineteenth century. Williams cannot understand why the picture has been sent to him by his regular supplier and resolves to return it. Before he can do so, the picture begins to change. Over the course of a weekend, a grim drama is enacted: a mysterious, black-garbed figure crosses the lawn to the house, enters through a window, and leaves bearing a child. After these events take place, the picture never changes again. Through some research Williams discovers that he has evidently seen a ghost steal a child; its father had engraved the picture, which is obviously haunted. In this story, James cleverly misdirects the tension: Williams is in no danger, although he feels he is. Since the tale is basically one of detection, the tension is resolved intellectually—and thus lingers, without full emotional discharge, in the reader's mind.

The stories in the later volumes repeat the themes and motifs of the first, with gradually diminishing effectiveness. In *More Ghost Stories*, James gives the reader a carefully balanced set of tales. Two involve haunted gardens; two others deal with the exposing of a murderer by his victim's ghost; two others, with the deaths of malefactors at the hands of injured ghosts; and one with the disturbing of a tomb. There is a good deal of ingenuity and wit in the stories—a necromancer conjures up a demon to have vengeance on writers of unfavorable reviews; a ghost haunts a library to prevent the discovery of an encrypted will; a schoolboy invents Latin exercise sentences that hint at knowledge of a murder. The stories possess the same sense of real locality and the same tone, but they are more clever and less intense than the original group. The ghosts of *A Thin Ghost*, the shortest volume, are nearly routine, as ghost tales go: two boys killed while dabbling in necromancy; a murdered man who induces significant dreams in his nephew and thus induces the punishment of his killers; the inhabitant of a cathedral tomb; and others. *A Warning to the Curious* tends toward the folkloristic (the ghostly guardians of the ancient Anglo-Saxon crowns), the macabre (a pair of field-glasses that can see into the past because they are made in part from dead men's eyes), and the self-imitative (a haunted doll's house reminiscent of the mezzotint of the first volume). The last tales—the ones collected for the omnibus volume— move away altogether from the world of the antiquary and are yet slighter. Each has some effect, but none has the compelling power of the first collection's understated, sinister stories.

The early stories and the best of the later ones can nevertheless still work their magic. The reader must be willing to sit and listen attentively to surprising horrors in the midst of rural scenery or tranquil universities. The voice that tells of them is cultivated, avuncular, quiet; it produces few screams, being content with a stifled gasp. The voice creates a lost England of gentility, calm, and rationality; then it shatters all these by telling of an intrusion of the irrational and the dangerous. The reader shudders involuntarily, as one does when one feels a touch on the shoulder when one is alone in a room. The antiquary ghost story has succeeded.

William H. Hardesty III

Bibliography

Briggs, Julia. *Night Visitors: The Rise and Fall of the English Ghost Story*, 1977.

Cox, J. Randolph. "Ghostly Antiquary: The Stories of Montague Rhodes James," in *English Literature in Transition*. XII (1969), pp. 197-202.

——————— . "Montague Rhodes James: An Annotated Bibliography of Writings About Him," in *English Literature in Transition*. XII (1969), pp. 203-210.

Neilson, Keith. "M. R. James," in *Critical Survey of Short Fiction*, 1981. Edited by Frank N. Magill.

Sullivan, Jack. *Elegant Nightmares: The English Ghost Story from Le Fanu to Blackwood*, 1978.

THE COLLECTED GHOST STORIES
OF OLIVER ONIONS

Author: Oliver Onions (George Oliver, 1873-1961)
First book publication: 1935
Type of work: Short stories and a novella

A chilling series of "daylight" ghost stories in which the vagaries of human perception and the vulnerability of the mind render the ambiguous ghostly presences even more fearsome

Although Oliver Onions treats many of the traditional genre subjects in his supernatural stories, such as haunted houses and rooms ("Beckoning Fair One," "A Rope in the Rafters"), clairvoyance and precognition ("The Accident," "The Rosewood Door"), time dislocations ("The Cigarette Case," "'John Gladwin Says . . .'"), lycanthropy ("The Master of the House"), otherworldly women ("The Honey in the Wall," "The Painted Face"), and, of course, ghostly apparitions, his approach is unique. Onions articulated the basis of this originality in the "Credo" he affixed to his *The Collected Ghost Stories of Oliver Onions*. Ghosts, he stated, "like the stars at noonday . . . are there all the time and it is we who cannot see them." He went on to suggest that "What the writer has in practice to investigate is the varying 'densities' of the ghostliness that is revealed when this surface of life, accepted for everyday purposes as stable, is jarred, and for the time of an experience does not recover its equilibrium." Moreover, the evidence of such presences comes not primarily by sight, but through the more subtle senses: "Who at some time or other has not walked into a room, known and familiar and presently to be known and familiar again, but that for a space has become a different room, informed with other influences and charged with other meanings?" On the other hand, Onions continues, there are "living" humans who, while participating actively in "this world," hover on the edge of the "secondary zone" and almost seem to belong to it; their presences and fates are every bit as unnerving as those of the unseen.

Onions completely blurs the lines between the living and the dead, the real and the unreal, and the present and the past and future. Man has his senses, his experiences, and his mind to utilize in scrutinizing this most precarious and dubious thing called reality, and all are quite unreliable. It follows, then, that the supernatural in Onions' best stories is subtle, ambiguous, and subjective. Characters feel the otherworldly intrusions into their reality, and become increasingly involved with them, but it is seldom clear whether such forces are supernatural agencies or are but the products of the characters' increasingly distorted perceptions and progressively unstable minds.

Thus, it is not surprising that Onions' weakest stories are those in which the supernaturalism is the most overt. "The Rosewood Door" is a good example of the blatantly occult story. The first night she sleeps in the room behind an ornate, curved rosewood door, recently acquired by the owner of the house, guest Agatha Croft sees an apparition; it is a handsome man in an archaic costume bearing a short sword. The ghost proves himself "real" by leaving the sword with Agatha. Later she meets an identical man in the flesh, Barty Paton, the long-lost adventurous brother of another houseguest. Agatha and Barty fall in love and are married. Agatha objects strongly to spending their wedding night in the room behind the rosewood door, but she is overruled. That night Barty appears in a daze and kills Agatha with the short sword. He has been possessed by the spirit of an ancestor who, upon returning from the Crusades, murdered his wife for infidelity. The story is clever and the character of Agatha is well drawn, but the overall effect is flat. The short sword magically appearing from the Middle Ages is just too palpable, and perhaps too trite, to belong in Onions' "secondary zone." Other stories with unambiguously supernatural intrusions—for example "The Cigarette Case" and "The Odd Sister"—suffer from similar problems. At best they are ingenious; at worst, simply contrived.

"The Accident," on the other hand, has only a touch of the supernatural, but that touch crystallizes the story into one of Onions' best. Romarin, a successful painter, waits in front of a restaurant where he is to have a reconciliation with Marsden, an antagonist of many years. He sees Marsden coming and then, Onions tells the reader, Romarin has his "accident"— although the author does not reveal the nature of that accident until the story's end. What follows is a long, brilliant dramatic set piece in which, over lunch, both characters are thoroughly revealed—Romarin as a sensible, decent man; Marsden as a bitter, erratic hedonist—and the nature of the conflict is gradually exposed. Tensions mount as Marsden recalls their old hostilities and exacerbates them, until Romarin explodes and stabs his luncheon partner in the neck. At that point, the "accident" is revealed; the entire lunch scene has been a precognitive vision existing only in Romarin's mind— or was it merely an example of the painter's lively imagination? In any event, Romarin turns and flees, breathing a sigh of relief which is shared by the reader. The story is vividly and economically told; the dialogue is sharp and subtle, with small details and gestures reinforcing and intensifying the dramatic conflict. The touch of the otherworldly, coming as and when it does, fuses everything together beautifully.

Thus Onions balances the objective and the subjective, the intensely realized dramatic scene and the evocatively rendered inner landscape, with the supernatural intrusion—which may or may not be "real"—crystallizing the experience. It is not irrelevant that Romarin is a painter; most of Onions' best stories involve artists of one sort or another. Indeed, it is the special place he gives to creative artists, to their especially acute perceptions, and to the relationship between themselves and their works, that gives Onions' ghostly fictions their most unusual thrust.

In "The Beckoning Fair One," Onions' best-known and most celebrated story, one that no less than Algernon Blackwood called "the best ghost story ever written," it is his acute sensitivity that makes the main character, novelist Paul Oleron, especially vulnerable to the growing influence of the female spectral presence that seems to occupy the set of rooms he rents. The story starts slowly and carefully traces the stages by which the malevolent yet seductive female spirit gradually possesses and destroys the protagonist—or is it simply a protracted dramatization of the final descent of a frustrated, solitary middle-aged writer into madness? The only overtly supernatural intrusion into the story is a noise, the sound of a woman's long hair being slowly, carefully, sensuously brushed, and that sound is heard by Oleron only after he is well on the way to emotional collapse. Yet Onions creates his atmosphere so deliberately and thoroughly with language and detail, and builds his effects with such subtlety and precision, that the reader is completely absorbed in the unnaturalness of the situation. Paradoxically, the power of the otherworldly becomes so overwhelming in the story because it is brought in so unobtrusively and indirectly. Like Paul Oleron, the reader is unaware of being absorbed by the beckoning fair one until it is too late.

Paul Oleron rents a new set of rooms for reasons of convenience. There is nothing supernatural evident in them; even the usual "exceptionally low rent" can be accounted for by the generally run-down condition of the rooms and the neighborhood. As he settles into his new and more convenient lodgings, he is poised to complete the novel, *Romilly Bishop*, that promises to win for him his long-awaited critical and commercial success. Yet, even on the purely realistic level, Oleron clearly has problems. Although he has received some critical recognition for his twenty years of effort, he makes at best a modest living as a writer. He seems to be in the midst of at least a mild "mid-life crisis," some second thoughts about his career as a fiction writer, and a general uneasiness about the indecisiveness of his life.

These feelings focus on his curiously irresolute relationship with Elsie Bengough, a "popular" writer in her mid-thirties. She is more than friend to him, but less than lover or potential mate; she gives him advice, counsel, and encouragement, along with hard criticism, and clearly loves him. He respects and needs her support, is quite fond of her without being willing to admit to deeper affections, and admires her as a person. She is, in fact, the model for "Romilly Bishop"; his shifting attitude toward that character reflects his changing feelings toward Elsie. Oleron's relationship to Elsie Bengough is, of course, but an indication of his general separation from other people, a voluntary isolation that makes him especially vulnerable to the spectral presence in his room—or to his own self-created demons.

"You'll never work here," Elsie tells Paul shortly after he moves in, and her hostility is the first real indication that something is awry. The rooms, in turn, react against her; on her first visit, she is severely scratched by nails Paul was sure he had removed; on her second, her foot goes through a stair that had seemed solid moments before. The pivot of the story becomes the conflict between Elsie and the rooms for Paul's spirit, and as the spectral presence makes itself more concretely known, the motive becomes clear: jealousy.

The most important developments throughout the story, however, are in Paul's personality, although most of them seem relatively harmless in the beginning. He grows indolent and puts off work on the novel. Then, as he considers the book, he decides he wants to change it, to scrap the chapters already written (modeled on Elsie) and create a new female character, although the precise character of the woman eludes him—until the very end of the story. His relationship to his rooms heightens, his sense of hearing becomes more acute, and he begins to listen consciously to the small sounds of the building. He finds himself unconsciously doing surprising things, most notably humming a song he has never, to his knowledge, heard before; his housekeeper identifies the tune as "The Beckoning Fair One."

As Paul becomes more occupied with his rooms, he becomes more isolated, more distant from Elsie, and more vaguely panicked, but when he finally hears the ghostly hairbrushing it is too late. His feeble attempts at escaping or finding a defense against "her"—by getting drunk at a local pub, by researching the "history" of the rooms—amount to nothing. Oleron declines quickly into confusion and psychosis. Then, with a most adroit shift in point of view, Onions gives the outcome of the story in a brief dramatized scene when the police search Oleron's rooms, finding him naked and demented in bed; Elsie has been murdered and stuffed into a cupboard.

Who is "the beckoning fair one?" The reader never learns. The history of the rooms reveals only that a previous tenant, a painter named Madley, had also gone insane. Early in the story Oleron had "amused himself with the farfetched fancy that he might so identify himself with the place that some future tenant, taking possession, might regard it as in a sense haunted." After hearing the mysterious brushing he wonders if "there might have been a similar merging and coalescence in the past." That is the closest thing to an explanation of the story that Onions offers. The "beckoning fair one" is perhaps the most seductive, malevolent, and *real* female ghost in the literature, although she is never seen. How much more awful than creaking doors and clanking chains is the sound of "the long sweep with the almost inaudible crackle in it. Again and again it came, with a curious insistence and urgency. It quickened a little as he became increasingly attentive . . . it seemed to Oleron that it grew louder."

Just as Oleron alters the main female character of his novel-in-progress as "she" alters his consciousness, so Aubrey Kneller, the writer/hero of "The Real People," alters the heroine of his novel in response to another female force. Or perhaps it is the other way around: the character in the story, operating in conjunction with a real woman, alters both the fictional story and the life of its author. Thus Onions presents another variation on the theme of the complex, ambiguous set of relationships, real and perhaps even supernatural, between the author and his work, and the author and the real world. "The Real People" demonstrates one additional facet of Onions' talents as well—his sharp comedic sense. What was fearsome in "The Beckoning Fair One" becomes charming, amusing, and provocative in "The Real People."

Aubrey Kneller has been a safe, proper, commercially successful author up until his most recent book, *Delia Vane*. That novel too had begun as a safe, respectable novel of manners, until a minor character, a waif named Annie, asserted herself, took over the book, renamed herself "Delia Vane," and altered the plot beyond recognition: the hero falls in love with her, drops his proper betrothed, and eventually loses her to an aristocratic playboy. Having just completed the book and mailed it off with trepidation to his publisher, Aubrey stumbles into an antique shop where he meets a salesgirl who seems to be Delia Vane in the flesh. Aubrey then, of course, retraces the route of his hero. The result is personal, social, and financial ruin, but not disintegration—the story is comic, not tragic, and Aubrey's final mood, for all of his problems, is downright euphoric.

Thus Oliver Onions' ghosts are as likely to be products of the creative imagination come to life as dead souls hovering about just out of sight, and either kind of specter can be stimulating or destructive or both. In the most extreme instances the artist may even become his work, figuratively or literally. In one completely realistic story, "Resurrection in Bronze," John Braydon becomes so obsessed with his potentially prize-winning piece of sculpture that he destroys his own humanity, first alienating himself from wife and child, then destroying his own health, and finally becoming so numb to other things that, when his wife is accidentally killed during the final bronzing process, he refuses to allow a pause in the work.

Less stark and more fantastic variants on the same theme are the stories "Benlian" and "Hic Jacket." Both stories center on the relationship between a "genius" and a "hack" in which the hack is gradually overwhelmed by the genius and his art until he almost becomes a part of the artist's metamorphosis into his own art work. The narrator of "Benlian," after initial skepticism, finally comes to believe that Benlian's work is, indeed, an extension of the man, and, when Benlian dies, almost as an act of will, the narrator *knows* that Benlian's spirit has passed into and animated his sculpture (at which point the narrator is incarcerated in a mental hospital). On the other hand, the hack-writer narrator of "Hic Jacket" is never able to establish a mystical connection with painter Michael Andriaovsky and so, thinking that he is writing the life of his painter friend, he discovers that he has only turned out another in his series of trashy novels.

Again, the ghosts are ghosts of the mind, spirit, and imagination. They are always "there," but one can never be sure whether "there" is in the surrounding atmosphere or in one's own mind and perceptions, or both. "We are not gods," Paul Oleron muses late in "The Beckoning Fair One." "We cannot drive out devils. We must see selfishly that devils do not enter into ourselves." Enter they do, however, and no modern ghost-story writer has made such devils more real or fearful than Oliver Onions.

Keith Neilson

Bibliography
Onions, Oliver. "Credo," in *The Collected Ghost Stories of Oliver Onions*, 1971.

THE CONAN SERIES

Author: Robert E. Howard (1906-1936)
First book publications: Conan the Conqueror: The Hyborian Age (1950); *The Sword of Conan* (1952); *King Conan* (1953); *The Coming of Conan* (1953); *Conan the Barbarian* (1955)
Type of work: Short stories, novellas, and novels
Time: The Hyborian Age, 18,000 years in the past
Locale: Ancient Europe, Africa, and Asia

    Conan the Cimmerian, a barbarian adventurer from the far North, rises from his beginnings as a thief and mercenary to become King of Aquilonia, the most powerful nation in the world

        Principal character:
        CONAN, a barbarian from Cimmeria

    Robert E. Howard is one of the most influential figures in the history of modern fantasy literature. He has been both praised and damned as the leading popularizer of the genre known as "sword and sorcery." While other earlier writers have been cited as having shaped the development of the field, there is no question that it is Howard who founded, defined, and developed the genre and who, despite modern competition, still remains its most popular writer.

    Howard's most famous character was Conan the Cimmerian, a barbarian adventurer who appeared in a series of novellas and short stories in the pulp magazine *Weird Tales* from 1932 until the author's suicide in 1936. An accomplished writer, Howard sold more than one hundred stories to various pulp publications in the period 1930 to 1936, with *Weird Tales* being his best market. It was in that magazine that he first gained a reputation with his earlier series stories about heroic characters. While the average quality of the Conan series was not as high as that of his other published series, the best Conan stories were better than the best of Howard's other writing.

    Conan, as described by his creator, is the composite of many rough, tough "he-men" the author had met during his life. The barbarian was also an amalgam of Howard's earlier fantasy heroes: Conan featured the moodiness and barbarism of King Kull, the chivalry and heroism of Solomon Kane, the leadership and battle skills of Bran Mak Morn, and the red rages of Turlogh Dubh. Howard was the typical "pulp cannibal" in that he used rejected stories and unpublished manuscripts to shape and fill out new stories. A King Kull unpublished adventure was rewritten into the first Conan story, and early Conan adventures were used to form the plots of later Conan stories. The Cimmerian resembled other Howard heroes because in several cases, he had originally been one of those heroes.

    In a letter to fellow author Clark Ashton Smith, Howard stated that for weeks after developing Conan he did nothing but write the adventures of the barbarian hero. Normally Howard was not a careful writer, and he rarely developed more than a sketchy outline of the history and geography of his imaginary worlds. For the Conan saga, however, he wrote an entire long essay, "The Hyborian Age," detailing the history of the Age of Conan, starting with the rise of civilization on Atlantis thousands of years before the Cimmerian's life, and describing the rise and fall of civilizations until the coming of the Ice Age which destroyed every trace of the Hyborian world. He mapped and sketched each kingdom of Conan's time and described its inhabitants for his own reference. He used a jumble of ancient history and mythology for names in order to give them a historic flavor. Thus, Conan (a heroic character from Irish myth) traveled from dark and cold Cimmeria to the distant south of Kush and Stygia, to far Vendhya, and even to far eastern Khitai. While this sort of world-making is not uncommon in contemporary fantasy, it was the best-developed scenario for any fantasy series of its time.

Nor did Howard focus on any one period of Conan's life. The first few stories in the series are about a middle-aged Conan as King of Aquilonia. The third story published, "The Tower of the Elephant," features Conan as a young man recently arrived in the civilized kingdoms. Later stories feature the Cimmerian as a thief, mercenary soldier, and pirate. The stories appeared in no particular order, giving the impression of an old veteran remembering his adventures. With its wide span of times and settings, the series managed to paint a broad picture of the Hyborian Age.

Howard was not a patient writer who spent hours or days on a single story, rewriting each line to achieve perfection; he dashed through his work and did little editing or revising. He wrote for pulp magazines, where pay was low and speed was the key to earning a living. He saved every line for later use and filled pages upon pages with the beginnings of stories and outlines of ideas.

It was from one of these discarded stories, "By This Axe I Rule," featuring King Kull, that Conan sprang into life. The original Kull story had a melodramatic love interest but no fantasy element; it did, however, have a strong plot and a vibrant fight scene. Howard dropped the girl, added a demon, and produced "The Phoenix on the Sword." First published in *Weird Tales* in December, 1932, this story is chronologically one of the last Conan adventures. The Cimmerian is King of Aquilonia. A year before the opening of the tale, Conan, at the head of the rebellious army, has slain the decadent King Numedides and set himself up as ruler. At first extremely popular with the people, Conan finds after a time that the crown does not always rest easily. A mad minstrel, Rinaldo, inates the common people against the Cimmerian, and plotters scheme to topple the throne.

Behind these devious plans is Ascalante, an outlawed nobleman who dreams of power. Aiding him is Thoth-Amon, a sorcerer from Stygia. Once a powerful wizard in the southern kingdom, Thoth has lost his ring of power and is in hiding from powerful, demoniac enemies. Thoth-Amon serves Ascalante as a slave and is treated as such. The Stygian hates the outlaw but fears his enemies more; he therefore serves in silence. Ascalante plans a midnight attack to kill King Conan.

Conan is visited in his sleep by an ancient sage who warns him of dire danger by etching a strange symbol on Conan's sword and then departing. The King awakens, hears the noise made by the plotters, and dons his armor. Therefore, when Ascalante and his puppets attack, they are confronted by an awake and armored Conan instead of a sleeping, unarmed man. In the meantime, Thoth-Amon, left behind by the plotters, finds his ring of power. His sorcerous powers restored, the Stygian sends a night demon to kill Ascalante and all those with him. Conan, in a barbaric rage, has killed all of the plotters except Ascalante. The King is off guard for an instant, and the outlaw is lunging forward to kill him when the demon arrives. Ascalante is killed in horrible fashion. The monster then turns on Conan, but the Cimmerian destroys it with his sword, aided by the magic of the phoenix on the blade.

Howard is at his best in this first Conan story. The characters, while not three-dimensional, are still much more lifelike than most of those appearing in pulp magazines; they have dreams, ambitions, and schemes. The plot is complex, and all of the subplots and odd elements are woven together to form a satisfactory conclusion. At the same time, Howard's faults are also apparent. Coincidence is strained to the utmost, especially in the scene in which Thoth-Amon recovers his ring, lost years earlier; nor is the arrival of the demon, staged just in time to save Conan, particularly believable. The scene featuring the ghost of Epemitreus the Sage has a comic-book effect and serves as little more than a *deus ex machina*.

This novella set the format for the adventures to follow. With rare exceptions, sorcery was kept to a minimum, usually only coming at the climax of the story. Magic and monsters were an integral part of the stories but did not dominate them. Instead, the personality and exploits of Conan completely controlled and motivated the adventures.

The basic theme that underlies all of Howard's work is the nobility of the savage. Conan is an idealized figure, a peculiarly American hero, yet there is more to the stories than mere wish fulfillment. The Conan stories all share a brooding sense of inevitability, while the best of the tales have a certain grimness unmatched by other authors in the genre. Howard's dark, romantic vision of life is filled with continual-strife heroics and everpresent death; in his cosmos, death is the only certainty.

One story that perfectly illustrates this grim atmosphere of inevitability, as well as Howard's belief in the noble savage, is "Queen of the Black Coast." Young Conan has an encounter with the law while looking for work in the river kingdom of Argos. With the police in close pursuit, Conan manages to

escape on a trading ship bound for the black kingdoms of Kush. Unfortunately, a few weeks later, the vessel is attacked by the dreaded pirate Belit
and her band of killers. While all of the Argosians are killed, Conan manages
to leap aboard Belit's ship and wreak havoc with his broadsword. Belit, a
white woman in command of black pirates, is awed by the Cimmerian and
his fighting skills and spares his life. Soon Conan is the most feared pirate
on the Black Coast and Belit's lover.

Following the rumor of a fabulous lost treasure city, the pirates travel up
a haunted river. In a ghostly jungle, they find an ancient megalopolis while
a giant, winged, apelike creature watches from afar. When the pirates go
searching for treasure, the flying monster destroys their water supply, so
Conan must take a party of men to search for more water. During the search,
he falls victim to the spores of the Black Lotus, which trap him in a drugged
slumber, and while he dreams, his men are killed by the ape-thing. In an
eerie vision, the Cimmerian learns that the beast is the last member of the
high race that built the stone city but then degenerated into monsters. It is
served by a horde of hyenas, men of Stygia whom the creature has transformed
into beasts by magic.

Awakening, Conan rushes back to the pirate ship to find all dead, including
Belit. In grim fury, the barbarian takes his revenge, killing all of the hyenas;
but he is then trapped by falling masonry during a collapse of the ruins. He
is inches away from his sword but cannot reach it because of a beam across
his legs. The flying monster attacks, but before it can reach Conan, Belit
appears between the two; her love for Conan is so great that she has returned
from death to protect him. The monster reels back in fear. A berserk Conan
throws off the column, snatches up his sword, and slays the last member of
a once majestic race. Belit is then given a pirate funeral: Conan builds a huge
pyre on the pirate ship, surrounds her body with jewels, and sends it, aflame,
out to sea. He then turns inland, having no more desire to roam the seas.

The concept of the noble savage is fundamental to the story. Conan is
forced to flee Argos because he will not betray a friend to the law, an act
that the "civilized" judge cannot understand. He fights the pirates out of
loyalty to his shipmates, even though he knows death is inevitable. There is
never a thought of deserting his comrades, whether they be Argosian sailors
or Belit's pirate crew. At the same time, the superiority of the barbarian over
the civilized man is evident in every reference to Conan. Even Belit, a dangerous pirate, is astonished by his fighting skills and wild bravery. The savages
on the pirate ship are in awe of Conan's single-handed attack on their boat.
Only the Cimmerian is not frightened by the evil tricks of the flying monster,
and only he of all its victims throughout the centuries is able to destroy it.

Grimness gives the story its drama and depth. Death is everywhere; by the
end of the story, only Conan is left alive. When the monster is killed, Howard
emphasizes again and again that this is the death of a proud civilization that

has sunk into degeneracy; the monster is the last of an elder race that was once great and that time made mad. In one particularly telling passage in "Queen of the Black Coast," Belit asks Conan about his gods. He replies, "Their chief is Crom. He dwells on a great mountain. What use to call on him? Little he cares if men live or die. He is grim and loveless, but at birth he breathes power to strive and slay into a man's soul." This grim, uncaring deity is basic to the series. Crom is not a god of warriors but of slayers; he is not a god to be worshiped, but to be feared. This grim air of fatalism and the presence of inescapable death haunts the best of Howard's work and sets it apart from that of his successors in the genre.

The same melancholy air of struggle against the inevitable collapse into barbarism is best exemplified in another long Conan story, "Beyond the Black River." Originally published as a two-part serial in *Weird Tales* in May and June of 1935 and remembered chiefly for its concluding scene, it also illustrates Howard's theme of the triumph of the savage over the civilized man and the inevitability of death and decay through constant strife and turmoil. The novel is a derivative of the Revolutionary War novels of Robert W. Chambers set in New York State. Conan is a scout on the Aquilonian border at the Black River, which separates that country from the Pictish wilderness. The settlers are comparable to the early American pioneers in the Chambers novels, with the Picts serving as the Indians. Fort Tuscelan is the only thing that protects the settlers on the river from the savages.

Conan and a secondary hero, Balthus, learn of a new leader, Zogar Sag, who is trying to unite the warring Pict tribes into one nation to drive the settlers back from the river. Knowing that Zogar Sag is a powerful wizard and that without his leadership the tribes would never pose a danger, Conan takes a party of soldiers from the Fort across the river to ambush the sorcerer. Unfortunately, the party is discovered by Picts; Balthus and another man are captured, and Conan disappears. The other captive is slain by sorcery, but before Zogar Sag can kill Balthus, the Aquilonian is rescued by Conan. While they escape through the wilderness, the Picts attack the Fort.

The destruction of Fort Tuscelan is at hand when Conan and Balthus make their way back across the river, so the two men separate to warn the settlers of the massacre planned by the Picts. Balthus and a savage dog, Slasher, make a valiant stand in a small settlement, buying time for the women to escape. Conan is confronted by a forest demon that turns out to be the magical brother of Zogar Sag and is linked by unholy bonds to the wizard. All material things are subject to cold steel, however, and Conan manages to kill the demon. In doing so, he also kills Zogar Sag. The death of the wizard from no apparent cause frightens the Picts and they abandon their attack. The land close to the Black River has been lost to the savages, however, and civilization is pushed a little farther back. Balthus' body is found, and he is given a hero's burial. Conan solemnly vows to slay ten Picts in revenge for his friend's death.

"Beyond the Black River" is a perfect illustration of why Howard's sword-and-sorcery fiction is superior to other works in the genre written since his death. The story does not adhere to all of the clichés that are supposedly necessary in the genre. There is no love interest in the story and no women at all in major roles. The magic is not the world-changing sorcery that is often present in other writers' fantasies; Zogar Sag is a mere village wizard. He does not scheme to rule the world or even Aquilonia; his only mission is to drive the settlers from a small area that the Picts feel is theirs. Howard's demon kills only a few men, and Conan is able to kill it with his sword, rather than with some potent magical weapon. The sorcery is an integral part of the story but does not dwarf the characters or their actions. It serves its purpose, as does the setting; but it is no more important than the scenery.

It is the conflict between civilization and barbarism which is central to the story and which makes it something more than a genre adventure. The Cimmerian is perfectly matched by the Picts, even though he serves their enemies. He is a barbarian among barbarians. When Conan leads a party of Aquilonian forest scouts to ambush Zogar Sag, Balthus reflects that the rangers are civilized men who have reverted to semibarbarism while Conan is a barbarian descended from a thousand generations of barbarians. Balthus thinks of the foresters as wolves, but of Conan as a tiger. This fundamental difference is the theme of "Beyond the Black River" and the entire Conan series. The Cimmerian is a barbarian, and in all of his adventures, from his days as a young thief to his reign as King of Aquilonia, he remains a barbarian at heart. He is a noble savage, free from the corrupting influences of civilization that make men weak. As Howard concludes at the end of "Beyond the Black River," "Barbarism is the natural state of mankind. Civilization is unnatural. It is a whim of circumstance. And barbarism must always ultimately triumph."

Unfortunately, not all of the Conan stories present this philosophy in such clearly defined terms. Howard often dashed through stories, and a number of Conan tales are inferior work—"The Slithering Shadow," "Pool of the Black One," and "Jewels of Gwahlur" are typical of these slapdash pieces. Some stories, including "A Witch Shall Be Born," contain effective passages mixed together with long stretches of barely competent work.

Excessive reliance on coincidence was Howard's greatest problem. Too often, he substituted it for plot, and it is a rare story that does not have some coincidence or strange turn of events crucial to the outcome of the action. In the longer adventures, one or two such occurrences can be overlooked, but in short stories, such excess is glaringly apparent. Women also caused problems for Howard. His female characters rarely serve as anything more than plot devices; too often they are in the story only for Conan to impress them with his barbarian strengths. The women are sketchy characters and tend to give the stories a cheerful, almost silly atmosphere that conflicts with their underlying grimness. The best of the Conan stories do not feature women at all. Even at his worst, however, Howard entertains. His dialogue is purple and unrealistic, yet it fits the characters who speak it. He was a natural storyteller with a boundless enthusiasm for his fiction and his fictional creations.

Howard's suicide ended the Conan saga. When readers of *Weird Tales* wrote to that magazine asking that the character be continued, editor Farnsworth Wright disagreed, stating that Howard was a unique talent and that no other author could capture the magic of Conan. Instead, other writers, including Clifford Ball and Henry Kuttner, tried to duplicate Conan's success with characters of their own, but none of these heroes was original or successful.

In the early 1950's, L. Sprague de Camp became interested in Howard's work and in Conan in particular. He took several unpublished Conan stories and edited them for publication in magazines. Later, when Gnome Press published the Conan series in five hardcover volumes, de Camp helped to prepare the stories for publication. De Camp then took four unpublished Howard adventure stories and rewrote them into Conan stories, changing the modern settings to the Hyborian Age and adding magic and monsters. The stories served as links between the major events in Conan's career and continued the saga as well. These early "collaborations" were competently done, with much of the content of the original Howard stories intact. They were also collected in book form by Gnome Press.

Another new Conan story appeared when Swedish fan Byorn Nyberg wrote an entirely new Conan story and submitted it to American markets. De Camp revised and enlarged the story, "The Return of Conan," which again appeared in hardcover from Gnome Press. Events in the Nyberg-de Camp novel take place after the adventures in the last story, chronologically speaking, of the Conan saga, "The Hour of the Dragon." In the new tale, Conan travels across the Hyborian world seeking his new bride, stolen from him by a Khitain sorcerer. The story, although it features numerous characters from Howard's Conan adventures, is a disappointing work. Except for a few nobles who provide links in the King Conan episodes, Howard rarely had Conan encounter characters from previous adventures because he realized that death and distance made such events extremely improbable. In the Nyberg adventure, every chapter seems to contain a shadow from the past. The characters in the new novel are pale imitations of the people Howard created with broad, bright strokes. The constant encounters make the story more of a parody than a pastiche.

Another problem is that de Camp is too conscious of the demands of plausibility and verisimilitude. In Howard stories, Conan can wade into a troop of assassins and emerge victorious, if somewhat bloodied. De Camp's Conan knows that one man could never defeat such odds and so uses trickery or strategy to defeat them. Howard's Conan is all passion, a grim and berserk killer with death at his side. The de Camp Conan is a much more intelligent, thoughtful, and cautious character; he is much too civilized.

This disparity grew worse in the 1960's. De Camp turned over the Conan series to the paperback publisher, Lancer Books. The original five Conan books by Howard, plus the two new Conan books, all done by Gnome Press, were expanded into eleven. Filling out the other books in the revised series are new Conan stories written by de Camp and Lin Carter. Some of the adventures are based on fragments left by Howard, while others are entirely new stories. Eventually, there were more Conan stories in print by people other than Howard than by the creator of Conan himself.

The Carter-de Camp collaborations and revisions helped to round out the saga of Conan the Cimmerian by presenting a more complete picture of his life. Whether the picture presented is the one Howard intended is a matter of speculation. None of the stories in the continued series has the basic underlying moodiness and grimness of the originals. The stories are better plotted but lack the force and drive of Howard's work. Often they descend to the level of parody, trying to tie up every loose end and kill off every villain who went unpunished in some earlier story. Howard rarely bothered to tie up loose ends in his stories; Carter and de Camp always did.

In the 1970's, Conan became one of the best-selling characters in the history of fantasy literature. The steady demand for more Conan stories was met by many new efforts. A series of new novels and story collections was done by a number of authors, including Andrew Offutt, Poul Anderson, Karl Wagner, and de Camp and Carter. Again, the stories are imitations and nothing more; all of the authors involved had done much better work on their own. While all of them could write a story in the style of Robert E. Howard, none of them could write a Robert E. Howard story.

The enduring popularity of the series is evident in the success of Conan's latest incarnation, the film *Conan the Barbarian* (1982). Despite the steady stream of imitations, pastiches, homages, and adaptations, Conan remains the unique creation of his originator, and his and his creator's names remain linked together in fantasy literature.

Robert Weinberg

Bibliography

de Camp, L. Sprague. "The Miscast Barbarian: Robert E. Howard," in *Literary Swordsmen and Sorcerers: The Makers of Heroic Fantasy*, 1976.

Schweitzer, Darrell. *Conan's World and Robert E. Howard*, 1978.

Weinberg, Robert E. *The Annotated Guide to Robert E. Howard's Swords & Sorcery*, 1976.

THE CONFIDENCE-MAN
His Masquerade

Author: Herman Melville (1819-1891)
First book publication: 1857
Type of work: Novel
Time: One April Fools' Day in the mid-nineteenth century
Locale: The riverboat *Fidèle*, steaming from St. Louis toward New Orleans

In a series of conversations and confrontations, a ship of fools on a pilgrimage of faith reveals the nature of the universe

Principal characters:
> A LAMBLIKE MAN, who is deaf and dumb and dressed in cream colors
> WILLIAM CREAM, the ship's barber
> BLACK GUINEA, a crippled black man
> PITCH, an ostensible misanthrope
> THE INDIAN-HATER, a man devoted to revenge
> THE COSMOPOLITAN, who is dressed in many colors and styles

For decades after his novels were published, Herman Melville was still known merely as a man who had lived among cannibals and written some sea-adventures: that the adventures concealed his vision of the universe was recognized neither by the reading public nor by the critics. *The Confidence-Man*, his last novel, remains his least-read and least-understood work. Anyone reading it for adventure will be disappointed: on the surface, it is a tedious series of conversations aboard a Mississippi riverboat. Beneath the surface lies Melville's humorous but depressing allegory of the power behind the universe, a power which is not really interested in human beings but nevertheless expects their faith.

There has been considerable diversity among specific interpretations of the allegory, however, and some critics even believe the novel to be unfinished. The Confidence-Man of the title has been identified in various ways, primarily as the Devil or as the American spirit, the latter specified as either optimism or materialism. More recently, the theological view seems to have superseded the sociological view. Some, however, see a more sinister meaning than either view might suggest. The theme of this novel is the same as that of Melville's other works: evil does exist in the world, and it is so inextricably bound up with the good that it cannot be removed. Blind faith that everything will necessarily turn out all right is unwise and, in this book, made to seem ridiculous.

The first character in the April Fools' Day fantasy-dance of strangers who appear, interact, and disappear is clearly a Christ-figure, a lamblike man dressed in cream colors. In an apparent attempt to distract attention from a sign warning of "a mysterious imposter, . . . quite an original genius in his vocation," he displays a series of Pauline messages about charity, beginning with "Charity thinketh no evil." Consistent with attitudes about God expressed elsewhere in Melville's writings, the lamblike man is deaf and dumb.

Meanwhile, the ship's barber (whose name is William Cream) hangs up his usual sign, "No trust." The use of the word "cream" for both the lamblike man and the barber presents an ambiguity that continues in the next character and, indeed, throughout the novel. The crippled black man who calls himself Black Guinea appears in the same place where the lamblike man was last seen; on the surface, they are opposites, but they are connected in other ways besides location. Black Guinea is, if not a lamb, at least a black sheep. Instead of a white fur hat of a fleecy nap, he has hair which is a nap of black fleece, and, like the con men who appear later, he can be said to fleece the other passengers. When asked if anyone aboard can vouch for him, he mentions a number of people, and his list forms the structure of the rest of the novel.

The first four on the list of eight appear as they are described and in the order given. They are a man with a weed in his hat, a man in a gray coat and white tie, a man with a big book, and a herb doctor. On first sight, each exudes benevolence, but ultimately there are suggestions of the Devil or of snakes about them. They are all confidence men in the traditional sense, but on another level, they are really after the people's confidence rather than their money.

The man with the weed (a black ribbon to indicate mourning) solicits funds with a personal sob story, and the man in a gray coat and white tie, with stories of social misery: he claims to work for charitable agencies. Both insist that they care less for the money than for the spirit behind it, and indeed, they seem satisfied with rather small sums. The man with the big book, a stock salesman, most clearly states that it is confidence he desires: he will not sell his shares until an unequivocal confidence in them is expressed. Similarly, the herb doctor specifically says that his medicine will not work without confidence. The confidence they are all after stands for faith in traditional religion. The first two con men ask for charity as well as confidence: the connection between faith and charity is self-evident. From the names of the salesman's companies, New Jerusalem and Black Rapids Coal, suggesting Heaven and hell, the reader understands that he is really selling stock in the world to come. The herb doctor offers hope, and he aligns himself with the others by giving part of his proceeds to charity.

So far, the progress of the novel has been orderly, determined by Black Guinea's list. One con man supersedes another, and they are neatly bridged by their victims, who are passed from one to the next. Once the reader is lulled into believing he perceives an order, however, the order is disrupted. In the second half of the book, the reader becomes progressively more confused.

The confusions inherent in the structure of this novel may well be intended to suggest the confused structure of the real world. There is no order in Melville's universe. Just as no theory can completely account for accidents and other unpredictables in the real world, so the theory which held up for the first part of the novel also begins to falter.

The next four character-references on Black Guinea's list are a man in a yellow vest, a man with a brass plate, a man in a violet robe, and a soldier. These do not appear in proper order; the soldier is only a fake soldier; and the yellow vest and the violet robe do not appear at all, unless one chooses to look beyond the literal.

The soldier represents a significant departure from the previous order not only by appearing next when he should appear last but also by appearing as a victim as well as a con man. He is conned by the herb doctor into buying medication, and the reader learns that he has also been victimized by society: his injuries were received in prison, where he had been sent unjustly. He, in turn, victimizes society by soliciting alms under the pretense of being an old soldier who lost his health in the Mexican War.

Once doubt is established regarding who is the con man and who the victim, the reader is introduced to two apparent misanthropes who blur the distinction between the misanthropic and the benevolent. The first is called Pitch and the second, the Indian-hater. Pitch follows the rule that in the world of this novel, nothing is what it seems to be. Unlike the genial con men, his manners are hostile; his name conjures up Satanic associations; he lives alone and carries a shotgun. Yet he reproves the herb doctor for taking advantage of a sick man; he allows the man with a brass plate to talk him into letting his good nature overcome his good judgment; and he exposes a third confidence man as a hypocrite, pretending to be a lover of humanity while actually a cynic.

Pitch, the apparent misanthrope who is truly kind, is identified by several distinct references with another character, decidedly not kind, called the Indian-hater. This character does not appear in the novel: his story is told by one con man to another. The story is of a man who, having lost all his loved ones in an Indian massacre, devotes his life to revenge. Both the listener and the teller express horror at the behavior of the Indian-hater, and their joint opinion does appear to be the humane one. As one of them exclaims, "How could a man of hate also be a man of love?" This, however, is precisely Melville's point. Just as Pitch's misanthropy grows out of his kindness, so the Indian-hater's love begets his hatred. Only those who really love have a basis for hate: only those who really care for people can detect hypocrisy. Good is inextricably mixed with evil in this world: it is not possible to separate them because the evil is so deeply rooted that it cannot be removed without destroying the world. As is pointed out to the herb doctor, some pains can be eased only by opium and eliminated only by death. In Melville's view, evil and good, hate and love, black and white are not opposites but different aspects of the same thing.

Early in the novel, black and white predominate, giving way to gray and other neutral shades; finally, in keeping with the growing moral complexity of the novel, there is a riot of colors. The prime example is the cosmopolitan, dressed in many hues and many styles, representing an affinity for all nationalities and all kinds of people. There is also a man in a violet vest, and the sunset hues of his clothing clash with his sallow complexion. Finally, there is a boy in a tattered red shirt and a grimy yellow coat.

All of these characters have been considered candidates for either the man in the violet robe or the man in the yellow vest. There is, in fact, no violet robe and no yellow vest: the vest is violet, and the cosmopolitan's predominating color is red. Moreover, the only robe mentioned is not on a person but in a picture of a man with a halo. (Should the Confidence-Man wear a halo?) Some critics attribute such discrepancies and blurring of details to the fact that Melville did not himself proofread the manuscript before it was sent to the printers. These apparent errors can also be accounted for, however, if one accepts that Melville chose to make his point in style as well as in content. Thus, they are demonstrations of the interrelatedness of all things.

The novel comes full circle in two ways. First, the cosmopolitan temporarily convinces the barber to take down his "No trust" sign and promptly cheats him out of a shave. Second, the Christ-figure in the opening chapter is balanced in the final chapter with an opposing image of Christianity: the Inquisition. The boy associated with *auto-da-fé* is not lamblike but resembles a leopard cub. He wears not cream colors but grimy yellow and red. Instead of entreating the people to ignore the warning about an impostor, his mission is to instill the trusting with distrust.

He provides a peaceful, Bible-reading old man with a safety lock, money-belt, and counterfeit-detector. The old man seems to be losing his confidence, but he is only transferring it. He transfers it to the cosmopolitan, who "kindly" leads him away from his Bible as the narrator remarks that "something further may follow of this Masquerade."

It is this depressing final note, as well as the fact that nineteenth century novels do not usually become more and more confusing as they end, that leads many critics to suppose that the novel is unfinished. Others suggest that the open-endedness is deliberate and is related to the existentialist and absurdist literature which came much later. Melville, however, did not believe in Nothing: he believed in a powerful force with which human beings cannot cope and certainly should not trust.

That force he here calls the Confidence-Man. It is generally agreed that the series of confidence men who appear in the novel are disguises, representatives, or manifestations of the single Confidence-Man. These separate manifestations are connected to each other in several ways. Often the connection is a mutual recommendation: one confidence man recommends another. At other times, the connection is more complex, as when the man with the weed knows the name and occupation of one of his victims because he possesses a business card that had been surreptitiously acquired by Black Guinea. Together these confidence men are perhaps simply avatars of the mysterious impostor warned about in the opening chapter.

The mysterious impostor is an "original genius." The phrase suggests Aristotle's First Cause, which set the universe going, as well as Thomas Carlyle's "originals," the human heroes who make the world what it is. Both are referred to in one of Melville's three interpolated chapters which are ostensibly about the art of creating fiction but actually about creation in general. In that chapter, it is stated that original characters in fiction are almost as rare "as in real history is a new law-giver, a revolutionizing philosopher, or the founder of a new religion." Such a character, however, would give an impression "akin to that which in Genesis attends upon the beginnings of things."

The Confidence-Man certainly shows demoniac qualities, and for Melville, the destructive spirit is merely another aspect of the creative spirit. Images suggesting God and images suggesting Satan are frequently brought together in this novel. One example (often given a different interpretation) is a solar lamp with a pattern on its glass shade in which a man with a halo alternates with a horned altar emitting flames. God and the Devil seem to work hand in hand, and the relationship between the cream-colored man and Black Guinea begins to make sense. The one who introduces the novel and the other who provides its structure are two aspects of the same original genius.

As April Fools' Day and the novel approach their end, the above-mentioned lamp is the only one still lit: the others are "barren planets." Amid hints of apocalypse, the cosmopolitan extinguishes this lamp. "Something further" still might follow, but that would be a different story.

Barbara L. Berman

Bibliography

Bowen, Merlin. "Tactics of Indirection in Melville's *The Confidence-Man,*" in *Studies in the Novel.* I (Winter, 1969), pp. 401-420.

Branch, Watson G. "The Genesis, Composition, and Structure of *The Confidence-Man,*" in *Nineteenth-Century Fiction.* XXVII (March, 1973), pp. 424-448.

Foster, Elizabeth S. "Introduction," in *The Confidence-Man: His Masquerade,* 1954.

Melville, Herman. *The Confidence-Man: His Masquerade,* 1971 (Norton Critical Edition).

Mitchell, Edward. "From Action to Essence: Some Notes on the Structure of Melville's *The Confidence-Man,*" in *American Literature.* XL (March,

1968), pp. 27-37.

Seltzes, Leon F. "Camus's Absurd and the World of Melville's *The Confidence-Man*," in *PMLA*. LXXXII (March, 1967), pp. 14-27.

Sten, Christopher W. "The Dialogue of Crisis in *The Confidence-Man*: Melville's 'New Novel,'" in *Studies in the Novel*. VI (Summer, 1974), pp. 165-185.

Tichi, Cecilia. "Melville's Craft and the Theme of Language Debased in *The Confidence-Man*," in *ELH*. XXXIX (December, 1972), pp. 639-658.

CONJURE WIFE

Author: Fritz Leiber, Jr. (1910-   )
First book publication: 1953
Type of work: Novel
Time: The 1950's
Locale: A small northeastern college town, not far from New York

A professor and his wife become exposed to and menaced by witchcraft directed by three women acquaintances

> *Principal characters:*
> NORMAN SAYLOR, professor of sociology at Hempnell College
> TANSY SAYLOR, his wife
> HAROLD GUNNISON, dean of men at Hempnell
> HULDA GUNNISON, his wife
> HERVEY SAWTELLE, professor of sociology
> EVELYN SAWTELLE, his wife
> LINTHICUM CARR, professor of mathematics at Hempnell
> FLORA CARR, his wife

Fritz Leiber, Jr., one of the masters of genre literature, may not be the best known, the most fashionable, or the most studied, but he has been the most honored of American fantasy writers. He has through his long career gathered six Hugo Awards at World Science Fiction conventions and three Nebula Awards from the Science Fiction Writers of America. Despite the names of these awarding bodies, many of his honors have been for his fantasies, not for his science fiction: his "Gonna Roll the Bones" (1968), a fine story about gambling with the Devil, won both a Hugo and a Nebula, as did "Ill Met in Lankhmar" (1971), one of the stories in his "Gray Mouser" series. In addition, his "Belsen Express" won both the World Fantasy Award and the August Derleth Fantasy Award in 1976. Leiber was named a Grand Master of Fantasy (the Gandalf Award) in 1975 and he received the World Fantasy Life Award the following year.

When Leiber wrote *Conjure Wife*, these honors were in the future. The story was first published in 1943 in the magazine *Unknown*, John W. Campbell's short-lived but respected companion in fantasy to *Astounding Science Fiction*. The novel was revised for its book publication in 1953 (for example, a reference to the atomic bomb was inserted), and has been reprinted at least five times in paperback since.

Leiber's competence in both fantasy and science fiction shows in *Conjure Wife*; the novel is something like a tripod, since Leiber furnishes not one but three possible explanations for the events of the book. Indeed, *Conjure Wife* is unique in that it can be read in any of three ways: as science fiction, as a realistic novel about abnormal mental states, or as the fantasy readers usually perceive. An outline of the plot will show the features of the book, which reflect so differently in these three different mirrors.

The central character, Norman Saylor, is a sociologist specializing in ethnology of primitive cultures—particularly their superstitions—teaching at Hempnell College, a small private institution. He is prospering in his work and stands in line for the chairmanship of the sociology department, a position which is to become open in the near future. After a difficult start, he and his wife Tansy have made a place for themselves in the tradition-ridden, fearful, and ambitious world of Hempnell. As the novel opens, Norman makes a discovery that snaps his pleasant mood: he finds that his wife has been practicing magic for some years. When he also discovers that she attributes his academic success and advancement to her conjuring, he doubts her sanity. Through a long and tension-filled afternoon and evening, Norman and Tansy debate the significance (and the question of the normality) of her actions, and the confrontation ends with Tansy convinced that she has been a fool. She gives up her magic, burns her papers, charms, and packets, and retires for the night.

Immediately, things begin to go wrong for Norman: within minutes of each other, he receives two late-night telephone calls. One is from a paranoid former student who accuses the professor of failing him because of prejudice and threatens to take revenge. The other is from Norman's student assistant, a girl whose sexual fantasies break through her repressions and who offers herself to him. He settles these two problems in dangerous scenes in the next few days, but others arrive to take their place. As Norman begins to encounter problems on every side, he slips from his position as the favorite candidate for the headship. There are also possible physical dangers that threaten: a stone figure on the roof of the building opposite his office window appears to move downward through the course of a few days. Almost unconsciously, Norman begins to believe that it is nearer the eave of the roof than he had noticed it to be earlier. Later, a storm shakes his house and lightning crashes outside; then, an especially violent bolt strikes something that seems to be moving on his porch. Investigation reveals it to be the stone figure, now inert. As his nerves fray, Norman loses his usually composed manner and even seems to antagonize his peers and superiors, endangering the delicate balance he has achieved through his years at the college.

Whether Norman is being bewitched or not, enough people hate him to wish him evil: Hulda Gunnison, wife of the dean of men, envies the influence Norman has over her husband; Evelyn Sawtelle sees Norman as the barrier to her husband heading the department; and Flora Carr, an elderly but libidinous faculty wife, combines a lust for Norman with a hatred of his tolerant attitude toward student social life.

Norman's problems reach a high pitch when Tansy, after a romantic evening, asks him if everything he has is hers. He assents, not realizing until later that she had regained her belief in magic and had attempted to draw onto herself any spells aimed at him. When he awakens the next morning, she has disappeared, either controlled by a spirit raised by Norman's three witch-enemies or unbalanced by the troubles lately so numerous. Now Norman begins magical countermeasures, instructed by notes from Tansy which he receives piece by piece throughout the day. The alternate explanations appear at this point, as Norman tries to find mentally satisfying causes for what has happened.

The first possibility, one always at the edge of Norman's mind, is that four women involved (and Norman too, if he ever believes the efficacy of what he does) have had their minds seized by a mania in which they all sincerely believe that their conjuring works. The effects that follow are then explainable either as the result of suggestion or simple coincidence. For example, the appearance of the stone figure on Norman's porch, so the college paper asserts, resulted from a prank by members of an athletic team, and nothing in the novel negates that possibility. To accept this first alternative, the reader must believe that Tansy's mind breaks under the strain midway through the book—that her belief that she has been bewitched leads her to something like schizophrenia. Even at the end of the book, the possibility remains. In their last conversation in the novel, Tansy asks Norman if his rationality has reasserted itself, if he now believes that he has "been spending the last week pretending to believe in witchcraft to cure your wife and three other psychotic old ladies." Norman replies, "I don't really know."

One can well imagine the story appearing in the "weird menace" magazines—*Thrilling Mystery*, for example, whose editorial policy required any seemingly supernatural event to be revealed as the result of natural causes. In that market, *Conjure Wife* would have had many of the same events and much of the dialogue that it in fact has; but it would have emphasized the psychological aberrations of the characters. Perhaps a friendly psychiatrist would have appeared at the end to explain the story exactly as Tansy suggests.

The second alternative is one that Norman explores when he is in the midst of his witchcraft. The hexes and charms, the soil from graveyards, and the strange herbs affront his rationality and he clutches for a "scientific" explanation for what he is doing. Perhaps, he concedes, magic has worked from time to time. He hypothesizes, however, that those successes demonstrate only that magic obeys natural laws not yet understood. He further considers what the situation would be if the laws governing magic were strongly dependent on their environment—he thinks, for example, of the usefulness of Euclidean geometry on Earth compared with its uselessness in space. Moreover, if the laws of magic changed rapidly, that change would account for the difficulty of replicating magical "experiments." As he tells himself, if the phenomena that led to Sir Isaac Newton's formulation of the laws of motion had changed several times in a thousand years, it would have been almost impossible to discover any physical laws at all. If that had been the case with magic, it is no wonder that magic has been regarded as superstition. Other parts of the occult arts, astrology, for example, have always been invalid, and their association with the magic that worked helped to discredit the whole.

In a scene that reads more like science fiction than fantasy, Norman collates magical spells to see if their comparison will reveal a common core of elements, parts that appear in all ages and cultures. Those elements, he supposes, must reflect the unchanging, effective parts of the spells, and the effective parts in turn must depend on physical laws. He converts the spells to formulas, substituting the symbols of logic for elements such as a flannel bag, a certain knot, and so on. He then approaches Professor Carr, the mathematician, with the covert spells, presents them as formulas for a new approach to sociology, and asks Dr. Carr if they appear to be workable. As he states the problem, "I'm wondering if one simple, underlying equation doesn't appear in each of the seventeen, jumbled up with a lot of nonessential terms and procedures. Each of the other sheets presents a similar problem." The mathematician accommodates him, presenting him with the derived equations that Norman seeks. If this portion of the story were emphasized and if Norman formulated a general theory to explain the phenomena, the book would be science fiction. Arthur C. Clarke has stated that any sufficiently advanced technology is indistinguishable from magic. If *Conjure Wife* followed the "science fiction" alternative, there would be a reversal of this dictum in which magic turned out to be an insufficiently developed technology.

Neither of these alternatives is presented forcefully enough to place the novel in their respective categories. Instead, the reader has the third alternative—magic by supernatural means—illustrated frequently and defended consistently throughout the book by all the characters except Norman. Even Norman must behave as if he believed in magic in order to help Tansy extricate them from their dangers. This thread, running consistently through the book, classifies it as fantasy of a traditional kind; but it is certainly not an ordinary fantasy.

Leiber's sure handling of the story makes it a notable example of the terror subcategory. The passage of years since its composition has not diminished its impact on the reader. Of course, some aspects of the book do seem a little old-fashioned: Hempnell College is exclusively male-run; Norman shares the prejudices of his colleagues, and at the beginning of the book patronizingly says of Tansy that "for a woman she was almost oddly free from irrationality." Yet the book is not disturbingly sexist; if anything, it illustrates the reverse, presenting Norman as a superrational creature, out of touch with important parts of the universe and blinded by his preconceptions from seeing what his senses present to him. In that sense, the novel tells of Norman's education in the range of human potential that women have preserved through centuries of male insensitivity.

Scholarly criticism has not yet discovered Leiber. Almost nothing has been said about his work in general, and on *Conjure Wife* only a retrospective review has appeared, in *Analog* of July, 1978. Hollywood has not been so slow to recognize the merits of the book, twice adapting it for the screen, bringing the story to millions who might better enjoy the stronger fantasy which the novel delivers.

Walter E. Meyers

Bibliography
Frane, Jeff. *Fritz Leiber*, 1980.
Grant, Charles J., and Foster Hirsch. "Introduction," in *Conjure Wife*, 1977.
Leiber, Fritz. "The Profession of Science Fiction: XII, Mysterious Island," in *Foundation*. No. 11/12 (March, 1977), pp. 29-38.
Leiber, Justin. "Fritz Leiber and Eyes," in *Starship*. XVI (Summer, 1979), pp. 9-18.
Merril, Judith. "Fritz Leiber," in *The Best from Fantasy and Science Fiction: A Special 25th Anniversary Anthology*, 1974.
Schweitzer, Darrell, ed. *Science Fiction Voices #1*, 1979.

A CONNECTICUT YANKEE IN KING ARTHUR'S COURT

Author: Mark Twain (Samuel Langhorne Clemens, 1835-1910)
First book publication: 1889
Type of work: Novel
Time: The early sixth century
Locale: Southern England

The story of a nineteenth century mechanic who finds himself in King Arthur's England and determines to make changes

Principal characters:
  HANK MORGAN, ALIAS THE BOSS, a Yankee mechanic
  ARTHUR, King of England
  AMYAS LE POULET, ALIAS CLARENCE, a page in Arthur's court
  ALISANDE LA CARTELOISE, ALIAS SANDY, a damsel in distress
  MERLIN, a wizard

Mark Twain purposed to write *A Connecticut Yankee in King Arthur's Court* a few days after he organized a company to develop and manufacture an automatic typesetting machine invented by James W. Paige. This machine, Twain hoped, would bring about a revolution in printing—a business in which he had some experience, having worked as an itinerant typesetter when he first left home in his late teens. Twain expressed his desire to finish his novel on the same day that the typesetting machine was perfected—a somewhat ironic desire, as events would prove. The typesetting machine never was perfected and was overtaken by Ottmar Mergenthaler's Linotype machine, which was better designed. Eventually, Twain rushed to finish the novel in 1889, needing money desperately to feed his doomed attempt to become an active force in the mechanical revolution that was changing the world.

There are, it seems, people who think that Miguel de Cervantes' *Don Quixote de la Mancha* (1605, 1615) is a comedy rather than a tragedy. There are people who make the same mistake about *A Connecticut Yankee in King Arthur's Court*, for much the same reasons. The two stories are counterparts: in one, a lone man tries to import the mythical past of knightly chivalry and courtly love into a crass, vulgar, and commercialized present; in the other, a lone man tries to import the mythical future of technological Utopia into a vicious, degraded, and poverty-stricken past. The nature of each project generates many absurd situations, which are inherently comic, and both authors made full use of their opportunities to play up such absurdities. In addition, the tone of each work is sarcastic and satirical. In spite of these facts, however, neither work taken as a whole can be considered to be a comic fantasy. They are essentially sad and bitter books. There is a point at which absurdity ceases to be funny and becomes awful, while sarcasm and satire always wear their humorous coat to disguise temporarily the taste of an acid pill.

Don Quixote and *A Connecticut Yankee in King Arthur's Court* have one important argumentative thrust in common: part of their purpose is to reveal chivalry as a sham. Neither has any patience with the mythical version of the feudal past and the romantic glorification of its social relationships. In both books, this determination to disenchant the past extends into a disenchantment of the present, whose ugliness and nastiness is brought inexorably, if subtly, into view, along with the "truth" behind the curtains of historical illusion. The main difference between the two projects is, of course, their sense of history. For Cervantes, past and present were much alike; no great gulf of time separated them, and social change was a mere matter of political tinkering. Twain, by contrast, was almost hyperconscious of the degree to which the world had been transformed. His thinking about social change was very different. He had not only read but had also visited Charles Darwin. He married an heiress whose family's fortune was made in coal, the fuel of the Industrial Revolution. He lived through the American Civil War. His hopes for the future America his daughters would inherit were no less boundless than those of Edward Bellamy, who was writing *Looking Backward: 2000-1887* (1888) while Twain was writing *A Connecticut Yankee in King Arthur's Court*. While he was thus engaged, however, Twain's ambition to play a personal role in the transformation was betrayed, and his general optimism came to be confused with a personal pessimism that was later to ruin his career.

The hero of Twain's novel is Hank Morgan, a superintendent in the Colt arms factory where, in real life, Paige was building the typesetting machine in which Twain invested so heavily. Morgan is a down-to-earth man, a nononsense exponent of homespun political philosophy and something of a wizard with machinery. Hit over the head by a crowbar, he finds himself in King Arthur's England, taken prisoner by Sir Kay and casually condemned to death as an ogre. He saves himself by pretending responsibility for a total eclipse of the sun and consolidates his reputation as a great wizard by blowing up Merlin's tower.

Morgan becomes a powerful man in Arthur's realm, but because he is not of noble birth, he remains simultaneously awe-inspiring and despicable. He coins his own title, styling himself "The Boss," and plans to civilize the world. Anticipating resistance, he begins his operations clandestinely, his most vital project being the establishment of a secret "man-factory" to train suitable agents and—more important—to educate children into an entirely new way of thinking. The latter is crucial because the people of the sixth century are virtually incapable of grasping new ideas, their minds already being set in certain ways. There is no reasoning with them; their stupidity is proof against the power of rational argument. This same stupidity, however, can be exploited—time and time again, the Boss constructs fatuous arguments of a kind *they* find acceptable, in order to get his own way.

The plot of the story is mostly taken up by two long journeys through Arthur's England. The first is an exploit in knight-errantry, to which the Boss is appointed in order that he may make himself worthy to face a challenge from a noble knight he has accidentally offended. He travels with Alisande la Carteloise, or Sandy, a girl who has come to Camelot begging the services of a knight who will save a bevy of princesses from cruel imprisonment. At the end of the quest, in the book's most Quixotic moment, the ogre's castle turns out to be a pigsty and all the "captives" swine, but on the way to this absurd rendezvous, the Boss is a guest of Morgan le Fay and on the way back, he has occasion to repair a miraculous well which has mysteriously gone dry. These experiences and others give him ample opportunity to observe and comment upon the horrors of a rigidly stratified, slave-owning society where the lower orders enjoy no rights at all.

This aspect of the novel becomes more pronounced when the Boss takes his second journey, incognito, in the company of Arthur himself. There is humor in this section, mostly arising out of Arthur's inability to adapt himself to his humble disguise, but it is basically a catalog of cruelties and stupidities. It ends with the Boss and the King about to be executed for the murder of an itinerant slave driver into whose possession they have fallen. The moment of high tension is punctured when Sir Launcelot and his knights arrive in the nick of time—a feat made possible by virtue of the fact that the Boss's first friend and loyal aide, Amyas le Poulet, or Clarence, has given them bicycles to replace their plodding horses.

Twain's vitriolic attack on the politics and mores of sixth century England may seem to some modern readers to be a careless shooting down of straw men. It must be remembered, however, that Twain grew up in a slave-owning society, and the morality of slavery was very much a live issue for him. He was drafted into the army of the Confederacy but deserted and went West to wait out the Civil War, working as a prospector and journalist. The fact that his political sympathies were with the North rather than the South was a matter of considerable personal importance in view of his birthplace, and the depth of feeling behind the condemnations of *A Connecticut Yankee in King Arthur's Court* is quite real. Similarly, when the Boss tries unsuccessfully to teach villagers in sixth century England the principles of political economy, the stupidities that are being pilloried are not those of imaginary history. The fact that the Boss continually acknowledges that his own thinking is set in ways determined by his own time adds an extra dimension of irony to the whole debate, and the argument is more open-ended than a superficial reading would imply.

The last sections of the novel are disjointed. Several humorous points are thrown in, rather as if Twain had figured them out earlier and did not want to waste them, but events move rapidly toward a violent and nasty conclusion.

The end is prefigured in the Boss's long-delayed duel with Sir Sagramor le Desirous, where he makes a mockery of the sacred institution of the Tournament. First he makes the armored knights look silly by unhorsing them with the aid of a lasso, then—when Merlin has stolen his rope and Sagramor comes to kill him with a sword—he whips out his revolvers to ram the lesson home.

Although time passes for the Boss, Twain rushes on from this point to the grand conclusion. The hero is lured away while the Established Church, which has at last realized what a menace he presents, gets to work. England is placed under an interdict, the aristocracy is shattered by war, and civilization is virtually shut down. When the Boss returns, he finds everything he has built up about to fall into ruin. Almost everyone has turned against him, except for his wife, Sandy (the erstwhile damsel in distress), and the faithful Clarence. Clarence has selected fifty-two youths educated within the Boss's system to constitute a small army. Fifty-four nineteenth century minds thus make ready to oppose the military might of all Christendom; the battle which ensues is, of course, a massacre. With an entrenched position, electrified fencing, a great water-trap, and Gatling guns, the Boss's force wipes out twenty-five thousand knights. Their victory, however, is a hollow one; they have no next step to take. When Merlin smuggles himself into their camp disguised as an old peasant woman and volunteers to do the cooking, his cleverness is really superfluous. Poisoning the Boss is really only a matter of providing the *coup de grace*. Morgan, returned to the nineteenth century, survives to pass on his story but dies eventually in tortured delirium.

In 1894, after a long struggle, Twain went bankrupt. He was already effectively exiled from his homeland. He paid off his debts mainly by lecturing and concluded his most successful tour only in time to see his favorite daughter die of meningitis. He was almost unhinged by grief and despair but came through the time of trial successfully. He returned to America in 1900 and remained a celebrity until his death. After *Pudd'nhead Wilson* (1894), however, he was never able to finish another major work. He made three attempts at *The Mysterious Stranger* (1916), but the version which eventually appeared was a fraudulent compilation. He left along with the fragments from which it was assembled a host of other oddments which are generally referred to as his "dark writings." In essence, if not in detail, all of this is foreshadowed in *A Connecticut Yankee in King Arthur's Court*. Like Don Quixote, the Yankee never *really* went into the world of chivalric romance at all; he was deluded by his inner vision into seeing his own world in terms of a new set of metaphors and living a frightfully transfigured version of his own life. He was cast away like Gulliver in a land of Yahoos, and he came to realize that the clothing of civilization could not entirely cover up the Yahoo that was in him by virtue of his own upbringing.

In purely aesthetic terms, *A Connecticut Yankee in King Arthur's Court* is not Mark Twain's best book. It is, however, considered to be a classic fantasy novel.

Brian Stableford

Bibliography

Baetzhold, Howard G. "The Course of Composition of *A Connecticut Yankee*: A Reinterpretation," in *American Literature.* XXXIII, no. 2 (1961), pp. 195-214.

Cummings, Sherwood. "*A Connecticut Yankee in King Arthur's Court,*" in *Survey of Science Fiction Literature*, 1979.

Kaplan, Justin. *Mr. Clemens and Mark Twain*, 1966.

Smith, Henry Nash. *Mark Twain's Fable of Progress: Political and Economic Ideas in "A Connecticut Yankee,"* 1964.

THE CROCK OF GOLD

Author: James Stephens (1882-1950)
First book publication: 1912
Type of work: Novel
Time: An unspecified past
Locale: Ireland

In trying to sort out complications caused by theft of the Leprecauns' crock of gold, the Philosopher comes to new wisdom, and the gods redeem Ireland

Principal characters:
THE PHILOSOPHER, a wise man who lives in Coilla Doraca
THE THIN WOMAN, his wife
SEUMAS BEG, their son
PAN, a Greek god
ANGUS OG, an Irish god
CAITILIN, the human girl who marries Angus Og

Hilarious and turgid, elfin and elephantine, *The Crock of Gold* is nothing if not Irish. It is a kind of brew, part satire and part fantasy, set partly in this world and partly in a secondary universe, although the boundaries between the two are insecure and generally unheeded. The Leprecauns who cause much of the trouble are straight out of folklore; the policemen who arrest the Philosopher are reflections, however comically they may be drawn, of the Irish Troubles—the religious and political conflicts that continue to savage that unhappy island. The gods who rescue the Philosopher (and Ireland) have Irish names but the physiques and philosophy of the gods as depicted by William Blake (1757-1827). In the figure of the Philosopher, Stephens affectionately parodies the contemporary Irish poet George Russell (1867-1935), who wrote under the name Æ. Pan comes straight from classical Greece. If the entangled theology of the book derives from Blake's *Jerusalem* (1804-1820), it can only partially obscure the love triangle between the human girl Caitilin and the two gods, Pan and Angus Og.

Finnian's Rainbow (1947), a Broadway musical, was based on *The Crock of Gold*, and when one of its characters performs the song "How Are Things in Glocca Mora?," the audience is cast straight into the warm, if slightly confused, heart of Stephens' inspiration. Two Philosophers and their termagant wives live in the dark wood of Coilla Doraca, very close to the Gort na Cloca Mora, where the Leprecauns live and where they keep buried their crock of gold, loss of which would take away their joy in living. After one of the Philosophers and his wife commit suicide because of reasoned boredom, the remaining Philosopher is approached by a neighbor, father of young Caitilin. Leprecauns have stolen his washboard. Foolishly, the Philosopher instructs him to steal the crock of gold in reprisal.

At this point, a conventional fantasist would get properly into narrative gear and depict, with a suitable sequence of events, the heavy costs of the Philosopher's bad advice and the long, strife-filled penance he must undergo before being forgiven. The pattern is familiar and deeply satisfying as structure and resolution; indeed, it is clear Stephens had something of the sort in mind and that he tried with some persistence to realize it in fact. His success was limited, although the book itself does not ultimately suffer.

The Leprecauns naturally blame the Philosopher for the loss of their crock of gold, and in appropriate and traditional retribution soon kidnap his children, Seumas Beg and Brigid. Out of fear, however, of the Philosopher's wife, the Thin Woman of Inis Magrath, who is something of a witch but also the children's mother, the Leprecauns soon bundle the children back home. It is at this point, only tenuously connected with anything that has preceded, that the main story of *The Crock of Gold* gets under way. Pan comes to Ireland and seduces young Caitilin, who follows him to a nearby cave where she sleeps with him, entranced by his goatish lower half, the like of which she has not yet seen in Ireland.

The Philosopher unsuccessfully sends his children after Caitilin, and they soon pass into the background of the novel, although Stephens would eventually express his sense of the importance of the innocent quest of the child in a volume of poems entitled *The Adventures of Seumas Beg* (1915), part of the contents of which already existed but which did not fit readily into *The Crock of Gold*. After Seumas Beg and Brigid return from their inconclusive visit with Pan and Caitilin, the Philosopher himself leaves Coilla Doraca to search for Angus Og, an Irish god who might see fit to intercede. This journey is the Philosopher's redemption. It has nothing to do with Leprecauns.

From an early age, James Stephens was engaged deeply in Irish life and letters. Such an engagement in 1905 (and later) bore a necessary political implication, since to be involved with Irish culture was to be an Irish nationalist. Stephens became identified early with the nationalist campaigns of the Sinn Fein conviction and published frequently in *Sinn Fein*, a paper which appeared, usually weekly, from 1906 to 1914. From January, 1909, up to the point that *The Crock of Gold* was ready for publication, Stephens contributed to *Sinn Fein* several pieces purporting to be disquisitions uttered by an Old Philosopher (in the unmistakable accents of the poet Æ, who had first discovered Stephens working as a clerk; Æ apparently did not resent the spoofing of his oracular style). These disquisitions, some of them running as long as fifteen pages, were incorporated into *The Crock of Gold* and support the assumption that in the character of the Philosopher, Stephens was attempting to create an exemplary Irish figure.

The Philosopher who trudges off in search of Angus Og may be a figure of fun, but he is clearly not that alone. Despite his interminable pontifications, his obsessive need to eviscerate everything that happens by peremptory, logic-chopping, philosophical discourse, and his incapacity to listen to others until it is almost too late, he is a man whose basic impulses, when properly aroused, are sound and life-affirming, although local rather than cosmopolitan. He needs only to learn how to marry his abstract philosophizing to the ancient powers of Imagination, and he will be saved; and if he can be saved, then perhaps Ireland can be saved as well.

Pan and Angus Og are both embodiments of the Eternal Will; Angus Og in particular can be seen as a representation of the Blakean concept of the God who weds Thought and Heart, a lonely God who needs Man to love him. After crossing the wilds of Ireland into the mountains, the Philosopher finds him at last and is granted an interview to which the reader is not invited. The result, however, is clear enough. Angus Og visits Pan and Caitilin, and his need for love convinces her that she must go with him. The Philosopher, for his part, leaves the cave of the God in a state of ecstacy. "From the wells of forgetfulness he regained the shining words and gay melodies which his childhood had delighted in, and these he sang loudly and unceasingly as he marched." He meets various people of the soil, all representatives of an Irish rebirth, and for each of them he has a preordained message from Angus Og that lifts their hearts. When he sees his wife he kisses her, and their marriage is saved; she becomes his protector.

Protection is certainly needed. Still desolate, the Leprecauns have betrayed the Philosopher to the police, telling them that he has murdered two people (the other Philosopher and his wife) and that the corpses are buried under the hearth. The police arrive. (In the meantime the Philosopher's children have returned the crock of gold, causing the Leprecauns some remorse; it should be noted that the crock of gold is actually a *MacGuffin*—Alfred Hitchcock's term for a device or gimmick whose nature is unimportant but which provides a motive for the quest or chase.) Soon the Philosopher is arrested and taken away in pitch dark from his home and family to await trial and inevitable execution. The journey of the Philosopher and the police through the terrors of the dark, in its hilarity and underlying melancholy, prefigures another astonishing Irish novel, Flann O'Brien's profound *The Third Policeman* (1967). In jail, the Philosopher's fellow prisoners tell him the sad stories of their lives, drab, oppressed, urban existences only possible, it would seem, under the inhumane trammels of an invidious political order.

For her part, the Thin Woman refuses to allow her husband's capture to go unchallenged. After an encounter with three Blakean deities, whose allurements she refuses, she finds Angus Og and Caitilin, who agree with her that the Philosopher must be saved. When they descend from the hills, they find that she has mobilized all of the traditional folk of Ireland—witches and Leprecauns and heroes long in retreat from the world of men—and together the assembled host marches to the rescue, as the novel closes:

> Down to the city they went dancing and singing; among the streets and the shops telling

their sunny tale; not heeding the malignant eyes and the cold brows and the sons of Balor looked sidewards. And they took the Philosopher from his prison, even the Intellect of Man they took from the hands of the doctors and lawyers, from the sly priests, from the professors whose mouths are gorged with sawdust, and the merchants who sell blades of grass—the awful people of the Fomor . . . and then they returned again, dancing and singing, to the country of the gods. . . .

This passage may well serve to illustrate the eloquence—amounting at times to blarney—of Stephens' style when he is in a singing mood. In this mood, when he is able to celebrate the language and lore of the Ireland he felt to be oppressed and to have been deprived of her heritage, he is capable of a high, glad richness not often found in prose. The confused philosophy, the disjointed plotting, and the slightly too self-conscious brogue of the style all fade into the background, and *The Crock of Gold* takes on the melancholy, polished glow of reinhabited legend. James Stephens wrote poetry, belles lettres, stories, and novels in some abundance, almost all of them about Ireland; and in almost all of them he didactically attempted to rekindle the Irish spirit. Only in *The Crock of Gold*, however, is the flame ignited and a pathway cleared to the country of the gods.

John Clute

Bibliography
Bramsbäck, Birgit. *James Stephens: A Literary and Bibliographical Study*, 1959.
Pyle, Hillary A. *James Stephens: His Work and an Account of His Life*, 1965.

A CRYSTAL AGE

Author: William Henry Hudson (1841-1922)
First book publication: 1887
Type of work: Novel
Time: The distant future
Locale: An earthly paradise

An account of a future era where men live in perfect ecological harmony with their pastoral environment

> Principal characters:
> SMITH, an Englishman
> YOLETTA, a young woman
> CHASTEL, the mother of the House

A Crystal Age is a difficult work to classify: it is a vision of an earthly paradise, but it is Arcadian rather than Utopian in character and by no means polemical. It carries no political message of exhortation, and might perhaps be better regarded as a defeatist parable lamenting the imperfections of contemporary man.

The narrator of the story, called Smith, identifies himself as an Englishman, but apart from this fact virtually nothing is learned about him. He cannot even remember where he was when the accident occurred that precipitated him into the strange world, which it is now his mission to describe. Awaking after an inestimable period of time, he wanders through a beautiful rural environment until he is discovered by its people. They are astonished by his appearance, and although they speak English they find most of what he has to say incomprehensible. They have not heard of England, or any person he can name; they have never seen clothes like his; and they do not know what money is. By comparison with them, Smith is uncouth in every way.

Smith is taken into the House which is the dwelling-place of the whole community (known as the House of the Harvest Melody), and he agrees to work with them in the fields in return for their hospitality. He is glad to be allowed to stay because he is captivated by Yoletta, a young girl who seems tồ be about seventeen years of age (although he later finds out that she is much older). He grows to love Yoletta passionately, but she and her people seem to be quite unfamiliar with the notion of erotic love, even though they are very affectionate in a quasifraternal fashion.

The whole world seems to be organized after the fashion of rural communes, everyone living in a house which has been constantly renewed through thousands of years. Each community is self-sufficient, and each is much devoted to the arts and to the business of maintaining family histories. The people know that there was once a very different social order—destroyed, apparently, by plague—but all detailed memory of it has been obliterated. They do not

connect Smith with their legends of it; they think him a visitor from a long-
lost island.

The people of the House acknowledge a masculine Creator, but otherwise
seem to practice a kind of matriolatry, holding the role of motherhood to be
sacred. Smith has been in the house for a month before he realizes that the
House has an actual mother, secluded because of illness. This mother, Chastel,
is the effective ruler of the community, and Smith repairs his most damaging
breach of etiquette by making himself known to her. At first, she treats him
harshly, but in time he comes to have a special place in her affections, although
he does not realize why.

Insofar as *A Crystal Age* may be said to have a plot, it is the story of Smith's
abominable stupidity. His references to himself give a modest account of his
intellect, but the real extent of his stupidity becomes apparent to the reader
only gradually. The reader must infer what Smith cannot, realizing the
implications of the fact that these people are very long-lived but not very
numerous, and thus understanding why each house has only one mother, and
why the other members of the household know nothing of sexual love. Once
this is deduced, it is easy for the reader to guess why Chastel takes a special
interest in Smith and his awkwardly confessed feelings for Yoletta: he is being
prepared for the role of father of the House, and she for the role of mother.
Smith, however, does not guess any of this.

Smith's failure to understand the situation ultimately leads him to disaster.
He finds a bottle whose label promises a cure for misery. The reader, noting
several references by Chastel and others to the fact that all but she are spared
the indignity of pain and old age, realizes that the liquid in the bottle is a
painless poison, but Smith does not. Instead, he jumps to the conclusion that
it is the means by which his hosts achieve the suppression of their sexual
desires. Despairing of the possibility that Yoletta might ever love him as he
loves her, he resolves to seek the same freedom from passion. Only after he
has drunk from the bottle does he find a book which tells him all that he
should have guessed, and only then does he realize what he has done to
himself. It is, of course, too late.

Smith, as his name suggests, is clearly intended to be an Everyman figure,
and his obvious stupidity is no mere idiosyncrasy, but rather a judgment
passed by William Henry Hudson upon his contemporaries. *A Crystal Age*
is, in fact, a bitterly misanthropic book: its message is that the ideal world
is not for the likes of modern man, because modern man is too brutal to adapt
to it. The lush descriptions of the marvels of the earthly paradise, whose
beauties Smith can appreciate enough to make him desire to share them, are
attractive enough; but their real purpose is to make the reader feel uncomfortable in his or her unworthiness.

While most nineteenth century visions of ideal states now seem quaint and
laughably naïve, *A Crystal Age* has worn very well, in that the notion of the

essential unworthiness of modern man remains popular, and the ecological mysticism which Hudson espoused well in advance of the founding of the science of ecology has at last attained fashionability.

A Crystal Age was written while Hudson was a poor man, long before he achieved success and security following the publication of *Green Mansions* (1904). It was, however, reprinted in 1906 to capitalize on the success of the latter novel, in an edition rather more handsome than the first. To this new edition Hudson put his name—the first was anonymous—and added a preface which piles further ironies upon those in the text. Hudson elects to belittle the book as mere pandering to the fascination with fantastic romance so prevalent in his day. He declares that although *A Crystal Age* is steeped in the ideas of its own day, he would still, if he were to write a new futuristic fantasy, imagine the human race in a "forest period." Even this expression of constancy, however, is rapidly sabotaged by his statement that the dream, of course, cannot command belief because "the ending of passion and strife is the beginning of decay"—an apparent reference to the Spencerian notion that progress is based on the struggle for existence and the "survival of the fittest." It is significant that Hudson should select this rather esoteric reason for his novel's being unbelievable (it contains several more commonplace impossibilities), for it is a key element in his own disillusionment.

Hudson, in *A Crystal Age* and *Green Mansions*, is a naturalist expressing the despair into which he has been cast by the Darwinian disenchantment of Nature, dreaming of a supernaturally reharmonized Creation by no means red in tooth and claw: Earth as a new Eden. Even while he dallied with such dreams and made them powerful enough eventually to win the acclaim of the reading public, he knew them to be the merest tissue of illusion; and yet— as he explains—he could not resist shaking one more pretty pattern out of the kaleidoscope.

Brian Stableford

Bibliography
Armytage, W. H. G. *Yesterday's Tomorrows*, 1968.
Clarke, I. F. *The Pattern of Expectation*, 1979.
Frederick, John Towner. *William Henry Hudson*, 1972.
Hamilton, Robert. *W. H. Hudson: The Vision of Earth*, 1946.
Haymaker, Richard E. *From Pampas to Hedgerows and Downs: A Study of W. H. Hudson*, 1954.
Mumford, Lewis. *The Story of Utopias*, 1922.
Ross, Harry. *Utopias Old and New*, 1938.

THE DARK IS RISING SERIES

Author: Susan Cooper (1935-   )
First book publications: Over Sea, Under Stone (1965); *The Dark Is Rising* (1973); *Greenwitch* (1974); *The Grey King* (1975); *Silver on the Tree* (1977)
Type of work: Novels
Time: The 1960's and 1970's
Locale: The British Isles

A sequence of five novels that demonstrate the validity and power of the Arthurian ideal in the contemporary world

Principal characters:
SIMON, JANE, AND BARNEY DREW, children who discover the long hidden Holy Grail
WILL STANTON, an "ordinary" English boy who realizes on his eleventh birthday that he is Merlin's youngest colleague
MERLIN, OR MERRIMAN LYON, the Old One who helps Will find and defend the six Signs of Power
THE LADY, Will and Merriman's loveliest and most powerful ally
THE WALKER, a miserable survivor from Merlin's thirteenth century circle who brings a crucial sign to the twentieth century
THE BLACK RIDER, the leader of the Dark's icy assault upon the modern world
BRAN DAVIES, King Arthur's son
THE GREY KING, a despotic Welsh ruler
JOHN ROWLANDS, a heroic Welsh shepherd

Some of the best twentieth century writing about the modern condition occurs in Arthurian fantasies. T. H. White's Once and Future King series brilliantly critiques the modern compulsion to make war instead of sense, and Mary Stewart's Merlin trilogy dramatizes the tragic shallowness of modern thinking, in which intuitive wisdom has given way to unenlightened pragmatism. Susan Cooper agrees with White and Stewart that modern selfhood and society essentially began in King Arthur's court but differs with them about the present role of Arthurian idealism. Instead of contrasting Camelot's lost glories with modern psychological and societal wastelands as White and Stewart do, Cooper celebrates the ongoing evolutionary influence of the Arthurian spirit. Her five Dark Is Rising novels propose that in the contemporary world a lively Arthurian energy impels children as well as adults to more responsible humanity.

Common sense suggests that Cooper's thesis is fantastically at odds with even the most easily observable facts of twentieth century life. To the contrary, each Dark Is Rising book is scrupulously realistic, grounded in Cooper's vivid, sharply focused perceptions of physical nature and human character. Her remarkable sensitivity to setting especially informs the series' opening volume, *Over Sea, Under Stone,* which is chiefly about Cornwall's landscape. It is because they attend closely to the telling details of the Cornish terrain that the three Drew children, Simon, Jane, and Barney, discover the Holy Grail, long sheltered "over sea, under stone." Cornwall compels the Drews' attention as it does the reader's, thanks to Cooper's evocative descriptions, which envelop one in an almost tangible sense of its physical presence and so awaken in the reader, as in the Drews, a first spark of Arthurian intelligence.

The quality that stirs in the Drews to such productive effect is intuition, the perception of inner, underlying truths. This is the quality that fully develops in Will Stanton, the eleven-year-old hero of *The Dark Is Rising*, second and title book in Cooper's series. Unlike the Drew children, whose plucky explorations express typical Boy Scout alertness and resourcefulness but not much more (until the series' third and fifth volumes), Will has depth. Seventh son of a seventh son, he suddenly finds on his eleventh birthday that there are crucial inner dimensions to his familiar English countryside and that inwardly, his family, friends, neighbors, and particularly he himself have profoundly meaningful lives. Appropriately, Will's birthday epiphany occurs at the winter solstice, during nature's most intensely "underground" season, so that in *The Dark Is Rising*, the external, physical setting dramatically reinforces the psychological action.

What most makes Will's experiences credible, however, is the astounding fact that he is an ordinary English boy who personally enacts two major heroic archetypes. As quest hero, he seeks the "Signs of Power" that explain and quicken natural phenomena; and he battles toward his goal by the initiation hero's process of transforming his thoughts, feelings, and wishes as wisely and responsibly as he can. On one level, the quest and initiation patterns give density and structure to Will's personality, showing his inner metamorphoses as he negotiates the modern adolescent's perilous passage from childhood to adulthood. On another, more significant level, Will's heroism indicates the goals and transformations all people need to survive the "Dark's" real onslaughts.

Cooper provides further information about practical heroism by making Will an Old One, a member of a vast worldwide network of warriors for the Light. As the youngest and last Old One, Will completes a major historical process which began with Merlin, many centuries before: the evolution of true community as a workable prospect for modern people. The Old Ones themselves constitute a model community, being a perfect circle of mutually supportive, thoroughly decent, utterly wise, kind, and capable kindred spirits, all "born with the same gift [for initiation], and for the same high purpose [or general quest]." They are not, however, finally human. Because each Old One's core, determinative selfhood *is* this community-building function, rather than a personality, he is immortal; ideas, after all, are deathless, and the Old Ones explicitly represent the power of the pure, enduring idea (the Arthurian concept of "civilization") to shape human experience. Through the

Old Ones' heroic commitment, the *idea* of community takes root in human consciousness. The responsibility for *being* civilized belongs to human beings, whose twentieth century tasks are the central concern of the last three Dark Is Rising books.

Merlin is the prototypical Old One. *Over Sea, Under Stone* introduces him in his modern persona of Merriman Lyon, eminent archaeologist and the Drew children's favorite "Great-Uncle Merry," but he remains merely a colorful enigma until *The Dark Is Rising*, where, as Will's chief tutor and closest companion, he discloses his innermost thoughts. From this inside perspective, Merriman/Merlin has the soul of a concerned physicist. He is absolutely dedicated to his enlightened conviction that the Arthurian impulse has both scientific validity and moral force, that it is the Tao of physics as well as mankind's best way to better living.

For this reason, Merriman has a good deal to say about the old Ones' view of the time-space continuum; knowing that time and space interpenetrate and that linear time is a human delusion, the Old Ones can appreciate why and how the Arthurian dream actually does live in multiple inner and outer realities. Merriman makes his mind-boggling wisdom real to Will by allowing him to read it in the occult *Book of Grammarye*, a compendium of visionary writings, and to live it in magical deeds such as traveling to various past times, transporting special objects back and forth in time, stopping time for an occasional human being, and stepping out of time into intuitive consciousness. Cooper brings the Old Ones' wisdom to life by incorporating it as the basic structural principle of the Dark Is Rising series. In her kaleidoscopic time-shifts and character-changes and her dazzling fusion of Celtic myth with modern realism, the reader imaginatively recognizes the truth of Merriman's teaching: "'all times co-exist, and the future can sometimes affect the past, even though the past is a road that leads to the future.'"

Although Merriman's outlook suggests post-Einsteinian physics in these important respects, in others it distinctly recalls the stirring sentiments of Henry Wadsworth Longfellow's "The Present Crisis": "Once to every man and nation comes the/ moment to decide,/ In the strife of Truth with Falsehood,/ for the good or evil side." Good is not the only shaping force in Merriman's universe. Since the beginning of time, the Light's community-building efforts have been countered by the equally substantive, dangerously effective opposing might of the Dark. Each side strives to direct, control, and animate human character, which is, like physical nature, inherently neutral, neither good nor evil; while the Light inspires people to live in harmony with the land and one another, the Dark fosters malevolent disunion. Its entropic energy scattered the Knights of King Arthur's Round Table and caused the Dark Ages. Now, swollen to totalitarian proportions, it threatens to extinguish the idea of civilization forever, as *The Dark Is Rising* vividly explains. Cooper's exploration of evil's real role in the war-filled twentieth century deepens as the series progresses, but for sheer dramatic power, she never surpasses Will's first chilling encounter with global hatred.

Two characters in *The Dark Is Rising* illustrate dangers that particularly beset the modern world, in which, as William Butler Yeats observed, "The best lack all conviction, while the worst/ Are full of passionate intensity." The Lady, who represents the ancient idea of *Natura naturans* (the ongoing creativity of organic nature), is exhausted. When she fades from view in this novel, Will and his contemporaries lose an extremely important weapon against the Dark, the ability to relate meaningfully to natural processes; the Lady's image is too attenuated and distant to be useful for modern thinkers. Meanwhile, the Walker suffers the tragic consequences of believing (in approved modern fashion) that personal caring transcends and nullifies all other commitments. Lacking an adequate concept of love, the Walker falls easy prey to spitefulness and resentment. He is the victim of the romantic fallacy.

Greenwitch, the third book in the Dark Is Rising series, shows how nature's, or the Lady's, vital, responsive presence can be rediscovered by modern people. Barney Drew reaches her imaginatively, via his strongly artistic sense of sight. Jane Drew uses feminine intuition and empathy to unlock the primal secrets that elude Will and even Merriman, with their predominantly masculine minds. On the other hand, Barney and Jane need the ideas which Will and Merriman articulate for them, just as earlier they needed the Arthurian map of Cornwall to locate the Holy Grail. Simon Drew's sturdy practicality and courage are also necessary. Their five-person community is a tiny twentieth century version of the Round Table. It is also a striking image of a healthy organism, for it liberates its individual members' complementary talents and thus, as an integrated total system, heals collectively the compartmentalized, fragmented, imbalanced consciousness in which Darkness breeds. In this way, the Drews, together with the Old Ones, translate *Natura naturans* into personal and societal growth; they learn to recognize the Lady within themselves as well as in exterior nature.

Developmental psychologists agree that being productive is one of the essential tasks involved in being mature; the other, they say, is achieving bonding, or intimacy. Having addressed productivity in *Greenwitch*, Cooper devotes the rest of the Dark Is Rising series to defining the true Arthurian character of bonding in modern times. In the fourth book, *The Grey King*, she desentimentalizes love by focusing on the bleak facts about "passionate intensity." This novel's central character is Bran Davies, King Arthur's son, whose life has been thoroughly disrupted by other people's passions. What happens to Bran parallels the argument of *Ich und Du* (1923, *I and Thou*), Martin Buber's masterly study of the modern condition. The heartless Grey King who dominates Bran's part of Wales epitomizes what Buber calls the "I-it" mentality: grasping, possessive, and manipulative, a travesty of love binding people not to one another but to the paralyzing sense of mortality and despair. At bottom, it is the spirit of materialism, for it reduces all beings to mere objects, or "its." By contrast, true loving frees potentials and opens horizons for everyone concerned, because it is the ultimate regard for the other's uniqueness. Thus Bran's I-thou relationships with his dog, Will, John Rowlands, and eventually his royal father enable him to outgrow his youthful alienation and self-absorption and commit himself wholeheartedly to destroying the Grey King's hold on twentieth century imaginations.

Silver on the Tree features John Rowlands, a Welsh shepherd who solves the problem that broke the Walker, how to be warmhearted and wise-minded at the same time. He does this by unflinchingly *thinking* through to the underlying truths of every emotional crisis. Rowlands' levelheaded reasonableness, absolute honesty, and unshakable conviction that "our choices are our own" emancipate him from his romantic delusions and make him the natural guardian of Arthurian freedom in modern society. He embodies the heroic potential of democratic man, who instinctively rejects totalitarian blandishments. The prejudiced, racist, antisocial, viciously tyrannical meanness which distinguishes the Dark in this final volume has no appeal at all for him.

The Dark Is Rising series ends in a mood of qualified optimism. As Merriman says in his farewell to his human colleagues, "The hope is always here, always alive, but only your fierce caring can fan it into a fire to warm the world."

Jane Hipolito

Bibliography
Cooper, Susan. "Newbery Award Acceptance," in *Horn Book*. LII (1976), pp. 361-366.

DARKER THAN YOU THINK

Author: Jack Williamson (1908-   )
First book publication: 1948
Type of work: Novel
Time: The late 1940's
Locale: The city of Clarendon, somewhere in mid-America

Will Barbee's romance with fellow reporter April Bell begins his initiation into a life of occult horror

Principal characters:
> WILL BARBEE, a reporter for the *Clarendon Call*
> APRIL BELL, a were-creature chosen to awaken and direct Will's dormant powers
> LAMARACK MONDRICK, an anthropologist who discovers the secret of the witch people and the key to their destruction
> ROWENA MONDRICK, his blind wife and a leader of those opposed to the ascendency of the witch people
> SAM QUAIN, a boyhood friend of Barbee and Mondrick's assistant
> DR. ARCHER GLENN, the director of Glennhaven Sanitarium, revealed as Barbee's half brother

Darker Than You Think appeared originally as a short novel in the December, 1940, edition of *Unknown*. It was an instant success and was in both style and treatment something of a departure for its author. Following World War II service in the army, Jack Williamson revised and expanded his original story to its present length and published it as a novel in 1948. The novel became a benchmark work in the history of horror fantasy, partly because of its effective combination of rational and occult fantasy blended with melodrama and a touch of science fiction. The addition of the psychotherapy and sanatorium scenes and the brooding, hallucinatory transitions in Will Barbee's consciousness between sleeping and waking and, more emphatically, between life as a human and as a were-creature undoubtedly owe something to Williamson's own experiences with therapy after the war.

Williamson's revision of his *Unknown* story accomplished other goals beyond the obvious one of expanded length. Originally set in prewar New York City, the story was shifted to a fictitious location somewhere in postwar mid-America. Some new characters were introduced; others, such as Rowena Mondrick and Nora Quain, became more fully developed. Considerably more exposition was added, especially in support of the rational fantasy. Perhaps most important of all the changes was the added development of the protagonist, Will Barbee, in his transition from a merely alienated, slightly alcoholic reporter for a small-town newspaper to the prophesied leader of the witch people. How and why this transformation happens is the essential argument of Williamson's novel.

Occult fantasy, of which this novel is an example, derives its materials mainly from oral and folk traditions that treat the existence of such magical creatures as witches, vampires, shapeshifters, and the like. Stories featuring such legendary types and their lore are among the most popular contemporary fantasies, especially in the film and broadcast media. The origins of such stories lie in the folk cultures of distant ages, but the lore that has developed around them in the fiction of the past two centuries amounts almost to a mythology in itself and continues to develop and evolve from one generation of writers to the next. The central conceit of occult fantasy is the representation of a natural order in which such extraordinary creatures may find a place—a fantastic extension of the familiar world. Unlike most fairy tales and science fiction, stories of this type begin with the ordinary and familiar, gradually transforming it into something strange and often terrifying.

Darker Than You Think begins at Clarendon's municipal airport, Trojan Field. On the scene are Will Barbee and April Bell, who identifies herself as a new reporter for a rival newspaper. Will is immediately attracted by what proves literally to be her animal magnetism. The occasion is the anticipated arrival of Professor Lamarack Mondrick's Mongolian expedition. Following extreme security precautions as the expedition cargo plane arrives, Professor Mondrick dies mysteriously while attempting to deliver a warning to the world, to the true human race, as he puts it, of a clandestine menace, evidence of which he has brought back from an excavation site in the Gobi desert.

Mondrick's death causes a sensation, naturally enough, and his assistants withdraw as though under siege, promising a report to the world at a later, more appropriate time. Following his reportorial instincts, Barbee demands that Sam Quain, his best friend in college and chief assistant to Mondrick, disclose the unfinished message. Instead, Quain evades the issue with a comment about Mondrick's obvious fatigue and failing health and an unwelcome reminder that Mondrick had refused to make Barbee one of his assistants, declaring that he was not to be trusted. The interview with Quain, however, does reveal to Barbee the probable cause of Mondrick's death. The professor was severely allergic to cat hair, and Barbee realizes that Mondrick's death was caused by anaphylactic shock from a kitten that April Bell had brought with her to the airport. Following up on his suspicions, Barbee discovers the dead cat in a handbag, pierced with a brooch belonging to Bell.

Confronted with Barbee's evidence, Bell not only admits her guilt but also confesses that she is a witch who was forced to defend herself and those like her from Mondrick's intention to destroy them. Bell explains that Mondrick had discovered evidence that witches did indeed exist as biological mutations of *homo sapiens*, that they were gathering their strength for an attempted takeover of the world, and that Mondrick had returned from the Gobi with incontrovertible evidence of the existence of a race of witches that once challenged humans for supremacy over the planet. Moreover, Barbee later discovers that Mondrick returned from the Gobi site of Ala-shan with a secret bane against the witch people. Mondrick had devoted his entire professional life to developing scientific proof of the existence of witches and witchcraft, and he had finally succeeded. Bell declares that such a revelation would mean the death of all witches like herself, since humans in the past had ruthlessly exterminated them upon far less compelling proof.

Bell's plea for understanding (after all, she did not ask to be born a witch) is met by Barbee's declaration that he is entirely under her spell. That night, he is called by Bell to change and join her. With the brooch as a talisman, Will changes into a werewolf at April's direction and the two go off to hunt down one of the assistants of Professor Mondrick and kill him. April explains to Barbee that he is one of the witch people, who are awaiting the appearance of the "Child of Night" to lead them to world dominance. The following day, Will is troubled by dreams of his evening's run as a werewolf and of their encounter with the defenses intended to keep them away from the mysterious box and its intimidating cargo. His recourse is to consult Dr. Archer Glenn, psychiatrist and director of Glennhaven Sanitarium. Glenn has been treating Barbee and reassures him that, however real the dreams may seem, they are nothing more than illusions. Barbee accepts Glenn's explanation although he is not satisfied by it, and, of course, the reader knows better.

The events that follow are orchestrated by Bell, although the extent of her direction is manifested to Barbee only at the conclusion. Each night, he is called by her to change and join her in opposing the enemies of the Child of Night, or, as he was called in the original version, the "Black Messiah." Barbee is changed again into a wolf, another night into a tiger, then a snake, and finally into a pterodactyl. Prompted by Bell in her wolf-form, Barbee murders in turn the remaining members of the expedition and Rowena Mondrick, the professor's wife. Bell even manages to provoke Barbee's own accidental death in a car crash so that he can be reborn as the Child of Night, destined by breeding and careful manipulation of events to become the leader of the witch people. Since Barbee succeeds in destroying the box and its contents (although he spares his last human friend, Sam Quain), the novel ends with the way prepared for the final, inevitable victory of the witch people over the human race—unless, of course, the main characters are either all mad or psychotic, and there is enough evidence of that hypothesis in the text to deserve at least some consideration.

Darker Than You Think is a typical example of the type of fantasy promoted by Campbell's *Unknown* and later by Horace Gold's *Beyond Fantasy Fiction*: it treats the occult in a speculative and pseudoscientific manner. In addition, there are other traces of the *Unknown* tradition still operative in the revised novel in the use of psi and rational fantasy. Williamson's own contribution to were-creature mythology is not so much in substance as in method, since shape-shifting is related to both psi and the fantastic science of what may be

termed occult anthropology. Bell possesses psi power by virtue of her attributes as a witch. Her explanation of how her power works and the connection
with shape-shifting is given to Barbee as an orientation lecture to his new
state. "The link between mind and matter," she tells him, "is probability."
Given the mind of a witch, probabilities can be anticipated and, to some
degree, matter can be controlled by the web of thought. Certain substances
such as silver, because of its molecular structure, and conditions such as
sunlight, because of its vibratory patterns, break down the mental web and
its power to control the vibrations of the atoms in the body "through the
linkage of atomic probability." This is all double-talk, of course, but Williamson handles it at least as well as Fritz Leiber in *Gather, Darkness!* (1950)
or Theodore Sturgeon in *More Than Human* (1953).

Underlying Bell's success as a mind reader and manipulator of human events
is Williamson's occult anthropology. The reader is briefed on the fabulous
history of *homo lycanthropus* from two points of view: first, Bell delivers her
apologia as a witch to Barbee after the murder of Professor Mondrick; later,
Sam Quain (gone into hiding with the Mondrick box) explains the professor's
theory of the rise of the witch people in the Pleistocene era following the first
Ice Age: "The witch folk sprang from another kindred type of Hominidae
who were trapped by the glaciers in the higher country southwest, toward
Tibet." Quain's account of Mondrick's discoveries covers the better part of
two chapters and is an entertaining and effective bit of fantastic speculative
reasoning. Quain ends his narrative with Mondrick's confirmed conviction
that the witch people have discovered a way to breed selectively and thus
control the randomness of the appearance of *homo lycanthropus* in history;
hence, the witch people's share of the human genetic pool has rapidly been
increasing. Beyond even that, Mondrick and Quain see the witch folk gradually taking control of the media and of scientific and political institutions in
a vast conspiracy that is about to achieve world domination.

One may speculate on the degree to which the cold war psychology of the
late 1940's is reflected in the Mondrick/Quain history of the rebirth of the
witch folk. Perhaps that psychology is reflected as well in the theme of paranoia that runs throughout the story. Of course, one may object that to the
extent so-called paranoia is justified, it cannot be properly considered aberrant
thinking. No one is to be trusted in the world of *Darker Than You Think*.
Dr. Glenn himself, who reassures Barbee that the correspondence between
his dreams of murder and the deaths of his friends is purely coincidental,
turns out to be the mastermind among the witch folk, a half brother of Barbee,
and the one responsible for awakening Bell to her special role in bringing
about the birth of the Child of Night and the final victory of *homo lycanthropus*. The logic of paranoia undercuts not only several sciences but also
the arts and, so it seems, nearly every creative human activity. The truly
human, those without the lycanthropic taint to their blood, neither see nor

presumably even suspect the existence of their predatory counterparts. The occult anthropology of Mondrick accounts for everything from myths and legends (Jupiter, Proteus, and so on) to all modern crime and insanity as the product of the conflict within the human personality between *homo sapiens* and *homo lycanthropus*. Those with lucky admixtures of the two turn out to be the creative geniuses of the race. Sam Quain's vision of history and human society has the weird logic of the insane.

Is it darker to think of the hegemony of *homo lycanthropus* or of the possible madness of the entire cast of characters? The consolation of the former is similar to that of Richard Matheson's *I Am Legend* (1954) or, in a mundane sort of way, that of Arthur C. Clarke's *Childhood's End* (1953) in the obligatory victory of the superior over the inferior species. Such orthodox Darwinism is amply supported in Williamson's narrative, and the fantastic historical revisionism creates a large part of the entertainment offered by the story. Perhaps such a view is a sufficiently dark one to dull the luster of the most manic reader, and it is without doubt the more obvious of the two possible readings. The second possibility persists, however, if only in the background: that the novel, in its guise of occultism and pulp fantasy, portrays a society gone mad, darker indeed than one may wish to think.

Donald L. Lawler

Bibliography

Moskowitz, Sam. "Jack Williamson," in *Seekers of Tomorrow*, 1966.

Myers, Robert E. *Jack Williamson: A Primary and Secondary Bibliography*, 1979.

Stewart, Alfred D. "Jack Williamson: The Comedy of Cosmic Evolution," in *Voices for the Future: Essays on Major Science Fiction Writers*, 1976. Edited by Thomas D. Clareson.

THE DARKOVER NOVELS

Author: Marion Zimmer Bradley (1930-   )
First book publications: The Heritage of Hastur (1975); *The Shattered Chain* (1976); *The Forbidden Tower* (1977); *Stormqueen!* (1978); *The Bloody Sun* (1979); *Two to Conquer* (1980); *Sharra's Exile* (1982)
Type of work: Novels
Time: About four thousand years in the future
Locale: A four-mooned planet, Darkover, orbiting a red sun, Cottman's Star (hence the Terran Survey name, Cottman IV)

A collection of novels that chronicle the history of the planet Darkover over the course of several centuries and the telekinetic powers of its inhabitants

Taken together, the seven Darkover novels published by Marion Zimmer Bradley since 1975 give a richer picture of Darkover than the eight which preceded them. In part this is owing to Bradley's growing literary sophistication, in part to the influence of her editors, who have realized that Bradley's readers want to know more about Darkover's telepathically gifted nobility and their psychic sciences.

As is generally the case in a long-running series, the sequence of composition of the Darkover novels is quite different from their internal chronology. The later novels, written over a seven-year period, would fall as follows in the chronology of Darkover: About six hundred years following the original settling of the planet by a lost Terran colonial ship, *Stormqueen!* takes place in the midst of the Age of Chaos, when telepathically powered weapons ran wild, and feudal kingdoms warred constantly among themselves. *Two to Conquer* is set at the end of the Ages of Chaos, when the signing of the Compact outlawed the use of psychic weapons on Darkover. Following the rediscovery of Darkover by the Terran Empire, *The Shattered Chain*, though written prior to the previous two works, is set some three hundred years later, during the building of the Terran spaceport at Thendara, Darkover's capital. A generation later comes *The Forbidden Tower* and the rediscovery of lost principles of matrix (telepathic amplifier) mechanics, and a generation after it, *The Bloody Sun* details the struggles of Darkovans and Terrans for the secrets of matrix mechanics. After another generation comes *The Heritage of Hastur*, with its theme of the conflict between Darkovans and Terrans for political control of Darkover. *Sharra's Exile* (a rewrite of *The Sword of Aldones*, 1962) depicts the last battle of the legendary matrix-weapons and a resolution of the Terran-Darkovan conflicts.

Much of the delight of the Darkover material arises from the creation of many of its elements before Bradley was fifteen, at an age when young people can wander for hours in the realms of imagination, literally dreaming up whatever suits their fancies. Drawing on a heady mix of "A. Merritt, Kuttner and Moore, Brackett and Hamilton, with a liberal splash of Graustark, the

Prisoner of Zenda, Zorro, and the lost races of H. Rider Haggard," Bradley created a world of swords and sorcery, bloody feuds and castles, lost races and exotic locales. The earlier novels in the Darkover series were long on adventure but relatively shy on character development, and the rationale behind the telepathic and psionic gifts of the Comyn lords was only sketchily explained. As the series progressed, Bradley deepened the characters, making them real people instead of fantasy heroes, and causing them to react realistically to the curse or blessing of their various gifts. Indeed, so thorough is her treatment of these psychic gifts in the later novels that the series could almost be read as science fiction. In one sense, their classification as fantasy depends on a quibble: Is their thought-wave amplifying matrix technology possible or not? Science-minded critics say "no," and yet have not raised the same objection to fiction premised on space travel at speeds exceeding the speed of light, although so far as science knows, such speeds are impossible. Yet the Darkover series *is* fantasy rather than science fiction, because of the dramatic and extreme form in which some of the psychic manifestations occur, such as a sword that produces firestorms and a woman who strikes her attacker with lightning. Such elements violate the commitment to logical extrapolation characteristic of pure science fiction.

Bradley's deepening of the fantastic elements in the later Darkover books goes in two directions. She has broadened and developed the actual technical applications of the *laran* (psychic) gifts, and she has probed sensitively into just how the possession of such gifts would affect human beings, both physically and psychologically. Both the technological and personal aspects of the psychic talents pose moral problems for her characters.

Some of the technological data relating to "matrix mechanics" are contradictory because Bradley seldom hesitates to change details if she sees that she has made an error in her original conception or if she feels that a new interpretation will work better; her refusal to be bound by the series has resulted in the strengthening of the individual books, and twice she has rewritten earlier works in the light of later developments.

The history of Darkover's matrix technology covers several hundred years. Soon after the settling of Darkover, some of the colonial families interbreed with psychically gifted natives, producing the "nobility" of the Comyn families. These families gain their preeminence through their ability to read minds and foresee future events, abilities which, in a hostile environment, help them to protect others who are not so endowed. Over several centuries a feudal society evolves, based on "matrix technology." The matrices are locally mined blue stones which amplify telepathic brain waves and psychic energies, so that a matrix-user can send thoughts over long distances or practice telekinesis. Single-stone personal matrices are "keyed" to their owners' brain wave patterns, and once keyed cannot be used by anyone else. Matrices can also be built into larger patterns, or matrix-screens, which must be powered by a circle of several telepaths; the "energons" (units of electrical energy) they produce are focused and controlled by an especially gifted and skilled telepath called a "Keeper."

Actual matrix technology is most fully detailed in *Stormqueen!* and *Two to Conquer*, the two "Ages of Chaos" novels, in *The Forbidden Tower*, and in some of the added parts of the second edition of *The Bloody Sun*. In *Stormqueen!*, matrix technology and a selective breeding program for telepaths are at their height, while the morals of the nobility have degenerated. The independent lords of the domains are able to have electric lights from matrix-charged batteries; aircars are similarly powered; and scarce metals mined molecule-by-molecule using focused psychic energy. They are served by genetically altered nonhuman slaves, and they have modified their own germ-plasm, combined it with that of the nonhuman species, and produced sterile subhuman concubines, *riyachiyas*, "too slender of waist and long of leg to be genuine women . . . as beautiful and unnatural as demon hags." Using telepathic power for levitation, individuals can soar long distances in gliderlike contraptions, riding the thermals like soaring birds. Matrix-workers have developed a wide range of weaponry, including *clingfire* for incendiary bombing, and homing explosive devices keyed to the brain waves of the target. Working together, a telepaths' circle can cause vibrations that topple castles, or can bring mass delusions on the garrison.

The moral problems raised by these technologies are major themes of both *Stormqueen!* and *Two to Conquer*. Appalled by the greediness and degeneracy of his father's friends, young Allart Hastur grudgingly leaves his monastic retreat to take up life in the war-torn domains. Cursing the breeding program that has produced the *laran* gifts, he wishes to die. Caught up in a war, he finds himself faced with responsibility: he must persuade an old man not to use the "ultimate weapon" of his daughter's horribly destructive gift. He does not succeed, but out of the war and failure he wins maturity enough to realize that if society does not suit him he must accept his responsibility to try to change it, even to the extent of accepting the terrible burden of a kingship he did not seek.

Two to Conquer, set some three hundred years later, during the time of the "Hundred Kingdoms," describes the general warfare again breaking out among the most powerful families. To the use of aircars and clingfire has been added the ability to make wide reaches of country radioactive by scattering "bonewater dust." In the field, *laran* workers ride with the armies, spying on enemy emplacements through the eyes of sentry-birds, casting spells of illusion on opposing armies. The telepaths who serve the lords are grieved by the suffering they cause and witness, yet no one seems inclined toward peace, until one of the factions drops *clingfire* on the telepath's tower at Hali. Instead of stopping their own hearts in painless death, the workers at Hali broadcast their pain to every telepath on Darkover, so that others sense "*A woman's body flaring like a torch, the smell of burning hair, burning flesh, agony searing*." The remaining towers refuse to manufacture any more *clingfire*, enabling Varzil the Good, Keeper of Neskaya tower, to forge the Compact that outlaws the use of any weapon whose reach is longer than a sword's. Agreement does not come easily, and the discussions among Darkover's leaders sound like contemporary disarmament debates: "We can't because they won't; if they do we have to. . . ." The sad fact is that Bradley is forced to use extraordinary means to end the conflict. Yet, there is a germ of hope in the solution. *If* men on Earth could learn to empathize with the suffering of others, perhaps they too could abandon their *clingfire*.

In *The Forbidden Tower*, Bradley gives perhaps her closest attention to what it might actually *feel like* to be gifted with telepathy. She uses both the point of view of a telepathic Terran, Andrew Carr, and of his Darkovan friend, Damon Ridenow, to demonstrate the sensations of being able to enter another's mind. The experience is at times almost too much for Andrew, raising questions about privacy and sexuality that disturb him deeply. Damon's adventures in the "overworld" as an out-of-body traveler are vivid and convincing, especially during a time-travel sequence in which he climbs an invisible staircase that leads him back to the time of Varzil. Formless unless formed by the thoughts of its travelers, the overworld is an easy place in which to lose oneself, cold and yet alluring, so that travelers must be monitored by other telepaths, lest the functions of their deserted bodies fail.

Bradley never portrays the gifts as unmixed blessings; rather, for the people who possess them, or are possessed by them, they may be more curse than anything else. The same breeding program that fixed the telepathic gifts in the Comyn families often produces lethal recessive genes and sex-linked characteristics that cause children to die in adolescence with the onset of "threshold sickness" as their powers develop, or cause a growing fetus to murder its mother in childbirth. The victims of the program suffer greatly. Allart Hastur of *Stormqueen!* possesses the ability to see the future, but he sees all the possible alternate futures, "fanning out ahead of him, every move he made spawning new choices." He suffers terrible nightmares, desires death, and vows never to have children until he slowly learns to unravel the probabilities and sees that some of his visions are much more probable than others. In this case, Bradley creates the fantasy-gift out of ordinary human capabilities. Most people have had the experience of seeing too many possibilities to be able to make a rational choice.

In the same novel, young Dorilys' ability to control storms and lightning (she is the Stormqueen of the title) dooms her to a difficult fate and severely tests the adults around her. Much of the novel centers around the attempts of Renata, a trained telepath, to teach Dorilys control of her power. Ultimately, Renata is unsuccessful, because the girl's father has never disciplined her. Lacking self-discipline, she cannot control the greater power that comes to her at her menarche. When her father, desperate to save his castle from seige, calls on her to cast lightning on the enemy, she does, against the advice of Renata and Allart, and the terrible gift unbalances her mind, taking over her brain. The father who would not control her when she was small must consent to see her placed in suspended animation and taken to Hali, where she must rest indefinitely, her consciousness trapped in isolation in the overworld. Overcome by her own power, Dorilys fails to mature to match her gift.

In contrast, successful human maturation on both psychic and emotional levels is beautifully portrayed in the major subplot of *The Heritage of Hastur*. Young Regis Hastur, whose gift wakens late, is sometimes frightened, sometimes surprised as he learns what it is like "to live with your skin off." Surviving the nausea, disorientation, fever, and convulsions of "threshold sickness," Regis learns that his talent can be used for good or ill, and that virtue is not in having ability but in using it wisely. Simultaneously, he has to deal with the fact that his awakening sexual desires are largely homosexual. Through the help of a friend who has been psychically abused by a sadistic homosexual, Regis discovers that it is not what he is but how he acts that will determine his worth as a human being. Bradley uses the telepathic experiences of Regis and his friend Danilo to paint an unusually poignant picture of adolescent friendship growing into love.

Both *The Heritage of Hastur* and its sequel, *Sharra's Exile* (a rewrite of *The Sword of Aldones*) have as their major plot-element the theme of human reactions to an "ultimate weapon." The great Sharra matrix, worshiped as a goddess of fire by the forge-folk of the Hellers, is a ninth-level stone, requiring a circle of at least nine telepaths for proper control. In *The Heritage of Hastur*, Lew Alton, with only five untrained matrix-workers at his command, succumbs to great temptation. He tries to use the ancient device as a power source, to convince the Terrans that Darkover has technology and power on a par with the rest of the Empire. The matrix, however, is only a weapon, which, once activated, draws its users to its destructive power, burning cities with the devastation of an atomic blast. Lew's good intentions are of no avail against it; he loses a hand and his young wife in a partially successful attempt to quench the thing temporarily.

In *Sharra's Exile*, Lew is able to obtain the only weapon powerful enough to overcome Sharra, the legendary Sword of Aldones. He gives it to Regis Hastur, heir of Darkover's ruling family, the only person who has the psychic power to use it. The lengthy novel culminates in a terrific battle of psychic forces as Regis, armed with the Sword and supported by the powers of an ancient Comyn Keeper, Ashara, confronts Sharra-maddened members of Lew's old group, led by a Comyn lord, Dyan Ardais, wielding the Sharra matrix. At last, Sharra is destroyed because the human antagonists both answer the question that rings through the Overworld, "Will you have the love of Power, or the Power of Love?" by not killing each other. Dyan dies in a backwash of power from Sharra; Regis is prematurely aged; Lew is freed from the image of Sharra which has dominated his life for years.

In this reworking of older material, Bradley sought to deepen and expand the human elements of the story. The characters of Lew, Regis, and Dyan are much more fully developed than they were in *The Sword of Aldones*. Dyan, especially, is changed from a stock villain to a complex individual, scarred by a difficult youth, motivated by loyalty to his country. Toward the end of the novel, however, the carried-over fantasy elements, the Sharra matrix and the mysterious Ashara, come to dominate the characters, turning them to cardboard at a time when they should be most human. Perhaps these elements were too close to Bradley's adolescent fantasy-adventures, which contained a good deal of stereotyping.

At her strongest, Bradley blends fantasy and human concerns in an effective, balanced mix, as she does in *Stormqueen!*, *Two to Conquer*, and *The Heritage of Hastur*, or concentrates on character development, as she does in *The Shattered Chain* and the rewritten *The Bloody Sun*. When the fantasy element dominates and edges into the supernatural, as it does in *Sharra's Exile*, it tends to weaken the structure.

For the aspiring writer of science fantasy, a reading of all fifteen of the Darkover novels will reveal how an author wrestles with and molds her material, and will demonstrate how fantasy can be too sketchy to be fully satisfying (most of the pre-1975 novels), how fantasy can be fully detailed but balanced by good characterization (most of the later novels) and how it can run away with even a carefully developed plot (for example, the last few chapters of *Sharra's Exile*). With the exception of the rewritten *Sharra's Exile*, all of Bradley's later Darkover novels are rich, successful, balanced works, shaping the strengths of youthful fantasy toward mature ends.

Lillian M. Heldreth

Bibliography
Breen, Walter. *The Darkover Concordance: A Reader's Guide*, 1979.
Leith, Linda. "Marion Zimmer Bradley and Darkover," in *Science-Fiction Studies*. VII (March, 1980), pp. 28-35.

THE DEAD FATHER

Author: Donald Barthelme (1931-   )
First book publication: 1975
Type of work: Novel
Time: The 1970's
Locale: An unidentified landscape

The story of an absurd journey during which the "children" of a Dead Father take him to his final resting place

> *Principal characters:*
> THE DEAD FATHER, a dead patriarch
> THOMAS, his son
> JULIE, Thomas' wife
> EMMA, a woman who joins the group
> PETER SCATTERPATTER, translator of *A Manual for Sons*

In *The Dead Father*, Donald Barthelme brings into play all the devices that he regularly employs in his many short stories. In some respects, this novel works like a series of interrelated short stories, bringing up bits of random action and loosely connected events, looking at them with a dispassionate eye, and casting them aside to move on to something new. The text opens with a prologue from the Dead Father's children. It seems that this enormous dead father figure does not wish to be dead; the children, of course, want nothing else. He rests, 3,200 cubits long, in the midst of their city. No one can remember when he was not there, but the city's residents set out to remove him.

The text proper describes the children's efforts to get rid of the Dead Father as they drag his huge body across the countryside to his waiting grave. The reader, of course, does not immediately know that this is the destination of the Dead Father and his entourage; he only knows that the journey itself involves disjointed, strangely out-of-focus events that may or may not be governed by the normal rules of logic. Barthelme is a master of the absurd, of yoking generally incompatible elements together in order to shock or confuse the reader. This novel with the journey it describes is no exception. One of his favorite vehicles for achieving this sense of disjuncture is the listing, seemingly *ad infinitum*, of catalogs of *things*. Ultimately these catalogs serve to reinforce the absurdity of the quasimythical journey; they do so by their very length. Lumping together, for example, a list of all the bizarre animals that the Dead Father murders when he gets into a "slaying" frenzy makes both his rage and the object of his fury appear foolish and inappropriate. Not only does the event appear as trivialized, but the quest itself becomes ridiculous.

The ridiculous, of course, is one of Barthelme's favorite topics, and in this novel no aspect of human relationships escapes his caustic wit. Barthelme pokes fun at such diverse things as the quest for the Golden Fleece and the problems created by too heavy a reliance on Freudian psychology. For example, at one point in the group's journey to the Dead Father's grave they encounter the Wends, a hostile tribe who will not let them enter their territory because fathers are illegal there. Their solution to the Oedipus complex has been to do away with fathers altogether and to have sons marry their mothers. Another encounter of this sort is the meeting between the Dead Father's group and a group of apes. No explanation is forthcoming for why they meet the apes or for where the apes come from—it would not be appropriate— and Barthelme uses this event to ridicule contemporary boredom with "the ways things are." One evening, Emma, one of the Dead Father's entourage, complains that she is bored, that there is nothing new to do, no new people to meet. Enter the apes. They begin to dance with the women of the group, one of whom conducts a ridiculous one-sided conversation with her ape dancing partner—a clever jab at contemporary partygoers.

The absurdist qualities of this novel are what will certainly cause many of its readers problems, since the ordinary touchstones the reader expects to be present in a conventional "realistic" novel are vigorously absent. The absence of conventional cause and effect, however, is one way in which Barthelme creates his fantasy world. Coming to terms with such a complex tangle of events is more difficult in a novel-length work than in a Barthelme short story. Yet most of the elements in this novel are no different from those in his short stories; and, if they were lacking in this text, it would no longer be a work of fantasy. Part of the problem with a novel such as *The Dead Father* is that it does not follow easily identifiable conventions that would allow the reader to describe what "kind" of fantasy it is. One thing this text certainly is *not* is formula fiction; but if the reader has taken the time to read some of Barthelme's short stories, he will be able to see a pattern in this novel.

The seemingly circular conversations or the events that turn back in upon themselves are common elements in the structure of a Barthelme work, and in *The Dead Father*, the author develops them at great length. For example, during several of the evenings that the Dead Father and his group are camped out, Barthelme reports snatches of their conversation. One cannot be certain exactly who is talking or which pieces of the many colloquies actually belong together; yet taken as a unit, this symphonic conversation serves to comment on the events and mock the trivia with which most people generally concern themselves. The conversations also reinforce the absurdist nature of the text by taking on the quality of a Greek chorus, recapitulating the many themes that surface and making "objective" comments on events during the journey. It is really not important that the reader be able to sort out who said what to whom; the general impression and combined picture of these vignettes is the important thing, since they capture both the jumbled nature of Bar-

thelme's world and the mundane fragments out of which his fantasy world is
built.

To add further to the discordant nature of his work, Barthelme includes a
pamphlet translated by Peter Scatterpatter entitled *A Manual for Sons*, in
which the reader is given such sundry information about the nature of fathers
as the colors of fathers (bay, liver chestnut, sorrel, blue roan), methods for
finding lost fathers, names of fathers (Af, Agwend, Balthral, and Boamiel),
and types of fathers' voices ("like film burning . . . the clash of paper clips
by night, lime seething in a lime pit, or batsong"). This subtext of Scatterpatter's only adds to the confusion.

The text ends as abruptly as it began. The group finally arrives at a cemetery
in which bulldozers have excavated a large grave for the Dead Father. He
climbs into the hole, reclines, asks if it will hurt, and the bulldozers move in
to cover him over. The reader is left with the question, "What does all this
mean?" Barthelme does not say—except that the journey from the everyday
world of recognizable events to the grave is plagued by absurdities that may
or may not relate to one another in some logical way. The incongruities and
the nonsense quality of Barthelme's textual world in *The Dead Father* are
precisely what make it a work of fantasy. Whether or not a reader has the
patience to struggle through this world is a matter of individual temperament;
The Dead Father is definitely not a text for everyone—precisely because it *is*
so bizarre.

Melissa E. Barth

Bibliography

Bellamy, Joe David, ed. *The New Fiction: Interviews with Innovative American Writers*, 1974.
Gass, William. "The Leading Edge of the Trash Phenomenon," in *Fictions and the Figures of Life*, 1970.
Gordon, Lois. *Donald Barthelme*, 1981.
Klinkowitz, Jerome. *Literary Disruptions: The Making of a Post-Contemporary American Fiction*, 1980.
_____ , et al, eds. *Donald Barthelme: A Comprehensive Bibliography & an Annotated Secondary Checklist*, 1977.
Tanner, Tony. *City of Words: American Fiction 1950-1970*, 1971.

THE DEAD ZONE

Author: Stephen King (1947-   )
First book publication: 1979
Type of work: Novel
Time: January, 1953, to August, 1979
Locale: New England

John Smith, a young schoolteacher, is plunged into a coma following an automobile accident; when he revives some four-and-one-half years later, he discovers that his injuries have enabled him to receive vivid psychic images, the most powerful of which dictates the course of his life

> *Principal characters:*
> JOHN SMITH, a teacher
> HERB SMITH, his father
> VERA SMITH, his mother
> GREGORY AMMAS STILLSON, a politician
> SARAH BRACKNELL HAZLETT, a teacher
> FRANK DODD, a murderer
> ROGER CHATSWORTH, a millionaire
> CHUCK CHATSWORTH, his son

While Stephen King is most often pigeonholed as a horror specialist, many of his readers have long been of the opinion that he could function equally well outside that genre. *The Dead Zone* both confirms this belief and demonstrates its author's versatility, for despite attempts to group it with King's more frightening works, it is *not* a horror novel. Rather, it is a tragic novel, the story of a common man overwhelmed by circumstances beyond his control and forced to perform in ways that he could never have anticipated. The novel bears a great resemblance to such horrifying fare as *Carrie* (1974), *Salem's Lot* (1975), and *The Shining* (1977), in part because King has scattered bits and pieces of his earlier works, including place names, titles, and recurring ideas, throughout the book. Indeed, beneath its tragic surface, *The Dead Zone* has something of the playful allusiveness usually associated with high modernist and postmodern writers such as James Joyce, Jorge Luis Borges, and Thomas Pynchon. In addition to littering the novel with references to his own fictional universe, King has created in *The Dead Zone* an elaborate homage to Ray Bradbury.

John Smith (he has no middle name or initial), the protagonist, is an ideal hero for a modern tragedy. Even his name, representing as it does the contemporary version of "Everyman," accents his commonality; he is the kind of young man one might expect to find living in the apartment next door or standing one line over in the supermarket. It is precisely this quality of ordinariness that Smith loses when he obtains his supernatural ability, and it is that loss, more than any other, which he comes to resent.

In the novel's Prologue, Smith is a normal, active six-year-old who accidentally skates into an ice-hockey game of some older boys. He is knocked down by one of the players and strikes his head on the ice hard enough to lose consciousness. While coming to, he first experiences his precognitive talent: he groggily warns one of the spectators not to "jump it again." Smith neither remembers issuing the warning nor makes any connection between the incident and an accident several months later which befalls the man he warned. (The man loses the sight of one eye when the battery in a car he is attempting to jump-start explodes.) Although "he would have been hard put to remember it by the time he finished grammar school," this brief blackout is a precursor to the much lengthier blackout Smith will experience as an adult.

The future career of Gregory Ammas Stillson, eventually to become a presidential candidate and Smith's nemesis, is also foreshadowed in the Prologue. Approximately two-and-one-half years after Smith's first accident, Stillson is selling Bibles door-to-door and dreaming of the far more important role he hopes to have later in life. Unfortunately, Stillson is no mere dreamer: he is a vicious, unbalanced young man who thinks nothing of spraying a farm dog with ammonia from a Flit gun, then kicking the animal to death afterward for daring to turn on him. His attitude toward human beings proves no gentler.

Bracknell, who had planned to spend the night with him for the first time, has become ill and forces herself to remain near the game only long enough for Smith to collect his winnings. His feelings of guilt about detaining her combine with Smith's unease about "found money"—something his mother, a devout Baptist, had long ago warned him against—to make him wonder whether this run of luck will prove to be good or ill.

After leaving his companion at her apartment, he discovers just how bad his luck has actually become. The taxi he has called to take him home is struck head-on by one of two drag-racing cars, and the cabbie, the driver of the other vehicle, and the passenger in that car are killed while Smith is thrown into the coma that will remove him from the world for fifty-five months.

While Smith lies in his coma, Vera Smith, shocked by her son's accident, withdraws further and further into religious fanaticism. Herb Smith gradually becomes so embittered by his double burden—his only child comatose, his wife nearly mad—that his initial hope for Smith's recovery sours into the hope that he will simply die and allow his parents to return to a normal life. Bracknell marries Walt Hazlett, a law student who reminds her of Smith, and the couple has a son. Stillson, now a successful businessman, carries on some of the most vicious political campaigning his state has ever seen, aided by a recruited cadre of motorcycle-gang members. In Castle Rock, Maine—a medium-sized town not far from Smith's own Pownal—an unidentified killer rapes and murders a number of young women, while across the state line, in New Hampshire, a traveling salesman fails to convince the owner of a roadhouse to invest in a few lightning rods for his roof.

Each of these seemingly unrelated events is part of a larger pattern, a pattern which requires Smith's participation to be complete. When he awakens from his coma and uses his newfound power for the first time (he learns how long his coma has lasted simply by touching the hand of an attending doctor), he is set against his will on an unavoidable course.

The publicity, positive and negative, which attends his miraculous recovery and the discovery of his psychic power propels Smith compulsively into his new life. He would very much prefer to let himself sink back into the unknown status he enjoyed before his accident (particularly when a small part of the publicity he has received appears to have caused his mother's fatal stroke), but the thrust of events will not permit him this relief. Instead, he finds himself compelled to help the Castle Rock sheriff track down the killer who is terrorizing that town. It is an exercise in which he initially refuses to engage, changing his mind only after the killer's most recent victim is discovered. Even if the effort will retard or prevent his return to normality, he cannot permit a nine-year-old girl's murderer and rapist to escape without trying to do something about it.

His work with the sheriff requires him to undergo great psychic stress, as does nearly every use of his power. The act of discovering the killer's identity, performed by visiting the site of the latest murder and handling a cigarette pack left there, results in an agonizing headache and other physical pains; nor does he receive unqualified thanks for his efforts. When the killer turns out to be Frank Dodd, a young man the sheriff has long treated as his own son, Smith senses that the man who has enlisted his aid is as horrified at learning the truth as he is relieved at having the case solved.

The Castle Rock case, however, costs Smith more than the affections of the town's sheriff. A teaching position he had lined up through a friend falls through when the school board decides a teacher as famous—or infamous— as Smith could be a source of trouble.

Smith finds employment as a private tutor, teaching Chuck Chatsworth reading skills. The seventeen-year-old, a bright boy suffering from a learning disability, and his father, Roger Chatsworth, a wealthy industrialist, offer Smith just the kind of sanctuary he has been seeking. The younger Chatsworth knows nothing about Smith's past, while the elder considers it unimportant to the job at hand, and Smith happily buckles down, doing the kind of work he does best and trying to forget the changes that have been made in his life.

Destiny, however, is not so easily escaped. It is during his stay with the Chatsworths that Smith meets Stillson in person, shaking his hand at a political rally. From the moment he makes contact with the other man, Smith recognizes him as the enemy, not only of himself, but of all human life. Unless Stillson is stopped, he will pick up the political momentum to be elected president, and will from that office manage to trigger a total cataclysm.

This, Smith begins to feel, is the explanation for what has happened to him. He has been gifted, or perhaps cursed, with the ability to see the future solely for the purpose of preventing the Stillson-poisoned future he has seen at the rally. Even so, Smith wavers, asking person after person what he comes to think of as "The Question": If you could jump into a time machine and go back to 1932 would you kill Hitler? The answers he receives unnerve him, but do not convince him to take immediate action, nor does the disaster which marks the end of his stay with the Chatsworths. Cathy's, the roadhouse where Smith's pupil plans to attend a graduation party, is struck by lightning and burns to the ground. Smith foresees the blaze, warns all who will listen to him about it, and manages to save some of the adolescents by convincing the Chatsworths to hold an alternative celebration at their home. Ironically, Cathy's would never have burned if its owner had purchased a set of lightning rods when he had the opportunity—years earlier, while Smith was still in his coma. The tragedy simply convinces him that he will not be able to take half-measures when the time comes to deal with Stillson.

The final impetus Smith needs, when it comes, is as much a part of the pattern controlling him as the events in Castle Rock, his obsession with The Question, and the fire, though it is not revealed to the reader until very near the story's end: the injured part of his brain, which Smith has thought of as the "dead zone," has developed a rapidly growing tumor.

Acting decisively at last, Smith manages to conceal himself in a building in which Stillson is scheduled to speak. He has armed himself with a rifle, mailed explanatory letters to his father and the woman he still loves, and is fully prepared to accept the probably fatal consequences of his action.

Though he does not escape being shot by members of Stillson's security force, Smith is allowed to carry out his mission without becoming a murderer. As Smith trains his rifle on Stillson following several misses, the politician seizes a small boy and holds him up as a shield. Smith, unable to kill the child in order to get to the man behind him, shoots no more and is quite confused when he touches Stillson once more before dying and realizes the other man's future has somehow been changed. A photographer has taken a picture of Stillson hiding behind the boy; the man has committed political suicide and is dangerous no longer.

As mentioned earlier, *The Dead Zone* is littered with references to King's other works. A place is described as being near Jerusalem's Lot, for example, and a hysterical girl accuses Smith of having started the fire at Cathy's "by his mind, just like in that book *Carrie*."

Far more pervasive, however, are the Bradbury influences. *The Dead Zone* is not King's first attempt at "homage"; *Salem's Lot*, predating it by several years, is in places a near-exact parallel to Bram Stoker's *Dracula* (1897). *The Dead Zone* is in many ways the more subtle tribute of the two, based largely on evocations of Bradbury's characteristic images and themes rather than on direct parallels. The episode with the lightning rods is, of course, sharply reminiscent of *Something Wicked This Way Comes* (1962), and throughout the novel King gives special weight to a time of year often associated with Bradbury. When Bracknell comes to meet Smith for their date at the fair, he is wearing a Halloween mask that frightens her. While Smith lies in his coma, his father finds October—the anniversary month of the accident—disquieting, the worst time of the year. All the associations with October are not painful, however; it is during the same month, almost exactly five years after their last date, that Smith's lost love, now married and a mother, comes to him for a single afternoon of lovemaking, her way of trying to compensate for everything the accident cost them both.

It is October, too, when Sarah Bracknell Hazlett visits Smith for the last time. Standing at his graveside, she remembers Smith's letter (written shortly before the attack on Stillson) and grows angry all over again at the way in which they were separated. As she weeps, she feels a hand touch the back of her neck, as Smith had spoken of doing in that letter, and is curiously comforted.

The reader, too, finds a strange comfort in that moment. It is as if King had infused Bradbury's often-sentimental tenderness with some of his own vigor, providing a conclusion to Smith's story which proves that the young man's death, while tragic, was not wasted.

Christine Watson

Bibliography

Alexander, Alex E. "Stephen King's *Carrie*—A Universal Fairy Tale," in *Journal of Popular Culture*. XIII, no. 2 (Fall, 1979), pp. 282-288.
King, Stephen. *Danse Macabre*, 1981.
_____ . "Foreword," in *Night Shift*, 1978.
Winter, Douglas E. *Stephen King*, 1982.

A DEAL WITH THE DEVIL

Author: Eden Phillpotts (1862-1960)
First book publication: 1895
Type of work: Novel
Time: The late nineteenth century
Locale: England

> *A one-hundred-year-old man gives his soul to the Devil in return for ten additional years of life during which he grows progressively younger*

> *Principal characters:*
> DANIEL DOLPHIN, a man who gives his soul to the Devil
> MARTHA DOLPHIN, the narrator, his granddaughter
> MRS. BANDLEY-BROWN,
> MARIE ROGERS,
> MABEL TALBOT,
> SUSAN MARKS, and
> PHYLLIS ROSE, Dolphin's various loves
> MR. PHIL MONTAGUE, a smooth-talking swindler

Toward the end of a long, dissipated life, Daniel Dolphin has reformed. He is miserable, although his spinster granddaughter, Martha, is delighted. On the eve of his hundredth birthday, however, the Devil awakens Daniel with a proposal. Instead of letting him die that night as scheduled, the Devil will give him ten more years of life in return for his soul—and instead of growing older, he will grow younger at the rate of ten years of age removed for each additional year he lives. Daniel accepts, and he decides that he might as well have fun with the time remaining to him. Accompanied by the disapproving Martha, he travels about the country, growing progressively younger, passing through the physical conditions and mental attitudes of life in reverse. Along the way, he leaves a string of jilted women who reflect his changing interests. Eventually, having reached the condition of a newborn baby, he vanishes among menacing spectral displays.

The most impressive thing about Eden Phillpotts' novel is the detail with which Daniel's regression is depicted. For example, Martha Dolphin's deep desire for a settled life makes her extremely sensitive to the mechanics of changing lodgings when her grandfather either becomes so altered in appearance that they would excite wonder if they stayed too long in one place, or, more frequently, when he becomes entangled with some all-too-willing woman. Martha also explains how other physical arrangements must be changed. What she calls the "New Scheme" of Daniel's aging complicates their lives immensely, and Phillpotts works out this basic idea in thorough, practical detail. He concentrates on such things as the way a man would alter his style of dress if regressing rapidly, how his speech and slang would vary, and how his attitude toward life would change; this is the more clearly done because Phillpotts' story is set within one lifetime and within one particular era.

That setting, the Victorian period, may complicate a modern reader's response to *A Deal with the Devil*. In particular, the novel's picture of Martha is disturbing. Daniel Dolphin announces that he intends to spend all his money before he fades away, leaving none of the inheritance he has intended for his granddaughter. She accepts this as a matter of course; after all, he is her grandfather, and she is only a woman. The women Daniel romances are either innocent ninnies or grasping shrews, and the novel takes a fairly uncomplicated view of them. In the case of Martha, who is neither ignorant nor selfish but who still considers herself essentially the property of her family, the novel's apparently callous attitude is bothersome. At the very least, Phillpotts created a character with more depth than he probably intended.

For the most part, the novel's intent appears to be humorous. Events are sometimes farcical, as when Martha begins to crack under the tension and starts drinking too much "medicinal" brandy; her determinedly euphemistic account of young Daniel rowing her home from an outing, while she collapses in the bottom of the boat, is genuinely funny. Sometimes Phillpotts seems to be attempting a more restrained type of comedy, showing in satiric scenes that Daniel's century-plus of experience has not made him less gullible whenever a pretty woman or a get-rich-quick scheme appears. Folly, Phillpotts, seems to be saying, is part of human nature, young or old. Yet the book's grim conclusion is presented straightforwardly. Daniel apparently is taken to hell, and he cries out in despair as he goes.

Martha, after Daniel's departure, has nothing left; her life has been ruined by the experiences over which readers may have been chuckling. Her stated intent at the book's end is highly serious: she wishes to warn others to avoid being trapped by "the principalities and powers by which mankind is secretly led and guided, blinded and befooled." Yet can this be done in view of the events Phillpotts has shown earlier? How seriously can a reader take Martha's thinking? Again, the matter is deeper and more complicated than Phillpotts probably intended. How a reader responds to *A Deal with the Devil* depends on his attitude toward the tone of the novel, and that may be complicated by uncertainty about how to view the characters and the action. Deftly constructed and smoothly written, the novel probably was not designed to entangle readers with these unresolved issues; nevertheless, they do exist.

Of the 250 books Phillpotts wrote in his lifetime, a few have recently been revived in reprint series of science fiction, fantasy, and mystery classics. While *A Deal with the Devil* is difficult to regard as a classic, it may still be read with pleasure if one can simply appreciate the ingenuity with which the basic idea is treated.

Joe Sanders

Bibliography
Girvan, Waveney. *Eden Phillpotts: An Assessment and a Tribute*, 1953.
Phillpotts, Eden. *From the Angle of 88*, 1951.

DEAR BRUTUS

Author: James M. Barrie (1860-1937)
First book publication: 1917
Type of work: Drama
Time: The early twentieth century
Locale: Lob's country house and the enchanted wood nearby

A play in which a number of people are shown what their lives might have been like in different circumstances

> Principal characters:
> LOB, a magic spirit, otherwise known as Robin Goodfellow, Hobgoblin, or Puck
> MATEY, a butler
> ALICE DEARTH, an intense young married woman
> WILL DEARTH, her husband, a painter
> MARGARET, their dream-child
> MABEL PURDIE, a young married woman
> JACK PURDIE, her husband
> JOANNA, a young single woman
> LADY CAROLINE, a young single woman

James Matthew Barrie is remembered chiefly for his invention of Peter Pan, the boy who never grows old. Peter Pan, the Lost Boys, Wendy, Nana, and Never-Never Land have all become part of the common currency of childhood; the revival of the play *Peter Pan* (1904) in the West End of London every Christmas is as essential to the festival as Santa Claus himself, and the chance to play the lead a coveted laurel for any young actress. His other works are for the most part forgotten, dismissed as sentimental trivia unworthy of further study. That is unfortunate, for although undeniably Victorian and Edwardian in tone, many of his plays, such as *The Admirable Crichton* (1903), *Dear Brutus*, and *Mary Rose* (1924) are well worth reading.

The title *Dear Brutus* comes from a line from William Shakespeare's *Julius Caesar* (1599-1600): "The fault, dear Brutus, is not in our stars,/ But in ourselves, that we are underlings." *Julius Caesar*, however, is not the only source of inspiration for the play; the primary source is *A Midsummer Night's Dream* (1595-1596). Barrie makes use of the element of magic and folklore in Shakespeare's comedy as the framework for his own drama, relying on the fact that the audience will be familiar enough with the concept of Puck or Lob as a mischievous sprite to understand fairly readily the strange events which he describes.

The play begins with all the female protagonists assembled in the drawing room of Lob's country house. It is revealed in conversation that it is the week of Midsummer's Eve; indeed, that very night is Midsummer's Eve. The women are all curious to know why they have been invited to a house-party at the home of someone they hardly know, and they try to blackmail Matey, the butler, into telling them. Apart from saying that it would have been better if they had not come, he refuses to give them any information, although he does warn them not to go beyond the garden if they are invited to go out on this particular night. There is some byplay between him and Lady Caroline which suggests that he is very much attracted to her and that possibly she is attracted to him; this paves the way for later events in the play, besides introducing the theme of class conflict into the action.

As it turns out, all the main characters are induced to venture beyond the confines of the garden, although not until after the audience has learned that Jack Purdie and Joanna are having an affair, that Alice Dearth was previously involved with a gentleman called the Honourable Freddy Finch-Fallowe, and that the whole company has been assembled because each member of the group is to be shown what his or her life might have been like in different circumstances. At the end of the first act, the audience sees that Lob's garden has been replaced by a wood of enormous trees. None of the characters genuinely seems to believe in the second chance which they are being offered yet rush into the wood as if they do. The act ends with Lob and Matey in the drawing room, and in a fit of malice, Lob pushes Matey into the wood.

The play's main dramatic tension lies in the first act. The final two acts show the protagonists combined in various permutations, and, most interestingly, introduce Margaret, the Dearths' dream-child. Of all the characters who are given a second chance at their lives, only the painter, Will Dearth, benefits from the experience. He and Alice are united in the loss of their dream-child, and their relationship is strengthened by their sojourn in Lob's enchanted wood. The plot is finally resolved with a weak explanation by Matey that Lob's experiment, although interesting, can be expected to have little permanent effect.

Although Barrie's play draws heavily upon *A Midsummer Night's Dream*, using Lob as a *deus ex machina* to contrive and ultimately to resolve the strange events which occur, there is nothing Shakespearean about Barrie's style. If the play has any close literary relatives, they must be John Boynton Priestley's Time plays (such as *Time and the Conways*, 1937, and *Dangerous Corner*, 1932). Although it does not contain any startling innovations or even any impressive *coups de theatre*, it is a work which interestingly illuminates many aspects of life in early twentieth century Britain. The play is especially effective when it is read rather than seen. Barrie puts so much into his stage directions that it is virtually impossible to present *Dear Brutus* on the stage in a fully satisfactory manner.

Vivien Stableford

Bibliography
Birkin, Andrew. *J. M. Barrie and the Lost Boys*, 1979.

THE DERYNI TRILOGY

Author: Katherine Kurtz (1944-   )
First book publications: Deryni Rising (1970); *Deryni Checkmate* (1972); *High Deryni* (1973)
Type of work: Novels
Time: 1120-1121
Locale: The kingdom of Gwynedd, occupying land in roughly the same geographical location as the British Isles, but in an alternate world

Several members of a race possessed of innate magical powers fight to save the political regime of Gwynedd against threats from others of their kind

Principal characters:
ALARIC MORGAN, Deryni Duke of Corwyn
KELSON HALDANE, the fourteen-year-old King of Gwynedd
DUNCAN MCLAIN, a priest, Morgan's cousin
SEAN DERRY, Morgan's military aide
CHARISSA, Countess of Tolan and would-be usurper
ARCHBISHOP LORIS, the Primate of Gwynedd
DENIS ARILAN, a bishop, secretly a member of the Camberian Council
WARIN DE GREY, a would-be messiah and enemy of the Deryni
WENCIT OF TORENTH, the principal enemy of Gwynedd
BRAN CORIS, Earl of Marley, defector to the cause of Wencit

Katherine Kurtz was the first writer to contribute original work to the Ballantine Adult Fantasy series edited by Lin Carter, the series which first hollowed out a niche in the paperback market for the genre which appropriated the term "fantasy" as its label. Kurtz thus became the first of many writers who moved in to occupy and expand this market space during the 1970's. She was followed by Joy Chant, Patricia McKillip, C. J. Cherryh, Janet E. Morris, Stephen R. Donaldson, Neil Hancock, and others. To some extent these writers were adapting a trend already established in juvenile fiction and moving with it "upmarket" into the field of adult publishing. Series fantasy was already well-established in the teenage market by courtesy of such writers as C. S. Lewis, Alan Garner, and Lloyd Alexander, and these writers had demonstrated the potential of imaginary worlds as vehicles for exciting adventures and parables of maturation.

There were two main factors which made this kind of work attractive to the paperback publishers of the 1970's. First, they were able to cash in on the sudden and spectacular fashionableness of a work first published some twenty years earlier: J. R. R. Tolkien's *The Lord of the Rings* (1954-1955). Second, partly because of Tolkien's exemplar, the characteristic form taken by these imaginary world adventure stories was the trilogy, and publishers were at that time realizing the potential of series books, which would help to support one another in the marketplace because each volume created a demand for the others.

This species of imaginary fiction is perhaps the most highly formalized of all popular genres. It has three principal themes which are almost invariably present. The first is the symbolization of a conflict between good and evil in terms of a war between black and white magic, often associated with bad kings (would-be tyrants and usurpers) and good kings (legitimate and benevolent rulers). The second is an argument about the propriety of the use of magic in human affairs; this problem produces wholly hypothetical moral dilemmas to replace more realistic ones, which tend to be squeezed out by the polarization of good and evil. (Magic works in all of these imaginary worlds, but it tends to be seen as a kind of cheating which is rarely cost-free and not to be undertaken lightly.) The third theme is that of the acceptance of responsibility—the movement from carefree childhood to mature adulthood (in the juvenile versions) or from relative passivity to heroic domination (in the adult versions which do not use adolescent heroes). Because of the association of the three themes, the learning process represented in the third theme does not consist of a conventional moral education, but rather the attainment of control over supernatural forces. In this way, the fantasies become parables of maturation, presenting analogues rather than realistic examples of the acquisition of mature responsibilities. This may seem perverse, but there may well be good psychological reasons for the utility of such substitutions.

Deryni Rising (1970), the first of Kurtz's series, adheres very closely to this formula and can easily stand as a paradigm case. How much this is a result of imitation of earlier models is not clear—the whole genre is stereotyped to the point that apparent plagiarism is commonplace—but there is also enough originality in the book to make it interesting in its own right. This first novel is complete within itself and was presumably written without the sequels in mind, but virtually all works of this kind lend themselves readily to continuation if commercial circumstances warrant it. The second and third volumes of the trilogy, *Deryni Checkmate* (1972) and *High Deryni* (1973), comprise a single subdivided narrative. When the initial trilogy was completed, Kurtz did not delay long before embarking on another set in the same imaginary world some 250 years earlier; this trilogy comprises *Camber of Culdi* (1976), *Saint Camber* (1978), and *Camber the Heretic* (1980).

Deryni Rising begins with the death of the King of Gwynedd, Brion Haldane, who is covertly murdered by magical means. The plot follows the political crisis which results. The rule of the Haldane dynasty is secured by virtue of the fact that its kings have been enabled to assume the magical powers which are the natural heritage of the Deryni race. The Deryni once ruled Gwynedd through a series of evil kings, but were overthrown through the agency of virtuous Deryni, including the briefly canonized Camber of Culdi. Camber established the Haldane dynasty so that one normal human, accepting the burden of magical power, might rule his own kind and preserve them from magical threats. Camber is now long-dead, however, and the Deryni are hated and feared by most normal men, especially by the hierarchy of the Church, which condemns the use of sorcery.

Brion's son Kelson is only fourteen, and many others hope to use him as a pawn. His mother, in particular, wants to force him to renounce the aid of Brion's trusted half-Deryni adviser Alaric Morgan. She and her allies do not realize that should they succeed, Gwynedd will fall into the power of the Deryni sorceress Charissa. It is she who has secured the death of Brion, although she has spread rumors blaming Morgan.

Alaric Morgan is the hero of the whole series. His role is partly a paternal one—he is the moral guide and guardian of the young king. There is a sense, however, in which he himself has much to learn: he has not yet "come to terms" with the full range of his own powers, and he is a social misfit caught between contending forces who has still to secure his own position within the scheme of things.

Deryni Rising is unusual among heroic fantasies in that its action is compressed into a few days. It moves along at a precipitous pace as Morgan is recalled to the capital city by Kelson and has to fight off attacks from right, left, and center—physical assaults, political challenges, and insidious traps. Nevertheless, he combines forces with his cousin Duncan McLain (a half-Deryni who has kept his power secret in order to win his way to an influential position within the Church) and Kelson to work the magic that will transfer the powers of the old king to the new. This involves the unraveling of a riddle and the disinterment of Brion's body to recover a vital talisman; the task is completed at the last possible moment, when the coronation ceremony is interrupted by Charissa and Kelson must face her in a magical duel. This climactic duel, involving illusory horrors and bolts of magical lightning, is perhaps the most disappointing part of the book and something of a letdown; it resembles the battles fought with colored light-beams and various sound effects in cinematic space-operas, and is equally silly.

The story contained in *Deryni Checkmate* and *High Deryni* is, of course, stamped from the same template: it is basically a long-winded reiteration. The opposition to Alaric Morgan is mobilized by Archbishop Loris, the Primate of Gwynedd. Loris is allied with a rebel named Warin de Grey, who considers himself to have been commissioned by God to destroy the Deryni. Circumstances quickly force Morgan into a situation in which his whole land of Corwyn is placed under interdict and he and his cousin are excommunicated. To add to his misfortunes, his sister and her intended husband are destroyed by a magic spell that goes wrong (although it never becomes clear how or why). Kelson, isolated from his adviser, appears to be in dire trouble as Gwynedd is about to be invaded by the evil Deryni King Wencit of Torenth; the first confrontation in this war is lost disastrously after the defection of

Bran Coris, one of Kelson's liege lords.

Deryni Checkmate ends with things in a parlous state, and in *High Deryni* they get worse. Morgan's aide Sean Derry is captured by Wencit and made a victim of a powerful spell which turns him into an unwilling agent of evil in Kelson's camp. Even the Camberian Council, a body set up by the one-time saint to regulate the affairs of the Deryni, seems to be working in Wencit's favor, although it is supposedly neutral.

Secret forces are, however, working in the cause of right. One member of the Camberian Council has actually emulated Duncan McLain in establishing himself in the higher echelons of the Church in Gwynedd, and he contrives to have Morgan's excommunication lifted. Morgan manages to convert Warin de Grey to his own cause by demonstrating that the powers he considers to be God's gift are actually Deryni powers. By the time the final confrontation between Kelson's forces and Wencit's comes about, the chances look about even. As in *Deryni Rising* the climax is set to be a magical duel, this time involving two teams of four, but Kurtz deliberately preempts the promised fight and cuts matters short. Possibly she was attempting in doing this to avoid the artificiality of the earlier climax, but she succeeds only in substituting a tame and unsatisfactory anticlimax which is no less of a letdown.

Although good has clearly won out, the ending of the trilogy is disappointingly weak. A frail element of romantic interest, built in late in the third volume when Alaric Morgan is allowed to fall in love with the estranged wife of the traitorous Bran Coris, comes to token fruition, although the real conclusion is a reminder that what has really been accomplished is the moral education of the leading characters—a reminder which takes the form of a few platitudinous remarks about the burden of kingship. It is worth noting, however, that weak endings are a typical feature of the genre (even *The Lord of the Rings* peters out in an awkward fashion, uncertain of how and when to leave off), and this flaw is not entirely a fault of the author.

The world in which the Deryni series is set is an alternate Earth. The map of Gwynedd and its neighboring kingdoms is clearly superimposed upon the map of the British Isles, although the Irish Sea and much of the North Sea are elevated above sea level and some extra mountain ranges appear to have sprung up in Ireland, Brittany, and elsewhere. Such vague similarity is, of course, reinforced by the borrowing of place-names in an erratic fashion. Gwynedd is but one of several Welsh names—Gwydion, Ifor, and Istelyn are also used—although some incorrectly rendered (such as "Gwyllim"). There is, however, no sign that in Kurtz's world there is a Welsh language, and this seems to isolate these names as arbitrary intrusions.

A similar confusion arises with respect to the Church. Lin Carter, in his Introduction to *Deryni Rising*, claims that Kurtz is an innovator in giving such a central role to religion—which, he claims, is entirely absent from Tolkien's Middle-earth and the realms of the most heroic fantasy writers. Actually,

however, Kurtz's Church functions entirely as a political institution; there is
never any reference to religious beliefs or to the effect of religion upon
people's lives. The Church is clearly Christian, and its chief ceremony is the
Latin mass, but these facts too are utterly without context. Despite the Latin
there is no mention of Rome (the Church in Gwynedd seems to be autonomous), and despite the acknowledgment of Christ there is no mention of the
Jewish people or of any place east of the desert which occupies most of the
land equivalent to France.

In fact, Kurtz's imaginary world is made up of a highly selective patchwork
of features borrowed haphazardly and promiscuously from earthly history.
The fact that they no longer make sense when ripped out of context is condemned to irrelevance by the demands placed on the reader by the author.
Kurtz similarly makes no real effort to accommodate the language used by
her characters to the presumed medieval setting, and the dialogue sometimes
strikes a highly eccentric note: "God's blood, Duncan, what have we gotten
ourselves into?," exclaims Morgan at one point.

Again, these things should not be held entirely against the author. Similar
things happen in many works of the same species, and within the context of
this type of work it is not entirely fair to condemn them as faults. Much of
the appeal of the genre lies in the establishment of fantasy worlds which have
the appearance of being detailed and coherent while nevertheless being comfortable and easily adaptable. The artificiality of these oversimplified other
worlds does not count against them in terms of their literary and psychological
function, and the apparently irrational pattern of Kurtz's borrowing may be
seen as sensible strategy in creating an illusion of a particular kind.

The appeal of these fantasy series is similar to the appeal of such role-
playing fantasy games as *Dungeons and Dragons* (and, indeed, the two have
evolved in association in recent years). They offer an opportunity for withdrawal into a world that is both socially and morally simplified, where serious
issues can arise in wholly symbolic form and be tackled in earnest by tried-
and-true rituals. The satisfaction they offer is obvious enough: the burdens
of responsibility can be accepted with dignity and carried off with style. In
worlds whose principal defining feature is that magic works, the power of
wishing is undeniable. One can safely acknowledge the awful difficulty of
coping with the problems of self-determination in a threatening world, because
at the end of the day the magic is always there, available to save any situation,
no matter how desperate.

It is hardly a surprise, therefore, to discover that Kurtz elected to follow
up the Deryni series by a further retreat into the depths of her fantasy world,
going back into its past to consolidate its detail and provide further "authen-
tification" for the events of *Deryni Rising* and its sequels. If she were working
in any other genre, the Camber trilogy would be a retrograde step, but in
heroic fantasy the move is practically *de rigeur*—few trilogies these days are

not supplemented by further volumes once they meet with reader approval. In such a stereotyped mode, more of the same is exactly what is needed, and to provide anything else would almost constitute a breach of faith.

The Camber series demonstrates some improvement in Kurtz's literary technique and displays the same ability to tell a fast-paced story; but this is a minor matter. There is perhaps no other form of writing to which literary values are less relevant. In essence, the second trilogy is an analogue of the first, with Camber playing the role taken in the Deryni trilogy by Morgan and the first of the Haldane kings replacing Kelson. The second trilogy should perhaps be seen as the repetition of a ritual sequence: a renewal of faith in and commitment to this particular version of the Protean dreamworld of heroic fantasy.

Brian Stableford

Bibliography
Kurtz, Katherine. *An Hour with Katherine: An Introduction to the Author and Her Work*, 1979 (cassette recording).
_____ . "The Historian as a Mythmaker and Vice Versa," in *Bulletin of the Science Fiction Writers of America*. XIII (1978), pp. 16-18.

DESCENT INTO HELL

Author: Charles Williams (1886-1945)
First book publication: 1937
Type of work: Novel
Time: The twentieth century
Locale: A suburb of London

While Lawrence Wentworth slips further into solipsism, turning his love inward toward a self-created succubus, Pauline Anstruther overcomes her fear of her Doppelgänger *and learns about the reciprocity of love*

Principal characters:
PETER STANHOPE, a poet
PAULINE ANSTRUTHER, a young woman haunted by her *Doppelgänger*
MARGARET ANSTRUTHER, her grandmother
LAWRENCE WENTWORTH, a military historian
ADELA HUNT, a young woman desired by Wentworth
A WORKMAN, a poor man who loses his job and commits suicide
LILY SAMMILE, a temptress modeled after Lilith

The work of Charles Williams is not as well known as that of his fellow "Inklings" C. S. Lewis and J. R. R. Tolkien. Although still in print, his seven supernatural thrillers have never achieved the mass cult of popularity attained by Lewis' Narnia books and Tolkien's Ring trilogy, perhaps because they are written in the tradition of the Gothic branch of fantasy. Akin to the dark psychological thrillers of Joseph Sheridan Le Fanu, one of the fathers of the detective story, they are only second cousins to the more idealized tradition of romantic fantasy inherited by Tolkien and Lewis from William Morris and George MacDonald. Williams' style is more demanding and philosophical; his passionate devotion to Dante, William Wordsworth, and John Milton reverberates in the dense melodies of his prose. Nevertheless, within his tradition and style, Williams demonstrates an utterly unique mastery. While his books take place in an England that H. G. Wells would have recognized as home, they at times reach an intensity of mystical experience approached only by poets such as Gerard Manley Hopkins.

Williams' reputation among the English literary elite of the 1930's and 1940's was high. At the time of Williams' death in 1945, C. S. Lewis, a close personal friend, suggested that Williams might be the greatest poet of the time. T. S. Eliot, who also knew Williams for a period of nearly twenty years, wrote an Introduction to *All Hallows' Eve* (1945) in which he admitted to having read all of Williams' novels with pleasure; it is often noted that both *The Four Quartets* (1943) and *The Cocktail Party* (1949) employ crucial elements from Williams. Dorothy Sayers commented extensively on how "greatly and imaginatively" Williams interpreted Dante in his novels. Influences on William

Butler Yeats and Dylan Thomas have also been suspected. W. H. Auden, discovering Williams' theological writings in the 1940's, wrote a Preface to *Descent of the Dove: A Short History of the Holy Spirit in the Church* (1939), in which he compared Williams to William Blake; he revealed debts to Williams in *New Year Letter* (1941), *The Age of Anxiety* (1947), and "Memorial from the City."

The man praised as an artist and a thinker was also loved by many. For most of his adult life, Williams worked at the Oxford University Press, and he seems to have inspired something near adoration in his coworkers, one of whom, Alice Hadfield, wrote the first full-length study of his life and works. Anne Ridler, a friend and former student, similarly describes the inspiring nature of his company and conversation in her Introduction to *The Image of the City* (1958), a posthumous collection of essays by Williams. Other testimonies—from friends such as C. S. Lewis, Owen Barfield, and Dylan Thomas—abound, and all suggest that Williams had a peculiarly charismatic personality, his ability to talk expressively being matched by his willingness to listen sympathetically. Even T. S. Eliot, not normally given to superlatives, declared in a memorial broadcast in 1946 that Williams "seemed to me to approximate, more nearly than any man I have ever known familiarly, the saint."

The hagiography that Williams inspired sits rather oddly upon the facts of his unremittingly ordinary middle-class life. His father was a clerk, although failing eyesight caused him to move the family out of London and open a shop in 1896, when Charles was eight. Educated at the Day School of St. Albans, Charles won a scholarship to University College in London when he was fifteen; after two years, however, the family could no longer contribute the additional money needed to keep him in school. Williams took a job as a clerk for four years and then in 1908 obtained a position as a proofreader for Oxford University Press. In that year, he met Frances Conway; they married nine years later and five years after that, in 1922, their only child, Michael, was born. For the next thirty-seven years, Williams continued to work for Oxford University Press, his knowledge of and passion for poetry earning him growing respect and responsibility.

What Williams added to this ordinary life—what made him extraordinary— was the life of the mind he composed from books. An omnivorous reader from an early age, he continued to absorb information and images from an astoundingly broad spectrum of sources. In his twenties, he joined the Rosicrucian group, the Order of the Golden Dawn, where he was introduced to a variety of esoteric and occult traditions. A few years later, he began giving lectures for the London County Council, which, along with his work on *The Oxford Dictionary of Quotations* (1941), deepened and crystallized his wide reading in English literature. Throughout his life, he studied and wrote in a wide variety of fields; in addition to his novels, poetry, plays, and literary criticism, he wrote popular histories of figures such as *Bacon* (1933), *James I* (1934), and *Queen Elizabeth I* (1936); a history entitled *Witchcraft* (1941); and several books on theological issues, including an investigation of *Religion and Love in Dante* (1941).

Williams was a prolific writer, but what impressed those who knew him and fascinates those who now study him is the remarkable consistency of concerns that unites virtually all of his works; his theology of romantic love is the basis for everything he wrote. The cornerstones of his theology are his view of the Incarnation and his Doctrine of Exchange, also known as Co-Inherence or Substitution. Actually, the two ideas are one: Williams saw the Incarnation of Christ as the exemplary manifestation of the integration of natural and supernatural realities; he interpreted this embodiment of God in man as the model for all relationships of exchange and love between human beings.

Williams was a phenomenological incarnationalist; he believed in the reality and validity of *both* the phenomenal world in which man pursues his daily activities and the noumenal world of grace which lies not only above but also inside this world. As T. S. Eliot explained in his Introduction to *All Hallows' Eve*, "For him there was no barrier between the material and the spiritual world."

Williams' seven supernatural thrillers embody the complete melding of the real and the fantastic that Williams accepted as a basic philosophical and religious tenet. In the first five novels, the supernatural intrudes into the mundane world, shattering expectations and provoking characters into making absolute choices between good and evil. In three of these novels, the supernatural force is concretized in a legendary object which is discovered in the midst of an ordinary, "Agatha Christie" village or the comforting familiarity of Edwardian London: the Holy Grail is recovered in the little town of Fardles (*War in Heaven*, 1930), the Philosopher's Stone makes its way to the conference tables of the British Foreign Office (*Many Dimensions*, 1931), and the original pack of tarot cards is kept at a country house before being sent to the British Museum (*The Greater Trumps*, 1932). The other two novels involve a collision between the conditions of morality and the forces of eternity: *Shadows of Ecstasy* (1933) describes a quest for immortality; *The Place of the Lion* (1931) envisions the revelation of angelic archetypes of the Platonic Ideas on Earth.

Descent into Hell (1937) is similar to these novels in its concern with the boundary between temporal and eternal worlds, but it differs from them in that the frontiers between the worlds are more easily crossed. As in his last novel, *All Hallows' Eve*, *Descent into Hell* takes place on a plain where realities meld; on Battle Hill, the living and the dead meet and mingle with one another. *Descent into Hell* is also unique in Williams' fictional oeuvre because it offers such a clear explication of the Doctrine of Substituted Love and such an explicit demonstration of its foundation in a phenomenal theory of the Incarnation.

All of Williams' novels center around a quest for spiritual power in which power is achieved only through obedience to the larger pattern of the universe. The good achieve this power through submission; the bad are destroyed by it when they seek to pervert it to selfish ends. What is at stake in all these spiritual quests is the law of incarnation and exchange. The good characters participate in the order of reciprocity and thus incarnate the spiritual in the temporal. The bad characters refuse to reciprocate; their selfishness separates them from the rest of the universe.

In *Descent into Hell*, this opposition between those who honor incarnation and accept exchange and those who refuse both is drawn with particular clarity. Setting, plot, and characters all reflect the dialectical structure of Williams' thinking. The novel is set on Battle Hill, a suburb of London: it is an intermediate environment, being between the city and the country, a place populated by both past and present inhabitants, a site of both death and life. The three threads of the plot embody a Hegelian model of thesis, antithesis, and synthesis. Lawrence Wentworth climbs down to his damnation; Pauline Anstruther rises up to her salvation; the anonymous workman wanders between worlds, learning to choose between the two paths.

The characters are also poised in an intricate structure of opposition. Peter Stanhope, the poet—mentor to Pauline Anstruther—takes on the burden of her fear of her *Doppelgänger* through the structure of disinterested love; Lawrence Wentworth, the military historian—mentor to Adela Hunt—creates a fantasy double or succubus in order to enjoy the simulacrum of her imagined love. Margaret Anstruther and Lily Sammile stand as the female hierophants of the plot's opposing movements. Margaret Anstruther's disciplined and obedient preparation for death allows her to cross the boundaries between worlds and to give the workman the love which begins his salvation; Lily Sammile, a contemporary manifestation of Lilith, tempts Pauline, the workman, and Wentworth to a selfishness which would damn them to a perpetual death-in-life and life-in-death.

On every level of thematic concern, *Descent into Hell* echoes these dialectics. The book opens with the juxtaposition of two central characters, both of whom have special access to a world apart from the natural realm. Peter Stanhope is a writer of verse dramas; his mastery of poetry puts him in touch with the structure of the universe. Stanhope seems to be a stand-in for Williams himself, who used the name as a pseudonym attached to his own verse play, *Judgement at Chelmsford* (1939). He is described as "contemplative"; his art is a "Thing of the soul" in which there is "no contention between the presences of life and death."

Pauline Anstruther is part of Stanhope's audience. Through no will of her own, she is dominated by her fear of meeting herself, a rupture in the structure of the ordinary world that she cannot bear to confront. She recognizes that

Stanhope has control over the very world of which she is afraid. When he speaks of "a different life" and "a terrible good," she begins to wonder about the difference and terror of her own existence.

The next movement of the book compares Stanhope and Pauline to two darker thematic opposites. Lawrence Wentworth is like Stanhope in that he, too, lives a life of the mind, but Wentworth's structures of military history have none of the universal lucidity of Stanhope's poetry. Instead of contemplating, he imposes his will: "His mind reduced the world to diagrams, and he saw to it that the diagrams fitted." The workman is like Pauline in that he, too, unwittingly crosses the frontier between worlds, but Pauline, however haunted she may be outdoors, has the sanctuary of a home, which the workman lacks. The workman is, in fact, totally alienated. He hangs himself because he has been cast off by society: "The Republic, of which he knew nothing, had betrayed him; all of the nourishment that comes from friendship and common pain was as much forbidden to him as the poor nourishment of his body." Pauline and the workman are on opposite sides of the same problem: she cannot live until she has integrated her selfhood; he cannot die until he has discovered his.

In the following section, the workman's experience of the limbo between worlds is compared to two other encounters with death: the obedient, disciplined vision accepted by Margaret Anstruther and the self-indulgent illusion chosen by Wentworth. The dominant characteristic of Margaret Anstruther's mind is its happiness with facts. Peter Stanhope's poetry is described as "the pure perfection of fact . . . free from desire or fear or distress," and this discipline of disinterested joy is what she seeks to perfect in herself. Williams describes this discipline as the art of love:

> The most perfect, since the most intimate and intelligent, art was pure love. The approach by love was the approach to fact; to love anything but fact was not love. Love was even more mathematical than poetry; it was the pure mathematics of the spirit.

Wentworth, on the other hand, does not respect fact. His nature is not like that of fellow historian Aston Moffatt, a scholar who would have sacrificed everything in life "for the discovery of one fact about the horse-boys of Edward Plantagenet." Instead, he twists the interpretation of facts to serve his own ego: "He identified scholarship with himself." When Moffatt receives a knighthood, Wentworth refuses to rejoice, thus opening himself up to the temptations of Lilith.

The center of *Descent into Hell* is the three versions of love depicted in Chapters VI through IX. Each of the three characters—Pauline, Wentworth, and the workman—makes a choice which determines his or her fate. The core of Williams' philosophy is articulated in Chapter VI as Stanhope explains the Doctrine of Substituted Love to Pauline. When she tells him of her haunting fear, he offers to take on the burden. At first she is suspicious, doubting that his acceptance of her burden will really change her emotions and being reluctant to surrender her self-respect enough to accept his help. Stanhope urges Pauline not to "insist on making a universe for yourself," telling her that the exchange of troubles is "a law of the universe" and explaining that "not to give up your parcel is as much to rebel as to not carry another's." Once Pauline submits to his generosity, she finds herself wonderfully free from dread. When Lily Sammile offers her the delicious prospect of living in a dream world where she will "never have to do anything for others any more," she recognizes the falseness of such egoistic greed.

Wentworth, however, falls completely into this trap. At the moment of his anger at Aston Moffatt, Lily appears. He takes her hand and she leads him deep into another world, a world which is actually the interior of his own body. There, in a parody of God's creation of Eve, she helps him form an image of the girl Adela, an inaccurate projection of his own needs which he takes home to serve his egotism. The succubus is an inversion of love, an incestuous fantasy of fulfillment.

The workman, whose life has been nearly completely lacking the possibility of the love available to Pauline and Wentworth, has the same choice before him; he is not dead precisely because he has never had the choice offered to him in life. As his moment of decision approaches, the fragmented landscape in which he wanders begins to take on shape and light. At first, he tries to run away; seeing the forms of his earlier existence, he seeks the comfort of darkness. Then he sees the shining face of Margaret Anstruther smiling tenderly down on him from a window. Feeling the energy of both her love and the added love of Pauline, the workman attempts to speak. He moans and, in that moment, begins his salvation, for his moan is answered across time by that of the crucified Christ: Godhead bearing the suffering of mortality.

The latter part of the novel depicts the fate to which the characters are led by their choices. Pauline and Wentworth are here contrasted as exemplars of love and solipsism, respectively. When Pauline's grandmother asks her to go into town in the middle of the night to "see if anyone wants you," she meets the workman. Having made his choice to join the Republic, he asks her the way to London. She wants to help him all she can; eagerly she tries to take on the burden of his troubles as Stanhope took on hers. The energy of her desire causes a merger of time in which the workman becomes her martyred ancestor who was burned at the stake; but the ancestor's fear of the fire is too much for Pauline to bear, and her generosity is paralyzed. Then she hears her own voice speaking behind her, accepting his fear. It is her *Doppelgänger*, completing the exchange of love which she could not accomplish alone. She turns and faces the phantom, discovering in that instant of integration the full joy of her selfhood.

Wentworth, meanwhile, has also moved farther into his selfhood, paradoxically disintegrating as he approaches the utter chaos of solipsism. He has become imprisoned in the precincts of what Stanhope calls "Gomorrah," that silent city where there is not even (as in Sodom) love between man and man. When the real Adela runs to him for help, terrified by the vision of opening graves that she witnesses on her own road to Gomorrah, he does not even recognize her. Wentworth's servants leave him, and he is forced to go to London and his club where he discovers a dinner in progress for Aston Moffatt. His watch has stopped, and during the course of the meal, he gradually loses his inner perception of time and, finally, space; the faces around him dissolve into meaningless forms and he falls into the void.

Both Pauline and Wentworth cross the frontiers of ordinary reality, experiencing epiphanal moments of timelessness, but their two supernatural states are diametrically opposed to each other. Williams consistently describes as deluded any attempt to reject time—to leave behind the particularity of each phenomenal moment. The epiphanal timelessness he seeks is supernatural not because it leaves the natural world of time behind but because it encompasses so many *more* moments and phenomena. The distinction is particularly clear in *Descent into Hell* where Wentworth's slide into the hell of total self-involvement is associated with a decreased awareness of time, whereas Pauline's triumphal discovery and unification of her selfhood involves a transcendence of time through a doubled awareness of both her own temporal existence and that of her ancestor. As always, Williams' supernaturalism achieves its fullest incarnation in phenomenal reality.

Elisa Kay Sparks

Bibliography
Carpenter, Humphrey. *The Inklings: C. S. Lewis, J. R. R. Tolkien, Charles Williams, and Their Friends*, 1979.
Glenn, Lois. *Charles W. S. Williams: A Checklist*, 1975.
Hadfield, Alice Mary. *An Introduction to Charles Williams*, 1959.
Hillegas, Mark R., ed. *Shadows of Imagination: The Fantasies of C. S. Lewis, J. R. R. Tolkien, and Charles Williams*, 1979.
Moorman, Charles. "Myth in the Novels of Charles Williams," in *Modern Fiction Studies*. III (1957-1958), pp. 321-327.
—————— . *Precincts of Felicity: The Augustinian City of the Oxford Christians*, 1966.
Morris, Lawrence Allen. *Charles Williams' Novels and Possibilities of Spiritual Transformation in the Twentieth Century*, 1978 (dissertation).
Reily, R. J. *Romantic Religion: A Study of Barfield, Lewis, Williams, and Tolkien*, 1971.
Rose, Ellen Cronan. "A Briefing for *Briefing*: Charles Williams' *Descent into*

Hell and Doris Lessing's *Briefing for a Descent into Hell*," in *Mythlore*. IV, no. 1 (September, 1976), pp. 10-13.

Shideler, Mary McDermott. *Charles Williams: A Critical Essay*, 1966.

_____ . *The Theology of Romantic Love: A Study in the Writings of Charles Williams*, 1962.

Urang, Gunner. *Shadows of Heaven: Religion and Fantasy in the Writings of C. S. Lewis, Charles Williams and J. R. R. Tolkien*, 1971.

THE DEVIL AND THE DOCTOR

Author: David H. Keller (1880-1966)
First book publication: 1940
Type of work: Novel
Time: The late 1920's
Locale: Stroudsburg and Voglertown, Pennsylvania; and New York

Befriended by a stranger who claims to be the Devil, Dr. Jacob Hubler finds himself mysteriously assisted in the achievement of his dearest dreams, but must contend with the hostility of neighbors who suspect him of making a pact with Satan

Principal characters:
  DR. JACOB HUBLER, a retired physician
  ROBIN GOODFELLOW, a mysterious stranger
  SUSAN GILMER (ANGELICA DEVENUE), an actress, later Mrs. Jacob
    Hubler
  MACNABE, a miller and a church elder

To readers who have been chilled by Dr. David H. Keller's horror stories or the grim prophecies of his science fiction, *The Devil and the Doctor* will come as a surprise: it is a supernatural comedy. As with all true comedy, its purpose is serious although its manner is cheerful.

The plot centers on two remarkable persons. Dr. Jacob Hubler's enigmatic visitor, Robin Goodfellow, claims to be the Devil—but not in the traditional sense. Heaven's propaganda, he says, has libeled him; his twin brother, the Judeo-Christian God, is a tyrant who has concealed from humanity the fact that Goodfellow desires only to help them. Genial and apparently harmless, the stranger charms the doctor with his reminiscences about the creation of the human race and about his exile into hell at the behest of his envious brother-god. Inexplicable events accompany Goodfellow; he seems to bring Hubler good fortune by supernatural means.

Hubler, even without claims to the supernatural, is at least as entertaining as Goodfellow. Retired from medical practice, he opens a bookstore simply because he is unwilling to sell an inherited library in bulk at five cents a volume. A bookworm and something of an intellectual, he takes special delight in works on demonology. Although kind and idealistic, he is an iron-willed individualist with a domineering streak and a touch of male chauvinism. Committed to traditional values of family, community, and simple decency, he is also cheerfully unconventional. He has his automobile modified so its top speed is twenty miles an hour, replaces the headlights with carriage lamps and the roof with an umbrella, and christens the result the "Flying Bitch." His greatest ambition, he says, is to spend his retirement building a stone fence. He has the project planned in detail, including the kind of meadow the fence will surround, the kind of house that will overlook the meadow, and the wife who will bring his lunch while he works. He wonders, though, if he will ever get around to making the dream come true.

What especially appeals to Goodfellow is the doctor's disrespect for aspects of church teaching that he cannot reconcile with common sense or with his compassion for human suffering. As Jehovah's adversary, Goodfellow finds in such iconoclasm grounds for putting his powers at Hubler's disposal. Thereafter he not only regales the doctor with stories of life in Heaven and hell, but provides uncanny assistance when Hubler woos an actress, seeks his ideal farm, risks his life going to a neighbor's aid during a blizzard, and undertakes to build the long-postponed Stone Fence. Goodfellow is always tactful and unobtrusive, but Hubler, a shrewd observer, deduces what is going on—with considerable doubt as to Goodfellow's real nature and methods.

The bright flow of whimsy is shadowed, however, as Goodfellow's apparently demoniac presence comes to the attention of narrow-minded villagers—especially the fanatical and ambitious miller, Macnabe. Hubler, an active churchman, despite his reservations on some points of doctrine, is not only denied the presidency of the consistory but is also subjected to physical threats for associating with the Devil. Tension rises, but in the end Goodfellow proves equal to the occasion, as to the others, and rewards Hubler's courageous stand in a finale that manages to be both dramatic and amusing.

The concept of the Devil as the maligned loser in a war with a tyrannical god owes much to Anatole France's *La Révolte des anges* (1914, *The Revolt of the Angels*). Yet Keller's handling of the theme is uniquely his own, in both content and style. The story is told with his strangely eloquent simplicity of language—a subordinate clause comes as a novelty. Supernatural events are set within an everyday background (mostly Pennsylvania locales well-known to Keller), cosmic ideas are scaled down to human intimacy, and serious intellectual and ethical elements are presented with a smile. Although the simplicity occasionally becomes banal, and the genial manner at times softens into sentimentality, the prose is usually pungent and the viewpoint realistic.

Keller includes many apparently irrelevant asides—anecdotes, reminiscences, even recipes—which are charming in themselves but which also enrich the flavor of traditional values. Whether Hubler is telling a tall story about his ancestors, giving advice on how to boil eggs or prepare sausages or choose the proper kind of mint, or describing in rhapsodic detail his plans for the Stone Fence, he gives the reader the taste of a way of life. Similarly, Goodfellow's tales of his celestial struggle and of his loving overseership of humanity reflect staunch old principles: freedom, honor, and kindness. This is a good-natured and humorous novel; yet it is filled with wistful awareness that the world changes although it does not necessarily progress.

Although Keller champions unchanging moral values and is nostalgic about a simpler way of life, he is neither a reactionary nor a conformist. The book glorifies the individualist, the outcast whose mind is too clear and whose ideals are too high for conventional society to tolerate. Through Goodfellow, Keller preaches enlightened change—change that is humane, that conserves the best of the old, and that enables mankind to develop its potential without the restraints of tyranny or dogma. Goodfellow's task is to encourage those who share that vision.

The Devil and the Doctor may distress the orthodox, but Goodfellow is far from satanic. Keller is not attacking Christianity as such; he is suggesting that if people are truly to follow the teachings of Christ, they must act less in the spirit of Macnabe and of the Devil's despotic brother, and more in the spirit of Hubler and Goodfellow. Goodfellow, in fact, is really Hubler's own best self, the best self of humanity, combining keenness of intellect with compassion of spirit—and the ability to work miracles. The delight of *The Devil and the Doctor* is that these ideas are expressed in a story as surprising and amusing as a fairy tale, yet grounded in the sober experience of a man who, as country doctor and psychiatrist, knew life to its roots.

Paul Spencer

Bibliography
Keller, David H. "Half a Century of Writing," in *The Last Magician: Nine Stories from "Weird Tales,"* 1978.
Moskowitz, Sam. "Introduction," in *Life Everlasting and Other Stories of Science, Fantasy, and Horror*, 1947.
Spencer, Paul. "In Memoriam: David Henry Keller," in *The Folsom Flint and Other Curious Tales*, 1969.
Stableford, Brian W. "David H. Keller, 1880-1966," in *Science Fiction Writers*, 1982. Edited by Everett F. Bleiler.

THE DEVIL IN CRYSTAL

Author: Louis Marlow (Louis Umfreville Wilkinson, 1881-1966)
First book publication: 1944
Type of work: Novel
Time: 1922
Locale: London

The story of a man who relives a few days of his earlier life

Principal characters:
    JAMES TIDBURNHOLME, a writer and gentleman of leisure
    JANETTA, a girl with unusual powers of perception

One of the most common daydreams consists of imagining one's mature consciousness taking control of one's earlier self, so that a part of life can be lived again with the aid of hindsight, with mistakes avoided, lost opportunities seized, and unappreciated pleasures savored to the full. Remarkably, there have been very few literary versions of this fantasy. The two most important novelistic versions appeared within a few years of each other: Louis Marlow's *The Devil in Crystal* in 1944 and P. D. Ouspensky's *Strange Life of Ivan Osokin* in 1947.

As with most literary reflections of common daydreams, both novels offer a rather reserved and cautionary account of the fulfillment of the wish, implying that its fulfillment would be less rewarding than might be assumed. Both imagine that the mature consciousness would find itself imprisoned within a determined pattern which can be broken, if at all, only with the utmost difficulty. Both novels refer to the Nietzschean doctrine of eternal recurrence, but Marlow's does so only in passing; unlike Ouspensky's, it is not committed to presenting a version of that thesis.

It is in the nature of the exercise that *The Devil in Crystal* should be an unusually intimate and rather claustrophobic narrative. The reader is eavesdropping on a stream of consciousness which reflects upon and tries to cope with wholly alien circumstances. The author takes his premise seriously, earnestly attempting to envision the sensations and ideas which might occur if the impossible were actually to happen. Marlow was always an idiosyncratic author, and his representation of the protagonist's feelings and thoughts will not seem plausible to all readers, but the account is not less interesting by virtue of its eccentricities.

James Tidburnholme, a man with a private income who supplements its provisions by writing essays of political commentary, wakes up on the morning of June 22, 1922, more or less as usual, except for the fact that the mind within his body has the memories and attitudes which Tidburnholme will not possess until 1943. He finds that the least lapse of attention will cause his body to perform like a robot the actions which first took him through that day, but that if he makes an effort of will, he can change at least a fraction of his behavior. Sometimes, although he does or says something different, people respond as if he had stuck to the "original" pattern, and he soon discovers that it is very difficult to make any alteration in his behavior that actually affects others significantly. He can detach himself completely from involvement with his actions and become a passive observer, but he finds this unduly disquieting. Equally upsetting is the fact that his mature consciousness suffers occasional lapses, so that he loses hours or days before he can reassert his peculiar presence.

At first, Tidburnholme imagines that he might use his opportunity to accomplish great things, perhaps even to avert the war that beset the world he left behind him. He soon realizes, however, that the mere fact of his foreknowledge will not help in such matters: he is altogether too inconsequential a person to affect the course of history. It becomes clear to him that if anything worthwhile is to come out of his experience, it must be something private and personal that will not substantially disturb the flow of worldly events. He is the victim of an odd loneliness and longs to be able to make clear to someone what curious kind of being he has become. He gets this opportunity when he meets a girl named Janetta, who (he remembers) is considered to be "odd" and slightly psychic. He determines to substitute a liaison with Janetta for the shallow and ill-fated romantic affair which fate and history will thrust upon him. It is not easy, but in some measure, he does succeed; he makes only a slight and temporary alteration of his personal history, but even this victory is crucial. When, inevitably, he returns from his extraordinary experience to the unchanged world of 1943, he is a little richer.

Although the story is essentially an elaboration of a daydream, it also has its nightmarish aspect. It is a tendency of human beings occasionally to imagine doing a better job if lives could be lived over again and to share the sensation of being a prisoner within a crystallized pattern of events, detached from the mainstream of change and impotent to alter the course within it. Man has the ability to take a mental step back from his daily existence, to watch himself performing social rituals from a viewpoint that makes them seem strange and slightly irrational. *The Devil in Crystal* presents a greatly exaggerated version of this kind of momentary alienation and has links with some of the surreal stream-of-consciousness ghost stories which are told from the viewpoint of the ghost (examples include Ashley Sampson's *The Ghost of Mr. Brown*, 1941, and G. W. Stonier's *The Memoirs of a Ghost*, 1947). James Tidburnholme's journey back into his earlier self is as much an uncomfortable revelation as it is an opportunity for gain.

The principal weakness of the novel is that it has as its protagonist a kind of character who hardly exists outside of "society novels" of the period between World War I and World War II. Tidburnholme's social world is nevertheless one which Marlow probably knew well, and part of the strength of the novel is a brooding background awareness of the fact that it is a doomed world, about to suffer its *coup de grâce* in World War II. Since that world has now virtually vanished into the mists of literary legend, the novel is badly dated; the contemporary reader will hardly be able to identify with the protagonist, and in a stream-of-consciousness novel, this causes awkward reading. Nevertheless, the novel's theme is sufficiently fascinating to warrant the reader's attention.

Brian Stableford

Bibliography
No listing.

THE DEVIL IS DEAD

Author: R. A. Lafferty (1914-   )
First book publication: 1971
Type of work: Novel
Time: The 1970's
Locale: The ship *Brunhilde* and various ports of call

> *Two factions of Neanderthal men, led by the Devil on one side and Finnegan on the other, fight a secret war to determine who will control the world*

Principal characters:
FINNEGAN, a Neanderthal seaman and artist
SAXON X. SEAWORTHY, the evil owner of the *Brunhilde*
PAPA DEVIL, the good grandson of the Devil, disguised as his evil twin
ANASTASIA DEMETRIADES, a mermaid
MR. X, a plotter on the good side
DOLL DELANCY, a *Homo sapiens sapiens*

R. A. Lafferty has gradually become convinced that the world ended sometime between 1912 and 1962; he is quite capable of maintaining that Earth and its inhabitants have been destroyed but have not noticed it yet. In this case, however, he means that there was a generally accepted world view in terms of which virtually everything could be explained but which has been abandoned. Nothing has yet taken its place. A look at history shows that if the world is to be replaced, it will be remade very soon. Lafferty has warned his audience that they have a chance to participate in this creation, shaping it to their liking; but they must act quickly. The point is not whether Lafferty's position has merit but rather what light it can shed on his writings. There are several recurring themes in Lafferty's work, and they are easier to understand if one is familiar with his views about the end of the world.

The word "recension" properly applies to edited texts, but Lafferty habitually applies it to differing versions (editions, as it were) of genus *Homo*. His reluctance to speak in terms of species or subspecies doubtless stems from two sources. First, the term "species" emphasizes differences rather than similarities; second and more important, the term "recension" suggests that there is, or was, an archetypal text which can be recovered. Lafferty suggests that there is a standard for humanity which various recensions of humankind resemble more or less closely.

Recensions of individuals are also common in Lafferty's writings. These *Doppelgänger* set one another off nicely by providing contrast in character. The two members of a pair will have contrasting strengths and weaknesses, and one will be able to accomplish what the other cannot; but both are doomed to failure because each combination of strength and weakness is fatally flawed. In *The Devil Is Dead*, Finnegan, Papa Devil, and a number of others have *Doppelgänger*.

Conspiracies are virtually inevitable in Lafferty's work, and rarely do they aim lower than at complete control of the world. Often plausible in detail, they are fundamentally absurd and intentionally so. Within this common absurdity there is a definite evolution in the way the conspiracies are treated, although there are regressions and false starts which sometimes make it difficult to discern what direction the evolution is taking. In earlier stories, the success or failure of the conspiracies could make a difference. As Lafferty gropes toward the conclusion that the world has ended, the conspiracies gradually lose their point, and their outcomes decline in importance until success or failure makes no difference at all because the prize, the world, has vanished.

Lafferty has the gift of creating believably tough heroes and believably deadly villains. Putting them in false situations reveals the absurdity of their preoccupations. The motive for absurdity, however, changes over time. In earlier stories, it stems from wanting something which, although attainable, is not something that any sensible person would want. In later stories, the absurdity lies in quarreling over something which does not exist and would not be desirable if it did. *The Devil Is Dead* falls in the late middle range. Doll Delancy practically tells Finnegan and Mr. X that their world has ended, but they pay no attention. At the time when *The Devil Is Dead* was written, Lafferty was not quite ready to admit that the world in which he thought he lived had ended too.

Lafferty makes extensive use of two kinds of fool figures. First, there are those who see so clearly and are so naïve that they are unaware of the layers of pretense in which most things are wrapped and do not have the sense to remain silent. Second, there are those who accept appearance as reality and act accordingly, with predictably bizarre results. A fool of either kind properly placed is admirably suited to reveal absurdity. Mr. X is a fool of the second kind. He serves his purpose with stunning earnestness. There are several other stock characters in Lafferty's writings who recur in various guises, somewhat in the manner of those in *commedia dell'arte*. The most important is a heavy-drinking, raffish hero who fights for the sheer joy of it. Such a man is Irish even when he is not; Finnegan is Italian, but he is a typical Lafferty hero.

None of these devices, nor even Lafferty's use of them in combination, is unique; what sets Lafferty apart is style, which is the source of both his strength and his weakness as a writer. Its hallmarks are auctorial intrusion, calculated digression, conspirators calling attention to their own slips of tongue, and passages of inspired nonsense. When this style works, it is a powerful device for portraying action taking place on several different levels at the same time. Unfortunately, it can easily get out of hand: the latter part of *The Devil Is Dead* bogs down in excessive digression, and the ending is

anticlimactic.

The Devil Is Dead is neither Lafferty's best work nor his worst; instead, the author has given readers a rough-cut gem which dazzles occasionally despite its flaws.

William M. Schuyler, Jr.

Bibliography

Lafferty, R. A. "The Case of the Moth-Eaten Magician," in *Fantastic Lives: Autobiographical Essays by Notable Science Fiction Writers*, 1981. Edited by Martin H. Greenberg.

_____. "The Day After the World Ended," in *Philosophical Speculations*. No. 2 (Summer, 1981), pp. 61-68.

_____. "The Profession of Science Fiction, 21: True Believers," in *Foundation*. XX (October, 1980), pp. 43-46.

THE DEVIL RIDES OUT

Author: Dennis Wheatley (1897-1977)
First book publication: 1935
Type of work: Novel
Time: The 1930's
Locale: England

The Duke de Richleau, knowledgeable in magic, persuades Rex Van Ryn that practicing black magicians have gained influence over their friend Simon Aron and that he must be rescued

Principal characters:
DUKE DE RICHLEAU, an exiled French art connoisseur
RICHARD EATON, an English "Musketeer"
MARIE LOU EATON, his Russian bride
SIMON ARON, an English Jew
REX VAN RYN, a young American visitor
TANITH, a beautiful clairvoyant
DAMIEN MOCATA, a black magician

Known as the "Prince of Thriller Writers," Dennis Wheatley wrote many best-sellers; and, to provide variety for his reading public, he maintained three series: the Duke de Richleau series, emphasizing magic and set in modern times; the Gregory Sallust series, about opposition to the Gestapo; and the Roger Brook series, covering the French Revolution and the Napoleonic Wars. In addition to these and other books on black magic, he wrote a variety of mysteries and a number of nonfiction books. His first novel, *The Forbidden Territory* (1933) was, according to his own statement, "reprinted seven times in seven weeks and within a year [was] translated into a dozen foreign languages." This novel introduced the character of the Duke de Richleau and his three companions, who later became known as *Those Modern Musketeers* (1939); the plot involved the Duke's rescue of Rex Van Ryn from a Soviet prison and Richard Eaton's acquiring of his Russian bride.

One of Dennis Wheatley's favorite themes is that magic exists, and that practitioners of black magic, greedy for power, threaten the lives and souls of people and even account for global wars. Wheatley claimed that not only a vast knowledge of occult subjects but also a mastery of "the theories accounting for supernatural manifestations" is necessary to write a successful satanic novel. Among his more than sixty books, which have been translated into twenty-six languages, *The Devil and All His Works* (1971) has been called a modern textbook on Satanism; enough occult lore fills the pages of *The Devil Rides Out* to earn it a similar distinction. The novel was made into the movie *The Devil's Bride* in 1968.

The Duke de Richleau and Rex Van Ryn, reunited in *The Devil Rides Out*, assume that Simon Aron's failure to keep their customary rendezvous means that he is in serious trouble. Rex Van Ryn, a large, muscular man who characteristically chooses action over caution, acts as the reader's consciousness for the unfolding bizarre events. Disbelieving at first, Rex gradually comes to realize, through the Duke's explanations and his own observations, that the powers of darkness in the world pit themselves in an unending battle against the powers of light. He provides the novel's romantic interest through his attraction to Tanith, already in the clutches of the evil Mocata.

Magic, an occult art utilizing complex symbols and rituals, requires exhaustive study and strenuous devotion; it was once a hobby of the Duke, a dilettante art connoisseur and exiled French loyalist. Its purpose, as the Duke explains, is to bring about change through the exertion of will. Through his role as victim, Simon Aron, once attracted to magic through the study of the *Qaballa* and *Zohar*, provides evidence that a black magician can exercise an evil influence on another person's will. Richard Eaton, happily domesticated on his English estate called Cardinals Folly, must also be convinced of the existence of magic. For him the costs may be great, for he and his wife Marie Lou are the fond parents of a sinless child, whose presence is required by many satanic rituals. The best of society—what the Powers of Light should protect—may be seen in this small family, whose beautiful daughter is appropriately named Fleur d'amore. To persuade his friends that the practice of magic influences events in the world, the Duke de Richleau provides information on specific topics such as alchemy, exorcism, witchcraft, lycanthropy, Manichaeanism, elementals, and astrology. Secondary characters support his theories by reporting on such related topics as numerology and vampirism. Additional information confirms that a body of knowledge, independent of any given religion, unites all religions.

Duke de Richleau begins his discussion of magic with the Persian myth of the contention of Ozamund and Ahriman, with Light symbolizing health, wisdom, growth, and life, and Darkness symbolizing disease, ignorance, death, and decay. Because the growth of the spirit toward Light is "long and arduous," the soul must be reborn through successive incarnations: Jesus Christ achieved perfection, and His message was that others might do so as well. Acceptance of the possibility that Christ and Buddha—"a sort of Indian Christ"—performed miracles leads to the admission that other mystics can also tap into the sources of special energy. The alchemists sought the elixir of life as a metaphor for eternal life, the changing of base metals into gold, and the transfusion of matter into light. Acceptance of reincarnation validates astrology; and, since words have special powers, the letters in one's given name reveal affinities with other people and also one's relationship to the universe (hence the science of numerology). Tanith explains that the followers of the right-hand path concern themselves only with the well-being of the universe as a whole, whereas the followers of the left-hand path work on human beings.

Astrology ensnares Simon, kidnaped by the followers of the left-hand path, because Mocata as a black magician needs Simon to perform the important ritual to Saturn, after which Simon will be permanently dedicated to Evil. Simon's birthday, at the certain hour of a certain year when Mars is in conjunction with Saturn, means that he can provide Mocata with the Talisman of Set. Tanith, more deeply entangled than Simon, bears the name of the Moon Goddess of the Carthaginians (known also as Isis or Astoroth), and she was born on May 2. Because her number and that of Mocata is two, the value of the Moon, the special vibrations between them make her an especially good medium for him. When the Duke and Rex Van Ryn use the power of their car's headlights to break up the Walpurgis Night, they rescue Simon for a time and save Tanith from a satanic baptism. She tells Rex, however, that her failure to cooperate with Mocata will mean that he will make her one of "the undead," a vampire. The Duke's frustration of Mocata's efforts by the powers of his own white magic seems successful until the four Musketeers discover that Mocata has captured a third victim: Richard Eaton's small daughter, Fleur d'amore. The blood of a child sacrificed to Satan will gain for Mocata the Talisman of Set and will enable him to release upon the world the Four Horsemen of the Apocalypse—War, Plague, Famine, and Death.

Mocata's successful projection of his black Malagasy servant's astral body frightens Rex sufficiently to make him a believer, but had he remain a skeptic, he would have been persuaded by the Walpurgis Night, when his otherwise dignified friend Simon takes part in the smashing of a crucifix, the gorging of food, climaxed by the eating of human flesh—the antithesis of the Blessed Sacrament—and wild nude dancing under the eyes of a materialized Goat of Mendes (Satan). Most fearful of all, however, is Mocata's evocation of elementals—evil materializations, usually of unnatural beasts. To protect Simon, the Duke practices his white magic, and the friends sit, at Cardinals Folly, with Simon inside a specially prepared pentacle, where they must fight off several attacks by the elementals. Simon escapes their good efforts to sacrifice himself after Mocata kidnaps Fleur. With Tanith dead, the Duke calls up her astral body to gain information concerning the wherabouts of Fleur and Simon.

Although the Duke recommends research in James Frazer's *Golden Bough* (1890), he improves upon it when he relates the history of the Talisman of Set, a history providing another variation of the perennial struggle of good versus evil, light versus darkness. The Egyptian dark brother Set planned the murder of his good and light brother Osiris, through the gift of a coffin which fit only Osiris, by a ruse nailed inside; and his death was accomplished with no blood spilled. Isis protected the coffin for some time until Set captured it and divided the body of Osiris into fourteen pieces. Years later, Isis erected temples to the memory of Osiris wherever she found one of the pieces and buried it; she did not find the phallus, which Set had kept for himself and had had embalmed as the most potent of all charms. It is frequently lost, but whenever it is found, world calamities occur.

The plot, having progressed unevenly and having climaxed early in the novel at the Walpurgis Night and again during the nightlong watch in the pentacle, now continues with supernatural intervention. At a ruined monastery in northern Greece, the four Musketeers and Marie Lou find Fleur outstretched on an altar about to be sacrificed by Mocata, who has cast around the would-be rescuers a magic circle which prevents their interference. Again Mocata calls up the Goat of Mendes to preside at another Black Mass. Even the prayers of the onlookers seem ineffectual, but then Marie Lou remembers a forgotten dream in which she had seen a page of one of the lost books. Now, reciting one sentence from that magical book, she causes the Talisman of Set to be swept out from between the horns of the Goat, and the magical apparatus dissolves. The Lord of Light momentarily takes the body of Fleur to materialize himself and assure the viewers that "The Adversary has been driven back to the dark Halls of Shaitan." The next scene seems somewhat superfluous; the rescuers arouse themselves inside the pentacle at Cardinals Folly, where Fleur sleeps peacefully and Tanith awakes. Mocata is found dead "of natural causes," and all the participants realize that they have shared the same dream.

Grace Eckley

Bibliography

Barclay, Glen St. John. *Anatomy of Horror: The Masters of Occult Fiction*, 1978.
Wheatley, Dennis. "The Way to Maintain Success," in *The Writer*. October, 1969, pp. 22-24.

THE DEVIL'S ELIXIRS
(DIE ELIXIERE DES TEUFELS)

Author: E. T. A. Hoffmann (1776-1822)
First book publication: 1815-1816
English translation: 1824
Type of work: Novel
Time: Presumably the eighteenth century
Locale: A monastery in Germany and various points between there and Rome

A youth reared by his mother for a life of piety to atone for the sins of his ancestors abuses a sacred relic entrusted to his care and encounters an ideal beloved, thereby undergoing an emotional crisis, with the result that his monastic superior sends him on a mission to Rome, whence he returns chastened in spirit and prepared to renounce earthly fulfillment of his love

> *Principal characters:*
> MEDARDUS, a monk
> AURELIA, his beloved
> LEONARDUS, his monastic superior
> VIKTORIN, his double
> EUPHEMIA, Aurelia's stepmother
> HERMOGEN, Aurelia's brother
> PETER SCHÖNFELD, a barber

With his short fiction, Ernst Theodor Amadeus Hoffmann emerged as an early—and perhaps world literature's greatest—master of the fantastic tale. *The Devil's Elixirs*, his first novel (if two youthful, unpublished, and unrecovered efforts are disregarded), was written near the beginning of his late-blooming literary career, when the success of his tales was not yet sufficiently apparent to persuade him fully that his future lay with that genre. This longer work thus offers important testimony regarding his potential talent as a novelist.

The Devil's Elixirs recommends itself on a number of counts. The depth and variety of its psychological portrayal and its richness of style make it one of the best products of the vogue of the Gothic novel (Hoffmann drew especially on Mathew G. Lewis' *Ambrosio: Or, The Monk*, 1796, and acknowledged this literary debt by making the heroine a reader of that novel). There is a mingling of scenes bordering on the comic with adventures as terrifying or gruesome as any found in Gothic romance. The handling of narrative perspective, moreover, is extremely subtle, leaving the reader in doubt as to how much of the hero's adventures is fact and how much is fantasy. Those familiar with Hoffmann's fantastic short fiction, however, may find that there is a falling-off of interest in this longer work.

Like Hoffmann's fantastic tales, his Gothic novel poses many tantalizing riddles. In particular, he does not invite simple suspension of disbelief, as other practitioners of the Gothic mode were in the habit of doing. Since the hero tells his own story, as an act of penance ordained by his monastic superior, the reader is thereby made aware that Medardus, whose mental stability is demonstrably not the best, remains the sole guarantor of its veracity—the more so in view of his having reportedly been dead so long that, by the time Hoffmann's editor, his Traveling Enthusiast from the earlier *Fantasiestücke in Callots Manier* (1814-1815, *Fantasy Pieces in Callot's Manner*), discovers the manuscript, there is no one still alive who was acquainted with Medardus. To be sure, there is a postscript by a monk who claims to have witnessed the uncanny circumstances of Medardus' death, but there is no survivor who appears to have known this "Pater Spiridion" either. Moreover, the editor reports that, together with the monk's memoir, he found a parchment manuscript purporting to be an account of the lives of the latter's ancestors, among whom the first was this manuscript's author—who thus must have written the account over the several centuries following his own death.

The reader is offered a degree of comfort insofar as the memoir is recognizably a tale of love. Even here, however, there is considerable uncertainty as to whether one is dealing with a factual or fictional account on the memoirist's part. As Medardus himself confesses, the beloved appears to enter his life almost as though she has stepped from a painting of St. Rosalia hung in his monastery; and in the end, he views their love as having been a test of the purity of his spirit, and her murder by his ghostly double as part of a divine plan that he be united with her, as St. Rosalia, in a higher realm.

The role of Medardus' double in his memoir is at once its most baffling element and the best hint regarding the nature of the spiritual crisis reflected in his weird adventures. The double, the ghost of a libertine aristocrat, Count Viktorin, obviously represents a role that Medardus both desires and fears to assume. In the end, he comes to view his involvement with Viktorin as having been the work of the Devil, but there is reason to believe that the double's entry into his life projects resentment over his having precipitously committed himself to monastic life when still a callow youth. In particular, his initially unwitting assumption of Viktorin's identity sets him on a path of compulsive, if intermittent, homicidal lust, indicating that his resentment centers upon the vow of chastity.

Medardus' decision to become a monk was occasioned by his embarrassment when, at age sixteen, a group of girls had noticed him passionately kissing a glove left on the piano bench by his music teacher's appealing young sister and had teasingly proceeded to ridicule him. His entry into monastic life appears, therefore, to have been undertaken as a panicked effort to escape the perils of desire, especially considering that the humiliating incident occurred after, on arriving for his music lesson, he had been greeted by the girl in her negligee and had subsequently, although unconnectedly, been questioned by Prior Leonardus concerning the degree of his innocence regarding sexual matters. Moreover, a final hint that Viktorin's role is a projection of Medardus' ambivalent feelings about his monastic vows and his guilt about lustful urges is given near the end in the mad ghostly double's otherwise irrational complaint that Medardus had literally pushed him into actually becoming a monk when he had meant only to assume that role for amorous purposes.

Medardus' career as a compulsively homicidal lover, real or imaginary, also involves self-identification with St. Anthony as having been tempted by Satan in the desert (the desert being, in Medardus' case, his Capuchin monastery). In particular, this identification concerns Medardus' irresistible, guilty urge to drink from the bottle of wine purported to be one of those with which the Devil tempted St. Anthony—a holy relic that Leonardus has entrusted to his care. (This act is suggested to him by the blasphemous remarks of a young nobleman, a visitor to the monastery, who, although not identical to Viktorin, is nevertheless a prefiguration of that role.) Medardus attributes his ensuing sinful career to his having drunk from this "Devil's elixir" (hence the title), but in Medardus' case, it would appear that desire (the elixir of love), not drink, is the great and dreaded temptation.

Once Medardus has left the monastery and, by chance, found himself thrust into Viktorin's role, his first adventure is with the arch seductress Euphemia, with whom the libertine double was engaged in an affair and who now mistakes Medardus for Viktorin. Her depravity fills him with revulsion and he escapes her snares, yet he simultaneously succumbs to equally lustful temptation regarding the ideal beloved, Aurelia, whose brother he kills in a fit of rage when the latter surprises him after he has entered the slumbering maiden's bedroom. In his subsequent adventures, Medardus is haunted by specters projecting his guilt over the murder of the brother, Hermogen, and over his passion to possess the sister—adventures which culminate in his mad struggle with the double as he is about to fulfill his dream of marrying Aurelia and in his resulting collapse. Then, after awakening to find himself in an insane asylum and after a troubled and terrifying sojourn in Rome, he returns to the security of his monastery, renounces the fulfillment of his dream of love in this life, and suffers one last moment of mad, guilty temptation when he witnesses Aurelia taking vows as a nun. Although he proves able to restrain his homicidal lust, the double fatally stabs the beloved.

The relative spiritual calm that Medardus finds in the end is owing to the vision of love's fulfillment in the beyond offered him by Aurelia as she is dying. Moreover, since having read in a monastery near Rome the family chronicle composed by his ghostly ancestor, he has come to interpret his temptations as a heroic struggle to overcome the effects of a hereditary curse and to view the ancestor's interventions in his life as an admonition to remain faithful to that calling. This vision of his destiny helps him to resist the temptation of surrender to insanity that was embodied in the advocacy of that course to him by his self-appointed friend and would-be angel of rescue, the zany German barber Peter Schönfeld, alias Pietro Belcampo.

In sum, Medardus' interpretation of his adventures is not necessarily to be accepted by the reader. His memoir is suspect—beginning with his departure from the monastery, at least—as a fantasy arising from his adolescent panic at the first experience of desire and from later feelings of guilt and resentment, which come to him at age twenty-one, over his earlier precipitous escape into monastic life. In this connection, it is noteworthy that the painting of St. Rosalia, from which Aurelia appears literally to step into his life, was done by the ancestor, who had studied with Leonardo da Vinci, at a time when the ancestor himself was torn between piety and guilty lust. The beloved's role, moreover, is suspect as having possibly been suggested to Medardus by Lewis' *Ambrosio: Or, The Monk*, since Aurelia confesses that the passion she has conceived for him originated in her reading of that novel in early adolescence. Furthermore, the ancestor's parchment manuscript, the family chronicle, would appear to be a fabrication, for the intervening generations listed there do not suffice to account for the time that must have elapsed between the ancestor's study with da Vinci and Medardus' adventures. Indeed, since Lewis' novel appeared only twenty years before Hoffmann's, the editor's report that no one at the monastery where Medardus' memoir was found had any knowledge of the persons or events concerned does not appear plausible. Medardus' story therefore would seem best described as a *roman fantastique*, in the special sense of a fantasy on the part of the principal character and on that of the fictive editor of the purported documents as well.

James M. McGlathery

Bibliography

Daemmrich, Horst S. *The Shattered Self: E. T. A. Hoffmann's Tragic Vision*, 1973.

Hewett-Thayer, Harvey W. *Hoffmann: Author of the Tales*, 1948.

Hoffmann, E. T. A. *The Devil's Elixirs*, 1963. Translated by Ronald Taylor.

McGlathery, James M. "Demon Love: E. T. A. Hoffmann's *Elixiere des Teufels*," in *Colloquia Germanica*. XII, no. 1/2 (1979), pp. 61-76.

Negus, Kenneth G. "The Family Tree in E. T. A. Hoffmann's *Die Elixiere des Teufels*," in *Publications of the Modern Language Association of America*. LXXIII, no. 5, pt. 1 (1958), pp. 516-520.

Passage, Charles E. "E. T. A. Hoffmann's *The Devil's Elixirs*: A Flawed Masterpiece," in *Journal of English and Germanic Philology*. LXXV, no. 4 (October, 1976), pp. 531-545.

DEVIL'S TOR

Author: David Lindsay (1876-1945)
First book publication: 1932
Type of work: Novel
Time: The 1930's
Locale: Dartmoor, England

The reuniting of two halves of an ancient, extraterrestrial stone brings together a man and a woman destined to found a new race beyond humanity

>   *Principal characters:*
>   INGRID FLEMING, a mystical young girl
>   HELGA, her mother
>   MAGNUS COLBORNE, her uncle
>   PETER COPPING, her fiancé, an artist
>   HUGH DRAPIER, her cousin
>   HENRY SALTFLEET, an explorer
>   STEPHEN ARSINAL, an archaeologist

Devil's Tor was the last of David Lindsay's works to be published during his lifetime, and it is apparent that he intended it as his masterpiece. He began work on it, under the title of *The Ancient Tragedy*, as early as 1922, only two years after the publication of his most famous work, *A Voyage to Arcturus*. After this version was rejected by a number of publishers during the 1920's, Lindsay began massive revisions in 1928 and eventually sold the manuscript to Putnam's in 1932 under its present title. Despite a few favorable reviews, the novel sold only some 650 copies and served only to cement Lindsay's growing reputation as a notoriously unmarketable writer. Largely as a result of this failure, Lindsay was unable to persuade Putnam's to reissue *A Voyage to Arcturus* in 1932, and two of his later novels, *The Violet Apple* and *The Witch* (both 1976), would remain unpublished until after Lindsay's death.

Devil's Tor is in many ways an even more demanding book than *A Voyage to Arcturus*. In place of the astonishing wealth of invention in that earlier novel, which sustained interest even when the meaning seemed unclear, Lindsay here chooses a domestic setting—a country house in Dartmoor—and a plot that is almost nonexistent, despite the novel's nearly five-hundred-page length. Most of the length is made up of detailed background exposition and endless philosophical dialogues, punctuated by moments of melodramatic action and at times overpowering visions; there are moments in *Devil's Tor* that are comparable to anything in *A Voyage to Arcturus*. To get to these moments, however, the reader has to be willing to plow through the often remarkably turgid prose in which Lindsay presents his various philosophical speculations.

These speculations, however, are far more explicit and detailed than are those in *A Voyage to Arcturus*, and there is much in the novel to suggest that Lindsay was seeking to compromise with the reader in order to make his ideas more accessible. In the first place, the very setting of the book gives the reader a dependable perspective such as is absent from *A Voyage to Arcturus*, and the limited action helps to avoid that earlier novel's problem of constantly forcing the reader to reconsider and reject whole worlds of morality. The cast of characters is also drastically more limited, and while Lindsay's characters are always strange, they are at least human in this novel. Moreover, Lindsay has this time cast the whole fiction in terms of a myth not of his own making, thus enabling him to draw on allusions and systems of belief already familiar to most readers. The myth that is central to *Devil's Tor* is that of the Great Mother, or the White Goddess.

This myth, as revealed in the novel through the researches of the archaeologist Stephen Arsinal and the visions of several other characters, is essentially as follows. Before the beginning of time, there existed only the Ancient, a lonely consciousness. From this Ancient came the Demiurge, or Eternal Feminine, which created the world and is known as the Great Mother. The Great Mother was originally a unity, like the Ancient, but at some time this unity was destroyed through a fall into sex, and two opposing forces, masculine and feminine, arose. The feminine principle is associated with the world of nature in its unspoiled state, but the masculine principle, through art and industry, has so degraded nature that it no longer provides access to the Eternal Feminine. Later myths such as that of Christ represent attempts to graft the principle of masculine dominance onto the myth of the Great Mother, with the result that Christ becomes an unsatisfactory androgynous figure while Mary dominates the iconography of Christian history. At some point in the distant past a meteorite landed in northern Europe and either created the blue-eyed peoples there or inspired them to their achievements in philosophy, art, and politics. The meteorite split into two fragments, and the rejoining of these fragments, according to ancient inscriptions, will bring together a man and a woman who will found a new race higher than man and reestablish the principle of the Eternal Feminine on Earth.

Arsinal, the archaeologist, has devoted his career to tracking down these stones, and with the aid of an experienced Tibetan explorer named Henry Saltfleet has finally located one and stolen it from a sacred temple in Tibet. While fleeing from the natives, Arsinal and Saltfleet entrust the stone to an adventurer named Hugh Drapier and arrange to recover it from him later.

As the novel opens, Hugh Drapier has arrived in Dartmoor to visit his cousin Ingrid Fleming, her mother Helga, and her uncle, the writer Magnus Colborne. Drapier, who carries with him the mysterious flint stone, cannot quite explain why he has been drawn to Dartmoor, or why he is even more strongly drawn to a nearby outcropping of stone called Devil's Tor. He visits Devil's Tor—so named because of a large stone in the shape of a devil's head—with Ingrid. During a sudden thunderstorm, a lightning bolt dislodges the stone, revealing an ancient tomb. Ingrid experiences a brief vision of a giant woman (the first of many visions of the Great Mother in the book). Drapier returns the following day to explore the tomb, but damages his flashlight, stumbles in the darkness, and picks up a small stone. Drapier believes this to be the Tibetan stone, which he dropped, but the reader will soon learn that it is actually the missing half of the ancient meteorite. An elaborate series of misunderstandings and confusions prevents the characters from realizing this, however, for the next few hundred pages. As Hugh leaves the tomb, a brief Earth tremor collapses and seals it.

Meanwhile, Saltfleet and Arsinal, who know of the legendary power of these stones, arrive determined to regain the Tibetan flint from Drapier at all costs. Saltfleet makes his wishes known to Helga and to Peter Copping, Ingrid's artist fiancé, and finds that Drapier has returned to Devil's Tor once more. Saltfleet finds Drapier there, dead but with the stone clutched in his hand. This stone turns out not to be the Tibetan flint, however, but rather its mate which Drapier had picked up in the tomb beneath Devil's Tor. After several chapters of arguing over which stone belongs to whom, Saltfleet and Arsinal agree to meet Ingrid and Peter Copping on Devil's Tor to rejoin the two stones.

When the meeting takes place, Copping, the sensitive artist, perceives an aura about Ingrid and Saltfleet. Taking this as a premonition of what is to come, he tells Ingrid she belongs not to him but to the Great Mother, and departs. Arsinal, the man of intellect, trained to "construct everything from surfaces," fails to perceive this spiritual light, and when he joins the two halves of the stone he is killed by the massive spiritual forces released. This leaves Ingrid and Saltfleet to be the founders of the new race. Ingrid experiences an overwhelming vision of the creation of life, of the Great Mother as a trinity of anguish, sacrifice, and love, and of the Ancient which exists at a deeper level of reality than even that of the Great Mother. With the joining of the stones, the Ancient once again begins to come into the world. Ingrid and Saltfleet are not to experience human love, but rather a higher agony, and the period of history that they institute will initially be one of discord, death, and madness. Saltfleet experiences similar visions, and at the end of the novel they leave the Tor together, Ingrid telling Saltfleet that she will go to live in the far north.

While these concluding chapters contain visionary passages of startling power and originality, they also emphasize the importance of action in Lindsay's universe. Of the three men who meet with Ingrid before the final apocalypse, it is Saltfleet, the explorer, the man of action, who emerges as the chosen father of the new race. In many ways Saltfleet resembles Maskull of *A Voyage to Arcturus*, and his rough, florid appearance seems to undercut the Nordic mystique that is part of the myth of the Great Mother as described

by Arsinal (Lindsay's attitudes on race are complex and sometimes contradictory, and Arsinal's speeches about the superiority of the Northern races
stand in opposition to notes Lindsay made in preparing the novel, in which
he viciously attacked *any* notions of racial purity). Copping, the artist, is
sensitive to the emanations of the other world, but he is limited in his understanding of this world in the same way that art is limited. Although Copping
is often the spokesman for Lindsay's views on art in the novel, he cannot
achieve the transcendence of feeling that is demanded by a higher order of
existence. Arsinal, the scientist and scholar, achieves intellectual understanding without feeling; his dedication to the surface structures of existence prevents him from perceiving what lies beneath.

Lindsay himself wrote that there appeared to be a number of contradictions
between the philosophy expressed in *Devil's Tor* and that of his earlier novel
A Voyage to Arcturus. Where the earlier work portrayed a never-ending,
cyclic struggle, the later one depicts a millennial new beginning. Where the
earlier work stressed isolation, the later one stresses union. Yet there are as
many similarities as differences. Both works concern a degraded world in
which reality is masked by illusion, and both contain symbolic representations
of this deeper reality: Muspel in *A Voyage to Arcturus* and the Ancient in
Devil's Tor. In many ways, the Demiurge or Eternal Feminine of *Devil's Tor*
fulfills a role similar to that of Crystalman in *A Voyage to Arcturus*, although
such a parallel is called into question by the fact that Lindsay does not treat
the Eternal Feminine with anything approaching the scathing contempt that
he holds for Crystalman in his earlier novel. In many ways, *Devil's Tor* is
more a continuation of the ideas laid out in *A Voyage to Arcturus* than a
recapitulation of them; if the earlier work was Lindsay's Passion play, this is
his Revelation.

Although the failure of *Devil's Tor* effectively ended Lindsay's career as a
writer, and although its length and frequent turgidity often come as a shock
to readers expecting more of the dramatic action and invention of *A Voyage
to Arcturus*, the work deserves a place in the history of modern fantasy as
well as in the history of Lindsay's development as a writer. The work is perhaps
the most thorough treatment of the Great Mother theme in all of modern
imaginative literature, and Lindsay's speculations on the origin, history, and
meaning of this archetype are often remarkably perceptive, presaging in many
ways the later work of depth psychologists and mythologists such as Erich
Neumann and Joseph Campbell. Read in this way—as a work of speculative
philosophy hung upon an almost minimal narrative frame—the novel can be
both stimulating and impressive. Read as a novel of character, even, it offers
more than *A Voyage to Arcturus* simply because of its more realistic setting;
and it is interesting to see how Lindsay integrates his often weighty mythical
notions with more conventional human characters. When approached as pure
story, however—as a tale of adventure and suspense—the novel fails. The

plot barely budges from one spot, the characters talk endlessly, and the action at times seems all but imperceptible. The style, too, is if anything even less felicitous than that of *A Voyage to Arcturus*. For those interested in Lindsay's ideas, or in the myth of the Great Mother, *Devil's Tor* can be a rewarding book; for those seeking anything resembling a traditional fantasy adventure, it may prove almost impenetrable.

Gary K. Wolfe

Bibliography
McClure, J. Derrick. "*Devil's Tor*: A Rehabilitation of David Lindsay's 'Monster,'" in *Extrapolation*. XXI, no. 4 (1980), pp. 367-378.
Pick, J. B., Colin Wilson, and E. H. Visiak. *The Strange Genius of David Lindsay*, 1970.
Sellin, Bernard. *The Life and Works of David Lindsay*, 1981. Translated by Kenneth Gunnell.

THE DILVISH SERIES

Author: Roger Zelazny (1937-   )
First book publications: The Changing Land (1981); *Dilvish the Damned* (1982)
Type of work: Short stories and a novel
Time: Infinity
Locale: A secondary universe

   A lively and essentially lighthearted series of episodes in Dilvish the Damned's quest for revenge

>   *Principal characters:*
>   DILVISH, a half-elf warrior and sorcerer
>   BLACK, a supernatural being who usually takes the form of a horse;
>   Dilvish's companion and steed
>   JELERAK, the mightiest and most evil sorcerer in the world
>   BARAN OF THE THIRD HAND, Jelerak's treacherous assistant
>   QUEEN SEMIRAMA, a long-dead but beautiful woman returned to
>   life by Jelerak
>   ARLETA, a virginal elf maiden

   Readers of *The Changing Land*, a novel by Roger Zelazny published early in 1981, may be excused for being somewhat puzzled: the book's action begins in the middle of a complex situation, racing along with Zelazny's customary brisk assurance. The reader may well wonder who these characters are and what they are doing; in fact, the novel concludes the saga of Dilvish the Damned before one might realize it had begun. This situation arises because the series of stories featuring the exploits of Dilvish had not yet been collected in a book at the time the novel was published; they had appeared in a wide variety of sometimes obscure publications over a wide span of years.
   Dilvish first appeared in "Passage to Dilfar" (*Fantastic*, February, 1965), and that story was soon followed by "Thelinde's Song" (*Fantastic*, June, 1965) and "The Bells of Shroedan" (*Fantastic*, March, 1966). At that point, outside factors intervened, as Cele Goldsmith was fired as editor of *Fantastic*. Goldsmith had been the first editor to encourage Zelazny and to buy his stories; Zelazny vowed to submit no more stories to *Fantastic* (or its sister magazine *Amazing*) while they were under their current ownership, although he realized the unlikelihood of another magazine taking up a series that had just been begun by a competitor. Consequently, after sending one last Dilvish story to a fanzine ("A Knight for Merytha" in *Kallikanzaros* #2, September, 1967), Zelazny turned to other projects. Dilvish, however, remained alive in the back of his mind, and from time to time he toyed with the idea of writing more stories; according to Lin Carter's *Imaginary Worlds* (1973), Zelazny conceived of writing enough Dilvish stories to make a book, *Nine Black Doves*.
   Zelazny actually returned to writing about Dilvish after a decade and a

half, however, when a semiprofessional magazine bought reprint rights to "A Knight for Merytha" and asked for another story. He wrote "A City Divided" (published in 1982 in *Eternity*). Then he wrote a story to connect "A City Divided" to Dilvish's earlier adventures ("The Places of Aache" in Roy Torgeson's anthology *Other Worlds 2*, 1980). He planned to conclude the short stories with a novella and wrote a brief story as a preface ("The White Beast" in *Whispers*, October, 1979), then the novella itself ("Tower of Ice" in Lin Carter's *Flashing Swords! #5*). Still later, however, he wrote two more Dilvish stories ("Garden of Blood" in *Sorcerer's Apprentice*, Summer, 1979, and "Devil and the Dancer," published in Torgeson's *Other Worlds*). Finally, he wrote the novel *The Changing Land*, using his ideas for *Nine Black Doves* as they had matured over the years; Ballantine published the novel in April of 1981, before several of the other stories were published. All the stories appear in the collection *Dilvish the Damned*, published in 1982. Their proper order, according to Zelazny, is as follows: "Passage to Dilfar," "Thelinde's Song," "The Bells of Shoredan," "A Knight for Merytha," "The Places of Aache," "A City Divided," "The White Beast," "Tower of Ice," "Garden of Blood," "Devil and the Dancer," "Dilvish the Damned," and *The Changing Land*.

The actual story of Dilvish is much less complicated than the history of the writing and publishing of stories about him. Initially, Dilvish interrupts the sorcerer Jelerak in a magical ceremony. In a fit of rage increased by Dilvish's physical resemblance to a hero who outshone Jelerak in several areas, Jelerak turns Dilvish's body into a statue and sends his soul to hell. After two centuries of torment, Dilvish escapes. Accompanied by Black, a being of supernatural powers and sardonic temper, Dilvish learns the Awful Sayings, incantations that produce unstoppable destruction, and returns for revenge. The stories show him taking care of obligations in familiar territory, then riding off in search of Jelerak. Finally, in *The Changing Land*, he penetrates Jelerak's mightiest stronghold and sees justice done—although not as he has planned.

The series has a very loose framework, capable of accommodating any number or type of adventures the author chooses. As he journeys along the road, Dilvish encounters such characters as a vampire, a werewolf, an elder god, or any other magical phenomenon that strikes the author's fancy. In fact, Zelazny acknowledges in a letter that he began the series with the idea of keeping it open-ended, so he could turn to it whenever he needed to write a story that would sell. The first stories in the series have the feel of being separate incidents, connected only by the presence of Dilvish and Black. It is only later that it is clear that the stories are written as part of a structure, so that they fit together and support one another. Even as the series draws to a close in *The Changing Land*, however, there is little of the intensity that makes some of Zelazny's other fantasy novels so impressive.

Nevertheless, the series as a whole and the novel in particular do provide some real pleasures. One such pleasure is Zelazny's writing. Almost from the beginning of his career, the author has shown a remarkably effective prose style. Its major quality is deceptive simplicity, relying on what looks like the flattest of statements that manage to suggest more color and motion than the florid strainings of some other fantasy writers. This quality can be seen in the following descriptive passage from *The Changing Land*:

> At that moment, a sound like laughter came out of the moaning of the wind. Lifting her eyes, Arleta beheld an enormous face formed out of a vortex of sand which had risen before her shelter. Its huge, hollow mouth was swirled in the form of a grin. Behind its eyeholes was a dark emptiness.

This passage displays the qualities of understatement and suggestion already mentioned, it is plain, with little imagery. Over the years, more confident in his skills, Zelazny has honed his talent for making direct statements that indicate a wealth of menace or delight. A reader may not be consciously aware of this stylistic development while reading the Dilvish series, but it is present and does help Zelazny achieve some stunning, unexpected effects.

Another of the series' pleasures is its humor. Virtually all of Zelazny's work is laced with humor, as he reverses direction suddenly, undercutting some apparently cherished principles with pratfalls. Zelazny believes in undercutting any system of belief that takes itself too seriously and claims to understand and control too much of life. In *The Changing Land*, for example, he offers an extremely ornate explanation of the nature of "The Castle Timeless," Jelerak's citadel, making the description even more imposing by using one immense, paragraph-long sentence. The next paragraph begins "This, of course, was all wrong, according to more practical-minded theorists." Humor may, in fact, be a basic part of Zelazny's purpose in all his work by showing how frequently reversals of situation and attitude can take place and how foolish it is to cling to one position.

Especially in the more recent episodes of the Dilvish series, humor is apparent in unexpectedly comic scenes and speeches. In the later stories, for example, the dialogue between Dilvish and Black relies less heavily on grim determination than on tongue-in-cheek posturing, put-ons, put-downs, and general straightfaced kidding. Zelazny delights in deflating emotion, often shattering the intensely serious mood of most sword-and-sorcery fiction with irrevernt anachronisms. For example, when two sorcerers are exchanging information by way of magic crystals, one suddenly exclaims: "The ether has ears as well as other appendages, I sometimes think. Let me take this on my other crystal." In another especially intense scene, Jelerak prepares to sacrifice Arleta to the elder god Tualua; with careful detail, Zelazny describes the helpless, seminude girl, the dark chamber, and the vermin swarming nearby. Then an intruder enters:

> "There you are, Jelerak, as I should have guessed I'd find you—surrounded by toads,

> bats, snakes, spiders, rats and noxious fumes ... about to tear out a girl's heart!"
> Jelerak lowered the blade.
> "These are a few of my favorite things," he said, smiling.

There is something immensely appealing about a villain who can quote saccharine lyrics from Howard Lindsay's and Russell Crouse's *The Sound of Music* (1960). In general, Jelerak is a disconcertingly humorous villain. After first trying to persuade Arleta to accompany him to the sacrifice voluntarily, he puts her in a trance, commenting, "So much for democracy." Thus humor complicates the reader's reaction to Jelerak and prepares for the book's outcome.

It is fitting that Jelerak's doom is not at Dilvish's hand, even though this frustrates Dilvish's desire for personal revenge. Life is never that straightforward, Zelazny believes. Moreover, such a conclusion is in line with the novel's swirl of plot and counterplot, reversal, and betrayals. In fact, although it may be camouflaging an emotional emptiness at its core, still another trademark of *The Changing Land* is its extreme liveliness. Clearly, as already noted, the novel is more than single- (and simple-) minded sword-and-sorcery fiction. In addition, Zelazny enjoys tossing in references to other works of fantasy. The major source is the fiction of William Hope Hodgson, to whom *The Changing Land* is dedicated. In particular, a troop of the swine creatures from Hodgson's *The House on the Borderland* (1908) prowl the dungeons beneath Castle Timeless, and the castle itself is a largely benign version of the doom-haunted structure in Hodgson's novel. For that matter, Zelazny uses the name Hodgson for one of the sorcerers who finally breaks the spell that holds the castle fixed at one place in time. In addition, the tentacled, whistling elder god Tualua has a strong resemblance to H. P. Lovecraft's pantheon of horrors.

All this is another element in an already formidably complicated structure. As noted earlier, the Dilvish series has a fundamentally loose plot; it can last as long as Zelazny continues to write the stories. After all, Jelerak could have any number of citadels, and there could be any number of strange beings waiting along the road for a traveler to encounter. There really is no special reason for the series to end when and how it does. Zelazny creates a sense of conclusion, however, by building a complex plot, as frantic activity builds to a peak and Castle Timeless is torn loose from its place in time and goes careening past the end of the universe and back, shedding and adding rooms as it goes. When it stops, the reader feels that since so much has happened, the story must be over. Zelazny will continue to write the Dilvish series; it is difficult to believe that Zelazny feels deep personal involvement with Dilvish, but it is also hard to believe that he has not had fun writing the stories. Without being at all profound, they do provide enjoyable, brain-teasing amusement.

Joe Sanders

Bibliography

Sanders, Joseph L. *Roger Zelazny: A Primary and Secondary Bibliography*, 1980.

_____ . "Zelazny: Unfinished Business," in *Voices for the Future: Essays on Major Science Fiction Writers, Vol. II*, 1979. Edited by Thomas Clareson.

Yoke, Carl. *Roger Zelazny*, 1979.

Zelazny, Roger. "Introduction to 'The Bells of Shoredan,'" in *Alternities*. Summer, 1981, p. 4.

DOC SAVAGE SERIES

Author: Kenneth Robeson (Lester Dent, 1904-1959)
First publications: 1933-1949 (more than 180 tales appearing in the *Doc Savage* magazine)
Type of work: Novels
Time: After World War I
Locale: New York City and various worldwide locations

Doc Savage and his five associates are lovers of adventure who are pitted against a never-ending series of master-criminals and their henchmen; when possible, they reclaim the villains for society rather than acting as self-appointed executioners

Principal characters:
  CLARK SAVAGE, JR. ("DOC"), trained by his father to develop all
    his mental and physical potential
  WILLIAM HARPER LITTLEJOHN ("JOHNNY"), an archaeologist
  COLONEL JOHN RENWICK ("RENNY"), an enormous engineer
  LIEUTENANT COLONEL ANDREW BLODGETT MAYFAIR ("MONK"),
    a homely chemist
  MAJOR THOMAS J. ROBERTS ("LONG TOM"), an electrical wizard
  BRIGADIER GENERAL THEODORE MARLEY BROOKS ("HAM"), a
    well-dressed Harvard lawyer with a sword cane
  PATRICIA SAVAGE ("PAT"), Doc's cousin, who frequently insists on
    being included in the adventures
  HABEAS CORPUS, Monk's pet pig
  CHEMISTRY, Ham's pet primate, a "monkey" of some sort

Beginning in 1933, in the midst of the Depression, the *Doc Savage* magazine filled a bleak time for many readers by providing a hero who was exceptional because of training from childhood and faithful adherence to the pattern set down for him by an extremely providential father. Not only does Doc follow his father to specialize in the field of medicine, but he also is more skilled than are his five associates in each of their specialties. Doc's father also left a legacy of enormous wealth for his use in putting a stop to evil plots. Doc is kind to the common man and has a sense of humor, appreciating the jokes that Monk and Ham love to play on each other, even to the point of tolerating their pets and finding them useful additions in solving many mysteries. Doc also makes use of an unlimited supply of wonderful gadgets developed from the very latest modern scientific research. The fantasy of having a new invention handy to solve the next crisis is one probably not so delightfully handled again until Ian Fleming's James Bond books. Doc has inventions ready to be used in each new adventure.

All of the characters, good and evil, are flat. Even though the identity of the leader of the villains is usually kept secret until the last chapter, the underlings who try to carry out the plots against Doc and his men are identified, and as a group, they are usually lower-class hirelings who exhibit such traits as low cunning, greed, cowardliness, and braggadocio. The leader is usually intelligent but unscrupulous and presents a sufficient challenge to test Doc's mettle. The characters of Doc and his men are so fixed that the descriptions of them are repeated verbatim, at length, from novel to novel. A reader new to the series is given knowledge of their skills and idiosyncrasies within the first few pages of each work and therefore may enjoy books quite late in the series without being disoriented by lack of knowledge of the earlier adventures.

The treatment of sex in the series follows a curious evasive pattern. Again and again, Doc encounters a beautiful young woman who might provide love interest but does not; usually there is a father or father figure with her. In *The Man of Bronze* (1933), Monja is the daughter of the Mayan leader, King Chaac, who will deliver the gold as Doc needs it; they are in danger from the warrior sect. In *Brand of the Werewolf*, Cere Oveja and her father are in danger from El Rabanos; their problem is compounded by her father's greed. India Allison is secretary to Lieber Von Zidney in *The Terror in the Navy*; Braun almost manages to make them seem the enemy whom Doc and his men must foil. In each instance, Doc must be stirred by the girl but must remain aloof in order to carry out his life's mission. Although the women all cling to him, Cere manages to kiss him on the lips. "The Señorita Oveja's lips were entirely delicious, Doc decided." This scene is probably one of the most passionate in the entire series.

Pat Savage is not the clinging woman even though she too is beautiful. Rescued from the gang who had murdered her father, Alex Savage, in *Brand of the Werewolf*, she is spunky and independent from the first. In later stories, such as *The Terror in the Navy*, she is both a resourceful companion and the butt of male-chauvinist humor. She flies her own plane, hears Doc's message in Mayan when Renny misses it, and is captured and taken aboard the submarine along with all the rest of Doc's assistants. She also fails to take the antidote to the laughing gas through her own stubbornness and appears very foolish when she is the only one of the group unable to control her laughing spasms. The gas, intended to reveal the hiding place of possible saboteurs, catches Pat as well.

The locations of these three adventures are typical of the variety in the series. Much of *The Man of Bronze* takes place in New York and later finishes in a hidden valley in Central America in which a remnant of the ancient Mayas still live, undiscovered even by the government of Hidalgo, the country in which it is located; the prize there is the Mayan gold supply. *Brand of the Werewolf* takes place in the Canadian wilderness near a large body of water through which an ancient Spanish galleon had tried to find the Northwest Passage; the prize is the ship's treasure. *The Terror in the Navy* (1937) is located around New York and the Connecticut seacoast; the United States government might have to pay a ransom. Lakehurst, the naval air station, and the destruction of an American dirigible, which halted the development of lighter-than-air flying ships, provides a timely reference: the German Zeppelin *Hindenburg* was destroyed at Lakehurst in 1937, and emphasis did shift to development of heavy air transport. Doc is skilled in taking the benefits of technology into remote areas; he and his associates each carry very compact kits in their specialties. Monk can produce an adequate chemical laboratory in the wilds of Canada, and Ham can write a message with ultraviolet chalk on the side of Habeas Corpus. Off the coast of Connecticut, Long Tom has a device to X-ray the mysterious box in their seaplane.

Doc Savage and his associates love the excitement of a good fight, but they abhor needless death. They are also skilled in combat, having been together in the war, but the development of most of the technology of mercy comes after they have the Mayan funding on which to draw. Late in the series, they use machine guns which shoot mercy bullets, a sleeping gas which immobilizes for two hours those who breathe it but which dissipates within a minute, so that Doc and his associates are able to hold their breath until their enemies are unconscious; they can also use their knowledge of anatomy to manipulate certain points in the neck to induce and later to remove paralysis. Doc also develops an institution to rehabilitate prisoners, where surgery, psychology, and retraining prepare them to become useful members of society.

In 1975, a film was released based on the first novel in the series, *The Man of Bronze*; the plot line is the same. Some changes are incorporated from later in the series. The main villain is no longer Don Rubio Gorro, who has become one of the hirelings, but the wealthy and still avaricious Captain Seas. The main villain is destroyed in the novel, but in the movie, he is rehabilitated to such an extent that he is last seen working for the Salvation Army. The method of death is changed from something brought into the hidden valley to an old Mayan secret which has fallen into the wrong hands: it is very much like the electrically charged vapor in *The Land of Terror* (1933). The film includes several other interesting plot elements not found in the original series: Monja is a working girl, employed in Don Rubio Gorro's office in the capital city of Hidalgo; she acts as Doc's guide to the lost valley. Don Rubio is a comically grotesque villain who sleeps in an enormous crib. Doc's single combat with Captain Seas adds immediacy to the demonstration of Doc's universal superiority and is true to the spirit of the series.

Elizabeth Sikes Davidson

Bibliography
Farmer, Philip José. *Doc Savage: His Apocalyptic Life*, 1975.
Weinberg, Robert, ed. *The Man Behind Doc Savage: A Tribute to Lester Dent*, 1974.

DRACULA

Author: Bram Stoker (1847-1912)
First book publication: 1897
Type of work: Novel
Time: The 1890's
Locale: Transylvania and England (mainly Whitby and London)

The most famous and influential of all vampire novels

> *Principal characters:*
> COUNT DRACULA, a Transylvanian landowner who decides to move
> to England
> JONATHAN HARKER, a solicitor's clerk sent to Transylvania to expe-
> dite the Count's plans
> MINA MURRAY, Harker's fiancée, later his wife
> DR. JOHN SEWARD, the owner of a lunatic asylum situated next to
> the Count's London *pied-à-terre*
> ARTHUR HOLMWOOD, later Lord Godalming, a friend of Seward
> LUCY WESTENRA, Holmwood's fiancée, a friend of Mina
> QUINCEY P. MORRIS, an American gentleman, a friend of Seward
> ABRAHAM VAN HELSING, the Amsterdam occultist summoned by
> Seward
> RENFIELD, a zoophagous resident in Seward's asylum

Although the name of Dracula is almost as well-known as Sigmund Freud's, most people know of the vampire Count only at secondhand. The novel, however, is more powerful than most of its derivatives. It is interestingly constructed, has considerable narrative strength, and incorporates a number of grisly scenes which, despite doses of melodrama and gore, operate on more than one level.

Bram Stoker was Irish, born in Dublin in 1847. *Dracula* contains echoes of works by Stoker's near-contemporary, another Dubliner, Joseph Sheridan Le Fanu, especially Le Fanu's superb vampire short story, "Carmilla." Although Le Fanu is the better writer, Stoker incorporates many of Le Fanu's techniques, such as able construction, ingenuity of plot, and a relish for the supernatural.

Like Le Fanu, Stoker attended Trinity College, Dublin, and, after a spell in the civil service, he became associated with the great actor Henry Irving. In 1878, the year that Irving took over the Lyceum Theatre in London, Stoker accepted the exacting position of manager. (Also in 1878, Stoker married Florence Balcombe, who bore him one son, Noel.) Stoker arranged all of Irving's tours and many other commitments, remaining a faithful lieutenant until Irving died after a performance in Bradford in 1905. During this long period, the large, amiable, red-haired Irishman traveled the world with Irving and produced a number of ephemeral novels; of these, only *Dracula* has remained.

One of Irving's most memorable performances was a weird and chilling impersonation of Mephistopheles in a version of *Faust* (1885-1887); Irving's Mephistopheles lives on in the theatrical character of Stoker's Count. Speculation suggests that Ellen Terry is personified, to some extent, in the characters of the two young women who fall victim to Dracula, Mina Murray and Lucy Westenra. This beautiful and famous actress was long associated with Irving, whom she joined at the Lyceum to play Ophelia opposite his Hamlet in 1878, the same eventful year that Stoker arrived. The beauty of Mina and Lucy and their clandestine intimacy with a powerful character that all but overwhelms the socially sanctioned relationships with their fiancés may be traced to the delectable Terry, who reportedly became Stoker's friend for life. Guesswork is prompted by the macabre relationships in the novel; these seem to determine the plot, rather than the other way around, as might be expected in a work designed merely to be sensational.

The opening chapters of *Dracula* are vividly memorable. They constitute Jonathan Harker's journalistic account of his difficulties with language and travel as he crosses Europe *en route* to the much-disputed territory of Transylvania, a mountainous region of Rumania. Here, in a land once ruled by the Turks, the Draculas have their castle. The coach drops Jonathan at Borgo Pass as daylight fades, and the locals cross themselves; once he transfers into Dracula's calèche, Jonathan will have moved into the region of Death. The symbolism of these passages is highly effective. Dracula's castle proves to be the epitome of all Gothic piles: "a vast ruined castle, from whose tall black windows came no ray of light, and whose broken battlements showed a jagged line against the moonlit sky." Thus the evil fairy tale begins.

Dracula greets Jonathan. His mouth is "fixed and rather cruel-looking, with peculiarly sharp white teeth"; he is extremely pale and has coarse hands, rank breath, and hairs on his palms. Then follow scenes with which most readers are familiar, if only through cinematic versions of the novel. Dracula does not eat or drink; he is absent by day; he casts no reflection in Jonathan's shaving mirror; most alarming of all, he climbs out his window at night and moves down the sheer façade like a lizard. Jonathan finds himself a prisoner in the castle. He is exploring a forbidden wing when three women materialize in the moonlight (one is reminded of Henry Fuseli's striking pen drawing of the three witches in *Macbeth*, a play which Irving revived in 1888). They make a lascivious approach to Jonathan, but Dracula appears and disperses them. Later, Jonathan finds that the evil Count is plotting his death.

The stage is thus dramatically set for a thriller which makes sense only in sexual terms. One of Dracula's most persuasive critics, Maurice Richardson, quotes Freud's dictum, "Morbid dread always signifies repressed sexual wishes." *Dracula* is an anthology of these wishes.

Nothing in the rest of the book entirely lives up to the curtain-raiser in Transylvania. Indeed, the Count makes only rare appearances on stage, although he remains an effectively threatening presence in the wings. The bulk of the novel belongs to Lucy and Mina and their mysterious ailments. Mina Murray is engaged to Jonathan; her friend Lucy Westenra is engaged to Arthur Holmwood, who becomes Lord Godalming at his father's death. Arthur is a friend of Dr. John Seward, who, at the age of twenty-nine, owns a lunatic asylum. (The asylum stands next to Carfax, a large house with grounds which Dracula has bought—it was in part to conduct these property negotiations that Mr. Hawkins, the solicitor, sent out his clerk, Jonathan, to Transylvania.) In this asylum is confined a fly-eating zoophagous lunatic named Renfield. Arthur, Seward, and his American friend Quincey P. Morris all propose to Lucy on the same day; she accepts Arthur. This is another of the strange triangular situations which emerge throughout the book.

Mina and Lucy then go to Whitby, a small port on the East Coast; they are in Whitby when Dracula's dead ship arrives with a freight of fifty huge boxes of consecrated earth. Transylvania, for reasons best known to the Count and his entourage, has become depopulated; Dracula's plan is to install himself in London, where there is a vast reservoir of people from which to draw. His first victim on shore is Lucy (he bestows his evil attentions only on women). Everyone is mystified by dear Lucy's neurasthenic illness, and Seward eventually summons Abraham van Helsing from Amsterdam.

Van Helsing bears Stoker's baptismal name; he is to play the role of the good father figure against Dracula's bad father figure in the psychic drama that follows. When Stoker was writing his novel, the stories of Sir Arthur Conan Doyle's great detective, Sherlock Holmes, were being published. Like Holmes, van Helsing baffles everyone with his superior knowledge. He is a lawyer as well as a doctor and anthropologist and is thus well equipped to recite vampire lore.

"My God, this is dreadful!" van Helsing exclaims, examining his fair patient and the marks on her throat. He eventually gives the weakened Lucy three blood transfusions—from Arthur, John, and himself—in a kind of mystical marriage. The blood, of course, pours through her veins into Dracula's. Despite the transfusions and the garlic flowers, Lucy dies later in lust and frustration, and van Helsing, not the most tactful of men, declares that "this so sweet maid is a polyandrist."

Later, in order to stop Lucy's vampire activities, the men go to her tomb and open the coffin. There lies the beautiful body, which van Helsing now examines; the white teeth are even sharper than at the time of her death. The others feel the sexual attraction of the corpse; as John Seward reports, "She was, if possible, more radiantly beautiful than ever." The next time they visit her, however, after Lucy's shade has been molesting small children, Seward shudders at "the whole carnal and unspiritual appearance" of the corpse. After van Helsing mutters a few religious words, Arthur proceeds to destroy the corpse. Just as Dracula's existence is a travesty of life and van

Helsing's ritual is a travesty of Christian tradition, so the killing of the "un-dead" woman is a travesty of sexual intercourse. This pornographic element must have done much for *Dracula*'s early popularity. Read today, nearly a century later, the novel can be appreciated as a compendium of the sexual fears which might have beset a respectable bourgeois Victorian household.

After Lucy's true death, the focus turns to Mina, who is exhibiting lassitude. Nobody can guess why, just as, for purposes of the plot, John Seward cannot deduce that Dracula has taken up residence next door to his asylum, despite continual promptings from Renfield, the resident lunatic. Now that Mina is threatened, the young men cluster about her, but they are all so noble and good that they cannot accept van Helsing's hints about the un-dead's love that dares not speak its name. While everyone is considerably perplexed, Dracula is also shown to be in a dilemma. He can do many things: he has power, even power over nature; he is, in a sense, immortal; he can come and go as he pleases and see in the dark. Yet his power ceases with the coming of day, and, while he can enslave others, he is himself a slave.

The men continue their investigations, from which they exclude Mina on the grounds of her female sensibility, although she proves courageous and shrewd. By now, although she shows all the stigmata of vampire attack, her faithful Jonathan is blind to the visits of her nocturnal lover. He, with the others, tracks down twenty-nine of the fifty earth-boxes, and the Count's methodical plans for the invasion of London are revealed. Despite the creaking implausibility of the story, the atmosphere of evil is somehow sustained.

Meanwhile, Renfield, the well-bred lunatic, is visited by Mina and then by the Count, with whom he wrestles with fatal results; he is found in a pool of blood. Having ignored Renfield's earlier warnings, the others now rush to Jonathan's room and break in to discover Mina with the Count and Jonathan lying in a stupor nearby. Dracula, in a fury, springs at the intruders, but they beat him back with crucifixes, and he disappears in a vapor. Mina admits to her rescuers that when Dracula approached, she "did not want to hinder him." Her story reads like vivid sexual fantasy, which it is, and she cries out that she is unclean and will not let Jonathan touch her when he awakens. (Chapters later, she is still crying that she is unclean and has the Burial Service for the Dead read over her.)

After the confrontation in Jonathan and Mina's room, Dracula escapes on a sailing ship bound for Turkey, home of the ancient enemy of his line, taking with him the last earth-box; the men follow with Mina. Finally, while the men go one way after Dracula, van Helsing rides with Mina to the castle in the Carpathians. She becomes suspiciously bright-eyed, and the three weird sisters materialize again, but the resourceful van Helsing dispatches them. In the climactic scene involving all the characters, who have converged on the horse-drawn wagon carrying Dracula in his earth-box, the Count is finally destroyed; "almost in the drawing of a breath, the whole body crumbled into dust." Jonathan and Mina survive to have a son and later actually take a holiday in Transylvania.

Despite annoyances of style and lurchings of plot, *Dracula* remains a compelling tale. As an anonymous critic writing in the 1966 *Times Literary Supplement* put it, "Stoker gave shape to a myth, and that is more than many more important writers can claim in a whole career devoted to the life of art." The same might be said of Mary Shelley's *Frankenstein* (1818); like *Frankenstein*, *Dracula* is considerably more complex than its many cinematic versions or its imitations. *Dracula*'s mysterious relationship with *Frankenstein* was noticed from the first. Stoker's formidable mother, Charlotte, wrote to him when his novel first appeared, "No book since Mary Shelley's 'Frankenstein' or indeed any other at all has come near yours in originality, or terror— Poe is nowhere."

For many years, the 1931 film versions of *Dracula* and *Frankenstein* customarily played together, with Bela Lugosi and Boris Karloff respectively in the leading roles. There is no doubt which is the better book, but both concern that fascinating area, the division between living and nonliving, between human and creature. Both rely for effect on a feeling for Christian doctrine, which is then set on end. Both have ineffectual heroes (if Jonathan Harker can even be styled a hero); the great attraction in both is a fiend whose hand is set against humanity. The difference between the two novels is that one can feel compassion for Victor Frankenstein's monster, while with Dracula, no such pity is possible.

Although Bram Stoker can never be regarded as a writer of first or even second rank, in Dracula he created a legendary monster which, despite van Helsing's savage ministrations, has risen from the pages of his book and seems destined for the immortality it fought so resourcefully to attain.

Brian W. Aldiss

Bibliography

Cawelti, John G. *Adventure, Mystery, and Romance: Formula Stories as Art and Popular Culture*, 1976.

Farson, Daniel. *The Man Who Wrote Dracula: A Biography of Bram Stoker*, 1975.

Ludlam, Harry. *A Biography of Dracula: The Life Story of Bram Stoker*, 1962.

McNally, Raymond, and Radu Florescu, eds. *The Essential Dracula: A Completely Illustrated and Annotated Edition of Bram Stoker's Classic Novel*, 1979.

Richardson, Maurice. "The Vampire Psychoanalyzed," in *The Observer*. December 22, 1957.

Twitchell, James B. *The Living Dead: A Study of the Vampire in Romantic Literature*, 1981.
Wolf, Leonard, ed. *The Annotated Dracula*, 1975.

THE DRACULA TAPE SERIES

Author: Fred Saberhagen (1930-   )
First book publications: The Dracula Tape (1975); *The Holmes-Dracula File* (1978);
  An Old Friend of the Family (1979); *Thorn* (1980); *Dominion* (1982)
Type of work: Novels
Time: The late nineteenth to the late twentieth century
Locale: Transylvania, England, and the United States

*A series of novels in which Count Dracula tells the "true" story of his career from
the time of Bram Stoker's novel to the late twentieth century*

Fred Saberhagen's series of novels featuring the familiar prince of vampires, Count Dracula, is a sequel to Bram Stoker's original *Dracula* (1897) with some fundamental modifications. Dracula is effectively rehabilitated in these novels from villain to hero and protector. Rather than humanizing the Count, Saberhagen turns him into a superhero with an old-world pedigree and manners to match. The result is melodramatic action with a modern flavor revolving around the demythologized Count, a heroic type of the old school.

The four novels of the series cover a century, beginning with the events recounted in Stoker's novel. In theory, the series could go on indefinitely. The critical reader will therefore approach these adventures of Dracula as a serial publication in the popular tradition of *The Seven-Per-Cent Solution* (1974). Saberhagen's Dracula revival is generally more successful than the numerous Sherlock Holmes sequels of the 1970's but perhaps not as good as the Flashman novels of George MacDonald Frazer.

The series begins with *The Dracula Tape*, in which the Count delivers his rebuttal to the characterization of his behavior recorded in the diaries and letters of Jonathan and Mina Harker and Dr. John Seward. The reader's enjoyment of *The Dracula Tape* will be greatly enhanced if he reads with a copy of Bram Stoker's *Dracula* open beside him. Saberhagen's modernist reinterpretation of Stoker's horror classic depends on a studied, anachronistic presentation of the Count, for beneath the fifteenth century aristocratic manners and the acquired speech patterns of the late Victorian Englishman, Saberhagen's Dracula has been given the mental outlook of a late twentieth century rationalist, with allowances for a certain preference for traditional modes of religious practice. (Indeed, one wonders whether Saberhagen's Count may not have fathered Anne Rice's Louis of *Interview with the Vampire*, 1976.) The effect of Dracula's revisions is the predictable demythologization of the legend but not of the character. Rather, Saberhagen offers contemporary readers a substitute for the mythology he chooses to have the Count systematically debunk.

The primary fantastic element of these novels is the acceptance of the imaginary world of Stoker's *Dracula* as though it were real. The Count insists in *The Dracula Tape* that he will set the record straight with an account of what really happened in 1887 Transylvania and England. The Count's rebuttal demythologizes the Stoker legend and then remythologizes true vampirism. Saberhagen's intention is to treat Dracula as a new type of superhero, a combination of the Byronic hero and Captain Marvel. Indeed, such combinations of adult and adolescent wonders and horrors are woven skillfully throughout the series.

Dracula is prepared to reveal much about his nature, his personal history, and his character in the course of his critique of the distorted accounts of 1887. Vampires, the reader learns, do not breathe and refer to humans as "breathers." Vampires can be created by other vampires through exchange of blood, but this process usually takes time and is rarely the result of a single encounter. Although vampires need blood for sustenance and strength, their life energies are supposed to come from unknown cosmic rays from the sun. Too much sun is, of course, debilitating to vampires and can even be fatal. Dracula insists that vampires ordinarily do not prey on humans; they feed on the blood of other mammals. Human blood is taken or exchanged for sexual reasons only. Only perverted or evil vampires prey on humans. Dracula's preference for young women as victims is thereby explained. He insists that he does not kill his victim-lovers. Lucy Westenra was actually killed by the crude medical methods of Van Helsing and Seward, who did not realize that blood transfusions could be dangerous or fatal among incompatible types. Dracula's action of making her a vampire, therefore, is seen as the Count's attempt to save the fearful Lucy from untimely death.

In the account of Saberhagen's Dracula, Mina Harker fears that she will be killed by her protectors to prevent her from becoming a vampire after she and Dracula become lovers. In self-defense and at the Count's suggestion, therefore, Mina writes a fictitious journal intended to convince her protectors that she is the innocent victim of the Count's mad attacks. *The Dracula Tape* presents Van Helsing as a religious fanatic and Mina's other male protectors as well-intentioned dupes. Mina's true enemy, according to Dracula, was the madman Renfield, who expected the Count to give Mina to him; when that design was frustrated by the Count's scornful rejection, Renfield vowed to rape and kill her. Dracula killed Renfield in self-defense, and most of the other killings for which he is responsible are similarly motivated. Occasionally, though, Dracula simply executes justice on malefactors who, the reader is assured, deserve their fate. Perhaps this decisiveness is another feature of the Count's appeal for the contemporary reader.

Dracula rejects the idea that Van Helsing's vampire banes had any effect on him; most of them are superstitious folly, according to the Count, and the use of crosses and consecrated hosts borders upon blasphemy. As a good Christian, of course, the Count has no use for even the suggestion of blasphemy. It seems that the Count was born into the Eastern Orthodox Church but converted to Catholicism (more for political than theological reasons) as a young man. Vampires do walk about in daylight when necessary, but prefer to sleep until night. Only young or weakened vampires are likely to die of exposure. It is true that vampires must sleep on their own earth if they are to have proper rest. Wood is harmful to them but running water, apparently, is not. Other conventions of fictional vampirism honored are the requirement that a vampire must be invited to enter a dwelling before he can pass inside and the fact that mirrors do not reflect the vampire image. Most cameras, however, can record their presence, although the Count objects to photographs. While vampires have superhuman recuperative powers, a good staking or a beheading will destroy them.

Dracula's powers are the key both to his personality and to his appeal. They are godlike and include immunity from natural death, hyperacute senses, the ability to change shape, superhuman strength and speed, and the ability to fly. Dracula also has the power to communicate with animals, to hypnotize, and to control weather. Dracula's adventures in the series are designed to display and sometimes to test these various powers for the reader's awe and delight. The rehabilitated Count, wise with the wisdom of centuries and a superior intellect, turns out to be one who must live alienated in a world populated with inferior beings who seek to destroy him out of ignorance and unreasoning fear.

Saberhagen's tale discards the allegorical dimensions of Stoker's novel, possessing none of the spiritual or psychological dimensions of the latter. Also lost is the folklore and mythology of vampirism, sacrificed to the method of rational fantasy. Instead, Saberhagen presents a vampire scaled down and rationalized enough to fit into the modern world.

The second novel of the series, *The Holmes-Dracula File*, follows up the successes of the first venture with some important similarities and some equally important differences. The novel is set in Victorian London, ten years later. Mina lives nearby in Exeter with her husband Jonathan and remains Dracula's lover, although the affair is not obvious in the story. The rationalizing tendencies of the first novel are largely transferred to Sherlock Holmes. The genre of *The Holmes-Dracula File* is the mystery-adventure melodrama, a form popularized by Arthur Conan Doyle and a close relation to Stoker's Gothic horror story. In addition, the second novel also operates within a fictional world compatible with the earlier one but one less morbid and more melodramatic. The overall effect is even better than that of Saberhagen's first effort.

Holmes and Watson are introduced with both tact and skill. Saberhagen's re-creations of the great detective and his companion are entirely believable and consistent with the originals. Their appearance is unforced and their eventual confrontations with Dracula are entirely within the scope of both characters and their preceding adventures. This is not to say that Saberhagen does not allow himself some liberties (particularly in the portrayal of Holmes), but with one very important exception, they are liberties invited by Doyle himself.

The premise of *The Holmes-Dracula File* lies in the Doyle story "The Adventure of the Sussex Vampire." Early in that tale, the giant rat of Sumatra is mentioned as the key to a "story for which the world is not yet prepared," according to Holmes. Doyle never wrote that story, but Saberhagen has: the novel is supposed to be the file kept by Watson on the adventure of the giant rat. The chief liberty taken by Saberhagen in connecting his Dracula with Holmes is to change the great detective from someone who would say that "the idea of a vampire was to me absurd" (in "The Adventure of the Sussex Vampire") to a man who has reason to believe in and dread vampires.

Saberhagen accounts for Holmes's willingness to believe in vampires as the result of an unhappy childhood, the consequence of his mother's notorious infidelities and premature death. Holmes, the reader is told, has always suspected that he is the child of one of his mother's Continental affairs. His remarkable similarity in appearance to Dracula suggests that the Count himself may have been his father. Dracula denies this possibility, since he was in another part of Europe at the time Holmes's mother was in Paris. The Count realizes, however, that his brother Radu, who was in Paris at the right time, may very well have been Holmes's progenitor, a speculation he does not mention because he fears Holmes's reaction might be harmful.

The Holmes-Dracula File is composed of two plot lines, and the narrative is presented from alternating viewpoints, first that of the Count and then that of Dr. Watson. (The technique was so successful that Saberhagen adopted it for the next two novels in the series.) Dracula's part in the affair of the giant rat of Sumatra begins in the Limehouse district of London near the East India dock. Dracula is shanghaied by agents of Dr. David Fitzroy for experimental purposes. Hit over the head in a strategic spot with a wooden club, the Count awakens a prisoner in a private clinic, suffering from amnesia. It is not until the end of the fifth chapter that he remembers his true identity and fully realizes the nature and extent of his powers. Meanwhile, he has escaped from the clinic the same way Edmond Dantes escaped the Château D'If. In the process, the Count attacks Frau Grafenstein, one of his cruel and odious keepers at the clinic, and drains her of blood.

It is this killing, justified by Frau Grafenstein's crimes and the Count's need to defend himself, that puts Holmes on the trail of a possible vampire loose in London. Meanwhile, Miss Sarah Tarlton appeals to the great detective to investigate the disappearance of her intended husband, Dr. John Scott, asking Holmes to verify Scott's reported reappearance on the East India docks. Scott, in fact, has died in Sumatra and is being impersonated by Dr. David Fitzroy, a look-alike. Under the direction of the archvillain Dr. Jack Seward, Fitzroy, who has brought the giant rat of Sumatra back to London as a living incubator of bubonic plague, plans to use it as a biological time bomb against the city unless ransom demands are met. Investigating the two cases leads Holmes into a desperate interview with the Count, a trap baited by Holmes with the Count's great trunk found at the docks.

The interview scene is the highlight of the story and leads to the strategy by which the evil doctors are foiled in their scheme to unleash the plague on London. Holmes and Dracula agree to switch places, taking advantage of Dracula's powers, for the detective anticipates Seward's plot to kidnap him in order to guarantee the success of his conspiracy. For his part, Holmes is willing to grant Dracula his revenge on his former captors, because he believes the Count to be both honorable and trustworthy within the limits of his own code.

There is a special gratification offered by sequels that re-create something of the original enchantment. Within the limits of its popular tradition, the pleasure is extended by Saberhagen's success in joining the legends of Holmes and Dracula, a fusion possible only within the framework of the fantastic. The effects of awe, wonder, and recovery are woven dexterously into the comfortable mold of the detective melodrama of which Doyle was a master.

The third novel of the series, *An Old Friend of the Family*, brings the Count to the New World. He is called to Chicago by Clarissa Southerland, the granddaughter of Dracula's beloved Mina Harker, who summons him by the use of a talisman. Naturally, she is unaware that Dr. Emile Corday, who arrives by air from London within a day of his summons, is Dracula, or even a vampire. Clarissa has been driven to the extreme of employing her grandmother's desperate remedy, because within a week's time, her granddaughter has been murdered and her grandson kidnaped and held for ransom.

Dracula arrives on the scene as an old friend of the family to offer counsel and investigative support. He finds his natural ally in Judy Southerland, the younger sister of the murdered Kate and a woman who greatly resembles Mina Harker, her great-grandmother. Dracula goes about investigating the supposed death of Kate and the abduction of Johnny, whose finger has been torn off and returned as a sign of the kidnapers' intent.

The plot is divided between Dracula's investigation and Kate Southerland's adventures as a modern damsel in distress, for Kate was not murdered in the traditional sense. Rather, she was turned into a vampire by the evil Enoch Wynter, one of a coven of Chicago vampires whose true intentions are to lure Dracula to Chicago. They plan to kill Dracula, whom they regard as an obstacle to their fiendish business of preying upon human victims for blood, a practice strictly forbidden in the vampire code which Dracula upholds. The new breed of lawless vampires is led by an ancient enemy of Dracula, a female vampire named Morgan. To them, Dracula is the most formidable of the "Old Ones." Their plan nearly succeeds.

In a visit to the morgue accompanied by Joe Keogh, Kate's fiancé, Dracula notices what the obtuse Chicago coroner has not seen: Kate is not dead; she has been transformed into a nonbreather, or vampire. Accordingly, the Count rescues the enchanted lady and brings her to her family mausoleum, where she can gain strength, adjust to her new nature, and learn something of her new powers under the guidance of the Count. While the Count is nurturing Kate, he also finds time to rescue her brother by hypnotizing Judy (who possesses psychic powers) and asking her to lead him and Joe to the white house she saw in her dream. The rescue places the outlaw vampires on guard, and they strike again. This time, they take Keogh hostage, kill Clarissa Southerland, discover the Count in his sarcophagus at rest, and leave him staked and pinned to the floor of the Southerland home to await his end. The Count is rescued by Judy, however, who removes the stake, closes the wound, and offers her own blood to save the Count's life.

With assistance from the other sister, Kate, Dracula launches a successful attack on the outlaw vampires' nest and destroys them. In the course of rescuing Keogh, Kate not only rediscovers her human, romantic love for Keogh but also unexpectedly transforms herself back into a breather by will-power, a phenomenon that Dracula explains as possible, especially for young vampires.

The narrative offers Saberhagen the opportunity to bring his character to his native Chicago, and his evocation of the city in the 1970's is convincing and effective. The plot is a display case for Dracula's personality and his powers in action. Kate's bizarre fate and the plot of the outlaw vampires introduce some interesting extensions and inventions of vampire lore. The emphasis in this tale, once again, is on rational fantasy, but there is enough of the occult and the unexplained remaining to keep the story from approaching anything like realism. The roles of the Count as a protector of Mina's descendants, as a superhero guided by his own code of honor, and as a detective fit together comfortably. Saberhagen has adapted the formulas and conventions of the comic-book or movie-serial heroic adventure to the adult-reader level.

In the fourth novel of the series, *Thorn*, the Count travels to the American Southwest in quest of an old masterpiece, which turns out to be a portrait of his second wife, Helen Hunyadi, sister of King Matthias of Hungary. The King, his captor, had sent him on a mission to apprehend Helen, Matthias' runaway sister, and either kill or marry her. Dracula chose the latter course, but Helen lived up to her reputation by running off with Perugino, a young painter. The portrait, at auction in Phoenix, was actually painted by the young Leonardo da Vinci and not by Verrocchio or one of his anonymous studio artists, as the art dealers believe. Unfortunately, the Seabright family, wealthy, powerful, and decadent, also suspect its true value and intend to have the painting at any cost.

The Count has assumed the identity of Jonathan Thorn for his latest adventure. His interest in the painting, in the fate of Helen Seabright (who seems to be the reincarnation of his second wife), and in the affairs of Mary Rogers draws Thorn into the machinations of the Seabrights. Their interests range from acquisition of the portrait to debauchery and murder. Mary Rogers claims inheritance rights to the portrait after the presumed death of Delaunay Seabright, but a bomb kills her and forces Thorn to dematerialize ahead of the shock wave. Thorn returns to stalk his would-be assassins, wreaking vengeance with the relish and polite brutality to which his pedigree as Dracula seems to entitle him.

The sordidness of his enemies makes the Count once again a hero by comparison, and his self-appointed avenger role is a recognized and well-established one in popular adventure and detective stories. It seems that Delaunay Seabright has cultivated an appetite for orgies involving drugs and runaways. He has even filmed some of them, keeping the tapes in a vault for private screening. He more than meets his match in Annie Chapman, a runaway with no sense of propriety. She turns out to be a vampire who transforms Delaunay into a vampire at his request. Annie, who plays the part of the murdered Helen Seabright, is actually the reincarnation of Helen Hunyadi, the fifteenth century Hungarian princess who was Dracula's second wife. The least contented of Dracula's conquests, she has retained for him a timeless fascination.

The Seabright plot and Thorn's attempt to solve the mystery of Delaunay's supposed kidnaping and presumed death is balanced by an account presented in alternate chapters of Dracula's early career as a captive Prince of Wallachia, the prisoner of Matthias, King of Hungary, and later the King's envoy and brother-in-law. More of Dracula's background as archetypal superhero is sketched in as a way of reinforcing the contemporary image of a demigod in disguise. At the hands of his original captors and torturers, the Turks, it seems that the Count lost all fear of pain or death. It was that state of mind that was to make him a vampire, for he was not bitten by another vampire. Rather, when dying of multiple wounds from his military enemies, the Turks, his will refused death, and somehow he lived on, transformed into a vampire, or nonbreather. (The generic name preferred by the nonbreathers is *nosferatu*.) These and other revisions and additions to vampire lore help make Saberhagen's Dracula novels entertaining reading for one whose taste lies in the way of action fantasy. Although the Count in his various guises does not pose as an existentialist vampire, such an outlook seems to be the basis of his original transformation and of his character. Like the strong, silent, granite-jawed lawmen of the West, Dracula fears no one, and for him death has no terrors.

Once again, Saberhagen's narrative counterpointing of two plot lines, tying them together at the end, is accomplished with skill. Unfortunately, the Renaissance characters are presented without much conviction, except for the Count and Helen. The modern plot line becomes rather murky toward the end, perhaps because it has to bear the overpowering weight of too many changed identities, competing groups of vampires who seem to arise from nowhere, and the largely undeveloped business of reincarnation.

The contemporary reader who seeks entertainment in Gothic adventure fantasy will not be disappointed in Saberhagen's sequels to the Dracula legend. The novels are well-written, fast-paced, and well-informed. The rational fantasy is successfully grafted onto the Dracula character, and the resultant transformations and reinterpretations of vampire lore are consistently pleasing. So long as the reader is prepared to accept the sequels as popular entertainments which have a place, of sorts, in the history of vampire stories and particularly in the bibliography of Dracula, he will not be disillusioned. Let him not expect the complexity, depth, or power of the original, however, for these further adventures of Dracula do not even aspire to offer such satisfactions. If one title of the first four had to be recommended over the others, the reader should consider beginning with *The Holmes-Dracula File*. In any case, the pleasures of reading the Dracula Tape series should be deferred until after the original has been digested.

Donald L. Lawler

Bibliography
Stewart, Alfred D. "Fred Saberhagen: Cybernetic Psychologist," in *Extrapolation*. XVIII (December, 1976), pp. 42-51.

THE DRAGON AND THE GEORGE

Author: Gordon R. Dickson (1923-   )
First book publication: 1976
Type of work: Novel
Time: 1976 and the Middle Ages
Locale: Minnesota and medieval England

In a parallel of medieval England, where magic is a natural law, James Eckert finds his consciousness placed in a dragon's body and seeks to free his fiancée, who has been physically transported to the same world

> Principal characters:
> JAMES ECKERT, a teaching assistant and historian
> S. CAROLINUS, a magician
> SIR BRIAN NEVILLE-SMYTHE, a knight
> ARAGH, an English wolf
> SMRGOL, a dragon
> DAFYDD AP HYWEL, a Welsh bowman
> DANIELLE O' THE WOLD, a wandering bow-woman

Gordon R. Dickson, best known for his stories of the Dorsai (the science-fiction works which comprise the published section of his Childe cycle), has taken a jaunt into the realm of magic and heroic fantasy with *The Dragon and the George*. The medieval world in which Dickson sets his tale reflects both his careful scholarship and his involvement with the Society for Creative Anachronisms (SCA). In this England, as within the SCA, chivalry is in full flower, and a knight's honor is something held exceedingly dear. Dragons exist, are intelligent, and speak as well as any other beings they encounter; mages practice a craft that may be seen as both art and science; and none of this is made any the less believable by contrasting it with the twentieth century environment that can be found in the first two chapters of the book. If anything, the petty intrigues and difficulties of the "real" world pale in the comparison.

The quest for justice—and for the valor needed to see that it is done—lies at the heart of the novel. Each new development places one or more of the protagonists in the position of having to choose between personal safety and the increasingly dangerous continuation of that quest. Nor are all of the obstacles involved external ones: pride, self-delusion, and fear are among the impediments that must be overcome in order for the quest to succeed.

James Eckert, a teaching assistant and historian at Riveroak College, is in the unpleasant position of wanting to marry without being able to afford it. Sharing this predicament is his fiancée, Angela Farrel, who also works at the college. Eckert's first call to heroic action is given when Farrel disappears during an experiment conducted by her superior at the school. The experimenter explains that Farrel was concentrating on dragons at the moment she "apported," and that he has no idea of how to retrieve her short of sending Eckert's mind in search of her. The young man agrees to the attempt, concentrates on his fiancée *and* dragons, and suddenly finds himself in the body of one Gorbash, a full-grown dragon.

Locating Farrel turns out to be a much easier matter than Eckert had anticipated: the dragons with whom his host resides have captured a female "george" (their generic word for humans) and are in bitter argument as to what should be done with it. Eckert arranges to take custody of the captive, ostensibly to negotiate with the other georges for her release, and discovers that returning both of them to their own world is going to be much more difficult. Trapped in the dragon-body, Eckert cannot simply will himself home, and Farrel refuses to be sent back without him. They are thus forced to learn more about their new environment.

Eckert is given an explanation of the seriousness of their intrusion when he confronts S. Carolinus, an elderly magician to whom Smrgol—an equally elderly dragon, grand-uncle to Eckert's host—has referred him. Carolinus first threatens Eckert with being turned into a beetle; then, upon realizing what sort of situation has arisen, warns him of its consequences:

> "The fact of your appearance—yours and this Angie's—has upset the balance between Chance and History. Upset it badly. Imagine a teeter-totter, Chance sitting on one end, History on the other, swinging back and forth—Chance up one moment, then Chance down and History up. The Dark Powers love that. They throw their weight at the right moment on a side that's already headed down, and either Chance or History ends permanently up. One way we get Chaos. The other we get Predictability and an end to Romance, Art, Magic and everything else interesting."

Those consequences are coming to fruition before the mage has fairly completed his explanation. Smrgol rushes in to announce that the dragon responsible for capturing Farrel initially has stolen her away. To free her and correct the imbalance he has helped to cause, Eckert must find a party of Companions and lead an attack on the Dark Powers and their allies at the Loathly Tower.

It is an endeavor far stranger than any he might have been called upon to perform in his own world, and he sets about the task with all the awkwardness that would be expected. His first Companion, Sir Brian Neville-Smythe, agrees to join him only after trying to engage his dragon-body in mortal combat. Aragh, an English wolf who is one of Gorbash's friends, agrees to travel with the oddly matched pair after he saves them from a horde of sandmirks.

The sandmirks are an interesting addition to the ranks of dangers generally found in heroic fantasy as well as an illustration of the internal/external obstacles the protagonists must face. Small and cowardly, these weasellike creatures possess a single, terrible weapon. Their chittering has the power to drive those they stalk mad with fear, to force them to run until they can move no more. It is then, when the victims are paralyzed by terror and exhaustion, that the sandmirks feed.

Aragh, like the rest of his kind, is immune to sandmirk-induced terror. His only response to the creatures is to kill as many of them as he can reach until the pack flees; this is the method he employs to rescue Eckert and the knight. He is far more susceptible, however, to his own feelings of independence and scorn for those weaker than himself, and it is only by keeping these feelings in check that he manages to cooperate with the rest of the Companions.

The three of them become four when Danielle o' the Wold, another of Aragh's friends and the only one capable of piercing the wolf's facade, accosts them in the Malvern woods. Their journey to the Loathly Tower has been detoured to Malvern Castle so that Neville-Smythe can obtain his lady's permission to join in freeing Farrel, and Danielle is so taken by "Sir James's" tale of enchantment that she decides to accompany them.

Their plans are thwarted this time by a set of far less supernatural enemies. A knight with designs on the castle and person of Neville-Smythe's lady has invaded her holdings and murdered the inhabitants of one of her villages. When the Companions approach an inn formerly protected by Malvern Castle, they learn the details of the raid on the castle as well as the identity of the last human to join their party. This is Dafydd ap Hywel, a Welsh bowman who has traveled to England to challenge Giles o' the Wold in bowmanship and stays to battle alongside his daughter's comrades instead.

The liberation of Malvern Castle serves as a sort of dry run for the Companions. Whether they can fight successfully against the Dark Powers and their minions remains to be seen, but they know they can better more mundane forces. This knowledge is costly, however: Eckert, ignoring the warnings given him by his access to Gorbash's memory, flies at the evil knight in a frontal attack which nearly costs him his life. This brush with death sobers him and takes away the sense of near-omnipotence his presence in the powerful dragon-body has given him. Eckert learns lessons about himself and his position in the strange world that he would rather not have had forced upon him, but they are lessons that will serve to help him in the final conflict which awaits.

It is the last battle that serves as the true measure of the Companions' valor. In addition to Eckert, Aragh, Neville-Smythe, ap Hywel, and Danielle, three others—Carolinus, Smrgol, and Secoh (a lesser dragon Smrgol has shamed into valor)—join forces at the Loathly Tower to battle the evil hiding there.

The force awaiting them is as varied as their own, and each faces the nemesis he or she is best equipped to fight. Carolinus uses his magic to fend off the Dark Powers and to keep them from overcoming the rest of his comrades. Neville-Smythe, deprived of his warhorse, battles a giant worm afoot. Ap Hywel and Danielle draw bows against a flock of harpies. Smrgol, aided by the smaller Secoh, tackles the dragon who originally helped the Dark Powers by bringing Farrel to them, while Aragh holds off the sandmirks that lie in wait for all of them outside the battlefield.

Eckert's opponent is an ogre similar to one Smrgol slew eighty-three years earlier, and he goes into the fight equipped with the strength of his dragon-body and a goodly amount of advice on the subject of ogres donated by that body's grand-uncle. Neither of these advantages serves to best his enemy, however, and the battle continues for such a long time that the Dark Powers are nearly able to win the contest by default when night falls. Eckert prevents this, and saves himself, by disregarding part of the advice he had received and allowing himself to be swept inside the ogre's guard; once there, he utilizes Gorbash's body in a way the dragon, thinking only in terms of tooth and claw, would never have attempted. Clumsy as the grip of the dragon's forepaws is, it suffices to hold a spear for long enough to use the weapon against the unsuspecting ogre, and the battle is ended.

None of the Companions emerges completely unscathed, but the consequences for some members of the party have been particularly bad. Aragh has been forced to fight on three legs, a casualty of an earlier ambush by the Mother of sandmirks (a creature built more on the lines of a bear than a weasel). Smrgol, locked in a final grip on his enemy's throat, has died, and ap Hywel, bitten by the one harpy who managed to reach him, appears doomed to a similar fate.

At this difficult moment, the balance of powers within the realm of magic, earlier mentioned by Carolinus, comes into play. Danielle reminds the fallen bowman that she had earlier declared him a knight, and that no knight may take leave of his lady without her permission. He rallies at this and announces that not even death is going to force him to do anything against his will. Carolinus affirms the Welshman's statement by explaining to Danielle that not even the Auditing Department—the mage's name for the force that controls the powers of both History and Chance—will exact such a price from ap Hywel for helping win the battle he never asked to join. The bowman will survive.

The Dark Powers, though defeated, stage one last attempt at thwarting justice, and this, too, is handled by the overseeing force. Carolinus has called for Farrel's release and, when his demand is ignored, for help:

> "Are we to be flouted? *Auditing Department!*" Something happened then that Jim was never to forget. The memorability of it lay not in what happened, but in the quality of the event. Without warning, the whole earth spoke—the sea spoke—the sky spoke! And they all spoke with the same, single bass voice that had responded from thin air to Carolinus before, when Jim was present. This time, however, nothing was apologetic or humorous about the voice. "DELIVER!" it said.

Not even the Dark Powers can ignore such an order. Farrel is returned immediately.

Balance is restored and justice is done in a number of other areas as well. Eckert, offered the choice between remaining in this new world (in his own body) and returning to the old, decides to stay. His fiancée wholeheartedly agrees, and Carolinus restores Eckert and his host to their proper conditions.

Secoh, the mere-dragon, has won a stout heart from *his* role in the battle and uses it to defend Eckert when the disgruntled Gorbash threatens the george who dared take control of his body. He is not Eckert's only defender, however; each of the Companions, in turn, takes the angry dragon to task, with Carolinus having the final word when he offers once again to see that Gorbash is turned into a beetle. In keeping with its dispensation of justice, however, the Auditing Department has seen to it that the host dragon will be reimbursed for his trouble. Gorbash, by participating in the battle at the Loathly Tower, has become the most famous of his kind.

Neville-Smythe, being a knight and not a philosopher, is seldom given to pronouncements, yet it is he who best summarizes the balance that has been restored in *The Dragon and the George*. Leading his comrades in for their first meal since the battle, he advises them:

> "Take seats, friends, and let us all be joyous, for we're given pains enough in life so that we should not lack will but make good use of pleasure such as this, when it is truly earned."

Christine Watson

Bibliography
No listing.

THE DREADFUL DRAGON OF HAY HILL

Author: Max Beerbohm (1872-1956)
First book publication: 1928
Type of work: Novel
Time: Thirty-nine thousand years B.C.
Locale: Hay Hill, London, England

A misanthropic moral tale

>
> *Principal characters:*
> THOL, a prehistoric man
> THIA, a prehistoric woman
> THE DRAGON

In *The Dreadful Dragon of Hay Hill*, Max Beerbohm steps outside his usual artistic persona of amusing dilettante and attempts something rather outside the normal compass of his talents. There is no element of parody in this novel, and only a little wry humor. It is not inspired by any events in his own private experience, but is instead a satire which puts forth a moral judgment on human nature in general. Because Beerbohm's strength lies in his ability as a parodist and humorist, the novel under discussion cannot be considered one of his better works.

The story is a simple one. Set in prehistoric London, it tells of the Homelanders, a small, discontented, quarrelsome community that is attacked by a dragon. In the face of this threat, people forget their differences and unite against the common enemy to become better and happier than they were before they were threatened. The hero, Thol, kills the dragon in order to win the love of Thia, the heroine. The result of this brave act is that, once the threat of the dragon's presence is removed, the Homelanders fall back into their old habits of strife and disunity. Thia, now married to Thol, soon tires of him. In order to regain her love, Thol devises a hoax whereby the Homelanders are led to believe that another dragon is threatening to attack them. His ruse succeeds, Thia returns to him, and together they maintain their deception. The Homelanders become united once more in the face of a threat to their community, until Thol and Thia die and the truth is revealed to them. When this happens, at the end of the book, the Homelanders relapse for the second time into their original condition.

At the end of the story, Beerbohm adds a comment which relates not only to the novel but also to his own world view, which was made ever more cynical by the events of World War I. He observes that human nature seems to be incapable of changing for the better or learning from its mistakes. Doing good must be enough reward in itself for the perpetrators, for it is useless to expect humanity *en masse* to make any improvement. There is also an optimistic note, however, when he says that the fact that in their last days on

Earth Thol and Thia enjoyed greater happiness than they had ever known should be enough to satisfy the reader. This remark suggests that the author is prepared to see a possible salvation for mankind in individual altruism rather than in wholesale improvement.

A moral satire with war as its subject is far removed from Beerbohm's usual range of interest. Caricature and parody, acid wit applied with a light touch, constitute Beerbohm's *forte*; when he strays from these styles to more didactic modes of expression, he is less successful. In his biography of Beerbohm, David Cecil compares *The Dreadful Dragon of Hay Hill* to Beerbohm's cartoon "Civilisation and the Industrial System." He observes that both the novel and the cartoon are failures and points out that they both have their artistic roots in the same basic fear—that of industrialism and the soulless, ruthless, profiteering forces of mechanization and greed that accompany it.

From a biographical standpoint, *The Dreadful Dragon of Hay Hill* is fascinating, as are all atypical works by great artists; it is well worth reading for the light it sheds upon aspects of the author's character that are unrevealed by his more successful work.

Vivien Stableford

Bibliography
Behrman, S. N. *Portrait of Max: An Intimate Memoir*, 1960.
Cecil, David. *Max: A Biography*, 1965.
Riewald, Jacobus G. *Sir Max Beerbohm: Man and Writer*, 1953.

DREAM

Author: S. Fowler Wright (1874-1965)
First book publication: 1931
Type of work: Novel
Time: Unspecified, but probably the early Pleistocene
Locale: Unspecified

Three people are sent back in time via a dream to inhabit the bodies of protohumans

Principal characters:
MARGUERITE LEINSTER, a young socialite
RITA, her alter ego, a tree-dwelling ape
STEPHEN CRANLEIGH, Marguerite's fiancé
STELE, his alter ego, a caveman
ELSIE, Stephen's sister
ELSYA, her alter ego, Stele's sister
THE KING, chief of a protohuman tribe
THELMO, his son
TEKLA, Thelmo's sister

Dream was the first of S. Fowler Wright's prehistoric romances; some years later he published a second, *The Vengeance of Gwa* (1945), under the name Anthoy Wingrave. *Dream* has subdued affinities with *The World Below* (1929), Wright's classic story of the remote future, and reflects the same absorbed interest in characters and environments very remote from the contemporary world. Late in life, Wright wrote a sequel to *Dream* that is structurally similar, dealing with an equally savage and remote world: *Spiders' War* (1954). Unfortunately, the latter work—his last novel, written at the age of eighty—testifies to the waning of the author's literary powers.

The central character of *Dream* (which bore, in its first edition, though not in a later one, the subtitle "The Simian Maid") is a young woman named Marguerite Leinster. Although little is said about her life or background, it is evident that she is a "free spirit": a liberated woman of the 1920's who, despite her engagement to Stephen Cranleigh, has little intention of retiring into wedlock. Before the story begins, she has visited Atlantis and ancient Babylon through the medium of "dreams" in which her body disappears to be reformed as an appropriate physical presence in another era. She has bought these experiences from a "magician" who gains funds for his research by pandering to her hunger for adventure.

Her present project is to visit a world more remote in time than Atlantis: a world inhabited by the remote ancestors of mankind. She is incarnated as a tree-dwelling furry primate, of a species that coexists with two others: the "cave-people" who have more elaborate tools and a more elaborate language than her own kind; and the Ogpurs, a savage and degraded race. Despite the cultural advantages enjoyed by the cave-people, Rita (who retains only the most fleeting memory of her former persona) considers her own kind to be the "higher" because they are less vulgar. As for the Ogpurs, they are called a "mongrel" race, and are reckoned the lowest of the low in this world— they, the author suggests, must be the direct ancestors of Homo sapiens. (Wright's fiction is full of such misanthropic remarks.)

The magician, having sent Marguerite on her adventure, is forced to send Stephen Cranleigh to follow her, and Cranleigh's sister Elsie to follow him. They enter the primeval world as Stele and Elsya, cave-people sent abroad from their own land in search of a mate for Stele. They encounter Rita and are drawn into a strange collusion with her, eventually arriving with her in a valley connected to the outer world only by a hazardous cave-system. There they receive sinister hospitality from a King who is also King of a tribe in the outer world. Elsya is married to the King's son Thelmo, while his daughter Tekla has designs on Stele, but there are ominous matters of family politics to be cleared up before any of the three strangers can be sure of their fate.

The outer lands ruled by the King are threatened by invasion by creatures like giant rats, and one of his tribes is eventually caught up in a desperate battle with these monsters. Meanwhile, the tribe in the valley foments rebellion, and the three outsiders are caught in the middle. Stele and Rita meet a tragic death in the caves, while Elsya reaches her husband only in time to die with him in the bloody conflict. The experience has its effect, once the three find themselves back in their own world, on the way that Marguerite and Cranleigh develop their relationship.

Like many prehistoric fantasies, *Dream* is not to be construed as an attempt to represent the actual conditions of prehistory, but rather as an attempt to use an imaginary study of man's ancestors to make a moral point relevant to modern man's concept of himself. In this respect, *Dream* is by no means as clear as such novels as J. Leslie Mitchell's *Three Go Back* (1932, which might almost be seen as an ideological reply to it) or William Golding's *The Inheritors* (1955), but it seems obvious that Wright is saying something about the essence of sexual relationships and glorifying, in a slightly perverse way, the Darwinian struggle for existence. "The time when mankind would become an earth-wide curse," he observes at one point, "from which all other life would crouch and flee, might be a million years ahead, but its shadow was beginning to move already upon the face of the world."

Despite the mild pretense of moral seriousness, though, *Dream* is basically an escapist fantasy—and if the world it describes is cruel, this does no more than remind the reader how much delight he can take, along with Wright himself, in the contemplation of savagery and war. Even escapist fantasy can be—and perhaps ought to be—unsettling. The lack of moral clarity about a story which seems so pregnant with moral implication is confusing, but at least it saves the work from being trivialized into a too-obvious allegory of dubious pertinence. *Dream* is not one of Wright's most powerful works, but it is by no means the least of them.

Brian Stableford

Bibliography
Bleiler, E. F. "S. Fowler Wright," in *Science Fiction Writers*, 1982.
Moskowitz, Sam. "Better the World Below than the World Above," in *Strange Horizons*, 1976.

A DREAM PLAY
(ETT DRÖMSPEL)

Author: August Strindberg (1849-1912)
First book publication: 1902; presented 1926
English translation: 1912
Type of work: Drama
Time: The early 1900's
Locale: The territory of dreams

The Daughter of Indra descends to Earth to see if man's cries of suffering are justified; her experiences with the Officer, the Attorney, and the Poet flow into one another like dreams and encompass the whole of human life, including love, death, poverty, the struggles for power, and the pains of guilt

Principal characters:
> THE DAUGHTER OF INDRA, OR AGNES, a goddess who descends to Earth to partake of man's suffering
> THE OFFICER, the first of her guides
> THE ATTORNEY, the second of her guides, who marries her and who is tainted with the evil of men but bravely defends the poor
> THE POET, her guide through the long last portion of her journey

A Dream Play, along with *Spöksonaten* (1907, *The Ghost Sonata*), stands as the epitome of August Strindberg's fantasy expressionist writing, and its magnificent sweep of human experience is cast in the most vivid and unforgettable poetic writing and symbolism. The Daughter of Indra's quest for the reasons behind human discontent is parallel to the Incarnation of Christ, although it is notably different in that she ascends in the image of a burning castle with a vast chrysanthemum bursting from its roof rather than offering herself as a "full, perfect and sufficient sacrifice." Moreover, she is known and almost expected in the world by several of those she visits, and all the characters share a principal idea which contrasts with the Christian message: every action and situation is a blending of light and dark, pleasure and pain, good and evil.

Perhaps the most effective way to grasp Strindberg's method, technique, and achievement is to examine one sequence of this vast quest odyssey in detail. Early in her stay on Earth, the Daughter of Indra opines that love conquers all; the scene suddenly shifts to an alley outside an opera house where the Officer, as a young suitor, awaits Victoria, the young singer who is to be his bride. Also in the scene is the Portress, keeping the gate to the stage and crocheting a star-studded bedspread which she had begun twenty-six years earlier when her lover had left her and she had lost her talent as a dancer. There is also a Billposter, cleaning a hoarding, who is happy because he has with him a green fishing net for which he has longed for more than thirty years. In keeping with Strindberg's strongly symbolic style, there is also on the set a dwarfed lime tree, from whose black branches hang a few pale green leaves, and a large blue aconite (or monkshood flower) standing in a green, sunlit space.

In this sequence, the Daughter of Indra replaces the Portress, who remains to explain to her how the various performers suffer when they are not chosen for the company. She and the Daughter watch together as—in a succession of quick blackouts—the flowers, including the roses in the hands of the suitor, wither, and the suitor grows older and more shabby. The seasons pass swiftly until the suitor is a very old man, left only with a desire to open a mysterious door in the wall which has a cloverleaf-shaped hole in hopes that it will explain the mystery of his lost love. This desire is frustrated by a policeman, the dream shifts to a scene with the Attorney, and another section of the play flows into being.

The sequence is typical in its dreamlike flow of action and the way in which all of its details converge on the mood of lost hope and desire. In the course of the suitor's futile vigil, the Portress' lost love is mentioned and the Daughter of Indra puts on the Portress' shawl, which holds all the sad memories of the Portress' thirty years of watching human sorrow. The Billposter even loses his joy, for his green fishing net is not the ideal shade of green of which he has dreamt for so many years. The human condition is portrayed as only loss and sorrow.

The play places absolutely no limits on the flexible imagination of its author. Successive scenes present Foulgut, where the plague combines with men working off their sins of excess in a gymnasium with strange equipment like torture devices, and Faircove, across a channel from Foulgut, where music and beauty predominate. In keeping with the theme of contrasts, one can see both locales in each scene, and even Faircove is marred by those overlooked in love and by the distinctions of class which keep the serving maids from joining in Faircove's merrymaking.

Through it all moves the Daughter of Indra, learning of the suffering and joy of human life, unable to explain why the world is full of lost joys and pain. Strindberg offers the entire richness of life in the transcendent symbolism of the flowers growing out of dung and the castle that grows daily and that finally bursts into bloom even as it is consumed by fire. The richness of life is found in the dream of life as it is lived, at once concrete and vivid in the domestic details of poverty and love, yet flowing with the dramatic symbolism of poetic language, setting, and action.

Peter Brigg

Bibliography
Johnson, Walter Gilbert. *August Strindberg*, 1976.

Lucas, Frank L. *The Drama of Ibsen and Strindberg*, 1962.
Mortensen, Brita M., and Brian Downs. *Strindberg: An Introduction to His Life and Work*, 1965.

THE DREAM-QUEST OF UNKNOWN KADATH

Author: H. P. Lovecraft (1890-1937)
First book publication: 1943
Type of work: Novel
Time: The early twentieth century
Locale: The realm of dreams

A New England dreamer voyages perilously through the abysses of nocturnal vision in search of a marvelous sunset city glimpsed in his dreams

> *Principal characters:*
> RANDOLPH CARTER, a dreamer
> ZOOGS, GUGS, AND GHASTS, various dreamland denizens
> RICHARD UPTON PICKMAN, Carter's friend-turned-ghoul
> GHOULS, dreamland compatriots of Carter
> SHANTAKS, large dreamland birdlike creatures
> NIGHT GAUNTS, dreamland flying horrors
> THE GREAT ONES, gods of Kadath
> NYARLATHOTEP, the Crawling Chaos

When H. P. Lovecraft wrote *The Dream-Quest of Unknown Kadath* (1926-1927), he demonstrated—at least for later generations; he never tried to get the work published—that his work cannot be thoroughly categorized without risk of oversimplification. Some critics have yielded to the temptation to divide Lovecraft's works exclusively into such categories as Dunsanian fantasy (after the fashion of Lord Dunsany: such works as "Celephaïs," 1920); dream narratives ("The Statement of Randolph Carter," 1919); New England horror tales ("The Colour Out of Space," 1927); and Lovecraft Mythos tales ("The Dunwich Horror," 1928), as if these categories were independent. It is tempting, also, to think of Lovecraft as having passed through distinct periods of influence, particularly a "Poe period" and a "Dunsany period." *The Dream-Quest of Unknown Kadath* puts the lie to such reductionist approaches to the Lovecraft canon. It is clearly a work heavily influenced by Lord Dunsany, with its lofty and sonorous language and its compelling treatment of man's relation to primordial gods, but it is a Dunsanian fantasy written several years after the period of Lovecraft's major experimentation with Dunsanian themes and style, in a period in which Lovecraft is primarily thought of as producing such non-Dunsanian Lovecraft Mythos works as "The Call of Cthulhu" (1926). The novel is much more than a late-arriving Dunsanian effort, however; by this time, Lovecraft, far from merely copying Lord Dunsany, had deeply assimilated what he had found of value in that author, transmuting his style to suit the purpose of expressing ideas and visions uniquely Lovecraftian.

The novel cuts across categories, for it is redolent also of the Lovecraft Mythos conception in that it deals with man's soul-chilling relationship with such ancient godlike entities as Nyarlathotep and Azathoth. It is obviously a dream narrative and, in a somewhat less obvious way, a New England tale as well—such quaint dreamland cities as Ulthar and Celephaïs are Love-craftian responses to favorite New England places, including Providence, Salem, and Marblehead. It is as if Lovecraft sought to express all of his major emotionalities—his admiration for Dunsany, his vicarious liking of bold adventure, his love of New England, his fondness for cats, his fascination with dreams, his sense of brooding horror, and his preoccupation with the Mythos notion of man's precarious position in the cosmos—in one work, a work not even divided into chapters but rather allowed to run as a free confluence of his fondest thoughts and feelings. Perhaps more than any other single Lovecraft work, *The Dream-Quest of Unknown Kadath* is a charming and prismatic self-portrait.

The novel nevertheless stands on its own merits apart from biographical considerations and is a deeply interpretable work. The setting alone places it apart from other such fantasy-adventure creations. Randolph Carter, a scarcely veiled Lovecraft persona "old in the land of dream," has glimpsed in his dreams a marvelous sunset city, and he yearns for it desperately; but further glimpses of it are not forthcoming, and Carter feels "the bondage of dream's tyrannous gods" who have denied him the vision. He descends into dreamland to carry on an epic quest for his beloved city. This realm of dream is portrayed as an actual domain accessible to deep dreamers. The domain of dream lies in part "not far from the gates of the waking world" but contains depths remote from the familiar haunts of humans and falls under the dominion of immemorial gods known as the Great Ones, who dwell in an onyx castle in Kadath in the Cold Waste. By setting this weirdly picaresque adventure in such a postulated dream world, rather than merely in a distant age or far spacial realm of the familiar waking universe, Lovecraft sets his protagonist upon a journey which literally has characteristics enjoyed only symbolically by similar protagonists elsewhere in literature. Carter, by sojourning in dreamland, literally indulges in a quest through the depths of the psyche. It is common in literature for some journey to be a *symbolic* quest through the psyche—Marlow in Joseph Conrad's *Heart of Darkness* (1902) journeys symbolically into the deep unconscious when he sails up the Congo River into the darkness of the jungle—but it is far from common for the psychic journey to be literal, as in the case of Randolph Carter.

The novel, in fact, lends itself well to Jungian interpretation, for at its heart lies the notion of dream, and dreams in Jungian theory obtrude upon the personal unconscious as a result of the activity of archetypes, those mysterious patternings which operate in the collective unconscious of the deep psyche. By journeying deep within the realm of dream, Carter traverses an inner cosmos; the novel is replete with symbolism to reinforce this view.

For example, when Carter descends the seven hundred steps to the Gate of Deeper Slumber and passes into the Enchanted Wood, the home of the piquant Zoogs, he finds "a circle of great mossy stones" left by "older and more terrible dwellers long forgotten," and one readily sees this circle in Jungian symbolic terms as the circle of individuation, the eternal mandala. To achieve psychic wholeness, the questing hero must plunge into the very depths of his psyche, confront his Shadow or counter-ego, come to terms with it, and return with an integrated, whole psychic identity, thus completing the circle and achieving the whole Self. The circle of stones in the novel signals that this is the nature of what lies ahead for Carter to accomplish. The fact of the stones being mossy and being left by old dwellers "long forgotten" nicely parallels the notion that the structure of the psyche is immemorially ancient and too deep, in part, to be consciously known—the mandala itself is an archetypal pattern implanted far down in the collective unconscious and often encountered as a symbol in dreams. Also, the Lovecraftian suggestion that his dreamland is a genuinely existing realm which is "down there" for people in general closely parallels Carl Jung's notion of the collectively or commonality of the unconscious mind's deepest patternings—the notion that there is a profound archetypal depth of being that humans all share, and that dreams symbolically illuminate its nature.

The necessity of Carter's confronting his counter-ego, the other and darker side of himself, is symbolized as well by the matter of the great carven face on Mount Ngranek in the land of dreams. Besides reflecting a probable Nathaniel Hawthorne influence (see Hawthorne's "The Great Stone Face"), this carven visage has much symbolic significance. Carter must look upon the stone face on the remote side of the mountain in order to learn to recognize the facial lineaments of the Great Ones, because these lineaments will be reflected in mortal faces near unknown Kadath—the gods often consort with humans. (The great carven face has long-lobed ears reminiscent of the carven faces on Easter Island, by which Lovecraft is known to have been fascinated.) The stone face lies on the mountainside facing away from the accessible world of humans, just as the ego and counter-ego "face" in opposite directions by being opposed forces in the psyche, but forces, nevertheless, which must be integrated. In the dreamland quest, Carter and the dreaded gods of Kadath must come to terms if he is to achieve wholeness, and the gods, symbolized by the stone face, operate as his counter-ego. Ultimately, the counter-ego or Shadow is oneself, and since the Great Ones hold court in the deep realm of dreams, they constitute an archetypal facet of Carter's own psyche. Jung identifies the "god archetype"—the pattern in the collective unconscious by which man formulates notions of gods—with the ego archetype, and by this pattern of identification, one comes around to the idea that the ego and counter-ego are opposite faces of the same coin, just as the opposite sides of Mount Ngranek represent bipolarities of one psychic reality.

Carter's adventures in dreamland are reminiscent of those of many a hero figure in literature. He is the mythic questing hero, whose quest in this case is not merely symbolically but literally a quest for the Self—he must satisfy his deepest need, the craving to find again the elusive sunset city. It is significant that although his quest is an exceedingly prideful one (in that he presumes to sway the gods), his motives are entirely aesthetic rather than being informed by greed, desire for adventure, or other such impulses. His beloved city is "a fever of the gods, a fanfare of supernal trumpets and a clash of immortal cymbals"—that is, an archetypally profound cornerstone of his very original being—and he yearns with the heart of a poet for the city's "walls, temples, colonnades and arched bridges of veined marble, silver-basined fountains of prismatic spray in broad squares and perfumed gardens, and wide streets marching between delicate trees and blossom-laden urns and ivory statues in gleaming rows." Clearly Lovecraft is reflecting here both his own love of New England beauty and his fascination with the delicacies of Greco-Roman antiquity.

Randolph Carter is an oneiric Ulysses, voyaging from peril to peril, doing battle with Gugs, Ghasts, and moon-beings as he perseveres in his single-minded quest of the marvelous city. He experiences moments of exquisite horror, as when the galley in which he sails passes through the Basalt Pillars of the West into an abyss and he glimpses as black, amorphous stirrings "the nameless larvae of the Other Gods." He forms an alliance with Pickman—an artist who vanishes in Lovecraft's slightly earlier tale "Pickman's Model" (1926)—with Pickman's fellow ghouls, and even with the dreaded night-gaunts. These creatures are flying horrors which were derived from Lovecraft's own childhood dreams. Clearly, *The Dream-Quest of Unknown Kadath* is a highly personal work, connecting with Lovecraft's earlier stories and expressing his various predilections.

The novel's conclusion, foreshadowed philosophically in Lovecraft's early Dunsanian tale "Celephaîs" (1920), comes when Carter, finally wafted into the onyx castle of the Great Ones atop Kadath, meets Nyarlathotep, the Crawling Chaos, who discloses to him the truth about the marvelous sunset city: that it is "only the sum of what you have seen and loved in youth," the remembered and accumulated charm of New England byways. Nyarlathotep nicely reinforces the Jungian interpretability of the novel by saying of the memory sources of Carter's sunset city: "These, Randolph Carter, are your city; for they are yourself." Carter returns to the waking world with the same sort of enlightenment as that imparted by a Zen master to a monk who had asked him how to seek one's original Buddha-nature; the master replied that to do so is like going off on an ox in search of the ox. This revelation goes a long way toward illuminating the beauty-charmed, reminiscing mind and heart of H. P. Lovecraft.

Donald R. Burleson

Bibliography

de Camp, L. Sprague. *Lovecraft: A Biography*, 1975.

Joshi, S. T. *H. P. Lovecraft and Lovecraft Criticism: An Annotated Bibliography*, 1981.

_____ , ed. *H. P. Lovecraft: Four Decades of Criticism*, 1980.

St. Armand, Barton Levi. *The Roots of Horror in the Fiction of H. P. Lovecraft*, 1977.

Shreffler, Philip A. *The H. P. Lovecraft Companion*, 1977.

DUNCTON WOOD

Author: William Horwood (1944-   )
First book publication: 1980
Type of work: Novel
Time: The 1970's
Locale: Various rural parts of central England and Wales

In a great saga of mole life, Bracken, a woodland mole who tries to maintain religious tradition in the face of intolerance, combats the forces of evil and restores the spiritual heritage of moles

> *Principal characters:*
> BRACKEN, *a great traveler and sometime leader at Duncton*
> REBECCA, *Bracken's mate and a healer*
> BOSWELL, *a scribemole of Uffington*
> MANDRAKE, *Rebecca's father and one-time leader at Duncton, an exceptionally large mole*
> RUNE, *the notoriously evil one-time leader at Duncton*
> ROSE, *a healer*
> COMFREY, *Bracken's son and a healer*
> MEDLAR, *an exceptional fighter and teacher*

For many years a newspaper journalist, William Horwood is English and lives near Oxford, England. Close by is the wood that he used as the major setting for his first novel, *Duncton Wood.* The novel is a massive saga (running to more than seven hundred pages) dealing exclusively with moles and covering generations of their brief lives.

In its contemporary English setting and concentration upon a particular common animal species whose members speak, *Duncton Wood* begs comparison with *Watership Down* (1972) by Richard Adams. While there is no denying that *Duncton Wood* is derivative of *Watership Down*, there is one crucial difference: Horwood's moles are far more intelligent than Adams' rabbits. The latter can converse only simply and are, for the most part, lacking in intellect or philosophy, while the former are of near human intelligence, possessing institutions, artifacts, written records, and a fully developed religion. In consequence, Adams never has a problem with credibility, his rabbits behaving in accordance with the reader's expectations.

Horwood, on the other hand, has immense problems in establishing and maintaining credibility; rather than mere moles, his characters seem like sentient aliens. It is surprising that they have not developed a higher level of technology and, given their books and carvings, do not possess weapons or badges of office. Why have such intelligent creatures not produced a mechanical or chemical defence against owls, their major enemies, and why have they never succeeded in communicating with mankind? It is true that both Walter Wangerin, Jr., in *The Book of the Dun Cow* (1978), and George

Orwell, in *Animal Farm* (1945), have produced novels about highly intelligent talking animals, but Wangerin's is a religious allegory set in a fantasy world, while Orwell's is a political satire. Horwood's novel is primarily an adventure story with a realistic setting, and it is that realism which makes his intelligent moles hard to accept.

There is an allegorical dimension to *Duncton Wood*, though this is far from being the author's major intention. The novel's quest for the seventh stillstone and for the seventh holy book of mole philosophy (which are known to be linked), is effectively a "Holy Grail" quest. Also, the various mole characters represent the forces of good and evil, and the fierce fights between individuals or groups, which are ostensibly mating disputes, leadership struggles, or territorial battles between neighboring systems of tunnels, can all be seen as part of the continuing war between good and evil. Furthermore, there are parallels with contemporary society in such areas as the generation gap, freedom of worship, and styles of leadership.

Not only are moles used as symbols of good and evil, but they themselves are also fully aware of these forces, possessing a highly evolved system of religion. This is not a Christian religion (though most if not all of its tenets are those of the Christian Church) but one that involves the worship of certain natural standing stones (or "Stones," as Horwood calls them). The headquarters of the mole church (and, in fact, the only place where the mole religion exists as an institution rather than being observed by lay believers) is at Uffington. This, though Horwood does not say so, is high up on the Berkshire Downs, at the site of a prehistoric White Horse figure and a prehistoric earthwork castle, and only a few miles from Adams' location for *Watership Down*.

Deep in the chalk hills is a mole-made library, the repository of all mole knowledge, staffed by the monklike scribemoles and presided over by the Holy Mole—the mole equivalent of the Pope. This is a highly secretive church, with many services and other rituals suggested. Away from Uffington, there is little religious observance except for the Midsummer Night service, which is conducted each year beside the Stone at Duncton and elsewhere, by lay believers. Despite the lack of scribemoles or of any formal religious teaching anywhere outside Uffington, most moles seem to possess an innate belief in the power of the Stone. Certainly there is a powerful religious strand extending throughout the novel.

A parallel strand, sometimes closely connected with the religious one and sometimes totally separate, is what can only be summed up as a kind of mysticism, the various manifestations of which are never satisfactorily accounted for during the course of the novel. On the religious side is the seventh stillstone, hidden at the heart of the Duncton tunnel system, which glows with white light and transforms in different ways any who touch it. No less mysterious are the psychological barriers that normally prevent moles from approaching the stillstone's hiding place. Then there is an Oriental mysticism—a kind of Samurai spiritualism—involved in the approach to fighting taught to Bracken and his companions by Medlar. In addition, several moles seem to possess forms of extrasensory perception. For example, there is telepathy (Rebecca knows when Bracken is badly wounded, even though he is miles away); clairvoyance (Bracken can sense the direction of the Stones); and precognition (of which there are several examples), though none of these gifts is consistently present, even in the most talented of moles.

The most interesting of these talents is healing, and healer moles are rare and highly revered. Much of their work is achieved with herbal remedies (though there is a suggestion that magic may be necessary when some herbs are picked, in order to ensure their efficacy), but in the most serious cases, psychic healing is practiced. This is not a simple and speedy laying on of paws; it is a very lengthy process involving close physical contact, in which the healer seems to pass some of her (healers are nearly always female) own life force to her patient. Prayer is also involved, and healers always appear to be very saintly moles.

Becoming a healer is the only means by which a female can avoid being a second-class citizen in mole society, where male chauvinism is rampant and virtually unchallenged. In a few instances, female healers become leaders of their respective tunnel systems, but these are exceptions to the rule. All other leaders and elders are male, and the scribemoles appear to be exclusively male. There is a logical reason for Horwood to have adopted this approach: mole dominance is based on size (the largest moles are better fighters and can have their choice of mates), and males are, on average, a little larger than females.

In contrast to *Watership Down*, *Duncton Wood* cannot be read and enjoyed by children. Mole society, in real life and in Horwood's book, is dominated by violence and sex. In the spring and, to a lesser extent, in the autumn, there is an urge to mate, and at these times male moles will fight to the death for the right to mate with the female of their choice. Both male and female are liable to fight at any time to preserve or acquire territory. Horwood depicts these fights frequently and in horrific detail, describing the deadly efficiency of teeth and claws. This savagery helps a little to counterbalance the image of moles as intelligent, civilized, talking creatures by showing them up as the wild animals they really are. It can be seen as a deliberate ploy by Horwood to improve credibility—and it succeeds. Moles who discuss philosophical concepts in multisyllabic words one moment and then leap at each other with intent to kill or inflict grievous bodily harm the next moment ought to appear so contradictory in their behavior as to be unbelievable, yet such behavior is acceptable in context. Human conduct is sometimes no more consistent, particularly in the case of children, whom these moles resemble in temperament.

Mole sex is also well portrayed and adds to the book's credibility. This is so because it is very different from human sex, being seasonal, almost wholly governed by a mating urge rather than by love, and fairly casual with no hint of marriage or even prolonged cohabitation. Because this state of affairs is so much an accepted part of life among Horwood's moles (even Rebecca, the saintly heroine, has litters by three different males without objecting), it can easily be accepted by the reader.

The characters of the moles in *Duncton Wood* are derived from humans and are often complex. Although Bracken is undeniably the novel's hero and is followed from birth to death, he is, for the most part, not a particularly heroic figure. (One of the author's themes is the manner in which legends are an exaggeration of reality; the legends connected with Bracken make him into a supermole.) He is a highly intelligent but physically weedy youth who is naturally opposed to violence and who drifts apart from the violent society of his birth. Living alone, he has sufficient imagination to make more than one conceptual breakthrough, and his strength of will enables him to undertake journeys that, he is told, are impossible. It is ironic that he does, through exercise and specialized training, become a great fighter. He never craves the power of leadership, and when it is thrust upon him he is like Winston Churchill, successful in war but not in peace. To the end, he remains impetuous and fallible, unable to understand Rebecca's great love for him.

Rebecca is a tomboy, who discovers at maturity that she is destined to become a healer. She is the leader of the Duncton moles for a while, in Bracken's absence. Her relationships with her father Mandrake, Bracken, the old healer Rose, and Bracken's son Comfrey are extremely well drawn. Boswell, the scribemole from Uffington who recognizes something exceptional in Bracken and eventually writes the story of Bracken and Rebecca, is intelligent, slightly crippled, and essentially a pacifist. He is perhaps a little too saintly, being content to move in Bracken's shadow and, apparently, to remain celibate throughout his life. Yet he does achieve his life's ambition of finding the seventh stillstone and the seventh book.

Mandrake survives terrible hardship at birth to become a physical giant among moles. He is an atheist and, after his takeover at Duncton, a strict and ruthless leader. He enjoys power and is, perhaps, corrupted by it, though he is not evil, and any evil present in his regime is the result of actions by Rune, one of his subordinates, who is portrayed as evil incarnate. Mandrake also has a great and very human love for his daughter Rebecca, though this is characterized by extreme possessiveness and at one point becomes incestuous. Comfrey, a weakling son of Bracken who is nursed by Rebecca, is important to the plot through his finding of the antidote to a plague that sweeps through Duncton, though he is a minor character and not particularly believable.

The countryside setting is authentic and can only be the result of both familiarity and research. Details of flora, fauna, and climate are well conveyed through the cycle of the seasons. Even the great drought which afflicted Great Britain during the summer of 1976 is carefully described. Horwood has chosen to make scant reference to any animals other than moles. This decision was, presumably, made in order to avoid the whimsicality of different animal species chatting to each other. Humans, too, are virtually excluded from the book, and in retrospect, it seems unreasonable that Bracken and Boswell, after their lengthy treks across England and Wales, should not have developed an appreciation of the true nature of human beings and their noisy machines. Yet they regard motor vehicles as a kind of owl.

Horwood's writing style is straightforward and uncomplicated, descriptive but full of incident. It has a considerable emotive quality, incorporating great joy and great sadness. Both these emotions are overdone for the sake of entertainment. It is not a subtle novel, having been aimed at the average reader rather than one who specializes in fantasy. The author seems to have become frightened (or perhaps exhausted) by the book's great length and to have cut down on characterization and description in the last fifth of the book, contriving to force his plot to a speedy conclusion.

It is difficult to assess the importance and staying power of *Duncton Wood*. Probably it will always lag some way behind *Watership Down* because of the latter's more universal appeal. Whether Horwood has more than one such novel in him and whether he will continue to produce work that can be considered as fantasy are questions that remain to be answered.

Chris Morgan

Bibliography
No listing.

THE DYING EARTH
and
THE EYES OF THE OVERWORLD

Author: Jack Vance (1920-   )
First book publications: The Dying Earth (1962); *The Eyes of the Overworld* (1966)
Type of work: Short stories and a novel
Time: The far future
Locale: Earth and Embelyon

*In the distant future, when Earth is a dying world and magic has replaced technology,
various characters vigorously pursue their own interests in the time remaining*

Principal characters:
The Dying Earth
TURJAN OF MIIR, a sorcerer wishing to create life
PANDELUME, a sorcerer who has already done so
T'SAIS, a woman Pandelume created imperfectly
T'SAIN, a corrected version of T'sais, created by Turjan
MAZIRIAN THE MAGICIAN, an enemy of Turjan
LIANE THE WAYFARER, a highwayman
GUYAL OF SFERE, an information-hunter

The Eyes of the Overworld
CUGEL THE CLEVER, a thief and confidence man
IUCOUNU THE LAUGHING MAGICIAN, Cugel's intended victim
FIRX, an alien parasite

In both *The Dying Earth* and *The Eyes of the Overworld*, Jack Vance has
conjured up a world both frightening and poignant. The world is Earth, but
an Earth set so far in the future that its name is practically the only similarity
it bears to the Earth of the present. Technology has given way to spells and
talismans; the sun has grown weary and dim; and the impending extinction
of humankind is accepted as a given by all parts of society. Nevertheless, the
individuals who inhabit Vance's Earth strive to fulfill their desires with as
great an avidity as those of any other period in the world's history—with
knowledge of their approaching fate seemingly driving them harder.

The Dying Earth is a collection of six interrelated short stories, while *The
Eyes of the Overworld* (though published almost in its entirety in six sections
in *The Magazine of Fantasy and Science Fiction* in 1965 and 1966) is structured
as a novel. The variance in form, however, does not account for all of the
differences between the two. There is a constant shifting of protagonists in
the first work that does not occur in the second, as well as a great difference
in the attitudes projected by the books at their conclusions.

The Dying Earth's first story begins with a search for knowledge. Turjan
of Miir, a studious and accomplished wizard, has succeeded many times over

in creating artificial life in his workroom. He has *not* succeeded in bringing to life creatures of "normal configuration," nor has he yet managed to duplicate humanity in his nutrient vats. These failures trouble him so badly that he seeks out Pandelume, a more knowledgeable wizard, intending to buy the secret of the "master-matrix" by serving the stronger magician.

Turjan gains the knowledge he craves by stealing an amulet for Pandelume. He also gains two things he did not originally seek: an introduction to T'sais, a lovely but flawed woman created by Pandelume, and the means of re-creating her without the flaw. T'sais can see beauty in nothing, and hates everyone and everything she encounters; T'sain, Turjan's creation, sees beauty everywhere and hates nothing.

The women accidentally meet during Turjan's and T'sain's preparations to return to Earth. (Pandelume lives in Embelyon, also referred to as the "Land None Knows Where.") Despite Turjan's dire warnings, T'sain takes no harm from the encounter. Instead, she tells her look-alike of her own beauty, as well as of the anticipated beauties of Earth. T'sais, disturbed by the notion that she might be insane but intrigued by her double's words, lets T'sain pass and resolves to have Pandelume send her, too, to Earth.

Earth is not without its own difficulties, as Turjan and his companion are reminded in the second story. Captured by a rival, Mazirian the Magician, Turjan is shrunk and placed in a maze with a small dragon. Mazirian uses the hungry beast to torture his captive while he is himself troubled by the repeated appearances of a beautiful woman who is immune to his spells. Even Turjan and the secrets Mazirian wishes to pry from him are forgotten in this new obsession.

The woman is T'sain, and she succeeds in leading Mazirian to his doom and returning to release her creator from his prison, though injuries sustained in that effort cost her her life. Turjan, now in possession of his enemy's workroom as well as his own, carries her body away and vows to create one equally as lovely to house T'sain's brain.

T'sais, sent to Earth by Pandelume in the third story, has no easy journey, either. She stumbles upon Liane the Wayfarer, an egocentric highwayman, and two of his victims, managing to wound him and permitting the one still-living captive to escape. She is then set upon by robbers, whom she kills; and a deodand—a hybrid of wolverine, basilisk, and man with an insatiable hunger for human flesh—whom she escapes by taking refuge with a most unfortunate young man.

T'sais's host, once handsome, now wears a hood to conceal the hideous demon-face a witch's curse inflicted on him. After they intrude on a Black Sabbath and capture the witch responsible for the curse, the pair force her to go with them before an ancient god known for dispensing justice. The young man's face is restored to him, T'sais is freed of the defect that made her beauty-blind, and the witch is left with the demoniac visage. "To each who comes, justice is done," explains the god.

Liane the Wayfarer, the subject of the fourth story, also meets with a kind of rough justice. Conceited, supremely self-confident, and determined to have his usual way with an emphatically uninterested woman, he goes on an errand of thievery for her as payment in advance for her favors. Too late, Liane discovers that the woman operates as a Judas goat for an entity far more powerful than he. It is this creature's pleasure to decorate his robes with the eyes of his murdered victims, and he finds Liane's a fine addition to his collection.

In the fifth story, Ulan Dhor is the nephew of a powerful wizard and wishes to ferret out new spells and incantations in order to strengthen both himself and his relative. He journeys to a faraway city, once ruled by a magician of legendary might, and labors to uncover the ancient ruler's secrets. In the process, he allies himself with a young woman of that city and together they find not only the ruler's magic but also the ruler himself, preserved in suspension for five thousand years. Dhor, having found more than he wanted, destroys the now-mad wizard and flees with the woman who has befriended him.

The central figure in *The Dying Earth*'s last tale is, once again, a seeker after knowledge. Unlike the others, however, Guyal of Sfere wishes to learn for learning's sake alone, rather than in any hope of professional or financial gain. He plagues his father with so many unanswerable questions that the man despairs of ever satisfying him, and the local villagers joke about part of Guyal's brain having been stolen during his mother's labor. When his exasperated sire finally refuses to submit to any further questioning, Guyal leaves his home to look for the Museum of Man. This legendary establishment, and its Curator, are said to possess the sum of all knowledge; through them, Guyal reasons, he may at last receive the wisdom he craves.

After overcoming many obstacles and gaining a young woman as traveling companion, Guyal gains entry to the Museum. The facility has been invaded by a demon, who has attempted to overthrow the Curator and who has been terrorizing the locals for many centuries. Aided by Guyal, the ancient Curator defeats the demon at last, though he also dies as a result of the battle. As he expires, the Curator tells Guyal how to unlock all of the Museum's information and reveals that information's true worth: "Attend: the stars are bright, the stars are fair; the banks know blessed magic to fleet you to youthful climes." Guyal, who wanted knowledge of his doomed world and race, has instead discovered the knowledge required to free humanity from its exhausted home. *The Dying Earth* ends on this optimistic note.

Less optimistic—but more humorously written—is Vance's *The Eyes of the Overworld*, a novel set in the same twilight period as the earlier work. Cugel the Clever, the central character in this book, is as determined and self-interested as any of the characters in *The Dying Earth*; where he differs from each of them, however, is in the roundabout and often comic way he pursues his goals.

Cugel, a petty thief and confidence man, is attempting (and failing) to sell bogus talismans at a fair when a nearby magician approaches him with an offer. If Cugel will burgle the manse of Iucounu the Laughing Magician, this lesser wizard will pay him handsomely for all the treasures he obtains. In addition, Cugel's adviser agrees to keep Iucounu busy at the fair long enough to permit the thief time to work.

Unfortunately for Cugel—who agrees to the enterprise—Iucounu has booby-trapped his home so well that escape with the stolen goods is impossible. When the magician returns from the fair, Cugel is still trapped inside the manse, literally holding the bag. After threatening him with such dire punishments as the Charm of Forlorn Encystment (an incantation which traps its victims in pores of rock some forty-five miles beneath the surface of the Earth), Iucounu decides to put Cugel to work for him instead.

The magician desires a small hemisphere of violet glass, mate to the one he already possesses, and declares that Cugel shall be the one to obtain it for him. To ensure the thief's arrival at the place where hemispheres can be found, Iucounu sends him off in a demon-powered cage; and to ensure Cugel's dedication to the task, he insinuates into the thief's body a small, alien creature from the star Achernar. Firx, as the creature is known, does not wish to leave the fellow alien remaining in Iucounu's vat, and will torment his host severely if Cugel dawdles in completing his mission.

After this inauspicious launching, Cugel finds that the next part of his work goes relatively smoothly. The cusps—actually demoniac relics called Eyes of the Overworld because they permit their wearers to view the next-highest level of existence—are distributed among the residents of a small village. Each pair, upon the death of its owner, is given to the peasant next in line who has labored the longest in supporting and feeding the village. (Those wearing the cusps, who fancy themselves princes and princesses, do no work at all.) Cugel arrives shortly before such a transfer is to take place and cunningly substitutes himself for the peasant who has toiled thirty-one years for his cusps.

Arranging his investiture is the last thing Cugel finds easy. Midway through the ceremony, when the thief is wearing only one cusp, the peasant he has cheated bursts in and demands that he be given his due. This causes no end of difficulty for the village leader, who finally declares that Cugel, now elevated, may not be returned to his cuspless status; the peasant will, instead, be given the remaining half of the pair. The peasant's wrath, and the peasant's equally wrathful fellows, are the first obstacles Cugel must overcome in order to return the cusp to Iucounu and free himself.

Overcome them he does. A local ruler, a woman, takes a fancy to the cusp and steals it from him; Cugel finds a bracelet which identifies him as the rightful liege of her country, uses it to gain access to the cusp, and must finally surrender the bracelet to its true owner to avoid becoming demon-food. He is tricked by the inhabitants of Vull, a small village in the Mountains of Magnatz, into becoming their permanent sentry, but manages (with considerable prompting from Firx) to escape the sentry tower, thus breaking the spell that has kept the creature called Magnatz at bay and leaving the village open to destruction.

Cugel also destroys the lifework of a wizard, tricks an unfortunate band of pilgrims into accompanying him through an area he could not pass without a large party, and is captured (after the last of the pilgrims has been killed) by rat-folk with a taste for human flesh. When he frees himself from his captors with a book of spells he has found in their tunnels, Cugel finds that he has also freed the book's owner. Grateful, the magician drives Firx from Cugel's body and transports the thief and his cusp back home.

Cugel has a duplicate of the cusp made and takes it to Iucounu's manse, planning one more attempt at cozening the Laughing Magician. He finds that matters stand in a far more favorable state for him than obtained when he left: Iucounu has been taken over by Firx's comrade and has virtually no will of his own left. Cugel drives the alien parasite from its host and imprisons Iucounu in a glass tube, his mouth sealed shut to prevent him from using any magic to escape.

With his enemy thus at his mercy, Cugel diverts himself by tormenting Iucounu with his own spells and exhibiting him to public ridicule. Cugel possesses no great native talent as a magician, however, and the spells he uses often go awry when he reverses their "pervulsions." Displaying his prisoner leads to further difficulties when it attracts the attention of the magician who sent him to rob Iucounu in the first place. Since he advised Cugel to pillage the more powerful magician's manse, this worthy declares, the thief is morally obligated to let him share in Iucounu's wealth.

A struggle ensues in which Iucounu, though still unable to speak, is freed from his tube. Furious, Cugel announces that he is done with them both and will now perform the Charm of Forlorn Encystment upon them. His lack of aptitude proves his undoing, however, for in attempting to send his enemies to prisons in the Earth, he frees all those who have ever been so cursed. Nor does a second attempt work better:

> "Appear, appear!" called Cugel. "The desination is as before: to the shore of the northern sea, where the cargo must be delivered alive and secure!"
> A great flapping buffeted the air; a black shape with a hideous visage peered down. It lowered a talon; Cugel was lifted and carried off to the north, betrayed a second time by a misplaced pervulsion.

Cugel's luck has run out on him for the last time, returning him to a part of the world in which he has managed to enrage almost everyone he encountered.

His prospects do not look good.

In *The Eyes of the Overworld*, then, Vance has shown his protagonist defeating himself with his own ineptitude and greed, while *The Dying Earth* ended with a promise of ultimate victory. In both cases, however, Vance has shown that human endeavor, whether for good or ill, continues undaunted even in the face of approaching doom. It is a welcome message.

Christine Watson

Bibliography

Levack, Daniel J. H., and Tim Underwood. *Fantasms: A Bibliography of the Literature of Jack Vance*, 1978.
Underwood, Tim, and Chuck Miller, eds. *Jack Vance*, 1980.

THE EARTHSEA TRILOGY

Author: Ursula K. Le Guin (1929-   )
First book publications: A Wizard of Earthsea (1968); *The Tombs of Atuan* (1971);
  The Farthest Shore (1972)
Type of work: Novels
Time: A legendary time roughly equivalent to the early Iron Age and the Mycenaean
  Age as recalled in classical Greek literature
Locale: The Terrestrial Archipelago of Earthsea and the surrounding Reaches and
  Open Sea

*In Earth's distant past, when magic was a practical craft and high art, the boy Duny
becomes the man-child Ged, who goes on to become a mage (wizard), a man, and then
the greatest of the Archmages of Earthsea*

Principal characters:
>   GED (CHILD-NAME, DUNY; USE-NAME, SPARROWHAWK), a wizard
>   of Earthsea
>   OGION THE SILENT, his master in his early apprenticeship in magic
>   VETCH, Ged's friend
>   JASPER, Ged's apparent rival at the school for wizards
>   TENAR (ARHA, THE EATEN ONE), the One Priestess of the tombs
>   of Atuan
>   KOSSIL, the High Priestess of the Godking of the Kargad Empire
>   and antagonist to Tenar
>   ARREN (TRUE-NAME, LENANNEN), the son of the Prince of Enlad
>   and ultimately King of All the Isles of Earthsea
>   COB, the powerful sorcerer who finds the secret of immortality and
>   nearly destroys the world
>   ORM EMBAR, the Dragon of Selidor and ally with Ged against Cob

Great art is widely accessible, pleasing and instructing an entire culture and making the basic truths of that culture lively, significant, and immediately relevant to people's lives. The greatest art also speaks to a wide audience and repeats and renews a culture's truisms; in addition, it teaches less familiar things—truths one should know and possibly does know but does not like to hear. By these criteria, Ursula K. Le Guin's Earthsea trilogy ranks with the greatest art.

The trilogy was written as juvenile literature and works well in that genre. The Earthsea trilogy will teach or reteach its readers things familiar from their cultural heritage: the dangers of overweening pride and the will to dominate others—to reduce the "Other" to a thing to be vanquished or manipulated, an "It" and not a "You"; the necessity for living in harmony with the physical environment; the importance of compassion and love, what Le Guin calls in her fiction "touch"; the centrality of the pair-bond, the loving connection between two people, for true human community. These are commonplace ideas but important ones. Great narratives use such commonplaces unabashedly, giving them local habitations and names, placing them within stories that make one feel the truth of such clichés—and, sometimes, making one realize their radical implications. Such ideas are embodied in the Earthsea trilogy, quite literally "informing" it, giving it artistic form. Other ideas, however, are here as well, ideas less familiar to Western readers, ideas radically opposed to some of the assumptions of what one of Le Guin's characters in *The Lathe of Heaven* (1971) calls "the Judeo-Christian-Rationalist West." The great trick of the trilogy is not so much getting readers to suspend their disbelief in magic and dragons as in getting Western readers to suspend their belief in several fundamental assumptions of their culture. While held in the spell of Le Guin's art, they learn of alternatives to their aggressive, overactive culture.

The Earthsea trilogy, then, is high art, and its overarching story is that of the development of an artist, the wizard Ged. The trilogy, however, is no futile exercise in "metafiction," glorying in elite irrelevance to the real world and to the lives of people who are not artists. Ged is an artist, the greatest practitioner of the art of magic in the history of Earthsea, but more important is the fact that Ged is a man: a great artist and hero indeed, but one who must endure the trials faced by any man who would become fully human. Ged's art as such is rarely a problem for him; except for the period just after he is attacked by his shadow, magic comes easily to him. His problem is learning how to use his gift, and when and for what purposes—a general human problem, not unique to art and artists. The Earthsea trilogy is Ged's story, covering his boyhood, youth, and passage to wholeness as a man in *A Wizard of Earthsea*; a crucial adventure of his vigorous young adulthood in *The Tombs of Atuan*; and the culminating adventure of his even more vigorous maturity in *The Farthest Shore*. Taken together, the three novels form a classically elegant *Bildungsroman* and, to a lesser extent, a *Künstlerroman*, a novel of the development of an artist.

A Wizard of Earthsea traces Ged's development into a youth who will release his shadow upon the world (manifested as a shape-changing monster of darkness), the release of the shadow, and Ged's development into a man, one who recognizes the shadow as part of himself: he frees the world and himself from the threat of the shadow by calling it by his own name and incorporating the shadow into his being, his self. The principal action of *The Tombs of Atuan* is Ged's rescue of the Priestess Arha from the sterile service of the Old Powers of the Earth and his bonding with her in symbolic marriage; together they restore to Earthsea the Ring of Erreth-Akbe, a great talisman which, once returned, will allow the development of truer, more complete community in Earthsea. In terms of the psychology of Carl Gustav Jung, the first book of the trilogy shows Ged's integration with his shadow to form a fuller "Self"; the second book, in part, shows Ged's coming to terms with his anima, the feminine principle in him (and every human male). In *The Farthest*

Shore, Ged must confront death, restoring the proper relationship between the worlds of life and death in Earthsea and establishing that proper relationship in the mind of Prince Arren, the boy whom he initiates into manhood and prepares for kingship.

A Wizard of Earthsea may be viewed almost totally from Ged's point of view without doing violence to its meaning, since—for all its exciting adventures and real threats to Ged's world—it is still primarily a symbolic story, an allegory of psychological conflict and reconciliation. *A Wizard of Earthsea* is about Ged's recognition that his shadow, the monster he releases, is *his* shadow: his arrogance, his presumptuous pride, his mortality—the shadow, in short, of all that men's conscious minds devoutly wish to deny is theirs, especially the recognition that death is something within each of them, personally. The second two books of the trilogy are more complex, and they forbid a reading of the trilogy as a single straight line of Ged's story from birth to retirement.

Indeed, neither *The Tombs of Atuan* nor *The Farthest Shore* is told from Ged's point of view; Ged does not even appear until the fifth chapter of *The Tombs of Atuan*. The viewpoint character in *The Tombs of Atuan* is Tenar, the anima-figure to be rescued; the viewpoint character in *The Farthest Shore* is Arren. This play between various points of view will come as no surprise to students of Le Guin's science fiction; *The Left Hand of Darkness* (1969) "is all one story," and it, too, is told from various points of view. "The truth," as the narrator of *The Farthest Shore* observes, "varies with the man." To fulfill art's obligation to truth, Le Guin often chooses multiple points of view. Additionally, telling the story of Ged's rescue of an anima-figure from that character's point of view allows Le Guin to present the anima-figure as a fully developed character, not merely a missing part of the hero in a psychological allegory.

Most important, however, the multiple viewpoints in the Earthsea trilogy allow Le Guin to deal three times with a major theme of the trilogy: coming of age. In *A Wizard of Earthsea*, one sees Ged's coming of age, the coming of age of a great wizard. In *The Tombs of Atuan*, one sees the coming of age of a girl as Tenar finds a man and symbolic sexuality, finds trust and very explicit (and painful) freedom. In *The Farthest Shore*, one sees the coming of age of Arren, a boy without any magic power but who is destined to be the King of All the Isles of Earthsea: the hero not as artist or sage but as man of action and king, the lord of himself, of others, and of life.

The multiple points of view create a circularity in the trilogy which complements the linearity of Ged's heroic and artistic career. Each individual comes into adulthood only once, but the process is repeated with each generation. Ged's relationship with Arren, that of the old man to the child, is a recapitulation of that archetype in *A Wizard of Earthsea*, where Ged was a rather stubborn child to Ogion's old man. Moreover, at the end of the trilogy,

Ged retires, his magic spent, to his home on the island of Gont, seeking Ogion and Ogion's life of "being" as opposed to "doing." The true journey, Le 'Guin insists, is the circular journey leading home, and Ged returns home, leaving Arren to carry on the life of action. The straight line of the individual's life combines with the cycles of nature and of the generations. With a good deal of luck, the combination of line and circle yields a spiral, one moving upward or onward to larger and better worlds, worlds more truly fit for human habitation. The Earthsea trilogy traces a beneficent spiral, leading to ever more complete integration.

These, briefly, are the major movements of the trilogy as a whole. With these in mind, one may proceed readily to the world of the trilogy and the plots, characters, images, diction, and themes of the individual novels as they work out their stories in Le Guin's godless yet ethically demanding universe.

The first characteristic that should strike most readers about the world of the trilogy is its flatness and small scale. Even readers familiar with medieval and Renaissance literature, who can adjust easily to the snug comfort of a Ptolemaic, Earth-centered universe, are accustomed to more depth and more space: the spheres of Heaven above, the Earth in the center, hell beneath. A wise wizard such as Ged may intuit the existence of other worlds beyond Earthsea and know that the stars will outlast his world, but such insights are relatively irrelevant in the world of the trilogy. For all practical purposes, Earthsea is covered with the dome of the sky; there is no Heaven above, but only the ancient starry heavens. There is also no hell below, not in the Christian sense of hell; there is only the Dry Land of the dead, and even that is not exactly "below." In Earthsea, the Dry Land touches the familiar world and is reached by a spirit journey, with the crucial step of the journey taken over a low wall of stones. If one wishes to take most of the trip physically, one sails toward the sunset, to the last shore in the West. From there, one travels in spirit down "a long slope of darkness going down into the dark." Rather than making a rapid descent like that of Christ or Dante or most other heroes, Ged and Arren sail west, as Odysseus did, and then go down a slope into a land that has its own dome of sky and that contains all the dead, virtuous and vicious alike. Even the domain of the chthonic Old Powers of the Earth is relatively shallow, shallow enough to break through to the surface in the area of the Tombs of Atuan. Below the underground parts of the Tombs of Atuan are inaccessible and ethically irrelevant strata of rock, strata leading down to the purely physical fires at the Earth's core.

Humans in Earthsea are, in Jean-Paul Sartre's words, "on a plane where there are only men." Above, there is only "the empty sky," with no God or gods, no Heaven as a final goal for the good. Below, there are the ancient realms of darkness, chaos, and madness, the womb of the Great Mother as seen by humans before they had personified their gods enough even to talk of Mother Earth. In the farthest West, and ever at hand, is what the Hebrews called Sheol and the ancient Greeks called the Realm of Hades: the Dry Land, or Death. In its largest outlines, the world of Earthsea is a classically heroic world: the world of the more philosophical pagans in Homer's epics and in *Beowulf* (c. 1000); the world of Job and the heroic philosopher Koheleth (the Preacher in Ecclesiastes); the uncertain, insecure world of William Shakespeare's *King Lear* (1605).

The social and cultural world of Earthsea is also heroic; it is the time of the last heroes, Ged and Arren, who bring the heroic age to an end with Arren's ascension as high King. In physical culture, Earthsea is in the early Iron Age, with some technology (such as compasses) that the historical Iron Age lacked. In one or two places, steel has been made, but in backward areas, such as Ged's native island of Gont, bronze is still the main metal. Outside of the school for wizards on Roke (necessarily a kind of meritocracy), the social organization is generally (and loosely) feudal. Before Ged and Tenar restore the Ring of Erreth-Akbe and when Cob reigns as Anti-King of Life and Death, there is piracy and slave-taking. In the early years of Ged's life, the Inter Lands are raided by semibarbaric, white-skinned, Viking-like warriors of the Kargad Lands. All in all, this is a world familiar to readers of the *Iliad* and the *Odyssey* (both c. 800 B.C.), *Beowulf*, and the Norse sagas. If the milieu seems different from the usual view of the heroic ages, that fact is largely the result of Le Guin's unusual ideas about heroism.

Le Guin's hero, Ged, becomes a mage; like Le Guin, he is an artist of words. Ordinary physical heroism would be easy for Ged; he needs to learn philosophical heroism to face his world with courage, seeking the ways in which he can contribute to life. Most immediately, he must learn what *not* to do and, more generally, *how* not to do; he must eventually learn Unaction, the action-yielding stillness of a Taoist sage.

The early portions of the plot of *A Wizard of Earthsea* show Ged as an arrogant youth, eager to use his inborn powers and newly learned skills of magic to earn fame and power. He begins his training as an apprentice to Ogion the Silent of Gont, a master who could teach Ged what he most needs to learn: patience, silence, following the order of things (the Balance, or Equilibrium—Yin-Yang, arising from the Tao, the Way). Ged, though, wants to force the world to obey his will. Ogion tries to teach Ged the advantages of a life of being over a life of doing. Ged wants action, however, and glory, as is clear when he tries to impress an aristocratic witch-girl by learning a spell for summoning the dead. Ged succeeds only in summoning a thing of darkness, the shadow of his shadow. Ogion then offers to send Ged to the school for wizards on Roke, and Ged leaps at the offer. Ged excels at Roke, and his abilities are adequately recoginized. Only the aristocratic older student Jasper withholds the respect that Ged sees as his due. When Jasper, a sorcerer, mocks Ged, Ged is so angered that he challenges Jasper to a contest in magic, thereby violating a wise rule on Roke and rejecting the urgent entreaties of his friend Vetch. On a night of great power, "the shortest night of full moon of the year," at a place of great power, Roke Knoll, Ged prepares to summon up the spirit of Elfarran, a legendary beauty who has been dead for a thousand years. On Roke Knoll, Ged's hatred for Jasper and his anger at Jasper's slights disappear and are "replaced by utter certainty. He need envy no one." Ged feels his great power on the Knoll: "He knew now that Jasper was far beneath him . . . no rival but a mere servant of Ged's destiny."

A sense of destiny is not necessarily a bad trait in Le Guin's universe, nor are certainty, pride, or anger necessarily bad; according to Le Guin, few things are good or bad unless their context makes them so. Such arrogant certainty, however, such a desire to demonstrate raw power for the purpose of humbling a perceived rival, is evil, and a great evil comes from Ged's succumbing to this temptation to demonstrate his power. Ged does summon Elfarran from the dead, but along with her comes Ged's shadow. This shadow-monster mauls Ged's face, marking him forever and almost killing him; only the immediate appearance of the Archmage Nemmerle and a feat of great magic banish the shadow from Roke. Nemmerle soon dies, exhausted by his deed. The rest of *A Wizard of Earthsea* consists of Ged's first fleeing and then hunting his shadow. The key parts of Ged's subsequent quest in this book are his resisting two temptations and making two important human contacts.

After Ged is attacked by his shadow, he falls into illness and then into despair. He is saved from despair by his friend Vetch, who comes to see him just before Vetch leaves Roke. Vetch gives Ged a great gift: he tells Ged his true name. Since in Earthsea the name of a thing is the essence of the thing, knowing a true name is a source of power over the thing or person named. When Vetch and Ged exchange names, they exchange a profound trust. This act of friendship gives Ged the will to survive.

Ged then faces two major temptations. In the first, he confronts the Old Dragon of Pendor, seeking to force the dragon to promise not to raid the Archipelago. The dragon tempts Ged by telling him that he can offer Ged safety by naming his shadow. Ged can have the shadow's name or the dragon's promise to leave humans in peace, not both. Ged resists the dragon's temptation, putting social duty above his personal desire to be rid of his shadow. A force of the Old Powers, the spirit of the Terrenon Stone, also may be able to supply the name of Ged's shadow. This temptation Ged also resists, knowing that the Old Powers of Earth are not for human use and that a bad means will yield a bad end.

Le Guin cannot be overly explicit in describing the danger Ged faces without giving away the ending of *A Wizard of Earthsea*, but upon rereading the book, one can note that Ged did well not to ask either the dragon or the Stone for his shadow's name. In naming the shadow, they would have named Ged, thereby gaining power over him.

Ged flees the forces of the Terrenon Stone and of the Lord of the Court and returns to Gont, having changed himself into a hawk. Ogion releases Ged from hawk form and receives from Ged recognition as Ged's true teacher (and substitute father). Ogion gives Ged some important advice: first, that the true nature of the threat of the shadow is its desire to take over Ged's being and, second, that the shadow has a name, a point doubted by the new Archmage and other masters on Roke, more reliable authorities than dragons or stones. Most important, Ogion tells Ged, "You must turn around." Now, Ogion says, the shadow drives Ged, choosing his way. If Ged is to save himself, he "must choose." A man, Ogion insists, cannot know his end

> if he does not turn, and return to his beginning, and hold that beginning in his being. If he would not be a stick whirled and whelmed in the stream, he must be the stream itself, all of it, from its spring to its sinking in the sea. You returned to Gont, you returned to me, Ged. Now turn clear round, and seek the very source, and that which lies before the source. There lies your hope of strength.

Ged follows this advice and later comes to understand it. Immediately, he sets off to hunt his shadow, a literal turning around and the turning point of the novel.

During his hunt, Ged is tricked by his shadow; shipwrecked on a reef, he discovers an old brother and sister who had been exposed there on orders of the Godking of the Kargad Empire. The woman gives him a gift, half of an old ring: it is half of the Ring of Erreth-Akbe. Later, Ged meets Vetch on Vetch's native island, and the two go together for the final confrontation between Ged and his shadow.

Ged and his shadow meet in a nowhere land, a sandy, "dry land" that forms upon the surface of the "living sea." In the moment of confrontation, Ged and the shadow speak simultaneously, together saying the word "Ged": "Light and darkness met, and joined, and were one." The narrator says that Ged's merging with his shadow was neither victory nor defeat for him. Ged, by naming "the shadow of his death with his own name, had made himself whole: a man: who, knowing his whole true self"—including its evil and its mortality—"cannot be used or possessed by any power other than himself, and whose life therefore is lived for life's sake and never in the service of ruin, or pain, or hatred, or the dark." This description of the merging of Ged with his shadow temporarily resolves a theme that will be completed in *The Farthest Shore* and completes in *A Wizard of Earthsea* the pattern suggested by the mark left by the shadow's initial attack on Ged. Ged's scars are white; his skin is dark. His face, then, becomes a Yin-Yang symbol in itself. This symbol gains psychological meaning in Ged's merging with his shadow. A whole man is light and dark, good and evil, ego and shadow. He draws strength from his full being, including the powerful, dark, amoral, subconscious shadow portion at the source of his being. Such a man can make significant choices; if he chooses well, he incorporates his being and his doing into what Ogion called "the stream": he goes with the Tao, the Way, which is nature and being itself.

Ged's newly attained wholeness and balance is put into this universal context immediately after his merging with his shadow. Vetch here, almost at the end of *A Wizard of Earthsea*, repeats the lines that are in its Epigraph: "Only in silence the word, only in dark the light, only in dying life: bright the hawk's flight on the empty sky." Both the immanent, undivine Tao (the source of Yin-Yang) and Le Guin's universe contain these oppositions; in merging with his shadow, the forever-scarred Ged comes to contain them as well. Paradoxically, the acceptance by Ged—the Sparrowhawk—of his darkness brightens his flight across that empty sky.

His flight eventually takes him to Atuan. Ged here is a young man, somewhere in his twenties or early thirties. It is time for him, as hero, to rescue a fair maiden (literally fair, since Tenar is Kargish and therefore white); but Le Guin persists in handling traditional motifs in unusual ways.

In *A Wizard of Earthsea*, Ged meets his monstrous enemy and comes to acknowledge this thing of darkness as his own: this wisdom is found in Shakespeare's Prospero and Walt Kelly's *Pogo* (1951) but rarely in heroic fiction, where evil is usually of the "Other": foreign foes, aliens, monsters. In *The Tombs of Atuan*, Le Guin tells a fairly standard rescue story, but does so from the maiden's point of view, providing the trilogy's second story of coming of age; Le Guin also asserts the rights of the Darkness.

The Darkness, the Old Powers, do *not* have a right to Tenar, nor do they have the right to the service, much less the worship, of any human being. They have, however, the right to be acknowledged: they are "the Ones whom we call Nameless, the ancient and holy Powers of the Earth before the Light." These are "the powers of the dark, or ruin, of madness"; they exist and are, as Ged tells Tenar, "holy."

The plot of *The Tombs of Atuan* is simple in structure, following Tenar's life from childhood through her perverted passage into full power as the One Priestess and on to her rescue by Ged and their arrival at Havnor, the political center and "heart" of Earthsea. The reader is also told that Ged will soon take Tenar to stay with Ogion until she is ready to face what is for her the huge new world of the Archipelago.

In Tenar's life, one sees the sterility of Atuan. The land around the tombs is a desert, a place of stasis. Atuan itself is part of an aggressive, militaristic, slave-keeping empire ruled by a Godking who holds power in small part through his people's superstitious awe of him and in larger part through military power and through the murder of enemies. The agent of these royal murders is Arha, the One Priestess. At Atuan, the powers of darkness have taken more than their due, and Ged steals from them what they have usurped—the Ring and Tenar—and indirectly brings about an earthquake that restores the Darkness to its proper place, correcting an imbalance. Ged does not, however, make any attempt to destroy the Old Powers, nor does he ravish Tenar or even marry her. Their sexual union is symbolized by Ged's penetration into Tenar's domain as Arha and his bringing light from his wizard's staff to the shallow underworld of the Undertomb. In addition, their marriage is symbolized by Ged's joining the two halves of the Ring of Erreth-Akbe as he reaches his black hand to touch the Ring on her white arm when Tenar doubts him and fears the despair and pain that comes with freedom.

Ged does not slay a monster at Atuan, marry a princess, and bring fertility to a wasteland. He refuses to interfere with the wasteland. He recognizes the rights of the Darkness, but he will rob the Darkness when it encroaches upon life and usurps things of Light. He brings Tenar to womanhood not by copulating with her but by forcing her to *choose*: she can come with him and be reborn as Tenar, or she can kill him and remain Arha. She chooses life and freedom.

The implications of Arha's choosing to be Tenar prepare the reader for important general themes in *The Farthest Shore*; the plot device of the Ring binds together the plots of the books in the trilogy. The castaways episode in *A Wizard of Earthsea* introduces the half-Ring and establishes the premise of *The Tombs of Atuan*; the newly joined Ring at the end of *The Tombs of Atuan* is ultimately for Arren, when he becomes King at the end of *The Farthest Shore*.

More specifically, *The Tombs of Atuan* introduces two ideas central to *The Farthest Shore*: not only the general rights of the Darkness but also the specific wrong of lusting after immortality. The Kargish people believe in gods (more or less) and in eternal life through eternal reincarnation. The mages, the Priestess Kossil says, are atheists, and, after their deaths, they "are not reborn. . . . They do not have immortal souls." Her first statement is correct; where mages dwell in Earthsea, there is no worship of the gods. Her other statements, however, are misleading. True, people in the trilogy do not have immortal souls in the traditional Christian understanding of immortality. There is in Earthsea no reincarnation of the dead and no Heaven, only the Dry Land, where there is no consciousness and where the individual becomes "a shadow and a name." Death receives all that remains of the essence one has created throughout one's life through one's choices. That essence, however, is nothing but "dust and shadows." Far more important is what remains of one on Earth. Ged tells Cob that Erreth-Akbe, though long dead, "is the earth and sunlight, the leaves of trees, the eagle's flight. He is alive. And all who ever died, live; they are reborn and have no end." This is immortality, but immortality in the sense that the Taoist philosopher Chuang Tzu talked of the immortality of Tzu Yu: the return of the body to the natural cycles. Ged refers elsewhere in *The Farthest Shore* to the participation in "being" by all who live and die: all people are like waves on the sea of being. The belief in immortality in the Kargad Empire is wrong, but it is important in that Tenar becomes the One Priestess because she is assumed to be the reincarnation of the former One Priestess; the Kargish belief in immortality helps to prepare the reader for *The Farthest Shore*, in which the notion of eternal life in the Christian sense is shown to be ultimately destructive.

Arren wants to be immortal; he fears death. Arren's desire and fear are blameless and rational, since most people dread death. Le Guin acknowledges death's horror, and everyone in *The Farthest Shore* can be tempted by immortality—everyone except, possibly, the masters on Roke, and Ged, who has learned wisdom and who desires nothing beyond his art.

In this book, Le Guin explicitly opposes not only the Judeo-Christian tradition but also all the other religious and philosophical traditions that seek or promise eternal life—all the traditions that promise the safety and certainty of absolutes. Le Guin insists upon a human sense of the sacred and upon the existence of the holy. Consistently, however, she has denied the easy absolutes that come from rationalized systems where there are gods to reward and punish, gods or vast abstractions even to allow and forbid. This denial is made explicit when Ged asks Arren, "Who allows? Who forbids?"; but it is implicit in Le Guin's writing throughout the trilogy and reflected even in her diction. On all its levels, the Earthsea trilogy rejects any system of absolutes.

For an example, despite the commonly accepted absolute that stealing is a crime, Ged steals, as does Tenar. More important, the reader approves of their thefts. "You will not lie" is a legitimate paraphrase of a key tenet of the genteel code still prevalent in America. It is a rule Tenar lives by as Priestess and a rule which Le Guin herself imposes on mages. Tenar, however, lies to save Ged, and the disguised Ged lies in his rescue of Tenar and on his quest with Arren; and the reader approves of their lying.

Le Guin will not even allow an absolute, context-free code within her own writing; she demonstrates the relativity of almost all of her important terms. She does, however, introduce a "must" in negative ways, where people feel obligated to do one thing or another and are quite wrong. Touch, for example, is a good thing in Le Guin's fiction, when two people touch each other in love; it would be wrong, however, for Ged to have touched "the Stone" at the Court of the Terrenon. Silence and speech, dark and light, death and life have been recurring oppositions in the trilogy's imagery and language. Silence is a good thing in *A Wizard of Earthsea*; it is what Ged needs to learn from Ogion. Silence, however, is not absolutely good, not unequivocally, unambiguously, universally good; it is not good at Atuan, where the silent Old Powers have grown ascendant. Silence is not good where speech is called for in *The Farthest Shore*. Light is a good thing in *The Tombs of Atuan*, where Ged's magelight illuminates the beauty of the great cave that is the Undertomb, but in *A Wizard of Earthsea*, Ged must come to accept his own darkness.

So it is with Le Guin's other operative terms, with the notable exceptions of gray (which is negative if not the color of hair) and joy (which is primarily positive). Balance is the norm, not the golden mean of prudent "gray" mediocrity or some absolute code of conduct. Balance is doing the right thing, the appropriate thing, for the context. One must follow the Way, become the stream; one must discover the nature of things as they exist in the world, especially the nature of things in one's immediate environment, the things one can act on consciously and effectively, even as a wizard can only work useful magic on his immediate surroundings, on things he can know and name exactly. These are true general rules for actions. Right and wrong, useful abstract categories of good and evil—these are not possible.

Of all the good things in the world, however, life seems most clearly to be absolutely good, and to each man individually, his own death seems most clearly to be absolutely evil. Such is Arren's perspective also. In *The Farthest Shore*, however, Arren must be taken into the dark, into the rightful realm of death; he must be reconciled with his mortality. The plot of *The Farthest Shore* moves toward death—but also toward renewal.

At about the time Ged becomes Archmage, the sorcerer Cob achieves immortality by opening the door between life and death. Light and vividness, distinction and joy slowly drain from the world of life, as if Cob had opened in it a great wound. One of the first results of this wounding is the loss of magic in the more remote areas of Earthsea. Arren comes to Roke on a commission from his father to seek the counsel of the wise. Ged invites Arren with him on the quest to find the source of what seems to be a strange contagion, a radical imbalance, something outside the natural order. *The Farthest Shore* is the story of that quest, as Ged seeks a guide to what he correctly believes is a single man responsible for this evil. The quest moves from Roke to Hort Town, from Hort Town to Lorbanery. At Lorbanery, Ged finds Sopli, formerly the Dyer of Lorbanery and a man of power but now utterly mad. Sopli cries "I found it! I found it!," but he has found "it"— the way to eternal life, bodily immortality—far less than Cob has found him. Cob can do evil on a great scale, because he can press people like Sopli into his service. Cob appeals, as Ged tells Arren, to the "little traitor soul" in those who can understand him: artists and heroes, makers of magic and beauty, "the ones who seek to be themselves." Cob appeals to "the self that cries I want to live; let the world burn so long as I can live!" Ged will not hear this appeal, but Sopli listens, and it drives him mad.

Sopli soon drowns, but Arren also hears Cob—who whispers to him in his dreams much as Ged's shadow whispered to him. Arren seeks Cob and thus becomes Ged's final guide, the child Ged follows.

This following comes in the final part of the quest, the spirit journey. The physical end of the quest precedes it, and the guide here is the dragon Orm Embar. Cob cannot precisely tempt the dragons, but he can madden them;

he can take away from them their language, the Old Speech which is the language of magic and the language which Segory, the Eldest Lord, spoke at the Making. As the potential lord of the "unMaking," Cob has a decorous antipathy to dragons and their language. The threat to even the dragons has grown so great that Orm Embar does something very unusual for dragons, possibly unique: he appeals to help from a man, Ged. Orm Embar leads Ged and Arren to Selidor, at the very end of the West Reach. There Orm Embar is deprived of speech by Cob, who then paralyzes Arren and Ged with a spell and reaches out to touch Ged with the wizard's staff he wields, the staff of the significantly named Grey Mage. Orm Embar has been deprived of his speech but not of his will or of his brute strength and animal wisdom. He throws himself upon Cob's body and upon the enchanted steel blade of the staff. Thus Orm Embar saves Ged and Arren at the cost of his life.

Arren and Ged—side by side and later in that order—then follow Cob on the slow descent of the spirit journey into the Dry Land. There, at last, Arren and Ged defeat Cob and close the door between Life and Death, saving the world. This act exhausts Ged's magic powers and his strength, and Arren must lead him and carry him over the Mountains of Pain back to life.

Arriving back on Selidor and assuming their bodies, Arren gives Ged water—usually a symbol of life in the trilogy—and the two fly to Roke on Kalessin, the eldest of the dragons. At Roke, Ged kneels to Arren, publicly recognizing him as King of All the Isles, the awaited fulfillment of the prophecy that the King must be one who has crossed the land of the dead while living and has arrived at the *"far shores of the day."* Ged then remounts Kalessin and returns to Gont. As the Master Doorkeeper of Roke says, "He has done with doing. He goes home."

Le Guin then gives two alternatives for Ged's final end. The version in *The Deed of Ged* has Ged attend Arren's coronation in Havnor and then leave in his boat, *Lookfar*; his boat takes him "from Harbor and from haven . . . westward over sea" to an unknown destination. In the version of Ged's story told on Gont, Arren comes to Gont to bring Ged to his coronation and learns that Ged has gone alone into the mountain forests. When people offer to search for Ged, Arren forbids them, saying, "He rules a greater kingdom than I do." The first version properly closes Ged's life as a hero, like Alfred, Lord Tennyson's Ulysses—but without Ulysses' companions—sailing out of safety toward death. The second version properly closes Ged's life as mage: no longer having his art, he becomes a sage alone in a mountain forest. Both versions have Ged finally alone and finished with doing—heroic or artistic— and going home to being, either the pure being of death or to a life of being as a sage in a mountain forest, ruling over his self.

Arren and his people, one may assume, all live happily ever after, for as long as they remain alive, to the extent that people can find happiness in a world of pain and mortality. This, however, *is* a happy ending. In Le Guin's fairly consistently Taoist and quite consistently unchristian world of Earthsea, in the romantic, existentialist, paradoxical world she has created for children and young adults, in this brilliantly subversive, radically uncertain world of high art, she allows triumph and joy in the midst of pain and death. As Ged tells Arren, "There is no safety. . . . The dance is always danced . . . above the terrible abyss"; but only above the abyss, only in uncertainty and pain, will people reach out in love to touch one another—only above the terrible abyss can people dance the dance of human life.

Richard D. Erlich

Bibliography

Barbour, Douglas. "On Ursula Le Guin's 'A Wizard of Earthsea' [sic]," in *Riverside Quarterly*. VI (April, 1974), pp. 119-123.

Bittner, James W. "Approaches to the Fiction of Ursula K. Le Guin," 1979 (dissertation).

De Bolt, Joe, ed. *Ursula K. Le Guin: Voyager to Inner Lands and to Outer Space*, 1979.

Extrapolation. XXI, no. 3 (Fall, 1980).

Le Guin, Ursula K. *The Language of the Night: Essays on Fantasy and Science Fiction*, 1979. Edited by Susan Wood.

Olander, Joseph D., and Martin Harry Greenberg, eds. *Ursula K. Le Guin*, 1979.

THE EATER OF DARKNESS

Author: Robert M. Coates (1897-1973)
First book publication: 1929
Type of work: Novel
Time: The twentieth century
Locale: New York

Charles Dograr wanders through a surrealist landscape as he tries to extricate himself from his part in a series of fantastically executed murders committed by a mysterious scientist called "The Eater of Darkness" who assumes a multitude of personalities and somehow controls Dograr's actions

Principal characters:
> CHARLES DOGRAR, the deracinated protagonist
> "THE EATER OF DARKNESS," a mysterious international criminal and scientist
> ADELINE, Dograr's temporary lover who becomes his deadly enemy
> "THE MAN WITH THE WALKING STICK," a mysterious voyeur who may be "The Eater of Darkness" in disguise

Robert Coates's father, an itinerant metalworker, was an unusually restless man who pursued his various private visions from state to state across America. While Coates's preference for solitude in later life may reflect this youthful experience, he was noted among his friends for the amiability and openness of his personality. In fact, it is this quality of amiability that connects the seemingly disparate halves of his life.

During the second half of his life, he was an essayist, the respected art critic for *The New Yorker*, and a member of the National Academy of the Arts. Before settling into middle-class respectability, however, he spent most of the decade of the 1920's living the bohemian life of the expatriate writer in Paris, where his closest friends were Ernest Hemingway and Gertrude Stein. He was in Paris in 1924 when André Breton's *Mainfeste du surréalisme* appeared, and it was under the combined influences of Dadaism and surrealism that he began his first published novel, *The Eater of Darkness*.

Although the intervening half century has accustomed the reading public to the frenetic and anarchic energies of Dadaist and surrealistic art, *The Eater of Darkness* is an impressive comic fantasy. In 1926, however, it was not appreciated and was even somewhat feared as anarchic by most Parisian publishing houses. It was only through the efforts of Gertrude Stein that *The Eater of Darkness* was able to see publication; it then quickly established itself as a major "underground" novel. Ford Madox Ford hailed it as a Dadaist achievement of merit, and Coates's American publisher later advertised it as the first surrealist novel by an American. It is an amiable tour de force of eccentric wit and stylistic experimentation, which makes all the more disappointing the fact that it has been out of print since 1959.

Coates's major theme is the deception of appearances; indeed, his "layered" technique proliferates surfaces of all kinds. The use of multiple styles and multiple and ambiguous points of view implies that human perception is inadequate to the task of sorting out and knowing the distinctions between the surfaces of things and their true meanings. Indeed, it calls into doubt the existence of "true meanings." The novel shifts intertextual perspectives rapidly and radically—from persona to persona, from style to style, and from one typological device to another. Coates's concern, then, is with perception, and especially with the vitalist theory, popular in his day, that experience cannot be rationally known nor controlled by logic but only experienced in all its multiform complexity. The novel's tone and technique are determined by Coates's youthful infatuation with the anarchic energies of Dadaism and the allied surrealist doctrine that the novel should express the imagination directly and with as little conscious control as possible.

An examination of *The Eater of Darkness* shows clearly why surrealism should be considered a subgenre of the fantastic. The standard surrealist techniques—juxtapositions of normally incongruous materials, plotlessness, and wandering point of view—create a fantastic otherworldly atmosphere that relies for its effects upon the reader's willingness to suspend his common sense and to experience an alternate world ruled by the vague and often random phantoms of dream and desire.

The novel focuses upon a few weeks in the life of the deracinated and intensely alienated protagonist, Charles Dograr, a Frenchman who has gone to New York City for reasons that are never explained. The dreamlike quality that marks all surrealist fiction is established in the opening pages. The story opens (and closes) as a reverie in the mind of Dograr's mistress in France and then shifts to his confused adventures in New York. To achieve the dream-reverie effect, Coates replaces the temporal and spatial coherence of traditional fiction with a kaleidoscopic jumble of memories occurring in the girl's mind. Nothing in the novel proceeds in a clearly causal fashion; events seem merely to occur in no particular sequence, and the narrative shifts back and forth from Europe to America in a seemingly random manner. For example, the memory of his mistress' affair with Dograr is repeatedly punctuated by other memories that occur by a process of free association, introduced as parenthetical material inside the original memory. At times these memory-clusters are so thick that Coates uses parentheses inside parentheses inside parentheses to indicate the simultaneous, rather than the linear, nature of memory. Toward the end of her reverie, she experiences several free-associations that Coates numbers out of sequence as one, seven, four/three, five, and six; he omits number two altogether.

Such devices create an eerie quality of unreality (or surreality) that was somewhat shocking in 1926 (although Marcel Proust, James Joyce, and William Faulkner were already performing similar narrative experiments). In part, Coates's narrative structure reveals the influence of Freudian dream-analysis as championed by surrealism. Sigmund Freud had noted that the various elements and images of the unconscious do not emerge into consciousness in a logical or causal (sequential) fashion but, rather, as a jumble of images that relate to one another by the principle of association: one image recalls another similar one even though the two (or more) images may represent fragments of memory from widely different times or places. Some images are permanently repressed (as the number two is repressed or omitted in the disorganized sequence mentioned above), while others are linked by similarities and juxtaposed against each other instead of following a causal or linear order of emergence. The novel's techniques, therefore, are in keeping with the psychological model used by all the surrealists.

Framed by the thoughts of Dograr's mistress is the narrative proper, the tale of Dograr's preoccupation "with the problem of solving what is perhaps the greatest murder mystery of all time." Coates uses this pretext to launch into an intensely comic parody of various literary genres, including the detective story. While the novel is an extremely entertaining parody, it is much more than that. A number of Coates's antirealistic devices are explicable in terms of surrealism's ambition to "derange the senses" programmatically and to use the novel as a record of the nonlogical structures of the subconscious. Other devices in Coates's novel, however, are not understandable in terms of psychological concepts.

Dograr is a modern antihero in a tradition already established, notably by T. S. Eliot and Franz Kafka, by the 1920's. So alienated is he, in fact, that he often thinks of himself as an echo or shadow of some more substantial but undiscovered self. He inexplicably finds himself in New York City in order to solve a crime that has not yet happened; he rents a cheap room, lives solely on crackers, and wanders aimlessly about the city until he inexplicably enters a room containing "an old gentleman" and an intricate mystery machine. The old man seems to have been expecting him and shows Dograr the fantastic power of his invention. The machine, which "eats darkness," can pierce any substance and focus with deadly intensity upon any unsuspecting target. The device is an early type of laser, and the old gentleman—who calls himself "The Eater of Darkness"—is a parody of Mary Shelley's mad scientist.

In demonstrating the machine's powers, the old man creates a "Dead Plane," a fantasy region outside time and space from which he and Dograr aim the weapon's "x-ray bullet" and "scallop the brains" of unsuspecting and randomly chosen victims. Dograr thus becomes an accomplice in a multiple murder spree that ends only with the old man's death and Dograr's return (unpunished) to France.

Coates uses a number of devices that have since become standard avant-garde techniques but which were relatively new at the time he wrote the novel. For example, some chapters are designed as film scenarios, complete with numbered scenes and directional cues such as "Fade Out" and "Iris In." Others are constructed as newspaper headlines with both dialogue and expository description appearing in a variety of sizes and kinds of typescript. Some long passages are set in two-column fashion, with the left column in the form of a fragmented newspaper editorial and the right as traditional narration (each column also comments upon the other). Still other passages are comic lists (three pages long in one case), including the names of common objects, parts of the anatomy, the names of celebrities, and even the names of Coates's friends. Further, Coates mingles parodies of *True Confessions*, Gothic horror, hard-boiled detective fiction, and pornography.

It is Coates's turning of fiction into reflexive "metafiction," however, that is the most interesting and contemporary feature of the text. Like novels by such current writers as John Barth and Donald Barthelme, *The Eater of Darkness* often slyly comments upon its own fictiveness. The old gentleman's body contains "geometric designs like a page from a mathematical textbook"; footnotes are used throughout in a parody of academic writing (one of these footnotes chides "Mr. Robert Coates" for his inability to plot a story); Dograr has a dream from which he learns that he "shall not live long not [sic] more than 250 pages"—the length of the novel; the story contains an interruption directing the reader to "see page 108"; Dograr feels "little brown eyes like lead pencils leaving marks all over him"; the author's voice often intrudes and identifies now with Dograr, now with the reader, now with both.

Such metafictional devices point to Coates's buried theme, which is the logocentric character of modern experience. This logocentric and reflexive quality creates the "sense of wonder" that marks the text as a fantasy. The technique of endlessly mixing styles, points of view, and genres, and the repeated demonstrations of what Julia Kristeva has called the "intertextuality" of experience—the possibility that the reader as well as Dograr is in some sense "fictive"—call into question the distinctions between fact and fiction, realism and fantasy that the reader normally makes. Coates, Dograr, Dograr's mistress, "The Eater of Darkness," and the reader finally seem to mingle in an indistinguishable unity. In this sense, the novel seems quite contemporary.

The novel is a mystery story, but the reader never "solves the mystery" because the true problem with which Coates struggles in his entertaining way is not this or that murder, nor even the problem of the proper way to write a detective story; rather, he is concerned with the "mystery" of identity itself, of the distinction between appearance and reality, fact and fiction. The text's sustained comic inventiveness, multilayered structure, and vision of human experience as surreal rather than logically ordered and conceptually pure make *The Eater of Darkness*, an ignored minor masterpiece of antirealistic fiction, a novel that deserves the attention of all students of fantasy literature.

R. E. Foust

Bibliography
Cowley, Malcolm. "Afterword," in *Yesterday's Burdens*, 1975.
Pehowski, Marian. "Coates," in *Contemporary Novelists*, 1972. Edited by
    James Vinson.
Pierce, Constance. "'Divinest Sense': Narrative Techniques in Robert Coates's
    Yesterday's Burdens," in *Critique: Studies in Modern Fiction*. XIX, no. 2
    (1977), pp. 44-52.
Thrall, William Foint, Addison Hibbard, and C. Hugh Holman. *A Handbook
    to Literature*, 1960.

ECHOES FROM THE MACABRE

Author: Daphne du Maurier (1907-   )
First book publication: 1976
Type of work: Short stories

Nine short stories that explore the danger and menace that lie beneath the ordinary and familiar

In her long, prolific, varied writing career that has included such impressive novels as *Jamaica Inn* (1936), *Rebecca* (1938), *My Cousin Rachel* (1951), and *The House on the Strand* (1969), as well as a number of significant historical and biographical works, Daphne du Maurier has produced a modest number of subtle, and erudite short stories. The best of these have been collected in a single volume, *Echoes from the Macabre*, published in 1976.

The title of the collection, "echoes from the macabre," suggests the feelings provoked by the stories: "macabre" because all of the stories except one— "Kiss Me Again, Stranger," a tale of suspense about a psychotic murderess told from the viewpoint of her confused, frustrated, would-be boyfriend— deal with the irrational, dark forces lying beneath the placid surface of everyday life; "echoes" because these forces are, for the most part, approached through indirection, suggestion, and irony, leaving the reader poised uncertainly between the real and the demoniac. The stories are written in a clear, precise, understated style and carefully modulated tone that convey a sense of mounting anxiety and suppressed emotion that sometimes breaks into overt, graphic violence. They are carefully structured and neatly developed, frequently ending in twists that are as surprising as they are necessary. While the dominant mood of the stories is bleak, they are laced with touches of subtle humor.

This humor can be seen in two of the lighter stories in the collection, "The Old Man" and "The Blue Lenses." Indeed, "The Old Man" is little more than a joke, a kind of literary shaggy-dog story. The narrator becomes interested in a family and begins to study it, only to be horrified when the "old man"—the father—kills his son. The punchline of the story is in the last paragraph: "suddenly I saw the old man stretch his neck and beat his wings, and he took off from the water. . . ." The old man is a swan, not a human being. As "The Old Man" is about birds described as if they were human, "The Blue Lenses" is about humans who take on animal characteristics. After the bandages are removed from Marda West's eyes, following an operation to restore her damaged eyesight with implanted lenses, she sees people's faces turned into those of animals, the particular type of beast corresponding to the character of the person. Thus, one nurse looks like a cow, another like a cat, her doctor like a fox, and, most ominously, her special nurse, Miss Ansel, like a snake, and her husband, Jim, like a vulture. Feeling herself the victim of a conspiracy and sensing an affair between Nurse Ansel and Jim, she tries to escape, but she collapses. Subsequently, her eyes are operated on again and permanent lenses are implanted, after which everybody seems normal—until she looks into the mirror and sees a sacrificial doe. Both of these stories are humorous and clever, but "The Old Man" is merely that, while "The Blue Lenses" mixes humor with the truly macabre. The ending of "The Blue Lenses" is scary, not only because of the cleverness, but also because Marda West is a real character, a sensitive, fragile, helpless victim.

As in most of the best macabre fiction, it is this interaction between character and situation that generates the real horror. Du Maurier's characters suffer as much from their own psychological vulnerabilities as they do from external threats. In one of the best and longest of the stories, "The Apple Tree," the reader never knows whether the old, gnarled tree that finally captures the aged husband in its tangled roots actually contains the soul of his dead, vengeful wife, or if he has simply projected those attributes onto it. "The Chamois" may or may not be the incarnation of a pagan god, but it is the vehicle through which Stephen overcomes his fears and becomes reconciled with his wife. Similarly, Mr. Stoll in "Not After Midnight" may or may not be Silenus the Satyr, but his fate traumatically affects Mr. Gordon, a stuffy schoolmaster. Finally, whether the pool that young Deborah magically enters at night is real or is the product of her overheated imagination, its loss is terrible and frightening.

Surprisingly, du Maurier's two most famous stories, "Don't Look Now" and "The Birds," are not at all ambiguous in their presentation of evil: it is a real, palpable, destructive thing. In the former, evil takes the form of an irrational murderer in a strange guise; in the latter, it is embodied in a sudden "rebellion" against man by one of nature's presumably benign species, the birds. The fantastic element in "Don't Look Now" is not in the killer, but in the psychic paraphernalia that attracts and finally overwhelms the main characters, John and Laura.

While vacationing in Venice in an attempt to assuage their sorrows over the death of their five-year-old daughter Christine, John and Laura are accosted by a pair of aged twin ladies who claim to be psychics with a message from the dead girl—a warning to leave Venice. John scoffs; Laura believes. A telegram that their son has been taken suddenly ill sends Laura home and apparently confirms the warning. John plans to follow the next day, but, when he "sees" his wife and the sisters in Venice, he remains to investigate. He finally discovers that what he saw was a scene from the future, not the present. He is, the twins tell him, psychic. Not completely convinced, but less skeptical, he plans a belated return home, but before he can leave Venice, he encounters an angry mob chasing a child. He rescues the child—who turns out to be a dwarf, a hunted killer. John realizes, as he dies from a knife wound, that what he had seen the previous day was his own funeral party. "Don't Look

Now" is an exciting, suspenseful, provocative short story that turns on a number of bitter ironies: it was his own lost child that set John up for the dwarf's attack, and it was his own psychic powers—which he denied—that made him vulnerable.

If it is John's denial of the irrational that costs him his life, it is Nat Hocken's acceptance of it that enables him to survive, at least for a time, in du Maurier's short-story masterpiece, "The Birds." Although not the first important treatment of the "revolt of nature" (that honor probably goes to Arthur Machen's "The Terror," 1917), it is the most famous, due in part to Alfred Hitchcock's classic 1963 film version of the story. Yet, despite the power and resources of the film, the short story is far more horrific in its implications. The rebellion of the birds in Hitchcock's version is, finally, no more than a local aberration; in du Maurier's short story, the catastrophe is worldwide. Nat Hocken's family may, at the end of it, be the last people alive on earth and their hours are numbered. By focusing on a single family and only hinting at what is going on in the rest of the world, du Maurier creates one of the bleakest end-of-the-world scenarios in the genre.

The real horror in "The Birds" is that the birds always remain birds—they never become monsters or mutants or any of the other grotesque creatures of pulp fiction—and that, while their behavior is never explained, there is a chilling logic to it that makes it seem, at least within the context of the story, quite possible: "Nat listened to the tearing sound of splintering wood, and wondered how many millions of years of memory were stored in those little brains, behind the stabbing beaks, the piercing eyes, now giving them this instinct to destroy mankind with all the deft precision of machines." Nat is a sharply drawn character, an "ordinary man" who becomes heroic in a crisis. His heroism, as well as the intensifying horror of the situation, is emphasized by the methodical, detailed, understated manner in which he goes about defending himself and his family against the onslaught of the birds, especially when contrasted with the behavior of those around him and given the probable futility of his actions.

Thus, in "The Birds" as in her other fine short stories, du Maurier shows that the most frightening possibilities exist in the most serene landscapes, familiar people, and ordinary objects. Even in a relatively visceral story such as "The Birds," the unseen is the most awful, a principle that has served horror writers well for centuries but is seldom found in current macabre fiction. With the possible exception of Robert Aickman, no other contemporary dark fantasy writer has produced stories as worthy of Jack Sullivan's term "elegant nightmares" as Daphne du Maurier.

Keith Neilson

Bibliography
du Maurier, Daphne. *Myself When Young*, 1967.

THE EDUCATION OF UNCLE PAUL

Author: Algernon Blackwood (1869-1951)
First book publication: 1909
Type of work: Novel
Time: The early twentieth century
Locale: A country house in the south of England

A novel that explores the discovery of one's Inner Reality through the fantastic imagination of a group of children

Principal characters:
  PAUL RIVERS ("UNCLE PAUL"), a "forest-traveller"
  MARGARET MESSENGER, his sister and the widow of his childhood friend
  JONAH (RICHARD JONATHAN),
  TOBY (ARABELLA LUCY), and
  NIXIE (MARGARET CHRISTINA), Margaret's children

The Education of Uncle Paul was an important book in Algernon Blackwood's life. First, it gave him the nickname, Uncle Paul, by which he wanted to be known by his friends, and more especially their children. The character of Uncle Paul in the book is modeled very closely on Blackwood's own background and beliefs. More important, the success of the novel was a significant factor in deciding the direction that much of Blackwood's later work would take. Blackwood discovered that he was able to identify closely with children, and he was never happier than when wandering off with them into the woods telling them stories. In effect, he lived the life of Uncle Paul, and many of his later books were aimed deliberately at children or the young-at-heart. The important fact to remember about *The Education of Uncle Paul*, however, is that it is not a children's book but a book about children and the importance of their fantasy worlds.

The book begins with Paul Rivers returning to England after twenty years in America where he had held the job of a "forest-traveller, *commis voyageur* of the primeval woods." He was responsible for surveying the vast forest owned by a lumber company and reporting upon the qualities and values of the timber. It was a job he loved because it brought him close to Nature:

. . . meeting the wild animals in their secret haunts; becoming intimate with dawns and sunsets, great winds, the magic of storms and stars, and being initiated into the profound mysteries of the clean and haunted regions of the world.

This was just the kind of life Blackwood had led when the opportunity arose, both in Canada, where he lived from 1890 to 1892, and subsequently in many of the wild, uncontaminated regions of Europe. Blackwood describes himself when he says of Paul Rivers: "He came to personify Nature as a matter of course."

The proximity to Nature had more than that effect on Paul Rivers. It kept him a dreamer and sustained within him a childlike enthusiasm for all that was wondrous and simple in the world:

> He was destitute of that nameless quality that constitutes a human being, not mature necessarily, but grown up. Sources of inner enthusiasm that most men lose when life brings them the fruit of the Tree of Good and Evil, had kept alive, and . . . he longed intensely for some means by which he could express them and relieve his burdened soul.

This, then, is the Paul Rivers at the age of forty-five, who, having inherited the fortune of his aunt, returns to England on a year's leave to stay with his widowed sister and help her look after her children.

Paul's natural shyness and reserve is soon overcome when he meets his sister and the children. He is also delighted with the big old rambling house in which they live and with the wildness of the surrounding countryside. Although it lacks the primitive splendor of his forests, it still has not been subjected to the conditioning and orderly arranging of so much of the landscape in southern England. The children, in descending order of age, are Nixie, Jonah, and Toby, two girls and a boy, known by the nicknames bestowed upon them by their father. Paul feels particularly close to the eldest, Nixie, who is approaching her teens, and the main thread of the novel traces their relationship.

Over the ensuing weeks, Paul becomes acquainted with the children but tries to keep some form of parental reserve. The children, however, recognize this as a sham, seeing through the pretense to the genuine, sympathetic nature within. One night, while walking in the woods, Paul is approached by Nixie, who tells him that he should drop this façade and be as he really wants to be—as one with them—and join them in their "aventures." Paul is thereupon summoned to a nocturnal secret meeting of the children who ordain Paul into their Society. Paul's official job is to record the "aventures" and read them aloud at meetings.

The first "aventure" is also the most vivid and stands alone as a short story. Paul and Nixie are on the lawn one hot afternoon in mid-June. Nixie is studying the clouds and thinking about how they move. "I suspect there are creatures that can see the wind," Paul remarks; and this is the spark that triggers the first "aventure." He and Nixie sink down and down "through soft darkness, and long, shadowy places" and enter a dream which they both share. They are in a lost forest just before dawn and are about to see the wind. Paul discovers that this is the land where the wind sleeps when it is not blowing, but as dawn arrives, the wind awakes. In passages of beautiful imagery, Blackwood brings to life dawn, the winds, and the forest.

The next "aventure," however, is the core of the novel. It happens one night during a thunderstorm while Paul is thinking about writing a new story for the children telling how he had climbed the Scaffold of the Night. His thoughts wander and he envisages a place where all yearnings find adequate expression and where all lost things are found. The land can be reached only at midnight, at that moment that is neither yesterday nor tomorrow and no longer today. At the stroke of midnight, a "crack" opens and Uncle Paul and the children pass into the timeless world beyond. Here, as Nixie explains, "Nothing 'xactly-*happens* . . . but everything—*is*." It is also the "heaven of broken things"—or rather of things broken accidentally and not deliberately.

The Land Between Yesterday and Tomorrow, as Paul calls it, gradually becomes more real. It is a dreamland where all one's desires can be attained. In describing the Land, Blackwood produces some wonderful imagery, such as when Paul and Nixie witness the migration of the trees, which, like the birds, go south in the autumn. The visible tree does not move but rather the inner tree, its spirit, which can only be seen by those with access to the Land, moves.

Blackwood uses the Land on two levels. Superficially it is a place for "very wonderfulindeed aventures" for the children, but it holds a greater significance. For Paul Rivers, it becomes

> . . . that timeless, deathless region where the spirit may always go when hunted by the world, fretted by the passion of unsatisfied yearnings, plagued by the remorseless tribes of sorrow and disaster.

This was only an intermediary level, however; there is an even greater significance to the Land. It is a means to an end, the route to self-discovery and self-realization: ". . . its rewards might vary immensely according to the courage and the need of the soul that sought it."

Paul, Nixie, and the others have a variety of "aventures" in the Land, but the novel now takes a somber turn. Paul decides to stay in England beyond his year's leave, but he first has to settle his affairs in America. When he returns to England a few weeks later, he finds that Nixie is terminally ill, and soon she dies. Paul is left lost and lonely, but philosophically he readjusts. He retreats more and more to the Land Through the Crack, and it is here that he first encounters the spirit of Nixie. That yearning for self-realization that Nixie represents is at last taking a firm hold on Paul, for he now discovers Nixie in the normal world. "Think of me as your centre," Nixie tells him. "That's the real way to get near." Such is the true education of Uncle Paul.

Outwardly, this is a novel about children's "aventures," but inwardly, it is an allegorical fantasy about the search for Reality and Inner Truth. The novel ends with a realization of the Reality of Death. Once again, it is the voice of Nixie that reveals the Truth:

> What you call Death is only slipping through the Crack to a great deal more memory, and a great deal more power of seeing and telling—towards the greatest Expression that

ever can be known. It is, I promise you faithfully, Uncle Paul, nothing but a verywon-
derfulindeed Aventure, after all!

The Education of Uncle Paul is thus a novel of hope, but only for those
with a "genuine yearning" and a "spirit which seeks ever for a resting-place
in the great beyond that reaches up to God." The novel was Blackwood's
first vehicle for the theme of self-realization that he would later use to greater
effect in *The Centaur* (1911). The latter, however, is a profound and mystical
novel, while *The Education of Uncle Paul* takes a parallel and less exacting
route. Blackwood's message is made all the more potent if the two books are
read in tandem.

As official record-keeper of the children's "aventures," Uncle Paul assembles a book within the novel which is called "Adventures of a Prisoner in
Fairyland." Following the success of *The Education of Uncle Paul*, Blackwood
felt both obliged and delighted to produce the book that Uncle Paul wrote,
which appeared as *A Prisoner in Fairyland* in 1913. With the assistance of
Violet Pearn, the two books were adapted and totally revised as children's
plays: *The Education of Uncle Paul* as *Through the Crack* (1925) and *A
Prisoner in Fairyland* as *The Starlight Express* (1915). Both are only very
loosely based on the novels and introduce many new characters which Blackwood was also to use in other novels such as *The Extra Day* (1916) and *The
Fruit Stoners* (1934). In a complete study of this cycle of novels, one should
not forget Blackwood's earlier book, *Jimbo* (1909), a psychological study of
an unconscious boy's delirious fantasy. All these books are quasi-allegorical/
moral tales for both children and adults that can be read on more than one
level.

Mike Ashley

Bibliography
Blackwood, Algernon. *The Collected Essays, Journalism, and Letters*, 1968.
Briggs, Julia. *Night Visitors: The Rise and Fall of the English Ghost Story*,
    1977.
Colombo, John Robert. *Blackwood's Books: A Bibliography Devoted to
    Algernon Blackwood*, 1981.
Sullivan, Jack. *Elegant Nightmares: The English Ghost Story from Le Fanu
    to Blackwood*, 1978.

ELIDOR

Author: Alan Garner (1934-   )
First book publication: 1965
Type of work: Novel
Time: The 1960's
Locale: Manchester and Elidor

> When the fantasy kingdom of Elidor is threatened with death, four Manchester children are burdened with the task of saving it, which they do at great cost

> Principal characters:
> ROLAND, the child protagonist
> NICHOLAS,
> DAVID, and
> HELEN, his three siblings
> FRANK AND GWEN, his parents
> MALEBRON, the maimed King of Elidor
> FINDHORN, the unicorn

Any attempt to come to terms with the work of Alan Garner must deal at length with the nature of children's literature, or work on the assumption—whether or not it can be properly tested—that a book for children can successfully meet adult criteria without provoking debilitating caveats about the nature of its intended audience. *Elidor* is a book published for children, and it is a tragedy. At its heart lies a fantasy land of castles and magic, but the children who are drawn into it are entirely justified in resisting the experience; the land of Elidor is blighted and dying, and a horrifyingly ambiguous death is the price for restoring light to it. Elidor represents not an escape into a secondary universe but the threat of death, and the child Roland who penetrates the Dark Tower at its center risks his sanity in doing so.

Footloose for the afternoon in the city of Manchester, a city blighted by bomb damage during World War II and cruelly transformed by later redevelopment, the four Watson children find themselves wandering seemingly at random into an area of slum clearance, where they come across an isolated and abandoned church. Their arrival at the church is not fortunate. Haunted and driven by the tunes of a lame fiddler, they one by one disappear into the church and one by one are transported into the land of Elidor. The youngest, Roland, who is the last to be torn from this world, turns out to be the key to their temporary rescue.

Roland finds himself beneath a ruined castle called Gorias, into which he climbs. The castle trembles. Through a window he sees a bleak country and the fiddler, whom he follows across the drawbridge and into Elidor. After willing himself free of a circle of stones, he finds, deeply embedded in rock that has crystallized around it (for time is different in Elidor), his sister's glove; it has been there for eons. The fiddler reappears, transformed into

Malebron, King of Elidor, but still lame. He draws Roland compulsively into "the heart of darkness" of his enforced quest, which is to penetrate with his unique human power of imagination the Mound of Vandwy, where his siblings lie entranced, and return with them and the four Treasures that will stave off darkness for a while, although for Elidor to be saved permanently, Findhorn the unicorn must sing.

Roland completes his quest and in so doing tastes death. Chased by nightmares of evil, the four siblings escape Elidor with their Treasures, arriving back in the slum as the church collapses. Roland's spear is transformed into an iron railing, Nicholas' stone of kingship into a keystone, David's sword into "two splintered laths," and Helen's cauldron (or Grail) into "an old cracked cup." They return home to the repressed and constricting proprieties of the middle-class home into which their parents have just moved, which is surrounded by working-class suburbs. They bury the Treasures because they interfere with radio and television transmissions. A year passes pretty much without incident.

Roland remains obsessed by the dark land buried in his memory, but his siblings try to ward off all recognition of its power. Eventually, however, terrifyingly, the boundary between the two worlds is breached by Malebron's enemies looking for the Treasure; and then Findhorn himself appears, harried and flecked with foam. Tracked by the enemy, the children make their way back (as though by accident) to the Manchester slum clearance site, where Roland finds the unicorn at bay. Roland is desperate for him to sing, but Findhorn will not. When Helen ("a makeless mayde": a virgin) appears, however, Findhorn nestles his head in her lap, as he must; an enemy spear pierces his heart, and he sings, in a "tongue of fire that rang beyond the streets, the city, the cold hills and the sky. The worlds shook at the song." Elidor can be seen reflected in the windows of abandoned buildings, golden; Elidor is saved. The vision shatters, and the children are left "alone with the broken windows of a slum." They have won—or have they lost? Certainly they have been *used*.

The sources of this tale in folklore and myth are complex and numerous and lend themselves to extremely detailed examination. It must suffice here to indicate that much of the underlying structure relates to Celtic lore; that the ancient Scots ballad, "Childe Roland and Burd Helen," provides essential underpinning to the relationship between Roland and his sister, as well as adding resonance to the virtual supplanting of Roland by Findhorn, who is a kind of secret sharer of Elidor worthy of Helen's love; and that, in the Treasures, deep though muffled echoes of the Arthurian Grail cycle can be perceived.

This intensity of mythic reference, much of it rather deeply buried, acts mainly to intensify the sense of pressure for which the text is so remarkable. In their ordinary lives, Roland and his siblings are under pressure, constrained by the smug proprieties of their suburban culture, a culture self-consciously threatened by the weight of working-class people vying for the same living space. Far from having adventures on a higher and freer plane in Elidor, however, the children are victims of a predestined story that almost destroys them, which forces their every move, which acts as a dark analogue of their growth from innocence to adulthood in a battered, disappointing world, and the conclusion of which leaves them desolate and abandoned in the secular wasteland of this world. If Malebron is a Fisher King, monarch of a Wasteland, then in saving himself and his country he has planted desolation in the hearts of the children who were his instruments of salvation. To go to the other world is to die; to remain in this one is to waste away. That is the tragic sense of life imparted by *Elidor*.

John Clute

Bibliography
Garner, Alan. "Inner Time," in *Science Fiction at Large*, 1976. Edited by Peter Nicholls.
Philip, Neil. *A Fine Anger: A Critical Introduction to the Work of Alan Garner*, 1981.

ELSIE VENNER

Author: Oliver Wendell Holmes (1809-1894)
First book publication: 1861
Type of work: Novel
Time: The late 1850's
Locale: Rockland, a small town in New England

> *The tragic story of a girl subject to a sinister prenatal influence*

Principal characters:
ELSIE VENNER, a pupil at the Apollinean Female Institute
DUDLEY VENNER, her father
RICHARD VENNER, her cousin
BERNARD LANGDON, a teacher at the Institute
HELEN DARLEY, a fellow teacher
THE REVEREND CHAUNCY FAIRWEATHER and
THE REVEREND DR. HONEYWOOD, ministers of rival churches

Elsie Venner was the first of the three "medicated" novels which Oliver Wendell Holmes was to write in the course of his varied career, and it remains the best known. It was first published in serial form during 1859 and 1860 as "The Professor's Story" in *The Atlantic Monthly*, a periodical which Holmes had helped to launch in 1857 and for which he produced the conversations that were collected into his most famous books: *The Autocrat of the Breakfast-Table* (1858), *The Professor at the Breakfast-Table* (1860), and so on. It was for his poetry that Holmes hoped to be remembered, but his literary career ran parallel with his work as professor of anatomy at Harvard University, and his medical essays, usually based on public lectures, made a notable contribution to the thought of the day, especially in the field of the philosophy of medical science. He wrote a classic paper on "Mechanism in Thought and Morals" in 1870.

The medicated novels have been represented as thought experiments in abnormal psychology. Clarence P. Obendorf, reintroducing abridged versions of them under the title *The Psychiatric Novels of Oliver Wendell Holmes* (1944), suggests that *Elsie Venner* should be seen as a study of schizophrenia, while *The Guardian Angel* (1867) examines multiple personality and *A Mortal Antipathy* (1885), an unusual case of phobia. This is certainly a misrepresentation of *Elsie Venner*, and it is something of a distortion of the other novels.

Elsie Venner is the story of a strangely beautiful girl who possesses a peculiar combination of character traits and also pseudohypnotic powers. She becomes enamored of Bernard Langdon, a young man who is forced by financial circumstance to interrupt his medical studies and take a post as a teacher in the school that she attends at Rockland, in New England. He, through no fault of his own, is no suitable object for such a passion, and the affair drags tragedy in its wake. Richard Venner, who has made up his mind to marry his cousin for her money, is driven by frustration to attack the young teacher, who narrowly escapes death. Elsie is not so fortunate, although her father, Dudley Venner (a widower since the time of her birth), does find happiness in a second marriage to another teacher at the school, Helen Darley.

Although it is never stated in so many words, Holmes makes abundantly clear by implication that Elsie's mother was bitten during her pregnancy by a rattlesnake and that Elsie inherited her peculiarities through the poison that mingled with her embryonic blood. Had Holmes really believed in the kind of prenatal influence that provides the premise of his fantasy, *Elsie Venner* might qualify as an eccentric, fictitious case study. Holmes, however, was careful to point out that although such an influence was impossible, he certainly did not wish to assert the reality of it.

The idea is used as a convenient literary device for dramatizing the real subject matter of the novel, which is the question of the extent of personal moral responsibility: a question that unites psychological speculations about behavioral determinism with theological disputes about the doctrine of original sin. Holmes may almost be seen as an intellectual ancestor of Clarence Darrow, the great American lawyer who frequently defended criminals by emphasizing that their behavior was caused as much as it was chosen, and who took on the Fundamentalist William Jennings Bryan in the Scopes trial. The real argument of Holmes's story is that the tragedy that visits Rockland is the product of forces working through the people concerned, who are victims of their heredity in a rather different way from what is implied in the doctrine of original sin. The novel is not so much a case study as an exercise in hypothetical moral philosophy.

Elsie Venner also contains a subplot involving matters of religious conscience, developed through an account of the rivalry between Rockland's two ministers and the eventual loss of faith suffered by one of them. This is construed by most readers as a satirical digression—a gibe at Calvinism inspired by the fact that Holmes's father Abiel had been ousted from his parish by Calvinists—but it is actually an essential part of the discussion that underlies the events. What eventually converts the Calvinist is his acceptance of a more humane view of sin as well as his more understanding doctrine of forgiveness.

Biographical sketches of Holmes tend to refer to the medicated novels in a half-embarrassed fashion, suggesting that there is slight merit in them because of the incidental description of New England life; but this says more about fashions in literary appreciation than it does about the true worth of the stories. *A Mortal Antipathy* is, in fact, rather poor, but the two earlier novels are, for their time, relatively sophisticated novels of ideas, which remain neglected largely because novels of ideas as a subgenre are considered unworthy of attention. Readers who are sympathetic to Holmes's project and who actually realize what he is trying to do (those who attend to the second Preface, added in 1883, should be in no doubt) ought to be able to evaluate *Elsie Venner* in terms of its own ambitions and to find it both intelligent and thought provoking.

Brian Stableford

Bibliography
Morse, John T., Jr., ed. *Life and Letters of Oliver Wendell Holmes*, 1896.
Small, Miriam R. *Oliver Wendell Holmes*, 1962.

EMPIRE OF THE EAST

Author: Fred Saberhagen (1930-   )
First book publication: 1979
Type of work: Novel
Time: The millennia after a nuclear war
Locale: Mountains, swamp, desert, grasslands, and walled cities

Because of his aptitude for technology in an age when magic rather than science is the means to power, Rolf, a young farm boy, becomes a key figure in an archetypal struggle between good (West) and evil (East)

Principal characters:
   ROLF, a farm boy-turned-swordsman
   THOMAS, leader of the forces of the West in their first two
      encounters
   LOFORD, a wizard for the West
   STRIJEEF, member of an intelligent species of giant birds who help
      the West
   CHUP, first an unpledged lord of the East, later a warrior for the
      West
   CHARMIAN, the beautiful but wicked daughter of Ekuman and trou-
      blesome wife of Chup
   SOM THE DEAD, the unliving ruler in the Black Mountains
   ZAPRANOTH, the Demon lord
   GRAY, a powerful wizard of the West, brother of Loford
   EMPEROR JOHN OMINOR, leader of the Eastern forces
   CATHERINE, slave to Charmian but later companion of Rolf
   ORCUS, the superpower of the East
   ARDNEH, the superpower of the West

An entertaining sword-and-sorcery fantasy in three parts, Fred Saberhagen's *Empire of the East* presents the two contending principles of good
and evil under the respective geographical designations of West and East.
Although the action in the novel moves progressively from west to east, more
important is the distinction between the moral understanding of the beings
involved with each of the two factions.

Service to the East produces enormous power but degrades the one who
is raised to such eminence. The formal act of pledging one's services eliminates
honorable servants, because those who cannot overcome a desire to deal
honorably with friend or enemy cannot commit the base act of betrayal necessary to be a true villain. Those who are rulers in the East, supported by
their demonic powers, must love torture for its own sake, delight in petty
malice, and hold no bond more sacred than their own greed. As a result, the
only Eastern loyalty is that of fear and slavery; the only safety is one's temporary usefulness in the maintenance of or rise to power of an even more evil
being. Service to the East also means an uneasy familiarity with demons,

whose very presence sickens the strongest of men. The very worst demon may be trapped and used for a time, but no man is ultimately his master. The only way demonic evil can be checked is by a major change in the world such as the one by which they had been created.

Service to the West involves no such formal commitment but is equally identifiable by moral characteristics. The West, in fact, has seemed at a disadvantage because those who support its principles encourage freedom, generosity to friend and enemy, personal courage, self-sufficiency, and loyalty to friends and family. The servants of the West must at last come together as a group to preserve their ability to practice such values. They have no formal organization, however, as does the East: no Emperor, no standing army, and no creatures quite like the demons. Their first efforts are guerrilla warfare and a mysterious connection with a being called Ardneh, whom no one, good or evil, understands. Although the army of the West grows larger and makes significant progress under the guidance of Ardneh, it has no direct involvement such as that of the demons with the East, and some marvel of ancient technology is forever destroyed for each step toward the West's reestablishment of freedom.

Three marvels from the technological Old World, even though not understood in the New World of magic, lend a touch of science to the struggle between good and evil. Two of them may even be used indiscriminately by either side. The struggle for the possession of the first, a tank called Elephant, brings on the first pitched battle between Ekuman's Eastern army and the Western guerrilla force led by Thomas. The boy, Rolf, can operate Elephant to attack the walls of Ekuman's citadel, but Ekuman is also able to operate it against the attackers. It is stopped by Rolf's careful observation and ingenuity. The second marvel, a lake of life-giving water, is being used by the chosen soldiers in service to Som the Dead. They wear metal bands around their necks, and when they are mortally wounded, flying machines like helicopters retrieve the corpses and transport them to the lake for revivification. At the time when Chup changes sides, he takes advantage of this process, in a sense dying that the people of the West (himself included) might have life. The third technological marvel is Ardneh itself, and from the beginning of the novel, Ardneh cannot be used by the forces of evil because they are also the forces of destruction. Ardneh tells Rolf and Catherine why it cannot be used by the East.

> I was built by war-planners of the Old World, as part of a system of defense. But not as a destructive device. My oldest purpose is to defend mankind, and so I am of the West today, though there was no East or West when I was built. My basic nature is peaceful, so it has taken me long to develop weapons of my own to enter battle.

Ardneh, however, is partly responsible for Orcus being what he is rather than what he was created. To preserve life from nuclear annihilation millennia in the past, the Automatic Restoration Director-National Executive Head-quarters had initiated the Change which allowed the development of sentience in what had been the ultimate bomb and also in himself. Destruction of Orcus means reversing the Change, letting the bomb detonate, and destroying Ard-neh, the most technologically complex machine supporting the West.

Equal in importance to the technological marvels is the development that magic has been able to make since the Change initiated by the machine Ardneh. Most obvious is the development of Ardneh as a being and the transformation of nuclear weapons into demons such as Orcus. Also, there are significant elements of magic that make wizards among the chief advisers of rulers and a necessity in any army. Men such as Elslood and Wood have sought to use demonic forces and ultimately are destroyed by them. Those such as Loford and Gray avoid them, using only those magical forces which are not demonic, such as elementals; gradually they strengthen the forces of the West even in the face of the seemingly omnipotent East. Magic, too, has parts which may be used by either side. Of equal importance with Elephant in opening the citadel to Thomas' tiny army are the two stones, the Thun-derstone and the Stone of Freedom. The first brings a storm with deadly lightning; the second releases whoever holds it from any form of imprison-ment, making locks on castle doors give way under some very remarkable circumstances. The elementals raised by Loford are generally directed suc-cessfully against the enemy, but they are mindless and can as easily turn against those who raised them.

Character development is not emphasized in *Empire of the East*, and most of the characters are flat and unchanging. The three characters who do change are Rolf, Chup, and Charmian. Rolf's principal change is that he ages from sixteen to nineteen; he moves beyond needing personal revenge for the destruction of his family to defending the cause of the West through com-mitment to its principles.

Chup's character develops from that of an unpledged Lord of the East, enjoying the benefits of its power without having committed himself to its ways of operation. When in Book Two he must either go through a pledging ceremony or refuse it, he refuses. As part of his early link with the East, he is married to Charmian in Book One and drawn to her in Book Two by a charm made of her hair. When he surrenders the charm and is no longer held in her service through enchantment, he still refuses to do her harm as she would have done to him. In Book Three, when she is defeated by what she fears most in all the world, Chup has grown to be able to care for her and to succor her in her utmost distress.

Change in the character of Charmian is gradual and subtly handled. A too-beautiful woman, she begins as a troublesome daughter of an evil father and delights in any malicious mischief that she can persuade her admirer, Elslood, to perform. Although married to Chup, she spurns him for Tarlenot, but, convinced that Chup is better able to help her achieve power over Som the Dead, she lures him into her evil plot. Even having used him thusly, she trusts him to save her from the revenge of Som. His nature, she trusts, will lead him to kill her quickly rather than to torture her. When her trust proves well-founded, she grows slightly and (perhaps) helps him to get to the lake of the Beast-Lord Draffut, an important step in destroying the Demon Lord Zapranoth. Although she is still troublesome and malicious, she does not make as much trouble for Chup as she could, perhaps buys him another day of life by persuading Wood not to make a quick sacrifice of him, and chooses to go with him rather than to stay in the camp of the East. It is not much change and it has been painful, but it does demonstrate Charmian's potential for growth.

Two nonhuman intelligent allies add to the fantastic nature of the struggle between East and West. The East is aided by flying reptiles who are active in the daylight, while the West has the cooperation of giant birds who operate only at night. Although the two species are natural enemies, their clashes occur during the sleeping time of one or the other. Thus, there can be no direct battle. None of the reptiles is treated as an individual, but two birds are distinguished from all the rest, Strijeef and Feathertip. Feathertip, the female bird, finds Elephant, and the two birds help Rolf jump to the cave opening above the tank. Although Featherstrip is killed, Strijeef becomes Rolf's link with the West when Rolf is imprisoned, delivers the Stone of Freedom to him, and sees him safely back to Elephant's cave. Although migrating South during the winter, at which time the reptiles are also absent in hibernation, Strijeef and the birds return to help Rolf and Catherine communicate with the forces of the West as they make their way to Ardneh's cave.

The forces of technology and magic, the armies, the demons, and the wizards are all brought together in a final confrontation which will mean the end of the world as they know it. Another Change occurs when Ardneh permits the nuclear bomb which is Orcus to explode, but that Change does not put an end to all the magic developed since the first Change. The wizard Gray explains:

> If there is anything impossible to men, it is going back to what has once been changed. True, the Old World energies of nuclear power are once more with us, like outlandish demons that only technologists can control. But the energies of magic remain in force, still much stronger than they were in the days of Ardneh's origin. The world we live in from this day hence is a blend of Old and New, and so is doubly new.

Although they do not inhabit an Eden and the serpentlike evil of war is still with them, the promise of a renewed world is clearly with them. The forming of two couples—Rolf and Catherine and the newly bonded Chup and Charmian—leaves hope for a brighter future. Although Charmian is a flawed prize, Chup emphasizes that she is not a prize of war. The end of *Empire of the East* is one marked by forgiveness, tenderness, and love.

Elizabeth Sikes Davidson

Bibliography
Stewart, Alfred D. "Fred Saberhagen: Cybernetic Psychologist," in *Extrapolation*. XVIII (December, 1976), pp. 42-51.

THE ENCHANTED CASTLE

Author: Edith Nesbit (Edith Nesbit Bland, 1858-1924)
First book publication: 1907
Type of work: Novel
Time: The early twentieth century
Locale: A British castle and garden

Four children discover a magical ring that not only grants wishes but also provides entry into an enchanted land where, in the moonlight, statues come alive and congregate to pay homage to light

> *Principal characters:*
> GERALD, a young boy
> JIMMY, his younger brother
> KATHLEEN, their sister
> MABEL, the daughter of the castle's caretaker
> MADEMOISELLE, a temporary nurse for the children
> LORD YALDING, the owner of Yalding Castle and gardens

It may be argued that out of all Edith Nesbit's book-length fantasies, *The Enchanted Castle* comes the closest to being a bona fide novel with its successful interweaving of two story lines—one concerning four children and their humorous and sometimes frightening escapades with magic, and the other, a conventional love story of two adults separated by a misunderstanding, who are brought together eventually by magic. Yet Nesbit's supposed success in writing a novel—a genre she did have difficulty mastering—is not the chief reason for the success of *The Enchanted Castle*; more significant reasons are her ability to create believable and attractive characters and to rationalize the existence of magic.

Four young children, Gerald, Jimmy, Kathleen, and their newly acquired friend Mabel are the main characters. As she had already demonstrated in the Psammead trilogy, Nesbit knew how to cast a web of plausibility over children's experience of magical adventures that take place in otherwise realistic settings. Hence, the four children are well-read, sensitive, resourceful, and intelligent; in other words, they are the kind of children likely to have adventures involving magic because they are prepared to believe in magic if they ever encounter it. Moreover, as is also true in the Psammead trilogy, the strength of Nesbit's characterization is the children's struggle to behave as ordinarily as possible when magic unexpectedly intervenes in their everyday affairs and to learn through a process of trial and error how magic works.

For *The Enchanted Castle*, furthermore, Nesbit devises an effective variation in the way she has her protagonists initially encounter magic. As the narrative begins, the children find a secret way into a garden that seems as magical as any created by their imaginations, which are fed by their extensive reading of fairy tales. Finding there what seems to be a sleeping princess, they prepare themselves to cope with the excitement of having finally stumbled upon what they know does exist but which they simply have not yet experienced. When the sleeping princess is revealed to be merely an ordinary girl, the daughter of the caretaker, and the garden and castle merely the large, well-taken-care-of property belonging to a lord, they are chagrined and keenly disappointed. At the very moment that the children have been rudely brought back into the prosaic, magicless world, they unexpectedly do discover a ring that dispenses magic. Afraid they may be disappointed a second time, they are skeptical until the invisibility of Mabel convinces them. In this fashion, Nesbit makes the children's encounter with magic very interesting and convincing.

As with the Psammead trilogy, much of the fun of *The Enchanted Castle* derives from watching the four children coping with a ring whose power (it soon becomes clear) is far greater than they first suspected or even could imagine; thus the difficulty they experience in discovering the rules by which the ring operates and then obeying them places the children in awkward, embarrassing, and even perilous circumstances. Perhaps the most striking instance of the ring's magic and its disconcerting effects is the coming-alive of the "characters" they have fashioned out of clothing and common household objects for a play they are producing. Once alive, the grotesque and aptly named Uglie Wuglies demand directions to a respectable hotel. When nearly all the Uglies have been tricked into believing that a mausoleum is a hotel and are about to enter it, they become hostile, inciting fear and inflicting bodily harm before they are shoved into it.

In *The Enchanted Castle*, as in *The Story of the Amulet* (1906), Nesbit treats magic seriously, explaining it and its laws by associating them with humanity's long-held dream of a Golden Age. Nevertheless, when magic is carelessly used, it can become merely a wishing ring that affects persons and situations in the everyday world: for example, Mabel becomes invisible, a statue of a marble dinosaur lives, and Kathleen turns into a marble giant. When the full scope of the ring's power is explained, however, the children learn that there is a land of magic which exists independently of their familiar world. Sometimes mortals can enter into that land through a gossamer curtain "that hangs forever between the world of magic and the world that seems . . . to be real." Because of "little weak spots" in the curtain, rings or amulets, for example, "almost anything can happen." In this land, manifested on the grounds of the "enchanted castle," statues can come alive whenever the moon shines. There is also one night during the year—the moon's rising on a month's fourteenth day—when all mortals can gain access to the land of magic; and the children successfully puzzle out what day this is. That special night becomes the moment when the two lovers are brought together and their misunderstandings disappear. More significantly, it is the time when all statues and what they represent come together to pay homage to the "light" in which "everything is revealed . . . every place that one has seen or dreamed of . . ." an "eternal" light which is "the center of the universe and . . . the universe itself."

In *The Enchanted Castle*, Nesbit consolidated the breakthrough into fantasy writing that she had made in the Psammead trilogy. In doing so, she showed other writers, particularly writers of children's books, that the everyday world and magic can be combined in fiction that is serious and entertaining without being solemn or trivial. Finally, for those writers of fantasy who for one reason or another choose not to follow the path of George MacDonald's mythic fantasy or of Lewis Carroll's highly cerebral nonsense, Nesbit provided a third path—that of mixed fantasy.

Francis J. Molson

Bibliography
Bell, Anthea. *E. Nesbit*, 1960.
Green, Roger Lancelyn. "E. Nesbit," in *Tellers of Tales*, 1965.
_____ . "E. Nesbit and the World of Enchantment," in *Five Children and It*, 1959.
Lochhead, Marion. "An Edwardian Successor: E. Nesbit," in *The Renaissance of Wonder in Children's Literature*, 1977.
Manlove, Colin N. "Fantasy as Witty Conceit: E. Nesbit," in *Mosaic*. X (Winter, 1977), pp. 109-130.
Prickett, Stephen. *Victorian Fantasy*, 1979.

ERIC BRIGHTEYES

Author: H. Rider Haggard (1856-1925)
First book publication: 1891
Type of work: Novel
Time: The tenth century
Locale: Iceland

A Victorian romance written in the mode of the Icelandic sagas

> *Principal characters:*
> ERIC BRIGHTEYES, son of Thorgrimur Iron-Toe
> GUDRUDA THE FAIR, daughter of Gudruda the Gentle and Asmund Asmundson
> SWANHILD THE FATHERLESS, daughter of Groa the Witch and half-sister to Gudruda the Fair
> OSPAKAR BLACKTOOTH, a northern chieftain

The books for which H. Rider Haggard is primarily remembered are *King Solomon's Mines* (1886) and *She* (1887); most of his other works have lapsed into obscurity, among them *Eric Brighteyes*. Yet *Eric Brighteyes* enjoyed considerable critical acclaim when it was first published: Andrew Lang was of the opinion that it was the best thing that Haggard had written, Rudyard Kipling described it as "strong as a wire rope," and the Prince of Wales is said to have preferred it to Haggard's other works. The fact remains, however, that the work is familiar neither to students of English literature in general, nor even to those of Victorian literature in particular. This is perhaps because of Haggard's own stated aim in writing a novel in the manner of the ancient Icelandic sagas, as much as because of the book's intrinsic qualities.

In his Introduction to *Eric Brighteyes*, Haggard states his intention of writing a saga tailored to the taste of the Victorian reader, devoid of irrelevant side-plots and genealogies. What he seems to achieve, far from being a powerful amalgam having the force of a saga and the literary quality to grip a reader, is a literary five-finger exercise with little but its curiosity value to recommend it. Having read and been captivated by such works as *King Solomon's Mines* and *She*, one is disappointed with *Eric Brighteyes*. It may be that what is lacking is the element of quest which gives impetus to many of Haggard's other novels. It may also be that in Eric, the Victorian reading public found an ideal, macho hero who supplied plenty of action, unhindered by too much thought, and who died (along with most of the other characters) heroically and appropriately by the last page.

The novel tells the tale of Eric Brighteyes and two women, half-sisters, who seek his love. It is obvious to the reader that the love of Eric and Gudruda the Fair is doomed from the outset, by virtue of the fact that Swanhild, the daughter of a witch, is also in love with him. This is made obvious in the early pages of the novel, when the prophetic dream of Asmund Asmundson, the priest, is related. This dream is allegorical and tells the tale of Eric Brighteyes, Gudruda, and Swanhild using animal symbolism; the point that the love of Eric and Gudruda is doomed is made once more by Asmund's wife as she lies dying. Thus, the reader embarks upon the novel prepared for what is to come.

Although Haggard claims to have dispensed with superfluous characters, those that remain are so undifferentiated in their addiction to violence that it is sometimes difficult to distinguish among them as they hack and stab their way through the plot. It is Swanhild's wickedness and her witchcraft which generates most of the action, coupled with Ospaker Blacktooth's declared intent to marry the most beautiful woman in Iceland—that is, Gudruda the Fair. Swanhild attempts to murder Gudruda by pushing her over the edge of the Golden Falls. Eric saves Gudruda, having on the same day already vanquished Ospakar Blacktooth and his henchmen on Horse-Head Heights, with the assistance of Skallagrim Lambstail, a Baresark.

As punishment for trying to murder Gudruda, Swanhild is made to marry Earl Atli the Good (a fate which she chooses in preference to taking her trial in the Doom-Ring) and goes away with him. By use of witchcraft, however, she succeeds in causing the shipwreck of Eric on Straumey's Isle, so that Eric and Skallagrim are stranded in Atli's hall for some time. By further deceit and treachery, Swanhild manages to convince Eric that Gudruda means to marry Ospakar Blacktooth. Consumed with grief, Eric is bewitched into betraying Gudruda with Swanhild. He also kills Earl Atli while under Swanhild's spell. Before long, it becomes clear to Eric that Swanhild has deceived him, and the book reaches its climax with a confrontation between Eric and Ospakar Blacktooth.

Although Eric vanquishes Ospakar and wins Gudruda, he is not destined for happiness. Swanhild's magic continues to work against him, and she arranges for Gudruda to be slain on her wedding night. It is outside the conventions of the saga that anyone should be permitted a happy ending or domestic felicity. Having caused the death of her rival, Swanhild then contrives the death in battle of Eric and Skallagrim. In the Viking tradition, Swanhild causes all the dead to be loaded into a longboat, and sails away in the teeth of a gale with her cargo of corpses.

It is not easy for the modern reader to identify with any of the protagonists of *Eric Brighteyes*; its literary style is said to be excellent, yet its content is so much of a historical curiosity that this may explain its lack of popularity. Whatever the reason for its lack of success, there is no doubt that this novel cannot compare with Haggard's more successful (and more conventional) works, which continue to be reprinted and reread.

Vivien Stableford

Bibliography
Cohen, Morton. *Rider Haggard: His Life and Works*, 1960.
Ellis, Peter Beresford. *H. Rider Haggard: A Voice from the Infinite*, 1978.

THE ETERNAL CHAMPION SERIES

Author: Michael Moorcock (1939-   )
First book publications: The Stealer of Souls (1963); *Stormbringer* (1965); *Warriors of Mars* (1965, later published as *The City of the Beast*); *Blades of Mars* (1965, later published as *The Lord of the Spiders*); *Barbarians of Mars* (1965, later published as *The Masters of the Pit*); *The Jewel in the Skull* (1967); *Sorcerer's Amulet* (1968, later published as *The Mad God's Amulet*); *The Sword of the Dawn* (1968); *The Secret of the Runestaff* (1969, later published as *The Runestaff*); *The Eternal Champion* (1970); *Phoenix in Obsidian* (1970, pulished in the United States as *The Silver Warriors*); *The Singing Citadel* (1970); *The Sleeping Sorceress* (1971, later published as *The Vanishing Tower*); *The Knight of the Swords* (1971); *The Queen of the Swords* (1971); *The King of the Swords* (1971); *Elric of Melniboné* (1972, published in the United States as *The Dreaming City*); *The Jade Man's Eyes* (1973); *Elric the Return to Melniboné* (1973); *Count Brass* (1973); *The Champion of Garathorn* (1973); *The Bull and the Spear* (1973); *The Oak and the Ram* (1973); *The Sword and the Stallion* (1974); *The Quest for Tanelorn* (1975); *The Sailor of the Seas of Fate* (1976); *The Weird of the White Wolf* (1977); *The Bane of the Black Sword* (1977)
Type of work: Short stories, novellas and novels

Five series of novels and short stories whose heroes fight against evil forces in an effort to balance the forces of law and chaos

It is easy and necessary to say of the works of Michael Moorcock that they are interrelated; all of the titles in his large oeuvre comprise one lengthy series. It is less easy, but equally as necessary, to make some usable distinctions in the great mass of titles and to winnow out from them some governing principles. The twenty-four volumes that make up the Eternal Champion sequence in its definitive form also comprise five smaller series which relate to the rest of Moorcock's work—to his science fiction, his romances, and his nongeneric novels—with varying degrees of closeness. Before examining his heroic fantasy, all of which is devoted explicitly to avatars of the Eternal Champion, it is important to point out the basic mechanisms by which these twenty-four volumes are related to Moorcock's more serious fiction. Two central ideas—the concept of the Eternal Champion himself and the concept of the multiverse—are central themes in the job of lacing together all of Moorcock's books, even those written before the major revision efforts in the 1970's, which were intended to tie together the volumes into a more unified whole.

Unwillingly called from mortal life, hibernation, another universe, another time, or from another self entirely, each avatar of the Eternal Champion must wage battle, wherever he finds himself, against threats to the cosmic balance— that precarious, shifting harmony between the forces of law and the forces of chaos. In the heroic fantasies, law and chaos are generally manifest as gods or lords, through whose mediation the Eternal Champion generally finds himself forcibly evoked to stand in battle. Never will the Eternal Champion fully plumb the significance of any of his actions in any one venue; it is at the heart of Moorcock's treatment of these figures, who in conventional heroic fantasies such as Robert E. Howard's Conan books would be figures of wish fulfillment, that fundamental ironies hedge their heroic status and their very identities.

Latent (but decipherable) in even the most straightforward of the heroic fantasies, these ironies visibly control the destinies of those avatars of the Eternal Champion who appear in the nonfantasy part of the oeuvre. Indeed, so corrosive are these ironies, and so thoroughly do they undermine the notion of an Eternal Champion manifesting himself throughout the multiverse to right wrongs, that it becomes impossible to think of Moorcock as affirming in his work any belief whatsoever in the value of heroic action. In later texts such as *Gloriana* (1978), *Byzantium Endures* (1981), and *The Brothel in Rosenstrasse* (1982), the more a character dominates the action, the less reliable are his credentials, his protestations, and his claims to self-knowledge, and the more devastating are the consequences of his behavior. All the same, although Ricky von Bek of *The Brothel in Rosenstrasse* is only a distant relation to Elric of Melniboné or Hawkmoon, he is nevertheless related. In Moorcock's complex lacing together of connections, it is sufficient to note that Ricky von Bek is a descendant of the von Bek who, in *The War Hound and the World's Pain* (1981), shows clear signs of being a secular avatar of the Eternal Champion.

The central coordinating character of an additional twelve titles, which are not considered a part of the heroic fantasy, is Jerry Cornelius, a contemporary antihero figure of very considerable complexity; he is Moorcock's most famous creation and a kind of solarized rendering of the Eternal Champion, with all values changed or at least mocked. Although the terms within which he was written had implications far outreaching this genesis, he originated as a direct parody of Elric of Melniboné, who himself represented an inversion of standard heroic fantasy values. The first third of *The Final Programme* (1968), in which Jerry Cornelius makes his first appearance with an antic jauntiness he is to lose as the years pass, shares its plot with that of the first of the Elric stories, "The Dreaming City" (1961), originally collected in *The Stealer of Souls* and appearing later, slightly revised, in *The Weird of the White Wolf*. Jerry Cornelius, who begins as a photographic negative of the albino Elric, serves as the source for more than one nonfantasy avatar of the Eternal Champion, most notably for Jherek Carnelian, who, like Jerry, operates as the coordinating figure for his own series, the six Dancers at the End of Time books.

The books centered on Jerry Cornelius and on Jherek Carnelian, plus the Eternal Champion heroic fantasies proper, make up a total of forty-two books, more than half of Moorcock's entire production. The central Eternal Champion figure, whether he is upright yet flawed or inverted yet often distressingly triumphant, is echoed in different ways in Moorcock's work, ranging from science-fiction novels to short-story collections. These books, however, along with the Jerry Cornelius and the Jherek Carnelian volumes, will not be discussed in this essay, yet they do provide some of Moorcock's richest work.

While the figure of the Eternal Champion stitches Moorcock's oeuvre together in one way, the concept of the multiverse provides a rationale for the shifting yet disturbingly similar venues in which he faces his destiny, laughs at it, or runs away from it. It is a concept perhaps more comprehensive than rigorous, but for this reason, it is well-adapted to the task of coordinating sixty or more novels and collections into one convincingly interconnected series. In other words, the concept of the multiverse is a kind of nesting device. It assumes a multiplicity of parallel and alternate universes, existing either side by side or as alternatives to one another, which is nothing new in fantasy literature; parallel and alternate universes have long been a stock-in-trade of both the science-fiction writer and the fantasist. The sophisticated concept of the multiverse, however, transcends these old devices in that Moorcock assumes that all conceivable universes simultaneously coexist and that access from one to the other is so constant a process that it generally passes almost unnoticed. The protagonists of novels such as *The English Assassin* (1972) and *The Adventures of Una Persson and Catherine Cornelius in the Twentieth Century* (1976) exist uniformly in a vast four-dimensional nest of alternate futures and pasts, traversing the boundaries according to aesthetic, political, or more frivolous impulses.

Here again, similar to his creation of the more sophisticated versions of the Eternal Champion, Moorcock engenders a sense of ever-mutating complexity beyond all hope of respite in any final resolution, even a catastrophic one. Although he writes comically and tragically, he writes neither comedies nor tragedies, both of which forms require a sense of ending. Moorcock never provides his readers with a genuine ending, and much of his writing is ambiguous in that there are few instances of a definite conclusion. In the mature works, this ambiguity may be taken as an analogue of the supernatural complexity of the cosmic balance, though refined into an art that does not require high-sounding props or Lords of Chaos to point the moral. In the heroic fantasies, on the other hand, this refusal to conclude a story though serious enough when decoded by reference to other works more often has the effect of a marketing device: it keeps the reader's attention; he must read on to discover the story's conclusion.

In the late works, characters traverse on hectic impulse the futures and pasts and alternatives of the multiverse, maskers in a dance of worlds. In the heroic fantasies, the Eternal Champion, bidden to battle from his temporary respite, generally finds himself bound to the wheel of one reality; his mask is frozen. Within the Eternal Champion sequence, each series posits one relatively stable primary universe in which the action takes place, though always within a framework that allows incursions from other phases of the unending struggle between law and chaos, so that characters from different series will sometimes visit one another, sometimes under their own names. All the same, the Eternal Champion himself is generally a prisoner of the series of which he is the hero, and the melancholia that afflicts and benumbs him in most of his embodiments may well attest the fact that, although he is a hero in the context that has been chosen for him by a Lord of Chaos or a Lord of Law, he is nevertheless, by being tied to one world, a victim of it.

Just as the Eternal Champion is tied to individual venues, so his overall sequence breaks into several formally separate series, each featuring the enlisted exploits of a different avatar. The Eternal Champion sequence consists of the following five series, which are named for their protagonists: Erekosë, Elric of Melniboné, Hawkmoon, Corum, and Michael Kane. The Erekosë works include *The Eternal Champion*, *Phoenix in Obsidian* (*The Silver Warriors*), and *The Quest for Tanelorn*. Elric of Melniboné is the principal hero in ten works in the Eternal Champion series, including *The Stealer of Souls*, *Stormbringer*, *The Singing Citadel*, *The Sleeping Sorceress*, *Elric of Melniboné* (*The Dreaming City*), *The Jade Man's Eyes*, *Elric the Return to Melniboné*, *The Sailor of the Seas of Fate*, *The Weird of the White Wolfe*, and *The Bane of the Black Sword*. The Hawkmoon works include *The Jewel in the Skull*, *Sorcerer's Amulet*, *The Sword of the Dawn*, *The Secret of the Runestaff*, *Count Brass*, and *The Champion of Garathorn*. The Corum series includes *The Knight of the Swords*, *The Queen of the Swords*, *The King of the Swords*, *The Bull and the Spear*, *The Oak and the Ram*, and *The Sword and the Stallion*, while the Michael Kane series, written by Moorcock under the pseudonym Edward P. Bradbury, includes: *Warriors of Mars*, *Blades of Mars*, and *Barbarians of Mars*.

As fiction, the three novels devoted to the travails of Erekosë are less satisfactory than the others in the sequence, with the probable exception of the swift-moving but ramshackle Michael Kane stories. It is significant, however, that the first Erekosë volume is entitled *The Eternal Champion* and that some of the material making up the tale first received copyright as early as 1957. *The Eternal Champion*—though revised as late as 1977—represents Moorcock's first and most explicit attempt at modeling the Eternal Champion, who initially comes to existence in a standardized heroic fantasy landscape replete with swords, sorcery, grandiose (but vague) contrasts of geography, dress, demeanor, and so on. The multiverse hardly exists as a governing principle, and in its primitive form, it is referred to as the Ghost Worlds. Erekosë himself remains the only avatar of the Eternal Champion actually conscious of his enforced destiny. (Throughout the twenty-four titles, characters who hint at an awareness of the multiplicity of worlds are often recognizable as being mutated incarnations of Jerry Cornelius—himself a mutated incarnation of Elric.) Erekosë knows he was once, in phrases reminicent of E. C. Tubb, a human being with human concerns: "There was a woman. A child. A city. An occupation. A name: John Daker. A sense of frustration. A need for fulfillment."

Yet he has nightmares in which he is summoned by the name Erekosë, and soon he is translated entirely from Earth:

> Had I hung for an eternity in limbo? Was I alive—dead? Was there a memory of a world that lay in the far past or the distant future? . . . Was I John Daker or Erekosë? Was I either of these? Many other names—Corum Jhaelen Irsei, Aubec, Elric, Rackhir, Simon, Bastable, Cornelius, Asquinol, Hawkmoon—fled away down the ghostly rivers of my memory.

This passage (from the 1978 revision) of *The Eternal Champion* represents in all its crudeness the only point at which the Eternal Champion makes a list of his previous selves. It is therefore appropriate that Erekosë, in *The Quest for Tanelorn*, the volume that claims to end the entire cycle of lives, serves Moorcock as a unifying device, though without much conviction. In that novel, he is fount, matrix, and final repose; but this can only be notional, for no repose can be permanent.

In the two novels devoted primarily to him, Erekosë, in a manner conformable to his forthright self-awareness and manly vigor, takes on tasks of organization and generalship of daunting complexity. Although troubled by vainglory and guilt, he manages to behave throughout as though selfhood and action were not divorced. Of all of Moorcock's creations, he is the most burly and primitive.

It is true that Erekosë is nothing like Elric of Melniboné, who is nothing if not internally riven by every sort of dichotomy. The traditional hero of sword-and-sorcery always acts first (with magical rightness, so that the world is saved) and thinks second (fatuously and with numbing self-complacency, as befits the muscular "lord of all he surveys"). Elric thinks his complex, introspective, melancholic, subtle thoughts before acting. A priest-king sworn to maintain his realm, he betrays Melniboné to his enemies and spends most of the series in anguished exile. Devoted to his wife, friends, and allies, he brings almost all of them to disaster, actually managing to kill them through the agency of his sword Stormbringer, which drinks the souls of both the good and the evil. It is as though his every action were performed in front of a mirror, but with his actions having no substance and only the disastrous reversals of the mirror affecting the world he loves, though bitterly and in a mutilating fashion. Elric's anguish is indeed precisely that he is a parody, a slave to Lord Arioch of Chaos, and that he can save his universe only by destroying it.

Sensitive and fairly intellectual, Elric is a romantic creation, despite the fact that he was conceived as a deliberate parody of Conan the Conqueror and his ilk; at the same time, Elric has the profound humorlessness of youth (his and Moorcock's). Moorcock betrayed Elric by turning him inside out into Jerry Cornelius, whose early gaiety is manic and whose lunges into action exhibit a bizarre selfishness. In a very recent novella, "Erlic at the End of Time" (1981), Moorcock places his anguished albino into a venue where aesthetic will is omnipotent, so that in a sense Elric can have nothing to complain about any longer. He duly continues to mourn, however, for the Eternal Champion needs enemies.

Enemies are generously supplied in the Hawkmoon series, which is set in a remote Europe eons hence, in which the war between chaos and law is more vigorously socialized than elsewhere in the overall sequence. Although he spends much of the series crippled by the jewel in his skull that provides the title for its first volume, Dorian Hawkmoon, Duke of Coln, engages with some fullness in a well-realized environment, which is centered on the small realm of Kamarg, in what is now southwestern France. The ruler of Kamarg, Count Brass, acts as a father figure to Hawkmoon, one of the few father figures Moorcock allows more than a few pages of existence; Hawkmoon woos, sleeps, weds, lives, rescues, and closes the series with Count Brass's daughter, Yisselda. Unlike the Elric books, whose conclusion was written first and the subsequent titles written to fill in Elric's earlier life, the Hawkmoon series was written in the order of its internal chronology, and Hawkmoon's career—despite some multiverse-ordained excursions—is Moorcock's most sustained presentation of a single life. In his heroic fantasies, although written deliberately within the limits of popular fiction, the Hawkmoon books present a remarkably successful contrast to the world of Elric.

Cursed by a poisonous jewel in his skull and by other threats from the bestial rulers of Granbretan, and burdened with a sequence of talismans he acquires from volume to volume, Hawkmoon is the most colorful and engaging of all the avatars of the Eternal Champion, though by no means the brightest intellect among them. The war he and his allies wage against Granbretan also seems comparatively unambiguous, for there is no questioning the evil of the foe, nor the positive values represented by the threatened homeland. There is an air of solidity about the world of the Hawkmoon series, a sense that in this aspect or plane of the multiverse something like a clearcut victory is possible. It is perhaps no mistake that some of the descriptions of the Kamarg could almost have been written by H. Rider Haggard, for whom a lawful empire did exist, though no individual man might fully comprehend its ramifications. One must not go too far, however: in Moorcock's oeuvre, despite his abiding nostalgia for the bright toy-soldier verities of a habitation whose boundaries are secure, there is no stable empire.

A kind of detached nostalgia infuses the stories about Corum, whose sense of the world he inhabits is constantly retrospective. He is the last surviving member of the Vadhagh, a race supplanted within his time by a ranting, vulgar humanity. Exiled through the genocide of his people and by a natural fastidiousness that finds mankind revolting as well as immoral, Corum is a combination of the destructive introversion of Elric and the acculturated dutifulness of Hawkmoon. Although he is in internal exile, as well as being exiled from his heritage, Corum can in no sense be thought of as a voluntary hero; nor does he ever volunteer. The world he is coerced into defending is a version of prehistoric Britain, but no attempt is made to enlist the reader's imaginative engagement with this circumstance; there is no sense that anything like the Matter of Britain is being forecast by Corum's solitary and nostalgic quests for partial victory against the Lords of Chaos. It is entirely typical of Moorcock's work that the Corum books inhabit a mythos whose terms do not extend beyond the oeuvre as a whole. In the Corum books, as elsewhere, Moorcock creates his own symbolic array of gods and demons with an effect both liberating and restricting. The reader is liberated from exegetical renderings of gods whose moral valencies have already been explored, recast, and stereotyped to the point of boredom. At the same time, he is restricted to a cosmogony whose resonances are necessarily superficial. Lord Arioch of Chaos, whom Corum fights successfully, has no resonances beyond the texts within which Moorcock confines him.

Of the Eternal Champion series, the six Corum novels are the most polished of Moorcock's heroic fantasies, being structured with a seemingly effortless control of rhythm, pace, and distance. Of these three, distance is the most significant. Where Elric glares at the reader through the pages of the text like a prisoner glaring through the bars of a cage, Corum has his back, aesthetically speaking, to the reader, just as he treats the shifting demands of the multiverse with disdain. Always he is trying to disappear from the reader's view, to retire. He does not wish to suffer any longer, or to help humans in their evolutionary rampage, or to create a new era. The ironies by which he is forced to do precisely all three are inherent in the impassive, distanced clarity of Moorcock's telling of his extremely violent life, during the course of which he loses an eye and a hand and outlives the mortal woman he loves; and the series closes with his abrupt, senseless (but distanced) murder.

The pseudonymous Michael Kane trilogy stands rather to one side and does not merit undue attention. Set on a florid Mars, it is a pastiche of the work of Edgar Rice Burroughs, and although Michael Kane has in retrospect been enlisted as an Eternal Champion figure, the trilogy adds nothing of significance to the portrait. Almost alone among Moorcock's 1960's heroic fantasies, the Michael Kane books have undergone no revisions; the books have gained little reputation as significant works and readers have found them to be of lesser quality than Moorcock's other books in the Eternal Champion series.

In a formal sense, the entire Eternal Champion sequence reaches its close with *The Quest for Tanelorn*, a volume not written until 1975, when Moorcock seemed to have lost interest in heroic fantasy. Indeed, there is a kind of inattentiveness about the novel which, despite its thematic import, is one of

Moorcock's shortest and most perfunctory works. All four primary avatars
of the Eternal Champion appear in the book: Erekosë, Elric, Hawkmoon,
and Corum. Tanelorn is an eternal city and offers repose for the heroes, the
reader is led to believe, and not only repose, but also answers to their questions, resolution of the problem of the trembling cosmic balance, judgment,
and closure. Unfortunately for the success of this title, all problems are solved
by marriage or death, fortunately, in a broader sense, Moorcock as a writer
seems constitutionally incapable of allowing the worlds of his imagination to
close themselves down in the bad faith of a terminal quietude. As Moorcock
renders it, quietude is a delusion, a face of the multiverse held still—as though
by a great cardsharp—just long enough to entrap the unwary. Then peace is
whipped aside, faster than the eye can see, and the catastrophe continues.
Although each avatar of the Eternal Champion longs for an island of peace,
for a still face of the world to rest upon, it is at the hard, mature heart of
the twenty-four books of the sequence, beneath their surface crudities and
morose rigmaroles, that repose can only be a dream of the moment, perhaps
sunlit. Always, before it can be laid to rest, however, the moment calls.

John Clute

Bibliography
Bilyeu, Richard. *The Tanelorn Archives: A Primary and Secondary Bibli-
ography of the Works of Michael Moorcock, 1949-1979*, 1981.
Moorcock, Michael. "Wit and Humour in Fantasy," in *Foundation*. XVI (May,
1979), pp. 16-22.
Pratt, Charles. "Michael Moorcock," in *Dream Makers*, 1980.

ETIDORHPA

Author: John Uri Lloyd (1849-1936)
First book publication: 1895
Type of work: Novel
Time: 1826-1827
Locale: New York and underground Kentucky

For exposing the secrets of a secret society, the "Man" is kidnaped and then led into the center of the Earth; he receives instruction in the possible advanced states of humanity and must pass tests proving him worthy of a higher consciousness

> *Principal characters:*
> LLEWELLYN DRURY, the narrator of the frame story
> THE MAN, the narrator of the story-within-a-story
> THE STRANGER, the Man's spiritual guide on Earth
> THE BEING, the Man's spiritual guide in Earth
> ETIDORHPA, the White Goddess, or soul of love

Etidorhpa offers a story within a story that, on the basis of scientific discourse, expands the imagination beyond the bounds of "materialistic" science and, in fact, scorns known science. The novel establishes Llewellyn Drury as an ordinary citizen who receives an extraordinary visitor—or visitant—who identifies himself only as "I am the man who did it" and who, like the Ancient Mariner, binds Drury to a promise to listen to a reading of his manuscript. Thereafter, the listener must lock the manuscript in a vault for thirty years, after which he must seek an illustrator and publish it for a limited audience. With the introduction of his mysterious visitor, Drury personally experiences telepathy, psychokinesis, and consciousness of duality. The only friend he consults dismisses these as hallucinations.

Except for the Drury role, *Etidorhpa* is a novel without names, a novel in which discussion of ideas, often in paragraphs two pages long, diminishes the effect of incident. *Etidorhpa*'s speculative scientific content grew out of both the vocation and the avocation of John Uri Lloyd, a famous and much-honored pharmacist who wrote eight scientific books and approximately five thousand scientific papers, developed new medicines, and invented many chemical apparatuses. The best known of his eight novels is *Stringtown on the Pike* (1900). He published *Etidorhpa*, his first literary work, privately; an edition for subscribers aroused interest and led to eight more editions the following year. The book was translated into Swedish and German and published in England. Reversing the letters in the book's title spells Aphrodite, the foam-born goddess of love here idealized as an affinity or harmony among all the laws of nature; its title, *Etidorhpa*, means "a future banquet." Lloyd withheld from the early editions three chapters which present Aristotle's ether as a scientific possibility and Professor Daniel Vaughn's ideas on gravitation, as well as a demonstration of water defying gravity.

The exact aim of the book seems to have been in doubt, for other editions present a confusing assortment of chapters deleted in chronological order and added at the end. The close parallels between narrator and listener in the frame story and in the story proper enabled subsequent publishers to shift chapters from Drury and the Man to the Man (as listener) and the underground "being" who acts as his guide. Three chapters omitted from some editions introduce a third party, a confidant sought by Drury to confirm the existence of the Man and to help him question the Man's astounding science; these chapters make the book read more like a novel and less like a scientific treatise. So carefully argued is the science of the book that later scientists saw in it predictions of X-rays—described as "vitalized darkness"—the airplane, the atomic bomb, argon, and other elements of the atmosphere.

The novel's complete title tells much about it: *Etidorhpa: Or, The End of Earth, the Strange History of a Mysterious Being and the Account of a Remarkable Journey*. A frontispiece shows the Man with long white hair and an even longer white beard; underneath, a scrawl identifies him: "I am the man." The many illustrations by J. Augustus Knapp, approved one by one by Lloyd, suggest the seriousness of the author's intent in making his own manuscript conform to the requirements of the Man.

Although the novel consists of many extended essays or explanations of "scientific" phenomena, the journey of the Man forms a dominant pattern remarkably consistent with that elaborated by Joseph Campbell in *The Hero with a Thousand Faces* (1949). The Man's character is quickly established as that of a seeker, a person whose search for knowledge and discontent with traditional science foster occult study. The published works of the alchemists lead him to membership in a secret fraternity, so that an anonymous "Alchemistic Letter" addressed "To the Brother Adept Who Dares Try to Discover Zoroaster's Cave, or the Philosopher's Intellectural Echoes, by Means of Which They Communicate to One Another from Their Caves" occasions no surprise. The letter's promise of even more secrets to be revealed carries a fateful challenge and an appeal to egotism in the guise of altruism, recalling the tantalizing "call to adventure" of Campbell's outline.

The description of the sacred order strongly suggests the Masons; although Lloyd was not a member of the Masons, he was a student of the occult. The story of "I Am the Man" was no doubt inspired in part by a well-publicized incident in New York State, the disappearance of a Mr. Morgan who was a Mason and who had revealed the order's secrets. In the novel, the Man's written confession prompts the sacred order he seeks to expose to have him jailed; mysterious kidnapers free him and drive him far from his New York village. He crosses the first threshold, in Campbell's terms, when he discovers that the person beside him is really a corpse, which provides the cover of a false death for him when it is thrown overboard, allowing him to assume a new identity. With some substance of the new science applied to his face and figure to make him appear an aged man, he tests the success of the application by his return to his village, where no one recognizes him. The Man's metaphoric death corresponds to what Campbell calls the "belly of the whale"; it means the permanent loss of his family and his former life. He becomes the aged man of the frontispiece: "I am the man who did it." The Man's earthly guide demonstrates and explains telepathy as well as human instinct greater than that of the homing pigeons; he explains both as sciences of the future. He explains time as tranquillity rather than sequence and life as disturbed energy. His doctrines, cut to the cloth of the archetypal hero, promise the Man eternal youth (even with an aged appearance) and a world mission.

Mammoth Cave provides entrance to the underworld at the center of the Earth, in that section of Kentucky which the guide proclaims "the most remarkable portion of the known world." The Man's "Road of Trials" begins with the loss of his earthly guide and the acquisition of a strange being having neither eyes nor nostrils; there follows a plunge into an underground river, reminiscent of the Styx, for here he must bid goodbye to sunshine. Ten miles into the Earth's interior, however, a kind of "epipolic dispersion" provides light, and the being lectures him on the limitations of science and of present human nature: "Man must yet learn to see with his skin, taste with his fingers, and hear with the surface of the body." The fantastic journey takes him through a forest of fungi among strange flowers, reptiles, and monstrous cubical crystals. The Man learns to accommodate himself to weightlessness and to accept the disappearance of objects, the transference of water downward by capillarity, and a new science of volcanoes and of primary colors. A fuelless motorboat is powered by the "inherent energy" of Earth and space.

The being explains matter as retarded motion and recites a long list of the failures of scientists. He says that the chemist of the future will provide man with the ability to commune with the spirit world, for "a study of true science is a study of God." This contrasts with the present world, in which man's spirit is "a slave to his body," with the lungs and heart seen as "antagonists of life," a philosophy that seems credible because the Man finds that he no longer needs to breathe. The matter of slavery to the body, however, proves to be the most exacting of the Man's tribulations on this Road of Trials. Four chapters of lecture and experience point to the evils of drink, using frighteningly grotesque examples of people with exaggerated limbs, such as a foot or a hand fully twelve feet in length. The Man nearly yields to the temptation to drink three times, then he sees behind the innocent tempter the face of a leering devil and strikes away the cup. Here occurs the meeting with the White Goddess, a fitting reward for the man induced—though unwillingly—to complete successfully a journey toward spiritual fulfillment.

Lloyd fully exploits his poetic talents in describing Etidorhpa, who in the approved Knapp illustration remarkably resembled his first bride of only eleven days. To confirm that she became for him "the spirit that elevates man, and subdues the most violent of passions" (in other words, the expression of the anima), she describes herself in the terms of mythology's conceptions as "the beginning and the end of earth." She embodies all women in their triple phases: "With the charm of maiden pure, I combine the devotion of wife and the holiness of mother." Confirming Lloyd's attacks on materialism, she insists, "I come from beyond the empty shell of a materialistic gold and silver conception of Heaven." The Road of Trials continues beyond this meeting with the Goddess; she warns the Man, "You cannot pass into the land of Etidorhpa until you have suffered as only the damned can suffer."

The traveler learns to appreciate the narcotic mushroom, to recognize man's time as the whiplash passing through the flesh, to confront what occultists call the Akashic record (the imprint of events on space), to consider life in Platonic terms as a shadow or illusion of a floating thought, to acquire for himself the skills of telepathy and existence without a heartbeat, to learn that earthbound conditions may be contradicted in areas not proscribed by them, to recognize that "there is a concave world beneath the outer convex world," and to exert the mind on a material force (psychokinesis). With these trials and accomplishments, the Man seemingly reaches Etidorhpa, or the End of Earth. He is ready now for immortality.

The interior story reaches an abrupt end. Although the Man has materialized unexpectedly in Drury's quarters and acts mainly like a spiritual being, he looks much like a human in his last meetings with Drury in chapters deleted from some editions. In "The Last Farewell," he breaks down as he remembers his wife and children; then a conversation with the invisible Etidorhpa reassures him that he must go on in his new spiritual identity. From her, he understands that love binds people to Earth and Earth's illusions, but his destiny lies beyond these things. As a last human touch, this person—who has read Drury's mind and accomplished wonders of Socratic dialogue in furthering his arguments about the future of science—now pleads that Drury will search out his abandoned family and provide for their needs. He himself exists in that in-between world, divested of his mortal body but not yet meriting the rewards of a spirit in eternity.

At the height of its popularity, *Etidorhpa* was likened to books by Victor Hugo, H. Rider Haggard, and Jules Verne. So convincing were the novel's occult contents that occultists experimented with applying its doctrines; at the same time, persons of serious scientific bent tried to descend to the Earth's center through the underground caverns of Kentucky's Mammoth Cave. Fantasy, in such a work, reverberates through reality.

Grace Eckley

Bibliography
Simons, Corinne Anna Miller. *John Uri Lloyd: His Life and Works*, 1972.

THE EXORCIST

Author: William Peter Blatty (1928-   )
First book publication: 1971
Type of work: Novel
Time: The 1970's
Locale: Washington, D.C.

The release of a demoniac spirit from an excavation near Nineveh sets in motion a sequence of events half a world away involving the demoniac possession of an eleven-year-old girl, murder, the desecration of religious shrines, and the involvement of a Jesuit psychiatrist in the ancient rite of exorcism

Principal characters:
CHRIS MACNEIL, an actress
REGAN MACNEIL, her daughter
DAMIEN KARRAS, a Jesuit priest and psychiatrist
BURKE DENNINGS, a witty but profane British producer
LIEUTENANT WILLIAM F. KINDERMAN, a Washington police
    investigator
LANKESTER MERRIN, a Jesuit paleontologist and exorcist
FATHER JOSEPH DYER, a friend of Karras

A best-selling novel of demoniac possession, *The Exorcist* has spawned a host of demoniac horror stories, beginning in the early 1970's and continuing unabated into the 1980's. Its effect on films has been no less dramatic. It is too soon to say whether its influence has been as baleful as critics claim. Certainly, *The Exorcist* has produced a legion of mutated and grotesque imitations. Its success is a literary and cultural phenomenon the effects of which will be felt for some time to come.

The key to the popularity of *The Exorcist* is not to be found in its workmanlike style or in its slick plotting. William Peter Blatty's characters, while competently drawn, are not exceptionally vivid. Indeed, Merrin, the exorcist, and Regan, the possessed girl who shares with him the novel's most memorable scenes, are not really characters at all. They are rather both masks through whom demoniac and divine powers act and engage in a horrifying but fascinating conflict. Whatever its other strengths or weaknesses may be, the key to this novel is its power to project a sense of the weird: that is, to produce the illusion of supernatural agents intruding into a thoroughly demythologized, secular society.

This rupture of the fabric of everyday life is dramatized in the transformation of a young girl into a vessel of malice and monstrous evil. Regan's youth, innocence, and essentially normal interests and behavior emphasize the preemptive power of the evil spirit, whose very existence is an affront to the modern mind. Much of the tension of the novel derives from the conflicting responses of various characters to this phenomenon. Regan's mother, Chris, is open-minded in the modern sense; that is, while she is skeptical of any spiritual remedy, she is prepared to try anything with a chance of success. The skepticism of Damien Karras is more complex and persuasive. He is a man divided between two professional selves, priest and psychiatrist, and the claims of each are such that he is unable to resolve the conflict. Instead, he bears the burdens of others as well as his own.

In his way, Damien Karras defines not only the limits of scientific thought when confronted with supernatural powers but also the limits of reason. Damien's Greek surname suggests that he is guided by the philosophical spirit and ideals of the Greek tradition. Karras' skepticism about demoniac possession, therefore, reflects the inner conflicts of the man. In the end, his triumph is emotional rather than intellectual. Fulfilling the promise of his given name, he challenges the demon who is not only torturing but also killing Regan to leave her spent body and take his own. His martyrdom is an impulsive, spontaneous gesture and a glorious, heroic fulfillment of his destiny. One of the strongest sections of the novel is that which details the ambiguous responses of Chris and Regan MacNeil to Damien's sacrifice, which lies beyond their spiritual frame of reference, and the uncertainty of Father Joe Dyer, Karras' closest friend in the Jesuit order. Unable to devise a wholly rational explanation of his friend's death (was it perhaps suicide? or was it caused by the demon?), Dyer must rely on what his heart tells him of his friend's dying responses: "'It's all right,' he said. Then he shrugged. 'I've got a feeling it's all right.'" The reader is in a position to know that Dyer's intuition is correct; one can only pity the weakness of his faith.

While Damien's crisis of belief in two competing systems of faith, one religious and the other scientific, is dramatically resolved, the other characters do not achieve such certainty. Neither Regan nor Chris is converted by the harrowing experience, although Chris acknowledges a newly formed, tentative belief in the Devil. Dyer's reaction is hopeful, suggesting that faith is not finally a matter of reason but of desire. These tenuous resolutions are supported by the bantering conversation between Dyer and Kinderman that ends the novel. Their newly formed friendship seems to be a continuation of the unfulfilled friendly relationship between Karras and Kinderman, and also, in a way, a representation of the undeveloped bond between Karras and Merrin. There is a certain irony, however, in Blatty's conclusion, for if a number of the characters retain their skepticism, the reader knows better. The reader, thus granted a privileged position, is subtly encouraged to feel superior to the characters. In the flood of novels and motion pictures which have followed the success of *The Exorcist*, this encouragement is far from subtle: instead of identifying with the characters, readers and viewers are urged to regard them with a sadistic sense of superiority.

The novel's presentation of demoniac possession as a reality, a reproach to self-assured unbelief, raises the issue of whether *The Exorcist* can rightly be classified as fantasy at all. The question also underlines the special power of the novel, which depends on the reader's sense that the horror of demoniac possession is or could be real. Indeed, the novel successfully defines the contradiction between civilized common sense, with its assumption of a controlled and sensible world order, and the peremptory challenges of evil which make a mockery of such pretensions. For the true materialist reader, *The Exorcist* will perhaps seem fantastic if not grotesque, stirring up the ghosts of old terrors. Henry James argued that such power was the distinctive attribute of the ghost story, and H. P. Lovecraft in *Supernatural Terror in Literature* (1927) defines the genre in terms of whether this effect is produced by the story. There should be little dispute that *The Exorcist* produces these effects and many others, including a convincing evocation of the ambience of Georgetown University in northwest Washington, D.C.

Once the shock of the reader's imagined encounter with Regan's demons wears off, there remains the memory of the grim triumph of Karras' martyrdom. Also, one leaves the book with a sense of an encounter with two strong authority figures: Kinderman and Merrin. The former is the spokesman for natural wisdom and the latter for supernatural wisdom. Each man in his own sphere has learned to deal with brutal and uncompromising evil. Each man has been scarred by it and has learned compassion for human suffering through those encounters. Neither man has any illusions about evil or its nature. Unlike Karras, neither tries to understand it in the abstract as a proposition of philosophy; for these true men of the world, evil is an inherent reality. In part, their stature as authority figures is a consequence of their competence in defending both reason and civilization from the anarchic forces that threaten them. It seems also a condition of their competence that each understands the limits of reason and politeness. Neither is squeamish. Each realizes that the human mind can approach truth, isolate it, perhaps even determine it; but truth itself remains mysterious.

The view of human nature and human history proposed by Blatty in *The Exorcist* is the view that once was taken for granted in the West: that the interface of body and soul, mind and spirit is essentially dynamic, involving supernatural powers of good and evil intimately in the encounter. It was an order in which souls are to be saved or lost. It was a world in which human beings counted for so much that God and the Devil sometimes chose mortals as an arena in which to join the struggle. The recovery and affirmation of this world view and its dynamic potential may be, after all, the hidden key to an appreciation of the popularity and the power of this unusual novel.

Donald L. Lawler

Bibliography
No listing.

THE FACE IN THE ABYSS

Author: Abraham Merritt (1884-1943)
First book publication: 1931
Type of work: Novel
Time: The twentieth century
Locale: The lost land of Yu-Atlanchi and the surrounding Andes mountains

Nicholas Graydon chances upon the lost land of Yu-Atlanchi, where he falls in love with the Princess Suarra and is drawn into a conflict between the forces of Good, represented by the Snake-Mother, and the forces of Evil, represented by the Shadow

> *Principal characters:*
> NICHOLAS GRAYDON, a young American adventurer
> SUARRA, his lover, Princess of Yu-Atlanchi
> ADANA, the Snake-Mother, leader of the forces of Good
> REGOR, Graydon's friend, a giant warrior who serves Adana
> NIMIR, the Shadow, leader of the forces of Evil
> LANTLU, a corrupt and sadistic Prince of Yu-Atlanchi, follower of
> Nimir

The work of Abraham Merritt is fantasy fiction of the first rank. Donald Wollheim's claim that Merritt was "the dean of fantasy writers, the very top" has been echoed by other enthusiasts such as Lin Carter and L. David Allen. In view of such praise, as well as the fact that Merritt was a popular writer whose novels sold well in their time (the 1920's and 1930's), it is astonishing that his works are now nearly inaccessible to the public, and even more puzzling that no study has been done either of the man or his fiction. The absence of any in-depth study of Merritt's work constitutes one of the largest gaps in the criticism of fantasy literature.

Too little is known of Merritt's private life to allow psychological speculation concerning his major literary themes. The facts of his public life are known, however, and can be quickly outlined. He was born into a Quaker family in Beverly, New Jersey, in 1884. He disliked school, quit as soon as possible, and got a job with the *Philadelphia Inquirer* at the age of nineteen. A very capable journalist, he became assistant editor of *The American Weekly* in 1912, was promoted to editor-in-chief in 1937, and held that position until his sudden death in 1943. In 1917, he published "Through the Dragon Glass," the story that launched his career as a fantasist.

Merritt's successful and very busy public life left him relatively little time for writing fiction; indeed, he seems to have written stories primarily to relax from the pressures of daily affairs. In addition, he was a stylistic perfectionist who carefully and repeatedly revised and polished his work, but who nevertheless was satisfied with only one story that he ever wrote. (That story, "The Woman of the Wood," long forgotten and only recently reprinted, is a classic of its kind.) For these reasons, Merritt's output was relatively slight—eight novels and a collection of stories—compared to contemporaries such as E. R. Burroughs who wrote on similar themes. On the other hand, his fiction is of unusually high quality, combining entertaining plotting with a vivid and dynamic style that is the result of his meticulous care. If by style the critical observer means the highly self-conscious attention that the writer brings to the task of fitting his language to its subject within the context of a given work's purpose, then it is not too much to say that his only stylistic rivals among American fantasists are James Branch Cabell and Peter Beagle.

The Face in the Abyss, which embodies the "lost race" theme that was his primary source of inspiration, is an excellent example of Merritt's artistry. The plot follows the fortunes of the young adventurer Nicholas Graydon, who stumbles onto the ancient lost city of Yu-Atlanchi (the myth of Atlantis remains the most fertile source of lost race novels) while seeking treasure in the Andes. He falls in love with the pagan princess Suarra, and their love, a standard component of lost civilization novels since H. R. Haggard, provides the motivation for his involvement in the power struggle between the forces of Good and Evil that threatens the existence of Yu-Atlanchi.

In his effort to escape with Suarra to modern civilization, Nicholas is forced to choose sides and to participate in the Armageddonlike conflict between Adana and her archenemy, Nimir, the Shadow. He is aided by several archetypal characters: Regor, a gigantic warrior; Kon, a spider-man with human emotions; and The Lord of Folly, an enigmatic sorcerer. He also confronts many obstacles and enemies: Lantli, aristocratic and sadistic lieutenant of the Shadow; Nimir, the vampiric Shadow whose malevolence and thirst for power know no bounds; a succession of lizard-men who are Nimir's slaves; and the stone "face in the abyss" which telepathically seduces and destroys all who encounter it through fantasies of limitless power. Merritt skillfully manipulates these and other characters in fine fashion, and the depiction of the final conflict, in which Adana and Nimir do battle with a multitude of supernatural allies and stratagems, matches the best writing of its kind in such literature (including the Armageddon scene in J. R. R. Tolkien's *The Return of the King*, 1955).

This plot summary cannot do justice to the suspense, the powerful imagery, and the seemingly inexhaustible diversity of conflict that mark each page of the text. The novel's value, however, does not lie in any technical innovation. At one point, the narrator speaks of the romance of discovering "lost civilizations and races, buried beyond trace under the dust of time." This theme is part of a tradition stretching back at least to medieval travel books, and perfected for modern audiences by H. Rider Haggard in his *King Solomon's Mines* (1886). There, and later in *She* (1887), Haggard introduced and developed the erotic element of the thinly disguised sexual love affair between the hero and a pagan princess that became a standard feature of the tale. To say that Edgar Rice Burroughs is the only American fantasist who both uses the lost race theme and matches Haggard in stature implies Merritt's importance. For, while Merritt pioneered no technical improvements in the use of the theme (no one since Haggard has), he is an incomparably better writer than Burroughs, Duffield Osborne, Edison Marshall, or the host of Haggard's epigoni.

The Face in the Abyss contains in abundance what is typical and valuable in all of Merritt's prose: the dynamic momentum of a strong plot, imagery that is simultaneously hard-edged and abstract, and a sentence cadence that is nearly poetic. For example, during the final conflict Graydon looks upon the universal carnage and sees "Shapes of flame that battled with slaying shadows . . . and Huon dead there at his feet beneath a crimson sky." More important, however, is Merritt's treatment of the alien; it is unique among writers on this theme since most of them treat the fabulous beings encountered either with a certain awe (as in Haggard) or as "bug-eyed monsters" to be subjugated or destroyed (as in Burroughs). Merritt, however, sees these beings—his spider-men and snake-women—in a more liberal and complex way as doubles of human experience; not as irremediably foreign but as somehow akin to the human protagonist, as exemplars of alternative evolutionary trends, as potential allies, or, at the very least, as enemies who are not entirely beyond the pale of the reader's sympathy. Thus the novel's center of power, Adana, is a composite of animal (snake) and woman who mingles the wisdom of nature with the rationality of humanity; the same is true of Kon, the spider-man, and even of Nimir's servants, the lizard-men, who are "if not men, at least semi-human." Indeed, Graydon admits that there is "no mistaking the human element in them," that they are "men and lizard inextricably, inexplicably, mingled—as man and spider had been mingled in . . . the Weaver." This visionary sensing of the complex and mixed nature of human experience makes Merritt's fiction more interesting than that of his better-remembered contemporaries such as Burroughs.

Although Abraham Merritt produced little, his best work—*The Moon Pool* (1919), *The Ship of Ishtar* (1924), *The Face in the Abyss; Dwellers in the Mirage* (1932), and *Burn Witch Burn* (1933)—deserves careful study. Merritt is the equal of both Haggard and Burroughs in inventiveness, and he is clearly their superior in style. It is time that students of fantasy literature rediscover this neglected modern master.

R. E. Foust

Bibliography
Atheling, William, Jr. [James Blioh]. "Exit Euphues: The Monstrosities of Merritt," in *More Issues at Hand*, 1970.
Foust, R. E. "Monstrous Image: Theory of Fantasy Antagonists," in *Genre*.

XIII (Winter, 1980), pp. 441-453.

Moskowitz, Sam. "The Marvelous A. Merritt," in *Explorers of the Infinite: Shapers of Science Fiction*, 1963.

THE FACE IN THE FROST

Author: John Bellairs (1938-   )
First book publication: 1969
Type of work: Novel
Time: The Middle Ages
Locale: The North Kingdom and the South Kingdom

Two magicians set out on a journey to save mankind from the evil spell of their enemy, Melichus, a corrupt warlock, and finally vanquish him through the help of the real world, a fantasy world to them

Principal characters:
> PROSPERO, a wizard
> ROGER BACON, his friend and fellow wizard
> MELICHUS, an evil wizard, former associate of Prospero
> M. MILLHORN, a magician from a future technological world

Sepharial, the professional name of Walter Gorn Old, has said in his book *The Kabala of Numbers* (1913) that "what we call an event is but a displacement and rearrangement of the parts of our own sphere of reality." This is an appropriate comment on John Bellairs' book, both because the author mentions the *Kabala* as the solution to his character's dilemma and because he has, in fact, utilized this concept of rearranging known historical facts as the basis for constructing an idealized medieval world of surpassing charm and beauty. Indeed, Bellairs' novel deals very directly with the question of the nature of reality—and who or what makes things real.

Prospero and Bacon, wizards and old friends, embark upon a journey to save mankind from the evil spell of their former colleague and fellow magician, Melichus. Melichus has found an old book written in curious ciphers that seem untranslatable; when he tries to decipher the strange writing, he can make out only tantalizing glimpses of some basic formulas of power. The more he pursues the question, the more entranced he becomes; what has begun as intellectual curiosity quickly becomes an obsession, first with the translation itself, and then with the power the spells might bring the translator. The formulas somehow contain the secret to another reality or series of realities; the master of these arcane symbols can literally destroy the world of the North and South Kingdoms. This Prospero and Bacon must prevent at any cost.

This is not the Roger Bacon who was the Franciscan monk in the "real world," a man known not only for his contributions to science ("It is the intention of philosophy to work out the nature and properties of things") but also as an alchemist and dabbler in magic. Yet he is clearly intended to be an analogue of the real Bacon in a world where magic works. Like his model, this alternate version is devoted to the truth, whatever it may be, wherever it may lie; like the real Bacon, Bellairs' wizard is a man of honor and courage. Prospero, on the other hand, is modeled after William Shakespeare's fictional sorcerer, the practitioner of "this rough magic." In *The Tempest* (1611), Prospero sets out to right the wrongs of his world, and in so doing, employs his magic one last time to bring about a proper balance of persons and events. Bellairs' character is also concerned with balance, with setting right *his* world; a bumbling and forgetful man, clearly no match for the brilliant and logical Melichus, he nevertheless sets forth with a desperate kind of courage to fight the good fight. His very lack of pretension, his refusal to fool himself by championing his own considerable abilities, are major assets in this struggle to the death.

The mark of Melichus' growing power over the land is the ever-recurring image of "the face in the frost," a yawning, vacant visage which, when glimpsed, evokes a nameless terror, a horror that cannot be dispelled by reason: "He felt very nervous, drowsily nervous, with prickling dark borders on his sight. A glass bell was ringing somewhere deep, deep in the forest. An icy green glass bell ridged with frost, trembling on a green willow branch." Time is growing short; the two friends begin their adventure by shrinking themselves and sailing a model ship down an underground stream that leads from Prospero's root cellar. In the ensuing chapters, the magicians defeat a troll, make use of a prophetic mirror (a looking-glass), ride in a pumpkin (squash) coach, fight off the spells cast by an enchanted forest, and climb a magical vine (beanstalk) to reach the fairy-tale-like cottage once shared by Prospero and Melichus in happier days. These images from common folk myths and childhood fairy tales weave a rich but dark tapestry of allusion and double entendre throughout Bellairs' tale.

At the cottage, Prospero retrieves the green glass paperweight that contains the magical powers of Prospero and Melichus combined. Like Zed in John Boorman's acclaimed motion picture *Zardoz*, Prospero enters the world of the prism, a strange place in which technology has prevailed, filled with electric lights, lawnmowers, and the accoutrements of modern civilization. Zed's crystal had contained all of man's knowledge; with it, and with the knowledge he gained of himself, Zed was able to destroy the prism itself, thus freeing man from the bonds of self-imposed technological shackles. In Bellairs' prism, Prospero encounters M. Millhorn, a true believer in the occult, a man who has been waiting all of his life for this moment. In exchange for the paperweight, Millhorn uses his knowledge of the *Kabala* to save Prospero from the pursuing Melichus; Prospero is returned to his own world, where he finally remembers the spell he must use to destroy Melichus and his evil book, thereby restoring reality. In the end, Prospero's world returns to normal, and he and Bacon celebrate their triumph with a party for their friends.

The Face in the Frost was published originally as a children's book, although it has been reprinted in paperback as an adult novel; it can be read on many different levels. What appears on the surface to be rather lighthearted adventures of two bumbling wizards on a quest becomes, on rereading, a darkly streaked tale of moral courage, tragedy, and the ultimate doom of the world. Everything in the book is seen through the two-sided mirror, a glass which, when held up to "reality," reflects fantasy and real life, the past and the present, humor and sorrow, the pursuit of power and a devotion to duty, in equal measures. The reader sees "through a glass darkly" to reach the truth on the other side. Prospero must pass out of his world through the glass before he can defeat Melichus; he must see his world—and see evil—for what it is, before he can remember the spell. He must recognize that good and evil are the only true constants.

Bellairs' powers of description bring this book alive; every leaf on every branch of every tree is limned in exquisite detail. His ability to make his readers see, smell, hear, taste, even touch the outlines of his fantasy creation makes it real for them. In the context of his story, this must surely be the ultimate paradox.

Mary A. Burgess

Bibliography
No listing.